D0221087

For Reference

Not to be taken from this room

Hispanics in Hollywood

Garland Reference Library of the Humanities
Vol. 1761

This book is dedicated to my wife, Ronda, and my son, Luis Ignacio Keonimana Reyes, who share the legacy of the movies; and to my mother, Maria, who taught me to appreciate the beauty of the performing arts in our lives, and my father, Pablo, who used to stay up late with me and watch all the westerns on TV.

Luis Reyes

For Jack, a fellow movie buff, brilliant guitarist, and the man who introduced me to the pleasures of computerized golf when I should have been working.

Peter Rubie

IRVINE VALLEY COLLEGE LIBRARY

DISCARD

PANICS
in Hollywood

An Encyclopedia of Film and Television

LUIS REYES and PETER RUBIE

GARLAND PUBLISHING, INC.
NEW YORK & LONDON / 1994

© 1994 by Luis Reyes and Peter Rubie

All rights reserved

Library of Congress Cataloging-in-Publication Data

Reyes, Luis, 1953–

   Hispanics in Hollywood: an encyclopedia of film and television/
Luis Reyes and Peter Rubie.

      p. cm.—(Garland reference library of the humanities: 1761)

      Includes bibliographical references and index.

      ISBN 0-8153-0827-2

      1. Hispanic Americans in motion pictures—Encyclopedias.
2. Hispanic Americans in television—Encyclopedias. 3. Hispanic American
actors—Biography—Encyclopedias. I. Rubie, Peter. II. Title. III. Series.

PN1995.9.H47R49   1994

791.43'08968—dc20   93-40607

Book design by Lisa Broderick

Printed on acid-free, 250-year-life paper

Manufactured in the United States of America

"*Cyrano* was such an important step in my career, such a turning point. I had borrowed money when I was 34 years old and produced it on Broadway, starring myself. Four years later, there I was making a movie of [it]."

Jose Ferrer, 1950 Best Actor Academy Award winner for
Cyrano de Bergerac, Dramalogue (10/8/87)

"I don't want to be typed as a Latin or anything else. . . . When the movies get a Latin girl they always try to make a spitfire out of her, another Lupe Velez. That's not any more typical of a Latin girl than Betty Hutton is of an American girl."

Lina Romay, as quoted in *Hollywood Studio Magazine* (April 1985)

"There's a whole new breed. . . . They are just well trained actors who just happen to be Hispanic. We're just playing people and not playing the results of people, especially negative people."

Elizabeth Pena, *Los Angeles Herald Examiner* (7/6/87)

"I'm Puerto Rican and that in itself seems to mean spitfire to so many people in Hollywood. It's tough enough getting roles being a woman, but being both female and Puerto Rican makes it all that much harder. I think the barriers, the stereotypes, actually are finally falling apart. I want to show that I can play several kinds of roles, not just Latinas, though I look forward to good Latina parts."

Rita Moreno, *San Francisco Chronicle* (9/14/76)

"Winning the Oscar for my first American film was like buying one ticket in the lottery and winning. It triggered [a] new [level to my] career in America and also bounced back into Europe."

Nestor Almendros, Academy Award–winning cinematographer
for *Days of Heaven* (1978), *Interview* (November 1984)

"When the few good Latin parts go to non-Hispanic actors, Hollywood is saying, 'You people are interesting enough to make films about, but you aren't good enough to play yourselves.'"

John Leguizamo, *Premiere* (August 1992)

"This film about our people [*Stand and Deliver*] will touch the nation. It shows we can achieve anything we want. Being able to make a film like this is the finest moment of my life."

Edward James Olmos, 1987 Best Actor Academy Award nominee
for *Stand and Deliver*, *Los Angeles Times* (3/27/88)

"I became a movie extra just to get money to eat and to lose myself as a face in the crowd. I never had that ambition to be an actor, but it was like a chain reaction. One day a director asked if I could say a line, and I did it."

Fernando Rey, Spanish-born actor, noted for his work with filmmaker
Luis Bunuel, and for his role as the Frenchman in *The French
Connection* (1971), *Los Angeles Times* (5/13/88)

"I have also been stubborn in refusing to do certain types of roles that feed into that distortion, that feed into that horrible misrepresentation [of Latinos]—the drug dealer of the month, that kind of garbage. I don't know if I wouldn't have done those roles if I had been starving, but it never quite came to it."

Hector Elizondo, *Los Angeles Times* (2/9/93)

"I am very hurt that I am not considered an American actor, extremely hurt by it. But I'm afraid the die has been cast, and I will have to play these ethnic roles—but I must say, I'm very happy, because I get to play Hungarians, I get to play Turkish, I get to play Chinese, I get to play Russians—I get to play a much wider scope of humanity than just, quote, American."

Anthony Quinn in an interview with Luis Reyes (1988)

"When we were in Argentina, my mother used to go to the movies three times a week. We spoke about movies, practically every day. It got into my blood."

Julio Macat, cinematographer for *Home Alone* (1990) and
Only the Lonely (1991), *Film and Video Monthly* (8/1991)

"My research showed that men in that period wore bloomers, ruffles and face powder. Errol [Flynn] took one look and said, 'Not for old Dad.' So I made up my own period. . . . I got an Academy Award and he was beautifully dressed. So much for authenticity."

Bill Travilla, five-time Academy Award nominee,
who won Best Costume Design for *The Adventures of
Don Juan* in 1949, *Los Angeles Times* (9/12/68)

CONTENTS

Acknowledgments   xi

Abbreviations   xiii

Bibliography   xv

Foreword   xvii

Introduction   xix

Movies   1

Television   261

   TV Series   269

   TV Movies and Miniseries   301

Zorro & The Cisco Kid   321

Biographies   347

Index   527

ACKNOWLEDGMENTS

Special thanks and appreciation to: Mike Hawks; Pete Bateman; Doug Hart; Critt Davis; Leith Adams, USC/Warner Bros. Archives; Frank Rodriguez, Universal Pictures; Louis Garcia, TriStar Pictures; Ann Lander/Teri Avanian, Orion Pictures; Halina Krukowski, Lucas Films; Jess Garcia, Warner Bros.; the Staff of the Academy of Motion Picture Arts and Sciences Library and Center for Research Study; Television Academy Library; Jeff Baskim, TriStar Pictures; Brian Robinette, NBC; Francisco Chico Day; Angelina Estrada; Gilbert Roland; Victor Millan; Anthony Quinn; Mel Ferrer; Ricardo Montalban; Edward James Olmos; Jesus Trevino; Pepe Serna; Alex Colon; Bart Andrews; Michael Donnelly; Margaret Ward and Rodney Mitchell of SAG; Selise Eisseman of the DGA Special Projects; Dolores Argo, HBO; Mona Lee Schilling; Bob Dickson; my taskmaster Peter Rubie; and, most of all, Lori Perkins, who never gave up the faith.

Luis Reyes

ABBREVIATIONS

AA	Allied Artists
AFD	American Film Distribution
AIP	American International Pictures
BV	Buena Vista
Col	Columbia Pictures
D	Director
Emb	Embassy Pictures
EP	Executive Producer
FN	First National
Fox	Fox Film Corp.
HBO	Home Box Office
MGM	Metro-Goldwyn-Mayer
Mi	Miramax
Mon	Monogram
NG	National General
Or	Orion Pictures
P	Producer
Par	Paramount Pictures
PBS	Public Broadcasting Service
Rep	Republic Pictures
RKO	RKO Radio Pictures
S	Screenplay
T	Touchstone
TCF	Twentieth Century–Fox
Te	Teleplay
TNT	Turner Network Television
TS	TriStar Pictures
U	Universal Pictures
UA	United Artists
UFD	United Film Distribution
WB	Warner Bros.

Note: If a film company or distributor is not a major studio or distribution or releasing company, the name is not abbreviated but is spelled out in the movie entry.

BIBLIOGRAPHY

Adams, Les, and Rainey, Buck—*Shoot Em Ups* (Arlington House: New Rochelle, NY, 1978).

Agan, Patrick—*The Decline and Fall of the Love Goddesses* (Pinnacle Books: Century City, CA, 1979).

Belafonte, Dennis, and Marill, Alvin H.—*The Films of Tyrone Power* (Citadel Press: New York, 1979).

Bell, Geoffrey—*The Golden Gate and the Silver Screen* (Cornwall Books: New York, 1984).

Boetticher, Budd—*When in Disgrace* (Neville Publishing: Santa Barbara, CA, 1989).

Buscombe, Edward—*The BFI Companion to the Western* (Atheneum: New York, 1988).

Cardoso, Abel, Jr.—*Carmen Miranda* (Simbolo S.A. Industria, Graficas: São Paulo, Brasil, 1978).

Crowther, Bruce—*Charlton Heston: The Epic Presence* (Columbus Books: London, 1986).

De Usabel, Gaizka—*The High Noon of American Film in Latin America* (UMI Research Press: Ann Arbor, MI, 1982).

Eames, John Douglas—*The MGM Story* (Crown Publishers: New York, 1976).

Eames, John Douglas—*The Paramount Story* (Crown Publishers: New York, 1985).

Everson, William K.—*The Films of Laurel and Hardy* (Citadel Press: New York, 1967).

Gallagher, Tag—*John Ford: The Man and His Films* (University of California Press: Los Angeles, 1986).

Gunning, Tom—*D.W. Griffith and the Origin of American Narrative Film* (University of Illinois Press: Urbana and Chicago, 1991).

Haskell, Molly—*From Reverence to Rape* (Holt, Rinehart & Winston: New York, 1974).

Hirschhorn, Clive—*The Columbia Story* (Crown Publishers: New York, 1989).

Hirschhorn, Clive—*The Warner Bros. Story* (Crown Publishers: New York, 1979).

Hurst, Richard Maurice—*Republic Studios: Between Poverty Row and the Majors* (Scarecrow Press: Metuchen, NJ, 1979).

Huston, John—*An Open Book* (Alfred A. Knopf: New York, 1980).

Jewell, Richard B., and Harbin, Vernon—*The RKO Story* (Arlington House: New York, 1982).

Koszarski, Diane Kaiser—*The Complete Films of William S. Hart* (Dover Publications: New York, 1980).

Langman, Larry—*A Guide to Silent Westerns* (Greenwood Press: Westport, CT, 1992).

McCarty, John—*The Complete Films of John Huston* (Citadel Press: New York, 1990).

Miller, Frank—*Casablanca: As Time Goes By* (Turner Publishing: Atlanta, GA, 1992).

Mora, Carl J.—*Mexican Cinema: Reflections of a Society, 1896–1988* (University of California Press: Los Angeles, 1989).

Nash, Jay R., and Ross, Stanley R.—*Motion Picture Guide,* 12 vols. (Bowker: New York, 1986).

Newman, Kim—*Wild West Movies* (Bloomsbury Publishing Limited: London, 1990).

Noriega, Chon—*Chicanos and Film* (Garland Publishing: New York, 1992)

Okuda, Ted—*The Monogram Checklist: The Films of Monogram Pictures Corporation, 1931–1958* (McFarland: Jefferson, NC, 1987).

Oshana, Maryann—*Women of Color: A Filmography of Minority and Third World Women* (Garland Publishing: New York, 1985).

Parish, James Robert—*The Paramount Pretties* (Arlington House: New Rochelle, NY, 1972).

Parish, James Robert—*The RKO Gals* (Arlington House: New Rochelle, NY, 1974).

Parish, James Robert, and Bowers, Robert L.—*The MGM Stock Company* (Arlington House: New Rochelle, NY, 1973).

Sennett, Ted—*Warner Bros. Presents* (Arlington House: New Rochelle, NY, 1971).

Shipman, David—*The Great Movie Stars: The International Years* (Hill and Wang: New York, 1980).

Vermilye, Jerry—*Burt Lancaster: A Pictorial Treasury* (Fallon Enterprises: New York, 1971).

Walsh, Raoul—*Each Man in His Own Time* (Farrar, Straus, & Giroux: New York, 1974).

Wiley, Mason, and Bona, Damien—*Inside Oscar: The Unofficial History of the Academy Awards* (Ballantine Books: New York, 1988).

Zmijewsky, Boris, and Pfeiffer, Lee—*The Films of Clint Eastwood* (Citadel Press: New York, 1982, 1988).

FOREWORD

In the 1940s, as a young actress under contract to MGM Studios, I could not have conceived of a publication documenting the careers and artistic achievements of Latino artists—not only because Latinos were few and far between in Hollywood films, but because we were virtually invisible in the eyes of the studio heads themselves.

Like many aspiring actresses, I came to Hollywood wanting nothing more than to be the next Lana Turner, but my education was to be abrupt and painful: the doors of opportunity were only open to me on strict conditions which the studios dictated. Like hundreds of other ethnic actors, I was relegated to playing a spate of nameless Indian maidens and Mexican spitfires. Latino contract players were afforded no options in the old studio system; we played the roles we were given no matter how demeaning they might have been.

Even with a certain amount of success under our belts, the struggle to be recognized as serious actors persisted. For example, after winning an Academy Award for playing Anita in *West Side Story* I spent years turning down roles that were veiled versions of the same role, but without the substance that *West Side Story* possessed. Thus, I turned to theater to practice my craft. I did everything in my power to seek out venues which were less inclined to typecasting.

Though the road has been quite rough, many Latino actors have attained success in the entertainment industry and, more importantly, have earned the respect of their peers. Those who did not allow the rigidity of the system to dishearten them persevered and, in many cases, achieved great successes when afforded the opportunity. I have progressed throughout a 40-plus-year career from playing Indian captives to starring in my own television series, "9 to 5," in which I played an all-American businesswoman.

Too long has it taken for the entertainment industry to embrace the scope of Latino talent. Nevertheless, throughout the years Latino actors have made many significant contributions to film and television and will undoubtedly continue to do so.

This book salutes both those who paved the way and those who broke down stereotype barriers with their talent and fortitude. The time is long overdue to recognize and celebrate the Latino contribution to Hollywood.

Rita Moreno

I really believe that the motion picture industry is an ideal place where actors and actresses can play any part. To me all actors are part of a universal nation called "Actor." I am part of that nation of actors and that is how I would like to be remembered.

Anthony Quinn

INTRODUCTION

I grew up on New York City's Upper West Side in the late 1950s and early 1960s, and the first Hispanic presence on television I can remember was Desi Arnaz as Ricky Ricardo on "I Love Lucy." He looked, acted, and talked just like my Dad, especially when he got mad and spoke Spanish to Lucy. Their home life resembled mine, for they lived in an apartment in New York and struggled every day to make ends meet. And even though Lucy was nothing like my Latin mother, she had that universal comic humanity in her characterization that we all could relate to.

Zorro and the Cisco Kid were Hispanic, but their shows were historical swash-bucklers and westerns. Although, like every other young boy, I loved cowboy films, it was shows like "Naked City" and "East Side, West Side," which were shot on location in New York, that had Puerto Rican tenement-dweller characters played by New York Puerto Rican or Latino talent with whom I could identify.

My first moviegoing memories are of stars like Charlton Heston in *El Cid* (1961) and John Wayne in *The Alamo* (1960), as well as endless Jerry Lewis comedies. The only actresses I ever really liked were Susan Hayward and Marilyn Monroe, though I was also drawn to the exotic and bosomy charms of Sophia Loren, Claudia Cardinale, and Brigitte Bardot.

I identified mainly with all the screen tough guys, including Kirk Douglas and Burt Lancaster, who grew up in Spanish Harlem when it wasn't Spanish, but apart from Gilbert Roland, who was always dashing, romantic, and sly and usually a friend to the leading man; Anthony Quinn, a towering screen presence who had a very vague ethnicity; and Ricardo Montalban, who has always somehow personi-fied the classic Spanish don, I saw very few Latinos on screen. When Puerto Ricans Rita Moreno and Jose Ferrer became Oscar winners, I was proud.

After seeing a film, I would stand in the lobby, perhaps of the RKO Nemo on 110th Street and Broadway, which was just one of many movie houses that were near our apartment on 109th Street, and stare at the movie posters and photos and displays in eager anticipation of coming attractions. Through these displays I would also relive what I had just seen.

I didn't think about race or ethnicity as an issue until I was a teenager during the civil rights movement of the 1960s. By then we had all become conscious of our own history. In my case, I began to learn about how my family had arrived in New York from Puerto Rico, and how our culture was melding with mainstream American culture, while sharing our neighborhood turf with the Irish, Jews, and Italians.

When I entered high school I began to wonder why there were so few Hispanics in the movies and even fewer on television. Mexicans were part of westerns, and I easily bought into the fantasy that Hollywood created. I wondered why television commercials didn't feature blacks or Hispanics; after all, I bought Nestle's choco-late and Cheerios and Pepsi just like Anglo kids. Our lives and Puerto Rican cul-ture in general were, I thought, just as dramatic and interesting as the Italian American or Jewish American experience. To this day, there has not been one major Puerto Rican–experience film made in Hollywood with a Puerto Rican direc-tor and star.

Through a New York Puerto Rican youth educational and leadership program called Aspira, I was exposed to many aspects of Puerto Rican culture of which I had not been aware. Through this organization in 1972 I was able to obtain a scholarship to Elbert Covell College in Stockton, California, at the time the only bilingual (Spanish/English) college in existence in the United States. I knew Stockton because it had been the location for the western TV series "The Big Valley" and the movies *All the King's Men* (1949) and *High Noon* (1952). It was there that I began to see how rich and variable Latino culture was. Half the student body and teachers were from Latin America, and from my upbringing I really knew only Puerto Rican, Cuban, and Dominican cultures.

After graduation, I went to Los Angeles and looked up the organization Nosotros, founded by Ricardo Montalban and others to fight stereotypic images and to improve opportunities for Hispanics in movies and television. Here, as in New York, I found a wealth of talented artists, writers, and directors who were enthusiastic and passionate about their art and considered their culture part of the American experience.

But Hollywood was interested only in the same old stereotypic images: maids, slum dwellers, drug addicts, gang members, and hot-blooded senoritas. Thankfully, since then actors like Raul Julia, Hector Elizondo, Edward James Olmos, Andy Garcia, Maria Conchita Alonso, Julie Carmen, Elizabeth Pena, Rachel Ticotin, and Rosana De Soto have risen to the forefront of their profession as the new generation who are at last beginning to be seen by both mainstream America and Hispanic America alike as Hispanic stars considered part of the mainstream of American culture.

Being a lifelong film buff and working in the public relations side of the film industry, I discovered a whole legacy of lesser-known Hispanic talent in Hollywood that seemed in danger of being lost if it wasn't documented somehow. Those who had forged a place in the film industry in the early days were dying or had already passed away, and as the years passed, their stories and inevitably the history of Hispanics in Hollywood were in danger of being forever lost.

Angela Gomez, a 93-year-old Hispanic extra player, once told me, "This show business is something I've always wanted to be a part of since my youth. Times and circumstances were much more difficult then and I am grateful for the opportunity it gave me and my husband to work and provide a decent living for our family. Just as important, it was an escape, a fantasy world, like storybooks come to life in which one took part."

This book is an attempt to show the way Hollywood has depicted Hispanic Americans and Latin America, while also pointing out the contributions to Hollywood movies and TV made by unsung Hispanic Americans like Angela Gomez, as well as by those more famous.

By way of an explicit definition, the term "Hispanic American" refers to all people living in the United States who can trace all or part of their background to Spain, Portugal, Latin America, and the Philippines. The book will deal only with the history of the Hispanic American in the Hollywood film and television industry. It will not attempt to deal with the cinema of Latin America and Spain, except in terms of how they affected Hispanic American images or artists in Hollywood.

The material is based on interviews conducted by Luis Reyes; previously published material in magazines, newspapers, and studio archives; press materials; and the viewing of the films by the authors when possible.

Nearly 400 films and TV shows are listed with credits, short synopses, production information pertaining to Hispanic elements, and critical commentary. For inclusion, the following criteria were used:

- The film or TV show contains Hispanic leading or supporting characters.
- The story takes place in Spain, Latin America, or the United States.
- It is a major Hollywood studio or independent U.S. production.
- The film or TV show deals with Hispanic subject matter.

Most of the films listed are from the sound period (post-1927) because many of the silent films are either unavailable (lost) or inaccessible.

Photograph by John R. Hamilton

Luis Reyes

INTRODUCTION

Hispanic Americans, like many other minority groups in the United States, suffer from damaging stereotyping in motion pictures and on TV. Yet while other minority groups are beginning to get a better (or perhaps broader) portrayal in the 1990s, the Hispanic American is still cast in the old cliches.

There are few films that explore the variety of Hispanic American experience— that is, very few feature affluent, educated, middle-class, or well-to-do Latinos; gay or non-Spanish-speaking Hispanics; or Jewish or Protestant (non-Catholic) Hispanics. The diversity of Hispanic Americans and their cultures and contribution to U.S. art and daily life has yet to be fully explored, particularly by Hollywood.

A breakthrough in reshaping a stereotyped image often comes when members of the minority group being portrayed on the screen are also prominently involved in the writing, acting, production, and direction of the movie as is the case with the fledgling Chicano cinema. Notable recent examples include *Zoot Suit* (1981), *Born in East L.A.* (1987), *La Bamba* (1987), *Stand and Deliver* (1988), and *Hangin' with the Homeboys* (1991). The irony is that Hispanic Americans have been involved in the Hollywood moviemaking process almost from its inception but are only now beginning to affect positively how they are portrayed in the movies.

By definition, a cliche or stereotype is based on a self-evident truth, but that truth is misleading because it is one-dimensionally repetitive and, more importantly, fails to find a person's humanity. Cliches and stereotypes, in the end, are lies because they use *partial* truths to give illusory weight to the racist's argument that (fill in the blanks) "all ___ are ___ because ___."

Hollywood argues that by and large its movies (and, to a lesser extent, television) are entertainments without any political bias, the only goal of which is to give us a few hours of harmless fun. This is not only untrue—*all* stories have a point of view and an implicit meaning—but also disingenuously dishonest because in the course of watching these entertainments we constantly see portrayals of characters that perpetuate stereotypical racist opinions considered acceptable because "everyone knows it's true." And why do we know it's true? Because we see examples of it in the movies or on TV all the time.

More and more, Hollywood movies and TV shows have become our filters for interpreting the world around us. We have become victims of the old adages "A picture is worth a thousand words" and "The camera doesn't lie." We should know better these days because modern technology *can* make the camera lie with frightening conviction; even without the use of this computerized technology, the "truth" is often twisted by capturing a moment out of context and presenting it as common reality. What's more, as Hitler and Goebbels discovered, if you tell people the same lie loud enough and long enough, they start to believe it.

There is a fine line between the artistic tyranny of "political correctness" and being sensitive to perpetuating a stereotype. It could be argued that the line is best walked with an honest awareness of and an attempt to portray the best in us, rather than accepting as truth stories and characters that continually reflect only the worst. Hollywood, however, has not been particularly sensitive to positive minority portrayals or to a positive approach to minority storytelling. TV is not much better, especially when it comes to portrayals of Hispanic Americans and their culture and way of life.

Instead, Hollywood hides behind a bottom line, a dollar mentality that often masks a form of passive racism that most people would be horrified to learn they were practicing. The insidiousness of racism is not so much the overt acts of the self-proclaimed fascist but the moral cowardice of those who avoid speaking out against off-the-cuff offensive remarks. Accepting unchallenged, stereotyped portrayals in the movies is such a form of passive racism.

Backlot Mexico

Most film portrayals of Hispanic and Latin American characters (i.e., those living south of the Mexico-U.S. border or those living in the U.S. having a Spanish heritage) by North Americans reflect the ignorance of the filmmakers and perpetuate myths that are for the most part negative. Banana republics, sleepy villages with lazy peons basking in the sun, uncivilized half-naked Indians, violent government coups spearheaded by cruel dictators, mustachioed bandits and beautiful senoritas, and the idea that one Anglo is worth ten Latinos are just some of the many stereotypical images most North Americans have of Latin America, Hispanics, and Hispanic Americans.

These negative images have not changed throughout much of the twentieth century and are alive and well in such movies as *The Alamo* (1960), *The Magnificent Seven* (1960), *Kings of the Sun* (1963), *Butch Cassidy and the Sundance Kid* (1969), *The Wild Bunch* (1969), and *Old Gringo* (1989). *Raiders of the Lost Ark* (1981), for example, shows Indiana Jones being chased by Indians in a South American rain forest after stealing a gold idol. Nick Nolte and Powers Boothe spar over drugs, the hand of Maria Conchita Alonso, and the right to be "gringo in charge" (benevolent or otherwise) in *Extreme Prejudice* (1987), in which the bandidos are now drug traffickers.

Although Hollywood has recently rediscovered Nicaragua, El Salvador, and Panama, Central and South America all seem to melt into a single, amorphous south-of-the-border culture. A great many North Americans could not even identify the names, let alone the locations, on a map of countries south of Mexico, yet they all have an opinion about them and the people who were born there. As recently as 1993, in Steven Spielberg's *Jurassic Park,* which is set on an island off the coast of Costa Rica, San Jose, the capital city, in reality a bustling metropolis, is depicted as a seedy backwater port, and Mexican music is heard incongruously playing in the background.

In the past, moviegoing audiences were treated to memorable images of Humphrey Bogart making his way through savage jungles while eluding bandits in his search for lost gold in Mexico (*The Treasure of the Sierra Madre* [1948]), Cesar Romero and Tyrone Power conquering the Aztecs and winning the women as well (*Captain from Castile* [1947]), Cary Grant flying mail over the Andes (*Only Angels Have Wings* [1939]), and Carmen Miranda dancing to a North American version of one type of Latin rhythm that became the stereotype for them all.

On a domestic level, the stereotypes have slowly evolved over the years from the bandido who terrorized the American West to the modern drug dealer or street gang member. Women have undergone very little change, from the jovial mamacita to the suffering mamacita, or the sexually provocative "spitfire" to the street hooker or girl gang member.

The primary source for our modern-day ideas about Hispanic Americans has been westerns and urban crime dramas, though these images have their roots in nineteenth-century yellow fiction and journalism. Somehow, all the land below the U.S. border is viewed as one giant Mexico, and all Spanish-speaking peoples are considered somehow Mexican.

Mexico: a place to escape from American law; a place of corrupt anarchy, overwhelming poverty, and cheap hedonism; a place where the American dollar can last a long time; and a place where dark-haired, copper-skinned beauties share their beds for a few pesos (paradoxically, this attitude is also characteristic of the Latin lover in films). At the same time, ". . . a piece of us expects to be murdered on holiday in Mexico, and the knife would come as no surprise," Octavio Paz commented in *Labyrinth of Solitude*. The place is dangerous and exotic, as are its people.

Mexico as an extension of the American West is an image that has been popular in the more recent adult westerns as contemporary filmmakers have focused on the closing days of the American frontier. This image has been underscored by the popularity, in the late 1960s and 1970s particularly, of the European "spaghetti western," often filmed in areas of Italy, Spain, or Mexico that look a lot like the Southwest.

B westerns produced in the 1930s and 1940s by such studios as Republic, Monogram, and Columbia and starring George O'Brien, Buck Jones, John Wayne, Hopalong Cassidy, Roy Rogers, and Gene Autry had a great deal to do with creating a backlot Mexico that has passed into movie mythology, helping define in the process stereotypical ideas of Hispanic Americans that are still with us. On the Republic Studios backlot or in most studios in Hollywood, there was a permanent standing set of a typical Mexican adobe town with a church, a plaza, a cantina, and a hacienda residence. This set was used to represent Mexico and the Southwest in hundreds of films. Writers like Ernest Hemingway created a picturesque view of exotic, tropical Cuba, and American tourists flocked there and to other South American and Caribbean countries during the Jazz Age and Prohibition. The infectious Latin rhythms of Afro-Caribbean music began to take hold in the United States with the success of bandleaders like Xavier Cugat, Desi Arnaz, Perez Prado, and many lesser-known musicians who influenced such American composers as Cole Porter, Aaron Copland, and, later, Leonard Bernstein.

John Huston created a modern version of the romantic image of Mexico with his 1964 film of Tennessee Williams's *The Night of the Iguana*. Taylor Hackford's *Against All Odds* (1984) (a remake of 1947's *Out of the Past*) features a Mexico that serves as an exotic backdrop for murder and romance among Anglos. Oliver Stone's *Born on the Fourth of July* (1989) offers a thinly sketched shantytown Mexico that is a sexual haven for paraplegic Vietnam War veterans. Unfortunately, making the setting Mexico, rather than, say, downtown USA, exploits the audience's stereotyped assumptions about Hispanics. These assumptions are so ingrained in the American consciousness and exert such a powerful hold over the imaginations of filmmakers the world over that they will be perpetuated in one form or another for years to come.

The Bandido and the Greaser

Long before the advent of motion pictures, many popular misconceptions and stereotypes about Hispanic Americans had been adopted. Much of this is seen in movies that deal with history. To read Carlos Fuentes's novel *The Old Gringo*, for example, and then to see how it was altered to fit not just a movie format but North American sensibilities as well is to gain some sense of the depths of the problem, even though matters are clearly improving.

The battle of the Alamo in 1836 and the Texas War of Independence left deep-seated prejudices between Anglo Americans and Mexicans still reflected over 100 years later in such movies as *Man of Conquest* (1939), *The Last Command* (1955), and John Wayne's *The Alamo* (1960).

The Mexican American War of 1846 and the resulting Treaty of Guadalupe Hidalgo, which ended the hostilities in 1848, ceded 51.2 percent of Mexican territory to the United States, including the present-day states, among others, of New Mexico, Arizona, and California. As a result, 100,000 former Mexican citizens quickly found themselves second-class citizens in the United States. Spanish noblemen saw their large landholdings slowly dwindle as a result of Anglo American encroachment, facilitated by murder, deceit, and legislation including the onerous "Greaser Law of 1855" (the epithet was actually written into the text of the law).

Throughout the 1850s, groups of bandits moved about the countryside raiding and pillaging. Their actions were in part a reaction against discrimination directed at the dark-skinned minorities of the gold regions. Such things as the Greaser Law and taxes on foreigners stirred deep anti-Anglo sentiment among Latinos. Resentment of Anglo domination was deep-seated and widespread, and many of the original bandidos had at least the tacit support of the Mexican American community.

The term "greaser" has several origins, but terms take on their own history over time and are used for differing political and ideological reasons. The term is a negative or derogatory one usually referring to a non-Anglo or lower-class individual. One meaning of the term applied to Mexican laborers in the Southwest who put grease on their backs to facilitate the unloading of hides and cargo. In the dime novels of the 1880s, "greaser" usually referred to an oily, dark, swarthy villain or bandit who, more often than not, was Mexican or of mixed blood. In the 1950s, "greaser" usually applied to ethnic teenagers, considered to be juvenile delinquents, with greased hair and black leather jackets.

Nineteenth-century melodramas and the stories of popular writer Bret Harte helped shape the image of the Mexican bandit. The popularizing of the American West in the dime novels of the 1880s, written mostly by easterners who had never been west of New Jersey, reinforced the images of bandits, beautiful senoritas, and sleepy peons in Mexican towns.

The Wild West shows of Buffalo Bill and others that toured the eastern cities compounded these images by featuring colorfully costumed Mexican *vaqueros* strumming their guitars and demonstrating rodeo techniques. The shows also presented them as bandits being apprehended by Texas Rangers, Buffalo Bill, or the U.S. Cavalry.

The era of President Teddy Roosevelt at the turn of the twentieth century, the building of the Panama Canal, the imperialistic expansion of the United States, and the concepts of "our little brown brothers" and "yellow journalism" practiced by the Hearst and Pulitzer newspapers all helped to foster misconceptions of our neighbors to the south.

The Spanish American War of 1898, the "yellow press," lurid stories of the sinking of the battleship *Maine*, and stories of Teddy Roosevelt's Rough Riders charging up San Juan Hill against the Spanish enemy in Cuba solidified an idea of manifest destiny.

As a result of that war, the United States acquired Puerto Rico, the Philippines, and Guam and gained temporary control of Cuba. The island country of Cuba after 1898 became a corrupt center of gambling, drugs, and prostitution controlled by the U.S. government and later by organized crime through a series of puppet dictatorships. Puerto Ricans were given American citizenship in 1917, while the U.S. Marines were involved several times in propping up dictatorships in places such as the Dominican Republic as late as 1965.

The revolution in Mexico (1910–1917) captured the American public's imagination because it was so close to home. It gave rise to the portrayal of the bandit in the form of Francisco "Pancho" Villa, whose daring exploits became legendary on both sides of the border. The writings of American journalist John Reed described Villa as a Mexican Robin Hood and the revolution as a romantic endeavor. American ambivalence to Villa was partly brought about by Villa's attack on Columbus, New Mexico, and the punitive military expedition, led by U.S. general John Pershing, sent into Mexico to capture him. In 1913, President Woodrow Wilson refused to recognize the revolutionary Mexican government and sent Marines and gunboats to seize temporarily the Mexican port of Vera Cruz.

The development of the movies from peep show nickelodeons to the relatively sophisticated psychological dramas of silent film directors such as Cecil B. DeMille and D.W. Griffith had a powerful impact on audiences.

Bandits and sleepy Mexican towns were a standard feature in many silent westerns, and the vicious greaser image came into being in these early silent films. *Bronco Billy and the Greaser* and *The Greaser's Revenge* (both 1914), for example, seemed to confirm the Mexican as an evil and sinister villain. In William S. Hart's *Hell's Hinges* (1916), the villain, Silk Miller, is described in the title card as "mingling the oily craftiness of a Mexican with the deadly treachery of a rattler." It was only rarely, such as in *The Mexican* (1914) starring Tom Mix, that a Mexican was treated sympathetically.

Most of the heads of the studios were Eastern European immigrants who had endured much in their homelands and in their newly adopted country and tried to integrate themselves into American society as best they could. Their films rarely reflect their ethnic experience. They simply bought into the American Dream and spun those fantasies and myths for millions of Americans, extending and reinforcing already established popular misconceptions.

After the revolution, the newly established Mexican government objected to the many film stereotypes by issuing an official protest in 1924, banning American films outright. Hispanic American groups in the States began expressing in their Spanish-language newspapers their opinions of negative Hollywood film portrayals.

By the end of World War I, the agricultural and industrial development of the Southwest and Midwest, coupled with the political and economic instability of the post-revolution Mexican government, resulted in the first significant migration of Mexicans into the United States. Setting a pattern that exists to the present, subsequent U.S. deportation policies and job opportunities (both legal and illegal)—which also affected resident Mexican Americans—set up a "push, pull" situation that brought millions of Mexican immigrants across the border.

Added to this was Pancho Villa's edict ordering all Spanish-born Mexicans to leave northern Mexico, which is what brought Gilbert Roland's family to El Paso and later California. Anthony Quinn's mother and father fought for Villa, then became disillusioned by the strife and came to the States.

The immigration of large numbers of Puerto Ricans and Cubans to the United States, on the other hand, started much later, mainly in the 1940s and 1950s, and more recently Central and South Americans have migrated to the United States via the Mexico-U.S. border in large numbers as a result of political turmoil in their countries.

These waves of immigration can be seen to correspond, very broadly, to portrayals of Hispanics in American films: Mexican American social problem films of the post–World War II period, the juvenile delinquent films of the late 1950s and 1960s, and more recently the drug dealer and gang stereotypes of the 1980s.

Antonio Moreno (in car) on the set
of a 1920s silent film.

Pioneers

The motion picture industry secured a living and a future for many Hispanic Americans by creating jobs and opportunities in the Los Angeles area. The history of Hispanics in Hollywood begins with the extra players in silent movies in the late teens and early 1920s. Extra work, along with wrangling and day labor, were the areas of moviemaking most accessible then.

Very early on, however, some Hispanics made it to the forefront of the industry. According to film historian Geoffrey Bell in *The Golden Gate and the Silver Screen* (New York: Cornwall Books, 1984), Hispanic actresses Beatriz Michelena and Myrtle Gonzales were among the first leading ladies of the silent screen, and Frank Padilla and Eustacio Montoya were two of the first silent film cinematographers. Film historian Antonio Rios-Bustamente in *Chicanos and Film* (Garland, 1992), edited by Chon Noriega, states that Myrtle Gonzales was the early film industry's "first Latina star." In 1911, she appeared in the film *Ghosts* and, until her sudden death from influenza in 1917, received star billing in more than 40 Vitagraph and Universal Pictures films. "In marked contrast to the experience of later Latinas who used their own names, Gonzalez portrayed vigorous outdoor heroines," says Rios-Bustamente.

Michelena was a star of the San Francisco musical stage at the turn of the century and appeared in her first film, *Salomy Jane*, produced by the California Motion Picture Corporation, in 1914. The next year the major trade paper *Motion Picture World* featured her on the cover with the caption, "Beatriz Michelena, Greatest and Most Beautiful Artist Now Appearing in Motion Pictures." Between 1914 and 1919 she appeared in 16 feature films. "The new industry's need for experienced and popular players created an opportunity for talented actors, including Latinos," concludes Rios-Bustamente, who adds, "unlike later Latino players, these early players were able to star with Spanish surnames, even prior to the Latin Lover craze which made Latinos temporarily fashionable."

Los Angeles, due to its historical antecedents, always had a large Mexican population, which became a great resource for the film studios. This population grew even more during the Mexican Revolution (1910–1917), when refugees immigrated to the United States to escape the violent turmoil across the border.

Hispanics on the East Coast, on the other hand, were relatively small in number and were virtually shut out from any kind of involvement in the early film industry that was developing there. During this early silent period their only documented involvement as extras and laborers was in films that were shot in Cuba and Puerto Rico. Instead, it was the European immigrant who provided the cheap labor on the East Coast. Duncan Renaldo (the actor who gained fame as the Cisco Kid) began as an extra at Paramount Studios in Astoria, Queens, when he first arrived in New York. He was promptly hired as an art director and artist when he resketched a set for a South Seas movie. The original, he told the director, was more typical of Cuba and the Caribbean.

Los Angeles became a popular spot for filmmakers because, among other things, there was plenty of sunshine and warm weather (a necessary bottom line asset in the silent days when films were made outside without lights). The area around Los Angeles also had a varied topography, including mountains, rivers, ocean beaches, and deserts, that could be utilized for many different story settings. Los Angeles was also a nonunion town with a plentiful supply of inexpensive Mexican (and Asian) workers, and labor costs were half what they were back East.

Frank Quinn, Anthony Quinn's father, worked as a laborer and propman at the old Selig Studios. Many Mexican *vaqueros* and ranch hands were employed as cowboys and wranglers for western movies. Mexicans, in general, found work as extra players in countless movies (especially the epics) of the silent era, such as D.W. Griffith's *The Birth of a Nation* (1915) and *Intolerance* (1916), Raoul Walsh's *The Thief of Bagdad* (1924), and the Valentino vehicles *The Four Horsemen of the Apocalypse* (1921), *The Sheik* (1921), and *Blood and Sand* (1922). Mexicans portrayed Arabs, Jews, Pacific Islanders, and Native Americans.

In a 1975 *TV Guide* article, Gilbert Roland wrote of his early days: "Central Casting called for Spanish and Mexican extras to report at Paramount Studios: three dollars a day and a box lunch. Over a thousand of us were hauled into trucks and driven through the narrow and dusty Cahuenga Pass to Lasky Ranch. The picture—*Blood and Sand*, the star playing the matador—Rudolph Valentino."

In 1983, a frail 92-year-old woman by the name of Angela Gomez, who was then the oldest living extra player, revealed some interesting facts about Hispanics and extra work during an interview with Luis Reyes. All told, she appeared in over 300 motion pictures, including the original silent and the sound remake of *Blood and Sand*.

Angela Gomez was born in 1891 in San Bernardino, California, but her family later moved to Arizona, where she married and raised a family of her own. She returned to San Bernardino in 1919 with her husband, Ralph Bauer, a Mexican of German descent. They settled in Los Angeles in 1920 around Sunset and Grand avenues, an area that was then an immigrant melting pot for Mexicans, Italians, Hawaiians, Filipinos, Jews, and Chinese.

"On Temple and Diamond Street," said Gomez, "lived a man named Gamboa who along with his brothers were runners for the motion picture studios. Runners were hired to gather extra players as needed in their respective ethnic areas.

"Pedro Carmona and Chris-Pin Martin (who went on to become a character actor), who lived in the Chavez Ravine area, supplied [Hispanic] extras. The studios would call the runners and tell them they would need two or three hundred Latin types, and they proceeded to gather the people. They would congregate around 'El Arbol,' a big tree outside the Gamboa home. You would take your friends, relatives, whomever, for they made big pictures then. Extras would earn two or three dollars a day and a box lunch. A runner would get 75 cents a head for each extra brought in that worked."

Angela Gomez soon placed her husband in the movies, where he also worked under the name Gomez. He started as an extra, but due to his physical abilities and a friendship with a director, he quickly became a stand-in and stuntman.

When there was no work by way of the runners, the extras would pile in someone's car or take the Red Car (a public transportation trolley) to the studios, lining up early at the studio extra casting gate. An assistant director or the director himself would come out and pick from among the crowd the types needed for the day.

This was a time before the unions and the guilds were formed. Extras were subjected to all kinds of abuses, including high employment agency fees, underpayment of wages, overwork, maltreatment, and sometimes their lives were needlessly put in danger. Central Casting was formed as a nonprofit entity in 1928 by the Association of Motion Picture Producers. It efficiently consolidated the extra casting efforts of all the studios into one central location, which effectively ended the days of nonunion extras.

Extras would be paid additional money for unusual pieces of action or business. These would be called silent bits, whammy, or double whammy. Extras would compete for space within the camera range or next to the stars and would be quick to size up the situation on the set. Angela Gomez explained, "If you were in a three shot or close to the stars or the main action, you would be used more, not only in the master shot but in close-ups or reaction shots, as in a fight scene, as opposed to being way in the background. This way you would be employed longer and also get more money for reactions or silent bits, which were great incentives for people."

"When I was six months old Angela got my brother and me in pictures," remembers her granddaughter, veteran actress Angelina Estrada (no relation to "CHiPs" TV star Erik Estrada). "She raised us, and some films I remember vividly like *Gunga Din* with Cary Grant, because they took us to the rocky and cold Sierra Lone Pine, California, location. I had to walk around barefoot and came back with the chicken pox."

Angela Gomez and her family were representative of many Hispanics who worked in the movie industry as extras. The father of director Luis Valdez worked as an extra driving a mule team and wagon in the Oklahoma land rush scene in the classic western *Cimarron* (1931), filmed near Bakersfield, California. Hispanic extras were an integral part of the Warner Bros. classic *Casablanca* (1942), for example. Eighty-seven-year-old Henry Carbajal, who worked as Henry Carr, remembers he got his first taste of extra work during a week-long night shoot at Paramount Studios and quit his job as a soda jerk at a downtown department store. "It was a cantina scene and I had a pretty girl on my lap and I made $47 for the week. At the time I was only making $18 a week as a soda jerk." Carr also recalls "working in the hot open California sun and having to wait in long lines for several hours to change into a Roman toga in a tent along with hundreds of other extras during the making of *Ben-Hur* with Ramon Novarro."

When playing themselves, however, Mexicans were still usually relegated to extra work. Male lead Mexican roles, for example, almost always went to Anglo actors wearing dark makeup and thick mustaches. Latin leading men did not come into vogue until Rudolph Valentino became a star in 1921. With the onset of the Latin lover, personified by Valentino, a niche was created that allowed actors such as Ramon Novarro and Gilbert Roland to rise to prominence from the ranks of extras.

The Latin lover image can be traced back to Don Juan, to the amorous exploits of nineteenth-century aristocratic Latin Americans in Europe who became popular figures in literature, and to the cultural clash between an extrovert Latin culture and a predominantly introverted Anglo-Saxon, puritan society. While there are many criticisms that may be leveled at the movie version of *Old Gringo*, its portrait of this cultural clash is well drawn and clearly seen through the characters of schoolteacher Harriet Winslow (Jane Fonda) and the Old Gringo, 71-year-old Hearst newspaper journalist Ambrose Bierce (Gregory Peck). This clash is particularly pointed up by their interaction with the character of the young revolutionary general Thomas Arroyo (Jimmy Smits), who plays a variation on the Latin lover, in particular by unleashing repressed passions in the virginal Winslow.

Dolores Del Rio has her palm read by an extra player while director Raoul Walsh looks on in amusement on the set of *The Loves of Carmen*.

The Latin lover as a screen type reached its zenith with Rudolph Valentino, who captivated audiences worldwide with his legendary silent screen portrayals during the 1920s. The phenomenon corresponded to the spirit of the times. The generation that survived and followed World War I became known as "The Lost Generation" and was typified in social customs, literature, and art by F. Scott Fitzgerald and Hemingway, Gertrude Lawrence, Gertrude Stein, Dorothy Parker, accusations of loose morals, the Charleston dance, "bathtub gin," and the decade or so of prohibition that began in 1920.

Valentino's popularity enabled a number of Hispanic actors to become major stars in an attempt to duplicate his "Latin lover" charm and success. Spaniard Antonio Moreno, in fact, had established himself prior to Valentino but was eclipsed by him. Soon followed Ramon Novarro, Ricardo Cortez (who was, ironically, an Eastern European who made a career out of being identified as Latin), and Gilbert Roland, who found themselves working in major motion pictures, though not necessarily in Latin roles. The Latin lover at this time was a Mediterranean-type character, not necessarily a Hispanic American one.

With the death of Valentino in 1926, the Latin lover as a major screen figure fell into decline, taking with it the careers of several actors who had followed in Valentino's footsteps. Several, however, surfaced some years later as character actors in supporting roles.

Novarro, however, was one of the actors discovered in the wake of Valentino's popularity who managed to become a superstar during the 1930s. Born in Durango, Mexico, he fled the Mexican Revolution in 1914, going to Los Angeles with his family. Once in L.A., he did odd jobs until he was discovered by a director who saw in Novarro some of the same qualities that women all over the world loved about Valentino.

Novarro played the title role in the epic *Ben-Hur* (1926), while Gilbert Roland, another discovery who used his Latin lover casting as a springboard to superstardom, played the young Frenchman Armand Duvalle in *Camille* (1927).

In the 1930s and 1940s, the Latin lover types, who included Don Alvarado and John Carroll, were eclipsed by the tall, strong American hero actors, typified by Clark Gable, Gary Cooper, and John Wayne.

Even so, there was still a popular Latin lover type of this period: Cesar Romero. Born in New York City of Cuban parents, Romero used a much lighter touch in his film portrayals, starring in a series of musicals with the likes of Alice Faye, Betty Grable, and Carmen Miranda while under contract at Twentieth Century–Fox.

By 1945, MGM was still promoting two major stars as Latin lover types: Argentinian Fernando Lamas and Mexican-born Ricardo Montalban. Both Lamas and Montalban had been established stars in their home countries before coming to Hollywood, partly as a result of President Franklin Roosevelt's Good Neighbor Policy. The idea was to exploit the Latin American movie market to replace the European film market, which, as a result of World War II, was almost nonexistent. Indeed, Montalban even starred in a 1953 movie called *Latin Lovers,* and despite some outstanding performances in movies like *Right Cross* (1950) and *Sayonara* (1957) was never totally able to escape the Latin lover movie star image that he caricatured so well later in his career in *Sweet Charity* (1969).

The Glamour Years

The premiere of Warner Bros.' *The Jazz Singer*, in October 1927, the first talking motion picture with synchronized sound on Vitaphone discs, ushered in a new era for motion pictures that caused major upheavals in the motion picture business.

In an April 20, 1958, *New York Times* interview with John P. Shanley, Dolores Del Rio recalled, "There was a dreadful anxiety about the talkies. I couldn't even speak English then, so I was in much worse shape than the others were." By the late 1920s, the major Hollywood production centers were concerned about the development of the new sound technology in particular because European film-makers could now begin to make films in their respective languages. This would result in less revenue for Hollywood films in an international marketplace they had once virtually dominated. United Artists stars and owners Mary Pickford, Douglas Fairbanks, and Charlie Chaplin, for example, were adored as much in Paris, France, and Berlin, Germany, as in Paris, Texas, and Berlin, Massachusetts.

Dolores Del Rio's provocative appearance as the French farm maid in *What Price Glory?* (1926) had brought her wide praise and immediate fame. She achieved a fashion-plate image coupled with an elegant, exotic aura that she put to good use in several musicals and costume dramas. A 1934 contract from the Warner Bros. archives showed her to have earned $100,000 for three pictures (*Wonder Bar* [1934], *In Caliente* [1935], and *I Live for You* [1935]) in the midst of the Great Depression.

In the May 24, 1931, edition of the Los Angeles Spanish-language newspaper *La Opinion*, it was reported that Del Rio had turned down a part in *The Broken Wing* because she found the role denigrating to Mexican identity. The role was that of a "cantina girl" who jilts a "Mexican bandit" for an American airline pilot. It eventually went to the lesser-known Lupe Velez, who began her career in silent films as Douglas Fairbanks's leading lady in *The Gaucho* (1927). She continued to play such typecast roles until she committed suicide in 1944. In between, she had a torrid romance with Gary Cooper and later married Olympic swimming champion and screen Tarzan Johnny Weissmuller. Mexican-born Raquel Torres, Rosita Moreno, and Lupita Tovar also found work as exotic types in silent films. Tovar later married producer and agent Paul Kohner.

These Hispanic American stars found themselves in the midst of Hollywood social life and were photographed and pampered wherever they went, earning extraordinary sums of money. They worked opposite some of the biggest stars of the era, including Clara Bow, Norma Talmadge, Greta Garbo, Edmund Lowe, Warner Baxter, and Victor McLaglen.

Gilbert Roland recalled, "To be a star with United Artists [as I was] was a great thing. The studio had John Barrymore and was owned by Mary Pickford, Douglas Fairbanks, and Charlie Chaplin."

Several studios, including Metro-Goldwyn-Mayer, Paramount, and Fox, decided to remake their original English-language productions in foreign-language versions for their principal overseas clients. They put a number of foreign writers, directors, and actors under contract. Paramount had a studio facility in Paris that was used to produce original foreign-language productions. The Spanish-speaking market, consisting of Spain and Latin America, was a lucrative one due to its combined population, which hovered at about 100 million.

With this in mind, a number of Spaniards and Latin Americans came to Hollywood in order to work in this new experiment. Just as with their Anglo counterparts, much of the new talent for sound films came from the theater. Some examples were, from the Spanish theater, Martinez Sierra, Lopez Rubio, Jardiel Pioncela, Catalina Barcena, and Ernesto Vilchez; from Mexico, although already established in Hollywood, Dolores Del Rio, Gilbert Roland, Rosita Moreno, Lupita Tovar, and Berta Singerman; from Argentina, Carlos Gardel, Mona Maris, and Barry Norton; from Brazil, Raul Roulien and Lia Tora (even though they speak Portuguese in Brazil, the transition to Spanish was easy for Brazilian performers, who worked throughout Latin America); from Chile, Carlos Borcosque and Robert Rey; and from Cuba, Rene Cardona and Luana Alcaniz.

Two types of films were produced, Spanish-language versions of original English-speaking Hollywood productions and original Spanish-language productions.

These pictures had a curious mixture of elements that did not always gel in the final result. The Spanish versions of English-speaking films were filmed at a very fast pace. The same sets, costumes, and locations were used, as were many of the same camera setups. Lines were written on chalkboards that were placed out of camera range. The director worked with a moviola at his side in order to reproduce the same camera angles.

A controversy surfaced over which kind of Spanish would be used in the Spanish versions: the Castilian Spanish of Spain or the Spanish of Latin America, which was spoken slightly differently in each of as many as 20 countries. The films became a mishmash of varying Spanish accents, which proved confusing if not laughable to Spanish-speaking audiences.

In the case of the Spanish-speaking version of *Dracula* (1931), however, produced by Paul Kohner for Universal and starring Carlos Villar and Lupita Tovar, cultural and creative differences made for a better film than the Bela Lugosi English version. Simultaneously working on the same sets and using the same costumes as the English-language version, they would commence filming at 7 o'clock at night, after the Lugosi production wrapped for the day, working until 6 the next morning.

Spanish-speaking roles were almost literal translations of their English equivalents. Juan de Landa played Wallace Beery's role in *El Presidio* (1930), in English, *The Big House*. Gilbert Roland had the lead role in both the English and Spanish productions of *Men of the North* (1931).

Gilbert Roland (second from left) stars in the Spanish- and English-language versions of *Men of the North*.

Spanish-language version of Laurel and Hardy comedy short subjects.

Photo courtesy of Critt Davis Archives.

Early on, Laurel and Hardy made several Spanish-language versions of their short comedies, in which they were to find lasting success as Flaco y Gordo (Skinny and Fat). *Tiembla y Titubea* (*Below Zero*) (1930); *De Bote en Bote* (*Pardon Us*) (1931); and *Politiquerias* (*Chickens Come Home*) (1931) are several examples. The comedians were not bilingual; they read their lines from chalkboards that were placed out of camera range, speaking their lines phonetically in Spanish with the help of vocal coaches and supporting actors who were Spanish-speaking. Even the extra players in the Spanish-language versions were Latin-looking as opposed to the English-version extras. Actress Linda Loredo appeared in most of their Spanish-speaking shorts, for example. The foreign-language shorts were a little longer in their running time than their English-speaking counterparts. Some of the added length is padding, to take advantage of the greater rental fees that could be charged to foreign theaters. Some of this padding, however, involved a cultural propensity toward more slapstick, or "business," in building up a gag than Anglo audiences wanted or were used to and a greater use of supporting foreign-language players.

By 1932, this foreign-language/English-language approach was being phased out. Foreign audiences wanted many of their English films in the original language. Besides, it was cheaper and easier to dub the original English-language version, once that technique was perfected, or subtitle it, after a practical system of superimposed subtitling was developed. However, while MGM began dubbing or subtitling its movies, Fox, Warner Bros., and Columbia Pictures continued to make original Spanish-language films well into the late 1930s.

At this time, some of the most successful Hispanic Americans in Hollywood were pioneers in behind-the-camera work. A good example was Francisco "Chico" Day, Gilbert Roland's brother. Like his famous brother, Chico began his Hollywood career as an extra. His behind-the-camera career started as a technical adviser on the Samuel Goldwyn production of *The Kid from Spain* in 1932. He advised on the bullfighting sequences and interpreted for the Spanish toreador who doubled for actor Eddie Cantor. Chico later applied for a job as an assistant director at Paramount but was turned down.

Undaunted, he got a job in the mailroom at $18 a week. That same year his knowledge of Spanish won him a job as a technical adviser on *The Last Train from Madrid* (1937), in which his brother starred. When the second assistant director (2nd AD) was promoted and given an assignment on another film, Chico was given the 2nd AD's position.

When director Mitchell Leisen needed an interpreter for a film with a Mexican background, he chose Chico. Leisen made Chico 2nd AD on all his films. In *Hold Back the Dawn* (1941), much of the action takes place on the Mexican border, and Chico researched in Mexicali, Tijuana, and other towns. A border street was constructed on Paramount's backlot, and Chico had it filled with all the details he had observed.

Chico became the first Hispanic American assistant director and worked for over 30 years at Paramount Studios on such films as *The Big Broadcast of 1938* (1938), *Lady in the Dark* (1944), *Whispering Smith* (1948), *Samson and Delilah* (1949), *Streets of Laredo* (1949), *Shane* (1953), and *The Ten Commandments* (1956). He later became a unit production manager on such films as *The Magnificent Seven* (1960), *Hello Dolly!* (1969), and *Patton* (1970).

Another good example of major behind-the-scenes contributions by Hispanic Americans was the 1933 RKO production of the classic *King Kong*. It utilized the talents of model makers Marcel and Victor Delgado, and of Mario Larrinaga, who was a background effects artist. The Delgados constructed several full-size sections of Kong for use in close-up scenes: a full-size bust of Kong with eyes that rolled; a mouth that snarled and eyebrows that moved; a full-size leg and foot, together with an all-important full-size hand, which would clutch Fay Wray in close-ups in the film. The Delgado brothers and Larrinaga were part of the creative team put together by Willis O'Brien, who was the man responsible for bringing Kong to life on screen. O'Brien evolved and perfected the technique of stop-motion animation, in which small, inanimate figures are made to move by photographing successive stages of their movement a frame at a time.

In 1934, Mexico and Mexicans were the subject of the first live-action short film, *La Cucaracha* (RKO), made in the new three-strip Technicolor process.

Eduardo Cansino (Rita Hayworth's father) and his family of Spanish dancers would quite often work for the studios by choreographing and performing Spanish and Mexican dance sequences in films. They owned and operated a dance school in Hollywood and performed in nightclubs.

Carlos Alvarado, brother of actor Don Alvarado, became an agent in Hollywood handling Hispanic talent almost exclusively, founding his own agency in 1943. Hispanic talent found it virtually impossible to find decent representation, for the talent agencies did not want performers of Latin heritage on a full-time basis. But if a studio needed a Latin actor, they would call Alvarado.

Brother Don, meanwhile, also known as Don Page, went on to become an assistant director at Warner Bros., and worked on such films as *East of Eden* (1955), *Auntie Mame* (1958), and *The Old Man and the Sea* (1958).

George Herrera was one of the founders of the Screen Extras Guild, while his brother Joe at first found employment as Errol Flynn's bodyguard during the 1940s and then, because of his association with Flynn, appeared in such Flynn films as *Objective, Burma!* (1945) and *San Antonio* (1945).

Bill Travilla won an Academy Award for Best Costume Design for 1949 for his work on *The Adventures of Don Juan* with Errol Flynn, and later designed many of the dresses worn by Marilyn Monroe in her films. Al Ybarra, a longtime Hollywood art director, has to his credit such notable films as *The High and the Mighty* (1954) and *The Alamo* (1960).

Famed guitarist Vicente Gomez tutored many Hollywood stars when they were required to play a guitar on camera.

In a little-known interlude between his early days as an avant-garde filmmaker in pre-Franco Spain and his more mainstream but substantial participation in the fledgling Mexican film industry, the brilliant writer/director Luis Bunuel worked as a dubbing producer at Loews, dubbing films for MGM. From 1941 to 1944 he worked in the film department at the Museum of Modern Art (MoMA) in New York City, and for another year he supervised Spanish dubbing of American films at Warner Bros. in Los Angeles.

The Good Neighbor Policy

By the late 1930s and throughout the 1940s, an increasing number of Hispanic actors and actresses appeared in Latin-themed films. These were aimed at exploiting the South American film market when it became apparent to the Hollywood studios that the rumblings and then the actuality of war in Europe, beginning with the loss of Spain in 1936, would cut off the lucrative European market for American films. The Nazis in Germany seized and banned Hollywood films and applied political pressure against U.S. movies in neutral countries or countries that sympathized with the Nazis.

In 1933, the United States had signed a pact with Latin American countries ending the "gunboat diplomacy" long practiced by the United States to protect its interests in Latin America. This new pact was known as the Good Neighbor Policy; exchange programs were set up, and business ventures were encouraged.

Although Hollywood films dominated Latin America, the market had never been fully exploited. The Production Code Administration (PCA) in Hollywood regulated the content of movies, and until 1939 there was no miscegenation or inter-marriage allowed on screen. The Office of Coordinator of Inter-American Affairs, the PCA, and the Motion Picture Society for the Americas carefully scrutinized portrayals of Latins in Hollywood films between 1939 and 1948. Mexicans and/or Latin Americans during the period of the Good Neighbor Policy were, for screen purposes, considered white. The Department of State aided Hollywood by creating the Office of the Coordinator of Inter-American Affairs (CIAA) in October 1940. The CIAA opened its Motion Picture Division almost immediately, under the directorship of John Hay Whitney. Whitney's goal was to convince Hollywood to abandon the stereotyped bloodthirsty Latin American villains in its movies and instead to produce films with Latin American themes and locales. Having achieved this, he would use the material to neutralize propaganda flowing into Argentina, Brazil, and Chile from Axis wire services, features, newsreels, and documentaries. Whitney created the Newsreel Section for this purpose, and by 1943, the CIAA had shipped to South America more than 200 newsreels produced in cooperation with all the studios and newsreel services. On April 26, 1942, the *New York Times* commented that while "the bulk of these 16mm films will reach influential Latin American persons through U.S. embassies, the Latin public will see in regular Hollywood entertainment films more subject matter and scenic atmosphere of a special interest to them."

A select group of Hollywood producers went on a 10-week tour of Latin America and came back with many ideas that could be incorporated in future Hollywood productions. However, there was a problem: Hollywood movies with Latin subject matter had always been a source of controversy in Latin America because of the ignorance of the filmmakers about Latin America, its history, its people, and its culture. Latin Americans would not accept films in which they were characterized absurdly; their manners, attitudes, and expressions were altogether neglected; their arts and folklore, native music and dances, grotesquely deformed; their environment not even considered. More insultingly, these "gringo fiascos" were presented as typical of the particular country being portrayed. Though successful in the States, these films were disasters in the countries whose spirit they only half-heartedly attempted to reproduce.

Orson Welles was sent by RKO to Brazil to make a documentary film that would foster cultural harmony between the Americas. *It's All True!* remained unfinished when RKO had a change in administration and abandoned Welles and the project.

Latin American populations reacted to these Hollywood films in many different ways. Many of the films were poorly attended or banned outright. Some nations made official protests, and many people openly demonstrated their disgust. In Argentina, for example, people rioted and threw stones at the theaters showing *Argentine Nights* (1940).

While most of these Hollywood concoctions were unpopular in Latin America, a number of films stand out for their effective use of regional dialect, Latin themes, and popular Latin American actors and musicians.

With *The Mark of Zorro* (1940), for example, Twentieth Century–Fox shrewdly dubbed the movie in six Spanish dialects (Mexican, Argentinian, Chileno [Chile], Venezuelan, Cuban, and the Castilian of Spain) to match the kind of Spanish spoken in each of the principal South American nations in order to win over more completely that market. The film was a major hit in Latin America, making Tyrone Power an idol south of the border.

In 1941, Walt Disney and his staff made a goodwill trip to Latin America, and a year later hundreds of sketches, photographs, and film recordings were reworked into a part-animated, part-live action travelogue called *Saludos Amigos*. The film was initially released in Latin America, where it was one of the few Hollywood films to enjoy wide acceptance and success.

Laurel and Hardy appeared to great acclaim at the Mexico City Film Festival in April 1941 as guests of President Manuel Avila Camacho. As mentioned earlier, their films continued to be very popular in Spain and Latin America.

MGM served up its own brand of Latin American flavor by hiring Xavier Cugat and his Orchestra and including them in many musicals of the day. Spanish pianist Jose Iturbi and singers Lina Romay and Carlos Ramirez were among other Latin performers featured in such MGM films of the period as *Bathing Beauty* (1944), *Music for Millions* (1944), and *Holiday in Mexico* (1946).

Paramount Pictures put Arturo De Cordova under contract. De Cordova was a Mexican actor of great stature who made his debut with an important role as Augustin in *For Whom the Bell Tolls* (1943). Olga San Juan, a Brooklyn-born Puerto Rican singer, became Paramount's answer to Carmen Miranda and was featured in a few musical/comedies. In *Blue Skies* (1946), San Juan danced with Fred Astaire in the torrid "Heat Wave" number. At Universal, Maria Montez, from the Dominican Republic, had a short reign as the Queen of the Technicolor Epics. Montez played Arabian beauties and native island girls, but rarely did she play a Latina.

Down Argentine Way (1940) is notable for being the first in a series of Technicolor musicals at Fox that utilized Latin backgrounds and themes. It also introduced Carmen Miranda, the "Brazilian Bombshell," to the movies. The combination of Betty Grable, Don Ameche, Cesar Romero, and Miranda proved to be unbeatable at the box office. The simple scripts placing an American in a Latin American locale were loaded with amusing situations (usually of the "fish-out-of-water" variety) and sumptuous musical numbers interspersed with stock location footage.

As a result of the American entry into World War II and the Good Neighbor Policy, Hollywood filmmakers began to seriously consider including Americans of Mexican or Spanish descent in dramatic motion pictures. The concept of the Mexican American was introduced in the action war movies produced during World War II. After all, as many as 500,000 Hispanics served in World War II, with 53,000 from Puerto Rico alone. Twelve Hispanics were awarded the Congressional Medal of Honor; this represented one of the highest proportions of any ethnic group.

These films, based on actual wartime incidents or battles, would often revolve around plot lines utilizing an ethnically balanced platoon or squad that represented a cross section of the U.S. population. The typical movie squad would have a hardened veteran sergeant leading a group of men, one from Brooklyn, either Italian or Irish, one from the Midwest, one from the South, one from California, and one from Chicago. The Mexican American began to be integrated into this group in such films as *Bataan* (1943), *Bombadier* (1943), *Guadalcanal Diary* (1943), and *Battleground* (1949).

This period also saw the further development of the Hispanic American actor in Hollywood, in particular the acceptance of stars like Cesar Romero, Rita Hayworth, Anthony Quinn, and Pedro Armendariz. They had no accents, were either born or raised in the United States, and portrayed ethnically diverse roles including American types. Rita Hayworth, in particular, became the epitome of the "All-American Girl" during the war years, and she married the "All-American Boy Genius" of American film, Orson Welles.

By 1944, Hollywood's foreign market had shrunk quite drastically. Realizing that the war would soon end but that it would be quite a few years before Europe would regain any kind of economic strength, Hollywood decided it would continue to exploit the Latin American market, avoiding many past difficulties by actually filming in Latin America and utilizing some of the stars of the Mexican cinema.

During the war years, the Mexican cinema had developed and bloomed into an industry to rival Hollywood. In 1943, Gilbert Johnson of Atlas Theaters opened two movie houses in New York City's Times Square to show Mexican movies. These movies were reviewed by the *New York Times* and *Variety* on a regular basis.

Mexican films gained serious attention both in the States and internationally for their unique style and visual expression, which reflected Mexican culture and history. This was best represented in the work of director Emilio Fernandez and cameraman Gabriel Figueroa. In many ways these films were the inspiration for what, in the 1980s, became known as the Chicano cinema. Mexican movies of the period helped to give a cultural identity to many Mexicans and Mexican Americans.

Maria Candelaria (1943), starring Dolores Del Rio and Pedro Armendariz, won the grand prize at the 1946 Cannes Film Festival. That same year, *Flor Silvestre* (1943) won at Locarno, and *La Perla* (1945) won at San Sebastian in 1946. (All three films were directed and photographed by Fernandez and Figueroa, respectively.)

In 1946, RKO Studios helped build Churubusco Studios in Mexico City, which became the leading state-of-the-art film production facility in Latin America. Many American films produced by RKO, set against exotic or Mexican backgrounds, utilized the Churubusco facilities.

Pedro Armendariz, one of the biggest stars in Mexican cinema, was put under contract by Mary Pickford of United Artists in 1945 and was immediately pressed into service in Hollywood films by director John Ford. Armendariz first worked with Ford in Mexico on *The Fugitive* (1947), starring Henry Fonda. Armendariz played a military officer in pursuit of a priest on the run in an anticlerical Central American country. The cast also included Dolores Del Rio, Leo Carrillo, Chris-Pin Martin, and Rafael Inclan. The cinematographer was Gabriel Figueroa, and Emilio Fernandez was the associate producer. *The Fugitive* became the first truly Mexican American co-production, combining the best talents on both sides of the border and, in the process, crossing artistic and cultural as well as geographic boundaries.

In August 1946, Tyrone Power and Cesar Romero were sent on a goodwill tour of Latin America by Twentieth Century–Fox which was a resounding success. They were mobbed wherever they went and were hosted by such dignitaries as Juan and Evita Peron.

In 1991, Cesar Romero talked to Luis Reyes about the tour: "The studio provided us with this twin engine beechcraft which we named *Saludos Amigos*. Tyrone did all the flying, because he'd been a Marine pilot during the war. We flew down through Mexico, then Central America, and all of South America except for Venezuela. We hit every capital city.

"The first person we had to meet [wherever we landed] was the American ambassador, and nine times out of ten times he would arrange a meeting with the president of the country. The most amusing was when we had lunch with the Perons in Buenos Aires, Argentina.

"Evita was a very attractive lady who never stopped talking. Talk, talk, talk, all the time. The others on the trip didn't speak Spanish, so I generally acted as interpreter. Juan was a very serious, quiet man who said 'Yes' to everything Evita said.

"I was sitting next to Evita during the luncheon, and she said to me, 'Why do the people in your country call my husband a dictator? He is not a dictator, he is a patriot.' She turned to her husband and said, 'Is not that right, Juan? You're not a dictator,' and he said, 'Yes, my dear.' She told me and Tyrone [Power] over dinner, 'You're fortunate, because in America they treat movie stars right. Here they spit at them. I should know. I was an artist. Would you like to see one of my movies? I can arrange a showing at the national theater.'

"Right then and there Juan said, 'My dear Evita, I'm sure that the last thing they want to do is go to the movies.' I'm sure that if Darryl F. Zanuck had offered her a contract she would have left Juan."

The Good Neighbor Policy began to fade when the war ended in 1945. By 1948, with the approaching recovery of the European market and with a backlog of American films waiting to be seen by European audiences, Latin America began to be deemphasized, and starting with *The Treasure of the Sierra Madre* (1948), the bandit figure and many of the old stereotypes began slowly to reappear. It became production as usual at the studios, and the tried-and-true formulas began to be recycled with some minor adjustments. Some actors were able to make the transition into better roles. Pedro Armendariz, for example, worked not only in his native Mexico but also in U.S. and European productions. Others, though, became bound by rigid typecasting and found it difficult to keep a diverse career going. Some, like Arturo De Cordova, who did not meet with wide audience acceptance even after starring with Joan Fontaine in the big-budget *Frenchman's Creek* (1944), left Hollywood and became big stars in the Spanish-speaking cinema, where they commanded huge salaries and were able to portray a wide variety of roles.

The Post-World War II Period

Mexican Americans who settled primarily in California and the Southwest during the Mexican Revolution had earned their U.S. citizenship with their own lives and the lives of their sons who had fought and in many cases died in World War II. Many Mexican Americans, however, still had memories of unjust harassment during the Zoot Suit riots in Los Angeles in the early days of the war and the racism that still prevailed back home. The nation's urban centers began teeming with new immigrants as a migration took place along the East Coast. Puerto Ricans, who are racially mixed Spanish-speaking American citizens from the Caribbean, were arriving in New York City, Newark, Boston, and farther west in Chicago in search of jobs and a better way of life.

Overseas, the Marshall Plan was instituted to help Europe get back on its feet economically. In 1948 President Harry S. Truman desegregated the U.S. Armed Forces. In the cinema, meanwhile, the European neorealist films, growing out of the sobering nihilism of the war, began to show the physical and psychological damage the violence of war inflicts on people.

Hollywood began to reflect some of these changes. A harder-looking, pseudo-documentary style of filmmaking began to emerge, and more difficult subject matter was tackled. Movies such as *The Best Years of Our Lives* (1946), *Gentleman's Agreement* (1947), *Broken Arrow* (1950), *The Men* (1950, aka *Battle Stripe*), and others dealt with such topics as war-traumatized veterans adjusting to civilian life, anti-Semitism, racial prejudice, paraplegic veterans, and the plight of the American Indian.

John Huston and many of his fellow Hollywood directors, including George Stevens, Frank Capra, and John Ford, were changed by the war, and this change was reflected in their postwar work.

Even the traditional heroes began to show darker, more complex sides, beginning with Bogart's Fred C. Dobbs character in Huston's *The Treasure of the Sierra Madre* (1948). Jimmy Stewart's easygoing Mr. Smith persona changed to the hard-nosed, vengeful, near antiheroes of *Winchester '73* (1950) and *Bend of the River* (1952). John Wayne showed a darker side as ruthless cattle baron Tom Dunson in *Red River* (1948). James Cagney played Cody Jarrett, a small-time gangster with a psychological mama fixation, in *White Heat* (1949).

The Treasure of the Sierra Madre (1948) signaled the end of the Good Neighbor Policy by both the reintroduction of Hispanic stereotypes and the reintroduction of location filming, largely abandoned since the silents, utilizing real-life Mexican landscapes and people. (Another movie, *The Naked City*, made the same year in New York City, also helped popularize the location shoot, which was aided by the development during the war of lighter camera equipment.)

Because of economic advantages, technical capabilities (RKO's Churubusco Studios in Mexico City, for example), and scenic locations, many Hollywood productions were filmed in Mexico in the late 1940s and throughout the 1950s. The areas of wide desert expanse proved irresistible to western filmmakers. Some of the films shot in Mexico include *Captain from Castile* (1947), *Blowing Wild* (1953), *Garden of Evil* (1954), *Vera Cruz* (1954), *Bandido* (1956), and *The Wonderful Country* (1959). This surge of film production in Mexico provided employment and long-term experience for Mexican and Hispanic American actors and technicians.

Several films, including *The Lady from Shanghai* (1948), *The Big Steal* (1949), *The Brave Bulls* (1951), and *The Bullfighter and the Lady* (1951), illustrated a progressive and modern image of Mexico. They featured contemporary Mexico City, Acapulco, and Taxco as story backdrops.

The western was transferred to two South American locales, Brazil for *The Americano* (1955), starring Glenn Ford, and Argentina for *Way of a Gaucho* (1952), starring Rory Calhoun.

Films made during the 1950s and early 1960s that brought a new consciousness of the Hispanic American as part of contemporary American society include *Border Incident* (1949), *The Lawless* (1950), *Right Cross* (1950), *My Man and I* (1952), *The Ring* (1952), *Salt of the Earth* (1954), *Blackboard Jungle* (1955), *Giant* (1956), *The Man from Del Rio* (1956), *Man in the Shadow* (1957), *Cry Tough* (1959), and *West Side Story* (1961).

Hispanic American veterans and older Hispanic civil rights organizations such as the League of United Latin American Citizens (LULAC) struggled for first-class citizenship through a policy of assimilation. By the 1950s, Hollywood had taken up the issues of racial injustice through "social problem" movies, though by the early 1960s and with the impact of rock 'n' roll the industry had shifted to an almost exploitive focus on juvenile delinquents. Warner Bros. had in fact pioneered social problem films as early as the 1930s, but *Bordertown* (1935) starring Paul Muni was one of the few sympathetic portraits of Mexican Americans made in that period.

Meanwhile, an older generation of Latino stars was passing from the screen, or becoming relegated to secondary character roles. Along with the dependable screen heroes of yesteryear like John Wayne, Clark Gable, and Humphrey Bogart, a new screen hero emerged. He was young, brooding, and vulnerable, and took the form of Marlon Brando, Montgomery Clift, and James Dean.

The successors of Latino stars such as Cesar Romero and Dolores Del Rio—actors like Ricardo Montalban and Rita Moreno—were never able to achieve quite the same stature or access to starring roles as their predecessors.

The Senorita and the Spitfire

The images of the Hispanic woman seem to divide into two types, the virginal senorita and the loose Latin spitfire. They are extensions of their Anglo counterparts, the fair-haired, virginlike Lillian Gish or Doris Day, and the vamp, a more voluptuous, and sultry figure, who, in the cases of Mae West or Marilyn Monroe, is also saucily independent. In their own way, these stereotypes are as stylized within American drama as the ritualistic characters in a Japanese Noh play.

The senorita is an extension of the virgin (indeed, the word implies virginity), and has long been a staple of Hollywood westerns and costume dramas. The sexually alluring and available spitfire (in other words, "the fallen woman") is the vamp. Both types were played alternately by such stars as Dolores Del Rio and Lupe Velez at the start of their careers and continued into and throughout the sound period.

Such characterizations caused actress Rita Cansino to toil for years in Hollywood B movies until she was cosmetically stripped of her ethnicity and became the all-American Rita Hayworth.

Maria Castenada, who achieved brief popularity when known as Movita, played a native girl in MGM's 1935 production of *Mutiny on the Bounty*. She went on to play assorted Polynesians, Indians, and Mexican types for the rest of her career.

To make matters worse, these roles were often played not by Latinas, but by Anglo actresses such as Linda Darnell, who in *The Mark of Zorro* (1940) played a senorita, and in *My Darling Clementine* (1946) played a Latin spitfire.

Because of Roosevelt's Good Neighbor Policy, more and more Latin actresses appeared on American screens, but they were usually limited to senorita or spitfire roles. For example, as she matured, Lupe Velez was forced into the "hot tamale" or Mexican-wildcat type in the popular *Mexican Spitfire* series at RKO. Brazilian Carmen Miranda with her dancing, cute accent, and wild fruits and banana costumes reached the epitome of the caricature of Latin women as hip-swinging, fractured-English-speaking, dizzy sex objects.

Another Hispanic actress who dominated the industry in the 1940s was Maria Montez. Born in the Dominican Republic, she starred in a series of extravagant Technicolor adventure films at Universal that exploited her undeniable sexuality and exotic beauty. However, typically, she too was limited to the roles of senorita and vamp, playing native girls and Arabian princesses.

In sum, Hispanic actresses could find plenty of work in films but only as part of a parade of hip-swinging, finger-snapping, raven-haired Marias and Rositas. There also developed the all-knowing "suffering mother" or jovial mamacita.

Such female stereotyping was not exclusive to Hispanics, however. Jane Darwell made a career out of such roles, one of her most famous portrayals being the mother in *The Grapes of Wrath* (1940), for which she won an Oscar. Hattie McDaniel, a black actress, usually played the mammy, housekeeper, or maid, a role which won her an Academy Award for *Gone with the Wind* (1939). As McDaniel commented, "It's better to get $7,000 a week for playing a servant than $7 a week for being one" (article on Hattie McDaniel by Eleanor Traylor in *Dictionary of American Negro Biography* [New York: Norton, 1982]).

Latinas were (and still are) portrayed as subservient to men and victims of male Hispanic and Anglo violence. They often betrayed their Hispanic men (who were depicted as wicked, violent, and stupid) when shown the error of their ways by the Anglo hero with whom they had fallen in love. At the film's end, the Anglo hero would ride off into the sunset with the promise that he would be back. But the audience, and the Latina, knew that once over the border, he would forget her and fall into the arms of his fair-haired Anglo girlfriend. Or, in another variation, the Latina would conveniently die.

Jennifer Jones as Pearl Chavez in *Duel in the Sun* (1946) is perhaps one of the strongest Latin-woman characterizations ever presented in a Hollywood film. Pearl is strong willed, a fully realized multidimensional character who is a virtual life force around whom the story revolves. There were a number of Hispanic actresses who could have played the role, but Jones was the producer's choice. Several years later, Mexican actress Katy Jurado impressed audiences with her striking features and acting ability as Helen Ramirez in *High Noon* (1952), and then was nominated for an Academy Award as Best Supporting Actress for her role as an Indian woman in *Broken Lance* (1954), opposite Spencer Tracy. Along with Jurado, Maria Elena Marques and Sarita Montiel appeared in several major Hollywood films.

Even though they played diverse roles in their native countries, Mexican actresses, no matter how talented, were relegated to roles as Indian squaws, beautiful senoritas, or spitfires in Hollywood films. This was true even as late as the 1960s. For example, after leaving Hollywood and becoming Mexico's first lady of the cinema, Dolores Del Rio returned to the States after a long absence to play Elvis Presley's Indian mother in *Flaming Star* (1960) and then played the dignified Cheyenne matriarch Spanish Woman in *Cheyenne Autumn* (1964).

Actress Rita Moreno captured critical attention as Tuptim in the celebrated movie version of the Broadway musical *The King and I* (1956) and won an Oscar as Best Supporting Actress for her portrayal of Anita in *West Side Story* (1961). Success was a double-edged sword, however.

An Oscar usually assures an actress a choice of the best roles and financial security. However, Moreno, a Puerto Rican, did not work in movies for seven years after winning her Oscar because she refused to continue accepting roles she felt were demeaning and artistically limiting. Her richly comic portrayal of Googie Gomez in *The Ritz* (1976) is a biting satire of all the roles she (and other talented Latinas) had to play at the beginning of their careers.

More recently, Mexican actress Elpidia Carrillo has become the all-purpose victimized native Latin girl in a series of major motion pictures in which she appeared opposite some of the world's most important leading men, beginning with *The Border* in 1982 starring Jack Nicholson. Elizabeth Pena played a sexually liberated, tough-talking maid in *Down and Out in Beverly Hills* (1986). Argentine actress Norma Aleandro, who first drew U.S. attention in 1985 in *The Official Story* (which won an Oscar for Best Foreign Language Film), was nominated for an Academy Award as Best Supporting Actress in *Gaby—A True Story* (1987), in which she played a Mexican Indian maid. Aleandro went on to other important roles in Hollywood films, as did sexy Brazilian Sonia Braga in *The Milagro Beanfield War* (1988) and *Moon over Parador* (1988). Madeleine Stowe played a very positive and modern Hispanic American woman as Maria McGuire in *Stakeout* (1987).

Luis Valdez's *La Bamba* (1987), the first major film of the Chicano cinema to achieve mainstream box-office success, has made the most dramatic statement about Hispanic women.

Connie Valenzuela (Rosana De Soto) is the all-suffering noble mother who watches over her family. De Soto brought to life a character with many complexities who, as the head of her family, has to work and keep her two boys, Ritchie (Lou Diamond Phillips) and Bob (Esai Morales), in line. Connie loves and defends her sons and is there with Ritchie through his first triumphs, taking an active part in his success. The record producer who wants to sign Ritchie assumes she is a simple Spanish woman and asks, "Habla Ingles?" She replies, "We speak business."

Rosie (Elizabeth Pena) in *La Bamba,* on the other hand, is a much darker character who starts out being the virginal senorita to Ritchie but is more attracted to his older brother, Bob. She runs off with Bob and becomes pregnant by him, becoming a victim of her own cultural upbringing in a cycle she is never likely to break.

Rosana De Soto has gone on to play a variety of characters such as Dustin Hoffman's Jewish wife in *Family Business* (1989) and a Klingon princess in *Star Trek IV: The Voyage Home* (1986).

In August 1992, a group of Hispanic American actresses in Los Angeles were outraged when it was announced that Laura San Giacomo would be cast in the role of Mexican artist Frida Kahlo in a film biography called *Frida and Diego* opposite Raul Julia as acclaimed Mexican muralist Diego Rivera. They were outraged because they had not been given the chance to audition and were effectively being blocked from access to this major leading role. When director Luis Valdez was reportedly told by the producers that a recognizable star name was required, they were harking back to an established Hollywood mind-set that prevented Hispanic actors and actresses from finding stardom or leading roles for years. But, the actresses figured, who was Laura San Giacomo before her sensational 1989 film debut in *sex, lies and videotape?*

New Line Cinema pulled out of its financing agreement on the film, which has yet to be made, just prior to the negative publicity. Writer/director Luis Valdez issued a press release that said in part: "Art is not a question of affirmative action. It is an affirmation of one's belief in human universality. I will not be intimidated into making my vision of America coincide with whatever is politically correct at the moment. I have helped to define the Latino identity in America through my plays and films, but I will not be coerced into limiting my artistic choices in violation of basic human principles. My social objective has always been to counteract racism in the world, not reinforce it." However, the actresses were protesting not Valdez's choice for the role, but the fact that the movie industry continues to block Latinas from even trying out for roles they are clearly ethnically as well as technically equipped to handle. Their point was that they were striving for equality of opportunity in the casting process, not guaranteed success.

Along with Hispanic actors such as Andy Garcia, Raul Julia, Hector Elizondo, Jimmy Smits, and others, Hispanic actresses are bit by bit managing to find nonstereotypical leading roles. Examples include Maria Conchita Alonso's immigrant Bloomingdale's shopgirl in Paul Mazursky's *Moscow on the Hudson* (1984), Elizabeth Pena as the sensuous Jezzie in *Jacob's Ladder* (1990); and Evelina Fernandez as a struggling single mother in the barrio in *American Me* (1992). Rachel Ticotin plays Melina, a Martian mystery woman, in the science fiction film *Total Recall* (1990), and played an Assistant U.S. Attorney on the television series "Ohara." Madeleine Stowe, of Costa Rican background, plays a Latin woman in *Revenge* (1990) and an English woman in Revolutionary War America in *The Last of the Mohicans* (1992). And let's not forget Rosie Perez's memorably feisty New York Latina in *White Men Can't Jump* (1992), who not only proves she is smart and determined enough to realize her dream, but remains true to herself even at the cost of abandoning her Anglo lover, a fascinating reversal of roles from the days when the Anglo hero rode off into the sunset, leaving his Latina dalliance in favor of the Anglo blonde who had been "waiting for him to come to his senses."

Coming of Age

North American Latino culture is not homogeneous. It is divided by nationality, class, geographical area, and degrees of assimilation. The three principal Latino groups in the United States are Mexicans, Puerto Ricans, and Cubans. There is also a growing population of immigrants from Spanish-speaking Caribbean islands, such as the Dominican Republic and Dominica, but they have not as yet been much recognized by Hollywood.

The coming of age of Hispanic Americans in the Hollywood motion picture industry is tied to the way Hispanic Americans have evolved as a part of American society. Their role and growing visibility in mainstream American society is being defined and reflected partly in cinematic terms. Most of the progressive work in this area has been initiated by independent filmmakers in such films as Jesus Trevino's *Raices de Sangre* (*Blood Roots*) (1979) and Robert Young's *Alambrista!* (1978) and *The Ballad of Gregorio Cortez* (1983). Other works, such as *Stand and Deliver* (1988, financed by PBS, released by Warner Bros.) and Robert Redford's *The Milagro Beanfield War* (1988, initiated by producer Moctezuma Esparza and financed and distributed by Universal) have come to fruition through a curious mixture of both independent and studio financing.

Considering the abundance of American films dealing with war, most, sadly, have overlooked the participation of the Hispanic American. Even in the Vietnam era the only exceptions are Oliver Stone's *Platoon* (1986), which had minor Hispanic characters in platoon members Rhah (Francesco Quinn) and Rodriguez (Chris Castillejo); Stanley Kubrick's *Full Metal Jacket* (1987), which featured one Hispanic Marine recruit (Sal Lopez); and Sidney J. Furie's *The Boys in Company C* (1978), which featured a Hispanic Marine drill instructor played by Santos Morales, although none of the recruits were Hispanic. The reality is that 13 Hispanics won Congressional Medals of Honor for service in Vietnam.

Taylor Hackford's *An Officer and a Gentleman* (1982), a romantic service drama about Top Gun pilots starring Richard Gere and Debra Winger, featured a multiethnic cast including Tony Plana as a recruit named De La Serra, whose character represented a minor breakthrough in that he was depicted as an intelligent, mainstream American rather than as a dim-witted working-class migrant worker, an artisan, or a thieving gang member.

As the 1960s progressed, the civil rights movement, led by African Americans, also encouraged other disenfranchised or ignored groups, such as women and Hispanic Americans, to recognize their own unsatisfactory condition. A rediscovery and reexamination of America's heritage began to take place as seen through the eyes of groups who had been either left out of the history books or relegated to a minor, often stereotyped role. Colleges and universities established black, Chicano, and Puerto Rican studies programs that filtered down to the high school level.

Out of this period of political unrest and great social movements came funding for public television and education-related programs, many of which were specifically designed to meet the needs of ethnic minorities. Young Hispanic Americans with an interest in the arts, education, and communication were able to use their talents to explore social consciousness. Forms of self-expression and -awareness manifested themselves through street-culture murals that popped up in barrios across the country, while *centro culturales* (cultural centers) began to be formed along with theater groups like El Teatro Campesino, El Teatro de la Esperanza, and the Puerto Rican Traveling Theatre. At public television stations, aspiring filmmakers gained access to 16mm cameras and equipment and set about recording the events of the day as they affected their communities, and produced documentaries about Hispanic American life in the United States.

In 1969, Nosotros (the Spanish word for "we, the people"), a Hispanic actors' organization, was formed in Hollywood by Ricardo Montalban, Richard Hernandez, Val DeVargas, Rudolfo Hoyos, Jr., Carlos Rivas, Tony DeMarco, and Henry Darrow.

Anthony Quinn, Gilbert Roland, and Ricardo Montalban at Nosotros Awards, 1980

Photo courtesy Satir Gonzalez

The organization is dedicated to improving the image of Hispanic Americans and Spanish-speaking peoples in general in movies, television, theater, and radio. The group also seeks to improve opportunities for Hispanic performing artists through training and workshops. At great personal cost to their careers, these few individuals, led by Ricardo Montalban, confronted studio heads, network heads, producers, and writers and urged them to reevaluate the problems of stereotypical depictions of Hispanics. These meetings and discussions came to a head when the Frito Bandito television commercials began to be broadcast in 1970.

The commercials had a stereotypical sombreroed and mustached cartoon bandit stealing corn chips. They were so offensive that various Mexican American communities and their leaders rallied around Nosotros and forced the advertiser to abandon the campaign. As Nosotros president Ricardo Montalban commented in an interview with Luis Reyes: "Why couldn't the cartoon have been the Frito Amigo, who gave the chips away instead of the negative image of the bandido who steals?" Perhaps there was such an outcry from the Latino community because the negative Frito Bandito image was directed toward children. The controversy focused national attention on the preponderance of negative, stereotypical images of Hispanics in the media. Hispanic American children had too few role models and on top of that were being fed negative images without any positive Hispanic images to balance them. Furthermore, the negative stereotyping of Hispanics was being reinforced in Anglo children, condemning yet another generation to perpetuate a worsening problem.

Hispanic actors found themselves in a dilemma: by accepting negative roles in order to work, they were sacrificing personal dignity and artistic growth; but if they protested too loudly, they could be blacklisted by producers. Nevertheless, through Nosotros and community-based groups, pressure was applied to the entertainment industry, and small yet significant changes began to take place.

By the 1970s, the acclaimed work of Spanish filmmaker Luis Bunuel and the cinema of Castro's Cuba like *Lucia* (1969, but first shown in the States in 1972), directed by Humberto Solas, and *Memories of Underdevelopment* (1968, first shown in the States in 1973), directed by Tomas Gutierrez Alea, were penetrating the American progressive moviegoing consciousness, especially on college campuses and the art house circuit. Such films had a profound influence, inspiring a new generation of Hispanic American filmmakers.

This new generation has ushered in Chicano cinema, which it is necessary to define. A Chicano is a Mexican American whose consciousness was born out of the civil rights movement of the 1960s and who is aware of his or her dual heritage. To qualify as true Chicano cinema, a movie should

- concern itself with Mexican American subject matter;
- express a Mexican American viewpoint on life in the United States;
- contain principal characters who are Mexican American;
- have creative forces (director, writer, producer) who are predominantly Mexican American; and/or
- be a film that speaks from a personal and unique vision that stems from a political base.

Hispanic American cinema subscribes to the same basic criteria except that the term "Hispanic American" is an umbrella title that includes Chicano, Cuban, Puerto Rican, and all other Hispanic groups living in the United States. *Raices de Sangre* (1979), *Zoot Suit* (1981), *Seguin* (1982), *The Ballad of Gregorio Cortez* (1983), *El Norte* (1983), *Born in East L.A.* (1987), *La Bamba* (1987), *Stand and Deliver* (1988), *Break of Dawn* (1989), and *American Me* (1992) would all be considered Chicano cinema. All of these titles, plus *El Super* (1979) and *Crossover Dreams* (1985), would also be considered Hispanic American cinema.

As of 1993, Chicano cinema is just over 14 years old, and so is still in its formative stage. It has had a slow, somewhat isolated development and owes much of its existence to organizations like the Corporation for Public Broadcasting and private investors. Grants, funding sources, and community-supported public television have acted as the economic genesis for many of these independent works.

Latin-themed films, on the other hand, are films produced in Hollywood that have Latin characters or situations (set in or out of the United States), but whose stories are generally told through Anglo protagonists. The 1980s saw a number of these films produced, and they usually fell into the conventional genres of gang films, border stories, westerns, and war-torn banana republic stories. In Latin-themed films, there is usually no Hispanic involvement in the key creative film-making positions. Examples of recent Latin-themed films are *Under Fire* (1983), *Havana* (1990), *The Mambo Kings* (1992), and *Bound by Honor* (1993).

These films signify a difference in the way Hollywood looks at Hispanic Americans. As filmmakers, Hispanic Americans are creating and defining their own images rather than allowing themselves to be defined by someone else. *Stand and Deliver, Born in East L.A.,* and *La Bamba* all share the common theme of the reaffirmation of the promise of the American Dream.

While the burgeoning black filmmaking movement generated 20 feature films in 1991, the same year Hispanic Americans produced only one: the low-budget *Hangin' with the Homeboys,* written and directed by Joseph B. Vasquez, who, because of the color of his skin, is perceived by the media as black when in fact he is of Puerto Rican descent.

The political and economic strength of the Hispanic American community is only now starting to be recognized as a major force in American society, and the entertainment industry is slowly beginning to reflect those concerns in films and television.

Though films do not have the responsibility, they do have the capability to educate and provoke thought as well as to entertain. With the new developing technologies (videocassettes, laser discs, cable and digital computer imaging), images created on film and videotape will be with us long after those who created them are gone.

A new generation of Hispanic filmmakers is following the imprints of many Hispanics in Hollywood who paved the way by overcoming many still-existing obstacles of ignorance and racism. They will eventually free themselves and other Hispanic Americans from the bondage of stereotypical images, although they must be wary of creating new or updated versions of these cliches while painting the changing face of America in light and shadow as we move into the twenty-first century.

MOVIES

Boldface type indicates individuals included in the Biographies section.

Aaron Loves Angela (1975 Col)

D: Gordon Parks, Jr.
S: Gerald Sanford
P: Robert J. Anderson
Cast: Kevin Hooks, **Irene Cara**

Set in New York City, this Romeo and Juliet love story between an African-American boy from Harlem and a Puerto Rican girl from Spanish Harlem stars engaging young performers and ends happily, despite the obstacles.

Kevin Hooks, son of actor Robert Hooks, after a successful acting career, is now directing television and feature films. Irene Cara went on to score a big hit in the film *Fame,* in which she also sang and danced.

Jose Feliciano scored the music.

The Addams Family (1991 Par)

D: Barry Sonnenfeld
S: Caroline Thompson and Larry Wilson
P: Scott Rudin
Cast: **Raul Julia**, Anjelica Huston, Christopher Lloyd

Based on the darkly humorous cartoons drawn by Charles Addams that were featured in *The New Yorker* magazine from the 1930s to the 1980s. This extended family of freaks and misfits caught the imagination of the American public when 64 half-hour films were produced as a series for ABC Television in 1964–1966 with John Astin playing the role of Gomez.

This film is a curious entry because it was a major studio-produced hit film whose leading male character, named Gomez, is played by actor Raul Julia in a flamboyant style. Gomez is an exotic romantic swashbuckler with his slicked-back hair, near-pencil-thin mustache, and trademark cigars. He fences with his accountant, wears satin and velvet smoking jackets, and is wildly in love with his wife, Morticia, and his family. Gomez backflips through windows, dances, and stages massive train wrecks with his toy locomotives. He tends to fly through life blinded by his own enthusiasm, which at times gets him in trouble. "Raul Julia plays Gomez as a Chivalrous Caballero," Patricia Dobson wrote in *Screen International* (11/21/91).

The plot concerns Gomez's yearning for the homecoming of his long-lost brother, Fester, and the arrival of someone who is a dead ringer for and claims to be Uncle Fester.

Adventure (1945 MGM)

D: Victor Fleming
S: Frederick Hazlitt Brennan and Vincent Lawrence, based on the novel by Clyde Brian Davis
P: Sam Zimbalist
Cast: Clark Gable, Greer Garson, Thomas Mitchell, **Lina Romay**, Tito Renaldo

Story of a romance between a rough-and-ready merchant seaman (Gable) and a librarian (Garson). The first ten minutes of the film take place in a port on the seacoast of Chile, where Gable has a brief romance with a native girl, Maria, played by Lina Romay, whom he leaves behind. Romay sings a couple of Spanish tunes.

The Adventurers (1970 Par)

  D: Lewis Gilbert
  S: Lewis Gilbert and Michael Hastings, based on the novel
     by Harold Robbins
  P: Lewis Gilbert
Cast: Bekim Fehmiu, Ernest Borgnine, Olivia de Havilland, **Fernando Rey**

Melodramatic potboiler about a Latin American ambassador's son (Yugoslavian actor Bekim Fehmiu), a jet-setting playboy who eventually returns to his native land to take revenge on the corrupt government official who raped and murdered his mother.

Although part of the film was shot in Colombia, Hispanics and Latins are noticeably absent except for Fernando Rey and thousands of Colombian extras. Brazilian Laurindo Almeida scored the music. The film subscribes to the banana republic in violent turmoil stereotype.

The Adventures of Don Juan (1949 WB)

  D: Vincent Sherman
  S: George Oppenheimer and Barry Kurnitz, based on a story
     by Herbert Dalmas
  P: Jerry Wald
Cast: Errol Flynn, Viveca Lindfors, Robert Douglas

Flynn comfortably played the role of the famous Latin lover Don Juan in this amusing Technicolor swashbuckler.

The movie was made with the usual Warner Bros. attention to accuracy and detail in costumes, sets, and props, though many were borrowed from the studio's previous historical outings.

Art director Edward Carrere designed one master set for the Madrid palace at Warner Bros. Studios in Burbank, California, with a floor area of 26,600 square feet. Mobile wall units were shifted to form backgrounds for 22 different sections of the palace.

The film won an Academy Award for Best Costume Design. Receiving it were Leah Rhodes, Marjorie Best, and a young Latino designer named Bill Travilla.

Concerned more with politics than tender passions, the film is about how Don Juan (Flynn) saves Queen Margaret (Lindfors) and the King (Romney Brent) from the treachery of the evil Duke de Lorca (Robert Douglas) in seventeenth-century Spain.

Don Juan has been the hero of many literary works and is supposedly modeled on the life of Don Juan Tenorio of Seville. Famous versions of his life include Tirso de Molina's *El Burlador de Sevilla*, Moliere's *Dom Juan*, and Mozart's opera *Don Giovanni*. Corneille, Dumas, Browning, and Shaw have also contributed their own chronicles of his life.

The basic story involves a Don Juan who seduces the daughter of the commander of Seville and kills her father in a duel. Then, while visiting the statue of the victim, he is seized by it and dragged off to hell.

Don Juan was previously filmed with great success in 1926 by Warner Bros., starring John Barrymore. The Flynn version met with only mild success in the United States but did tremendously well overseas, especially in Europe and South America. Neither version is true to the story's origins, however, as the screenplays were concocted to serve as swashbuckling vehicles for what the studio's stars did best.

Affair in Havana (1957 AA)

- D: Laslo Benedek
- S: Burton Lane and Maurice Zimm, based on a story by Janet Green
- P: Richard Goldstone
- Cast: John Cassavetes, Sara Shane, Raymond Burr, Sergio Pena, Lilia Lazo, Celia Cruz, Jose Antonio Rivero

A young musician, Nick (Cassavetes), has an affair with Lorna (Shane), the wife of a paralyzed Cuban plantation owner, Mallabee (Burr, before his "Ironside" TV series days). Mallabee is drowned by a man-servant (Pena), long infatuated with Lorna, and the man-servant's wife (Lazo) proceeds to avenge Mallabee by knifing Lorna. Nick returns to his piano playing.

This dreary melodramatic film relies on the scenic beauty of Cuba and its Afro-Cuban music, which is highlighted in a fiesta sequence featuring some of Cuba's best musical talents of the time, including famed singer Celia Cruz in one of her first film appearances. The film was produced by Dudley Pictures of Cuba as the first in a planned series of English-language films jointly financed through an agreement with the Agricultural and Industrial Development Bank of Cuba (BANFAIC), which set up a $1 million revolving fund. *Affair in Havana* was produced and filmed entirely on location in and around Havana and the resort town Varadero.

Alambrista! (1978 Filmhaus)

- D: Robert M. Young
- S: Robert M. Young
- P: Michael Hausman and Irwin W. Young
- Cast: **Domingo Ambriz, Trinidad Silva**

Alambrista! (Wirejumper) provides a gritty and realistic look at the lonely and frightening encounters of Roberto (Ambriz), an illegal Mexican farmworker in the United States.

The film won the Palme d'Or Award at Cannes for Best First Feature and the San Sebastian Film Festival Gran Concha de Oro award. It played numerous U.S. film festivals, even though it had been commissioned as part of the "Visions" Public Broadcasting Service series and had previously aired on public television in 1977. The project originated when Young was filming a documentary in Arizona on migrant farmworkers and their children.

It is a small, beautifully made film with many touching and amusing scenes that illustrate the human cost of illegal immigration, such as having to buy forged green cards, picking crops for meager earnings only to be run off by immigration officials just before payday, and coping with the fears and loneliness of being in a foreign country.

Domingo Ambriz as Roberto gives a brilliantly realized performance using body language and facial expressions to communicate what he is going through. Trinidad Silva as Joe, a farmworker, gives a Chaplinesque lesson to Roberto on how to act like a gringo.

In the last scene of the movie, a Mexican woman in the process of being deported by American authorities at a border crossing gives birth to a baby while still on the American side. She shouts hysterically, "He was born on American soil! He will need no papers," as Roberto watches from a bus that is returning him to Mexico.

Alambrista! had a limited U.S. art house release in 1979.

The Alamo (1960 UA)

D: John Wayne
S: James Edward Grant
P: John Wayne
AP: James Edward Grant
Cast: John Wayne, Richard Widmark, Laurence Harvey, Frankie Avalon, **Linda Cristal**, Richard Boone, Carlos Arruza

It took John Wayne over 12 years to bring his epic movie *The Alamo* to the screen. The movie centers around the historical conflict in March 1836 between 180 Texas settlers and the Mexican general Santa Anna's army. Against this historical canvas are woven the personal stories of the Alamo defenders, highlighted by the conflict over command between Col. Jim Bowie (Widmark) and Col. William Travis (Harvey). Wayne starred as Davy Crockett and directed and produced the film.

In 1951 Wayne received script approval for an Alamo movie from the Mexican government and permission from the Mexican craft unions to shoot in Mexico. The script for the final 1960 production, however, filmed in the United States, was vastly different from the original script, developed while Wayne was under contract to Republic Pictures. He parted company with Republic when the studio decided not to make the Alamo movie, and then in 1952 Republic president Herbert J. Yates rushed into production with *The Last Command* (1955), utilizing major elements from the original 1951 script.

Beginning in 1951, Wayne and Alfred Ybarra, art director for Wayne's company (first called Wayne-Fellows, then Batjac), searched for locations in Peru, Panama, and Mexico. Wayne and Ybarra could not find financing for the project, despite Wayne's box-office prominence, because of the film's projected high production costs and Wayne's insistence on directing the film. It eventually cost over $12 million to make.

In 1957, Happy Shahan's ranch in Brackettville, Texas, was chosen as a location. Financing was finally arranged with United Artists and several independent Texas businessmen.

Ybarra's set re-creating San Antonio and the Alamo mission combined authenticity, practicality, dramatic invention, and imagination. It took over a year to construct and eventually sprawled over 400 acres.

Filming took place from September through December 1959. Cinematographer William H. Clothier captured strikingly beautiful images and action sequences, some of which are the most exciting ever put on film.

James Edward Grant's script avoided the complexities of the real historical situation, however, and became a simplistic patriotic spectacle. Wayne did feature Tejano historical figures such as Juan Seguin, portrayed by Joseph Calleia, but they are not developed characters. Surprisingly, however, even though Santa Anna and his army are never personalized, they are treated as a dignified and gallant enemy. At one point in the film, one of the Alamo defenders says, "It sure is the prettiest army I ever did see," while another replies, "Don't be fooled, they've been putting down rebellions for over two years and have marched over a thousand miles."

Over 1,500 Mexican extras were used to represent Santa Anna's army, townspeople, and some Alamo defenders.

Spanish bullfighter Carlos Arruza portrayed Lt. Reyes, messenger for General Santa Anna. Linda Cristal, an Argentina-born actress, played a variation of the traditional Mexican senorita in her role as Flaca (Spanish for "skinny," although that's an unfair description of her), Crockett's love interest.

Flaca is landed, widowed, beautiful, and educated and it is ironic (because she is Mexican) that she becomes the one chosen by Crockett to help spread the word about the Alamo and the fight for freedom against tyranny.

Richard Widmark, Linda Cristal,
Laurence Harvey, and producer/director/
star John Wayne on the set of *The Alamo*.

Wayne's love of the Mexican people is well shown by Crockett's benevolent if paternalistic attitude toward Flaca and a young boy. In an introductory scene, Crockett helps Flaca avoid an unwanted suitor and insists that the boy be given a tip for carrying the suitor's luggage, despite the fact that Crockett carries both the luggage and the boy up the stairs.

In a letter reproduced in the *Hollywood Citizen News* dated November 11, 1960, Wayne wrote, "Because of my close friendship with many wonderful Mexicans and my honest love for the people of our neighbor country, . . . I knew that a great piece of drama could be told about this incident without in any way disparaging Mexico. Ours is a picture of heroics and within its chapters we have shown not only the bravery of its defenders but also of its attackers."

There are touching scenes of the Mexicans removing their dead from the battlefield and of Santa Anna permitting Mrs. Dickinson, a woman survivor, and her children to depart safely after all the Alamo defenders are killed.

It is worth noting, though, that the long-held myth of U.S. Manifest Destiny in foreign policy, with regard to Latin America in particular, and the idea that it takes many Mexicans to equal or best one Yankee, had their origins in the Alamo legend. Both are faithfully rendered in the movie, released when the cold war was at its height, and American involvement in Vietnam was just beginning.

In 1960, the Mexican government banned *The Alamo*, but this seems in no way to have hurt Wayne or his relationship with the Mexican government or film industry, which continued to support his filmmaking activities. Many of his later films were made in Durango, Mexico.

Alive (1993 T)

    D: Frank Marshall
    S: John Patrick Shanley
    P: Robert Watts and Kathleen Kennedy
 Cast: Vincent Spano, Ethan Hawke

Based on the true story of the Uruguayan rugby team whose plane crashed in the snow-covered Andes Mountains between Argentina and Chile in 1972. Of the 27 who lived through the crash, only 16 made it off the mountain. Those who survived had to resort to eating the dead in order to stay alive for the 72 days spent trying to get off the remote mountain site.

Alvarez Kelly (1966 Col)

    D: Edward Dmytryk
    S: Franklin Coen and Elliott Arnold, based on a story by Coen
    P: Sol C. Siegel
 Cast: William Holden, Richard Widmark, Janice Rule

In 1864 a group of American drovers and Mexican *vaqueros* led by Mexican Irish Alvarez Kelly (Holden) attempt to bring a herd of 5,000 cattle from Mexico to Virginia in order to feed Union Army forces during the Civil War but are intercepted by Confederate Army troops. This average western features Pepe Callahan, Roberto Contreras, and Pedro Regas.

American Me (1992 U)

    D: **Edward James Olmos**
    S: Desmond Nakano and Floyd Mutrux
    P: Sean Daniel, Robert M. Young, **Edward James Olmos**
 Cast: **Edward James Olmos**, William Forsythe, **Pepe Serna,**
        Evelina Fernandez, Sal Lopez, Danny De La Paz, Daniel Villarreal,
        Vira Montes

A brutal, relentless, unflinching, and grimly honest look at 30 years in the life of a Hispanic American family living in East Los Angeles, focusing on one of its members, Santana (Olmos), from teenager to adult caught in a vicious cycle of violence and imprisonment that consumes his soul.

Olmos not only stars and produces but makes a forceful theatrical feature film directorial debut with this harrowing documentarylike drama. *American Me* is a powerful, richly textured film that is both satisfying and disturbing.

Santana becomes a ruthless crime lord whose power over life and death emanates from his prison cell and extends to the streets. The movie is structured like a memoir, with Santana narrating his life as he contemplates old photographs while waiting for his shocking but inevitable death.

We meet Santana's ill-fated parents on the night of the 1943 Los Angeles Zoot Suit riots. American soldiers and sailors, fueled by racism and war hysteria, attack and brutally beat Santana's zoot-suited father, Pedro (Lopez), and rape his mother, Esperanza (Montes).

American Me then follows the youthful Santana and his friends J.D. and Mundo (Panchito Gomez, Steve Wilcox, and Richard Coca) through a long journey that begins with their first stay at juvenile hall (as a result of a show of machismo in which they cross a rival gang's turf and are forced to break into a restaurant to escape the gang's wrath) and the first of many murders, which leads to the maximum security cells at Folsom Prison.

Fifteen years later, they are grown men, still in Folsom Prison (and now played by Olmos, Forsythe, and Serna). Santana shrewdly gains power when he organizes the prisoners along racial lines in order to control illegal activities both in and out of prison. Three years later he is released from prison and finds himself ill at ease in the outside world. He is trying to pick up his life from where it was cut off at the age of 15.

There are no visible rewards for the criminal in this film; no money is ever seen, and Santana returns to live in the impoverished barrio neighborhood where he grew up. It is even his friend Mundo (which means "world" in Spanish) who causes Santana's demise.

Santana slowly begins to find his humanity as he tentatively develops a relationship with Julie (Fernandez), a single mother he meets at a fiesta. (It is, ironically, this late but welcome effort to change and do something positive with his life that proves to be Santana's downfall.) Julie represents the only glimmer of hope in the community as she tries to turn her life around by going back to school, but the boys in the neighborhood are involved in the same cycle of violence and drugs that first entrapped Santana. She is the only one who dares to tell him the truth: "You're nothing but a dope dealer," she tells him. "Your business kills kids."

The film failed to win over a large segment of the audience. Its characters and situation are not sympathetically portrayed, and the grim, violent nature of the piece kept audiences away except for the Chicano community and Olmos's fans, primarily in California and the Southwest, who showed up at the box office to the tune of $15 million.

Olmos dreamed of making *American Me* for 18 years, ever since he read the original script by Mutrux in 1974 when he played a bit part in Mutrux's *aloha, bobby and rose* (1975). *American Me* has a long history; at one point it was going to be filmed with Al Pacino, as a more romanticized, traditional prison drama. Pacino went on to play a Hispanic crime lord in *Scarface* (1983), and *American Me* languished. Edward James Olmos, the bit player, reached stardom over a 10-year period

Edward James Olmos—director, producer, and star of *American Me*.

beginning with his role in 1978 as El Pachuco in the acclaimed hit play *Zoot Suit*, followed by his Emmy award–winning performance as the sullen, no-nonsense Lt. Castillo in the television series "Miami Vice," culminating in his 1988 Oscar-nominated performance as the quirky math teacher Jaime Escalante in *Stand and Deliver.*

Ironically, as the years went by, the script for *American Me* grew more relevant as the problem of gang violence escalated. "A segment of our nation's youth is growing up in a self-perpetuating lifestyle spent in and out of prison, resulting in violent crime, drugs, and certain death," said Olmos to Luis Reyes in an interview. "*American Me* [was] made with the hope that the lives of some of the children will be redirected toward more positive goals."

The movie represents the largest gathering of Hispanic American talent in Hollywood, beginning with Olmos as star, director, and producer; Reynaldo Villalobos as director of photography; Joe Aubel, production designer; Sylvia Vega Vasquez, costume designer; Bob Morones, casting director; and Richard Espinoza, first assistant director. Among the ensemble cast, fine performances are given by Pepe Serna as Mundo, Evelina Fernandez as Julie, Sal Lopez as the father who carries unresolved pain and resentment, and Danny De La Paz as Puppet, a gang member who is torn between his loyalty to the crime syndicate and his love for the younger brother, Little Puppet (Villarreal), whom he must kill.

The filming locations included Folsom Prison, Chino Men's Institution, Los Angeles County Juvenile Hall, and areas of East Los Angeles. The Mercado, an outdoor market, brought Olmos back to a location that is on the doorstep of his boyhood home. On the backlot of Universal Studios, Hollywood, the New York street set was redesigned and redressed to stand in for downtown Los Angeles circa 1943 in the elaborate re-creation of the city's notorious Zoot Suit riots seen in the opening sequence of the film.

John Anderson in *Newsday* (3/13/92) said, "*American Me* is about death, not only of men but of dreams. A Chicano *Godfather,* it is about the violence men do and why they do it; how a criminal enterprise, born out of the need to protect one's own, grows beyond control; how once noble intentions are perverted by power and bring friends and brothers to betray each other."

David Elliot of the *San Diego Union* (3/13/92) commented, "Olmos has star power. His pitted face glows with macho presence lit well by Reynaldo Villalobos, and his tense aura of command is both creepy and sexy. He's like a deadlier, Mayan-faced Bogart."

However, in the *New York Times* (3/13/92) Janet Maslin said, "Violent as it is, *American Me* is seldom dramatic enough to bring its material to life."

The film is a journey to a place most audiences have never been and will probably, one hopes, never go.

The Americano (1955 RKO)

    D: William Castle
    S: Guy Trosper, based on an original story by Leslie T. White
    P: Robert Stillman
 Cast: Glenn Ford, Abbe Lane, Ursula Thiess, Frank Lovejoy, **Cesar Romero, Rudolfo Hoyos, Jr.**, Salvador Baguez

An American cowboy (Ford) is asked to deliver some Brahma bulls to a powerful, land-hungry rancher (Lovejoy) in Brazil. During his adventure Ford encounters rough terrain, bandidos, the rancher, and some lovely ladies.

Cesar Romero turned in a colorful performance as a bandit leader in this above-average western with a switch in locale (Brazil) and a good cast and Technicolor location footage.

Shooting began in 1953 with Glenn Ford, Cesar Romero, and Sarita Montiel. The cast and crew arrived in Brazil but a combination of bad weather and customs red tape made it nearly impossible to film there. By the time the weather cleared up and the equipment was finally released, Ford's contract had run out.

Director William Castle shot what footage he could and returned to Hollywood. Production resumed a year later when Ford was again available, but the rest of the film was shot at RKO and at a ranch in Riverside, California. Sarita Montiel could not return to the film and was replaced by Abbe Lane.

And Now Miguel (1966 U)

D: James B. Clark
S: Ted Sherdeman and Jane Klove, based on the award-winning
    novel by Joseph Krumgold
P: Robert B. Radnitz
Cast: Pat Cardi, Michael Ansara, **Pilar Del Rey**, Guy Stockwell, Clu Gulager

Story of a ten-year-old boy, Miguel Chavez (Cardi), coming of age in the American Southwest, filmed on location on a 23,000-acre ranch of one-time sheep-grazing land in the Chama River valley of New Mexico near the small town of Abiqui.

The Chavez family have been for generations successful sheepherders who live near the Sangre de Cristo Mountains in the high plateau country of north central New Mexico. Young Miguel's burning desire is to gain stature in his father's eyes so that he may accompany him to the mountains in the summertime with the herd. Miguel's father, Blas (Ansara), believes Miguel is too young to do a man's work. An itinerant sheepherder (Gulager) gives Miguel a chance to show what he can do. Miguel proves his courage and resourcefulness in the face of emergency when he has a chance encounter with a deadly snake and when he protects the herd from a pack of coyotes.

Ansara (a Lebanese American) personifies strength and dignity as the father, and received especially good notices for his work in the film. Good performances and outstanding Technicolor photography highlight this simple story that focuses on the Spanish Indian peoples of the American Southwest. The award-winning book and the film reveal sensitively, if somewhat idealistically, a little-known part of American life and culture to young moviegoing audiences.

Robert Radnitz made a name for himself producing family films such as *A Dog of Flanders* (1959), *Misty* (1961), and *Island of the Blue Dolphins* (1964). Radnitz's 1972 production, *Sounder,* a Depression-era story about a family of black share-croppers in the American South, was nominated for four Academy Awards including Best Picture.

The Appaloosa (1966 U)

D: Sidney J. Furie
S: James Bridges and Roland Kibbee, based on the novel
    by Robert MacLeod
P: Alan Miller
Cast: Marlon Brando, **Anjanette Comer, John Saxon, Emilio Fernandez,
    Miriam Colon, Rafael Campos**

Interesting, intense, but slow psychological western drama starring Marlon Brando as Matt Fletcher, a gringo saddle tramp who is determined to settle down and breed Appaloosa horses. He is thwarted in this desire when a magnificent Appaloosa stallion he plans to use as a stud is stolen from him by Mexican bandit Chuy Medina (Saxon).

He sets off across the Texas border to retrieve his horse from the bandit's stronghold in the Mexican village of Cocatlan. Medina subjects Fletcher to indignities and tests of strength, highlighted by an arm wrestling match. Matt retrieves the horse and heads back across the border with Medina in pursuit. In a climactic gun battle on a snow-covered mountain, Fletcher kills Medina. He and the horse ride off into the sunset.

Director Furie fills the screen with tables littered with tequila bottles, extreme close-ups of the bandits, moody landscapes, interiors, and sweaty faces. The film is full of stereotypes, from Mexican bandits to the noble peasant farmers to the fiery young senorita.

Trini is the archetypal fiery senorita, played by Anjanette Comer.

Beginning with his role in *The Appaloosa*, Emilio "El Indio" Fernandez (who plays the bandit Lazaro) portrayed despicable Mexican bandits and ruffians in a number of Hollywood films, but he had previously directed some classic Mexican films with beautifully stirring images of Mexico.

There are similarities to Brando's self-directed western *One-Eyed Jacks* (1961), particularly the theme of a loner on the trail of revenge. *One-Eyed Jacks*'s more romantic and civil view of Monterey and its citizens along with the strong portrayals by Katy Jurado and Pina Pellicer as mother and daughter give way to a more hellish fantasy of Mexico in *The Appaloosa*. The Mexican bandit in *One-Eyed Jacks* (played by Larry Duran) is Rio's (Brando's) friend and companion, not the greaser *Appaloosa*'s Medina is made to be.

Appointment in Honduras (1953 RKO)

D: Jacques Tourneur
S: Karen De Wolf, based on a story by Mario Silveira and Jack Cornall
P: Benedict Bogeaus
Cast: Glenn Ford, Ann Sheridan, Zachary Scott, **Rodolfo Acosta**

Set in 1910, this escapist entertainment consists mainly of a grueling trek through the Central American jungles.

Steve Corbett (Ford) is bringing money to the deposed president of Honduras and his loyal followers. When the ship's captain refuses to dock at Honduras, passenger Corbett frees a Nicaragua-bound group of criminals, led by Reyes (Acosta), and enlists their aid in the takeover of the ship. They grab a lifeboat, taking two passengers, Harry and Sylvia Sheppard (Scott and Sheridan), as hostages, and the couple are forced to accompany the troop through the jungle. Harry Sheppard successfully manages to worsen the discord between Corbett and the bandit Reyes. Besides each other, Corbett and Reyes also have to contend with assorted jungle menaces such as tiger fish, alligators, snakes, and torrential rain. Eventually a showdown between Corbett and Reyes occurs, with Corbett the victor. Harry is also killed, and Sylvia and Corbett ride off together into the Central American sunset.

The cast also features Ric Roman, Rico Alaniz, Julian Rivero, Pepe Hern, Henry Escalante, and Victor Ottero.

Argentine Love (1924 Par)

D: Allan Dwan
S: John Russell, based on the story by **Vicente Blasco Ibanez**
P: Allan Dwan
Cast: Bebe Daniels, **Ricardo Cortez**, James Rennie, Mark Gonzales, Aurelio Garcia

Juan Martin (Cortez), the refined local Argentinian strongman, awaits the homecoming of his betrothed, Consuelo (Daniels). She, however, falls in love with an American engineer, Phillip Sears (Rennie), who is building a bridge in her native Argentina. Typical melodrama of its time.

Argentine Nights (1940 U)
D: Albert S. Rogell
S: Arthur T. Horman, Ray Golden, and Sid Kuller, based on a story
   by J. Robert Bren and Gladys Atwater
P: Ken Goldsmith
Cast: The Ritz Brothers, The Andrews Sisters, George Reeves, Constance Moore

A lightweight musical/comedy about three unemployed American girl singers who run off to Argentina on a cruise ship with their managers in search of new opportunities.

The film made fun of the conventional Latin American stereotypes as seen in most American movies, but Latins were not amused. The Andrews Sisters sing "Rumboogie," which combines the rumba and boogie woogie, and "Brooklynonga," a Brooklyn name for a gaucho conga line. Unfortunately, the rumba is from Cuba as is the conga; both have Afro-Caribbean influences, unrelated to Argentina.

The Argentine consul was sent to Hollywood by the Argentine government as a technical adviser. At first, he was welcomed by the studio but was ignored once the film went into production.

Stills from the movie were shown to the consul, who remarked, "In the first place, the rumba is unknown in Argentina. It is a Cuban folk dance. Furthermore the costume is one that used to be worn by women in Cuban houses of prostitution and even they don't wear them anymore."

Argentine Nights was well received by audiences in the States, but in South America, particularly in Buenos Aires, the film caused riots, and people stoned the theaters in which the film was shown. Such Hollywood productions were presented as "typical" of Latin countries, but Latin Americans would not accept films in which the characterizations of themselves were totally absurd.

Hollywood was alarmed by the official government outcries. The U.S. State Department aided Hollywood by creating the Office of the Coordinator of Inter-American Affairs (CIAA), which opened a motion picture division headed by John Hay Whitney. It advised Hollywood to take more care with its productions set in Latin America if it wanted to win over the Latin American markets. Even with the activation of this office, the studios paid only lip service for the most part.

Actor George Reeves, who later became famous as TV's Superman during the 1950s, here plays Eduardo, a wealthy Argentine polo player and Latin lover.

Around the World in 80 Days (1956 UA)
D: Michael Anderson
S: S.J. Perelman, with James Poe and John Farrow, from the novel by Jules Verne
P: Michael Todd
Cast: David Niven, **Cantinflas**, Shirley MacLaine

This film recounts a journey around the world in 1872 by Phileas Fogg (Niven) and his faithful servant Passepartout (Cantinflas) on a bet wagered by fellow members of London's prestigious Reform Club. In the course of their race against time, Fogg and his servant experience all sorts of wild adventures. The film introduced Mexico's superb comedian Cantinflas to an international audience in his first English-speaking role. Cantinflas used his well-known Spanish clown characterization in the film, but no mention was made of his ethnicity.

Winner of five Academy Awards, including Best Picture, and based on the novel by Jules Verne, the film was a tremendous hit and broke worldwide movie attendance records up to that time. It is a grand entertainment made with the international film market in mind, filmed in seven countries, two U.S. locations, and the backlots of five major Hollywood studios. The cast featured 50 international stars in cameo roles. Latin stars included Gilbert Roland, Cesar Romero, Jose Greco, and Luis Miguel Dominguin. The production was conceived, produced, and supervised by the tireless millionaire showman and creative genius Mike Todd, who died in a plane crash in 1958.

At Play in the Fields of the Lord (1991 U)

   D: **Hector Babenco**
   S: Jean-Claude Carrière and **Hector Babenco**, based on the novel
      by Peter Matthiessen
   P: Saul Zaentz
Cast: Tom Berenger, John Lithgow, Daryl Hannah, Aidan Quinn, Tom Waits,
      Kathy Bates, Stenio Garcia

Two Protestant Christian missionaries (Quinn and Bates) arrive in the Amazon jungle to work under the direction of the missionary director and his wife (Lithgow and Hannah). Their task is to reactivate a Catholic mission in the heart of the jungle and convert the local natives before the Brazilian army moves in and drives the natives off their land in a brutal fashion. Meanwhile, American Indian pilot Moon (Berenger) resolves to find his roots. He parachutes from his plane and, stripping himself naked—quite literally—walks into the Indians' camp and is mistaken for a god.

The jungle, however, far from the Eden it seems to be, begins to take its toll on the outsiders. Instead of "civilizing" the jungle and its inhabitants, the outsiders begin to be changed by the jungle and its inhabitants, losing the thin veneer of civilization they brought with them, which they shed as easily as Berenger's Indian shed his clothes.

The meddling of both the missionaries and Moon leads to disaster for the Indians and the outsiders. There are terrific performances from Aidan Quinn and Kathy Bates in a generally well-acted and beautifully photographed piece that is perhaps a little too long in the end.

Stenio Garcia plays the police chief in the village where Lithgow is based, who is all set to illegally bomb the Amazon Indians out of their homes if Lithgow and Quinn can't convert the Indians and make them move peacefully.

Back to Bataan (1945 RKO)

   D: Edward Dmytryk
   S: Ben Barzman and Richard Landau
   P: Robert Fellows
Cast: John Wayne, **Anthony Quinn**, Fely Franquelli

In this patriotic World War II action/drama, Anthony Quinn co-stars as Filipino guerrilla leader Captain Andres Bonifacio, grandson of the legendary Filipino patriot, who, along with American Col. Madden (Wayne), helps to fight the Japanese enemy in the Philippines in anticipation of General MacArthur's return. Hollywood recognized the culture and background of the Filipino people, and for once a clearly Spanish-surnamed hero played by a Hispanic American actor figures in a leading role.

The Bad and the Beautiful (1952 MGM)

   D: Vincente Minnelli
   S: Charles Schnee
   P: John Houseman
Cast: Kirk Douglas, Lana Turner, Dick Powell, **Gilbert Roland**, Gloria Grahame

The story of the 18-year rise and fall of an independent producer from the Depression to the early 1950s. Jonathan Shields (Douglas) is a deceased and unlamented producer whose legacy is a deathbed letter to three protégés reminding them that, for all his sins, they owe their careers to his genius.

Gilbert Roland plays Victor "Gaucho" Ribera, an easygoing Latin lover movie star. Shields helps a screenwriter (Powell) with his unbearable southern wife (Grahame) by arranging for Ribera to take her on a plane ride, which ends disastrously.

Roland's portrayal of a character associated with his own real-life career acknowledged the contributions made by Hispanics, even in limited roles, as part of Hollywood's legendary past.

The movie won five Oscars, including Best Supporting Actress (Grahame) and Best Screenplay (Schnee).

Bad Boys (1983 U)
    D: Richard Rosenthal
    S: Richard Dilello
    P: Robert Solo
  Cast: Sean Penn, **Reni Santoni**, Jim Moody, Eric Gurry, **Esai Morales**

Gritty tale full of ethnic stereotypes and predictable situations. While escaping from a robbery in a stolen car, a youthful hoodlum, Mick (Penn), causes the death of his best friend and the eight-year-old brother of a Hispanic gang leader, Paco (Morales). For his crime, Mick is sent to a juvenile detention center where he's placed in a life-or-death situation among other young felons. Paco, who has vowed to avenge his brother's death, is later sent to the same penal institution for having raped Mick's girlfriend on the outside. The eventual violent confrontation between the two settles the score.

Esai Morales plays Paco, a hot-blooded Latin hood with few apparent redeeming qualities. Reni Santoni plays Ramon Herrera, a youth counselor who takes an interest in Mick but not in Paco. In an interesting twist on the traditional role of the Anglo saving the Hispanic, Herrera the Hispanic saves Mick the Anglo.

The Bad Man (1930 FN)
    D: Clarence Badger
    S: Howard Estabrook (English version), based on the play by Porter Emerson Browne; Baltazar Fernandez Cue (Spanish version)
  Cast: Walter Huston (English version); **Antonio Moreno** (Spanish version)

Story of the outlaw bandit Pancho Lopez (Huston) and his exploits until he is killed by a Texas Ranger.

With the advent of sound, in an attempt to reach the non-English-speaking countries, a number of English-language Hollywood motion pictures were filmed simultaneously in different languages, including Spanish, with different casts.

The English version, with Walter Huston in the lead, was shot in 24 days at a cost of $253,561. Huston earned $5,000 per week. The Spanish version was shot in 18 days at a cost of $73,027, with an all-Spanish-speaking cast headed by Antonio Moreno, who earned $2,000 per week. Baltazar Fernandez Cue was employed to write the Spanish version of the script for $10,000, and he eliminated some of the derogatory elements inherent in the English version. Huston played Pancho as a vicious greaser; Moreno played him as a devil-may-care character, which he enhanced with his own charismatic personality.

Badge 373 (1973 Par)
    D: Howard W. Koch
    S: Pete Hamill
    P: Howard W. Koch
  Cast: Robert Duvall, Verna Bloom, Felipe Luciano, **Luis Avalos**, Chico Martinez, Marina Durell, **Henry Darrow**

A sequel of sorts to *The French Connection* in that it further follows the exploits of real-life New York City cop Eddie Egan, who as the character of Popeye Doyle in the earlier film had become a big sensation.

The original story, as written by Egan, took place with Castro and Batista in Cuba, but the film shifted the locale to New York's Puerto Rican community and substituted a radical liberation group (more than likely for budget reasons—a period film is much more expensive to make).

Columnist and author Pete Hamill wrote the script, which moves through the seamy, oppressed Puerto Rican world of New York City. Eddie Ryan (Duvall) discovers that his dead partner knew of the plans of the cultured Puerto Rican gangster Sweet William (Darrow) to sell stolen guns to radicals to mount a rebellion on the island.

Richard Cuskelly in the *L.A. Herald Examiner* of August 3, 1973, summed up the movie: "Puerto Ricans are portrayed as either animalistic, violence prone thugs, or as foolish also violence prone, would-be revolutionaries. The police aren't treated much better unless we're supposed to admire their unnecessary manhandling of suspected criminals and unabashed racism."

Real-life Puerto Rican activist Felipe Luciano, a member of the then radical group the Young Lords, played a character like himself with fierce intensity, but the Puerto Rican community turned on him when the film came out. Luciano agreed to do the film because the script included a speech on Puerto Rican independence; however, the speech as shot in a rally at the Central Park bandshell was lost in the intercutting of a chase sequence.

Representatives of various New York–based Puerto Rican groups demanded that Paramount withdraw the film, publicly apologize for it, and increase the number of Puerto Rican technicians employed in the production end of the business. The protesters claimed that the film portrayed all Puerto Ricans as prostitutes, thieves, or bomb-throwing radicals. The one Puerto Rican cop in the movie (Chico Martinez, as Frankie Diaz) turns out to be crooked and is humiliated by Duvall in front of his family.

The head gangster, Sweet William, is a Puerto Rican Harvard graduate who makes every effort to let you know it by quoting famous poets. Puerto Rican actor Henry Darrow had made a name for himself on television as the lovable rogue son of a Mexican land baron on the successful series "The High Chaparral." It was disappointing to see him in such a role. Marina Durell (as Rita Garcia) is a junkie prostitute who gets murdered for what she knows. Luis Avalos (as Chico) plays a junkie whom Egan brutalizes into falling off a roof. Salsa musician Johnny Pacheco and his music are featured in the film.

The Ballad of Gregorio Cortez (1983 Emb)

D: Robert M. Young
S: Victor Villasenor, based on the novel *With His Pistol in His Hand* by Americo Paredes
P: Michael Hausman
AP: **Richard Soto**
Cast: **Edward James Olmos**, Tom Bower, **Pepe Serna, Rosana De Soto,** James Gammon

True story, set in 1901 Texas, of a legendary Mexican cowboy who shoots and kills a sheriff in self-defense after a tragic misunderstanding, the result of a mistranslation from English to Spanish. Cortez is not your typical Hollywood hero, but is presented as an ordinary human being who, fearing for his life, draws on his own resourcefulness, commonsense, and extraordinary horsemanship to outwit and outride a formidable posse sent out after him, until he is captured.

Young's work reflects a sensitivity that transcends boundaries and goes to the heart of the human condition. Young says of his work, "All my stories are about people to whom life gives a raw deal. But they are not losers. They have dignity and they find out who they are."

When he was approached for his participation, actor Edward James Olmos suggested Young be brought in as director; based on his previous work, Young was overwhelmingly approved. Olmos, who masterfully portrays Cortez, states, "*The Ballad of Gregorio Cortez* is a film about humanity. It never tries to polarize the audience. Just as the shooting evolves out of cultural and linguistic misunderstanding, in other encounters between Anglos and Cortez who have the same language barrier, they unite through their common humanity." In one scene Cortez's hunger overcomes his suspicion, fear, and curiosity when a lonely Anglo cowboy offers him food. Olmos's silent gratitude is as memorable as his look of total defeat and despair when he discovers his wife and children have been jailed.

The film was produced under the auspices of the National Council of La Raza, PBS, CPB, and Moctezuma Esparza. Though the film takes place in Texas, it was filmed in New Mexico on a $1.3 million budget. The production captured a strong feeling of authenticity and turn-of-the-century western ambiance. The striking visual images were by cameraman Reynaldo Villalobos. Robert M. Young and Olmos wrote the *Rashomon*-like screenplay (but did not receive credit) with Victor Villasenor based on the Americo Paredes novel *With His Pistol in His Hand.*

Olmos calls Cortez the first Hispanic American hero figure ever in American cinema based on a true person and actual events. "Films like this are meant to enhance the image of Hispanics and especially Chicanos. But at the same time they have a universal appeal that makes them important to American society as a whole," said Olmos during an interview with Luis Reyes.

The film aired on PBS television as part of the "American Playhouse" series. Edward Olmos obtained rights to the movie and started screening it theatrically in movie houses first in Los Angeles then across the country free of charge. He also screened it at theaters and community halls with 35mm film equipment. Olmos and a dedicated group of friends believed in the film and wanted as many people as possible to see it. PBS only reaches a certain viewership, and Olmos wanted to take the film out to the general public. Through persistence and hard work, which resulted in wide exposure and a rave review from leading *L.A. Times* film critic Charles Champlin, it was soon picked up for distribution by Embassy Pictures in a limited theatrical release.

Bananas (1971 UA)

D: Woody Allen
S: Woody Allen and Mickey Rose
P: Charles H. Joffe and Jack Grossberg
Cast: Woody Allen, Louise Lasser, **Carlos Montalban, Jacobo Morales, Miguel Suarez, Rene Enriquez**

Wild, satirical, and funny treatment of Latin American politics and culture as viewed through the eyes of Woody Allen in his second motion picture feature as a director. The film also takes pot shots at American politics and policies at home and abroad.

The new dictator of the banana republic of San Marcos island is General Vargas (Montalban), who promises to shut down the newspapers, train his soldiers, and fight off a new band of rebels.

Woody Allen is Fielding Mellish, a mousy young products tester living in New York who falls in love with a radical college student, Nancy (Lasser). She believes he doesn't have leadership qualities and breaks off the affair. Disillusioned, he quits his job and heads off to San Marcos.

Upon his arrival, Fielding becomes the object of an assassination plot. The dictator plans to have Fielding murdered but to blame the killing on the rebels. The dictator believes that the American government, outraged over the murder of one of its citizens, will send in American armed forces to quell the rebels and back the ruling dictator. The killing doesn't go as planned, however, and Fielding winds up with the real rebel forces in their mountain hideout. He meets Esposito (Morales), the rebel leader (who resembles Cuba's Castro), and is taken in by the rebels.

Fielding quickly becomes a rebel and reluctantly exerts the very leadership qualities he was told he lacked. He defeats the dictator and the rebel leader and eventually becomes president of San Marcos. Fielding turns to the United States for aid for San Marcos, which is in dire economic shape. He travels to New York in disguise, where his ruse is uncovered by the FBI. He meets the girl who rejected him, who is awed by his incarnation as the president of San Marcos. Fielding reveals his true identity to her, and they eventually fall in love and marry. The FBI drops its case against Fielding.

The movie is brilliantly realized by Allen, who shot the San Marcos sequences in Puerto Rico using many Hispanic actors, which brought a sense of realism and naturalism to the proceedings. The film cleverly combines quick-witted humor with slapstick. It is rooted in American 1960s-era counterculture and politics, which may seem a little dated in some situations and very contemporary in others.

Bandido (1956 UA)

D: Richard Fleischer
S: Earl Felton
P: Robert L. Jacks
Cast: Robert Mitchum, **Gilbert Roland**, Zachary Scott, Ursula Thiess, **Rodolfo Acosta**, Victor Juncos, Alfonso Sanchez Tello

A gringo gunslinger (Mitchum) sells his services for adventure and hard cash and drifts into Mexico in 1916 with weapons in hopes of taking advantage of reports of an impending revolution. The gringo meets a local rebel bandido (Roland) and helps him win several battles.

Mitchum is the gringo hero who sees Mexico as a land of adventure and brings his superior technology in the form of weapons to help the rebel bandits. Filmed on location in Mexico, the film offers plenty of action in a tongue-in-cheek style. Mitchum and Roland are excellent in their respective roles.

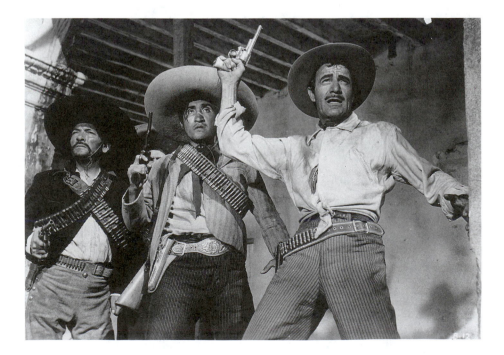

Victor Junco, Rodolfo Acosta, and Gilbert Roland in *Bandido*.

Raquel Welch portrays Maria Stoner, a young Mexican widow, in *Bandolero!*

Bandolero! (1968 TCF)

D: Andrew V. McLaglen
S: James Lee Barrett, based on a story by Stanley L. Hough
P: Robert L. Jacks
Cast: James Stewart, Dean Martin, **Raquel Welch**, George Kennedy, **Perry Lopez**, Rudy Diaz

Action/adventure set in Texas and Mexico in the post–Civil War period. Raquel Welch portrays Maria, a young Mexican woman widowed by Dee's (Martin) band during a bank holdup and taken hostage on the way out of town. When she is kidnapped she shows her strong character by standing up to the outlaws.

The film perpetuates the worst Mexican stereotypes as a posse chases outlaws into a Mexico of endless barren desert landscapes peopled by bandidos whose only purpose in life is to kill gringos.

In the middle of a climactic skirmish, the Mexican bandit Munoz (Diaz) spots Maria, drops everything, and runs toward her; he rips her blouse, and his hand disappears up her skirt. The greaser image returns, portraying the Mexican as someone of uncontrollable bursts of violence and lust. On the other hand, the Anglo outlaws aren't much better, even with the so-called heroes (Stewart and Martin) keeping them in check. Welch's Maria is a woman with a past, a former prostitute, who is not out of place with her outlaw captors.

Barbarosa (1982 U)

D: Fred Schepisi
S: William D. Wittliff
P: Paul N. Lazarus III
Cast: Willie Nelson, Gary Busey, **Gilbert Roland, Isela Vega, Danny De La Paz, Alma Martinez**

Willie Nelson is Barbarosa ("Red Beard" in Spanish), a notorious outlaw whose name is both feared and hated by residents of a Mexican village. He is married to Josephina (Vega) but her father, Don Braulio (Roland), despises him—so much so, in fact, that he has given his sons the mission of killing Barbarosa. Undaunted, Barbarosa creeps into the village by night to see his wife, while by day he outruns and outtrails his would-be assassins. When Barbarosa meets Karl (Busey), a naive farmhand also on the run for an accidental killing, he decides to teach him the tricks of the trade.

Brilliantly realized western with an extraordinary visual quality in which Mexicans are seen as noble ranchers, bandidos, and superstitious, stalwart peons. Roland, in his last theatrical feature film appearance to date, is excellent as the patriarch Don Braulio. Willie Nelson is adequate but is the weakest link in the film. Mexican actress Isela Vega contributes a strong portrayal as Josephina. De La Paz is convincing as the youthful son who goes after Barbarosa.

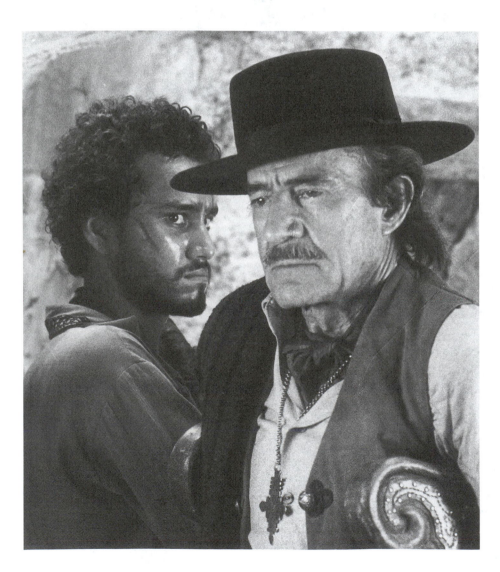

Gilbert Roland as Don Braulio and Danny De La Paz as the son in the beautifully photographed western *Barbarosa*.

The Barefoot Contessa (1954 UA)

D: Joseph L. Mankiewicz
S: Joseph L. Mankiewicz
P: Joseph L. Mankiewicz
Cast: Ava Gardner, Humphrey Bogart, Warren Stevens, Edmond O'Brien

Three American movie executives discover an extraordinary Spanish dancer, Maria Vargas (Gardner), in Spain. They bring her to Hollywood, "launch" her as a star, and rename her Maria d'Amata.

The producer, Kirk (Stevens), is a dictatorial sexist bigot who courts her. She despises him and finds herself at ease among truck drivers, gypsies, and handsome young men. She agrees to a meeting with a South American millionaire (Marius Goring) and goes to Rome with him, where she encounters an older Italian count (Rossano Brazzi), whom she marries. Her discovery on the wedding night that her husband is impotent helps to bring about the contessa's tragic end.

François Truffaut called *The Barefoot Contessa* "the most beautiful portrait of a woman ever filmed, in the person of Ava Gardner." Top stars, a good adult story, and resourceful direction are skillfully blended in a beautiful production filmed in Italy and Spain. The film is supposed to be somewhat based on the life of Rita Hayworth. The mystique of the exotic, sexual, and beautiful Latin woman was certainly exploited in this film. Ava Gardner was captivating and perfect in the role. Humphrey Bogart (as Harry Dawes) was never better as her friend and director, while Edmond O'Brien won an Academy Award for his role as press agent Oscar Muldoon.

Bataan (1943 MGM)

D: Tay Garnett
S: Robert Andrews
P: Irving Starr
Cast: Robert Taylor, Thomas Mitchell, George Murphy, Robert Walker, **Desi Arnaz**

Story of the American and Filipino troops who hopelessly defend Manila during the first days of World War II, after the Japanese invasion.

Many of the real-life Bataan defenders were Mexican Americans from New Mexico, and the ones that surrendered faced the infamous "Bataan Death March." This film is one of the first to recognize the Mexican American as part of the U.S. fighting force during World War II and thus as part of the American society. Desi Arnaz portrays Private Ramirez, a Mexican American from California's Salinas Valley. Representative cross sections of the United States were a popular mainstay in World War II films of the era, quickly becoming a cliched device.

Battle Cry (1955 WB)

D: **Raoul Walsh**
S: Leon Uris, based on his novel
P: Henry Blanke
Cast: Van Heflin, Tab Hunter, Aldo Ray, Anne Francis, Dorothy Malone, **Perry Lopez, Victor Millan**

Raoul Walsh directed *Battle Cry* as a broad, exciting picture of U.S. Marines in action and as a series of touching stories of men and their relationships with the women in their lives. It follows the men through camp training, romances, and problems, and then takes them to the bitter, bloody battles of the South Pacific theater of World War II.

Battle Cry was filmed on the island of Vieques, Puerto Rico, where the armed services maintain a base, with the film crew receiving the assistance and full cooperation of the U.S. Navy and the U.S. Marines. Battle scenes re-created the invasions of Guadalcanal, Tarawa, and Saipan. The cast roughed it and lived in tents like the Marines on the island location.

Three of the prominently featured soldiers were larcenous Spanish Joe Gomez (played by Perry Lopez), Pedro (played by Victor Millan), and the Native American Marine called Crazy Horse (played by Felix Noriego).

Actor Victor Millan told Luis Reyes in an interview in 1992 that the role of Pedro was more substantial in Leon Uris's original novel. Pedro was a Silver Star war hero who had to deal with a redneck Texan in his platoon. There was a scene in the film during liberty in a bar in which Pedro relates his feelings to platoon sergeant Mac, played by James Whitmore, and makes friendly overtures to the redneck Speedy, played by Fess Parker. Speedy rejects these overtures and throws beer on Pedro, causing a fight. The scene was cut from the final film because the U.S. Marine Corps insisted there was no racial prejudice in the Corps. Warner Bros., which relied heavily on the assistance of the Marine Corps, bowed to the pressure.

Aldo Ray, Victor Millan, James Whitmore, Fess Parker, and Bill Campbell (head down on table) in a scene that was cut from *Battle Cry* because the Marines demanded it be removed from the film, citing that there was "no racial prejudice in U.S. Marine Corps."
Photo courtesy of Victor Millan.

Battleground (1949 MGM)

D: William Wellman
S: Robert Pirosh
P: Dore Schary
Cast: John Hodiak, Van Johnson, **Ricardo Montalban**, George Murphy, Marshall Thompson, Leon Ames, James Whitmore, Don Taylor

This story of American G.I.s during the World War II Battle of the Bulge, forcefully directed by William Wellman, was a big commercial hit. Ricardo Montalban played Roderigues, a Mexican American G.I. in one of those representative squads, recognizing the valiant efforts and sacrifices made by Mexican Americans during the war.

From a commercial standpoint the studio was building up Montalban as a star. For Latin American audiences Montalban's participation in the cast carried vestiges of the Good Neighbor Policy and marquee value to be exploited: Montalban had made a number of films in Mexico prior to his arrival at MGM. From a public relations standpoint it was reassuring to see American citizens of Latin origin fighting for freedom in a U.S.-made World War II movie. The real-life American survivors of the battle were employed as extras to play themselves.

The Beast of Hollow Mountain (1956 UA)

D: Edward Nassour and Ismael Rodriguez
S: Robert Hill, based on a story by Willis O'Brien
P: William and Edward Nassour
Cast: Guy Madison, **Carlos Rivas**, **Patricia Medina**, Mario Navarro

Guy Madison is partnered with Carlos Rivas on a Mexican ranch in this science-fiction western filmed in Mexico. A wealthy rancher develops a dislike for Madison when his fiancée demonstrates an interest in the gringo. The love story and the cattle rustling soon take a back seat when they are all menaced by a prehistoric Tyrannosaurus rex that lives in the mountains near the ranch.

Behold a Pale Horse (1964 Col)

D: Fred Zinnemann
S: J.P. Miller, based on the novel *Killing a Mouse on Sunday* by Emeric Pressburger
P: Fred Zinnemann
Cast: Gregory Peck, **Anthony Quinn**, Omar Sharif

A post–Spanish Civil War story in which Peck plays Manuel Artiguez, a Loyalist hero who is now a bandit in exile. At his dying mother's request, he returns from his retreat on the French side of the Pyrenees to his native village in Spain. His implacable enemy is police chief Vinolas (Quinn) of the Guardia Civil, who has sworn for 20 years to capture Artiguez dead or alive.

The picture was filmed in southern France, because a movie in which a member of Franco's Guardia Civil is the villain would never have been allowed to be shot in Spain while Franco was still in power. While some might argue that Peck is miscast as a Spaniard, he brings an air of tired integrity to the portrayal of a man whose burning passions as a guerrilla leader fighting Franco's fascists in the Spanish Civil War have been transformed into the hollow emotions of a commonplace bandido. It is Quinn's excellent portrayal of the obsessive police chief that stands out, however. Omar Sharif as a village priest with divided loyalties is also effective. The story never has any real dramatic tension, however, and never captured general audience interest.

The Believers (1987 Or)
    D: John Schlesinger
    S: Mark Frost
    P: John Schlesinger
 Cast: **Martin Sheen**, Robert Loggia, **Jimmy Smits**

Cal Jamison (Sheen) arrives in New York to start a new life with his young son, after his wife is killed in a freak accident. Hired by the New York Police Department to help stressed-out cops, he's asked by Lt. McTaggert (Loggia) to treat a young detective (Smits) who is acting as strange as the series of ritualistic child murders he is investigating. Jamison is soon plunged into a frightening world of strange religious worshippers.

The film deals with the Caribbean religion of Santeria, portraying it as a black magic cult practiced by superstitious, bloodthirsty, and simpleminded blacks and Puerto Ricans in New York City. The notion of the white man saving the poor minorities from themselves is prevalent in this film.

Beyond the Limit (1983 Par)
    D: John MacKenzie
    S: Christopher Hampton, based on the novel *The Honorary Consul* by Graham Greene
    P: Norma Heyman
 Cast: Michael Caine, Richard Gere, **Elpidia Carrillo**, Bob Hoskins, **A Martinez**, Joaquin De Almeida

Filmed in Mexico, this is an adaptation of Graham Greene's novel *The Honorary Consul*, in which Gere plays a Paraguayan doctor in an Argentina-Paraguay bordertown who gets caught up in the kidnapping of an alcoholic British consul (Caine) by revolutionaries. He also falls in love with the consul's wife, a former native hooker played by Elpidia Carrillo. *Beyond the Limit* has similarities to John Huston's 1984 film adaptation of Malcolm Lowry's *Under the Volcano*. Both deal with an alcoholic British consul in a Latin American country, a three-way love affair, and the death of the consul as a result of political unrest.

The Big Boodle (1957 UA)
    D: Richard Wilson
    S: Jo Eisinger, based on the novel by Robert Sylvester
    P: Lewis F. Blumberg
 Cast: Errol Flynn, **Pedro Armendariz**, **Carlos Rivas**, Rossana Rory, Gia Scala, Sandro Giglio

Good crime/melodrama, concerned with a search by the Havana police for $3 million in counterfeit pesos and the plates that made them. Flynn is a casino blackjack dealer who finds himself involved in intrigue when he is passed a 500 peso note by a blonde and is caught between the police and the gang of counterfeiters.

Filmed against the background of Batista's (pre-Castro) Havana, the film features an exciting chase and gun battle along the walls of a sixteenth-century Spanish fortress. Flynn is good in the role of a world-weary American blackjack dealer, as is Pedro Armendariz as the police chief and Carlos Rivas as one of the heavies. Cuban actors featured include Guillermo Alvarez Guedes, Carlos Mas, Rogelio Hernandez, and Velia Martinez.

The Big Country (1958 UA)

D: William Wyler
S: James R. Webb, Sy Bartlett, and Robert Wilder
P: William Wyler and Gregory Peck
Cast: Gregory Peck, Charlton Heston, Carroll Baker, Jean Simmons, Charles Bickford, Burl Ives, Chuck Connors, **Alfonso Bedoya**

A big-budget western entertainment with a visual scope to match the important big-name cast and sprawling epic story line. James McKay (Peck) is a retired sailor from Baltimore who comes out to the western town of San Rafael to marry Pat Terrill (Baker), the pampered daughter of a cattle rancher, Major Terrill (Bickford). McKay finds himself caught in the middle of a local feud between the major and his nemesis, an adjacent rancher, Hannassey (Ives), and his family.

Alfonso Bedoya has an important role as Ramon Guttierrez, a Mexican wrangler on the Terrill spread who has been with the family for a long time and who is amused by the antics of McKay and quickly comes to respect his gentle, nonviolent way of proving himself. Terrill berates Ramon and calls him an idiot for letting McKay ride out alone in the expansive ranch country. McKay, however, has a compass and knows exactly where he is going, and the true idiot is Terrill. Mexicans are seen in traditional roles as house servants and ranch hands. The Spanish heritage of the Southwest is acknowledged when the schoolteacher (Simmons) tells McKay that the land was originally a present from the king of Spain to her great-grandfather.

The Big Fix (1978 U)

D: Jeremy Paul Kagan
S: Roger L. Simon, based on his novel
P: Carl Borack and Richard Dreyfuss
Cast: Richard Dreyfuss, Susan Anspach, Bonnie Bedelia, Ofelia Medina

Moses Wine (Dreyfuss), a private detective who has left his radical campus ideals behind him at Berkeley and who can barely make a living, is asked by a one-time campus activist (Anspach) to investigate the attempts to discredit a gubernatorial candidate. Ofelia Medina co-stars as a sensitive and intelligent Chicana student movement leader.

The Big Steal (1949 RKO)

D: Don Siegel
S: Geoffrey Homes and Gerald Drayson Adams, based on a story by Richard Wormser
P: Jack J. Gross
Cast: Robert Mitchum, Jane Greer, Patric Knowles, William Bendix, **Ramon Novarro**, **Don Alvarado**, Pascual Garcia Pena

Story of a thief who has stolen a U.S. Army payroll and is being pursued across Mexico, from the port of Vera Cruz through the surrounding villages.

This is a first-rate thriller that owes much to its atmospheric Mexican locations.

Blackboard Jungle (1955 MGM)

D: **Richard Brooks**
S: **Richard Brooks**, based on the novel by Evan Hunter
P: Pandro S. Berman
Cast: Glenn Ford, Anne Francis, Louis Calhern, Sidney Poitier, Vic Morrow, Richard Kiley, Paul Mazursky, **Rafael Campos**

Richard Dadier (Ford) is a struggling young teacher assigned to a tough inner-city American high school. He faces a school whose staff is made up mostly of indifferent teachers and whose racially mixed student body is dominated by a group of juvenile delinquents with disrespect for learning and any authority figure.

Although his pregnant wife (Francis) urges him to get out, Dadier withstands the students' taunts and is able to reach some of them. He faces a showdown with the head of a group of toughs (Morrow) in the classroom. Dadier overcomes him by sheer brute strength with the assistance of Miller (Poitier), one of the students he has been trying to reach. Writer/director Richard Brooks displayed strong direction showing the anguish and pain of urban American educational institutions of the mid-1950s.

The Puerto Rican as part of the American scene was introduced to films through the character of Pete Morales, one of Dadier's students, played by Dominican actor Rafael Campos in his feature film debut.

The film ushered in a whole new era for a generation of young Americans with its use of rock 'n' roll on the film's soundtrack, featuring "Rock Around the Clock," by Bill Haley and the Comets.

A tremendous hit at the box office, the film became a hotbed of controversy over its so-called unflattering portrayal of American youth and the American inner-city school system.

Blackboard Jungle started the filmic convention of having an Anglo schoolteacher help the poor inner-city minority kids to better their lives through education, perseverance, and acceptance of middle-class American values. In these earlier outings minority meant not only blacks and Hispanics but also Italians, Irish, and Poles.

Many of the young actors portraying the high school students went on to carve a niche for themselves in Hollywood. Sidney Poitier became Hollywood's first black superstar, an Academy Award–winning actor. Rafael Campos went on to become a well-established character actor. Paul Mazursky has become one of Hollywood's most important writer/directors. Jameel Farah (Jamie Farr) years later found fame as Klinger on television's hit series "M*A*S*H," as did Vic Morrow on the long-running series "Combat."

Blame It on Rio (1984 TCF)

D: Stanley Donen
S: Charles Peters and Larry Gelbart
P: Stanley Donen
Cast: Michael Caine, Joe Bologna, Valerie Harper, Demi Moore

Comedy about a coffee executive whose teenage daughter has a romantic fling with his best friend, which turns their vacation in exotic Rio de Janeiro upside-down. Americans' passions are unleashed in the more primal atmosphere of Rio through their exposure to native rituals and music. Reynaldo Villalobos's lush cinematography captures the colors of Rio and Brazil.

Blockade (1938 UA)

D: William Dieterle
S: John Howard Lawson
P: Walter Wanger
Cast: Madeleine Carroll, Henry Fonda, **Leo Carrillo, Lupita Tovar, Carlos de Valdez**

Arriving in Spain after a year of travel, a young English woman (Carroll) finds that her father and his associate have been fomenting civil war in Spain. Marco (Fonda), whom the young woman has met and fallen in love with, becomes a soldier when war breaks out. After killing her father in a pistol duel, Marco follows her every movement because he suspects her of being a spy. After a series of dramatic events, she is instrumental in saving a city from starvation and destruction, and exposes the real war makers.

This muddled film stirred controversy at the time of its release because it was set during the then-contemporary Spanish Civil War. Conservative, isolationist, Depression-era America saw it as an appeal for the Spanish Loyalist cause, some saw it as Marxist propaganda, and the Catholic church managed to ban the film in many American cities and towns.

The producers took precautions not to name the Spanish region specifically, and the viewer doesn't quite know which side the hero is fighting on. The wardrobe was not specific to any Spanish region.

Carlos de Valdez plays Major Del Rio, Lupita Tovar plays a palm reader, and Leo Carrillo plays Luis.

Blondie Goes Latin (1941 Col)

D: Frank R. Strayer
S: Richard Flournoy and Karen De Wolf, based on a story by Quinn Martin
P: Robert Sparks
Cast: Penny Singleton, Arthur Lake, Larry Simms, Irving Bacon, Ruth Terry, **Tito Guizar**

Chic Young's famous syndicated comic strip about an all-American middle-class family made its way to the movies in a long and popular series at Columbia starring Penny Singleton as Blondie. The eighth entry in the series had a half-dozen songs in a plot that found the Bumsteads at sea on a trip to South America with Dagwood's ailing boss.

Blondie doesn't get to a Latin country in this story, but the film has plenty of atmosphere, including Tito Guizar as a South American romancing Blondie. Five musical numbers, dances by Singleton, and singing by Ruth Terry and Guizar enhance the entertainment value.

Blood and Sand (1922 Par)

D: Fred Niblo
S: June Mathis, based on the novel *Sangre y Arena* by **Vicente Blasco Ibanez**
P: Famous Players—Lasky
Cast: Rudolph Valentino, Lila Lee, Nita Naldi

Silent. Story of an awkward small-town lad, Juan Gallardo, who becomes Spain's greatest matador. He marries his childhood sweetheart, Carmen, but soon falls under the spell of the alluring and aristocratic Dona Sol, who draws him into a reckless affair and humiliates his wife. Remorseful at having betrayed Carmen, the anguished Juan faces death in his dangerous profession.

Every care was taken to make *Blood and Sand* a special film, when Valentino came over to Paramount following three films at Metro, where he was never under contract.

June Mathis, who had scripted *The Four Horsemen of the Apocalypse* (1921), was hired to do the adaptation. Costumes and bullfighting equipment were imported from Spain and Mexico. A retired matador coached Valentino in the art of the *corrida* as did a young extra named Luis Alonzo, who later found fame as Gilbert Roland. Valentino immersed himself in the characters, and the role was a perfect vehicle for his talents.

"With a seemingly authentic Spanish background, a cast of people who both look and act like Spaniards, and a director capable of painting his pictures with veracity, *Blood and Sand* at The Rivoli this week could not fail to be entertaining," *New York Times* (8/7/22).

Blood and Sand (1941 TCF)

  D: Rouben Mamoulian
  S: Jo Swerling, based on the novel *Sangre y Arena* by **Vicente Blasco Ibanez**
  P: Darryl F. Zanuck
 AP: Robert Kane
Cast: Tyrone Power, Linda Darnell, **Rita Hayworth**, Alla Nazimova,
     J. Carroll Naish, Anthony Quinn

Tyrone Power plays Juan Gallardo, the ragged urchin who becomes Spain's greatest matador and succumbs to the adulation of the mob and the temptations of an international adventuress. Rita Hayworth is the statuesque but porcelain-hearted Dona Sol. Linda Darnell is Carmen, Gallardo's sweetheart, who remains faithful to him until death. Anthony Quinn plays Gallardo's rival in the arena, Manolo, and J. Carroll Naish, Garabato, a matador who ends up as a beggar.

For Power, the role was his second as a Spaniard, and he turned in a believable performance as the young bullfighter. Anthony Quinn found himself in the most demanding and showiest role of his career up to that time. As a rival of Gallardo's both for the affection of Dona Sol and the cheers of the arena mob, he plays in a score of passionate love scenes, paces through beautiful capework in the ring, and does a sensational dance with Dona Sol. The young Quinn demonstrated range and ability in a fully realized role, not the stock characters he had been playing and to which he would return.

The film made a certifiable star out of Rita Hayworth in her sexy performance as Dona Sol. According to a studio press item, Hayworth, to save herself embarrassment, started learning Spanish during the filming. Although of Spanish blood, she was born and raised in the United States. Darnell spoke a little Spanish and was in Mexico with her mother and a family friend who also spoke Spanish.

The film marked the fourth romantic screen teaming of Power and Darnell in much the same way that Errol Flynn and Olivia de Havilland were teamed at Warner Bros.

The film isn't entirely satisfactory as forceful drama, but it is gorgeous to look at. Director Rouben Mamoulian attempted three innovations in this version of *Blood and Sand*. He painted the picture instead of merely photographing it; he used as little dialogue as possible, letting the action tell his story; and he insisted that the studio sign Vicente Gomez, the famous Spanish composer and guitarist, to write and record authentic Gypsy songs in the true flamenco style.

Mamoulian set about "painting" the Blasco Ibanez story by drawing on the coloring and composition of the famous Spanish masters for the spirit of his scenes. He went to Murillo for the browns and sepias that dominate the early romance between Gallardo and Carmen; to Sorolla, the great master of light and shadows, for the filming of market scenes; to El Greco, famed for his religious paintings, for the episode where Gallardo dies in a chapel with Carmen by his side. During Gallardo's struggles for fame, the director drew on Goya, noted for his studies of the lower classes. When Dona Sol, an aristocrat by birth, enters the picture, the style of Velazquez provided the motif for the sets.

The director had two of Hollywood's best color cinematographers, Ernest Palmer and Ray Rennahan, to help him achieve his desired look in the three-strip Technicolor process. They won Academy Awards for their work on the film. Mamoulian used spray guns and several chests of bright cloths for his palettes. He would draw on his chests to put a blue ribbon in Linda's hair to accentuate a feeling of serenity or drape a brown shawl around Gallardo's mother to intensify her despair. Cloth at the time usually photographed flatly, so the spray guns were used in order to accentuate an oil texture such as characterizes many of the old master paintings.

The film builds dramatically with color, opening with subdued shades and progressing through brighter and brighter hues until the red climax in the arena.

Even though the story takes place in Spain, it was filmed in Mexico and in Hollywood. (With Spain coming out of a civil war and Europe engulfed in World War II, a location trip was out of the question.) A troupe of 300 went to Mexico City for 4 weeks, spending most of the time in the Plaza de Toros, where crowds of more than 30,000 people gathered to watch the filming and in turn be shot as extras.

The studio signed Armillita, then one of the world's greatest bullfighters, to act as a technical advisor and double for Power in the bullring. Armillita taught Power and the others the secrets of his profession. Budd Boetticher, casting director for Hal Roach, a feature film director, and a bullfighter in his own right, who had become enamored of the sport on a trip to Mexico years earlier, also acted as technical advisor. Quick to learn, Power mastered sufficiently for movie purposes the very intricate and difficult cape passes of a matador.

Blood In . . . Blood Out . . . (1993 BV)

See *Bound by Honor.*

Blowing Wild (1953 WB)

D: **Hugo Fregonese**
S: Philip Yordan
P: Milton Sperling
Cast: Gary Cooper, Barbara Stanwyck, Ruth Roman, **Anthony Quinn**

Old-fashioned melodrama set in the early 1930s, when Americans sought sudden wealth in Mexico's oil fields.

Jeff Dawson (Cooper) and his partner are discouraged from their oil claim by Mexican bandits and head to Mexico City. There they meet Paco Conway (Quinn), whose present wife, Marina (Stanwyck), had been in love with Dawson some time before. They decide to return to the oil fields. Dawson has no desire to resume any relationship with Marina. Infuriated at Dawson's coldness, Marina pushes Paco into an oil well pump. In turn, raiding bandits kill Marina and blow up the oil works, which makes for the action climax of the film.

The actors are much better than their material. Both Quinn and Cooper, Oscar-nominated for other films, found themselves unable to attend the Oscar ceremonies because of filming on location near Cuernavaca, Mexico, in the spring of 1952. Quinn won the Academy Award for Best Supporting Actor for his work in *Viva Zapata!,* and Cooper won as Best Actor for his performance in *High Noon.*

Blue (1968 Par)

D: Silvio Narizzano
S: Ronald M. Cohen and Meade Roberts, based on a story by Cohen
P: Judd Bernard and Irwin Winkler
Cast: Terence Stamp, Joanna Pettet, **Ricardo Montalban**

An American (British actor Terence Stamp), raised by Mexicans in the Old West, is resented by his adoptive brothers and violently conflicts with their bandit chief father (Montalban). He learns to trust when bullet wounds force him to depend on a woman. Stamp is convincing neither as an American nor as a Mexican, and the film isn't much better.

Bombardier (1943 RKO)

D: Richard Wallace
S: John Twist, based on a story by Twist and Martin Rackin
P: Robert Fellows
Cast: Pat O'Brien, Randolph Scott, Eddie Albert, Robert Ryan, **Richard Martin**

Story of the training of American bombardiers for combat duty at the outbreak of World War II. Richard Martin plays Chito Rafferty, an Irish Mexican, one of the bombsight trainees. Martin later developed this character as a sidekick to Tim Holt in a series of westerns made by RKO.

The Border (1983 U)

D: Tony Richardson
S: Deric Washburn, Walon Green, and David Freeman
P: Edgar Bronfman, Jr.
Cast: Jack Nicholson, Valerie Perrine, Warren Oates, Harvey Keitel, **Elpidia Carrillo, Mike Gomez**

Story of a border patrolman (Nicholson) who refuses to go along with the corruption and complacency of his fellow officers when he gets emotionally involved with an illegal alien woman (Carrillo) whose baby is kidnapped by a drug-smuggling ring. He comes to her aid at the expense of exposing his fellow patrolmen.

This is a traditional western in the guise of a contemporary action drama. Mike Gomez plays a sleazy, mousy greaser type. This violent film was shot on location in El Paso, Texas, and features a strong portrayal by Nicholson and an interesting American film debut for Carrillo as the exotic Guatemalan madonna he rescues.

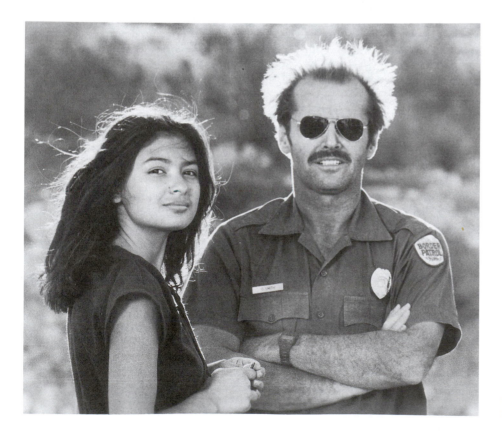

Elpidia Carrillo and Jack Nicholson in *The Border*.

Ricardo Montalban (center) as secret
agent Pablo Rodriguez in a scene from
Border Incident.

Border Incident (1949 MGM)

    D: Anthony Mann
    S: John C. Higgins, based on a story by Higgins and George Zuckerman
    P: Nicholas Nayfack
Cast: George Murphy, **Ricardo Montalban, Howard da Silva**

Pablo Rodriguez (Montalban) and Jack Bearnes (Murphy) are secret agents of the Mexican and U.S. governments who volunteer to uncover the methods of a band of crooks who are smuggling truckloads of undocumented Mexican nationals across the border from Mexicali to the Imperial Valley in California to work as field laborers.

Rodriguez disguises himself as a worker, or *bracero*, and buys transportation from the crooks, while Bearnes poses as a man wanted by the law in the United States who has work permits to sell. Bearnes's true identity is discovered, and he is tortured and brutally murdered. Rodriguez is saved from a horrible death only by the timely arrival of the Border Patrol.

The film shows the abuse and suffering of the workers, who have no legal redress and who are underpaid, robbed, and killed. After working in the fields they are dumped in the Canyon of Death, a morass of quicksand that swallows its victims.

The pairing of Montalban and Murphy as equal representatives of their governments provides human interest in the background of the story. These were change-of-pace roles for both actors, who previously were associated with musicals.

The stark documentary look of the film was unusual for glossy MGM. The film was relegated to the bottom half of double bills at theaters, where it played as a B film, but the reviews were uniformly good. The cast also included Alfonso Bedoya, Teresa Celi, and Jose Torvay.

Border River (1954 U)

   D: George Sherman
   S: William Sackheim and Louis Stevens, based on a story by Stevens
   P: Albert J. Cohen
Cast: Joel McCrea, **Pedro Armendariz**, Yvonne De Carlo, **Alfonso Bedoya**

With the South's plight growing more desperate in the closing days of the Civil War, a Confederate major (McCrea) and a band of cohorts steal $2 million in gold bullion from a Union mint. The major crosses the Rio Grande and in the anything-goes-for-cash town of Zona Libre seeks to make a deal for ammunition and supplies for the rebel army. During the course of events he has to deal with a renegade Mexican general (Armendariz) and his girlfriend (De Carlo).

This is a good Technicolor action/western with the usual bandido stereotypes, but at least this time out they are wearing uniforms and have major roles to play. Armendariz is effective as the cruel and sinister general. Bedoya scores as one of the general's aides. The name of the town, Zona Libre (free zone), suggests the North American bordertown fantasy of a Mexican village. There are plenty of Hispanics cast in this one, including Felipe Turich, Nacho Galindo, George J. Lewis, Martin Garralaga, Salvador Baguez, Pilar Del Rey, Orlando Beltran, Zarco Carreno, Estelita Zarco, and Jack Del Rio.

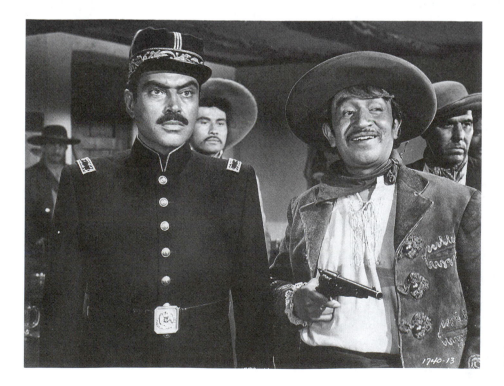

Pedro Armendariz and Alfonso Bedoya in a scene from *Border River*.

Borderline (1950 U)

D: William A. Seiter
S: Devery Freeman
P: Milton H. Bren and William A. Seiter
Cast: Fred MacMurray, Claire Trevor, **Nacho Galindo, Jose Torvay, Pepe Hern**

A female L.A. police officer (Trevor) and a Treasury agent (MacMurray) are sent to Mexico to uncover a nest of dope smugglers and bring them back to the United States. This routine B thriller has some interesting Mexican scenery.

Borderline (1980 AFD)

D: Jerrold Freedman
S: Steve Kline and Jerrold Freedman
P: James Nelson
Cast: Charles Bronson, Bruno Kirby, Ed Harris, Michael Lerner, Bert Remsen, **Karmin Murcelo, Enrique Castillo, James Victor, Panchito Gomez**

A contemporary action/melodrama that depicts the plight of illegal Mexican aliens and the problems encountered by the U.S. Border Patrol.

A veteran Border Patrol officer, Jeb Maynard (Bronson), is on the trail of the people responsible for his longtime partner's death on the U.S.-Mexico border. The murderer is a former Vietnam vet (Harris), who is part of an illegal-alien smuggling ring headed by a corporate mogul (Lerner) and operated by a rancher (Remsen).

A clue leads Maynard to Elena (Murcelo), an illegal worker employed as a maid in the California town of La Jolla, whose young son (Gomez) was shot alongside the border patrolman. She bravely leads Maynard, disguised as an illegal, back to Tijuana through northern Mexico and onto the smugglers' route.

They look at a traffic jam of cars awaiting entry into the States, only to hear howls of pain emanating from under the hood of a Mercedes-Benz. The Anglo woman at the steering wheel rushes to the hood and unlatches it, and a Mexican woman emerges screaming from radiator burns. She is carted off by the U.S. officials for attempting illegal entry. Elena observes, "So they let the gringa go and next week she'll be back to smuggle a new maid."

A young New York agent (Kirby), sent out to assist the Border Patrol, is horrified when he investigates some shantytowns while in pursuit of the killers. He is unable to arrest illegals because, he realizes, "How can you bust people for trying to better themselves." These are the real and honest moments in a film that is essentially a mediocre modern-day revenge western, in which the illegal alien has no face, no history, no motivation. These immigrant masses, huddled in trucks beneath flats of tomatoes, seem to have no other reason for coming across than to give the Border Patrol something to do. The filmmakers use them as bodies, as nonentities.

Bordertown (1935 WB)

D: Archie Mayo
S: Laird Doyle and Wallace Smith, from an adaptation by Robert Lord, based on a novel by Carroll Graham
P: Robert Lord
EP: Jack L. Warner
Cast: Paul Muni, Bette Davis, Margaret Lindsay, Eugene Pallette, **Soledad Jimenez**

Shooting began on *Bordertown* on September 17, 1934, on a tight, four-week schedule. The opening sequences were shot on a roped-off Olvera Street in downtown Los Angeles. Paul Muni plays Mexican American self-made lawyer Johnny Ramierez from the Los Angeles barrio in this socially oriented melodrama. Indignation at

Paul Muni as the Mexican American lawyer Johnny Ramierez plays opposite the flirtatious Bette Davis in *Bordertown*.

patronizing treatment causes him to strike a member of the law bar's fraternity. He runs off to a bordertown, where he becomes the manager of a nightclub. In the end, a murder, the madness of Davis, and the death of his dream girl as she attempts to flee from him convince Ramierez that his place is with his people.

In his review in the *New York Herald Examiner* (11/24/35), Richard Watts, Jr., said, "Upon occasion it seems to hint that Americans of Mexican parentage should keep their place and not try to mingle with their superiors. Chiefly, though, its more race conscious moments have a way of looking with proper disapproval on California snobbishness, which, the work tells you, has fine words and cruel treatment for Mexican immigrants who attempt to achieve success in the sacred practice of the law."

Born in East L.A. (1987 U)

    D: **Cheech Marin**
    S: **Cheech Marin**
    P: **Peter MacGregor-Scott**
Cast: **Cheech Marin**, Daniel Stern, Jan-Michael Vincent, **Daniel Valdez, Paul Rodriguez, Kamala Lopez, Lupe Ontiveros**

Based on a hit video and song Cheech and Chong had produced a year earlier, inspired by the Bruce Springsteen song "Born in the USA" and a newspaper account of a young Mexican American who had been illegally deported to Mexico.

Cheech decided to go without Chong and explore his own charismatic comic persona in an insightful, comic, and satirical look at what it means to be an American of dual heritage in contemporary America.

While in Tijuana, Cheech Marin as Rudy falls in love with the spirited Salvadoran refugee Dolores (Kamala Lopez) in *Born in East L.A.*

Rudy is a Chicano living in L.A. who is mistakenly arrested during an immigration raid and deported to Mexico. The bulk of the film revolves around Rudy's attempts to prove his identity and citizenship and return to the United States. In the process he rediscovers who he truly is and some basic truths surrounding the dual nature of being a Hispanic in the United States. The film reveals an important emerging artist at work in a somewhat uneven comedy. There are some hilarious and touching scenes that show Marin at his best, such as Rudy trying to show illegals how to be Chicanos, a border crossing featuring hundreds of undocumented workers crossing in broad daylight to the tune of Neil Diamond's "Coming to America," and Rudy trying to prove his citizenship to disbelieving U.S. immigration authorities. The irony is that Rudy can't even speak Spanish. Paul Rodriguez is featured as a recently arrived illegal cousin who visits the family in East L.A. and finds no one home.

Boulevard Nights (1979 WB)
 D: Michael Pressman
 S: Desmond Nakano
 P: Bill Benenson
 EP: Tony Bill
Cast: **Richard Yniguez, Danny De La Paz, Marta Du Bois**

A trendsetter for the 1980s with its dark, dismal, and disturbing view of gang life in the L.A. barrios. Richard Yniguez as Raymond and Danny De La Paz as Chuco (making his screen debut) star as brothers involved in gang activities, and Marta Du Bois is Raymond's girl, Shady. Raymond, who has long since abandoned gang life, promises his mother (Betty Carvalho) that he will take care of his younger brother Chuco and keep him away from gangs.

The stylistic, innovative lighting and camera work, coupled with sensitive performances from a largely Latino cast filmed on actual East L.A. locations, give *Boulevard Nights* an uncompromising realism. Director Michael Pressman and

Executive Producer Tony Bill deserve credit for their work, but ultimately the film proved too much of a downer for most audiences. The Chicano community in the southwestern United States protested against the unflattering and violent portrayal of a portion of its community. First-time screenwriter Japanese American Desmond Nakano wrote the script, which was optioned by Bill when Nakano was still studying at UCLA under the tutelage of Paul Schrader. Tony Bill at the time stated, "What makes *Boulevard Nights* special is that it is not an exploitation film but rather the story of two brothers and their family ties, told realistically and with humanity. It is also the first film of its kind with an all Latino cast. We've broken some new ground."

Bound by Honor [aka: *Blood In . . . Blood Out . . .*] (1993 BV)

    D: Taylor Hackford
    S: Jimmy Santiago Baca, Jeremy Iacone, Floyd Mutrux
    P: Taylor Hackford and Jerry Gershwin
 Cast: Benjamin Bratt, **Jesse Borrego**, **Enrique Castillo**, **Damian Chapa**

A 12-year saga that follows the lives of 3 cousins from East Los Angeles—a gifted painter who turns to narcotics after a brutal beating, a short-tempered boxer who becomes an undercover cop in his old neighborhood, and a half-Chicano gang member who goes to San Quentin and gets caught up in an interracial prison gang war.

The story is a variation on themes and ideas first explored in Edward James Olmos's *American Me* (1992) and shares a writer, Floyd Mutrux. The films were in production at the same time (the summer of 1991) and were filmed in many of the same East L.A. locations. Olmos filmed at Folsom Prison, and Hackford filmed at San Quentin. Hackford's saga is the more ambitious in terms of story and characters (Hackford envisioned two epic films); running almost three hours it went into general release as *Bound by Honor*, though it was known under its original shooting title, *Blood In . . . Blood Out . . .*, up until the month before national release. The film actually opened and was test marketed in various smaller markets around the country under its original title and was reviewed by *The Hollywood Reporter* as such. The original title was restored for the video release in early 1994.

Branded (1950 Par)

    D: Rudolph Mate
    S: Cyril Hume and Sydney Boehm
    P: Mel Epstein
 Cast: Alan Ladd, Mona Freeman, Charles Bickford, Robert Keith,
       Joseph Calleia, Peter Hansen, **Felipe Turich**, Joe Dominguez,
       Salvador Baguez

Choya (Ladd), a wandering gunfighter in Texas and Mexico during the 1890s, poses as the long-lost son of a rancher (Bickford) as part of a conspiracy to steal the man's land. However, once Choya meets Bickford's daughter (Freeman) and finds himself accepted by the family, he changes his mind and refuses to go through with the plot. Subsequently, Choya learns that the real son (Hansen) is alive in Mexico. He goes after the man and succeeds in bringing him home. In so doing he antagonizes the Mexican bandit Mateo Rubriz (Calleia), who has adopted the real heir. After a chase and a battle, all-around reconciliations are effected.

This is an entertaining Technicolor action/western that includes an unusual bandit portrayal by Joseph Calleia as a cultured Mexican bandit with a possessive devotion to his adopted son.

The Bravados (1958 TCF)

    D: Henry King
    S: Philip Yordan, based on the novel by Frank O'Rourke
    P: Henry B. Swope, Jr.
Cast: Gregory Peck, Joan Collins, **Henry Silva**, Lee Van Cleef, Ada Carrasco

Jim Douglass (Peck) rides into a small bordertown and chases into Mexico four escaped outlaws who he believes were responsible for the rape-murder of his wife. One by one he guns the men down, and the last man (Silva) confesses to him that they had nothing to do with the murder. Douglass, now remorseful over killing innocent men, suspects his ranch neighbor and returns home to confront him. This strong western features Peck in fine form and Henry Silva in a sympathetic portrayal as a Mexican Indian outlaw.

The Brave Bulls (1951 Col)

    D: Robert Rossen
    S: John Bright, based on the novel by Tom Lea
    P: Robert Rossen
Cast: **Mel Ferrer, Anthony Quinn, Miroslava, Eugene Iglesias**

Mel Ferrer is Luis Bello, a young Mexican peasant who rises to eminence as a matador. He begins to doubt his own abilities, and thus loses his courage, after he enters into a passionate romance with a high-toned tramp (Miroslava) who double-crosses him with his rough-hewn manager (Quinn) and then dies in a tragic car crash.

Filming on location in Mexico City, Rossen achieved the strong sense of Mexican culture and life in modern-day Mexico City that was also present in the novel.

Quinn is excellent as the rough manager. Ferrer as the matador gives a convincing performance. The Yugoslavian-born, Mexican-raised actress Miroslava committed suicide soon after the film was completed. Eugene Iglesias, a Puerto Rican–born actor, plays Bello's young bullfighter brother.

The details of bullfighting and the action in the bullring were captured to a degree even though the production code at the time would not allow the killing of the bulls to be shown. The cinematographers were Floyd Crosby and James Wong Howe.

The Brave One (1956 RKO)

    D: Irving Rapper
    S: Robert Rich [Dalton Trumbo]
    P: Maurice and Frank King
Cast: Michel Ray, **Rudolfo Hoyos, Jr., Elsa Cardenas**, Carlos Navarro

The Brave One remains the King brothers' most prestigious and highly regarded achievement. Starting from scratch in the 1940s, the three brothers, Frank, Maurice, and Herman, made a quickie exploitation film, *Paper Bullets* (1941), which was a modest box-office success. They continued to produce, specializing in exploitation-type pictures, each successive film boasting a slightly bigger budget. Among their tremendously successful films, are *Dillinger* (1945), *Mutiny* (1952), *Southside 1-1000* (1950), *Drums in the Deep South* (1951), *The Ring* (1952), and *Carnival Story* (1954).

The Brave One was their first film in Technicolor and CinemaScope with stereophonic sound. The original story was entitled "The Boy and the Bull," and was to have been directed by Kurt Neumann. Irving Rapper, the director of some of Warner Bros.' human drama stories (*Now, Voyager* [1942] and *The Corn Is Green* [1945] among them), wound up directing the picture, and in an interview with Charles Higham expressed his fondness for the film: "One picture of mine wasn't compromised: *The Brave One*. They all said, 'What do you see in it?' And I said, 'It's simple, it reads like a fairy tale, it cost $430,000 to make and grossed $8.5 million.'"

Rudolfo Hoyos, Jr., and Elsa Cardenas play father and sister to Michel Ray (center) in *The Brave One*, a story of a boy's love for his pet.

The extensive search by the King brothers to find the right star for the film ended when they saw an English picture called *The Divided Heart* (1954), featuring a young boy called Michel Ray. After a screen test, the 12-year-old was cast in the major role.

The film deals with the fierce love of a Mexican boy for his pet. The animal happens to be a prize-fighting bull nurtured from birth to full-grown magnificence by the youngster, who vehemently refuses to permit the killing of his lifelong companion in the bullring.

Jack Cardiff, Academy Award–winning cinematographer for *The Red Shoes* (1948), photographed the film on location in Mexico City and surrounding areas. The Mexican government gave the film company special permission to film scenes at historic Chapultepec Castle and other locations, including the vast Plaza de Mexico bullring in Mexico City. Celebrated matador Fermin Rivera played himself in the climactic arena sequences.

Out of a cast of 150 speaking parts, 148 Latin roles were cast in Mexico. Michel Ray is of French-German parentage and a naturalized British citizen. Mexican-born but U.S.-raised Rudolfo Hoyos, Jr., plays the father. Hoyos, Jr., had been featured in a number of Hollywood films including *The Fighter* (1952), *Second Chance* (1953), *The Americano* (1955), and *Timetable* (1956). Mexican actress Elsa Cardenas plays the boy's sister. An established actress in Mexico, Cardenas was signed by a Hollywood talent scout based on her work in *The Brave One* for a major role in Warner Bros.' *Giant* (1956).

The film won an Academy Award for Best Motion Picture Story in 1956, at which time it was discovered that there was no writer named Robert Rich. At the time there was considerable suspicion that blacklisted writer Dalton Trumbo was the author, and he admitted it publicly two years later when the Academy repealed the blacklist ruling. In May 1975, Trumbo was given his belated Oscar by Academy president Walter Mirisch, about a year before the acclaimed screenwriter died.

Brazil (1944 Rep) [aka: *Stars and Guitars* (1951)]

    D: Joseph Santley
    S: Frank Gill, Jr., and Laura Kerr, based on a story by Richard English
    P: Robert North
Cast: **Tito Guizar**, Virginia Bruce, Veloz and Yolanda, **Frank Puglia, Fortunio Bonanova, Aurora Miranda**

A young Brazilian composer attempts to capture the heart of an American woman who has written a book called *Why Marry a Latin?* She finds herself the victim of her own book when she travels to Brazil to write another one.

This pleasant musical/comedy is dominated by Tito Guizar, who is an engaging personality and sings quite a few songs. Ary Barroso, the distinguished Brazilian composer and author of the song "Brazil," wrote the musical score for the film. Roy Rogers makes an appearance singing "Hands Across the Border," by Hoagy Carmichael. Aurora Miranda is seen briefly as a dancer, and Veloz and Yolanda do a specialty dance number. *Brazil* was filmed at Republic Studios in Hollywood with background scenes filmed by a second unit on location in Brazil. The film was reedited and rereleased in 1951 as *Stars and Guitars*.

Break of Dawn (1989 Platform Releasing)

    D: Isaac Artenstein
    S: Isaac Artenstein
    P: Jude Eberhard
Cast: Oscar Chavez, Maria Rojo, **Pepe Serna**, **Tony Plana**, Socorro Valdez

The true story of Pedro Gonzalez, the first Spanish-language radio and recording star on the West Coast of the United States, who in 1934 was sent to San Quentin Prison on trumped-up charges.

The film documents Gonzalez's rise in popularity during the Golden Age of Radio with his original and romantic ballads and his daily commentary on radio station KMPC in Los Angeles. Gonzalez's rise and success occur during the Depression, when nearly half a million people of Mexican descent were deported to Mexico.

He becomes an outspoken critic of the unjust scapegoating of Mexicans in a stagnant U.S. economy. Gonzalez refuses to heed the warnings of the authorities and is framed on rape charges by a fearful and power-hungry district attorney. Gonzalez is convicted and sent to San Quentin. The film culminates with his wife, Maria, organizing the Mexican community in the United States to free her husband and clear his name.

Break of Dawn was written and directed by Isaac Artenstein, a Mexican of Jewish ancestry who resides in San Diego. It was produced by his longtime associate Jude Eberhard, and the project had its beginnings in a documentary on the life of Gonzalez, *Ballad of an Unsung Hero*, which aired nationally on PBS and won numerous awards, including an Emmy.

Break of Dawn was shown at the 1989 U.S. Film Festival and represented the United States at the 1989 Moscow Film Festival. The bilingual film was released in art houses and English-language theaters in the Southwest for limited runs. Critical response to the film was respectful but lukewarm, charging that the script lacked depth and was not clear as to the events. It was filmed on a budget of less than $1 million in and around San Diego, which doubled for 1930s Los Angeles. Artenstein and Eberhard were able to raise the money for the modestly budgeted feature from private investors largely because of the success of other independent features such as *Heartland* (1979) and *El Norte* (1984). "The restrictions of a small independent feature like this have one big advantage, complete creative responsibility," remarked Artenstein during an interview with Luis Reyes.

The cast was headed by noted Mexican folksinger Oscar Chavez as Pedro J. Gonzalez and Maria Rojo as his wife. Chavez as Gonzalez had the singing voice but lacked charisma and strong acting ability. Pepe Serna turned in one of his dependable supporting portrayals as a relative. Tony Plana was excellent as an ambitious police official. The film is an alternative view, another voice in documenting a piece of Hispanic American history, though it cannot overcome the first-time director's script and limited budget.

Breakout (1975 Col)
    D: Tom Gries
    S: Howard B. Kreitsek, Marc Norman, and Elliot Baker
    P: Robert Chartoff and Irwin Winkler
 Cast: Charles Bronson, Robert Duvall, Randy Quaid, **Alejandro Rey**, Jill Ireland, **John Huston, Emilio Fernandez**

Action/drama in which American aviator Nick Colton (Bronson) is hired to engineer the daring helicopter rescue from a Mexican prison yard of an American citizen, Jay Wagner (Duvall), who has been framed by his father-in-law (Huston).

The Bridge of San Luis Rey (1929 MGM)
    D: Charles Brabin
    S: Alice Duer Miller, Ruth Cummings, and Marian Ainslee, based on the novel by Thornton Wilder
    P: Unknown
 Cast: Lily Damita, Ernest Torrence, **Raquel Torres, Don Alvarado, Duncan Renaldo**

Based on the classic Thornton Wilder novel set in Peru that explores how the five victims of a bridge collapse happen to be there at the same time.

The Bridge of San Luis Rey (1944 UA)
    D: Rowland V. Lee
    S: Herman Weissman and Howard Estabrook, based on the novel by Thornton Wilder
    P: Benedict Bogeaus
 Cast: Lynn Bari, Alla Nazimova, Louis Calhern, Akim Tamiroff, Francis Lederer, Donald Woods

Remake of Wilder's moody story about five people meeting doom on a rickety bridge.

The Bright Shawl (1923 FN)
    D: John S. Richardson
    S: Edmund Goulding, based on a 1922 novel by Joseph Hergesheimer
    P: Charles H. Duell
 Cast: Richard Barthelmess, Dorothy Gish, Mary Astor, Edward G. Robinson, George Humbert, William Powell

Silent. Romance and adventure in the 1850s, when Cuba sought its independence from Spain. A wealthy New Yorker accompanies a Cuban friend to Cuba and is thrust into dangerous adventures and two romances. This silent drama was filmed on location in Cuba.

Bring Me the Head of Alfredo Garcia (1974 UA)
    D: **Sam Peckinpah**
    S: **Sam Peckinpah** and Gordon Dawson, based on a story by Frank Kowalski
    P: Martin Baum
 Cast: Warren Oates, **Isela Vega**, Gig Young, **Emilio Fernandez**

A down-and-out gringo soldier of fortune (Oates) becomes entangled in a web of murder and deceit when a wealthy Mexican (Fernandez) patron offers a $10,000 reward for the head of a young hustler who has made his daughter pregnant. The film opens beautifully and ambiguously with the father's confrontation of his wayward daughter in what appears to be nineteenth-century Mexico, then unexpectedly cuts to modern limousines roaring out of hacienda gates and jets taking off from airports.

This ugly, ultraviolent film is full of Mexican stereotypes and harsh Mexican scenery. Isela Vega, an attractive Mexican actress, plays a whore companion who gives the film's lead (Oates) crabs and is raped by a biker.

The Mexican government co-produced this film, and apparently the stereotypes did not bother them, as in reality many of the character types were frequently featured in Mexican films of the period. The film met with a cool reception at U.S. box offices.

The Buddy Holly Story (1978 Col)

D: Steve Rash
S: Robert Gittler, based on the book by John Coldrosen
P: Fred Bauer
Cast: Gary Busey, **Maria Richwine**, Charles Martin Smith, Don Stroud, **Gloria Irrizary**

The story of Texas-born rock 'n' roll legend Buddy Holly, who, at the beginning of his rise to fame in 1959, died in a plane crash. This superior, sparse film was produced as a heartwarming, sentimental bio-pic, which found favor with critics and audiences alike. All the actors played their own music, and Busey sang. The music was recorded live during the shooting of the scenes, which helped to capture the energy of early rock 'n' roll.

The film sensitively handles Holly's courtship and marriage to a Puerto Rican girl from New York, Maria Elena (Richwine), who worked at the record company for which he recorded.

Busey earned an Academy Award nomination as Best Actor for his performance. The Colombian-born, U.S.-raised Maria Richwine played a variation of the traditional senorita in her film debut. Her career never quite took off the way it should have. She was stymied for a time, after an altercation with the film's influential casting director, Joyce Selznick. Since then she has been featured in a number of low-budget films and guest shots on television. Gloria Irrizary played Maria Elena's aunt.

Teen rock 'n' rollers the Big Bopper and Ritchie Valens were also killed in the plane crash. Valens, who is a minor figure in this film, was played by Gilbert Melgar. Valens was later immortalized in the film *La Bamba* almost ten years later, in 1987.

Maria Richwine portrays Buddy Holly's wife in *The Buddy Holly Story*. Gary Busey (right) stars in the title role.

The Bullfighter and the Lady (1951 Rep)
   D: **Budd Boetticher**
   S: James Edward Grant, based on a story by **Budd Boetticher** and
      Ray Nazarro
   P: John Wayne
Cast: Robert Stack, **Joy Page**, **Gilbert Roland**, Virginia Grey, John Hubbard,
      Rodolfo Acosta, **Katy Jurado**

The story of an American, Chuck Regan (Stack), vacationing in Mexico with two friends (Grey and Hubbard). He falls in love with a Mexican girl, Anita de la Vega (Page), and, in order to impress her, persuades a matador, Manolo Estrada (Roland), to instruct him on the use of the cape and sword. When the matador dies in the ring saving Regan's life, Regan must vindicate his honor and courage in the face of a hostile crowd.

Like his hero, director Budd Boetticher had studied bullfighting in Mexico as a young American. Earlier in his film career, he had been technical advisor for the bullfight sequences in Rouben Mamoulian's *Blood and Sand* (1941). After *The Bullfighter and the Lady* he went on to make *The Magnificent Matador* (1955) and *Arruza* (1972). *The Bullfighter and the Lady* has a great feeling for the land and can be compared favorably to Robert Rossen's *The Brave Bulls*, which came out the same year.

Produced by John Wayne for Republic, it was originally to star Wayne, who felt himself too big physically to play a matador believably and therefore gave the role to Robert Stack. Eight of Mexico's leading matadors appear in the film as themselves, and two of them, the Briones brothers, also double for Stack and Roland in the bullfighting scenes. Katy Jurado played Chelo, wife of the matador. It was filmed entirely in Mexico over seven weeks on a $400,000 budget.

The project lent itself to bilingual treatment, and Boetticher believes he succeeded in obtaining complete linguistic realism, English and Spanish being used by the characters, without any sacrifice of intelligibility, exactly as they would use them in actuality. Boetticher had to emasculate the great Latin fiesta at its three climaxes—the impact of the toro and the pic, the insertion of the banderillas, and the final sword thrust—to mollify the Society for the Prevention of Cruelty to Animals.

The film was originally released in an 87-minute version edited by director John Ford, who admired Boetticher's work and thought the editing would improve the film's chances of commercial success. In 1987 the UCLA Film Archive restored the film to its original 124-minute length with the assistance of Boetticher.

Gilbert Roland received excellent notices for his portrayal of the aging bullfighter: "The most exciting performance in a collection of good ones is that of Gilbert Roland, who plays the popular matador, the teacher of Stack," Darr Smith, *L.A. Daily News* (4/26/51).

"Without overplaying, [Roland] gives his matador character color and vigor, bravery without bravado, and dignity. Katy Jurado, as Roland's wife, is another who makes a very strong impression," *Variety* (5/2/51).

The Bullfighters (1945 TCF)
   D: Malcolm St. Clair
   S: W. Scott Darling
   P: William Girard
Cast: Stan Laurel, Oliver Hardy

Laurel and Hardy in Mexico as private detectives in search of a lady criminal.

Butch Cassidy and the Sundance Kid (1969 TCF)

D: George Roy Hill
S: William Goldman
P: Paul Monash and John Foreman
Cast: Paul Newman, Robert Redford, Katharine Ross, **Jose Torvay**

Story of turn-of-the-century outlaws Butch Cassidy (Newman) and the Sundance Kid (Redford). This clever, well-acted western depends a great deal on the offbeat casting and striking chemistry of its two stars. In this buddy picture, the relationship of the two characters is explored through numerous adventurous, sometimes funny, escapades.

Robbing banks and being chased by the law throughout the American Southwest, the pair decide to go to Bolivia in order to escape the American authorities and start a new life. Upon their arrival they quickly discover that the pickings are meager and the territory and language present insurmountable problems. The two are besieged by a band of bandidos led by Jose Torvay, whom they are forced to kill. Butch and the Kid meet their deaths in a gun battle with 200 Bolivian army soldiers. While the climax echoes the "truth" of the end of the two antiheroes in real life, it can be argued that the ending continues the time-honored North American film tradition of having a whole army of Latinos kill the two gringos.

The Bolivian scenes were actually shot in Taxco and Cuernavaca, Mexico. It was reported that when director George Roy Hill was informed that the Bolivia of the film looked nothing like the Bolivia of real life, he replied, "Well, it does now."

Bye, Bye Birdie (1963 Col)

D: George Sidney
S: Irving Brecher, based on the stage play by Michael Stewart, Charles Strouse, and Lee Adams
P: Fred Kohlmar
Cast: Janet Leigh, Dick Van Dyke, Ann-Margret, Maureen Stapleton

Film version of the hit 1960 Broadway musical, in which Chita Rivera originated the role of Rosie. Conrad Birdie, rock 'n' roll idol, is about to be drafted into the U.S. Army, which spells doom for Albert Peterson (Van Dyke), a bankrupt songwriter who has written the title tune for the singer's new movie. Now there will be no movie, no title tune, no royalties. Adding to Albert's woes is a possessive mother, Mae (Stapleton), intent on breaking up his romance with Rosie DeLeon (Leigh). Rosie schemes to have Albert write a special farewell song for Birdie in an effort to make Albert rich and pry him away from Mama. A small-town USA television extravaganza results when Birdie visits the hometown of a fan and complications ensue.

In an offbeat casting venture, blonde star Janet Leigh was given a black wig and asked to sing and dance as Rosie DeLeon, the Spanish secretary and girlfriend of Dick Van Dyke.

California (1946 Par)

D: John Farrow
S: Frank Butler and Theodore Strauss, based on a story by Boris Ingster
P: Seton I. Miller
Cast: Ray Milland, Barbara Stanwyck, **Anthony Quinn**

Ray Milland is a cowboy who meets a lady gambler (Stanwyck) while en route to nineteenth-century California and gets involved in foiling an attempt by a former slave trader to establish California as a separate empire.

In this film loosely based on history, Anthony Quinn is featured as Don Luis Rivera y Hernandez, who is asked to support the attempt to usurp power while the Anglo settlers are deciding on California statehood.

California Conquest (1952 Col)
   D: Lew Landers
   S: Robert E. Kent
   P: Sam Katzman
   Cast: Cornel Wilde, Teresa Wright, **Alfonso Bedoya, Eugene Iglesias,**
   Tito Renaldo, Rico Alaniz, **Alex Montoya**

Action melodrama with historical overtones with the emphasis on action. Young Arturo Bordega (Wilde) is the leader of a group of well-to-do Spanish Californians who, tired of Mexican rule and fearing British, French, and Russian claims on their homeland, are hoping for peace and freedom under U.S. rule. Bordega disguises himself as a peon in order to evade capture and gain entrance to a Russian fortress. Wright is an American girl whose father has been slain by the Russians.

The film is representative of the McCarthy-era Cold War paranoia that permeated America in the 1950s, in that the heavies turn out to be Russians. Wilde, who had played suave Latinos previously, was excellent as the California don. Alfonso Bedoya contributed his patented bandit portrayal to good effect.

The Californian [aka: *The Gentleman from California*] (1937 TCF)
   D: Gus Meins
   S: Gilbert Wright, based on a story by Harold Bell Wright, adapted
      by Gordon Newell
   P: Sol Lesser
   Cast: **Ricardo Cortez**, Katherine DeMille, Marjorie Weaver

The story of Ramon Escobar (Cortez), an early California patriot. The film's plot revolves around a Robin Hood theme, and the villains are early American settlers from back East who by force and connivance steal the rich landholdings from the dons.

Of B movie quality with no originality, the film is dull and cliched despite its potentially provocative themes.

Cannery Row (1982 UA/MGM)
   D: David S. Ward
   S: David S. Ward, based on novels by John Steinbeck
   P: Michael Phillips
   Cast: Nick Nolte, Debra Winger, **Santos Morales, Rosana De Soto**

The script by David S. Ward (who had previously won an Academy Award for his script of *The Sting* [1973], and later scripted *The Milagro Beanfield War* [1988]) is based on John Steinbeck's *Cannery Row* and its sequel, *Sweet Thursday*. Set in a boisterous waterfront haven for derelicts, dreamers, and nonconformists, the film focuses on the love affair between an ex-baseball star, Doc (Nolte), and a feisty prostitute, Suzy (Winger). The couple triumph over harsh realities with their compassion and good humor. Santos Morales plays the Mexican American storekeeper Joseph and Mary Rivas. Rosana De Soto plays Ellen. The film got off to a shaky start when Raquel Welch, who was to play Suzy, was fired after several days of filming and was replaced by Debra Winger. The final film received mixed reviews and a poor box-office response.

Captain from Castile (1947 TCF)

   D: Henry King
   S: Lamar Trotti, based on the novel by Samuel Shellabarger
   P: Lamar Trotti
Cast: Tyrone Power, Jean Peters, Lee J. Cobb, **Cesar Romero**, **Thomas Gomez**, John Sutton, **Antonio Moreno**

The first and only major Hollywood film to date on the conquest of Mexico actually filmed in Mexico. *Captain from Castile* is a sumptuously romantic, entertaining film produced at the pinnacle of Hollywood's Golden Age. Any resemblance to history in this account of the conquest of the Aztecs is a swashbuckling, Technicolored coincidence. The story is a partial telling of the Spanish Inquisition and the conquest in 1519 from a Spanish point of view. Only the first part of Shellabarger's massive popular novel was filmed.

Pedro De Vargas (Power) is a young Spanish nobleman who flees to the New World when his family is persecuted by the Inquisition, headed by the brutal and arrogant Diego De Silva (Sutton). While still in Spain, Pedro forgets his vows to a Spanish lady and instead finds romance with the beautiful peasant girl Catana Perez (Peters, in her movie debut), whom he befriends. Catana becomes consumed by a burning love for Pedro, helps him escape from Spain, and follows him to the New World.

Vargas joins Hernando Cortez (Romero) and his expedition at Hispaniola in the exploration of and the conquest of the Aztec nation. Aided by a brave but alcoholic and guilt-ridden soldier of fortune, Juan Garcia (Cobb), Pedro rises to power in Cortez's army. Amidst innumerable hardships, inspired by his love for Catana and driven by his hatred of De Silva, Pedro covers himself with glory yet is unable to wreak his revenge. Finally, justice comes to the fanatic Inquisitor, but from an entirely unsuspected source.

Jean Peters was given the star buildup in her first role after winning a talent contest. Cesar Romero played Cortez, giving a strong performance, which he considered his favorite. He was chosen for the role during a visit to Darryl Zanuck's home when friend Tyrone Power suggested him for the part and Zanuck agreed.

Cesar Romero as Cortez is pleased with Dona Marina (Stella Inda) and with what he sees of the representatives of Montezuma's Aztec Empire in *Captain from Castile*. Jay Silverheels (rear right) portrays Coatl. (Unidentified man in head dress.)

This was the third and final time Power played a Spaniard. He was a big star in Mexico from his previous Spanish outings in *The Mark of Zorro* (1940) and *Blood and Sand* (1941) and he was mobbed wherever he went in Mexico. Before commencing work on *Captain from Castile*, Power made a personal appearance tour of South America along with Cesar Romero, in his own aircraft, *Saludos Amigos*, which, as a former U.S. Marine air pilot, he flew himself.

Silent screen veteran Antonio Moreno plays Power's father, Don Francisco. Stella Inda, a prominent Mexico City stage and screen actress, portrays Dona Marina, the Indian girl who was the interpreter for Cortez and who aided him immensely in his conquest. Dolly Arriaga plays Pedro's sister who dies a victim of the Inquisition. Jay Silverheels, a Native American actor (later famous as Tonto, the Lone Ranger's sidekick, on television in the 1950s), plays the Aztec nobleman Coatl, who is taken as a slave to Spain and escapes back to the New World.

The Mexican government approved the script and cooperated with the film company, which employed many Mexican film technicians.

Filming on a $3.5 million budget on a 106-day shooting schedule beginning on November 15, 1946, the company did not return to the States until March 1, 1947. In the almost four months spent filming in Mexico, three major locations were utilized: Morelia for six weeks, in which the interiors of 300-year-old homes were used to represent Spain; Uruapan for five weeks; and Acapulco for four. The company returned to Los Angeles for an additional 30 days of filming interiors at the Fox studio, where 20 sets were erected.

A special train of eight railroad cars was sent to Mexico City from Los Angeles. One car contained some 5,000 Aztec lances, 6,000 Indian shields, and 400 crossbows. Another car carried lighting and grip equipment as well as refrigerator units to preserve the Technicolor film from the heat and humidity of the remote locations. Also included were wardrobe for extras as well as costumes for the leading and supporting players. The Mexico City Museum cooperated with the Twentieth Century–Fox research department in researching details of culture and time period.

Four thousand extras in Mexico, including Tarascan Indians, were employed to portray Aztecs and Spaniards for the final sequences of the film. An Aztec temple, 40 feet high and 20 feet long, surrounded by a village of 40 huts, was built inland from Acapulco in Uruapan with the then-active volcano Parícutin in the background.

Mexican artists were hired to re-create on the walls inside the temple chambers murals that were exact copies of the ones preserved in the museum in Mexico City.

James Basevi, an art director on the film, recalled one intentional error in an interview with Virginia Wright in the *Daily News* (4/30/47):

> Every student of history knows that Cortez landed on the East Coast of Mexico, but in the movie we have him landing on the West Coast. We had two reasons for the shift. The locations were enough of an undertaking without the added complications of transporting actors and equipment all the way across Mexico. Then, weather is uncertain on the East Coast at the time of the year we wanted to shoot. There is very little difference in the tropical foliage. Both locations have coconut palms. More fortunate for our purposes the coastal contours at Acapulco are such that the sun actually rises over the water. We photographed a sunrise and nobody would be able to tell we shot the other ocean.

One of the film's highlights is a rousing, now-classic music score by Alfred Newman. The "March Conquest," which serves as the film's finale, is one of the most stirring compositions for the screen and is still played today by college and high school marching bands, especially at football games.

Captain from Castile has an irritating ending because the film ends before Cortez establishes diplomatic relations with Montezuma and before the ensuing clash of cultures. It ends with the conquistadors being led by Aztec messengers into the Valley of Mexico in a triumphant march into the sunset with a voice-over by Fray Bartolome de las Casas (Gomez) expressing hopes that the Spaniards are less interested in gold than in opening up a great new world to Old World civilization.

Captain Thunder (1931 WB)

D: Alan Crosland
S: Original story by Hal Davitt and Pierre Couderc; adaptation by Gordon Rigby; dialogue by William K. Web
P: Warner Bros.
Cast: Victor Varconi, Fay Wray, Charles Judels, Robert Elliott, **Don Alvarado**

A Mexican Robin Hood called Capt. Thunder (Varconi) always keeps his word to friend or foe. He has fun when Commandante Ruiz dispatches soldiers to capture him for a 50,000 peso reward. Thunder sends them back, bound and gagged on horses. Fay Wray plays Inez Dominguez. The Italian Varconi's accent is not quite Spanish in this early sound film.

Captains Courageous (1937 MGM)

D: Victor Fleming
S: John Lee Mahin, Marc Connelly, and Dale Van Evers, based on the novel by Rudyard Kipling
P: Louis D. Lighton
Cast: Spencer Tracy, Freddie Bartholomew, Lionel Barrymore

Based on Rudyard Kipling's classic nineteenth-century story of the developing friendship between a spoiled rich boy and a simple Portuguese fisherman named Manuel.

Spencer Tracy, of Irish descent, born near Milwaukee, Wisconsin, plays a Portuguese fisherman. Although his attempts at an accent are inconsistent, he projects sincerity and understanding coupled with infectious good humor and a joy for life that melt the boy's prejudice against an environment and people strange to him.

Tracy was at first reluctant to tackle the part, for he did not want to have his hair curled or to attempt a dialect role, but in the end he won the 1937 Academy Award for Best Actor for his performance.

Carlito's Way (1993 U)

D: Brian De Palma
S: David Koepp, based on the novels by **Edwin Torres**
P: Martin Bregman, Willi Baer, and Michael S. Bregman
Cast: Al Pacino, Sean Penn, Penelope Ann Miller, **John Leguizamo**, **Luis Guzman**, Viggo Mortensen, Jorje Porcel, **Jaime Sanchez**, John Ortiz, **Al Israel**

Al Pacino reteams with *Scarface* filmmakers Brian De Palma and Martin Bregman to star as Carlito Brigante, a once-notorious Puerto Rican gangster who, after winning his release from prison, tries desperately to retire from his life of crime. Although he dreams of settling down in the Bahamas, the treachery of old friends and rivals inevitably forces him onto a path of destruction.

The film is full of the Hispanic/Puerto Rican stereotype of the violent, inarticulate, poverty-stricken urban dweller who deals in drugs. There are no positive Puerto Rican characters, and the script meanders all over the place. There are no Hispanic women in the film except the sex object salsa dance queens who hang out at an after-hours club. There is no character development that reflects Carlito's ethnic background, and whatever there is of Spanish Harlem life is painted in very broad, superficial strokes. He has an Anglo dream girl, Gail (Miller), who is not all she makes herself out to be and who does

71

not acknowledge Carlito's ethnicity, calling him Charley instead of Carlito. Rather than go to Puerto Rico, Carlito wants to retire to the Bahamas and open a car rental agency, as if the character is rejecting his roots. The filmmakers had a chance to make an interesting film about the New York–Puerto Rican experience but instead made a crime saga devoid of a genuine ethnic or sociological point of view. John Leguizamo as Benny Blanco from the Bronx makes an impression but is essentially wasted in a small role, and Luis Guzman as Carlito's thickheaded bodyguard Pachanga gives a good character performance grounded in reality. Viggo Mortensen gives a chilling, heartfelt performance as Lali, a wheelchair-bound former crony of Carlito. Jaime Sanchez plays a waiter at the club.

Carnival in Costa Rica (1947 TCF)

   D: Gregory Ratoff
   S: John Larkin, Samuel Hoffenstein, and Elizabeth Reinhardt
   P: William A. Bacher
Cast: **Cesar Romero**, Vera-Ellen, Celeste Holm, **Dick Haymes,**
       J. Carroll Naish, Pedro De Cordoba

Pleasant, diverting little musical/comedy in which two well-to-do families have betrothed their children (Romero and Vera-Ellen) without taking their wishes into consideration. He is in love with an American nightclub singer (Holm), and she is in love with a young American visitor (Haymes). The fathers (Naish and De Cordoba) are left to straighten out the situation. Full of music and songs, the picture was filmed on the Fox backlot and studio. A film crew was sent to Costa Rica without the cast to gather background footage of the country for insertion in the film.

Casualties of War (1989 Col)

   D: Brian De Palma
   S: David Rabe, based on the book by Daniel Lang
   P: Art Linson amd Fred Caruso
Cast: Michael J. Fox, Sean Penn, **John Leguizamo**

American soldiers during the Vietnam conflict on a long-range reconnaissance mission abduct, brutally rape, and then murder a South Vietnamese village girl. A battle of wills ensues between the rookie Eriksson (Fox) and the deranged squad leader, Sgt. Maserve (Penn), over the incident. Leguizamo plays Diaz, the newest member of the squad, who vacillates between Eriksson and Maserve, which takes its toll on him.

Cat Chaser (1990 Vestron)

   D: Abel Ferrara
   S: Jim Borrelli and Alan Sharp, based on the novel by Elmore Leonard
   P: Peter S. Davis and William Panzer
Cast: Peter Weller, Kelly McGillis, **Tomas Milian, Juan Fernandez,**
       Frederic Forrest, Charles Durning, **Victor Rivers**

An overly complex caper movie about a former marine, George Moran (Weller), involved in the U.S. invasion of Santo Domingo (now Dominican Republic) during the 1960s, who returns to the island to try to find the woman who taunted him with the name "Cat Chaser" but also saved his life when he was captured by the guerrillas. His search involves him in an affair with Mary DeBoya (McGillis), who happens to be married to Andres DeBoya (Milian), the former head of the Santo Domingo secret police now living in Miami, and a plot by Nolan Tyner (Forrest) and Jiggs (Durning) to steal Andres DeBoya's money.

Catlow [aka: *Maverick Gold*] (1971 MGM)
  D: Sam Wanamaker
  S: Scot Finch and J.J. Griffith, based on the novel by Louis L'Amour
  P: Euan Lloyd
Cast: Yul Brynner, Richard Crenna, Daliah Lavi

Tongue-in-cheek western about Catlow (Brynner), a cattle rustler pursued by a longtime friend and lawman (Crenna). Catlow gets involved in Mexico with a Mexican spitfire (Lavi) and the lawman finds romance with the aristocratic Mexican woman Christina, all the while eluding Indians and Mexican cavalry.

This fair-to-amusing western with stereotyped characterizations all the way around was filmed in Spain, representing the Texas-Mexico border area.

Cha-Cha-Cha Boom (1956 Col)
  D: Fred F. Sears
  S: James B. Gordon and Benjamin H. Kline
  P: Sam Katzman
Cast: Steve Dunn, Alix Talton

Low-budget film designed to capitalize on the cha-cha and mambo dance crazes that spread across the United States in the mid-1950s. A disc jockey attempts to sign new talent from Cuba for his own recording company. The plot is an excuse to string together a number of musical acts.

The only value the movie has today is its musical and visual record of the legendary Perez Prado, the Mary Kaye Trio, Helen Grayco, and the bands of Luis Acaraz and Manny Lopez. Comic actor Jose Gonzalez-Gonzalez provided the comedy relief. Director Fred Sears also helmed the first rock 'n' roll movie, *Rock Around the Clock*, the same year.

Charlie Chan in Panama (1940 TCF)
  D: Norman Foster
  S: John Larkin and Lester Ziffren, based on the character created by Earl Derr Biggers
  P: Sol M. Wurtzel
Cast: Sidney Toler, Jean Rogers, Lionel Atwill, **Chris-Pin Martin**

Charlie Chan (Toler) works for the American government thwarting a spy plot to destroy the American naval fleet as it passes through the Panama Canal on its way to the Pacific.

Charlie Chan in Rio (1941 TCF)
  D: Harry Lachman
  S: Samuel G. Engel and Lester Ziffren, based on the character created by Earl Derr Biggers
  P: Sol M. Wurtzel
Cast: Sidney Toler, Mary Beth Hughes, Cobina Wright, Jr.

In Rio de Janeiro, Chan works with the local police to solve a pair of murders. The locale allowed for music and romance in doses unusual for a Chan picture in line with the studio's first attempts at the Good Neighbor Policy. This is a reworking of *The Black Camel* (1931), an early Charlie Chan film starring Warner Oland. Hamilton MacFadden, who directed *The Black Camel*, appears in this movie as Bill Kellogg.

Charro! (1969 NG)

    D: Charles Marquis Warren
    S: Charles Marquis Warren, based on a story by Frederic Louis Fox
    P: Harry Caplan and Charles Marquis Warren
Cast: Elvis Presley, Ina Balin, Victor French

A tedious, melodramatic action western in which an outlaw and his henchmen steal from the Mexicans a gold-and-silver-adorned victory cannon, which fired the last shot against the emperor Maximilian.

Former outlaw Jesse Wade (Presley) is branded and falsely accused of being the cannon-stealing culprit. Soon soldiers on both sides of the border are hunting down Wade. He must prove his innocence and protect a bordertown from being ravaged by the outlaw gang.

Ina Balin is Tracy, a saloon keeper with whom Wade renews a friendship. Balin's character could be Mexican based on her appearance and the location of the story, but she plays the role without an accent. The bearded Presley, who plays it straight, is named Jesse Wade, yet is called Charro, the name for a Mexican cowboy. Presley's dark looks suggest he could be a Mexican or a "half-breed," like the characters he had played in *Flaming Star* (1960) and *Stay Away, Joe* (1968). Tony Young plays Lt. Rivera and James Almanzar plays Sheriff Ramsey.

Che! (1969 TCF)

    D: Richard Fleischer
    S: Michael Wilson and Sy Bartlett, based on a story by Bartlett and David Karp
    P: Sy Bartlett
Cast: Omar Sharif, Jack Palance, Cesare Danova, Robert Loggia, Woody Strode, **Perry Lopez**, Rudy Diaz, **Barbara Luna**, **Frank Silvera**, Sarita Vara

Soon after the death of controversial Latin American revolutionary Dr. Ernesto (Che) Guevara, Twentieth Century–Fox chief Darryl F. Zanuck sent a request to Richard D. Zanuck, executive vice president in charge of production, to explore the possibility of producing a biographical film about the famous guerrilla fighter. Producer Sy Bartlett was assigned to the project because of his long record of association with Latin American people and their countries and because of his knowledge of the Spanish language. Bartlett then interviewed more than 100 persons, traveled thousands of miles, and used his contacts through governmental and military sources in the United States and Latin America to gather his material. Two months after Che's death and some 45 days after he had started his extensive research program, Bartlett turned in two voluminous reports that became the basis of a treatment.

Michael Wilson and Bartlett wrote a screenplay that covers the period from Che's landing with Castro in Cuba through the successful revolution and takeover of Cuba, which swept the Batista regime from power, and on to the futile guerrilla campaigns on the rugged Andean slopes and his death in Bolivia at the hands of Bolivian army rangers.

Omar Sharif, who had scored heavily in English-speaking films since *Lawrence of Arabia* (1962), his first, and cemented his reputation with *Doctor Zhivago* (1965) and *Funny Girl* (1968), was cast as Guevara. With beard and mustache he bears an uncanny resemblance to Che. Jack Palance plays Fidel Castro. Luna is Nurse Anita Marquez, who aids in doctoring guerrillas, Cuban peasants, and army soldiers alike. Near the end of the film, Silvera appears as an old goatherd who tells Che and an officer that he doesn't want what either of them pretend to offer. The film also features Sarita Vara, Perry Lopez, and Rudy Diaz in small roles.

Che! was filmed in Puerto Rico, subbing for Cuba, and in Hollywood with the Fox Ranch as Bolivia. Many actors from Puerto Rico were cast in small roles.

This middle-of-the-road film, which does not delve deeply into its subject matter, presents its story in a haphazard flashback narrative style.

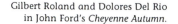

Gilbert Roland and Dolores Del Rio
in John Ford's *Cheyenne Autumn*.

Cheyenne Autumn (1964 WB)

    D: **John Ford**
    S: James R. Webb, based on the novel by Mari Sandoz
    P: Bernard Smith
Cast: Richard Widmark, Carroll Baker, **Gilbert Roland, Ricardo Montalban, Dolores Del Rio**, Sal Mineo, Karl Malden

A curious entry in that this tale of the long trek of the Cheyenne nation forced off their lands by the U.S. government in 1876 afforded the opportunity for three of Hollywood's legendary Hispanic American actors (Roland, Del Rio, and Montalban) to work together in starring roles for the only time, playing Native Americans, under the direction of John Ford.

Though these kinds of roles have often previously gone to Hispanic or other ethnic players for limited, one-dimensional characterizations (e.g., Henry Brandon in *The Searchers* [1956] as Chief Scar), these three actors brought enormous weight, dignity, and presence to a movie that affords an unusually epic and sympathetic view of Native Americans.

Roland plays Chief Dull Knife, who takes his people on a trek back to their homeland rather than face starvation and humiliation on a reservation. Ricardo Montalban plays Little Wolf, whose desire is to lead his people in a fight to the death with the white man. Dolores Del Rio plays Spanish Woman.

Roland, Del Rio, and director Ford had begun their careers in the silents and understood intuitively what was needed before the cameras. Montalban had proven himself a serious actor, not just a Latin lover type. After a successful career in Mexico, Del Rio had returned to Hollywood four years earlier to play Elvis Presley's Native American mother in *Flaming Star* (1960). Del Rio had had a close relationship with Ford since her early days in Hollywood and had worked with him previously in *The Fugitive* (1948).

In *Life* magazine (11/27/64), Richard Oulahan in his review said that "[though Del Rio] may be the handsomest woman of the 20th century[,] in this 3 ½ hour Trojan horse opera, she seldom gets a chance to show her acting skill. All she is allowed to do is look noble or sad while the camera gazes fondly at her classic face from any angle."

Perhaps for Ford these icons of both the silent and sound cinema represented a symbolic acknowledgment of a passing of the Hollywood he had helped to create, both on screen and off, a passing of a way of life that paralleled the experience of the Native Americans in the film.

Italian American Sal Mineo, then Hollywood's all-purpose ethnic teenager, was cast as a Native American along with another screen veteran, Victor Jory, as an old medicine man. The film's sympathies clearly lie with the Native Americans, but you never really get to know them as individual human beings. Much too much screen time is devoted to the white cavalry officer (Widmark), well-intentioned and scheming whites, and the bureaucratic red tape of Washington's policies. As with any Ford film, *Cheyenne Autumn* has some masterful moments highlighted by William H. Clothier's cinematography.

The Children of Sanchez (1978 Lone Star Int.)

D: Hall Bartlett
S: Cesare Zavattini and Hall Bartlett, based on the book by Oscar Lewis
P: Hall Bartlett
Cast: **Anthony Quinn, Dolores Del Rio**, Lupita Ferrer, **Katy Jurado**

After many years of trying to produce a feature film from the classic 1961 book about Oscar and Ruth Lewis's experiences living with Jesus Sanchez and his family in a Mexico City slum, Hall Bartlett was able to overcome Mexican government objections to its negative depiction of Mexican urban life in order to produce, write, and direct this bleak, disjointed, depressing film.

The talented cast of Latino performers could not overcome the script and the directorial weaknesses. Gabriel Figueroa's color lighting was inappropriate for this story of slum life. The film featured all the typical Latin stereotypes, without depth or understanding. Anthony Quinn's performance is the strongest element in the film, but even he can't overcome the movie's shortcomings despite the fact that for many years Quinn had also longed to do a film of this story. *The Children of Sanchez* was a co-production with the Mexican government. Popular jazz artist Chuck Mangione scored the film, and the theme from the movie became a popular seller and more widely known than the movie itself, which had an extremely limited U.S. release through a small distribution company, Lone Star International, that quickly folded.

"Earnest but flawed attempt to flesh out Oscar Lewis book," *Variety* (9/20/78).

"*The Children of Sanchez* is a heartbreaker, but not in the sense it was intended to be. The sadness, which ends up not much short of heartbreak, is that so monumentally important a work has been so abysmally translated into a movie. It is amateurish, stiff, uncinematic and unmoving," Charles Champlin, *L.A. Times* (9/22/78).

Perry Lopez (right) co-stars with
Jack Nicholson in *Chinatown*.

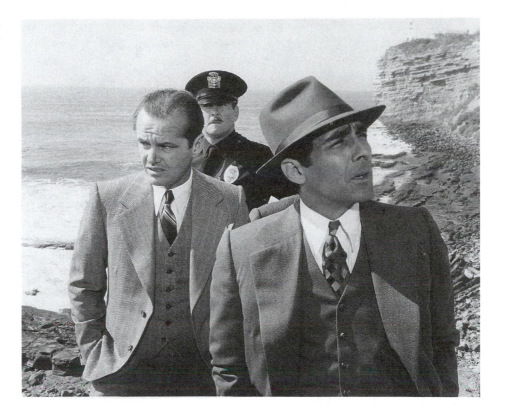

Chinatown (1974 Par)

D: Roman Polanski
S: Robert Towne
P: Robert Evans
Cast: Jack Nicholson, Faye Dunaway, **John Huston, Perry Lopez**

Perry Lopez played Mexican American police detective Lt. Luis Escobar, friend to Jack Nicholson's detective character, Jake Gittes, in what is considered by many a classic mystery thriller. Lopez's role was a major one in an important motion picture, which found favor with critics and audiences alike. It was unusual to find a Mexican American detective as a positive law enforcement figure, free from stereotypical restraints, in a film set in 1930s Los Angeles. More unusual was that the role was played by a Hispanic. Lopez, a screen veteran, seized the opportunity and gave a memorable flesh-and-blood portrayal opposite Nicholson.

Sixteen years later he re-created the role in the long-awaited but disappointing sequel, *The Two Jakes* (1990), written and directed by and starring Jack Nicholson. The story continues ten years later, but the character of Escobar, now a captain, lacks the vitality and the importance he had in the original film. The film does explain Escobar's loss of a leg due to a war injury, acknowledging the valiant sacrifices made by Mexican Americans in World War II.

Christopher Columbus (1949 U)

D: David MacDonald
S: Sydney and Muriel Box and Cyril Roberts
P: A. Frank Bundy
Cast: Fredric March, Florence Eldridge, Francis L. Sullivan

Sumptuous, handsome Technicolor production with March as a Columbus without much vitality in a weak script. The ocean voyage ship exteriors were photographed in the studio against painted backdrops.

"Often heavy handed, lumbering and far too prosaic in setting forth its story. The Anglo-Saxon approach to fervid Latin emotions is inept," Edwin Schallert, *L.A. Times* (11/9/49).

Christopher Columbus: The Discovery (1992 WB)

D: John Glen
S: Mario Puzo, John Briley, and Cary Bates
P: Ilya Salkind
Cast: Marlon Brando, Tom Selleck, Rachel Ward, George Corraface

Sweeping, lightweight, one-dimensional saga of a man who challenged the limits of his own universe and became the world's most influential explorer. The evil Spanish Inquisitor Torquemada, played by Marlon Brando, is softened, and the only Hispanic in the cast, Beneicio Del Toro, plays a dastardly villain. Rachel Ward plays Queen Isabella, and Tom Selleck, King Ferdinand. Filmed on location in Spain and in the West Indies, this film presents history as you might expect from the makers of *Superman*. Plenty of bare-breasted Indian women are on display at Columbus's landing in the New World. The unrealistic and unlikely image of the engine of the Spanish Inquisition, Torquemada, waving Columbus bye-bye from the dock probably best sums up this movie's "dedication" to historical accuracy. This is a movie whose motto is clearly "Never let the facts interfere with a good story."

Cisco Pike (1971 Col)

D: B.W.L. Norton
S: B.W.L. Norton
P: Gerald Ayres
Cast: Kris Kristofferson, Karen Black, Gene Hackman, **Antonio Fargas**

Dramatic film debut of Kris Kristofferson as Cisco Pike, a former folk rock composer and an ex-con who is being blackmailed by a corrupt narcotics detective (Hackman) into dealing drugs. Fargas has a small role as a dope dealer.

Nothing in the film indicates the lead character to be Hispanic except for his first name.

City Across the River (1949 U)

D: Maxwell Shane
S: Maxwell Shane, Dennis Cooper, and Irving Shulman, based on a novel by Shulman
P: Maxwell Shane
Cast: Stephen McNally, Richard Benedict, Luis Van Rooten, Peter Fernandez, Anthony (Tony) Curtis, Thelma Ritter, Richard Jaeckel

Adapted from Irving Shulman's novel *The Amboy Dukes* about juvenile delinquency and youth gangs in a Brooklyn slum, *City Across the River* is quite possibly the first so-called youth gang film. The 19-year-old Peter Fernandez, of Irish-Cuban descent, with 10 years of stage and radio experience, plays a Polish youth, Frankie Cusack, who, because of living in slum conditions and being neglected by parents who both work, joins a gang of tough Brooklyn boys calling themselves the Amboy Dukes (after Amboy Street).

Violent and somewhat simplistic, *City Across the River* has a semidocumentary tone: much of it was shot on location and it features many young unknown actors, with the unusual casting turn of a Hispanic, Fernandez, playing a Polish character.

Though he played the central character here, Fernandez apparently made no other films. Several years later Anthony Curtis would emerge a full-fledged star under the name of Tony Curtis, Richard Benedict went on to become a successful TV director, and Richard Jaeckel works often as an accomplished supporting player.

The Cockeyed World (1929 Fox)

    D: **Raoul Walsh**
    S: **Raoul Walsh** and William K. Wells
    P: William Fox
Cast: Edmund Lowe, Victor McLaglen, Lily Damita

Originally released in both sound and silent versions. The characters of Capt. Flagg and Sgt. Quirk originally appeared in Laurence Stallings and Maxwell Anderson's play and subsequent hit film version *What Price Glory?* (1926).

The Cockeyed World concerns the adventures of two bawdy U.S. Marines that take them from Russia to Brooklyn to Nicaragua. Lily Damita is Mariana, a Nicaraguan woman of easy virtue, which indicates the way Latin women are viewed in the film—as easily available sexual creatures. One Marine even refers to a woman as having found "the lay of the land."

Code of Silence (1985 Or)

    D: Andy Davis
    S: Michael Butler, Dennis Shryack, and Mike Gray
    P: Raymond Wagner
Cast: Chuck Norris, **Henry Silva,** Mike Genovese, Ron Henriquez

In Chicago, the daughter of an underworld don is kidnapped and used as a pawn in an escalating drug war between the dangerous South American Comacho family and the Luna organized crime family. Dectective Sgt. Eddie Cusack (Norris) must settle the situation, which also involves a detective who is responsible for the shooting of a Hispanic teenager. Henry Silva plays Luis Comacho, head of the Comacho family.

Colors (1988 Or)

    D: Dennis Hopper
    S: Michael Schiffer and Richard Dilello
    P: Robert Solo
Cast: Robert Duvall, Sean Penn, **Maria Conchita Alonso, Trinidad Silva, Rudy Ramos**

Bob Hodges (Duvall) and Danny "Pacman" McGavin (Penn) are two Los Angeles policemen fighting black and Mexican American street gang violence. Hodges is a 20-year veteran cop about to retire who is trying to teach the ropes to his know-it-all rookie partner, McGavin, until finally the younger cop learns his lesson, but too late to save his partner.

Colors is a highly emotionally charged film that offers nothing new except some style, music, and two seasoned leading actors. Chicanos and blacks are seen as street gang members with little subtlety or depth except for the character of Frog, played by Trinidad Silva. There are a few minority policemen, but they are relegated to the background. The film comes off to some as a black-and-white racist statement, feeding off the fears of the white American middle class toward inner-city minorities.

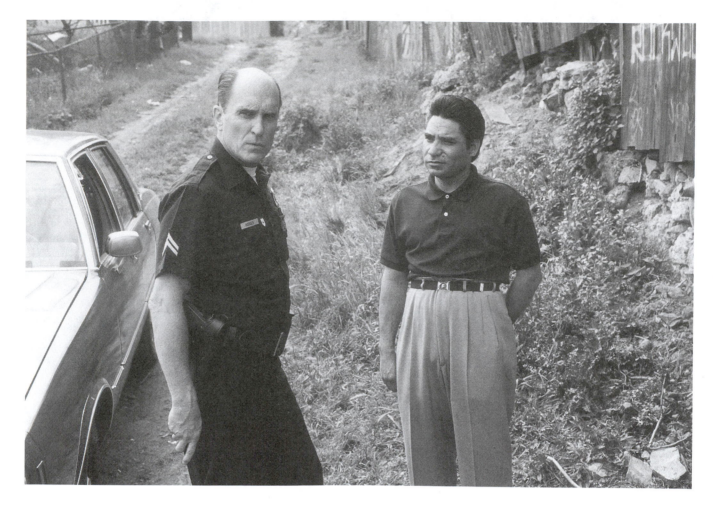

Trinidad Silva (right) as gang member Frog
meets Hodges (Robert Duvall) in order to
discuss upcoming gang activities in *Colors*.

It is more complex than that, however. It is perhaps more accurate to say that
the film falls victim to its intent, through the specific viewpoints of Hodges and
McGavin, to trace the development of a racist cop (Penn) and the efforts of his
older partner (Duvall) and girlfriend (Alonso) to save him from himself.

In one telling scene, Penn, who has had an ongoing affair with a Mexican
American girl (Alonso), discovers her all painted up as a street gang girl when he
is called to the scene of a party where a drive-by shooting has occurred. He is
almost visibly sickened when he realizes she has apparently been making love to
a black man in the room.

It could also be argued, however, that the viewpoint of the movie (Penn's) made
the harsh, almost stereotyped presentation of minorities as violent gang members
inevitable. It is interesting to compare *Colors* to Edward James Olmos's *American
Me* (1992) or to the much more obviously stereotyped *Badge 373* (1973).

To the film's credit, through the death of his partner "Pacman" does appear to
learn his lesson, to the betterment of the situation.

The Comancheros (1961 TCF)

    D: Michael Curtiz
    S: James Edward Grant and Clair Huffaker, based on the novel
       by Paul I. Wellman
    P: George Sherman
Cast: John Wayne, Stuart Whitman, Ina Balin, Nehemiah Persoff, Lee Marvin

A rough-and-tumble, larger-than-life oater filled with rowdy western types. The story is set in 1860s Texas when renegade whites, Native Americans, and Mexicans were selling whiskey and arms along the Texas-Mexico border.

John Wayne is a Texas Ranger on the trail of a gentleman gambler (Whitman) wanted for a murder in Louisiana. A set of circumstances leads them to the Comancheros' secret encampment, where in order to stay alive, they form an uneasy alliance. They are spared an unkind fate by the Comanchero chieftain's young daughter (Ina Balin), who has an interest in the gambler and whose betrayal of her father eventually leads to his demise.

The trio make their escape from the encampment, holding the Comanchero chieftain hostage, and they are saved by a detachment of Texas Rangers who arrive just in the nick of time. Nehemiah Persoff gives an interesting performance as the educated, wheelchair-bound Comanchero chieftain. In the Comanchero stronghold some Hispanic American history is interjected when a Native American called Iron Shirt is shown wearing a Spanish conquistador breastplate. It is explained that his grandfather fought the Spaniards in what was then Mexico. Michael Ansara plays Amflung, a Mexican bandit. *The Comancheros* was the last film directed by master director Michael Curtiz (*Captain Blood* [1935], *Casablanca* [1942], *Mildred Pierce* [1945]).

Commando (1985 TCF)

  D: Mark Lester
  S: Steven De Souza
  P: Joel Silver
Cast: Arnold Schwarzenegger, Rae Dawn Chong, Dan Hedaya

A retired special operations officer, Matrix (Schwarzenegger), is forced to return to the country of Val Verde by a dictator he helped depose when his daughter is kidnapped by the revenge-seeking ousted dictator. The dictator wants Matrix to undertake one last mission—to kill the democratically elected President Velasquez so that General Arius (Hedaya) can take over. Schwarzenegger is a one-man American killing machine running around a Latin American country overrun by dictators and gun-toting Latin thugs trying to keep down a helpless, freedom-loving populace.

Compromising Positions (1985 Par)

  D: Frank Perry
  S: Susan Isaacs, based on her novel
  P: Frank Perry
Cast: Susan Sarandon, **Raul Julia**, Joe Mantegna, Judith Ivey

Story of Judith Singer (Sarandon), a former newspaper reporter whose long-dormant writer's instinct is triggered by the murder of Dr. Bruce Fleckstein, her dentist. Detective David Suarez (Julia) of the Suffolk County (New York) Police is the divorced law officer in charge of the investigation, which brings him unexpectedly into a love relationship with Singer.

It is refreshing and fairly new to see a nonstereotypical Hispanic American law officer in this essentially upper-middle-class white suburban tale. Suarez's growing attraction to Singer is balanced by his respect for her investigative skills. Julia turns in a good performance.

Copacabana (1947 UA)

 D: Alfred E. Green
 S: Laslo Vadnay, Allen Boretz, and Howard Harris, based on
    a story by Vadnay
 P: Sam Coslow
Cast: Groucho Marx, **Carmen Miranda**, Steve Cochran

Groucho without the other Marx Brothers in a low-budget, mostly unfunny musical/comedy that has little to do with the reality of the famed legendary New York nightclub of the title, except for the name. Lionel Devereaux (Groucho) is Carmen Novarro's (Miranda's) agent. In his desperation to book his sole client in a nightclub, Devereaux convinces the Copa manager (Cochran) that he has another client available for a second booking. Novarro auditions for and lands both jobs, forcing her to take up the guise of a blonde French singer as well as her usual Brazilian bombshell self.

A Covenant with Death (1966 WB)

 D: Lamont Johnson
 S: Larry Marcus and Saul Levitt, based on a novel by Stephen Becker
 P: William Conrad
Cast: George Maharis, Laura Devon, **Katy Jurado**, Earl Holliman,
    Arthur O'Connell, Sidney Blackmer, Wende Wagner, **Emilio Fernandez**,
    Gene Hackman

Hypocrisy, sex, murder, and racism form the background of this story, which takes place in a small southwestern town in the 1920s. An innocent man (Holliman), accused of murdering his wife, is sentenced to hang. Amid a frenzy of protests, he leaps from the gallows, accidentally causing the hangman's death. The sentenced man is returned to his cell, and then another man confesses to the first killing. Will justice be served in the death of the hangman?

George Maharis is Ben Lewis, a young Mexican American judge who finds himself on trial before the community when he is faced with this taxing and unprecedented legal predicament. He has philosophical differences with an older judge and altercations with a D.A. who wanted Lewis's appointment and bitterly resents Lewis because of his inexperience and mixed ancestry. All through this Lewis is juggling romances with a Swedish woman (Laura Devon) and a Mexican woman (Wende Wagner).

A Covenant with Death is frequently interesting but never achieves the high-tension drama or excitement its subject matter promises. It is frequently slow, and there is much dialogue that does not advance the story line. The film plays like a 1930s Warner Bros. social melodrama reminiscent of actor Paul Muni's *Bordertown* (1935), without the conviction or social punch. There are various similarities to *Bordertown* in that both protagonists, Paul Muni's Johnny and Maharis's Ben Lewis, are caught between two worlds, the Anglo and the Mexican. Both are lawyers and both have Anglo love interests. The endings are similar: Muni loses the Anglo girl and returns to the barrio; Maharis loses the Anglo girl and marries the Mexican girl in a symbolic return to his own kind.

Maharis is adequate in the role of the young judge. A Greek American, he was a popular star of the "Route 66" television series of a few years earlier. Katy Jurado plays Eulalia, his domineering, cigar-smoking Mexican mother. Emilio Fernandez plays Ignacio, his hearty uncle. The film was shot on location in Santa Fe, New Mexico, and at Warner Bros. studios.

Cowboy (1958 Col)

    D: Delmer Daves
    S: Edmund H. North
    P: Julian Blaustein
Cast: Glenn Ford, Jack Lemmon, Anna Kashfi, Dick York

The story of a Chicago hotel clerk, Frank Harris (Lemmon), who decides to become a cowboy and joins cattleman Tom Reece (Ford) and his crew on a trek across the Southwest into Mexico. After an arduous journey of several weeks in which Harris learns the ways of a cowboy, the outfit crosses the Rio Grande and arrives at the Vidal Ranch to purchase cattle from a wealthy Mexican land baron, with whose lovely daughter, Maria (Kashfi), Harris had struck up a romance in Chicago. While Reece bargains for Vidal's cattle, Harris seeks out Maria and learns to his dismay that she has married Manuel (Eugene Iglesias) to satisfy the wishes of her family. During the Fiesta of San Margarita, characterized by violence, at nearby Guadalupe, the gringos win respect for their marksmanship and Reece's daring in which he bests Manuel in the dangerous "Game of the Bulls," a form of bullfighting. One of the cowboys gets himself in trouble chasing Mexican women. His fellow cowpokes refuse to come to his aid when he is apprehended by four tough Mexican hombres.

The Cowboys (1972 WB)

    D: Mark Rydell
    S: Irving Ravetch, Harriet Frank, Jr., and William Dale Jennings, based on a novel by Jennings
    P: Mark Rydell
Cast: John Wayne, Roscoe Lee Browne, Bruce Dern, **A Martinez**

A cattle rancher (Wayne) is forced to recruit 11 teenaged boys to help him on a cattle drive when his own men desert him upon hearing of a local gold strike. On the way, the trail becomes a rite of passage to manhood for the boys. They are left on their own when the rancher is murdered before their eyes by a gang of cutthroats. The boys then decide to avenge his death and retrieve the cattle.

The film was popular, but controversy ensued due to its ending, which finds the boys shooting down the rancher's murderers in a spree of violence.

A Martinez plays Cimarron, a young Mexican American cowboy (of course he is hot tempered and carries a knife) who joins Wayne and proves himself. The film also toplined a black trail cook played by Roscoe Lee Browne. These were obvious signs of the liberal social changes taking place in the late 1960s and 1970s, offering the inclusion of black and other minority characters in a more accurate historical context, from which previously they had been omitted.

Crisis (1950 MGM)

    D: **Richard Brooks**
    S: **Richard Brooks**, based on the story "The Doubters" by George Tabori
    P: Arthur Freed
Cast: Cary Grant, **Jose Ferrer**, Paula Raymond, Signe Hasso, **Antonio Moreno, Gilbert Roland, Ramon Novarro, Pedro De Cordoba, Vicente Gomez, Martin Garralaga, Rudolfo Hoyos, Jr., Roque Ybarra, Felipe Turich, Soledad Jimenez,** Jose Dominguez

An American surgeon (Grant) on his honeymoon in a fictional South American country must perform an emergency brain operation on ruling dictator Raoul Farrago (Ferrer) in order to save his life.

One-time matinee idols Ramon Novarro and Antonio Moreno appear together in *Crisis*. Here they are rehearsing for their next scene.

The fictional Latin American country in this gripping but talky story seems to be more of a Peron-like Argentina than the traditional banana republic.

Writer/director Brooks (in his debut movie) had the idea of bringing together in supporting roles such former silent screen matinee idols as Antonio Moreno, Ramon Novarro, and Gilbert Roland. He also had the Spanish-speaking characters converse in their own language when they were alone and in English when they weren't.

Crossover Dreams (1985 Mi)

    D: **Leon Ichaso**
    S: **Leon Ichaso**, Manuel Arce, and **Ruben Blades**
    P: Manuel Arce
Cast: **Ruben Blades, Elizabeth Pena**, Shawn Elliott

Rise and fall and redemption of Salsa singer Rudy Veloz (Blades), who yearns to hit it big in the Anglo pop music business. It's an old-fashioned morality tale with a contemporary New York Latin perspective. Rudy betrays his heritage by chasing success in the American record business. He signs with a big producer, compromises his music (by working with white musicians), and loses his devoted Latin girlfriend (for a white party girl).

"It is not only their talent and intelligence that makes the work of Mr. Ichaso and Mr. Arce so special, it's also their particular experiences as emigres (from Cuba) which enables them to interpret, for better or worse, aspects of our culture that have become invisible to the rest of us," Vincent Canby, *New York Times* (9/1/85).

Cry Tough (1959 UA)

D: Paul Stanley
S: Harry Kleiner, based on the novel *Children of the Dark* by Irving Shulman
P: Harry Kleiner
Cast: **John Saxon, Linda Cristal, Perry Lopez, Joseph Calleia, Barbara Luna**

Miguel Estrada (Saxon) is a Puerto Rican youth determined to break out of the Spanish Harlem barrio. Fresh out of prison after serving a year for armed robbery, he tries to resist efforts to have him rejoin his old street gang. Fate turns against him when he gets involved with Sarita (Cristal), a Cuban dance hall hostess who is picked up by immigration authorities for being in the country illegally. The gang chief provides Estrada with money for the girl's bail provided that he rejoins the gang. Estrada double-crosses the gang, and the girl walks out on him when he cannot provide her with the lifestyle she wants. Distraught, he asks the gang leader's forgiveness and again pursues a life of crime, which ends in tragedy.

This is the first Hollywood film that used the problems of second-generation Puerto Ricans in New York as a backdrop for a juvenile delinquent gang movie, filmed on the backlot New York street of MGM studios.

Producer/screenwriter Harry Kleiner spent several weeks researching the story in New York's Spanish Harlem, where he amassed 400 pages of notes before returning to Hollywood to put the screenplay together. In an *L.A. Examiner* interview with Neil Rau (10/12/58), Kleiner remarked, "I roamed the streets of the district every free moment I had, but most of the time I spent with two secretaries interviewing hundreds of people from the neighborhood on every level of life."

The resulting screenplay and film did not do justice to the research, however. Saxon gave value to his performance as did Linda Cristal, Perry Lopez, and Barbara Luna. Brazilian Laurindo Almeida provided the musical score. "What starts out a promising picture about poor Puerto Ricans in New York and the obviously circumscribed endeavors of one young fellow 'to belong' ends up as a routine gangster melodrama. . . . More's the pity, because this whole matter of the environment and economic patterns in which the masses of Puerto Ricans live in this city,

Linda Cristal and John Saxon in *Cry Tough*.

and the motivations that agitate their minds, cry for illumination and enlight-ened sympathy," Bosley Crowther, *New York Times* (9/17/59).

"There is no obvious evidence that anybody concerned with making *Cry Tough* bothered to look behind the headlines to understand or feel the background of New York's West Side or to catch the idiom or quality of the Puerto Ricans with which it makes such a point of dealing," Paul V. Beckley, *New York Herald Tribune* (9/17/59).

Cuba (1979 UA)
D: Richard Lester
S: Charles Wood
P: Arlene Sellers and Alex Winitsky
Cast: Sean Connery, Brooke Adams, Martin Balsam, **Hector Elizondo**, **Danny De La Paz**, Lonette McKee, Louisa Moritz, **Alejandro Rey**

In Havana on the eve of Castro's revolution, Robert Dapes (Connery), an English mercenary, is brought in by the Batista government to squash the guerrillas hiding out in the Sierra Madre.

Fifteen years earlier, Dapes had an affair with Alexandra Pulido (Adams), an American woman now married to a weak-willed Cuban tobacco factory owner, Juan Pulido (Chris Sarandon). Dapes and Alexandra Pulido are reunited. He finds himself still in love with her as he grows increasingly aware of the corruption and brutality of the regime and of the enormous discrepancy between Cuba's wealthy and poor.

Danny De La Paz is Julio, a Fidelista who runs guns for the revolutionaries out of the Pulido cigar factory and is sworn to revenge against Pulido for the rape of his sister. Hector Elizondo is Ramirez, a Cuban army officer who is assigned to maintain vigilance over Dapes but who understands what is happening to his country. The film has many points of similarity with *Havana* (1990) as they were written around the same time but produced ten years apart. Filmed in Spain.

Cuban Love Song (1931 MGM)
D: W.S. Van Dyke
S: John Lynch, John Colton, Gilbert Emery, Robert E. Hopkins, and Paul Hervey Fox, based on a story by Gardner Sullivan and Bess Meredyth
P: Metro Pictures
Cast: Lawrence Tibbett, **Lupe Velez**, Jimmy Durante

Typical musical of the 1930s set in turn-of-the-century Cuba and involving the romance of Terry (Tibbett), a U.S. Marine, with Nenita (Velez), a Havana peanut vendor. Filmed on soundstages and on the backlot at MGM, the film creates a Cuba of the popular imagination.

World War I interrupts the romance, and after the war Terry returns and marries his sweetheart in the States. When he returns to Cuba, the former Marine discovers the peanut vendor has died but left him a son born out of wedlock, whom he takes back to the States.

Cuban Pete (1946 U)
D: Jean Yarbrough
S: Robert Presnell, Sr., and M. Coates Webster, based on a story by Bernard Feins
P: Howard Welsch and Will Cowen
Cast: **Desi Arnaz**

An advertising executive attempts to lure a Cuban band onto an American radio program. The film was a low-budget romantic musical/comedy produced to play as the bottom half of a double bill.

Deal of the Century (1983 WB)

D: William Friedkin
S: Paul Brickman
P: Bud Yorkin
Cast: Chevy Chase, Sigourney Weaver, Gregory Hines, Vince Edwards, **William Marquez, Pepe Serna, Tony Plana, Loyda Ramos,** Eduardo Ricard, Wallace Shawn, Richard Libertini, **Alex Colon**

Eddie Muntz (Chase), a second-hand arms dealer, is selling weapons to local rebels somewhere in Central America, where he gets involved with the widow of an arms dealer. Back in the States, when an expensive war plane begins to act like a lemon, a representative of the military-industrial complex recruits Muntz to unload the plane on a Latin American dictator, General Arturo Cordosa (Marquez), and his country.

The movie can't make up its mind whether it's a satire or a farce, and as a result it is an obnoxious and offensive mishmash. Expert production design creates a most believable Central American atmosphere in an opening sequence filmed on downtown L.A.'s Olvera Street.

"We begin to notice how Friedkin was taking cheap shots at all Latins. San Miguel is merely an updated version of Al Capp's El Ignoranto, with chickens in the presidential palace and 'La Cucaracha' on the soundtrack. All those Latins on the screen give the characters a certain authenticity, but their roles as preening colonels, menacing Indian soldiers and raggedy assed rebels are ethnic caricatures like the bespectacled, bucktoothed Japanese of old war movies or the whole ignominious roster of Hollywood shuffling negroes," Enrique Fernandez, *Village Voice* (11/15/83).

Death of a Gunfighter (1969 U)

D: Alan Smithee
S: Joseph Calvelli, based on the novel by Lewis B. Patten
P: Richard E. Lyons
Cast: Richard Widmark, Lena Horne, **John Saxon**

Marshal Frank Patch (Widmark) is a man past his time whom the citizens of the town consider an embarrassment and a relic of the past. Patch and his kind of law and order are viewed as a detriment to the community and as standing in the way of eastern business interests. When they ask him to resign, he refuses and becomes the target of a death plot by the people of the town. Tough, shrewd county sheriff Lou Trinidad (Saxon), a Mexican whom Patch once had to force his town to accept, is now charged with bringing in the man to whom he owes the most. Not wanting to take sides, he leaves on the next train.

The citizens of the town are shown to be vehemently anti-Mexican, referring to Trinidad as a "greaseball." Lena Horne is Claire Quintana, the marshal's faithful mistress and the hotel madame. Quintana is supposedly a Mexican woman, though she is played by a light-skinned black actress, and Horne makes no obvious attempt at a cliched Mexican spitfire portrayal. This slow-moving story with potentially interesting but muddled themes was directed by Robert Totten (first half) and Don Siegel (second half) and credited to a fictitious Smithee.

Death of an Angel (1986 TCF)

D: Petru Popescu
S: Petru Popescu
P: Peter Burrell
Cast: Bonnie Bedelia, Nick Mancuso, Pamela Ludwig, **Alex Colon, Abel Franco,** Irma Garcia

Grace Mackenzie (Bedelia), an ordained Episcopal minister with a wheelchair-bound daughter, one day discovers that her daughter and her Mexican housekeeper are missing. A mysterious stranger (Colon) in a white suit takes her to her daughter, who is with a religious faith healer named Angel (Mancuso), whom Grace comes to believe is a fake. His following is largely comprised of infirm and disabled Mexican peasants. Don Tarjetas (Franco), a big bad Mexican ranchero who smuggles undocumented aliens across the border, believes Angel is turning against him. This is a dull and incomprehensible film.

Defiance (1980 AIP)

D: John Flynn
S: Thomas Michael Donnelly, based on a story by Donnelly and
   Mark Tulin
P: William S. Gilmore, Jr., and Jerry Bruckheimer
Cast: Jan-Michael Vincent, **Theresa Saldana, Rudy Ramos, Santos Morales, East Carlo**

Merchant seaman Tommy (Vincent) moves into a Lower East Side New York City neighborhood that is being terrorized by Puerto Rican gang members. He is threatened by the gang and decides to fight them head-on, inspiring the neighborhood people to join in the fight to reclaim their neighborhood. In stereotypical fashion, the Anglo protagonist comes to save the poor minorities from themselves.

Delta Force 2: Operation Stranglehold (1990 MGM)

D: Aaron Norris
S: Lee Reynolds
P: Yoram Globus and Christopher Pearce
Cast: Chuck Norris, Billy Drago, **Begonia Plaza, Hector Mercado**

Col. McCoy (Norris) is the leader of an American assault squad sent into a Latin American country to apprehend Ramon Cota (Drago), an underworld drug tsar who wreaks terror from his jungle fortress. He is helped by Quincana (Plaza), a beautiful native woman who is a victim of Cota's cruelty. The film features a typical paternalistic, jingoistic Anglo-American in Latin America saving the helpless natives from an international, home-grown drug tsar. It was filmed in the Philippines.

The Devil Is a Woman (1935 Par)

D: Josef von Sternberg
S: John Dos Passos and Sam Winston, based on the novel *The Woman and the Puppet* by Pierre Louys
P: Unknown
Cast: Marlene Dietrich, Lionel Atwill, **Cesar Romero**

Set against the backdrop of the nineteenth-century Spanish revolution, this is the story of Concha Perez (Dietrich) and the men she ruins. Cesar Romero, in one of his first major film roles, is effective in a part largely requiring a handsome appearance. The movie was not well received by audiences, and Franco's Fascist Spanish government protested the film on the grounds that it made fun of the Guardia Civil and threatened to ban all of Paramount's films in Spain if the film was not withdrawn. Paramount capitulated and the film was eventually withdrawn from worldwide distribution.

Dime with a Halo (1963 MGM)

  D: Boris Sagal
  S: Laslo Vadney and Hans Wilhelm
  P: Laslo Vadney and Hans Wilhelm
Cast: **Barbara Luna**, Roger Mobley, Paul Langton, **Manuel Padilla, Jr., Rafael Lopez, Tina Menard, Robert Carricart**

Offbeat, endearing low-budget B comedy/melodrama about five street urchins in Tijuana, Mexico, who take a dime from a church collection box to help buy a ticket in the big pool at the Caliente race track. They win a fortune, but because of their age, they cannot cash in the ticket. This leads to adventures and misadventures until the story reaches its unusual climax. Barbara Luna plays Juanita, the orphaned American sister of one of the five, who, in an attempt to keep her brother (Mobley) with her, moves to Tijuana and becomes an entertainer in a small nightclub. Luna, who is of Filipino descent, started her career on Broadway as a child actress in *South Pacific*. She attracted attention in her role as the blind nurse who marries Frank Sinatra in *The Devil at 4 O'Clock* (1961) and in *Five Weeks in a Balloon* (1962). Rafael Lopez, the 16-year-old leader of the boys in this film, was born in Mexico City and started his career as a child dancer with Perez Prado's Orchestra. He came to the United States at age 11 and appeared in the feature film *The Young Savages* (1961) and in many television shows. Manuel Padilla, Jr., was a seven-year-old discovery who went on to work in several motion pictures as a child, including *The Young and the Brave* (1963), and co-starred on the "Tarzan" TV series starring Ron Ely. Robert Carricart, Tina Menard, and Raymond Sanchez were also featured in supporting roles.

The Dirty Dozen (1967 MGM)

  D: **Robert Aldrich**
  S: Nunnally Johnson and Lukas Heller, based on the novel by E.M. Nathanson
  P: Kenneth Hyman
Cast: Lee Marvin, Robert Ryan, Ernest Borgnine, Jim Brown, John Cassavetes, Charles Bronson, Clint Walker, **Trini Lopez**

Singer Trini Lopez was one of *The Dirty Dozen* in a throwback to one of those representative World War II squads with a touch of 1960s social consciousness. The stellar cast included Lopez as Mexican American Pedro Jimenez and Jim Brown as black soldier Robert Jefferson, two of the twelve condemned men led by Col. Reisman (Marvin) on a suicide mission behind enemy lines on the eve of D day. The film was very popular with audiences but was described as "entertaining as a blow torch" by the *New York Times*.

Down and Out in Beverly Hills (1986 T)

  D: Paul Mazursky
  S: Paul Mazursky and Leon Capetanos, based on the play *Boudu Sauvé des Eaux* by Rene Fauchois
  P: Paul Mazursky
Cast: Richard Dreyfuss, Bette Midler, Nick Nolte, **Elizabeth Pena**

In this loose remake of Jean Renoir's *Boudu Saved from Drowning* (1932), Jerry Baskin (Nolte), a homeless bum who wanders Beverly Hills for food and shelter, decides to end his life by drowning himself in a swimming pool at the Whitemans' (Dreyfuss and Midler) home but is saved by Mr. Whiteman. Baskin's subsequent presence in the household changes and disrupts their lives. Elizabeth Pena plays the sexy, smart-mouthed Hispanic maid Carmen, who is made politically aware by Jerry. The actress had to relearn a Spanish accent for the role. "After thousands of dollars trying to get rid of my Spanish accent and having acquired a New York accent, I had to go back to my original way of speaking," recalls Pena, who attracted attention in the role.

Down Argentine Way (1940 TCF)

    D: Irving Cummings
    S: Darrell Ware and Karl Tunberg, based on a story by Rian James and Ralph Spence
    P: Darryl F. Zanuck
Cast: Don Ameche, Betty Grable, **Carmen Miranda**, **J. Carroll Naish**, **Chris-Pin Martin**

Notable for being the first in a series of popular Technicolor musicals at Fox, starring Betty Grable and Don Ameche, and for introducing Carmen Miranda, the "Brazilian Bombshell," to film audiences. The film was also an attempt by Fox to increase business in Latin and South America.

Horse-loving American heiress Grable falls for rich Argentine horse breeder Don Ameche. Ameche's proud father (Henry Stephenson) is still bitter over losing a girl to Grable's father when they were both students in Paris long ago. The picture was filmed entirely on Twentieth Century–Fox soundstages; a special crew flew to Buenos Aires without the principals to get the necessary exterior and atmosphere shots. Another crew flew from Hollywood to New York to spend five weeks photographing Carmen Miranda and recording the songs she sings in the picture. She is the only cast member to appear in the picture without having set foot in Hollywood. The unusual arrangement was made because Miranda was under contract to a New York nightclub and found it impossible to come to Hollywood.

Musical songs and splendid travelogue color photography made the film popular with stateside audiences, but in Argentina it found disfavor. Someone must have confused Buenos Aires with Cuba, since the music sounds more like the Cuban rumba than the Argentinean tango.

Duck, You Sucker! [aka: *A Fistful of Dynamite; A Fistful of Revolution*] (1972 UA)

    D: Sergio Leone
    S: Luciano Vincenzoni, Sergio Donati, and Sergio Leone, based on a story by Leone
    P: Fulvio Morsella
Cast: Rod Steiger, James Coburn

The story is set in 1913 Mexico and concerns a rascally Mexican peon, Juan Miranda (Steiger), who is unwillingly goaded into heroism in his people's revolution by Sean Mallory (Coburn), an Irish man haunted by the ghosts of his own people's revolution. Together they join forces to rob a bank. This was Steiger's first screen appearance as a Mexican. Steiger recalls, "It was unlike anything I've ever done before. I've never played a Mexican although I've worked with just about every other type of accent and nationality."

In a revealing interview with *Take One Magazine* (January–February 1972), Leone is quoted as saying about the film, "The Mexican Revolution in the film is only a symbol and not *the* Mexican Revolution. . . . It's a real myth. To avoid misunderstanding, I rejected the romance of the sombrero, preferring to deal with the theme of friendship which is so dear to me." There is plenty of action in the Leone style.

Jennifer Jones as Pearl Chavez co-stars with
Joseph Cotten as Jess in *Duel in the Sun*.

Duel in the Sun (1946 Selznick Int.)

    D: King Vidor
    S: Oliver H.P. Garrett and David O. Selznick, based on the novel by Niven Busch
    P: David O. Selznick
 Cast: Jennifer Jones, Gregory Peck, Joseph Cotten, Herbert Marshall,
       Lillian Gish, Lionel Barrymore, Walter Huston

Passion and furor swirl in this lurid tale of a young woman and the renegade son
of an empire builder. The film has much to offer, including florid acting, spectacular action sequences, and superb color photography.

Pearl Chavez (Jones) is left orphaned when her Confederate father, Scott Chavez
(Marshall), is sentenced to hang for murdering his Indian wife and her lover. Before he hangs he arranges to ship his daughter off to the household of the cousin
he should have married.

Chavez goes to live with Texas senator McCanles (Charles Bickford) and his
family. The senator resents Pearl's Indian heritage, as well as the fact that Laura
Belle (Gish), his wife, was once in love with Pearl's father. She is attracted to his
two sons, the charming Jess (Cotten), who is banished for contesting his father's
opposition to the railroad, and Lewton (Peck), whose virile arrogance eventually
overwhelms her. Lewton guns down her fiancé on the eve of the wedding and
escapes into exile. Pearl accepts an invitation from Lewton to join him at his hideout, where the two engage in a shoot-out resulting in each other's demise.

Selznick, who produced *Gone with the Wind*, was determined to outdo himself with this epic western tale, showcasing the talents of his wife, actress Jennifer Jones, who had won an Academy Award as Best Actress for her role in *The Song of Bernadette* (1943).

It is unusual that a Spanish-surnamed female character had the leading role in a western motion picture in which she is a virtual life force. Pearl Chavez may be the most liberated, free-spirited Hispanic American female ever portrayed on film. Chavez belongs to the heel-clicking spitfire school, except for the critical difference that this film revolves around her.

Though she is referred to as a "half-breed," her Confederate gambler father is described in the program notes as a "renegade ne'er do well, ill fated son of Creole ancestry," so we can suppose he had some Spanish and French blood with a name like Chavez.

A prologue involving Pearl's mother and father in a spectacular bordertown café scene is quite moving. Pearl dances to the music of the Mexican hat dance outside a presidio, while inside her Indian mother is dancing a very different kind of dance, the Orizaba. It is generally considered a Mexican native fertility dance and, as used in the film, a sexual act. Tilly Losch, who had played the dancing girl in *The Garden of Allah* (1936), did much the same thing in her portrayal of the mother, only in a more flamboyantly sexual manner. Scott Chavez's gambling companions taunt him over his wife's infidelity, and he proceeds to shoot her and her lover. This prologue sets up the premise and themes of the movie.

As Ed Lowry perceptively states:

> Like her father, Pearl inevitably will die for her acts of violence but in her sacrifice she will have insured the survival of the only happy couple in the film, Jess and Helen. Pearl makes the moral decision to protect them from Lewton by destroying both Lewton and herself. It is this decision to function as a protector which makes Pearl, in the most essential sense, the Western hero of *Duel in the Sun*. She is placed in the classic position of defending a civilized society too weak to stand up for itself from the lawless savage (Lewton). (*Cinema Texas Program Notes*, Vol. 10, No. 2, March 2, 1976)

Though panned by the critics, *Duel in the Sun* was a popular success, eventually grossing $17 million at the nation's box offices. It was the most expensive film of its day, made at a cost of $6 million, and shot over a year's time in Hollywood and on locations near Phoenix and Tucson, Arizona.

Jones received an Academy Award nomination as Best Actress for her role. Lillian Gish as Laura Belle was nominated as Best Supporting Actress.

"The audience eventually learns (thanks to the Johnston office) that illicit love doesn't really pay in the long run but for about 134 minutes it has appeared to be loads of fun," *Time* (3/17/47).

Eating Raoul (1982 Fox Classics Div.)

D: Paul Bartel
S: Richard Blackburn and Paul Bartel
P: Anne Kimmel
Cast: Paul Bartel, Mary Woronov, **Robert Beltran**

A middle-class couple disgusted with the violence of city life dream of opening a suburban restaurant but are beset by financial woes. They think their prayers have been answered when they accidentally kill a would-be rapist "swinger" neighbor with a swat to the head with a frying pan and his fat wallet falls to the floor.

In a local newspaper, they advertise for swingers and successively do them in. It looks like they will soon be working in the valley until a Latino burglar named Raoul discovers their bulging trash bags. Raoul turns a profit by selling the jewelry and clothes of the victims and, being one hot number, becomes the wife's lover. When Raoul's tricks become too much for the couple, they are forced to make their first big dish a Latin stew, its main ingredient being Raoul.

Paul Bartel describes his movie this way:

> [It] touches on many things, the perversion of middle class values, the resurgence of Nixonism, Latin machismo versus Wasp fastidiousness, film noir. *Eating Raoul* is a title with several meanings, one of which is that the Paul and Marys of this world can figuratively (or even literally) eat the Raouls of this world whenever it suits them. I don't mean to imply that Raoul deserves to be eaten, in fact he is probably the most sympathetic character in the story for all his peccadillos. He's so forthright, so full of life. It's just that in our society, the Paul and Marys are the kickers and he's usually the kicked. Paul and Mary share an aversion to sex and provide a haven for each other until the snake comes in, in the form of the hot Latin sexuality of Raoul.

Though the film is meant to be taken as a wild, cleverly disarming spoof, and a very dark cartoon, nevertheless Raoul as portrayed by Robert Beltran is a cocksure, leather-jacketed Latin lover stud, opportunistic thief, and hustler who reinforces stereotypes and a negative image. In truth, however, the Anglos come out of this movie looking just as shallow and vampyric. The difference here is that the Anglos seem to be satirized and the Hispanic stereotyped. The film, in limited art house release and in film festivals, met with enthusiastic audiences and critical reaction and has become a cult film with a huge following.

El Cid (1961 AA)

D: Anthony Mann
S: Philip Yordan and Frederic M. Frank
P: Samuel Bronston and Anthony Mann
Cast: Charlton Heston, Sophia Loren, Hurd Hatfield, Gary Raymond, Herbert Lom

Epic and sweeping saga of romance and adventure filmed on location against authentic backgrounds of Spain's breathtaking countryside and ancient castles and featuring an international cast. Charlton Heston stars as the eleventh-century Spanish hero Rodrigo Diaz de Bivar, better known as El Cid, who devotes his life to driving the Moors out of Spain.

The fabled Christian liberator of the Spanish nation was in fact a professional soldier who once hired himself out to a local Muslim leader to fight his fellow Christians. Even after reconciling with his Christian king, he pursued his own course, taking the territories he conquered for his own. Poets, writers, monks, and historians through the centuries have contributed to the myth of El Cid as national hero.

Heston was the logical choice for the role of El Cid after his success in such epic costume dramas as *The Ten Commandments* (1956) and his Academy Award–winning role in *Ben-Hur* (1959). Sophia Loren, the most popular international actress of the time, was cast as his wife, Chimene, which also helped in the complicated international financing agreements for the production of the film.

Producer Samuel Bronston took advantage of inexpensive labor and production costs in Spain. His success caused a boom in foreign film production in Spain during the 1960s and 1970s, creating a cottage industry that afforded a very poor country necessary capital and an international filmmaking experience on a grandiose scale that has served it well ever since.

Spaniard Jose Lopez Rodero was an assistant director on the film, which featured thousands of Spanish extras and many Spanish actors in small roles. Directed by Anthony Mann and handsomely photographed by Milton Krasner, *El Cid* was a tremendous international success and made many lists of the 10 Best Films of the Year in the United States.

El Condor (1970 Carthay Continental/NG)

   D: John Guillermin
   S: Larry Cohen and Steven Carabatsos, based on a story by Carabatsos
   P: Andre de Toth
Cast: Jim Brown, Mariana Hill, Lee Van Cleef

Two fortune hunters, Luke (Brown) and Jaroo (Van Cleef), plan to rob gold stored in a Mexican fort commanded by a powerful Mexican general (Patrick O'Neal) following the American Civil War.

Mindless action western filmed in Spain, chock full of sex and violence, an unreal melange of Apaches, convicts, sleepy Mexican villages, and Juaristas (followers of Indian Zapotec leader Benito Juarez during French occupation of Mexico). A whole army battalion rapes a town's female inhabitants, and the two fortune hunters wait patiently on a hill, moving in to shoot the soldiers while they are copulating. At the fort, a Mexican woman (Mariana Hill) distracts the soldiers so the fortune hunters can gain entrance unnoticed.

The film subscribes to a fantasy Mexico, where women are sex objects and the people are violence-prone. This is not a new idea, but it is taken to an extreme under the influence of Italian filmmakers in the era of the "spaghetti western." It also mirrors social changes of the late 1960s in America by having Jim Brown, a black American, co-star with Van Cleef, white, as the so-called antiheroes, reflecting their established international box-office popularity in the action market.

El Mariachi (1993 Col)

   D: **Robert Rodriguez**
   S: **Robert Rodriguez**
   P: **Robert Rodriguez** and Carlos Gallardo
Cast: Carlos Gallardo, Consuelo Gomez, Peter Marquardt

The remarkable $7,000 debut film from 24-year-old writer/director Robert Rodriguez. An impressive, effective entertainment breakthrough in mainstream Hispanic American filmmaking in the United States, *El Mariachi* is true to its Mexican setting and characters, without being preachy or constrictive, in a genre piece of Hollywood B moviemaking at its best visual fun. The action/adventure story is set in a Mexican bordertown and concerns a lone musician who dreams of being a respected mariachi singer like his father and grandfather before him. He enters a small town at the same time as a hit man. They both wear black and carry similar guitar cases, except that the mariachi's contains his beloved guitar and the hit man's contains a weapon. The mariachi falls in love with a beautiful bar owner who takes him in after he is accidentally confused with the hit man. The mariachi finds himself ushered into a violent underworld, battling the evil that lurks around him. There are strange story twists, and the gringo is the bad guy here. The supermacho hit man guzzles beer and sleeps with three machine-gun-toting women at the same time.

To finance part of the film, Rodriguez checked himself into a medical research program, which afforded him the time to write the script while he earned $3,000. He borrowed a 16mm nonsynchronized camera and a tape recorder and shot the film in the Mexican bordertown of Ciudad Acuña, near Del Rio, Texas, where his lead actor grew up and had access to several locations. He used nonprofessional

Writer, director, producer, and cameraman Robert Rodriguez gives direction to Carlos Gallardo in *El Mariachi*.

actors and rarely shot more than one take. He transferred the film to videotape and edited on videotape using two VCRs. On a trip to Los Angeles he sent an edited tape to an agent whose name he had seen in *Premiere* magazine. The agent was impressed with the work and secured a development deal for Rodriguez at Columbia Pictures, which released the film after visually enhancing it up to 35mm and improving the soundtrack. In January 1993 *El Mariachi* won the Audience Award at the Sundance Film Festival. The film was released in theaters in February 1993.

El Norte (1983 Cinecom–Island Alive)

D: **Gregory Nava**
S: **Gregory Nava** and Anna Thomas
P: Anna Thomas
Cast: Zaide Silvia Gutierrez, David Villalpando, Ernesto Gomez Cruz, **Trinidad Silva, Abel Franco, Lupe Ontiveros, Tony Plana, Enrique Castillo**

El Norte is Spanish for "the North," but it means more than that to sister and brother Rosa (Gutierrez) and Enrique (Villalpando), two Indians from Guatemala. To them it means "the United States," a mythical paradise where even the poor have private toilets and every person has the right to earn a decent wage. The story traces the plight of the two Guatemalan refugees as they strive to enter the United States illegally to seek a better life.

After their mother is taken prisoner and their father is killed by government troops, Rosa and Enrique are forced to leave their village to avoid a similar fate.

Posing as Mexicans, they make a cruel odyssey from Guatemala's pastoral highlands to Tijuana's infested shantytowns and finally to Los Angeles. They enter the United States by crawling through a rat-infested sewage tunnel, a circumstance that leads to tragic consequences.

El Norte explores the ignorance, poverty, and exploitation of the poor in overpopulated and underdeveloped as well as developed countries. Director Nava thoroughly immerses the viewer in the world of Latin immigrants and their individual experiences in this country. Upon arriving in downtown Los Angeles, Rosa asks in bewilderment, "Where are all the gringos?" All she sees around her is a sea of Latin faces. Nacha, a woman she has befriended, tells her, "The gringos don't like to live with us, they live in a separate area far away."

This powerful drama has a style of photography that approaches modern Latin American literature's fascination with magical realism. The imagery juxtaposes a dreamlike world and reality: Rosa, sitting in her adobe hut with its open cooking fire, pages through an old *Good Housekeeping* magazine and marvels at the modern kitchens; Enrique on his first day as a busboy in an upscale restaurant stares at the patrons and their dinners; busboys eat croissants instead of tortillas; and Rosa washes clothes by hand at a swimming pool at a Beverly Hills home when she can't figure out how to use the washing machine. Their tiny run-down room in Los Angeles is a far cry from what they saw in *Good Housekeeping,* but it nonetheless has a private toilet and electricity.

David Villalpando and
Zaide Silvia Gutierrez in *El Norte*.

Director Gregory Nava is of Mexican Basque ancestry, grew up in San Diego, and attended UCLA Film School. He talked about the long struggle to get the film made in an interview with Luis Reyes: "We kept hearing, again and again, that we should make Americans the main characters, that we would never get the film financed otherwise. We have nothing against films like *Missing* or *Under Fire*, but we wanted to make a film where Latin American people were the protagonists. We wanted the film to be true to their customs, their way of life, and we wanted the characters to speak in their own language."

Working with a limited budget, Nava and crew went to Chiapas in southern Mexico. Nava recalls, "We took a professional 35mm crew and a lot of complicated equipment into areas that were difficult to reach and film in. We shot in places where no one ever shot before and probably no one will shoot again, . . . like the sacred burial ground of Romerillo." They also shot in the state of Morelos near Mexico City, Tijuana, San Diego, and Los Angeles.

The film, funded by the "American Playhouse" series, aired on PBS, but received theatrical distribution prior to its airing. Primarily playing the art-house circuit in the States, the film received good reviews and was a modest financial success. Nava and Thomas had the distinction of having their screenplay nominated for an Oscar for Best Original Screenplay by the Academy of Motion Picture Arts and Sciences. The film is in Spanish with English subtitles.

"What makes it unique, especially to American audiences so used to hearing about the influx of illegal aliens and the problems they cause in the Southwest, is its humane explanation of the plight of these people from their point of view," Marylynn Uricchio, *Pittsburgh Post-Gazette* (2/24/84).

"A small, personal independently made film with the sweep of *El Norte*, with solid, sympathetic performances by unknown actors and a visual style of astonishing vibrancy must be regarded as a remarkable accomplishment," Janet Maslin, *New York Times* (1/11/84).

"What gives this film substance is the manner in which the characters are developed. They become real people and down to earth friends to one another as well as to those of us who put ourselves in their shoes. We like them, care about them and that means we become genuinely engrossed in their situations," Bob Polunsky, *San Antonio Express News* (3/16/84).

El Super (1979 Max Mambru Films Ltd.)

D: **Leon Ichaso** and Orlando Jimenez-Leal
S: **Leon Ichaso** and Manuel Arce, based on a play by Ivan Acosta
P: Manuel Arce and **Leon Ichaso**
Cast: Raymundo Hidalgo-Gato, Zully Montero, Raynaldo Medina, **Elizabeth Pena**

In Spanish, with English subtitles, this is the first film to depict the American experience of Cuban refugees, written, produced, and directed by Cuban refugees and released to warm critical praise. Heading the cast of Cuban and Puerto Rican actors are Raymundo Hidalgo-Gato as the "el super" of the title and Zully Montero, Raynaldo Medina, Elizabeth Pena, and Efrain Lopez Neri.

Filmed in New York City on a low budget ($250,000), *El Super* is the story of Roberto (Raymundo Hidalgo-Gato), a Cuban exile who is a superintendent of a large tenement building on Manhattan's Upper West Side. Roberto is fed up with his life in New York's harsh, cold environment, where he tends the boiler to provide heat for the tenants, makes minor repairs, and plays dominoes with his friends. He faces the challenges and dreams of most immigrants in America today and hopes to return to Cuba someday but sees life in Miami as a more attainable alternative. He has also to contend with his wife, Aurelia (Zully Montero), and his teenaged daughter, Aurelita (Elizabeth Pena), who are assimilating into the American lifestyle with ease.

Filmed with insight, intelligence, and humor, this was the first feature to be co-directed by Leon Ichaso and Orlando Jimenez-Leal. The motion picture was based on the play by Ivan Acosta, which was originally produced by the Cuban Cultural Center in New York City.

El Super is not a political film, though it does deal with working-class people who fled Castro's Cuba. Several political statements are made while the superintendents are sitting around talking and playing dominoes, when thoughts of returning to Cuba and the like emerge as natural conversation rather than heavy-handed statements.

El Super represented a labor of love for the filmmakers. Ichaso spent ten years making commercials before filming this first feature. It took a year to complete, though only three weeks were spent shooting and two months editing. Money was hard to come by and came from private investors while payments and salaries were deferred. *El Super* was a critical and financial success, playing in limited art-house release and in film festivals throughout the United States. "When you can laugh at the tragedy of being displaced . . . you're saved," said Ichaso, who hoped this film would give audiences insight into Cubans adjusting to life in the United States.

"This topic, long overdue for film treatment, is explored with insight and gentle humor in *El Super*, an engaging new movie made by Cuban exiles," Candice Russell, *Miami Herald* (2/4/79).

"*El Super* is not just for Cuban viewing, it is for everybody. Anglos will learn more about their Cuban friends in 90 minutes with *El Super* than they can learn in seminars, lectures or inter-community programs," Bill von Maurern, *Miami News* (2/2/79).

The Emerald Forest (1985 EMB)

D: John Boorman
S: Rospo Pallenberg
P: John Boorman
Cast: Powers Boothe, Meg Foster, Charley Boorman, Dira Pass

Powers Boothe is Bill Markham, an engineer helping civilization conquer the world's last frontier, the Brazilian Amazon, through the construction of the trans-Amazonian highway. Charley Boorman is Markham's young son, who disappears one day at the jungle's edge. Markham returns to the Amazon year after year in the hope of finding his son. Then after ten years, Markham finds the boy, now a Brazilian Indian warrior, who he must help survive. Director John Boorman's brilliant visualization breathes life, danger, and mysticism into this captivating, beautifully photographed adventure, based on a true story. Terrific music score by Junior Homrich. Native peoples threatened by civilization is the theme of this story.

Extreme Prejudice (1987 TS)

D: Walter Hill
S: Deric Washburn and Harry Kleiner, based on a story by John Milius and Fred Rexer
P: Buzz Feitshans
Cast: Nick Nolte, Powers Boothe, **Maria Conchita Alonso**, William Forsythe, **Luis Contreras, Rick Garcia, Carlos Cervantes**

Two friends, one a Texas Ranger (Nolte), the other a drug dealer (Boothe), on opposite sides of the law and the border are in love with the same woman, who happens to be a Mexican cantina singer. Maria Conchita Alonso is the Latin spitfire torn between the two men, who are both Anglo.

In *Extreme Prejudice,* Maria Conchita Alonso (right) portrays Sarita, a Mexican cantina singer torn between the love of two men on opposite sides of the law and the border. Nick Nolte (left) portrays Jack Benteen.

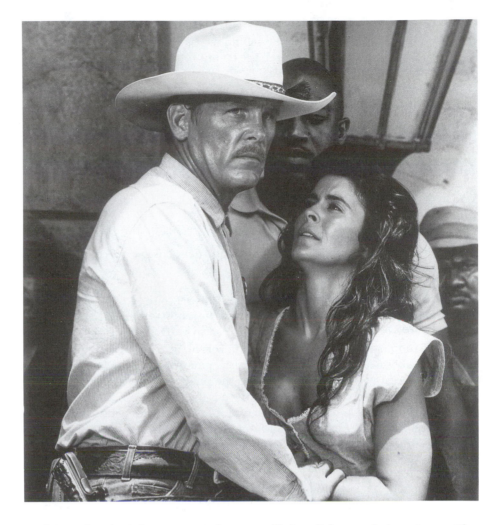

This updated, violent western features all the cliches and stereotypes. The bandidos are well played, though they fall more into the category of the vicious greaser of the silent era.

The Fabulous Senorita (1952 Rep)

D: R.G. Springsteen
S: Charles E. Roberts and Jack Townley, based on a story by Charles R. Marion and Townley
P: Sidney Picker
Cast: **Estelita**, Robert Clarke, **Nestor Paiva**, Marvin Kaplan, **Rita Moreno**, Tito Renaldo, **Martin Garralaga**, Nita del Rey

Amusing romantic comedy about Cuban businessman Jose Rodriguez's (Paiva's) two daughters, Estelita (Estelita) and Manuela (Moreno), who are sent to school in the United States. Manuela uses the opportunity to get married, and Estelita tries to cover for her by playing two roles, while at the same time falling for a young college professor (Clarke).

The Falcon and the Snowman (1985 Or)

D: John Schlesinger
S: Steven Zaillian
P: Gabriel Katzka and John Schlesinger
Cast: Sean Penn, Timothy Hutton

Based on the nonfiction account by Robert Lindsay, and largely filmed in Mexico City, this is the true story of an unstable young American idealist, Christopher

Boyce (Hutton), disillusioned by the CIA's covert intervention in foreign lands, who decides to punish his country by selling secrets to Soviet agents. He achieves this through a dope-smuggling friend, Lee (Penn), who has escaped American authorities by running away to Mexico.

With Lee as his go-between, Boyce manages to contact the Russian Embassy in Mexico and pulls off a number of deals until the Mexican police arrest and brutally interrogate him before giving him up to American authorities.

Mexican police are seen as efficient but brutal in an interrogation sequence that had to be filmed in the United States because the Mexican government objected to the negative image it presented of its police force.

The Falcon in Mexico (1944 RKO)

D: William Berke
S: Gerald Geraghty and George Worthing Yates, based on a character created by Michael Arlen
P: Maurice Geraghty
Cast: Tom Conway, Cecilia Callejo, **Nestor Paiva, Mona Maris, Fernando Alvarado, George J. Lewis, Julian Rivero, Pedro De Cordoba**

The suave amateur sleuth of the screen, the Falcon, untangles a murder mystery south of the border. It involves a dead artist's paintings and the attempts of the beautiful Mexican woman who posed for the paintings to recover them, which result in a gallery owner's death. The trail leads the Falcon from New York City to Mexico City and to the artist's daughter. Since the film shows effective work by Mexican police and the criminal is an American, the Hays Office gave the film a special commendation as one designed to cement Good Neighbor standing between the United States and Mexico.

Fatal Beauty (1987 MGM)

D: Tom Holland
S: Hilary Henkin and Dean Riesner, based on a story by Bill Svanoe
P: Leonard Kroll
Cast: Whoopi Goldberg, **Ruben Blades**, Sam Elliott

A disappointing and predictable melodrama laced with action and sophomoric humor as police detectives Rizzoli (Goldberg) and Carl Jimenez (Blades) search for those making and selling the lethal drug called "Fatal Beauty."

The film includes the usual assortment of Hispanic and black drug dealers and bad guys, somewhat balanced with the multiethnic casting of the leads, who also include Anglo Sam Elliott.

Fearless (1993 WB)

D: Peter Weir
S: Rafael Iglesias, based on his novel
P: Paula Weinstein and Mark Rosenberg
Cast: Jeff Bridges, Isabella Rossellini, **Rosie Perez**, Tom Hulce, **Benicio del Toro**

Story of a man, Max (Bridges), whose perspective on life undergoes a dramatic change after he survives an airplane crash. Rosie Perez plays Carla Rodrigo, a woman whose baby died in the air crash. For this role, Perez was nominated for an Academy Award as Best Supporting Actress.

A Few Good Men (1992 Col)

    D: Rob Reiner
    S: Aaron Sorkin, based on his play
    P: David Brown, Rob Reiner, and Andrew Scheiman
 Cast: Tom Cruise, Jack Nicholson, Demi Moore

On the U.S. naval base at Guantánamo Bay in Cuba, two young Marines are accused of murdering PFC William T. Santiago, a member of their platoon, during an unconventional disciplinary action known as a "Code Red." Naval lawyer Kaffee (Cruise) is determined to unravel the mystery behind the death and bring those responsible to justice.

This critically acclaimed film based on a Broadway play revolves around the death of a Hispanic U.S. Marine, but ethnicity and race are not the real issues. However, since the Marines are in Cuba and the murder victim is Latin and is viewed as the "enemy," Santiago's life is devalued and it is considered to be okay for him to die. (This issue is somewhat diffused, however, because one of the defendants is black.) Although Michael De Lorenzo, who plays Santiago, is seen only briefly at the beginning of the film, his Hispanic presence is felt every time his name is mentioned in this highly charged courtroom drama.

Fiesta [aka: *Gaiety*] (1941 UA)

    D: Leroy Prinz
    S: Cortland Fitzsimmons
    P: Hal Roach
 Cast: Anne Ayars, Jorje Negrete, **Armida, Antonio Moreno**

A Mexican rancher's daughter returns home from Mexico City for her approaching marriage, although she is engaged to another man. This Technicolor musical is stage bound and is peopled with stereotyped characters. One in a series of 50-minute B movies produced by Hal Roach for United Artists, the movie marks the only Hollywood film appearance of Mexican singing film star Jorje Negrete, who is billed as George Negrete. Armida ably and comically sings a song called "Never Trust a Jumping Bean." Also featured are Nick Moro, Carlos Valadez, Jose Arias and his Mexican dancers, and The Guadalajara Trio.

Fiesta (1947 MGM)

    D: Richard Thorpe
    S: George Bruce and Lester Cole
    P: Jack Cummings
 Cast: **Ricardo Montalban**, Esther Williams, Cyd Charisse,
         Mary Astor, **Fortunio Bonanova, Alex Montoya, Nacho Galindo,
         Carlos Ramirez**

Filmed in Mexico. Featuring gorgeous scenery, music, and charming singing and dancing, this film introduced a new screen personality to American audiences, Ricardo Montalban. He danced so ably with Cyd Charisse on film that many thought him a professional dancer.

Though born in Mexico, Montalban spent his teen years in Los Angeles. After a brief stint on Broadway, he returned to Mexico and starred in over 20 Mexican films before being put under contract to MGM.

The plot concerns a lady matador, Maria Morales (Williams), and her twin brother, Mario (Montalban).

The Mexican locations were Puebla and Telacala. Aaron Copland's composition "El Salon Mexico" was used in the film, renamed "Fantasia Mexican" and adapted and orchestrated by Johnny Green. The movie also featured Carlos Ramirez, who appeared and sang in a number of MGM musicals of the era.

The Fighter [aka: *The First Time*] (1952 UA)

    D: Herbert Kline
    S: Aben Kandel and Herbert Kline, based on a story by Jack London
    P: Alex Gottlieb
 Cast: Richard Conte, Lee J. Cobb, **Frank Silvera, Rudolfo Hoyos, Jr.,** Margaret Padilla, Paul Fierro, Rico Alaniz

Taken from the Jack London short story "The Mexican," this film concerns a Mexican fisherman who becomes a prizefighter in 1910 El Paso to provide funds for a revolutionary movement south of the border.

After his family is massacred by the Federales, Felipe Rivera (Conte) travels to the United States and pledges to fight against the Diaz regime. He swims across the Rio Grande to El Paso and joins the Madero forces in exile. Felipe earns money by sparring with prizefighters and then turns the money over to his fellow exiles. He wins a main event against a formidable boxer and uses the $5,000 purse to buy badly needed rifles for the Madero cause.

In this competently made B film, Richard Conte gives a strong performance supported by such actors as Lee J. Cobb as a Mexican revolutionary leader. The film utilizes some documentary footage of the village of Janitzio on Pátzcuaro Island in the Puebla area shot by Herbert Kline for his film *The Forgotten Village*.

The Firebrand (1962 TCF)

    D: Maury Dexter
    S: Harry Spalding
    P: Maury Dexter
 Cast: Valentin De Vargas, Kent Taylor

Mexican Robin Hood Joaquin Murieta (De Vargas) robs the gold-crazed American settlers in Old California. A determined California ranger, Major Tim Bancroft (Taylor), kills another man, lops off his head, and starts rumors that it is the head of Joaquin. He charges admission to see it in order to draw Murieta into the open. Joaquin has a showdown with the major and then rides off into the sunset. This dismal low-budget film is below the level even of a B western, but it has the distinction of having a Hispanic in the lead role.

Fires Within (1992 MGM/Pathé)

    D: Gillian Armstrong
    S: Cynthia Cidre and Peter Barsocchini
    P: Wallis Nicita and Lauren Lloyd
 Cast: **Jimmy Smits**, Greta Scacchi, Vincent D'Onofrio, Bri Hathaway

A family is separated in Cuba by Fidel Castro's oppressive government. The husband, Nestor (Smits), is imprisoned for life for his writings about the injustice and inhumanity of the revolution he once fervently believed in. He insists that his wife, Isabel (Scacchi), and their infant daughter escape to Miami, Florida.

Nearly dying at sea, they are rescued by Sam (D'Onofrio), an American fisherman. He and Isabel meet again in Miami several years later and fall in love. Looking after Isabel and the now seven-year-old Maribel (Hathaway), Sam is convinced that he and Isabel will eventually marry.

Eight years following Isabel's escape from Cuba, Nestor is unexpectedly released from prison and arrives in Miami to reclaim his family, unaware that he will force his wife to choose between him and the man she has grown to depend on and in whom she has invested her future.

This romantic drama about Cuban exiles in America was filmed on location in Miami and co-written by Cuban-born, Miami-raised screenwriter Cynthia Cidre.

Firewalker (1986 Cannon)

D: J. Lee Thompson
S: Robert Gosnell, based on a story by Gosnell, Jeffrey Rosenbaum, and Norman Aladjem
P: Menahem Golan and Yoram Globus
Cast: Chuck Norris, Louis Gossett, Jr., Melody Anderson

Americans in exotic Mexico in an escapist adventure/fantasy. After ten years of life-threatening, money-losing schemes and expeditions, fortune hunters Max Donigan (Norris) and Leo Porter (Gossett) are about to call it quits. Then a beautiful young woman (Anderson) appears with a map to the long-lost gold hoards of the ancient Aztecs. Dollar signs in their eyes, the trio embark on a journey to Guatemala, where they battle merciless mercenaries and the Aztec medicine man El Coyote (Will Sampson). Zaide Silvia Gutierrez is featured as an Indian girl.

The First Texan (1956 AA)

D: Byron Haskin
S: Daniel B. Ullman
P: Walter Mirisch
Cast: Joel McCrea, Felicia Farr, Wallace Ford, Jeff Morrow, **Rudolfo Hoyos, Jr.**

Story of Sam Houston (McCrea) and the independence movement led by resolute Mexicans and Americans determined to free themselves from oppressive Mexican rule and the events leading up to the battle of San Jacinto. Houston's army wins decisively against superior Mexican forces, capturing General Santa Anna and eventually winning independence for Texas.

Rudolfo Hoyos, Jr., portrays Cos; David Silva is Gen. Santa Anna; Frank Puglia is Pepe; and Salvador Baguez is Veramendi. The film also features Maurice Jara as Pablo, Nestor Paiva as a priest, and George J. Lewis as a Mexican doctor.

The First Time

See *The Fighter*.

A Fistful of Dollars (1964 UA)

D: Sergio Leone
S: Sergio Leone and Duccio Tessari
P: Arrigo Columbo and Giorgio Papi
Cast: Clint Eastwood, John Wells, Marianne Koch, Antonio Prieto, Jose Calvo

International cult phenomenon that launched the film careers of Italian writer/ director/producer Sergio Leone, composer Ennio Morricone, and little-known American television actor Clint Eastwood. A western remake of Kurosawa's *Yojimbo* (1961), this film created the genre of "spaghetti westerns." Both films are adaptations of Dashiell Hammett's novel *Red Harvest*.

Eastwood is the "Man with No Name," a greedy, amoral drifter of a gunfighter who arrives in a hellhole of a frontier community, where two gangs of bandits are vying for power. John Wells plays Ramon Rojo, the bandit and the leader of one of the gangs.

It is a western taken to the extreme with unremitting violence, gritty realism, and at times tongue-in-cheek antics. Leone used breathtaking panoramas as well as extreme closeups of the quivering lips and darting eyes of the international cast just before a shoot-out. Mexican bandidos, sleepy villages, and beautiful senoritas inhabit this western (much of which was shot in Spain and Italy). Ennio Morricone's haunting and quirky musical score became a signature theme.

A Fistful of Dynamite [aka: *A Fistful of Revolution*]

See *Duck, You Sucker!*

Flying Down to Rio (1933 RKO)
   D: Thornton Freeland
   S: Cyril Hume, H.W. Hanemann, and Erwin Gelsey, based on a play by
      Anne Caldwell from an original story by Brock
   P: Lou Brock
 Cast: Gene Raymond, **Dolores Del Rio**, Fred Astaire, Ginger Rogers, **Raul Roulien**

This musical/comedy stars Dolores Del Rio and Gene Raymond, but it was a new dance team that stole the film, Fred Astaire and Ginger Rogers in their first screen teaming.

Del Rio plays a beautiful Brazilian woman who is engaged to a wealthy Brazilian, played by Raul Roulien. Into her life comes aerialist and songwriter Roger Bond (Raymond), and complications ensue.

One of the great production numbers featured an aerial ballet in which scores of chorus girls anchored to the wings of old bi-planes dance and remove their clothes to the delight of the inhabitants of Rio de Janeiro below.

Dolores Del Rio and Fred Astaire dance to "Orchids in the Moonlight" in *Flying Down to Rio*.

Del Rio actually danced with Fred Astaire before Rogers in the film, but in the "Carioca" number, Astaire and Rogers emerged as one of the screen's greatest dance teams. The film was shot entirely on soundstages at RKO Studios in Hollywood, which re-created the look of Rio as an escapist postcard fantasy for a Depression-era America.

For a Few Dollars More (1965 UA)

  D: Sergio Leone
  S: Sergio Leone and Luciano Vincenzoni
  P: Alberto Grimaldi
Cast: Clint Eastwood, Lee Van Cleef, Gian Marie Volonte

Eastwood, the "Man with No Name," and Van Cleef as Col. Mortimer, an aging bounty hunter, form an uneasy alliance in quest of the reward money offered for the bandit El Indio (Gian Marie Volonte) and his band of desperados. During the climactic shoot-out it is revealed that Col. Mortimer's reason for hunting El Indio is not the reward money but vengeance for the murder of a family member.

This was the second film in the successful "Man with No Name" series, a "spaghetti western" trilogy that also included *A Fistful of Dollars* (1964) and *The Good, the Bad, and the Ugly* (1967).

For Whom the Bell Tolls (1943 Par)

  D: Sam Wood
  S: Dudley Nichols, based on the novel by Ernest Hemingway
  P: Sam Wood
Cast: Gary Cooper, Ingrid Bergman, Akim Tamiroff, **Fortunio Bonanova,** Katina Paxinou, **Arturo De Cordova, Joseph Calleia, Duncan Renaldo, Pedro De Cordoba**

Many films have been adapted from Hemingway's stories and novels, including *A Farewell to Arms* (1932 and 1957) and *The Old Man and the Sea* (1958). *For Whom the Bell Tolls* made its debut in 1943 after three years of prerelease publicity, second only to the publicity buildup for *Gone with the Wind.* Paramount bought the film rights to Hemingway's controversial best-seller shortly after its publication in 1940.

It is the story of an American university professor turned dynamiter on the side of the Loyalists in the 1936 Spanish Civil War. The demolition of a strategic bridge and the love of Robert Jordan (Cooper) for a lovely Spanish girl, Maria (Bergman), were the main dramatic thrusts of the movie.

Cooper was Hemingway's and the public's choice for the role of Robert Jordan. The movie script let go of the political overtones of the Spanish Civil War, thus robbing the film of its timely power and sense of a specific place and time. Except in terms of good guys and bad guys, the modern viewer is never quite sure who and what the characters are fighting for.

The film is overly long yet entertaining and distinguished by good acting and beautiful camera work. It features a terrific supporting cast, including Joseph Calleia as El Sordo, a guerrilla fighter; Akim Tamiroff as Pablo; Katina Paxinou (winner of the Best Supporting Actress Oscar) as Pilar, Pablo's woman; and Arturo De Cordova as Agustin. A young Yvonne De Carlo (a starlet and later a star at Universal in the late 1940s and 1950s) plays a dancer in a café sequence. In smaller supporting roles are Fortunio Bonanova as Fernando, Duncan Renaldo as Lt. Berendo, Pedro De Cordoba as Col. Miranda, Frank Puglia as Capt. Gomez, and Martin Garralaga as Capt. Mora. Bit parts were played by Trini Varela, Alberto Morin, Pedro Regas, Soledad Jimenez, and Tito Renaldo.

Left to right: Arturo De Cordova, Gary Cooper, Ingrid Bergman, and Katina Paxinou in a scene from *For Whom the Bell Tolls*.

Location scenes were filmed in the Sierra Nevada near Tuolumne, California. William Cameron Menzies was the production designer (he served in a similar capacity on *Gone with the Wind*). Ray Rennahan was the color cinematographer.

"It is a great picture without political significance. We are not for or against anybody," stated Adolph Zukor, head of Paramount Studios. "Love story set against a brutal backdrop" is how director Sam Wood described the movie.

Forever Darling (1956 MGM)

 D: Alexander Hall
 S: Helen Deutsch
 P: **Desi Arnaz**
Cast: Lucille Ball, **Desi Arnaz**, James Mason, Louis Calhern

Lucy and Desi play Susan and Larry Vega, a couple who experience difficulty in their marriage. Larry's job as a chemist keeps him burning the midnight oil, so Susan spends time with friends whom Larry finds distasteful.

Soon the couple find themselves growing steadily apart. But when Susan's guardian angel (Mason) appears, he encourages her to try to put the romance back in her marriage. She decides to accompany Larry on a camping trip, but after a sleepless night and disastrous morning, Susan and Larry are really on the rocks. Just when it seems that the couple will part ways, a few surprises send them traveling down the road to marital bliss.

Produced by Desi and Lucy's production company, Desilu, the film presented a modern Hispanic American married couple as the leads. In their first theatrical feature film outing, *The Long, Long Trailer* (1954), they presented themselves as a nondescript, presumably Italian American couple. By the time of *Forever Darling*, however, following their success in television, it was not necessary to disguise Desi's Latin heritage.

Fort Apache, The Bronx (1981 TCF)

D: Daniel Petrie
S: Heywood Gould
P: Martin Richards and Tom Fiorello
Cast: Paul Newman, Ken Wahl, Edward Asner, Pam Grier, **Rachel Ticotin, Gloria Irrizary**

Similar in spirit to *Colors* (1988), this film is about a veteran Irish American cop, Murphy (Newman), who teaches a young rookie cop, Corelli (Wahl), about life on the harsh streets of New York City's crime- and poverty-ridden South Bronx, instead of South Central and East Los Angeles as in *Colors*.

During a riot, a cop throws a young Hispanic boy from a rooftop to his death. Feeling justified in his actions, the cop causes a crisis of conscience in fellow policeman Murphy, who has witnessed the murder. Murphy exposes what happened and causes a rift among his fellow officers.

Since *Fort Apache, The Bronx* predates *Colors* by seven years, it is interesting to note the plot similarities. In both movies, the police station stands as an outpost of law, order, and white European civilization against the savages (meaning Hispanics and blacks). In *Fort Apache*, Murphy falls for a Puerto Rican nurse (Ticotin) who turns out to be a heroin addict and dies of an overdose, betraying his trust; in *Colors*, the rookie cop falls for a Chicana (Maria Conchita Alonso) who works at a burger stand and who betrays him by sleeping with a black gang member.

Blacks and Puerto Ricans are seen as prostitutes, junkies, and lowlifes. There are no positive black or Puerto Rican characters in the film. The white cops protect society from inner-city minorities.

During production, the film met with protests from a coalition of black and Puerto Rican South Bronx residents, who cited the exaggerated violence in the script, the lack of positive Spanish-surnamed or black characters, and the film's failure to explain how racial bias and poverty entrap many residents of the South Bronx.

The producers declined to make changes in the script. How easy and more interesting it would have been to make Murphy's Italian American rookie partner a Puerto Rican and achieve a balance of sorts.

Playwright Miguel Pinero (*Short Eyes*) plays a junkie with stinging veracity. Tito Goya and Gloria Irrizary are also featured.

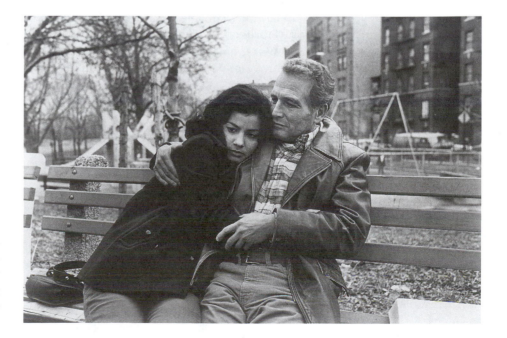

A nurse, Rachel Ticotin, is comforted by a compassionate cop, played by Paul Newman. The two are involved in a bittersweet romance in this powerful account of an embattled police precinct in a devastated, violent neighborhood in *Fort Apache, The Bronx*.

The Four Horsemen of the Apocalypse (1921 Metro)

    D: Rex Ingram
    S: June Mathis, based on the novel by **Vicente Blasco Ibanez**
    P: Rex Ingram for Metro Pictures
 Cast: Rudolph Valentino, Alice Terry, Pomeroy Cannon

Silent. Rudolph Valentino became a star when he danced the tango in a seedy Buenos Aires cabaret in the role of Julio Desnoyers, a young South American in Paris on the eve of World War I.

Filmgoers remember Valentino dressed as a gaucho boldly interrupting a couple on the dance floor and claiming the woman (Beatrice Dominguez) for a tango, and the mystical note on which the film ends.

Madariaga (Cannon), a wealthy old cattle owner of Argentina who despises his German son-in-law, lavishes all his affections on Julio. After Madariaga's death, the estate is divided, and the family disperses to Europe, the von Hartrotts to Germany and the Desnoyers to France. Julio buys a castle on the Marne and opens a studio, where he entertains, paints pictures, and soon falls desperately in love with Marguerite Laurier (Terry), the youthful wife of a jurist. World War I breaks out, and Marguerite joins the Red Cross, while her husband enlists. Finding her husband wounded and blinded in action, Marguerite resists the attentions of Julio. Spurred on by the words of a stranger who invokes the symbols of the Four Horsemen of the Apocalypse—war, conquest, famine, and death—Julio enlists. After distinguishing himself for bravery in the French army, he is killed in an exchange with his cousin, an officer in the German army.

The Four Horsemen of the Apocalypse (1962 MGM)

    D: Vincente Minnelli
    S: Robert Ardrey and John Gay, based on the novel by **Vicente Blasco Ibanez**
    P: Julian Blaustein
 Cast: Glenn Ford, **Yvette Mimieux**, Lee J. Cobb, Paul Henreid

In an attempt to duplicate the success of 40 years earlier, this costly and important production for MGM was both a critical and commercial failure. Comparison with the famed silent version starring Rudolph Valentino could not have been helpful, but they were two entirely different films similar only in superficial terms. Nevertheless, silent director Ingram's approach to the story was considerably less imaginative than Minnelli's, who had the benefit of all the technical advancements made in photography, directing, and acting techniques since the original was shot. Glenn Ford played Julio in a characterization totally different from Valentino's.

The story was updated to World War II and centers around Julio in Paris and his efforts as a French Resistance fighter. Filming took place on location in France and at MGM Studios.

1492: Conquest of Paradise (1992 Par)

    D: Ridley Scott
    S: Roselyne Bosch
    P: Ridley Scott and Alain Goldman
 Cast: Gerard Depardieu, Armand Assante, Sigourney Weaver

A handsomely photographed and visually striking but dull and disjointed production. Depardieu is a lumbering, heavily French-accented English-speaking Italian Columbus. A lot of attention is paid to historical accuracy, however, even if the four voyages are condensed into two.

Freebie and the Bean (1974 WB)

 D: Richard Rush
 S: Robert Kaufman, based on a story by Floyd Mutrux
 P: Richard Rush
Cast: James Caan, Alan Arkin

Comedy/action movie starring James Caan as Freebie Waters and Alan Arkin as Benito "Bean" Vasquez, a pair of plainclothes cops in San Francisco tracking down a numbers racketeer. The "Bean" is a Mexican American who puts up with the ethnic slurs of his partner and friend Freebie, including being called a "spick" and "wetback."

This supposedly comic bantering between the two makes up much of the humor of the film, which also includes broad car chases and crashes. Against this, however, is the contemporary characterization by Arkin of a Mexican American policeman as a positive, if new, kind of hero figure. Valerie Harper (later of TV's "Rhoda" fame) plays Arkin's Hispanic wife, whom he suspects of infidelity.

The Fugitive (1947 RKO)

 D: **John Ford**
 S: Dudley Nichols, based on the novel *The Power and the Glory* by Graham Greene
 P: Merian C. Cooper and **John Ford**
Cast: Henry Fonda, **Dolores Del Rio, Pedro Armendariz, Leo Carrillo, J. Carroll Naish, Fortunio Bonanova**, Miguel Inclan, **Chris-Pin Martin, Jose Torvay**

Fonda plays the lone surviving priest in a fictional Latin American country that has become a police state with a severely anticlerical stance. Del Rio plays the beautiful Magdalena figure Indian woman who helps the priest and is the cast-off mistress of the pursuing police lieutenant (Armendariz).

Filmed in Mexico, *The Fugitive* is truly the first Mexican American co-production in terms of bringing together the best and most celebrated filmmaking talents of both countries—director John Ford, associate producer Emilio Fernandez, cinematographer Gabriel Figueroa, actors Henry Fonda, Pedro Armendariz, and Dolores Del Rio. Mel Ferrer was an assistant to director John Ford. Figueroa's cinematography captured images of Latin America in its churches, its countryside, and its people. A cast of mostly Latin actors was gathered from both Mexico and the United States. Armendariz gives a stunning performance as an Indian who is hard on his own people, with a demonstrable antipathy toward the Catholic religion.

Fun in Acapulco (1963 Par)

 D: Richard Thorpe
 S: Allan Weiss
 P: Hal Wallis
Cast: Elvis Presley, Ursula Andress, **Elsa Cardenas, Alejandro Rey, Robert Carricart**

Soft, lush, and inviting backgrounds of Acapulco frame the setting of Presley's romp in Mexico, complete with the King singing in Spanish and diving off the high cliffs of La Quebrada into the ocean surf.

This light tale concerns a young man with a psychological problem as well as a romantic one. Having been a trapeze artist, Mike Windgren (Presley) is terrified of heights due to his failure years before to catch his partner, for whose death he blames himself. A local shoeshine boy, Raoul Almeido (Larry Domasin), with a head for business happens to overhear Mike's singing and appoints himself his manager.

He gets Mike a job as a part-time singer and lifeguard at a swank hotel. Mike soon becomes romantically involved with Margarita Dauphine (Andress), the

Elvis Presley sang (in Spanish) in the Mexican romp *Fun in Acapulco*.

daughter of a European immigrant, and Dolores Gomez (Cardenas), a lady bull-fighter. Another lifeguard and high-dive specialist, Moreno (Rey), becomes jealous of Mike's attention to Margarita. Eventually, Mike overcomes his fear of heights. Alberto Morin is featured as the hotel manager, and Robert Carricart plays Jose.

The film was shot largely on Paramount Studios soundstages, with a second-unit crew shooting all the Acapulco exteriors on location with doubles standing in for the stars. All the attention and publicity surrounding an Elvis Presley picture certainly helped to create a fun image of the Mexican resort for youths all over the world, who would later, as adults, want to make Acapulco a vacation travel destination.

Fun with Dick and Jane (1977 Col)
    D: Ted Kotcheff
    S: David Giler, Jerry Belson, and Mordecai Richler
    P: Hank Bart and Max Palevsky
  Cast: George Segal, Jane Fonda, Ed McMahon, Dick Gautier

An upwardly mobile young couple's dreams come crashing down when the husband loses his job. Their attempts to deal with the situation and the desperate lengths to which they go to maintain their upper-middle-class lifestyle are the basis of this comedy. Desperate for work, college-educated aerospace engineer Dick (Segal) turns for help to the Chicano janitor who used to clean his office. Stand-up comedian Hank Garcia plays Raoul Esteban, the janitor who becomes Segal's streetwise counsel on such matters as unemployment insurance and food stamps.

The Furies (1950 Par)

    D: Anthony Mann
    S: Charles Schnee, based on the novel by Niven Busch
    P: Hal B. Wallis
 Cast: Barbara Stanwyck, Walter Huston, Wendell Corey, **Gilbert Roland,
       Thomas Gomez**, Blanche Yurka, **Movita**

T.C. Jeffords (Huston), pioneer cattle baron, is the larger-than-life figure who finally meets his match in his own daughter, Vance (Stanwyck), a strong-willed woman who upsets her father by choosing Rip Darrow (Corey), a sworn enemy, as her boyfriend.

T.C. chooses a San Francisco widow as his new wife, and Vance in a rage attacks her. T.C. goes off on a rampage and hangs Juan Herrera (Roland), Vance's childhood sweetheart and sometime lover. This incident sets up Jeffords's own death at the finale at the hands of Herrera's avenging mother (Yurka). Thomas Gomez plays the ranch foreman El Tigre, and Movita Castenada plays Chiquita. Pepe Hern and Joe Dominguez are also featured.

This strong, well-acted western was directed by Anthony Mann, who would gain prominence with a series of mostly western action/outdoor melodramas of which this was the first.

Gaby—A True Story (1987 TS)

    D: **Luis Mandoki**
    S: Martin Salinas and Michael James Love, based on a story developed by Mandoki from events narrated to him by Gabriela Brimmer
    P: Pinchas Perry and Luis Mandoki
 Cast: Liv Ullmann, **Norma Aleandro**, Robert Loggia, Rachel Levin, Lawrence Monoson, **Robert Beltran**, Tony Goldwyn, **Danny De La Paz**

The true story of a young woman with cerebral palsy who becomes a professional writer. The movie is drawn from the 1979 autobiography of Gaby Brimmer, then the 34-year-old daughter of Jewish refugees in Mexico City. Gaby had the good fortune to be raised by an extremely understanding nurse, Florencia, who became her friend and companion.

Norma Aleandro plays Florencia, who, according to director Luis Mandoki in an interview with Luis Reyes, "represents the heart and soul of the Mexican people." Mandoki waited five years to get the production made the way he wished it to be. It is a modern-day look at life in Mexico. Norma Aleandro as the Indian maid in a white European household in Mexico gives evidence of a racist legacy in Mexico in which Eurocentric values are nurtured at the expense of mother Mexico. Florencia serves almost the same function as did the black mammy/nurse in such films as *Gone with the Wind*. Aleandro received an Academy Award nomination for Best Supporting Actress.

Filmed on location in Cuernavaca, Mexico, it was an international co-production with the Mexican government.

"Norma Aleandro, the fine Argentine actress (*The Official Story*), gives a quietly complex performance as the withdrawn servant who simply took charge of the child Gaby one night—and never left," Julie Salamon, *Wall Street Journal* (10/2/87).

"A superb performance by Norma Aleandro, the Argentine actress who . . . is a real standout, and . . . contributes greatly to the film's verisimilitude," Janet Maslin, *New York Times* (10/30/87).

"Luis Mandoki's treatment is blunt, outspoken and full of strong emotions. He receives immeasurable help from a sublime casting stroke that pairs two powerhouse actresses," Deborah Kunk, *L.A. Herald* (11/13/87).

Gaiety

See *Fiesta* (1941).

Gang

See *Walk Proud.*

The Gang's All Here (1943 TCF)

  D: Busby Berkeley
  S: Walter Bullock, based on a story by Nancy Winter, George Root, Jr., and Tom Bridges
  P: William LeBaron
Cast: Alice Faye, Phil Baker, **Carmen Miranda**, Benny Goodman

A soldier goes off to war and leaves behind two young women who believe they are engaged to him. One of them (Faye) is a chorus girl at a New York nightclub where Dorita (Miranda) is the star. Miranda steals every scene she is in. Miranda's version of the song and production number "The Lady in the Tutti Frutti Hat" has Mae West–type comic sexual overtones that are difficult to ignore when 60 chorus girls prance about with giant phallic bananas. It was Busby Berkeley's first color film and a high point in his career as a choreographer and director. Dancer Tony DeMarco, an Italian American, is also featured.

Garden of Evil (1954 TCF)

  D: Henry Hathaway
  S: Frank Fenton, based on a story by Fred Freiberger and William Tunberg
  P: Charles Brackett
Cast: Gary Cooper, Richard Widmark, Susan Hayward, Cameron Mitchell, **Rita Moreno**, Hugh Marlowe, Victor Manuel Mendoza

Three American adventurers (Cooper, Widmark, and Mitchell) and one Mexican (Mendoza) in a Mexican port agree to help a beautiful American woman (Hayward) rescue her husband (Marlowe), who is trapped in a gold mine deep in the wilds of Mexico. They rescue the husband but have to battle Indians on the way back. The movie was filmed on location in Mexico in CinemaScope and Technicolor.

The Mexican character comes off as courageous but dumb. For example, when Widmark asks Mendoza to cut the cards in a card game, he literally does so, using a machete. Rita Moreno plays a seductive dancing cantina girl in the opening sequence.

The Gaucho (1928 UA)

  D: F. Richard Jones
  S: Lotta Woods, based on a story by Elton Thomas [Fairbanks]
  P: Douglas Fairbanks
Cast: Douglas Fairbanks, **Lupe Velez**

In Argentina, the Gaucho (Fairbanks) fights against the evil usurper Ruiz (Gustave von Seyfferitz) in the town of Milagros.

Lupe Velez made her major film debut in *The Gaucho* as the female lead. She replaced Dolores Del Rio, who had been previously announced for the role but who had to drop out due to personal problems. Lupe got excellent notices, and the film made her a star. She matches Fairbanks in athletic prowess, acting, and humor.

In the *L.A. Record* (4/12/27), columnist Dan Thomas quoted Fairbanks's views on film production, shared by most of his colleagues at that time: "In this picture

I will be a gaucho, a South American cowboy. There will be no time element in the story, which might have taken place any time during the last century. Naturally it will be colorful, showing the South Americans as we think of them rather than as they are." He continued, "A film depicting the southern continent as it actually is today would be very uninteresting. We have to show the gauchos in colorful costumes and romantic village settings in order to make them interesting. This is what we call movie license."

The Gay Defender (1927 Par)
    D: Gregory La Cava
    S: Lay Harris, Sam Mintz, and Kenneth Raisbeck
    P: Adolph Zukor and Jesse L. Lasky
 Cast: Richard Dix

Fictionalized silent film biography of the legendary California bandit Joaquin Murieta. Some location scenes were filmed near Mission San Juan Capistrano in southern California's Orange County.

"Dix has side burns and a mustache, but it's still a tough job for him to look Spanish. He ought to remain on this side of the border. Other than that neither Mexico nor Spain will have anything to squawk about because the villain is an American. *Gay Defender* is just a western and not a good one," *Variety* (12/28/27).

The Gay Desperado (1936 UA)
    D: Rouben Mamoulian
    S: Wallace Smith, based on a story by Leo Birinski
    P: Mary Pickford and Jesse L. Lasky
 Cast: Nino Martini, **Leo Carrillo**, Ida Lupino, **Allan Garcia, Chris-Pin Martin**

A musical/comedy based on a popular Broadway show that spoofed the western and gangster genres and served as a film vehicle for then-popular Italian Metropolitan Opera singer Nino Martini.

Leo Carrillo, Ida Lupino, and Nino Martini pose for a picture in their costumes from *The Gay Desperado*.

The plot follows a Mexican bandit (Carrillo) who kidnaps Martini because he likes his singing and an American heiress (Lupino) in order to extract a ransom. As expected, Carrillo got the best notices for his wild, fun interpretation of a bandit. He even does a takeoff of gangster portrayals by James Cagney and George Raft.

The Gay Senorita (1946 Col)

    D: Arthur Dreifuss
    S: Edward Eliscu
    P: Jay Gorney
Cast: Jinx Falkenburg, Steve Cochran

The story revolves around the efforts of big businessman J.J. Frontess (Thurston Hall) to take over a historic city district and convert the area into a huge warehouse. Its Mexican American population, descended from those early Californians who founded the city on that very spot, refuse to sell. Dona Maria de Sandoval (Marguerita Sylva) dreams of the time when Sandoval Lane can be rebuilt and stand as a monument to the spirit of the early Mexican pioneers.

J.J. lets his nephew Phil (Jim Bannon) try his hand at acquiring the properties. The usual romantic complications arise when Phil falls for Elena (Falkenburg), daughter of Dona Maria, and turns against his uncle. He meets old friend Tim O'Brian (Cochran), now a bandleader who works under the name Tim Obrion. While J.J. is on a business trip, Phil uses company money to completely rebuild Sandoval Lane. Surprised and upset at what he sees upon his return, J.J., treated with nothing but kindness by the local citizenry, relents and decides to build the warehouse somewhere else.

This modest-budget musical offering sheds light on and acknowledges the history and contributions of Mexican Americans in the Southwest and their pride in that accomplishment. It could be called one of the first Chicano consciousness movies because of its theme of people banding together to save the remnants of their cultural heritage. Based on the actual efforts of citizens to save historic Olvera Street in downtown Los Angeles, *The Gay Senorita* features numerous Hispanic actors and performers including Corinna Maura, Isabelita, Luisita Triana, Lola Montes, Nina Bara, and Leander de Cordova.

The Ghost Breakers (1940 Par)

    D: George Marshall
    S: Walter De Leon
    P: Arthur Hornblow, Jr.
Cast: Bob Hope, Paulette Goddard, **Pedro De Cordoba, Anthony Quinn**

Larry Lawrence (Hope) is a breezy radio columnist who innocently becomes involved in a murder. Mary Carter (Goddard) saves him from the police and helps him escape in a trunk to a ship sailing for Cuba. They get romantically involved during the trip, and when Mary discovers she has inherited a spooky island castle called Castillo Maldito in Cuba, Larry offers to help her rid the castle of evil spirits.

Bob Hope and Paulette Goddard had been teamed previously in the popular *The Cat and the Canary* (1939). The comedy/thriller *The Ghost Breakers* helped establish Bob Hope as a top film comedian at Paramount. A young Anthony Quinn played two roles as Cuban twin brothers, Ramon and Francisco Maderos. Willie Best plays the eye-popping black sidekick.

The action takes place mainly in the haunted castle on an island off the coast of Cuba, and Paramount constructed the castle on two huge soundstages. The film was based on a play by Paul Dickey and Charles W. Goddard. There were two previous silent film versions, one in 1914 and the other in 1922, starring Wallace Reid.

Elsa Cardenas portrays Juana (center), a beautiful Mexican girl who marries the son (Dennis Hopper, in trench coat) of a wealthy Anglo rancher in *Giant*.

Giant (1956 WB)

D: George Stevens

S: Fred Guiol and Ivan Moffat, based on the novel by Edna Ferber

P: George Stevens and Henry Ginsberg

Cast: Rock Hudson, Elizabeth Taylor, James Dean, Dennis Hopper, **Elsa Cardenas, Victor Millan, Pilar Del Rey, Felipe Turich, Tina Menard, Natividad Vacio,** Maurice Jara

A multigenerational saga based on the novel by Edna Ferber that tells the story of a ranch dynasty as it encounters the sweeping changes brought on by the twentieth century. This was Dean's last movie, and Stevens won an Oscar for Best Director.

Henry Ginsberg commented in a 1973 interview in *Condo-News* (Palm Beach, Florida) that it was tough at first to get the book made into a film. "*Giant* was a forerunner of the black and white situation of today. It dealt with, in some parts, the attitudes of the Texans towards the Mexicans and the Industry may have been scared off at first by the inherent social issues."

The Benedicts are a cattle dynasty, and the head of the family, Bick Benedict (Hudson, in one of his best performances), chooses a wife from Virginia and so introduces a subversive influence into the extraordinary house set in the middle of the Texas plains. Wife Leslie, played by Elizabeth Taylor, finds it strange that, among other things, Mexican servants and their children should be allowed to die because a "white doctor cannot possibly attend to those people."

Years later, during a big reception at the Benedict ranch, Reata, Jordy Benedict III (Hopper) announces that he has married Juana (Cardenas), a beautiful Mexican girl. Bick is outraged at the idea of a Mexican being Mrs. Jordan Benedict III. Before a banquet for the opening of a new hotel, Juana is refused service at a beauty salon and is not allowed to enter the banquet hall with Jordan and their baby.

The climax of the film finds Bick accompanying his family to a burger joint, where the owner scowls at the fact that Bick has entered with Juana and the baby. Shortly thereafter, some Mexican workers enter the café and are ordered out by the owner. Bick intercedes and becomes involved in a fight. He loses the fight, but gains respect for having defended the Mexicans.

Based on a best-selling book, *Giant* was a major Hollywood production with a well-respected director and an all-star cast. The film proved big at the box office but received mixed critical notices.

Marfa, Texas, was headquarters for the location shooting. The Mexican village was constructed in the town of Valentine, 40 miles from Marfa.

The film features a number of Mexican American actors including Victor Millan as Angel Obregon; Pilar Del Rey as Mrs. Obregon; Felipe Turich as Gomez, head of the Mexican village; Maurice Jara as Dr. Guerra; and Tina Menard as Lupe. Menard was also responsible for casting the many Mexican American extras used in the film, both on location and at the studio. Sal Mineo plays Angel Obregon III, the son of one of the Benedicts' ranch hands, who was saved during an illness as a baby at the intervention of Leslie Benedict and who later dies a hero in World War II.

The importance of *Giant* to Hispanic Americans is that it was the first major film to expose the racism that Mexican Americans suffered in the Southwest and at the same time highlighted the problem of racism in general in the United States to audiences on the national and international levels. The problem was presented in a sympathetic liberal light in which the Mexicans were not the main players. The ending of the film, with its fusing of the Anglo and Mexican through intermarriage and the birth of their baby, signaled hope for a better future through integration and understanding. The film's importance as a catalyst for discussion in the media, however, was overshadowed by the death of its young star, James Dean, prior to the film's release.

Gilda (1946 Col)

D: Charles Vidor
S: Marion Parsonnet, based on an adaptation by Jo Eisinger of E.A. Ellington's original story
P: Virginia Van Upp
Cast: Glenn Ford, **Rita Hayworth**, George Macready, **Joseph Calleia**

From the moment she appears on screen, hair disheveled and cascading down her naked shoulders, Rita Hayworth as Gilda exudes an almost explosive sexual electricity that brings together her best qualities as a star. The image of Gilda is the one that Hayworth has come to be most identified with over the years.

The plot has something to do with entrepreneur Ballin Mundson's (Macready's) efforts to establish a tungsten cartel involved with the atomic bomb. Johnny Farrell (Ford), from the gutter, makes it to the top in Buenos Aires' posh casinos working for Ballin. Johnny meets Gilda, whom he knew previously. She is now married to Ballin, and a love/hate relationship develops between Johnny and Gilda, which Ballin soon notes.

Gilda turned out to be durably profitable for Columbia and was reissued twice with international success before being made available to television. Another Hayworth-Ford teaming, *Affair in Trinidad* (1952), a similar film, made even more money at the box office. *Gilda* was filmed at Columbia Studios in Hollywood.

Rita Hayworth in the lead role in *Gilda*.

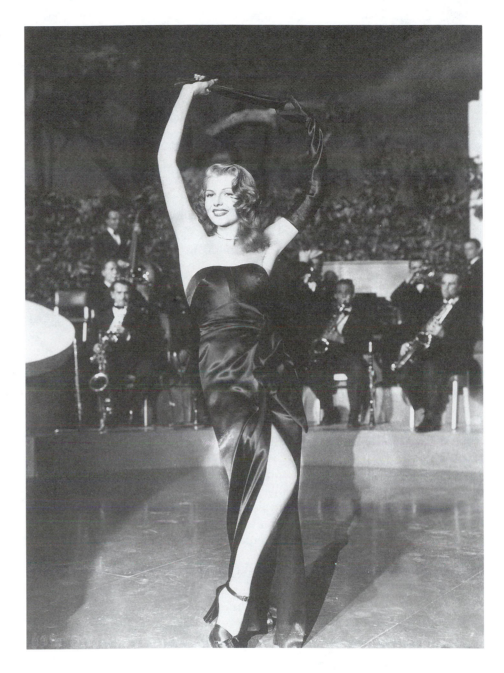

"When things get trite and far fetched, somehow, at the drop of a shoulder strap, there is always Rita Hayworth to excite the moviegoer," *Variety* (3/20/46).

"Has its setting in that hot spot, The Argentine. It is always a hot spot in the movies, because it can be thick with secret agents, soft spoken Latin Lotharios and tango tunes, and *Gilda* makes the most of this," Edwin Schallert, *L.A. Times* (4/27/46).

The Girl from Mexico (1939 RKO)

D: Leslie Goodwins
S: Lionel Houser and Joseph A. Fields
P: Cliff Reid
Cast: **Lupe Velez**

Madcap comedy starring Lupe Velez as Carmelita, a fiery Latin nightclub entertainer in New York City.

Girl of the Rio (1932 RKO)

   D: Herbert Brenon
   S: Elizabeth Meehan, based on the Willard Mack play *The Dove*
   P: Herbert Brenon
Cast: **Dolores Del Rio, Leo Carrillo,** Norman Foster

The egotistical, wealthy, and politically influential Don Jose (Carrillo) makes unwelcome advances to cantina dancer Dolores (Del Rio), whose sweetheart, Johnny (Foster), runs a gambling operation in a Mexican town. When Don Jose frames Johnny on a murder charge, Dolores is forced to offer herself to Don Jose in order to save her lover. This indifferent film of the border was banned by the Mexican government because of the story line and Carrillo's despicable portrayal. The story had been filmed before in a 1928 silent version with Norma Shearer in a Sicilian island setting. Norman Foster later became a noted director in Mexico and the United States.

Gloria (1980 Col)

   D: John Cassavetes
   S: John Cassavetes
   P: John Cassavetes
Cast: Gena Rowlands, John Adames, Buck Henry, **Julie Carmen**

A mobster's ex-mistress, Gloria (Rowlands), tries to protect a six-year-old Puerto Rican boy, Phil Dawn (Adames), who is the sole survivor of the gangland execution of his family. Gloria becomes the reluctant protector of a kid her mobster cronies want to rub out because he possesses the diary of illegal business transactions that his father, an ex-Mafia accountant, had kept. This gripping, if somewhat melodramatic, action movie follows the developing relationship between a tough-as-nails woman and a wise-ass six-year-old kid as they run for their lives. Cassavetes's production at times seems tongue in cheek.

   Julie Carmen plays Jeri Dawn, the young wife of Jack Dawn (Buck Henry), a mousy former Mafia accountant who squeals to the FBI. New York–based casting director Vic Ramos did the casting, and the saxophone playing over the opening scenes is by Tony Ortega. Adames is the New York–born son of parents from the Dominican Republic.

   Gloria received the 1980 Golden Lion Award for Best Picture at the Venice Film Festival. Rowlands was named Best Actress for her role by the Italian Network Commentators, who also honored Julie Carmen as Best Supporting Actress and Basilo Franchina as Best Supporting Actor.

Goldfinger (1964 UA)

   D: Guy Hamilton
   S: Richard Maibaum and Paul Dehn
   P: Harry Saltzman and Albert R. Broccoli
Cast: Sean Connery, Gert Frobe, Honor Blackman, Shirley Eaton, Harold Sakata

The third film in the popular James Bond adventure series full of villains, gadgetry, sex, humor, and action, *Goldfinger* was the first of the blockbuster Bond films. The furor with which moviegoers greeted the film was unprecedented.

   The five-minute pre-credit opening sequence is racy, violent, sexist, and brutal. In it, Bond (Connery) emerges from the sea to wreak havoc on a drug-dealing revolutionary called Ramirez by blowing up his South American compound. After his mission is accomplished, Bond enters the smoke-filled interior of a local nightclub, where he meets his contact. Dancer Bonita (Naja Regin) sets Bond up for a fall: as she steps out of her hot bath to give him a warm, sexy welcome, Bond spies an approaching South American heavy reflected in the girl's eyes. Bond soon dispatches his assailant in a crackling flurry of sparks and steam.

The Good, the Bad, and the Ugly (1967 UA)

- D: Sergio Leone
- S: Sergio Leone and Luciano Vincenzoni, based on a story by Age-Scarpelli, Vincenzoni, and Leone
- P: Alberto Grimaldi
- Cast: Clint Eastwood, Lee Van Cleef, Eli Wallach

Eli Wallach turns in a scene-stealing, hammy, outrageous performance as Mexican bandit Tuco the Terrible in this quintessential "spaghetti western," the third and final "Man with No Name" adventure, which became an international hit and helped rocket Clint Eastwood to stardom. Lee Van Cleef lends his evil black-clad presence as the sadistic Angel Eyes. This unholy trio's lethal pursuit of $200,000 in gold bullion forms the core of this action-filled tale, which covers the period of the American Civil War.

Green Mansions (1959 MGM)

- D: **Mel Ferrer**
- S: Dorothy Kingsley
- P: Edmund Grainger
- Cast: Audrey Hepburn, Anthony Perkins, Lee J. Cobb, **Henry Silva,** Sessue Hayakawa

This immortal romance of the savage wilderness, based on the popular novel by W.H. Hudson, is the story of Rima (Hepburn), the bird girl, who is found in the Venezuelan jungles by the political refugee Abel (Perkins). The superstitious natives want to kill Rima, whom they consider an evil spirit because she is able to communicate with nature. The girl is finally destroyed by the Indians, who kill her in a fire when she is trapped atop a huge hollow tree.

MGM and director Ferrer went on a 25,000-mile location trip through Venezuela, Colombia, and British Guiana (now known as Belize) for some exterior filming. Famed Brazilian composer Heitor Villa-Lobos scored special music for the film.

Guadalcanal Diary (1943 TCF)

- D: Lewis Seiler
- S: Lamar Trotti and Jerry Cady, based on the novel by Richard Tregaskis
- P: Bryan Foy
- Cast: Preston Foster, William Bendix, Lloyd Nolan, **Anthony Quinn**

Factual account of a group of U.S. Marines from varied backgrounds fighting the Japanese after landing in the Solomon Islands during a bloody World War II battle. Anthony Quinn was prominently featured as Soose (short for Jesus), a Mexican American Marine private who is the lone survivor of a dangerous patrol.

Guns for San Sebastian (1968 MGM)

- D: Henri Verneuil
- S: James R. Webb
- P: Jacques Bar
- Cast: **Anthony Quinn,** Charles Bronson, **Anjanette Comer,** Sam Jaffe, Silvia Pinal, Jorge Russek, **Pedro Armendariz, Jr.**

Based on the novel *A Wall for San Sebastian,* written by William Barby Flaherty, a Jesuit priest. Flaherty based his story on Father Keno, who established missions in Sonora and Arizona in the late 1700s. Quinn plays Leon Alastray, a rebel outcast and thief who is taken by desert villagers for a priest when he wears the clothes of a dead priest. Alastray helps the villagers rebuild their church and village and staves off vicious Yaqui Indian attacks. In the process he restores the faith of the villagers and of himself. This violent action western, filmed in Durango, Mexico, and at Churubusco Studios in Mexico City, was a U.S., French, Mexican, and Italian co-production.

Guns of the Magnificent Seven (1969 UA)

  D: Paul Wendkos
  S: Herman Hoffman
  P: Vincent M. Fennelly
Cast: George Kennedy, James Whitmore, **Reni Santoni, Frank Silvera,** Bernie Casey, **Fernando Rey**

George Kennedy takes over the Yul Brynner role of Chris, the strong, silent gun-fighter and leader of men, in this second sequel to *The Magnificent Seven* (1960). Persuaded by a fervent young Mexican revolutionary (Santoni) to help free his noble leader (Rey) from a Mexican prison, Chris recruits a team of the deadliest men in the West, experts with gun, knife, rope, and explosives. Little Tony Davis plays Emiliano Zapata as a child. The picture was filmed in Spain.

Hangin' with the Homeboys (1991 New Line Cinema)

  D: **Joseph B. Vasquez**
  S: **Joseph B. Vasquez**
  P: Richard Brick
Cast: **John Leguizamo,** Doug E. Doug, Mario Joyner, Nestor Serrano

Four young men from the South Bronx, two black and two Puerto Rican, head for Manhattan on a Friday night. They crash a party and a car, go after women, get nabbed jumping subway turnstiles, squeeze into a single booth to watch a peep show in Times Square, and discover a few truths about life and themselves along the way.

   The writing is sharp and the characters sure, brought alive by a young cast of actors. Writer/director Vasquez manages to unpretentiously show contemporary New York City life through a lighthearted boys' night out. In the process we discover the various social pressures the characters labor under (the Latino who insists his name is "Vinny" and rejects his heritage because he finds discrimination too difficult to deal with; the black who challenges people with, "it's because I'm black" every time he doesn't get his own way) and their effects on shaping character and attitudes. This is a well-made movie by a talented writer and director.

The Harder They Fall (1956 Col)

  D: Mark Robson
  S: Philip Yordan, based on the novel by Budd Schulberg
  P: Philip Yordan
Cast: Humphrey Bogart, Rod Steiger, Jan Sterling, Mike Lane, **Carlos Montalban**

The Harder They Fall is a study of corruption within the fight game. The film has an unyielding harshness in exposing a machine of deceit in which each individual has a place and in which the fighter himself is more spectacle than man.

   The syndicate secures a hulking figure from Argentina, Toro Moreno, who is manipulated by a gambling promoter (Steiger) and sports columnist-turned-press agent named Willis (Bogart). The duped Toro Moreno is not the principal character (although he is an effectively realized presence as played by the hulking and somber Mike Lane).

The pitifully inadequate Toro is built into a contender for the heavyweight championship. Bout after bout is fixed until the final fight, which can't be fixed. However, because of the big buildup the syndicate has given the South American wonderman, they are counting on a big take from the bets placed on his adversary. The fight becomes one of the messiest ever when the innocent Toro, who does not lack courage or pride, takes a terrible beating. While Toro is lying battered in the hospital, Willis tries to collect Toro's share of the million-dollar purse. He is informed that after expenses, Toro's share is exactly forty-nine dollars.

Havana (1990 U)

    D: Sydney Pollack
    S: Judith Rascoe and David Rayfiel
    P: Sydney Pollack and Richard Roth
Cast: Robert Redford, Lena Olin, **Raul Julia, Tomas Milian**, Alan Arkin, **Tony Plana**

Love triangle reminiscent of *Casablanca* between cynical gambler Jack Weil (Redford), impassioned freedom fighter "Bobby" Duran (Olin), and her well-born revolutionist doctor husband Arturo (Julia) on the eve of the Cuban Revolution.

Jack, in Havana in 1959 for the biggest card game of his life, finds himself falling in love and finding his true self. Bobby and Jack first meet en route to Cuba. Later, she is arrested and sought out by Weil, who buys her release from

Raul Julia and Lena Olin star as Arturo and Roberta "Bobby" Duran in *Havana*.

prison. Believing her husband dead, she returns to the rebels, and Weil goes after her, risking his life in rebel territory. Returning to Havana, he discovers Duran is alive and tells her. He buys Duran's release, and she goes to him, leaving Weil. An epilogue set four years later has Weil on the beach in Miami still thinking of the woman he loved and lost in Havana.

Pollack moves his story along, cutting between casinos and torture chambers, strippers and shootings, and garish neon flashing lights and nightclubs. There is no real feeling of impending doom or acknowledgment of what Fidel and the Revolution mean, except in expository speeches. The main character has an apolitical attitude, the rebels are unseen for the most part, and politics are avoided in the grand Hollywood tradition of moral cowardice. The film features large lavish set pieces, gorgeously lit by cinematographer Owen Roizman, but it loses steam in the second half with its unsuspenseful resolution.

Mark Rydell as Meyer Lansky, head of the organized crime syndicate, sums up the American position on Cuba and Batista. "We invented Havana and we can goddamn well move it someplace else if he can't control it."

Robert Redford plays the world-weary Jack effectively, and Lena Olin is excellent as the Swedish-born American wife of the revolutionary Duran, well played by Raul Julia. Cuban-born actor Tomas Milian does a nice job as secret policeman Col. Menocan. Tony Plana as alcoholic journalist Felix Ramos does as well as can be expected with an inadequate role.

The movie was filmed in Santo Domingo in the Dominican Republic, the second-largest island in the Caribbean after Cuba itself, since the filmmakers could not shoot in Cuba due to the existing trade embargo. The main exterior set of Havana's famous wide boulevard, El Prado, was constructed on the Dominican Air Force base. This quarter-mile-long street, surrounded by facades representing casinos, restaurants, and hotels, was one of the largest and most comprehensive sets constructed in contemporary cinema.

Both *Havana* and *Casablanca* share the same basic story, though this film is depressing and its lack of political stance is emasculating. Plot similarities include having a Swedish actress, Lena Olin, in a role similar to that played by another Swedish actress, Ingrid Bergman. *Havana* is, in an obvious way, a tribute to the movies of the past, in which American protagonists find love and adventure in exotic locales. *Havana* also has similarities to another film, *Cuba*, starring Sean Connery. It was also written in the late 1970s, but *Havana* took much longer to reach the screen.

Heartbreak Ridge (1986 WB)

D: Clint Eastwood
S: Jim Carabatsos
P: Clint Eastwood
Cast: Clint Eastwood, Marsha Mason, Everett McGill, Moses Gunn, Eileen Heckart, Mario Van Peebles, **Ramon Franco**

Gunnery Sgt. Tom Highway (Eastwood) is a Marine veteran of Korea and Vietnam who rejoins his old unit and takes the usual assortment of sloppy recruits (black, Hispanic, Italian), earning their hatred and then their respect as he whips them into an efficient fighting force in time for the liberation of the Caribbean island of Grenada in 1983. Two of the recruits are Hispanic: Aponte (Ramon Franco) is a distant, brooding individual with family problems. Quinones (Mike Gomez) is a competitive lifer with a discipline problem. One telling sequence has Aponte coming face to face with a dead Cuban soldier whom he realizes looks just like him.

Heartbreaker (1983 Emerson/Monorex)

- D: **Frank Zuniga**
- S: Vincente Gutierrez
- P: Chris D. Nebe and Chris Anders
- Cast: **Fernando Allende**, Dawn Dunlap, Peter Gonzales Falcon, **Miguel Ferrer, Pepe Serna**

This silly, low-budget film with no style is reminiscent of the drive-in movies of the late 1950s and 1960s that Roger Corman made for American International Pictures.

Beto (Allende), the handsome, 25-year-old president of a low-rider customized car club, falls in love with an Anglo girl from outside the area. Beto has his share of troubles from Hector (Gonzales Falcon), with whom he has an ongoing rivalry that dates back to their childhoods. Hector tries to undermine everything Beto achieves. The film features positive Latin characters free of the barrio gang stereotype trappings.

"Conflict in the script, written by former Samuel Goldwyn writing award winner Vincente Gutierrez, develops much too slowly and fails, given the chance, to really render any social insights to life in a Latin-dominated community beyond belonging to a car club," *Daily Variety* (5/6/83).

Heat (1987 New Century–Vista)

- D: R.M. Richards
- S: William Goldman, based on his novel
- P: Keith Rotman and George Pappas
- Cast: **Burt Reynolds**, Karen Young, Peter MacNicol

In Las Vegas, Nick Escalante (Reynolds), known as "Mex," is a professional bodyguard who is out to protect his friends. When a mobster's son savagely beats an old girlfriend of Escalante's, the incident ignites a violent series of events that pit him against the mob and culminate in a vicious cat-and-mouse climax. Burt Reynolds makes a believable Mexican American, which is the only redeeming feature of this ugly and violent story.

Hell to Eternity (1960 AA)

- D: Phil Karlson
- S: Ted Sherdeman and Walter Roeber Schmidt, based on a story by Gil Doud
- P: Irving H. Levin
- Cast: Jeffrey Hunter, David Janssen, Sessue Hayakawa, George Takei, Tsuru Aoki

True story of U.S. Marine war hero Guy Gabaldon, a Mexican American orphan from East Los Angeles who was adopted by a Japanese American family prior to World War II. His knowledge of the Japanese language and culture, coupled with his fighting ability, constituted a huge asset during the crucial battle of Saipan in the Pacific theater of war. The real-life Gabaldon faced a crisis of conscience when his Japanese American family was forcibly interned in a stateside prison camp during the war.

This was the first dramatic feature film to show the stateside internment of Japanese Americans under Executive Order 366 during World War II. The film presents sensitive story elements and plenty of battle action, though from watching the movie you would never have known that Gabaldon was Mexican American. All-American, blue-eyed Jeffrey Hunter played Gabaldon, which in retrospect is not that unusual since Hunter also played Native Americans and "half-breeds"

Marine hero Guy Gabaldon (right) was a real-life Mexican American orphan from East Los Angeles who was adopted by a Japanese American family before World War II. Here he is seen with Tsuru Aoki, who plays his adoptive mother in *Hell to Eternity*.

in several films. The movie never explores Gabaldon's own racial identity, only his adoptive Japanese American family. East L.A. looked like any Depression-era neighborhood as seen in the movies, when, in fact, at that time East L.A. was a very ethnically mixed area. Gabaldon is one of the few true-life Mexican American hero figures portrayed on screen.

Hellfighters (1968 U)

D: Andrew V. McLaglen
S: Clair Huffaker
P: Robert Arthur
Cast: John Wayne, Jim Hutton, Katharine Ross, Vera Miles, **Alberto Morin, Pedro Gonzalez-Gonzalez**

American oil-well firefighting movie, loosely inspired by the exploits of "Red" Adair, which climaxes with an oil fire at Venezuelan oil fields under attack by rebels.

Herbie Goes Bananas (1980 BV)

D: Vincent McEveety
S: Don Tait, based on characters created by Gordon Buford
P: Ron Miller
Cast: Cloris Leachman, Charles Martin Smith, John Vernon, **Joaquin Garay III**

The fourth film in the Herbie the Love Bug (Volkswagen) car series, which was popular with young audiences in the late 1960s and 1970s. Herbie sets sail for Rio de Janeiro's Grande Premio auto racing competition with his two new owners. En route they get sidetracked by a smuggling syndicate, pestered by a pint-sized Mexican pickpocket, and bullied by a raging bull. The movie was filmed in Puerto Vallarta and Guadalajara, Mexico, with background shots filmed in the Panama Canal Zone. Other Latin cast members from the United States include Ruben Moreno, Tina Menard, Jorge Moreno, Dante D'Andre, Alma Beltran, and Bert Santos.

High Noon (1952 UA)

- D: Fred Zinnemann
- S: Carl Foreman
- P: Stanley Kramer
- Cast: Gary Cooper, Grace Kelly, **Katy Jurado**, Lloyd Bridges

Mexican actress Katy Jurado made an impression on audiences with her striking features and acting ability in *High Noon* as Helen Ramirez, the owner of the town saloon and general store. Helen is unmarried and is looked down upon by the rest of the town because of her race and her illicit past. She was involved with Marshal Will Kane (Cooper) and an ex-con, just released from prison, who is now out to get Kane. Kane is left alone to fight Miller (Ian MacDonald) and his gang when none of the townspeople are willing to lend a hand to the marshal who put Miller away and brought peace and tranquility to their frontier community.

One of the strongest and most complex Mexican American female characters ever portrayed on film, Helen is relatively wealthy, but still endures the prejudiced attitudes of a town she is willing to exploit rather than to be exploited by. She tells the puritan Grace Kelly to fight for her man, something she herself cannot do, for Kane, though once her lover, is no longer hers. Jurado won praise for her work.

Lloyd Bridges, Katy Jurado, Gary Cooper, and Grace Kelly, the stars of the legendary western *High Noon*.

In an interview with Luis Reyes in 1992, Jurado said that producer Stanley Kramer had seen her in *The Bullfighter and the Lady* (1951) and asked her to come to Hollywood for a screen test. Jurado politely refused, telling Kramer she was an established actress in Mexico with five years of film work to her credit. If Kramer wanted to see how well she could act, all he had to do was go to downtown L.A. and catch one of her Mexican films. He did, and she got the part.

Jurado knew little English and learned her lines phonetically. She had actor friend Antonio Moreno translate the script for her on her arrival in Los Angeles, and he told her it was a fabulous part, though it called for someone slightly older than the 25-year-old actress. Jurado won the New York Film Critics Award for Best Supporting Actress. Academy Awards went to Gary Cooper as Best Actor, Elmo Williams and Henry Gerstad for Best Film Editing, Dmitri Tiomkin and Ned Washington for the theme song, "Do Not Forsake Me, Oh My Darlin'," and Tiomkin for Best Score. It was filmed at the Columbia Ranch in Burbank and near Sonora, California.

A High Wind in Jamaica (1965 TCF)
   D: Alexander Mackendrick
   S: Stanley Mann, Ronald Harwood, and Denis Cannan, based on the novel by Richard Hughes
   P: John Croyden
Cast: **Anthony Quinn**, James Coburn, Lila Kedrova

Anthony Quinn stars as pirate Juan Chavez in a tale about a family of British youngsters kidnapped by Caribbean pirates in the 1870s.

Hold Back the Dawn (1941 Par)
   D: Mitchell Leisen
   S: Billy Wilder and Charles Brackett, based on a story by Ketti Frings
   P: Arthur Hornblow, Jr.
Cast: Charles Boyer, Olivia de Havilland, Paulette Goddard, **Nestor Paiva**

European refugees are stuck in a Mexican bordertown awaiting permission to enter the United States just prior to American entry into World War II. One refugee, a suave Rumanian dancer, Iscovescu (Boyer), desperate to enter the United States, takes the advice of his former dance partner (Goddard) and decides to marry his way into the States. He meets a naive American schoolteacher (de Havilland) on a field trip with her students in Mexico, and the ensuing complications brought on by the affair make up most of the drama.

This was Paramount's most honored film of the year, receiving Academy Award nominations for Best Picture, Best Actress, Best Screenplay, Best Cinematography, and Best Score. Every effort was made to show Mexico in its best light. The Mexican border patrol were shown to be uniformed, neat, and clean shaven. A Mexican street facade resembling a bordertown was constructed on the Paramount lot.

Holiday for Lovers (1959 TCF)
   D: Henry Levin
   S: Luther Davis, based on the play by Ronald Alexander
   P: David Weisbart
Cast: Clifton Webb, Jane Wyman, Jill St. John, Nico Minardos, **Jose Greco**, Nestor Amaral and his Orchestra

A Boston psychiatrist (Webb) and his wife (Wyman) take their daughters on a trip to South America and find that most of their time is spent keeping the attractive young daughters away from men. The film takes them to Rio de Janeiro and São Paulo, Brazil, and Lima, Peru, with stock footage in CinemaScope. A very late entry for the Good Neighbor Policy, the film has the feel of a 1940s script that got shelved.

A young actor by the name of Henry Delgado, later known as Henry Darrow (of TV's "The High Chaparral" fame), made his film debut in a small role as a bus driver.

Holiday in Mexico (1946 MGM)

D: George Sidney
S: Isobel Lennart, based on a story by William Kozlenko
P: Joe Pasternak
Cast: Walter Pidgeon, **Jose Iturbi**, Jane Powell, Ilona Massey, **Xavier Cugat**

Slight musical that offers a little something for everyone, from opera to boogie woogie with Jose Iturbi and Xavier Cugat.

The daughter of an American ambassador (Pidgeon) in Mexico is planning a garden party to which Xavier Cugat and his Orchestra are invited along with a soloist (Massey), a Hungarian who is an old flame of the ambassador's. The child also imagines herself in love with Jose Iturbi, who plays himself.

Jane Powell, as the daughter, sings and romps her way through the film, shot in Hollywood at MGM Studios. Iturbi plays classics and jazz on elaborately photographed pianos.

"The likeliest Mexicans who appear in *Holiday in Mexico* are the impassioned maraca shakers in Xavier Cugat's band. Non-Mexican accents abound, however, Jose Iturbi (Spanish), Ilona Massey (Hungarian), Roddy McDowall (English), Walter Pidgeon (Canadian), and Jane Powell (American). The Technicolor film itself speaks in MGM's expensive accents. It is lavish, intensely musical and occasionally funny," *Life* (9/9/46).

Hombre (1967 TCF)

D: Martin Ritt
S: Irving Ravetch and Harriet Frank, Jr., based on the novel by Elmore Leonard
P: Martin Ritt and Irving Ravetch
Cast: Paul Newman, Diane Cilento, Fredric March, Richard Boone, **Frank Silvera**, Martin Balsam

John Russell (Newman), a white man raised by Apache Indians, finds himself on a long journey on a stagecoach, which is held up by outlaws. The very passengers who shunned him because of his Indian appearance soon find they need him to protect them from the outlaws.

The ensuing interrelationships among passengers and outlaws make up the crux of this superbly acted adult western featuring an all-star cast. James Wong Howe's harsh photography of the Arizona desert location added to the starkness of the story.

Frank Silvera comes over strongly as a humorous but deadly Mexican outlaw.

Hour of the Gun (1967 UA)

D: John Sturges
S: Edward Anhalt
P: John Sturges
Cast: James Garner, Jason Robards, Jr., Robert Ryan, Jorge Russek

Beginning with the showdown at the O.K. Corral in Tombstone, Arizona, in the 1880s, the movie goes on to relate what happens to the surviving participants, centering on Wyatt Earp (Garner). Ike Clanton (Ryan) is finally tracked down by Earp in Mexico, where he has returned to cattle rustling. In a small village, Earp

Wyatt Earp (James Garner, right) and Doc Holliday (Jason Robards, right center) search for Ike Clanton in Mexico in *Hour of the Gun.*

kills Clanton. On locations throughout northern Mexico, including Torreón and San Miguel de Allende, the Arizona Territory of the 1880s was re-created by famed art director Alfred C. Ybarra. Mexican actor Jorge Russek plays Latigo, one of Clanton's henchmen.

Human Cargo (1936 TCF)

D: Allan Dwan
S: Jefferson Parker and Doris Malloy, based on the novel *I Will Be Faithful* by Kathleen Shepard
P: Sol M. Wurtzel
Cast: Brian Donlevy, Claire Trevor, **Rita Cansino [Hayworth]**

A newspaper melodrama about rival reporters (Donlevy and Trevor) exposing a smuggling ring that transports illegal aliens into the United States from Canada and then blackmails them. The film also highlights Rita Cansino (soon to become Rita Hayworth) as Carmen, a Mexican dancer who is blackmailed by the smugglers and eventually killed.

In Caliente (1935 WB)

D: Lloyd Bacon
S: Jerry Wald and Julius Epstein, based on the story "Caliente" by Ralph Black and Warren Duff
P: First National
Cast: **Dolores Del Rio**, Pat O'Brien, **Leo Carrillo**

Larry MacArthur (O'Brien), a magazine editor whose review infuriates "La Espanita," a Spanish dancer named Rita Gomez (Del Rio), is sent to Agua Caliente, where he falls in love with the dancer he unmercifully panned. In the process of exacting her revenge, Rita falls in love with him.

This lightweight musical/comedy is a commercial endorsement for the popular-with-the-Hollywood-crowd Mexican resort and casino across the border from

Dolores Del Rio as the Spanish dancer Rita Gomez in *In Caliente*.

San Diego. Del Rio looked ravishing in her gowns and dresses. Leo Carrillo lent solid support, while Soledad Jimenez played a maid, Martin Garralaga, a waiter, and Chris-Pin Martin, the leader of a Mexican quartet. Judy Canova had a bit as a Mexican hillbilly, and the film also showcased the Sally and Tony Marco dance team. Busby Berkeley arranged the dance numbers.

In Old Arizona (1929 Fox)

See "Zorro & the Cisco Kid" listings.

Incendiary Blonde (1945 Par)

    D: George Marshall
    S: Claude Binyon and Frank Butler
    P: Joseph Sistroms
Cast: Betty Hutton, **Arturo De Cordova**

Based on the life of Texas Guinan (Hutton), a famous nightclub entertainer of the 1920s. Texas is the star of a rodeo show who falls in love with an Irish Mexican, Bill Romero Kilgannon (De Cordova), who is the married owner of the show. He becomes the love of her life, and their lives become entwined again years later when she finds stardom on Broadway and in Hollywood and he becomes a gangster. Audiences and theater owners in the southern United States objected to Kilgannon's character being changed to an Irish Mexican in order to accommodate the actor playing the role, Arturo De Cordova. The actual Kilgannon character was Irish, and notwithstanding the Good Neighbor Policy, it was considered objectionable to have a Mexican making on-screen love to an Anglo woman, particularly in the state of Texas.

The In-Laws (1979 WB)

    D: Arthur Hiller
    S: Andrew Bergman
    P: Arthur Hiller and William Sackheim
 Cast: Alan Arkin, Peter Falk, Richard Libertini

The daughter of a New York Jewish dentist is about to marry the son of a guy who claims to be in the CIA. The two prospective fathers-in-law (Arkin and Falk) meet. The CIA man gets the dentist involved in a series of incredible adventures that send them on a bullet-riddled chase from Manhattan to a South American banana republic. Richard Libertini is General Garcia, the nutty dictator of the fictional capital Tijada. Upon their arrival the fathers-in-law are welcomed by one of Tijada's leading statesmen, who is gunned down as he steps across the tarmac to greet them. This unpredictable and otherwise enjoyable comedy is marred by stereotyped Latin images. The Latin scenes were filmed in Cuernavaca, Mexico.

Internal Affairs (1990 Par)

    D: Mike Figgis
    S: Henry Bean
    P: Frank Mancuso, Jr.
 Cast: Richard Gere, **Andy Garcia**, Nancy Travis, Laurie Metcalf

Raymond Avila (Garcia) is a detective who has been promoted to the Internal Affairs Division of the Los Angeles County Police. While researching a misconduct case, Avila becomes convinced that a respected street cop named Dennis Peck (Gere, playing well against type) is involved in a complicated web of criminal activities. When Avila begins to investigate him, Peck retaliates by drawing Avila's wife, Kathleen (Travis), into what becomes an intense psychological struggle between the two men.

    This is a landmark film in that it shows a Hispanic American leading character, Avila, as played by Cuban American Andy Garcia, in a perceptive, complex portrayal, free from stereotypes, as an integral part of American society. In the role of a law enforcement officer, Garcia offered a positive role model, and the role proved to be a major step in his own rise to stardom. The film also features one of Richard Gere's best performances to date.

Jivaro (1954 Par)

    D: Edward Ludwig
    S: Winston Miller, based on a story by David Duncan
    P: William H. Pine and William C. Thomas
 Cast: **Fernando Lamas, Rita Moreno**, Pascual Garcia Pena, **Nestor Paiva**

Lamas is well cast as a rugged trader and Amazon riverboat captain who goes in search of lost missionaries and treasure seekers in the treacherous Jivaro Indian country. Pascual Pena plays Lamas's Indian assistant, and Rita Moreno plays a native girl.

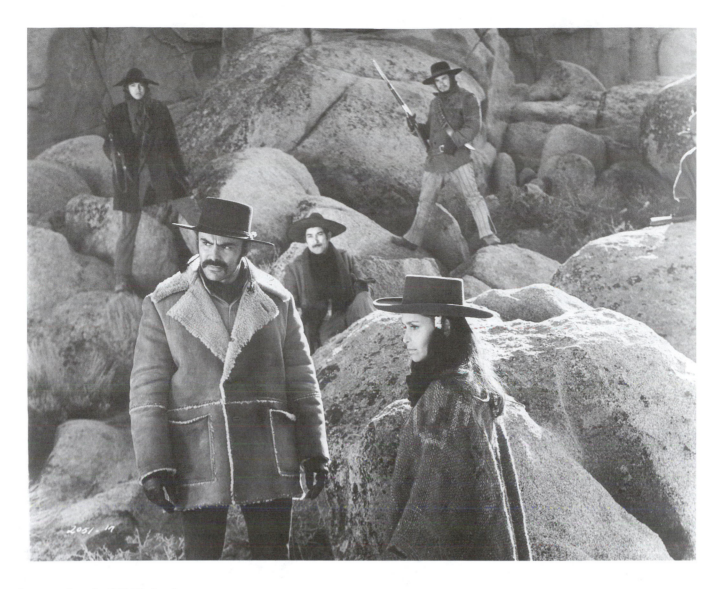

In a scene from *Joe Kidd*, Rita Sanchez (Stella Garcia) is disillusioned to discover that Luis Chama (John Saxon) refuses to disarm his men and return to a small town to face a prejudiced judge.

Joe Kidd (1972 U)

D: John Sturges
S: Elmore Leonard
P: Sidney Beckerman
Cast: Clint Eastwood, Robert Duvall, **John Saxon**, **Stella Garcia**, **Joaquin Martinez**

In New Mexico at the turn of the century, a loner, Joe Kidd (Eastwood), is hired by an American landowner, Harlan (Duvall), to lead a party of gunmen against rebel Luis Chama (Saxon), a Mexican American trying to save the original Spanish land grants handed to his people. The loner soon changes sides and joins Chama's forces in a climactic gun battle, in which the Mexicans eventually win. Kidd forces Chama to surrender and face a fair trial, leaving his fate in the hands of the Anglo. Pepe Hern has a supporting role as a priest.

"It forthrightly depicts injustices to Mexican-Americans, which strikes a note of contemporary awareness without seeming to strain for it," Kevin Thomas, *L.A. Times* (7/19/72).

Juarez (1939 WB)

D: William Dieterle

S: Aeneas MacKenzie, Wolfgang Reinhardt, and **John Huston**, based on the novel *The Phantom Crown* by Bertita Harding and the play *Juarez & Maximilian* by Franz Werfel

P: Hal B. Wallis and Henry Blanke

Cast: Paul Muni, Bette Davis, Brian Aherne, John Garfield, Claude Rains, **Gilbert Roland, Joseph Calleia, Pedro De Cordoba, Martin Garralaga,** Manny Diaz

Considered one of Hollywood's best Latin American films of the period, *Juarez* is a reverential treatment of its subject. In reality, however, it was two films in one—the story of Juarez and the story of Maximilian and Carlotta von Habsburg. The film ultimately suffered from this duality. Performances were good all around, except for John Garfield as Porfirio Diaz, whose New York accent kept getting in the way. Muni as Juarez was an incredible re-creation of the man as drawn from books and pictures. Considered the Mexican Abraham Lincoln, Juarez reportedly admired Lincoln, who was then President of the United States and who was himself going through a Civil War.

The film was popular everywhere except Mexico. When *Juarez* went into production, it was reported that the technical adviser pointed out that the Porfirio Diaz character was historically incorrect. His advice was ignored. In the eyes of Mexicans, Hollywood was doing something as wrong as placing Abraham Lincoln at the Battle of Bunker Hill.

Hundreds of Mexican American extras listen to the "Mexican Abraham Lincoln" (played by Paul Muni) in *Juarez.*

In the fall of 1937, Jack L. Warner and Hal B. Wallis began an intensive search for popular actor Paul Muni's next starring vehicle. Writer Wolfgang Reinhardt suggested that Wallis consider the story of Mexico's legendary liberal president, Benito Pablo Juarez. Reinhardt felt that Juarez's struggle against the Habsburg monarchy backed by French emperor Napoleon III would make exciting and topical screen fare. Muni liked the idea and agreed to do the film. He felt that the parallel world situation at the time (the recently ended Spanish Civil War and impending World War II) would make the film timely and hoped that the film might influence people against dictatorships no matter how benevolent. The studio research department assembled as complete a bibliography as possible on Juarez and the abortive reign of Maximilian and Carlotta.

The film went into production in September 1938 with a budget of $1,750,000 and a cast of 1,186. Art director Anton Grot and his assistant Leo Kuder drew 3,643 sketches of sets, from which the construction department built 54, the largest being an 11-acre re-creation of Mexico at the Warner Ranch in Calabasas, California.

Muni, along with Wallis and director William Dieterle, went on a six-week tour of Mexico prior to filming. They delved into every possible area of Juarez's life and times, steeping themselves in the atmosphere of the country. Muni wanted to know how Juarez looked, walked, and talked and wanted to learn any mannerisms that were particularly noticeable. Returning to the studio, they went through a series of makeup tests with different rubber masks in an attempt to make Muni resemble Juarez. It was agreed that it would be most believable to let Muni play with a minimum of structural change. Perc Westmore, head of Warner's makeup department, accentuated Muni's bone structure, made his jaws appear wider, squared his forehead, and gave him an Indian nose. He had to be darker than anyone else in the picture, since the film was in black-and-white, so they used a dark reddish-brown makeup highlighted by yellow. More than 3,500 extras were used in total during the 80 days of actual production. Gilbert Roland plays Col. Lopez, Joseph Calleia plays Urad, Pedro De Cordoba plays Palacio, and Manny Diaz plays Pepe.

Key Witness (1960 MGM)

D: Phil Karlson
S: Alfred Brenner and Sidney Michaels, based on the novel by Frank Kane
P: Kathryn Hereford
Cast: Jeffrey Hunter, Pat Crowley, Dennis Hopper, Corey Allen, **Frank Silvera**

A suburbanite, Fred Morrow (Hunter), stops in an East Los Angeles bar to make a phone call. He witnesses a brutal stabbing and discovers that none of the other onlookers are willing to testify. Regardless of the consequences, Morrow decides to appear in court, but it is not long before he regrets his decision. The alleged assailant, "Cowboy" (Hopper), and his gang begin to terrorize Morrow and his family. The problem of witness intimidation is one many residents in gang-infested areas of East L.A. still face today, over 30 years later.

Mexican American detective Rafael Torno is played by Frank Silvera. The highlight of the film is a night chase on foot in which Torno corners "Cowboy" on a freeway.

This film presents gang life superficially, in a way typical of the 1950s juvenile delinquent movies (with switchblades, sports cars, dope, and sex). The gang members are multiethnic.

The Kid from Spain (1932 UA)

   D: Leo McCarey
   S: William Anthony McGuire, Bert Kalmar, and Harry Ruby
   P: Samuel Goldwyn
Cast: Eddie Cantor, Lyda Roberti, Robert Young, **J. Carroll Naish**,
   Paul Porcasi, **Julian Rivero**

Eddie (Cantor) and his Mexican playmate Ricardo (Young) are expelled from college. They inadvertently get mixed up in a stateside bank robbery, which forces Eddie to go south of the border as an innocent fugitive from American law. He impersonates Don Sebastian II, son of a famous bullfighting family, and complications arise.

The movie is a dated musical/comedy based on the true story of Sydney Franklin, a pop-eyed Jewish boy from Brooklyn who became one of the world's greatest bullfighters. Many funny scenes include a bullfight in which Eddie is chased all over the arena. Francisco "Chico" Day, later a famed assistant director, worked on the film as an interpreter for the Mexican bullfighter brought from Mexico City to double Cantor. Frank Leyva handled all the Mexican extras during shooting in Hollywood.

Actor Robert Young, who plays Ricardo, later found greater fame on television, starring in the 1950s in the long-running "Father Knows Best" series and in the 1970s in the "Marcus Welby, M.D." series.

Why it is called *The Kid from Spain* when the story takes place in Mexico is anyone's guess.

Kings of the Sun (1963 UA)

   D: J. Lee Thompson
   S: Elliott Arnold and James R. Webb, based on a story by Arnold
   P: Lewis J. Rachmil
Cast: Yul Brynner, George Chakiris, Richard Basehart, Shirley Anne Field,
   Armando Silvestre

Superficial approach to a potentially fascinating subject, the ancient Mayan civilization at a point of crisis.

Ancient Mayan tribes of Mexico are menaced by fierce warriors from the north. The Mayan king is killed by invaders, and his young son, Balam (Chakiris), becomes the new Mayan ruler. The Mayans are forced to flee to the coast, where they commandeer boats owned by fishermen and sail to what is now North America, where they settle and start to build a new civilization. Black Eagle (Brynner), chief of a local tribe of Indians who resent the "invasion," decides to attack these people, but the Mayans capture him. Balam spares Black Eagle's life, and they decide to live in harmony. The Mayan high priest (Basehart) prepares Black Eagle for a sacrifice to their gods, and when Balam refuses this, the high priest sacrifices himself. Later, another group of Indians attack the Mayans, and Black Eagle is killed.

Brynner is excellent as the Indian chief, but Chakiris, Field, Basehart, and Leo V. Gordon as Mayans stretch credibility, especially when you put them alongside authentic Mexican Indian extras. (It is interesting to speculate what the Mexicans must have thought of a Hollywood production featuring American actors impersonating their descendants and heritage.) The only Mexican with a major role was actor Armando Silvestre, who plays a heavy.

Art director Alfred Ybarra and his assistant, Lynn Sparhawk, along with construction coordinator Bill Maldonado designed and built Mayan cities, fishing villages, Mayan homes, and other sets, including pyramids and ruins of the Mayan civilization.

Several major outdoor locations were used for the filming. Shooting began in Chichén Itzá in Yucatán, where the ruins of the pyramids still stand. The Mexican government gave special permission to the film company to shoot among the actual pyramids and ruins. The company later moved to Mazatlán. All interior sequences were filmed on soundstages at Churubusco Studios in Mexico City. One hundred fifty Mexican film technicians and a total of 5,000 Mexican extras were employed during the filming.

Kinjite: Forbidden Subjects (1989 Cannon)

    D: J. Lee Thompson
    S: Harold Nebenzal
    P: Pancho Kohner
 Cast: Charles Bronson, **Perry Lopez, Juan Fernandez**

Veteran L.A. cop Crowe (Bronson) and his partner Rios (Lopez) attempt to catch a sinister pimp (Fernandez) who has kidnapped the daughter of an L.A.-based Japanese businessman in this violent police drama.

Kiss Me a Killer (1990 Concorde)

    D: **Marcus De Leon**
    S: **Marcus De Leon**
    P: Catherine Ryan
 Cast: **Robert Beltran, Julie Carmen**

A young Latina woman (Carmen) married to an Anglo nightclub owner finds passion and freedom with a mysterious and handsome young musician (Beltran) who comes to work at the club. They soon plot to kill her husband and become entangled in a web of murder and deceit. The film marked a promising beginning for writer/director De Leon. Beltran and Carmen exude the appropriate sexual steam in this low-budget barrio version of *The Postman Always Rings Twice*.

Kiss of Fire (1955 U)

    D: Joseph M. Newman
    S: Franklin Coen and Richard Collins
    P: Samuel Marx
 Cast: Jack Palance, Barbara Rush, Rex Reason, Martha Hyer

Uneven mixture of period swashbuckler and western. A Spanish nobleman known as El Tigre (Palance) is engaged to lead a royal party from Santa Fe, New Mexico, to Monterey, California, where a ship awaits to take the heir apparent to the Spanish throne, Princess Lucia (Rush), to Spain when it is learned that Charles V is on his deathbed. Spanish hirelings and Indians try to stop the party before they reach their destination, and the princess finds true love with El Tigre and renounces the throne. Jack Palance is miscast in a role better suited to Errol Flynn or Cornel Wilde. Soundstage night exteriors clash with outdoor exteriors, and water doesn't seem to be a problem for people crossing desert landscapes.

Kiss of the Spider Woman (1985 Island)

    D: **Hector Babenco**
    S: Leonard Schrader, based on the novel by Manuel Puig
    P: David Weisman
 Cast: William Hurt, **Raul Julia, Sonia Braga**

Based on the 1976 novel by Manuel Puig, the movie is described by director Hector Babenco in the *L.A Times* (11/23/83) as "a story about . . . the slowly growing friendship between two men of totally different emotional, cultural and social backgrounds. The South American prison cell they share is the boxing ring where they resolve their conflicts before arriving at a stage of mutual affection."

Director Hector Babenco (center) helps
William Hurt (left) and Raul Julia prepare
a scene from *Kiss of the Spider Woman*,
a complex story about two men
with radically different perspectives
on life who share a prison cell.

This was the first Brazilian-made film to star American actors. The film stars William Hurt as Molina, a homosexual convicted on morals charges, and Raul Julia as Valentin, a highly disciplined and intellectual political prisoner. Molina lives in a fantasy world of glamour movies and romantic screen heroes and heroines that at first disgusts Valentin, then later hypnotizes him.

Little by little the two men form a bond of friendship and love. The two actors dominate the film, but Brazilian actress Sonia Braga is notable in not one but three roles. She is the captivating Spider Woman of the title, and a French chanteuse, both of whom are part of Molina's fantasy, as well as Valentin's girlfriend.

Kiss of the Spider Woman was a tremendous worldwide success and reaped enormous box-office and critical raves in the United States. William Hurt won the Academy Award as Best Actor.

"*The Kiss of the Spider Woman* succeeds on a deep emotional level and as spellbinding entertainment as well," Sheila Benson, *L.A. Times* (8/23/85).

"[There aren't] sufficient clues in the previous film careers of the director, Hector Babenco (the highly praised *Pixote*) and the two stars, William Hurt and Raul Julia, to anticipate the stature of the work they do here. *Kiss of the Spider Woman* is a brilliant achievement for all of them, staged with the perfect control and fierce originality that makes it one of the best films in a long time," Janet Maslin, *New York Times* (7/26/85).

"Filmed in Brazil (in English), directed by the Argentine born Hector Babenco from a script by the American Leonard Schrader and a novel by Argentine Manuel Puig. . . . This time the artistic melting pot bubbled to perfection," Richard Schickel, *Time* (8/5/85).

The Kissing Bandit (1948 MGM)

D: Laslo Benedek
S: Isobel Lennart and John Briard Harding
P: Joe Pasternak
Cast: Frank Sinatra, Kathryn Grayson, **J. Carroll Naish, Vicente Gomez, Alberto Morin, Julian Rivero, Ricardo Montalban,** Jose Dominguez

This movie chronicles the efforts of Ricardo (Sinatra), just returned to California from learning the hotel trade in Boston, to step into his father's romantic boots. Before he was killed, dad was known as "The Kissing Bandit" because he kissed every female he held up. A specialty dance number directed by Stanley Donen called the "Dance of Fury" featured Ricardo Montalban, Cyd Charisse, and Ann Miller. Vicente Gomez played Mexican guitar tunes. This muddled spoof of Zorro, adventure, and musical/comedy plots is not helped by uneven direction.

La Bamba (1987 Col)

D: **Luis Valdez**
S: **Luis Valdez**
P: Taylor Hackford and Bill Borden
AP: **Daniel Valdez**
Cast: **Lou Diamond Phillips, Esai Morales, Rosana De Soto, Elizabeth Pena, Daniel Valdez**

La Bamba was the brainchild of Daniel Valdez, brother of writer/director Luis Valdez, who had wanted to make a musical biography of the late Chicano rock 'n' roll star Ritchie Valens for over 10 years. With the success of the theatrical musical *Zoot Suit* and with a film version of it being readied at Universal, Valdez approached Universal Studios in 1981 but found no interest because *The Buddy Holly Story* (1978) had gone over similar ground and had not been a box-office success, even though it did win critical acclaim and an Oscar nomination for its star, Gary Busey.

Ritchie Valens, whose real name was Ricardo Valenzuela, was born and raised in Pacoima, California, in the San Fernando Valley. His meteoric rise as a rock 'n' roll star lasted only 8 months and delivered 3 hit records when he died at the age of 17 in the same 1959 plane crash that also killed Buddy Holly and disc jockey J.P. Richardson, known as The Big Bopper, during a snowstorm in Iowa. Valens has been overshadowed by Holly, and his life was shrouded in mystery. "I went and tried to research this guy and couldn't get anything, zero. I only had a hint he was Latin," recalls Daniel Valdez in press notes for the movie's release.

Undaunted, Daniel tracked down the Valens family and convinced them of his artistic intentions. He secured a five-year option on the Valens story and began to search for avenues of production. Meanwhile, he enlisted the aid of his brother Luis, who wrote a screenplay. The project was brought to Taylor Hackford, writer/director of such hit films as *The Idolmaker*, *Against All Odds*, and *An Officer and a Gentleman*, whose career the Valdez brothers had followed since Hackford's early documentary work at PBS television station KCET in Los Angeles.

Hackford had started a production company called New Visions that was to produce modest-budget features, and *La Bamba*, as the Ritchie Valens script was now called, was put into development. The film went into production in the summer of 1986 with Luis Valdez as writer/director and Daniel as associate producer. It was filmed on location in and around Los Angeles on a $6.5 million budget with a 45-day shooting schedule. The opening farmworker labor camp scenes were filmed near Hollister, California.

An intense talent search was launched to find the right young actor to play Ritchie Valens. When casting director Junie Lowry returned from a search of Texas and the Southwest, she thought she had found the ideal actor to play Ritchie's brother Bob. Lou Diamond Phillips was flown to California, but the more he audi-

Luis Valdez directs Lou Diamond Phillips
in his starring role as Ritchie Valens
in *La Bamba*

tioned with other actors, the more clear it became that they had found the man for the starring role instead. Phillips recalls in press notes, "I was a nobody from Texas, the entire time I was auditioning. I thought I would walk away with a good attitude and my head held high, and even though I wouldn't get the role it would pay off down the line. I just couldn't comprehend that I was to land this one."

A reverse situation occurred when it came time to cast the role of Ritchie's brother Bob. Esai Morales, who was initially considered for Ritchie, was quickly found to be the right actor to play Bob. "Bob was the dark side of Ritchie," says Morales in press notes. "He didn't know how to fight his own feelings of resentment toward his brother's success."

The final script had at its core the turbulent relationship between Ritchie and his brother Bob during Ritchie's eight-month rise to stardom. Luis recalls in press notes, "In writing the screenplay I stayed close to a reality I know . . . capturing . . . certain images that . . . were a part of Valens' life as much as they were a part of mine." He continued, "We all understand love/hate relationships between two brothers and the difficulties of a single mother trying to raise her children."

La Bamba became a smash success during the summer of 1987, earning $60 million and favorable critical response. Valens's hit song was re-recorded for the movie by the popular Mexican American group Los Lobos, who made the song "La Bamba" an even greater hit for Valens in death than it ever was when he was alive.

In an interview with Luis Reyes, Valdez remarked on his work, "I like to think that there's a core that's constant. . . . I'm not just a Mexican farm worker. I'm an American with roots in Mayan culture. I can resonate and unlock some of the mysteries of this land which reside in all of us."

La Cucaracha (1934 RKO)

D: Lloyd Corrigan
S: Jack Wagner and John Twist
P: Kenneth MacGowan
Cast: **Don Alvarado**, Steffi Duna, Paul Porcasi

In 1934, Mexico and Mexicans were the subject of this film, the first live-action short film made in the three-strip Technicolor process. The 20-minute short showcased dancers and extras in a cantina alive with music and colors swirling to the song "La Cucaracha."

RKO brought to Hollywood Robert Edmond Jones, the famous stage designer whose use of color lighting had revolutionized Broadway in the 1920s. Jones felt that color, used properly, could affect the emotional and psychological content of a film, and in *La Cucaracha*, he utilized all manner of stylized devices to heighten the dramatic and comedic aspects of the story.

The story line revolves around a cantina girl, played by Steffi Duna, and her problems with her dancer lover, played by Don Alvarado. Paul Porcasi plays a Mexico City impresario.

The jealousy, the quarreling, and the comedy are skillfully blended in this truly colorful romantic fantasy of Mexico and Mexicans.

The film was an immediate success with critics and the public, receiving more attention than most of the features it played with. It won an Academy Award for Best Comedy Short in 1934.

Lambada (1989 WB)

D: Joel Silberg
S: Sheldon Renan and Joel Silberg
P: Peter Shepard
Cast: J. Eddie Peck, Melora Hardin, Adolfo "Shabba Doo" Quinones

An East Los Angeles teacher spends his days motivating students and his nights at a nightclub where he engages in lambada dancing.

Lambada—The Forbidden Dance (1990 Col)

D: Greydon Clark
S: Albert Goldman
P: Marc Fisher
Cast: **Laura Martinez Herring**

Quickly produced youth-oriented movie designed to take advantage of the short-lived Brazilian lambada dance craze that began in Europe and found temporary favor with Hispanic populations in the United States. The film starred Laura Martinez Herring, a former Miss USA. The plot, such as it was, concerned a young Brazilian Indian girl sent by her tribe to the United States to try to save the Amazon rain forest. The film distorted the fact that lambada had its origins among the black people of Brazil and not among the Indians—another case of Hollywood misrepresenting a Latin American culture and its people through convenient filmic conventions and dramatic license.

The Lash (1931 WB)

D: Frank Lloyd
S: Bradley King, based on the story "Adios" by Lanier Bartlett
P: Warner Bros.
Cast: Richard Barthelmess, James Rennie, Mary Astor

A young Spanish nobleman, Don Francisco Delfina (Barthelmess), in 1848 Baja California, is duped out of his cattle by a swindling American land commissioner and becomes a desperado, assuming the sobriquet of "El Puma." He fights the Americanos, who are cheating and stealing to obtain Spanish/Mexican lands through crooked land commissioners. In the end, "El Puma" disbands his followers and crosses the border into Mexico, where he makes his new home. This is another variation on the Robin Hood, Zorro, and Joaquin Murieta legends in which, for once, the Americanos are not placed in a very good light. Highlighted by panoramic scenery and good action sequences, this is an average western set in the Spanish/Mexican era.

The Last Command (1955 Rep)

    D: Frank Lloyd
    S: Warren Duff
    P: Herbert J. Yates
 Cast: Sterling Hayden, Anna Maria Alberghetti, Richard Carlson, Arthur Hunnicutt, Ernest Borgnine, **J. Carroll Naish**

Jim Bowie (Hayden) is a personal friend of Santa Anna (Naish) until the latter's despotic actions lead Bowie to the siege of the Alamo. Bowie is torn between his love of Mexico and his U.S. citizenry during the fight for Texas independence. Italian singer Anna Maria Alberghetti portrays Consuela, the daughter of a Spanish-born Texas landowner.

General Santa Anna is depicted by Naish as a three-dimensional character who insists on calling Bowie "Jimmy." The film is slow to build to its climax but is interesting in its characterizations and point of view.

The Last Command, like *The Alamo* (1960), utilizes the racial imagery of the Anglo versus the Mexican less than prior films made on the subject. World War II and the Good Neighbor Policy kept blatant negative stereotypes of Latin Americans in check for a while.

Filmed on location in Texas and at Republic Studios in Hollywood, the film includes many Hispanic actors in featured roles, including Vincent Padula, Argentina Brunetti, Alex Montoya, Pepe Hern, Rico Alaniz, George Novarro, Fernando Alvarado, Abel Fernandez, Tom Hernandez, and Alberto Morin.

The Last of the Fast Guns (1958 U)

    D: George Sherman
    S: David P. Harmon
    P: Howard Christie
 Cast: Jock Mahoney, **Gilbert Roland, Linda Cristal**, Lorne Greene, Carl Benton Reid

An average oater gorgeously photographed in Cuernavaca, Mexico, made by Hollywood and Mexico's top craftsmen.

In the 1880s, gunfighter Brad Ellison (played by former stuntman Jock Mahoney) accepts an offer from wealthy John Forbes (Reid) to locate his brother, who disappeared into Mexico 30 years before. In the course of his search Ellison learns that the brother is now a well-respected local priest.

Nineteen of the 28 speaking roles went to Mexican actors and actresses. Argentina-born actress Linda Cristal made her American film debut and was signed by Universal to an exclusive long-term contract. Many of Mexico's finest English-speaking actors were recruited to play supporting roles. Prominent among them were Eduardo Noriega, who played important roles in such American productions as *Serenade* (1956), *The Beast of Hollow Mountain* (1956), and *The Sun Also Rises* (1957); roly-poly George Trevino, who is known to TV fans as Desi Arnaz's comical Cuban uncle in the "I Love Lucy" series; Francisco Reyguera, a film veteran whose career dates back to Mack Sennett comedies; and pretty Gilda Fontana, an American actress who transferred her career from Hollywood to Mexico. Gilbert Roland, a veteran actor since silent films, plays a double-dealing ranch foreman.

Last Plane Out (1983 Shapiro-Glickenhaus)

D: David Nelson
S: Ernest Tidyman
P: Jack Cox and David Nelson
Cast: Jan-Michael Vincent, **Julie Carmen**, Mary Crosby, Lloyd Batista

Routine, uninspired treatment of an American journalist in Nicaragua during the end of the Somoza regime. This film is filled with negative stereotypes—from cute kids who run a taxi service in a war-torn country to a rebel leader Nicaraguan woman, Maria Cardena (Carmen), who falls for the journalist. Similar material was handled much better in *Under Fire* (1983) and *Salvador* (1986).

Based on the real-life experiences of conservative journalist Jack Cox (played by Vincent), the movie is politically slanted to the right. Cox gets to talk to both Somoza and the rebels, and the rebels put a price on Cox's head because of his pro-Somoza government pieces and alleged connection to the CIA. As the Sandinistas close in on the capital, Cox and his TV crew find themselves struggling to reach the airport to catch the last plane out before the rebels succeed in killing them. The movie was filmed in southern Florida.

Last Rites (1988 MGM/UA)

D: Don P. Bellisario
S: Don P. Bellisario
P: Don P. Bellisario and Patrick McCormick
Cast: Tom Berenger, **Daphne Zuniga**

A Mexican woman named Angela (Zuniga) witnesses the murder of a mobster in an elegant New York hotel and escapes, eventually coming under the protection of a streetwise New York priest, Father Michael Pace (Berenger). His task of protecting her is complicated by their erotic attraction to each other and the fact that the murderer is his sister and the victim his brother-in-law, killed for fooling around with Angela. He finally takes her to Mexico to rid her of her pursuers.

The Last Train from Madrid (1937 Par)

D: James Hogan
S: Louis Stevens and Robert Wyler, based on a story by Paul Hervey Fox and Elsie Fox
P: George M. Arthur
Cast: Dorothy Lamour, Lew Ayres, **Gilbert Roland, Anthony Quinn**

It was inevitable that the powerful drama of the Spanish Civil War would be seized upon by Hollywood in 1937. However, *The Last Train from Madrid,* like *For Whom the Bell Tolls* (1943), is devoid of any politics and became instead a simple *Grand Hotel*–type of melodrama in which the lives of different people intersect when they all try to leave on the last train from Madrid to Valencia.

The film marked the first major role for Anthony Quinn and his only teaming with Gilbert Roland, of whom he said at the time he was "in awe." Dorothy Lamour, who made her screen debut in the title role in *The Jungle Princess* (1936), was cast in her first dramatic role. Her exotic beauty and charm led to her playing Latins several times in her long career. She had previously worked with Quinn in *Swing High, Swing Low* (1937), in which he played a Panamanian, with all his dialogue spoken in Spanish.

The story takes 10 people, most of whom do not know each other, and throws them together for 12 feverish hours from the time it is announced that a train will leave the war-stricken Spanish capital and the hour when it steams out for Valencia and safety. During those hours the potential passengers live a lifetime of emotions, bringing out the best and worst in them. Quinn is Capt. Ricardo Alvarez, an army officer who manages to get passes for his sweetheart Carmelita Castillo (Lamour) and his pal Eduardo (Roland). The cast also includes Lew Ayres as Bill Dexter, an American reporter who finds the love he has been seeking in the flaming city; Olympe Bradna as Maria, a member of the Spanish women's battalion; Karen Morley as an adventuress; and Frank Leyva.

It was filmed at Paramount Studios in Hollywood with the use of hundreds of Latin-looking extras. Francisco "Chico" Day worked as a second assistant director on this, his first film in that official capacity.

Latin Lovers (1953 MGM)
   D: Mervyn LeRoy
   S: Isobel Lennart
   P: Joe Pasternak
   Cast: **Ricardo Montalban**, Lana Turner, **Joaquin Garay**, **Rita Moreno**

Embarrassing musical featuring a suave Ricardo Montalban as a Latin lover in Rio de Janeiro involved with a rich American (Turner) who wants to live it up. Montalban dances with Rita Moreno in one scene.

Latino (1985 Cinecom)
   D: Haskell Wexler
   S: Haskell Wexler
   P: Benjamin Berg
   Cast: **Robert Beltran, Tony Plana, Annette Cardona**

Sixteen years after he made *Medium Cool* (1969), a "faction" about the violent 1968 Democratic National Convention in Chicago, Haskell Wexler returned as a feature film director with *Latino,* an overtly left-wing melodrama about the U.S.-backed Contras fighting the Sandinista government in Nicaragua.

Eddie Guerrero (Beltran), a Chicano Green Beret from East Los Angeles, is sent by the U.S. Army to Honduras to train CIA-sponsored Contra counterrevolutionaries. Through Eddie's eyes, Wexler tells the story of one man's awakening to the quagmire of self-destruction that can develop when a soldier believes in "my country right or wrong" without questioning the morality of his actions.

Eddie falls in love with a Nicaraguan woman (Cardona) living in Honduras, and is thus forced to face the ethical questions raised by his participation in the undeclared war his government is waging.

While naively idealizing the Sandinista movement in a way reminiscent of Sergei Eisenstein's early Soviet movies such as *The Battleship Potemkin* (1925), the film nevertheless raises thorny questions about covert American foreign policy, particularly in Latin America. It also brings up the cultural conflict of a Chicano soldier's struggle with self-identity when he is ordered to fight people who look like him, speak Spanish like him, and eat tortillas just like his mom makes back home.

Latino was filmed on a budget of $4 million on location in Honduras in February 1984. Lucas Films provided post-production facilities. The film had an extremely limited release in the States because it could not find a major distributor.

"There's a potency and fiber about *Latino* that you have to admire, [and] at its best it has moments of beauty, of power. But the simple minded pro-war action movie it wants to recall and deflate may have left too big a strain on its style," Michael Wilmington, *L.A. Times* (11/13/85).

"Although doubtlessly not intended as such, *Latino* comes off distressingly like a left wing [version of John Wayne's] *The Green Berets,*" *Variety* (5/15/85).

The Lawless (1950 Par)

D: Joseph Losey
S: Geoffrey Homes, based on his [Daniel Mainwaring's] book
P: William H. Pine and William C. Thomas
Cast: Macdonald Carey, **Lalo Rios**, Gail Russell, **Argentina Brunetti**, **Felipe Turich**, Pedro De Cordoba

In an agricultural northern California community with a sizable Mexican American farmworker population, a hysterical manhunt begins for a 19-year-old Latino (Rios) accused of attacking a policeman at a dance.

Frightened by his actions, the youth flees in an ice cream truck and steals a car at a roadside café before he is captured. A series of events lead to the youth being charged with crimes he didn't commit, and the press, reflecting the sentiments of the Anglo townspeople, sensationalizes and distorts the facts even further. Only the editor of the local paper will stand up for the young Mexican, and as a result the angry farmworkers turn on him. While they wreck his publishing plant, he manages to save the youth from a lynching.

Gail Russell plays Sunny Garcia, the youth's lawyer, and Argentina Brunetti and Felipe Turich play the boy's parents.

The film received generally good reviews and made a nice profit for Paramount and producers Pine and Thomas. It was filmed in 18 days in Marysville and Grass Valley, California, and at Paramount Studios at a cost of $385,000.

In the October 1950 issue of *Holiday* magazine, William Pine said of the film, "I [just] couldn't get the right Mexican girl for the lead. So we got Gail Russell who

Lalo Rios (left) portrays a young Latino falsely accused of attacking a policeman (Ian MacDonald) in *The Lawless*.

isn't Mexican but . . . has dark hair and . . . knows how to work." (By this he meant that she was used to working at the fast pace of B pictures.) Director Losey discovered Lalo Rios working as a housepainter in Los Angeles.

"It is the first picture to be made about discrimination against Mexican-Americans," said screenwriter Homes, in a *New York Times* story (3/5/50). "I laid the story in the farm country north of Sacramento where a great number of migratory workers, at least a third of them Mexican or Mexican American, are employed during the various fruit harvests."

The Lawless was considered a B picture. The reviewers cited the film for its subject matter and Lalo Rios's performance. It was two years before Rios, who had never acted prior to making the movie, got another chance at a major role, in the King brothers' *The Ring* (1952). That both films deal with the issues of Mexican Americans, were filmed on low budgets, and share the same starring actor make them fine companion pieces. Along with such movies as *A Medal for Benny* (1945), they are among the American cinema's first statements on the condition of the Hispanic American in American society. The success of *Gentleman's Agreement* (1947), *Home of the Brave* (1949), and other films dealing with ethnic or racial prejudice in America made this film possible.

That Sunny Garcia was a Latina lawyer in a small town was a progressive step for the time and marks one of the first modern Chicana images on the screen.

The Left-Handed Gun (1958 WB)
D: Arthur Penn
S: Leslie Stevens, based on the teleplay *The Death of Billy the Kid* by Gore Vidal
P: Fred Coe
Cast: Paul Newman, Lita Milan, John Dehner, Hurd Hatfield, **Martin Garralaga, Nestor Paiva, Tina Menard**

Memorable for Paul Newman's intense portrayal of the legendary western outlaw Billy the Kid in a film interestingly combining elements of action and psychology.

Billy resembles a juvenile delinquent who has violent, uncontrollable rages in this story of an unbalanced youth whose lust for revenge is born of the killing of his benefactor, an English cattleman, during a range war. Running from the law, he takes sanctuary in a small Mexican town, where he meets and falls in love with a Mexican girl, Celsa, played by Lita Milan, an actress of Hungarian-Polish ancestry. When he returns home, he finds a second father figure in lawman Pat Garrett (Dehner), who is eventually forced to kill the Kid.

The movie was filmed on a low budget in black and white by Warner Bros. at its standing Mexican set (built for *Juarez* [1939]) at the Warner Ranch in Calabasas and the Janss Ranch near Thousand Oaks, California. It was the first film for famed director Arthur Penn (*Bonnie and Clyde* [1967]). Hispanic cast members in featured roles include Nestor Paiva, Martin Garralaga, Tina Menard, and Frank Leyva.

The Leopard Man (1943 RKO)
D: Jacques Tourneur
S: Ardel Wray and Edward Dein, based on the novel *Black Alibi* by Cornell Woolrich
P: Val Lewton
Cast: Dennis O'Keefe, **Margo, Richard Martin**, Eliso Gamboa, Joe Dominguez

New Mexico background for an uneven but interesting and ambitious mystery thriller shot entirely at RKO Studios. A New Mexico nightclub uses a tame leopard for a publicity stunt, which backfires when the leopard escapes and presumably kills a girl. Margo plays Clo-Clo, a Spanish dancer. The local religious Penitente sect parade at the end is as weird a procession as anything you'll ever see in a film.

Let's Get Harry (1987 TS)

- D: Alan Smithee [Stuart Rosenberg]
- S: Charles Robert Carner, based on a story by Mark Feldberg and Samuel Fuller
- P: Daniel H. Blatt and Robert Singer
- Cast: Mark Harmon, Robert Duvall, Gary Busey, **Elpidia Carrillo, Gregory Sierra**

A group of small-town American blue-collar workers find out that their best friend, Harry, a pipeline worker, has been kidnapped by terrorists and drug runners in South America and decide to do something about it.

They demand action from Washington and when thwarted by an uncaring bureaucracy hire a mercenary to lead them on a renegade recovery mission. Inexperienced, naive, and brash, they soon find themselves face to face with real bullets.

This barely competent action flick saw limited U.S. theatrical release. Stereotypes include Latin bad guy drug dealers/terrorists, double-crossers, and violent, corrupt police and army officials. It was filmed in Mexico (subbing for Colombia) with Elpidia Carrillo, Gregory Sierra, and Guillermo Rios, who plays drug kingpin Ochobar. Director Stuart Rosenberg had his name removed from the credits.

Licence to Kill (1989 MGM/UA)

- D: John Glen
- S: Michael G. Wilson and Richard Maibaum, based on the characters created by Ian Fleming
- P: Albert R. Broccoli and Michael G. Wilson
- Cast: Timothy Dalton, Robert Davi, Carey Lowell, **Talisa Soto, Pedro Armendariz, Jr.**

James Bond (Dalton) is in Florida for his old friend Felix Leiter's (David Hedison's) marriage. On the eve of the wedding, Bond and Felix capture South America's most ruthless drug lord, Franz Sanchez (Davi). But after a $2 million bribe, Sanchez is a free man and exacts revenge by murdering Felix and his new bride.

The usually cool Bond is enraged, but Her Majesty's Government doesn't approve of secret agents with personal vendettas. When Bond refuses to obey, his Licence to Kill is revoked and he heads to a fictional South American country in search of Sanchez. Puerto Rican model turned actress Talisa Soto is one of the celebrated Bond girls. Filmed in Mexico with all the usual big-budget James Bond action, beautiful women, and thrilling stunts and car chases, it is surprisingly free of Hispanic stereotypes, except for the drug lord.

A Life in the Balance (1955 TCF)

- D: Harry Horner
- P: Leonard Goldstein
- S: Robert Presnell, Jr., and Leo Townsend, based on a story by Georges Simenon
- Cast: **Ricardo Montalban**, Anne Bancroft, Lee Marvin, **Jose Perez, Rodolfo Acosta, Jose Torvay**

A murder mystery filmed in Mexico City, *A Life in the Balance* is unusual in that it offers a very modern and nonstereotypical view of life in Mexico City with Mexican leading characters.

A young boy (Perez) tracks down a psychopathic killer (Marvin) in order to prove the innocence of his musician father, who has been arrested for the murder of a woman who lives in the same building. Well paced and well done, it gave Ricardo Montalban an escape from the Latin lover portrayals with which he had become saddled.

Ricardo Montalban, Jose Perez, and
Anne Bancroft in *A Life in the Balance*.

The film features a young Anne Bancroft as Montalban's lover in one of a series of ethnic portrayals early in her career. Rodolfo Acosta, usually cast as a heavy in American films, portrays the police detective. Puerto Rican Jose Perez went on to work on the Broadway stage and, as an adult, in many film and television shows.

The Life of Villa (1914 Mutual Film Corp.) [aka: *A Tragedy in the Life of General Villa* (1915)]

   D: **Raoul Walsh**
   P: **D.W. Griffith**

Silent. In 1914, Pancho Villa sold the movie rights for the revolution he was fighting in Mexico for his own personal gain. Though he could not read or write, Villa understood the power of the moving pictures he saw in El Paso.

Journalists and photographers from around the world came to Mexico to meet Villa and cover the colorful hero of the Revolution. In January 1914 in a hotel room in Juarez, Mexico, Villa met with Frank M. Thayer, a representative of the Los Angeles–based Mutual Film Corporation headed by D.W. Griffith, and signed a contract for $25,000 in gold and 50 percent of the profits. (Griffith felt that the story of this celebrated figure who made headlines in all the American newspapers would be surefire film material.) In a stunning piece of early "photo-op" thinking, the major contract stipulation was that the general would have to fight all his battles during the day so that they could be photographed using the slow film stocks of the period.

Young director/actor Raoul Walsh directed the film troupe, which included famed cameraman L.M. Burrud. After many months of personal tribulations and adverse shooting conditions, all at the mercy of the whims of General Villa, they returned to Hollywood exhausted. Finding most of the footage unusable as a narrative, cohesive whole, Griffith ordered a script written. Additional footage was shot with actors and dozens of extras at a ranch in the nearby San Fernando Valley with Walsh playing Villa, complete with sombrero, six-guns, and a sinister moustache.

Released in 1915 as *A Tragedy in the Life of General Villa*, the film was never a hit, but it did play in enough theaters to recoup the investment. Some of the actual Villa footage made it into the final film.

Life with Mikey (1993 BV)

D: James Lapine
S: Marc Lawrence
P: Ted Schwartz
Cast: Michael J. Fox, **Christina Vidal**, Nathan Lane, **Ruben Blades**

Michael Chapman (Fox), a former child star turned agent, discovers a tough homeless 10-year-old street kid, Angie Vega (Vidal), whom he catches picking his pocket. She turns out to be a natural in front of the camera, so he decides to represent her and to take her into his home. Angie is later reunited with her father, played by Ruben Blades.

The Littlest Outlaw (1955 BV)

D: Roberto Gavaldon
S: Bill Walsh, based on a story by Lansburgh
P: Larry Lansburgh
Cast: **Pedro Armendariz**, Andres Velasquez, **Joseph Calleia**, **Rodolfo Acosta**, **Jose Torvay**

Pedro Armendariz stars in this Walt Disney production about a little boy who runs away with his horse rather than see it killed.

Andres Velasquez plays the youngster, Little Pablito. The cast also includes Rodolfo Acosta and Joseph Calleia. It was filmed in English and Spanish on location in and around San Miguel de Allende, Mexico.

Director Roberto Gavaldon was one of the leading directors in Mexico from the 1940s until the early 1960s and was responsible for such classics of the Golden Age of Mexican Cinema as *The Count of Monte Cristo* (1941), *La Barraca* (1944), *La Otra* (1946), *La Rosa Blanca* (1961), and *Macario* (1959). His other English-language films include *The Adventures of Casanova* (1948) and *Beyond All Limits* (1957).

Lone Wolf McQuade (1983 Or)

D: Steve Carver
S: B.J. Nelson, based on a story by H. Kaye Dyal and Nelson
P: Yoram Ben-Ami and Steve Carver
Cast: Chuck Norris, David Carradine, **Barbara Carrera**, Robert Beltran, **Jorge Cervera, Jr.**

McQuade (Norris) is a renegade Texas Ranger who is assigned a Mexican American rookie partner (Beltran) by his superiors. They become embroiled in stopping a crime spree led by Rawley (Carradine).

This typical Chuck Norris vehicle is a violent and well-made action film combining a contemporary western with martial arts. Beltran is good as the rookie partner in a role free of stereotypical action or dialogue. Barbara Carrera is a strong presence as the bad guy's Native American girlfriend who falls for McQuade.

Losin' It (1983 Emb)

D: Curtis Hanson
S: B.W.L. Norton
P: Bryan Gindoff and Hannah Hempstead
Cast: Tom Cruise, Jackie Earle Haley, John Stockwell, Shelley Long, **Henry Darrow, Enrique Castillo, Santos Morales**

In 1963, four fun-loving American teenagers head south of the border to Tijuana for fun, sex, and excitement. One boy, Dave (Haley), leads his friends in search of the boisterous nightlife, and another brings his red Chevy convertible in hopes of having his car cheaply reupholstered. Instead, the car falls prey to the eye of a local police chief. Shelley Long plays Kathy, an American housewife in search of a Mexican divorce.

The film is every Southwest American kid's fantasy of what happens during a wild weekend in a Mexican bordertown. Included in this fantasy is every conceivable Mexican border stereotype, including corrupt police officials, prostitutes, saloon barkers, pimps, switchblade-wielding toughs, and smart-alecky taxi drivers. "You come to Mexico to do things you wouldn't do in your own country," points out one of the Mexicans to the boys.

The Loves of Carmen (1948 Col)

D: Charles Vidor
S: Helen Deutsch
P: Charles Vidor
Cast: **Rita Hayworth**, Glenn Ford, Ron Randell, Victor Jory, Luther Adler, Arnold Moss, **Natividad Vacio, Rosa Turich**

Rita Hayworth as the ultimate spitfire heroine in Prosper Mérimée's famous story of passion and death. Carmen (Hayworth) convinces Don Jose (Ford) to desert his duties, kill her husband in a fight for her love, and take over the leadership of a gang of mountain-dwelling outlaws.

Hayworth made the film for her own Beckworth corporation in Technicolor at a cost of $2.5 million. She tried to ensure box-office success by teaming with Glenn Ford again after *Gilda* (1946), who was miscast as Don Jose, and with *Gilda* director Charles Vidor. Ford was never able to make audiences believe he was a Spaniard. He himself referred to it as "a Rembrandt of miscasting, with me as a Spanish Gypsy" at a Directors Guild of America tribute to Richard Brooks in 1991.

Hayworth replaced Bizet's music with that of a contemporary composer. Her father, Eduardo Cansino, assisted Robert Sidney in choreographing the dance numbers, which replaced the ballet of the opera. The movie was filmed on location in Lone Pine, California, and at Columbia Studios, locations which did not correspond with Seville and the surrounding Spanish countryside. Despite a lukewarm critical reception, *The Loves of Carmen* was a commercial success.

Machete (1958 UA)

D: Kurt Neumann
S: Carroll Young and Kurt Neumann
P: Kurt Neumann
Cast: Mari Blanchard, Albert Dekker, **Juano Hernandez, Carlos Rivas**, Lee Van Cleef, Ruth Cains

Standard melodrama about a middle-aged plantation owner in Puerto Rico, Don Luis Montoya (Dekker), whose young bride, Jean (Blanchard), very quickly tries to seduce Carlos (Rivas), the foreman, whom Montoya has raised since childhood. Miguel (Van Cleef) is a troublemaking cousin who has his own designs on the plantation. Miguel sets fire to the plantation but is killed, while Carlos saves Montoya's life. Jean perishes in the fire, but Carlos is consoled by his true love,

Rita (Cains). The most notable aspect of the production is that it was filmed entirely on location in Puerto Rico.

Mackenna's Gold (1969 Col)

    D: J. Lee Thompson
    S: Carl Foreman, based on the novel by Will Henry
    P: Carl Foreman
 Cast: Gregory Peck, Omar Sharif, Lee J. Cobb, Telly Savalas, Camilla Sparv,
        Eduardo Ciannelli, Julie Newmar, Rudy Diaz

Overproduced, cliche-ridden big-budget western starring Gregory Peck as a drifter who is given a map to the secret location of lost gold in the Canon del Oro by a dying Indian in the desert. Omar Sharif plays Peck's Mexican bandit adversary Colorado and Keenan Wynn plays Sanchez, Colorado's second in command. The film features Rudy Diaz and Pepe Callahan as outlaws.

The Magnificent Fraud (1939 Par)

    D: Robert Florey
    S: Gilbert Gabriel and Walter Ferris, based on a play by Charles G. Booth
    P: Harlan Thompson
 Cast: Akim Tamiroff, Lloyd Nolan, Patricia Morison, Steffi Duna

A dramatic actor impersonates the drunken dictator of a fictional South American country until a large American loan can be completed. Akim Tamiroff plays actor Jules LaCroix and President Alvarado. The film never reaches the comic potential of the premise. This comedy spoof was remade more successfully five decades later as *Moon over Parador* (1988) by Paul Mazursky.

The Magnificent Matador (1955 TCF)

    D: **Budd Boetticher**
    S: Charles Lang, based on a story by **Boetticher**
    P: Edward L. Alperson
 Cast: **Anthony Quinn**, Maureen O'Hara, **Thomas Gomez**, Manuel Rojas

The Magnificent Matador captures the pageantry and heroic excitement of the bullring in this love story set in Mexico. In a Technicolor framework of haciendas, mountains, and plateaus, matador Quinn, an idol in the arena, superstitiously deserts the bullring because of an ill omen. Pursued by a rich American (O'Hara), he finally proves his fear is not for himself but for a younger bullfighter, his illegitimate son Rafael, played by Manuel Rojas. In a stirring climax, father and son enter the bullring in turn, proudly displaying their skill and bravery.

"Anthony Quinn as the Matador hero . . . is, as always, a capable and convincing player. . . . Mexico, in fact and film, is a beautiful country, and *Matador* does it justice," Jesse Zunser, *Cue Magazine* (5/28/55).

The Magnificent Seven (1960 UA)

    D: John Sturges
    S: William Roberts
    P: John Sturges
 Cast: Yul Brynner, Steve McQueen, Eli Wallach, James Coburn,
        Charles Bronson, Horst Buchholz, Robert Vaughn, Brad Dexter

In the Kurosawa film *The Seven Samurai* (1954), which this movie was based on, the villagers and bandits are all Japanese. In the American version, six of the seven professional killers were to be American gunmen who are recruited by village elders to help the villagers rid themselves of marauding Mexican bandidos, a notable difference to which even the Mexican government took exception. They pointed out that Mexican gunfighters were perfectly capable of helping the villagers rid themselves of Mexican bandidos.

Anxious to make the film on a budget, director Sturges made two of the seven gunmen Mexican (Bronson and Buchholz), and the Mexican government okayed the script.

Nevertheless, Americans in Mexico killing Mexicans is a critical but subtle difference that carries cultural and political implications of implied superiority, marring what is otherwise a landmark western.

Many of the original film's characters and situations are retained in William Roberts's screenplay. The Seven Samurai (i.e., the Magnificent Seven) are out-of-work gunmen and fugitives in a bordertown. Each of the gunmen is individualized: Chris (Brynner), the leader; Vin (McQueen), who is restless and seeks action and employment; Harry (Dexter), who is seeking a fortune; Britt (Coburn), an opportunist who tests his skills to their limit; O'Reilly (Bronson), half Mexican Indian, a wanderer who sympathizes with his people; Lee (Vaughn), a fugitive gunman who is looking for asylum and an escape from failing ability; and Chico (Buchholz), the young Mexican who denies his heritage in order to gain prestige by joining the group. Calvera, the Mexican bandit leader, is played with hammy exuberance by Eli Wallach. Four of the seven die in the savage fighting.

Yul Brynner as Chris (center), a hired gunman, confronts a gang of Mexican bandidos in *The Magnificent Seven*.

Future Hollywood cameraman John Alonzo played one of the bandidos as did actor Larry Duran. The main speaking roles of the villagers were played by Mexican actors Juan Martin de Hoyos and Elsa Monteros and Mexican American actor Natividad Vacio. Francisco "Chico" Day was the unit production manager on the film, which employed 150 Mexican film technicians and hundreds of Mexican extras.

The Magnificent Seven was filmed near Tepotzlan, Mexico, and became one of the first so-called international westerns. The casting of Yul Brynner, among others, in a western, a genre he was not generally associated with up to then, was innovative. Brynner makes a perfect samurai gunfighter, a role he later repeats in the movie *Westworld* (1973). His black outfit, previously associated with villains, was perfectly in tune with the antihero movies that were to follow in the 1960s and early 1970s.

With the exception of Brynner, who was already well known, the film's relatively little-known main players (with the possible exception of Dexter) went on to become stars. A popular and semiclassical music score was provided by Elmer Bernstein.

The film also started a 1960s preoccupation with the displacement of the men who tamed the West as civilization took over. This theme continued in such movies as *The Man Who Shot Liberty Valance* (1962), *The Wild Bunch* (1969), and *Butch Cassidy and the Sundance Kid* (1969).

The Magnificent Seven spawned three sequels, each using a variation of the same basic plot (*Return of the Seven* [1966], *Guns of the Magnificent Seven* [1969], and *The Magnificent Seven Ride* [1972]).

The Magnificent Seven Ride (1972 UA)

D: George McGowan
S: Arthur Rowe
P: William A. Calihan
Cast: Lee Van Cleef, Luke Askew, **Pedro Armendariz, Jr., Rodolfo Acosta**

Notable for managing to rip off two films at the same time and still failing: *The Dirty Dozen* (1967) and the original *The Magnificent Seven* (1960). Lee Van Cleef is Chris, the Bulletproof. Rodolfo Acosta took his turn as the bandit chieftain, and Pedro Armendariz, Jr., is one of the Seven, who are now convicts.

Major Dundee (1965 Col)

D: **Sam Peckinpah**
S: Harry Julian Fink, Oscar Saul, and **Sam Peckinpah**, based on a story by Fink
P: Jerry Bresler
Cast: Charlton Heston, Richard Harris, Senta Berger, James Coburn, Mario Adorf

Union Army major Dundee (Heston) forms an uneasy alliance with Confederate prisoners of war led by Capt. Tyreen (Harris) in order to ride into Mexico and track down a renegade Apache chief and his band of followers, even though he has no authority there.

During their pursuit in Mexico, Union and Confederate soldiers must overcome their hatred, suspicion, and fear of each other to band together to fight Apaches and French occupation troops under Maximilian. Freeing a Mexican village from French troops adds to the responsibilities of Dundee, who must protect various Mexicans and Teresa Santiago (Berger), the beautiful Austrian-born widow of a Mexican doctor. Dundee and Tyreen find themselves in competition for her favors.

A seriously wounded Dundee finds solace in the bottle and whores when he loses his confidence. He regains it in time for a final confrontation with the Apaches and French soldiers before heading back across the border.

Sam Peckinpah directed and co-wrote this strong, rousing western, which was filmed in and around Durango, Mexico, though he later disowned the film, which was truncated and recut by others. Mario Adorf plays a Union Army man.

The Mambo Kings (1992 WB)

  D: Arne Glimcher
  S: Cynthia Cidre, based on a novel by Oscar Hijuelos
  P: Arne Glimcher and Arnon Milchan
Cast: Armand Assante, **Antonio Banderas**, Cathy Moriarty, **Desi Arnaz, Jr.**, Maruschka Detmers, **Talisa Soto**, **Tito Puente**

Film version of Oscar Hijuelos's Pulitzer Prize–winning novel *The Mambo Kings Play Songs of Love* (1989) about two musician brothers, Nestor and Cesar Castillo, from Havana, Cuba, who come to New York during the Latin mambo dance craze of the 1950s.

The story lost much of its subtle cultural atmosphere and character nuance in its transition to the screen and is more like a typical musician's rise-and-fall-type movie of the 1930s.

Working in a meat processing plant during the day, the brothers try to make their mark on the Latin dance club circuit of New York, and after some success, they run up against the Cuban gangsters who control the circuit. The fact that these Cuban gangsters are black and would never have been allowed in the clubs, except as musicians, let alone been in control, is completely ignored.

The brothers are offered a contract for a long run at a preferred nightclub but refuse the offer, thus upsetting the gangsters, who put out the word. No one else will hire the boys. However, they are given a temporary reprieve when Desi Arnaz (played by Desi Arnaz, Jr.) catches their act, and later offers them a guest appearance on his "I Love Lucy" television show. Nestor (Banderas), who pines for his lost love in Cuba, does not share his brother's burning determination to "make it" unless on their own terms. He just wants to play music. As a result, he sells out to the gangsters without Cesar's (Assante's) knowledge, regrets his decision, and ultimately pays for his sins with his life.

Armand Assante overplays his character of the older brother, Cesar, who wants to be his own man; Antonio Banderas, however, is a quiet surprise as the brooding younger brother, Nestor.

The musical numbers are truncated, and the sense of what the music means to the people and the personalities involved is never fully explored. The women in the brothers' lives and their interactions are very superficial and get very short shrift. Tito Puente, the original Mambo King, appears as himself.

Director Arne Glimcher, a millionaire art dealer in New York, is not a director, and this film puts the lie to the idea that anyone can direct a movie. The film is driven by its music and its colorful, stylized art direction, and by the cinematography by Michael Ballhaus.

Nevertheless, with all its flaws, the movie does somewhat introduce mainstream America to the reality of Hispanic Americans as an established, historical presence in American society—a reality that was ignored for many years and has only recently been touched upon by much better movies such as *Zoot Suit* (1981) or the far superior *Stand and Deliver* (1988) and *La Bamba* (1987)—counterbalancing the stereotypical view that all Hispanic men are knife-wielding drug dealers and that their women are hip-swinging hookers.

The "I Love Lucy" re-creation was cleverly staged, intercutting film footage of the original show with shots of Lucille Ball and new footage with Arnaz, Jr., and the Castillos in the skit. Desi Arnaz, Jr., however, is but a pale imitation of his father.

The Man Behind the Gun (1953 WB)

D: Felix Feist
S: John Twist, based on a story by Robert Buckner
P: Robert Sisk
Cast: Randolph Scott, Patrice Wymore, **Lina Romay**, Alan Hale, Jr.,
    Robert Cabal

Randolph Scott is an Army major sent in disguise to prevent armed insurrection and the setting up of a separate state by proslavery elements in southern California of the 1850s. Lina Romay is effective as Chona Degnon, the proprietress of the Palacio saloon and gambling den. Romay sings two songs, "La Paloma" and "Adios Mi Amor."

Robert Cabal makes a brief but memorable appearance as the boy Joaquin Murieta.

The Man from Del Rio (1956 UA)

D: Harry Horner
S: Richard Carr
P: Robert L. Jacks
Cast: **Anthony Quinn, Katy Jurado**, Peter Whitney

An unusual, modest-budget western starring Anthony Quinn, significant for the fact that he played a Mexican American sheriff and co-starred with Katy Jurado as Estella, a nurse to the town doctor.

In order to rid itself of some outlaws, a frontier town swallows its prejudice and makes drifter Dave Robles (Quinn) sheriff. He expects to be accepted by the town when he takes the dangerous job as sheriff but discovers that he has been hired as a gunman and not acknowledged as a man.

Man in the Shadow (1957 U)

D: Jack Arnold
S: Gene L. Coon
P: Albert Zugsmith
Cast: Jeff Chandler, Orson Welles, **Martin Garralaga**

Contemporary but routine western drama in which Chandler plays a sheriff in an agricultural community who investigates the death of a Mexican laborer on a powerful rancher's land despite his and the townspeople's objections. In the end, the murderer is discovered to be the ranch foreman.

Man of Conquest (1939 Rep)

D: George Nicholls
S: Wells Root, E.E. Paramor, Jr., and Jan Fortune, based on an original
    story by Harold Shumate and Root
P: Sol C. Siegel
Cast: Richard Dix, Joan Fontaine

The rousing story of Sam Houston from his start in Tennessee politics under Andrew Jackson to his election as governor, his journey to Arkansas, his adoption by the Cherokee Indians, and finally his part in the Texas Wars for Independence. No Hispanics appear in major roles in this one except for Pedro De Cordoba as an old Indian. Plenty of Mexican extras were recruited near Stockton, California, and the Salt Springs Reservoir, where much of the film was shot.

Man of La Mancha (1972 UA)

D: Arthur Hiller
S: Dale Wasserman
P: Arthur Hiller
Cast: Peter O'Toole, Sophia Loren, James Coco

Overblown, big-budget screen version of the hit Broadway musical based on Cervantes's *Don Quixote* with no Hispanics in the cast and filmed in Italy largely on studio sets.

It stars Peter O'Toole in the dual role of Cervantes and Don Quixote, Sophia Loren as Aldonza, and James Coco as Sancho Panza. The singing voices of O'Toole and Loren were dubbed.

Maracaibo (1958 Par)

D: Cornel Wilde
S: Ted Sherdeman
P: Cornel Wilde
Cast: Cornel Wilde, Jean Wallace, Abbe Lane, Francis Lederer, Michael Landon

Set in the oil fields of Lake Maracaibo and Caracas, the capital of Venezuela, where most of the film was shot on location by producer/director/star Cornel Wilde. Vic Scott (Wilde), an American vacationing in Venezuela and romantically interested in novelist Laura Kingsley (Wallace), is called upon to extinguish a treacherous offshore oil well fire on Lake Maracaibo. The land belongs to a wealthy deaf mute, Miguel Orlando (Lederer), who is engaged to a former girlfriend of Scott, Elena (Lane). The rugged American finally extinguishes the fire in a spectacular sequence, but Orlando's close friend and interpreter, Lago (Landon), is killed by accident.

Wilde went on to produce and direct such films as the romantic *Lancelot and Guinevere* (1963), the critically acclaimed *The Naked Prey* (1965), the antiwar drama *Beach Red* (1967), and the post-*Jaws* shark adventure *Shark's Treasure* (1975). Michael Landon went on to find stardom on television's long-running "Bonanza" series soon after this.

Maria Candelaria [aka: *Portrait of Maria*] (1946 MGM)

D: **Emilio Fernandez**
S: **Emilio Fernandez** and Mauricio Magdaleno
P: Agustin J. Fink
Cast: **Dolores Del Rio, Pedro Armendariz**

Though actually filmed in 1943, *Maria Candelaria* was picked up for release by MGM International in 1946 to little U.S. box-office success, though it did well internationally. Originally shot in Spanish, the movie was dubbed into English.

Dolores Del Rio became a top star in Mexico soon after returning home from Hollywood. Del Rio's Maria was a perfect piece of film acting, and she found Emilio Fernandez to be a director who helped her realize her potential to the full for the first time.

Maria is a simple and deeply spiritual peasant girl who lives in beautiful and isolated Lake Xochimilco. She is stoned to death by her fellow villagers, who mistrust and fear her innate goodness. Maria and Lorenzo (Armendariz), her Indian lover, represent innocence corrupted and destroyed by civilization.

Gabriel Figueroa's brilliant black-and-white photography brought out the spirituality of Del Rio's beauty in a way no Hollywood film had ever done. Though playing a young girl, Del Rio was almost 40 years old at the time.

With this, her second Mexican film (the first being *Flor Silvestre* [1943]), Del Rio, her co-star Pedro Armendariz, director Fernandez, and cameraman Figueroa established themselves as the "big four" of the Mexican film industry.

Maria Candelaria was the first Mexican film to make an impact in Europe after World War II. It won the Grand Prize at the Cannes Film Festival in 1947 and helped initiate what is now called the Golden Age of Mexican Cinema.

Fernandez's films were immediately seen as uniquely Mexican, both in style and subject matter. Mexico's colorful folklore, expansive landscapes, coastlines, dramatic skies, vibrant cloud patterns, and the ethereal presence and passionate Indian beauty of the actors were fully realized under Fernandez's direction and Figueroa's masterful cinematography.

The Mark of Zorro (1940 TCF)

See "Zorro & The Cisco Kid" listings.

Masquerade in Mexico (1945 Par)

D: Mitchell Leisen
S: Karl Tunberg, based on a story by Edwin Justus Mayer and Franz Spencer
P: Karl Tunberg
Cast: Dorothy Lamour, **Arturo De Cordova**, Patric Knowles, Ann Dvorak, The Guadalajara Trio, **Martin Garralaga**

American nightclub singer Angel O'Reilly (Lamour) as part of a jewel theft impersonates a Spanish countess in Mexico. An entertainer in a Mexico City nightclub, she is then engaged by banker Thomas Grant (Knowles) to divert the attention of matador Manolo Segovia (De Cordova) from the banker's wife (Dvorak) to herself.

Pleasant, entertaining romantic musical shot at Paramount Studios in Hollywood. Lamour recalled in a *Saturday Evening Post* (1/18/47) interview, "Even the atmosphere of the set helped make *Masquerade in Mexico* a delight. I had never been south of the border, but had often dreamed of such a trip. The atmosphere of our neighbor nation was simulated so convincingly on the set that working there was like being in Mexico."

Lamour sings songs from a garlanded gondola on a simulated Lake Xochimilco, and a gigantic ballet is performed in a rural Mexican hacienda. This is clearly the Mexico of the popular American romantic imagination, and it is delivered with good dancing and singing, amid lavish settings and costumes.

The Latin cast members were headed by Arturo De Cordova as the warm-hearted matador who falls madly in love with Lamour. Other Latin cast members include Martin Garralaga, Enrique Valadez, Rita Lupino, Elisa Gamboa, Ray Beltran, Roque Ybarra, Juan Torena, Felipe Turich, Pepito Perez, Leon Lombardo, Primo Lopez (Cushion Boy), Rodolfo Hoyos, Sr. and Jr., Julian Rivero, and Frank Leyva.

The Master Gunfighter (1975 Billy Jack Enterprises)

D: Frank [Tom] Laughlin
S: Harold Lapland
P: Philip Parslow
Cast: Tom Laughlin, Ron O'Neal, **Barbara Carrera**, Hector Elias, **Victor Campos**

Set in California during the 1850s, this film deals with the conflicts between native Spanish Californians and encroaching American land grabbers.

In order to fight off efforts by the Americans to foreclose on their land, Spanish Californians need gold; but when an Indian village that the Spanish have enslaved tries to return some illegally obtained gold to the Americans, one of the leaders of the haciendas, Paulo (O'Neal), has the Indians slaughtered so they cannot reveal the source of their wealth. Finley (Laughlin) objects to the massacre and leaves for Mexico but returns for a fight with Paulo when he is about to massacre another village.

A stylized western, it is a cross between a Kung Fu epic and a "spaghetti western." Its star had an unprecedented box-office success with his character of Billy Jack in the film of the same name (1971). One of the best things about the movie is the creative casting. Paulo is played by Ron O'Neal, a black actor who had gained popularity in 1972 with *Superfly*. Fashion model turned actress Barbara Carrera made her film debut as Eula, an elegant Spanish noblewoman who marries Finley. GeoAnn Sosa plays Chorika, a young Indian woman who is the sole survivor of a massacre. Victor Campos is Maltese and Hector Elias is Juan, two henchmen. The film was shot on location in Big Sur and Malibu, California.

Maverick Gold

See *Catlow*.

A Medal for Benny (1945 Par)

   D: Irving Pichel
   S: Frank Butler and Jack Wagner, based on a story by John Steinbeck and Wagner
   P: Paul Jones
Cast: **J. Carroll Naish**, **Arturo De Cordova**, Dorothy Lamour, Mikhail Rasumny, Frank McHugh, **Rosita Moreno**, Charles Dingle, **Nestor Paiva**, **Fernando Alvarado**, **Pepito Perez**, **Martin Garralaga**, **Julian Rivero**

Based on a 20-page story idea by John Steinbeck and Jack Wagner, *A Medal for Benny* was the first Hollywood motion picture to deal somewhat sensitively with the problems of Mexican Americans living in the United States, recognizing them as part of the American scene. The film well illustrates the effects of racism and poverty in a subtle, inoffensive way that audiences of the time could accept.

J. Carroll Naish (left) and Arturo De Cordova (right) in *A Medal for Benny*.

Although he never appears in the film, Benny's presence is always felt, for he is the lovable renegade of the paisano colony who is ordered out of town by the police. He disappears for a year, and when he is next heard of, Benny has died on a Pacific battlefield in World War II and is posthumously awarded the Congressional Medal of Honor.

The town fathers go crazy with civic joy, as do the members of the Chamber of Commerce. A general, along with reporters and newsreel cameramen, will soon arrive and the town will be the center of national attention. The town fathers can't find Benny's family to receive the medal. Benny's last name was Martin, and by the time they realize with horror that it is pronounced "Marteen" and that Benny comes from the other side of the tracks, it is too late to give him a creditable background.

When the dignitaries first visit Benny's father, he thinks they are trying to evict him for nonpayment of rent. When he finally realizes what is going on, he proudly receives his son's medal.

One of the finest and most versatile character actors in the business, J. Carroll Naish, received an Academy Award nomination as Best Supporting Actor for his portrayal of the Mexican American father of Benny. Arturo De Cordova was excellent as the young fisherman, Joe Morales, who vies for the affection of the dead hero's girlfriend, Lolita Sierra, believably played by Dorothy Lamour. Along with De Cordova, the cast featured many Mexican American actors in principal roles and as extras.

During World War II, Hispanic soldiers won more Congressional Medals of Honor (12) than any other group in the U.S. armed forces.

Medicine Man (1992 BV)

D: John McTiernan
S: Tom Schulman and Sally Robinson
P: Andrew Vajna and Donna Dubrow
Cast: Sean Connery, Lorraine Bracco

Deep in the Amazon rain forest, a brilliant but eccentric research scientist, Dr. Campbell (Connery), is on the verge of astonishing the world with a major medical breakthrough, a cancer cure, but he's lost the formula and must now reinvent the elusive serum. The corporation sponsoring his research sends another biochemist, Dr. Crane (Bracco), to investigate the reclusive Campbell. They become caught up in a race against time to find the antidote before the coming destruction of their section of the rain forest to make way for a highway. Though it takes place in the Amazon, it was filmed in the jungles of Catemaco, Mexico, with some additional second-unit work in Brazil.

Although a great idea, the film was woefully lackluster in its direction and script, despite the efforts of Connery and Bracco to make it work, and suffers from one of the worst, most artificial, and unbelievable upbeat endings in years.

Mexican Hayride (1948 U)

D: Charles T. Barton
S: Oscar Brodney and John Grant
P: Robert Arthur
Cast: Bud Abbott, Lou Costello, Virginia Grey, Luba Malina, **Pedro De Cordoba**

Uninspired but mildly amusing Abbott and Costello romp through Universal's backlot Mexican street with Costello the fall guy for a group of con men with a fake mining operation in Mexico.

Joe Bascom (Costello), an American fugitive from justice, goes to Mexico to get Harry Lambert (Abbott) to confess. Joe is being pursued by two American detectives, and his old girlfriend Mary (Grey) is now a bullfighter working under the name of Montana in Mexico. Montana is about to throw a hat to a group of American tourists when she sees Joe, and in a rage she throws the hat at him. Because he catches the hat, Joe becomes the "Amigo Americano" and tours Mexico as an honored guest to symbolize Mexican American goodwill. Harry and his accomplice Dagmar (Malina), a Mexican spitfire type, use Joe's fame to put over another phony deal. The action culminates in a bullfight, with Joe making a very unlikely matador.

One of the highlights is Costello dancing a samba with a bull with the aid of trick photography. Costello also assumes a variety of disguises including a female tortilla vendor and a mariachi performer. Hispanic actors Chris-Pin Martin, Argentina Brunetti, Julian Rivero, Roque Ybarra, Felipe Turich, and Alex Montoya, among others, have supporting roles in the film.

Mexican Spitfire (1939 RKO)
 D: Leslie Goodwins
 S: Joseph A. Fields and Charles E. Roberts, based on a story by Fields
 P: Cliff Reid
Cast: **Lupe Velez**, Leon Errol

Actress Lupe Velez's career was revitalized in the B movie *Mexican Spitfire* series. In the first film in the series, made at RKO in 1939, a follow-up to *The Girl from Mexico* (1939), Velez introduced the character Carmelita, an exaggerated comedic stereotype of a Mexican woman living and dealing with life in the United States. Leon Errol co-starred in a dual role as Uncle Matt and Lord Basil. They made a very popular comic teaming, which wasn't originally planned as such. This was the second film in the series.

Mexican Spitfire at Sea (1942 RKO)
 D: Leslie Goodwins
 S: Jerry Cady and Charles E. Roberts
 P: Cliff Reid
Cast: **Lupe Velez**, Leon Errol

The "Mexican Spitfire" (Velez) gets herself and Uncle Matt (Errol) involved in all kinds of madcap situations on an ocean liner bound for Hawaii.

Mexican Spitfire Out West (1940 RKO)
 D: Leslie Goodwins
 S: Charles E. Roberts and Jack Townley, based on a story by Roberts
 P: Cliff Reid
Cast: **Lupe Velez**, Leon Errol

Carmelita's (Velez's) craving for more attention from her husband (Donald Woods) leads her to threaten divorce and run off to Reno, with Uncle Matt (Errol) in tow.

Mexican Spitfire Sees a Ghost (1942 RKO)
 D: Leslie Goodwins
 S: Charles E. Roberts and Monte Brice
 P: Cliff Reid
Cast: **Lupe Velez**, Leon Errol

The "Mexican Spitfire" in a haunted house that turns out to be the secret hideout of enemy agents making nitroglycerin.

Mexican Spitfire's Baby (1941 RKO)

D: Leslie Goodwins
S: Jerry Cady, Charles E. Roberts, and James Casey, based on a story by Roberts
P: Cliff Reid
Cast: **Lupe Velez**, Leon Errol

Uncle Matt (Errol) imports a French war orphan, who turns out to be a voluptuous young woman, in an attempt to calm the discord between his nephew (Charles "Buddy" Rogers) and his explosive niece (Velez).

Mexican Spitfire's Blessed Event (1943 RKO)

D: Leslie Goodwins
S: Charles E. Roberts and Dane Lussier, based on a story by Roberts
P: Bert Gilroy
Cast: **Lupe Velez**, Leon Errol

A garbled telegram indicates the birth of a baby to the "Mexican Spitfire," which prompts Lord Epping (Errol) to award a big business contract to the baby's father. In truth, the baby is really a baby ocelot and Carmelita (Velez) borrows a real baby in order to fool Lord Epping and help keep her husband's contract. This was the final film in the *Mexican Spitfire* series. A year after completion of the film, Lupe Velez found herself pregnant after a failed affair and committed suicide.

Mexican Spitfire's Elephant (1942 RKO)

D: Leslie Goodwins
S: Charles E. Roberts, based on a story by Goodwins and Roberts
P: Bert Gilroy
Cast: **Lupe Velez**, Leon Errol

Nutty plot about a smuggled toy elephant used as a hiding place for a valuable gem.

Mexicana (1945 Rep)

D: Alfred Santell
S: Frank Gill, Jr.
P: Alfred Santell
Cast: **Tito Guizar, Leo Carrillo**, Constance Moore, **Estelita Rodriguez**

The love-hate relationship between Mexican crooner "Pepe" Villarreal (Guizar) and American New York musical/comedy star Alison Calvert (Moore) in Mexico City. It was reissued in 1951 as *Beyond the Border*.

"The Hollywood version of the Good Neighbor Policy continues to portray Latin America in the standard plot and surreal satin and gloss of the routine studio musical," John T. McManus, *PM Exclusive* (10/18/45).

The Milagro Beanfield War (1988 U)

D: Robert Redford
S: David S. Ward, based on a novel by John Nichols
P: **Moctezuma Esparza**
Cast: Chick Vennera, **Julie Carmen**, Christopher Walken, **Ruben Blades, Sonia Braga**, Carlos Riquelme, **Natividad Vacio, Alberto Morin, Robert Carricart**, Freddy Fender

Contemporary tale of Joe Mondragon (Vennera), a lone New Mexico handyman who illegally irrigates his parched beanfield using water that has been earmarked for development. This tiny act snowballs, setting in motion a chain of events that have overwhelming consequences for both Joe and the people of his town.

The Milagro Beanfield War was based on a novel by John Nichols that was published in 1974. Producer Moctezuma Esparza acquired the rights to the novel in 1979 and actor/director Robert Redford expressed interest in making a film version (his second directorial effort) after his Academy Award–winning *Ordinary People* (1980).

"One of the things Bob and I talked about when we got together," says Esparza, in press notes on the movie's release, "was the importance of treating this with integrity, to try and open up opportunities for Hispanics."

Their approach extended behind the camera as well as in front of it. Many talented Chicanos got important production team jobs, including art director Joe Aubel, production manager David Wisnievitz, and construction coordinator Bill Maldonado.

The cast highlights some of the leading talents in the Latino acting community, including Chick Vennera as Joe Mondragon, Ruben Blades as Sheriff Bernabe Montoya, Sonia Braga as Ruby Archuleta, and Julie Carmen as Joe's wife, Nancy. Mexican comic actor Carlos Riquelme plays his first and only major role in an English-language production as Amarante.

Filming began in Las Truchas, New Mexico, in early August 1986 and finished in late November.

The film attempted to portray on the screen the Latin American literary tradition of "Magic Realism." In any event, however, it became an uneven blend of fantasy and reality and presented Hispanics as cute and slightly inept. Joe Mondragon was not presented with a strong enough characterization to ground the movie. Vennera as Mondragon did not suggest a salt-of-the-earth type of individual, coming off instead as weak and indecisive. His New York accent also got in the way of his believability as a New Mexico farmer. Sonia Braga was uncomfortable as Ruby Archuleta, and Carlos Riquelme almost stole the film with his portrayal of Amarante, the old man.

The film was much anticipated due to Redford's helming of the project along with David Ward's (*The Sting*) screenplay. It was hoped that it would be a watershed film for Hispanics in the film industry the way Steven Spielberg's *The Color Purple* (1985) was for blacks. The latter film was instrumental in launching the careers of Whoopi Goldberg, Oprah Winfrey, and Danny Glover. This did not happen with *The Milagro Beanfield War*, though Ruben Blades and Sonia Braga have gone on to successful Hollywood acting careers. The film received generally favorable reviews, but met with a lukewarm reception at the box office.

The Miracle of Our Lady of Fatima (1952 WB)

D: John Brahm
S: Cran Wilbur and James O'Hanlon
P: Bryan Foy
Cast: **Gilbert Roland**, Angela Clark, **Frank Silvera**

Reverent, affectionate, literate, and elaborate film of the true story of three small children who reported that they saw a vision of the Virgin Mary in a field near the village of Fatima, Portugal, in 1917.

Roland plays Hugo Da Silva, a disbeliever and a rascal who once was an aristocrat and follower of the church. He has a wry sense of humor, and he believes the children.

Fatima has become one of the greatest shrines in Christendom since the three children reported the apparition. The Virgin reportedly predicted the end of World War I and the beginning of World War II, and countless miracles and cures have been reported over the years. Filmed at the Warner Bros. Studios and at the Warner Bros. Ranch permanent Mexican village, with some alterations to make it pass for Portugal.

Gilbert Roland as Hugo Da Silva, a man who believes the children of Fatima when they say they have seen a vision of the Virgin Mary in *The Miracle of Our Lady of Fatima*.

Missing (1982 U)

    D: Constantin Costa-Gavras
    S: Donald Stewart and Constantin Costa-Gavras
    P: Edward Lewis and Constantin Costa-Gavras
  Cast: Jack Lemmon, Sissy Spacek

Greek director Costa-Gavras, known for political thrillers such as *State of Siege* (1973) and *Z* (1969), in his first American film tells the real-life story of Charles Horman, an American journalist who disappeared during the 1973 coup in Chile along with 2,500 Chileans. Horman was part of a band of Americans who were essentially trying to avoid the Vietnam War and other domestic turmoil, who moved to Chile to work for social reform and became trapped in the midst of a coup.

Sissy Spacek and Jack Lemmon portray Horman's wife and father, who battle the Chilean government and a complacent U.S. State Department (which led the protests and stirred controversy when the film was released) for word about the missing man. The American diplomats pretend to be helping but seem to know all along that the Chilean military authorities have already murdered young Horman.

Though the movie is based on actual events, Chile and Allende are never mentioned, in much the same way that the Greek colonels are never specifically mentioned in *Z*. This is a very European-style American movie eschewing brash challenge in favor of subversive whispers. Costa-Gavras chillingly captured the oppressive atmosphere and intense terror of a social system in upheaval through understated documentary-like texture and poetic imagery. For example, a frightened white horse is seen racing through the embattled streets at sunrise followed by an armed troop carrier, impersonal helicopters hold captured victims in searchlights before machine guns cut them down, and the killing becomes so overwhelming they must use a soccer stadium to retain prisoners and house the corpses. Although it reinforced the image of Latin America as a place of violent social upheaval, the film dealt very effectively with historic truth and managed to steer away from blatant stereotypes. It was filmed in studios in Mexico City, Acapulco, and Churubusco.

However, Stanley Kauffmann in the February 17, 1982, edition of the *New Republic* commented, "[While] Costa Gavras wanted to make a film attacking U.S. interference in Chile, using the Horman story as his focus, . . . that intent got watered down. . . . It never comes close to excitement. Whatever your views on the anti-Allende coup, it's boring to watch a film obviously on the subject in which Allende is never named and which carefully avoids having any view."

The Mission (1986 WB)

    D: Roland Joffé
    S: Robert Bolt
    P: Fernando Ghia and David Puttnam
 Cast: Robert De Niro, Jeremy Irons, Monirak Sisowath, Asuncion Ontiveros,
         Ray McAnally, Ronald Pickup, Cherie Lunghi, Liam Neeson

The story of the power struggle between church, in particular the Jesuit order, and state in colonial South America, *The Mission* dramatizes a period of colonization never before treated on film and about which very little has been written. The screenplay is by Robert Bolt (*Lawrence of Arabia* and *A Man for All Seasons*). The protagonists are Mendoza (De Niro), a Spanish mercenary and slave trader who kills his brother (a cameo appearance by Aidan Quinn) and then renounces his former life and decides to enter the priesthood to atone for his past misdeeds, and a Jesuit priest, Father Gabriel (Irons), with whom Mendoza tries to protect the Guarani Indians (even though the church has forbidden such actions).

The film was shot entirely in Argentina at the monumental Iguassú Falls and in Colombia in the sixteenth-century walled city of Cartagena and the jungle near Santa Marta. Director Roland Joffé used some 350 Waunana Indians from the Chaco region of Colombia, who were housed in a specially built village close to the location. In addition to salary, a trust fund for health and education was set up for them by the film's producers. Monirak Sisowath, a Cambodian who appeared in *The Killing Fields*, plays Ibaye, a Guarani Indian who becomes a Jesuit priest. Asuncion Ontiveros, who was born in Argentina and who is an Indian rights activist, also has a major role.

Joffé stated in press notes at the movie's release, "It's about South America, but it's about people. It's about choice, about power, about redemption, a luminous story on many levels."

The Mission won the Palme d'Or prize at the Cannes Film Festival and was nominated for seven Academy Awards including Best Picture of 1986, but won only a single Oscar, for Best Cinematography (Chris Menges).

Reviews for the film were mixed and widely divergent, but generally agreed about the majesty of the scenery and the earnestness and ambition of the themes presented. Irons and De Niro are very good, though De Niro's Mendoza is not quite believably Spanish.

Mr. Majestyk (1974 UA)

D: Richard Fleischer
S: Elmore Leonard
P: Walter Mirisch
Cast: Charles Bronson, **Linda Cristal, Alejandro Rey**

The Colorado melon farmer Mr. Majestyk (Bronson), an ex-Vietnam vet, hunts down and kills the Mafia gang that has terrorized the Mexican American farmworkers and ruined his crops. Leonard's script, however, delivers a better-than-average revenge movie that has its lighter moments.

With a name like Mr. Majestyk, we're not quite certain if Bronson is Mexican American or just the "Immigrant Everyman" with its echoes of Eastern European immigrants of days gone by, trying to suggest that Latin immigrants are no different from the Poles and Italians of the turn of the century, and treated as badly. Bronson does look the part of the Latin farmworker, and seems to sympathize with the farmworkers' plight. This is a typical Charles Bronson violent action movie with a bit of social relevance. Linda Cristal plays a Chicana activist who works with the farmworkers, a potentially interesting character that is given short shrift once the macho action gets going. Alejandro Rey is a friendly farmworker who gets his legs crushed for siding with Bronson.

Moon over Parador (1988 U)

D: Paul Mazursky
S: Leon Capetanos and Paul Mazursky, based on a story by Charles Booth
P: Paul Mazursky
Cast: Richard Dreyfuss, **Raul Julia, Sonia Braga, Fernando Rey, Charo**

This sophisticated, humorous farce is reminiscent of Anthony Hope's novel *The Prisoner of Zenda* and Mark Twain's novel *The Prince and the Pauper.*

On location in the fictional Latin American country of Parador, a struggling New York actor (Dreyfuss) is kidnapped and forced to impersonate the country's late dictator, creating outlandish consequences.

Richard Dreyfuss plays Jack Noah, who gets the role of his life when Parador's fascist strongman drinks himself to death the day before the elections. The chief of police (Julia) then forces Noah under threat of death to assume the role of president. Noah's confidence grows with each speech and with personal support from the dead leader's sultry mistress (Braga), a champion of Parador's downtrodden masses. But when guerrilla fighters strike, Noah wonders if it might be time to move on to a new role.

This film somewhat subscribes to the tired notion of an American being needed to save a Latin American country from itself. The movie was filmed in Brazil.

Murieta (1965 WB)

D: George Sherman
S: James O'Hanlon, based on a story by O'Hanlon
P: Jose Sainz de Vicuna
Cast: Jeffrey Hunter

Jeffrey Hunter plays the legendary Mexican bandit Joaquin Murieta, who seeks revenge during the 1849 Gold Rush in California when his young wife is killed by three racist American miners. Murieta swears vengeance and sets out to find the killers. Made in Spain against desert backgrounds although the story actually took place in the foothills of the High Sierras of California, it has the trappings of a "spaghetti western." Slow moving and ponderous, there is nothing special or out of the ordinary in its execution.

The story of Murieta cries out to be produced with a top-notch cast and intelligent scripting, in an authentic manner, in much the same way as Robert Altman's *McCabe and Mrs. Miller* (1971) or Robert Young's *Ballad of Gregorio Cortez* (1983).

My Darling Clementine (1946 TCF)

D: **John Ford**

S: Samuel G. Engel and Winston Miller, based on a story by Sam Hellman from the novel *Wyatt Earp, Frontier Marshall* by Stuart N. Lake

P: Samuel G. Engel

Cast: Henry Fonda, Victor Mature, Walter Brennan, Linda Darnell

My Darling Clementine centers on the true story of the Earp brothers, the Clanton gang, Doc Holliday, and the famous gunfight at the O.K. Corral in Tombstone, Arizona, in the 1880s.

The Wyatt Earp–Doc Holliday partnership in the Earp-Clanton feud had been a popular subject for westerns since the mid-1930s. Cesar Romero played Wyatt Earp in *Frontier Marshall* in 1939, also for Fox.

Director John Ford chose to emphasize the polarity between good and evil, adding the fictional women Chihuahua and Clementine, the archetypal dark and fair women of American fiction, and portraying the Earps as heroes, when both the Earps and Clantons were probably equally corrupt in real life.

Chihuahua (Darnell), a Mexican prostitute, is petulant, scheming, dishonest, and unfaithful. She dies at the end of the film in typical Hollywood code justice. This is the third film in which Darnell plays a Latin.

When Wyatt (Fonda) first takes the job as marshal of Tombstone, she tells him, "This is Doc Holiday's town." As the plot develops it becomes Earp's town. Chihuahua dotes on Doc (Mature) and turns jealous when Doc's ex-fiancée from the East, Clementine (Cathy Downs), arrives in town. Clementine meets Wyatt, and he becomes smitten with her. Things turn serious when Wyatt notices Chihuahua wearing a medallion that belonged to his murdered brother, Jim. She confesses that it was given to her by Billy Clanton (John Ireland), who then shoots Chihuahua.

Linda Darnell (left) as Chihuahua, a Mexican prostitute, and Victor Mature (right) as Doc Holliday, in John Ford's *My Darling Clementine*.

Doc resumes some of his former medical status when he operates on Chihuahua. She dies a few hours later, and Doc then sides with the Earps in their battle with the Clantons at the O.K. Corral. All the Clantons die as does Doc. The town moves away from outlaws like the Clantons and social misfits like Chihuahua and Doc Holliday to ordinary folks and civilization in the form of Earp and Clementine.

This was Ford's first film after serving in World War II, and also the first in which he exhibits doubts as to the nature of heroism and the American experience of western history.

My Man and I (1952 MGM)

D: William Wellman
S: John Fante and Jack Leonard
P: Stephen Ames
Cast: **Ricardo Montalban**, Claire Trevor, Wendell Corey, Shelley Winters, **Jose Torvay**, Jack Elam, Pascual Garcia Pena

Ricardo Montalban plays Chu Chu, a Mexican American farmworker in California who has just become a citizen and whose prized possession is a letter from the President congratulating him on his achievement. He spends his money not on drink (as so many of his compatriots are pictured doing) but on encyclopedias.

He takes a farm job with Mexican-hating Ansel Ames (Corey). Mrs. Ames (Trevor), a sultry and neglected woman, makes advances toward Chu Chu, which he rebuffs. He is in love with a suicidal taxi dancer named Nancy (Winters). Upon completion of the job, Ames pays him with a bad check, and Chu Chu tries unsuccessfully to collect. In the struggle, Ames is accidentally wounded with his own gun and coerces his wife to testify that Chu Chu shot him.

Chu Chu is convicted, but his friends force the Ameses to confess their perjury. Chu Chu is cleared of the charges and reunited with his true love, Nancy.

Jose Torvay, Jack Elam, and Pascual Garcia Pena lend fun to the script as Chu Chu's buddies, at one point using his volumes of encyclopedias to sit on during a poker game.

The fact that Chu Chu believes in the American system and that his friends take matters into their own hands by psychologically pressing the Ameses refreshingly demonstrates a nonpassive role for the Mexican American. The subject of integration is introduced through Chu Chu's love for Nancy, but the suggestion is that it is possible only with the poor white trash which Nancy seems to represent. Superior acting saves a script that is fairly mediocre, despite its clear echoes of John Steinbeck's fiction.

Mystery Street (1950 MGM)

D: John Sturges
S: Sydney Boehm and Richard Brooks, based on an unpublished story by Leonard Spigelgass
P: Frank E. Taylor
Cast: **Ricardo Montalban**, Sally Forrest, Elsa Lanchester

Ricardo Montalban is Pete Moralas, a Portuguese-American Boston police detective investigating the murder of a well-to-do amateur hooker known to socialize with members of the Cape Cod–Harvard blue-blood set. Moralas gets involved with the case because the body of the dead girl is found in the Portuguese section of the town in which he works. The thrust of the film is the demonstration of scientific techniques as applied to crime detection through the pioneering work of the Harvard University Department of Forensic Medicine. It was filmed partly in and around Boston and is a refreshing change-of-pace mystery/drama with Montalban as a Latin investigating Boston's high society, a character out of his element who is characterized without being patronized or condescended to.

The Naked Dawn (1955 U)

    D: Edgar G. Ulmer
    S: Nina and Herman Schneider
    P: James Q. Radford
Cast: Arthur Kennedy, Betta St. John, **Eugene Iglesias**

This film explores the corrosive effect the prospect of easy money has on a Mexican farmer (Iglesias) and his wife (St. John).

Santiago (Kennedy) hires the farmer to help him collect on the money from a freight train holdup, thus putting temptation in the way of the indigent farmer. Previously satisfied with his modest lot, the farmer now plans Kennedy's death in order to obtain the ill-gotten loot.

The film plays like a mixture of *The Pearl* (1948) and *The Treasure of the Sierra Madre* (1948) with good performances in a very downbeat story that lacks the emotional and artistic punch of its predecessors.

The Naked Jungle (1954 Par)

    D: Byron Haskin
    S: Ranald MacDougall and Philip Yordan, based on the story "Leiningen Versus the Ants" by Carl Stephenson
    P: George Pal
Cast: Charlton Heston, Eleanor Parker, William Conrad

Drama about a mail order bride (Parker) arriving at a South American plantation run by a lonely American (Heston) who comes into conflict with her. However, they must all band together when an army of killer ants threatens to destroy everything in its path, including the plantation. Heston refers to having civilized the Indians by taking them out of the jungle, giving them jobs, and developing the land, though he acknowledges their strength and intelligence as descendants of the Mayas.

The Naked Maja (1959 UA)

    D: Henry Koster and Mario Russo
    S: Georgio Prosperi and Norman Corwin, based on a story by Oscar Saul and Talbot Jennings
    P: Goffredo Lombardo
Cast: Anthony Franciosa, Ava Gardner

Tempestuous love affair between famous Spanish painter Goya (Franciosa) and the Duchess of Alba (Gardner). His painting of the noblewoman in the nude scandalized eighteenth-century Spain.

This was an American-Italian co-production filmed in Spain. Gardner and Franciosa were fine in their roles, though the film is uninvolving and slow moving, but spectacularly photographed.

Nancy Goes to Rio (1949 MGM)

    D: Robert Z. Leonard
    S: Sidney Sheldon, based on a story by Jane Hall, Frederick Kohner, and Ralph Block
    P: Joe Pasternak
Cast: Ann Sothern, Jane Powell, **Xavier Cugat, Carmen Miranda**, Barry Sullivan, **Fortunio Bonanova**

A mother (Sothern) and daughter (Powell), both actresses, are unwilling competitors for the same part in a Rio theatrical production and for the same man (Sullivan). There is a glaring error on a painted studio backdrop: the Corcovado and Sugarloaf

Mountain, two of Rio's most famous sights, are joined together even though they are geographically separate.

To this fluffy musical/comedy filmed at MGM Studios, Miranda adds a musical bright spot.

The Navy Comes Through (1942 RKO)

    D: A. Edward Sutherland
    S: Roy Chanslor and Aeneas MacKenzie
    P: Islin Aurtes
 Cast: Pat O'Brien, George Murphy, Jackie Cooper, **Desi Arnaz**

Story of a naval gun crew aboard a freighter in the Atlantic during World War II. Desi Arnaz plays Tarriba, a Cuban enlistee who hopes to do what he can to serve America.

The Night of the Iguana (1964 MGM)

    D: **John Huston**
    S: Anthony Veiller and **John Huston**, based on the play by Tennessee Williams
    P: Ray Stark
 Cast: Richard Burton, Deborah Kerr, Ava Gardner

John Huston created a modern and adult version of the romantic image of Mexico with his film of Tennessee Williams's *The Night of the Iguana*.

Director John Huston and cinematographer Gabriel Figueroa provide a romantic and visually stunning image of Mexico in *The Night of the Iguana*, with Richard Burton as a defrocked minister and Ava Gardner (center) as a voluptuous innkeeper who has two Mexican maraca boys at her beck and call.

It paints Mexico as an exotic land of unbridled passions, steamy sex, exotic tropical vistas, friendly natives, and a refuge in a primal setting from the problems of civilized white society.

The story is of a defrocked American minister (Burton) who conducts tours for lonely women out of a run-down Mexican hotel. Complex psychological interactions form the basis of the drama. Ava Gardner is the sexy, boozy hotel owner who has two Mexican maraca muscle boys at her sexual beck and call.

The publicity surrounding the off-screen and on-screen antics of Huston, Williams, Burton and his then wife Elizabeth Taylor, and Gardner in the Ray Stark production fueled the imaginations of a generation of moviegoers.

Puerto Vallarta and Mismaloya beach became synonymous with an adult romantic Mexico, which turned the location from a tiny fishing village to a much sought-after world-class vacation destination. It was filmed largely with a Mexican crew with Gabriel Figueroa as the cinematographer.

In a 1984 interview with Luis Reyes, Huston revealed his feelings about Mexico. "I never wanted to make a travelogue of cliches about Mexico. Usually Americans see only one aspect of Mexico, the tourism. Mexico is a country with so many faces, and only through living there and going around can you get to know everything about its heart, or hearts I should say." He continued, "There's a savage face to Mexico, and another, benign and gentle, a deep humanity."

Notorious (1946 RKO)
 D: Alfred Hitchcock
 S: Ben Hecht, based on a theme by Hitchcock
 P: Alfred Hitchcock
 Cast: Cary Grant, Ingrid Bergman, Claude Rains, **Antonio Moreno**, Luis Serrano, **Tina Menard**

Brazil is the background, but this is not a film about rumbas, congas, and tropical romance. T.R. Devlin (Grant) is an American agent who enlists a Nazi's daughter, Alicia Huberman (Bergman), for an espionage mission in Rio de Janeiro. The plan is for her to infiltrate a Nazi spy ring operating out of Brazil by marrying its leader (Rains) in order to betray him to the OSS.

This melodramatic love story features Hitchcock's stylish grace of execution and mastery of film form. Antonio Moreno plays Senor Ortiza and Luis Serrano plays Dr. Silva. Tina Menard plays a maid.

Old Gringo (1989 Col)
 D: **Luis Puenzo**
 S: **Luis Puenzo** and Aida Batnik, based on the novel *El Gringo Viejo* by Carlos Fuentes
 P: Lois Bonfiglio
 Cast: Jane Fonda, Gregory Peck, **Jimmy Smits**, **Pedro Armendariz, Jr.**

Directed by Luis Puenzo (director of the 1985 Best Foreign Language Film Oscar winner, *The Official Story*), *Old Gringo* is a curious film, directed and written by an Argentinian (Puenzo) from a novel by Mexican novelist Carlos Fuentes. Yet the film seems to support the idea of Americans finding Mexico a place to live out their fantasies at the expense of the Mexicans. Jane Fonda starred in and produced the film.

It is the story of a romantic triangle between the aging writer Ambrose Bierce (Peck), a spinster schoolteacher (Fonda) in Mexico during the height of the Mexican Revolution, and a young general for Pancho Villa (Smits).

It is based loosely on the last days of turn-of-the-century writer and newspaperman Ambrose Bierce, who crossed the border into Mexico not long after the Mexican

Gregory Peck, Jane Fonda, and Jimmy Smits (right), who portrays a young Mexican general, are involved in a romantic triangle in *Old Gringo*, an epic adventure story of passion and power set against the backdrop of the Mexican Revolution.

Revolution erupted in 1910 and was never heard from again. *Old Gringo* would probably never have been made had not Jane Fonda been captivated by the fictional character of Harriet Winslow. She is a prim and proper Washington schoolteacher who goes to Mexico as a tutor for the children of a rich *hacendado* and finds herself in the middle of a revolution while falling in love with the illiterate peasant General Arroyo.

Old Gringo was budgeted at $25 million and required hundreds of extras, period costumes, horses, and wranglers. It was filmed on soundstages at Churubusco Studios in Mexico City and at a hacienda just north of the city and in the cities of Zacatecas and Torreón.

The Old Gringo as played by Gregory Peck seeks the peace of death, while Harriet Winslow (Fonda) seeks the challenge of a new life. General Arroyo (Smits) represents vitality, a pure macho stud, and Harriet is interested in the sexuality and mystique of the Latin male. As a general, however, he is indecisive and ineffectual in leading his people. Luna, his woman, does not even make an attempt to take her man back from the Winslow character. Mexicans come off as brutal and barbaric (savage, unwashed, and uneducated), and the Americans are noble, loyal, and sensitive. The predominant image of Mexican women in the film is as whores. Certain cultural differences are clearly emphasized, but there is more to Mexican culture than peasant revolutionaries, corridas, eating tortillas, and giving in to your passions even in time of war and chaos.

Old Gringo has a historical sweep and epic grandeur that are true to the spirit of the way the Revolution caught the imagination of the American public.

Winslow, however, is not profoundly changed by her experiences in Mexico, and she returns to the United States somewhat chastened. Because of the intrusion of these gringos in a land where they don't belong, General Arroyo loses his life. He is a troubled soul who wallows in indecision over his past and his future.

Harriet Winslow's request to have the body of Ambrose Bierce, the Old Gringo, results in the death of Arroyo. In the film, American authorities find Villa (Armendariz) quickly and exert pressure on him in the midst of the revolution to return the body of the American. In fact, the U.S. government sent General Pershing and an army of cavalry to find Villa, and after six months of riding all over northern Mexico, the expedition returned to the States exhausted and empty-handed.

The Old Man and the Sea (1958 WB)

D: John Sturges
S: Peter Viertel
P: Leland Hayward
Cast: Spencer Tracy, Felipe Pazos, Harry Bellaver

This film is based on the novel by Ernest Hemingway published in 1952, which won the Pulitzer Prize for fiction. Spencer Tracy stars as Santiago, an old Cuban fisherman. Tracy, of Irish descent, had previously played a Portuguese in *Captains Courageous* (1937) and a Mexican American in *Tortilla Flat* (1942).

An old Cuban sailor, Santiago is reduced in his old age to making a living as a fisherman. For 84 days he has had no luck and has lived on the charity of a small boy (Pazos) who idolizes him. Seeking to defy this string of bad luck, the old man ventures far from coastal waters and hooks a great marlin. He pits his failing strength against his deep-sea antagonist. In his lonely vigil he feels a kinship with the vastness of the ocean and its creatures. When the climax comes, he is strong enough to pull in the marlin, which is longer than his boat and harpoon. With the prized fish lashed to his frail craft he sets sail for home. But the carcass is repeatedly attacked by sharks. In a nightmare struggle he loses his knife and harpoon but beats off the sharks. Weary and exhausted, he beaches his craft with nothing to show for his exertions but the bare spine and useless tail. He gains a brief moment of fame, for his fellows exclaim after seeing the remains, "There never was such a fish."

Spencer Tracy as Santiago, an old Cuban fisherman, befriends a young boy, played by Felipe Pazos, in *The Old Man and the Sea*.

The film began production in 1956 with Fred Zinnemann as director near Cojimar, Cuba, the setting of the original story. Tracy arrived five weeks prior to shooting to get in shape and to get his face tanned and properly weather beaten. A young 11-year-old Cuban boy with no prior acting experience, Felipe Pazos, won the role of the young boy after an extensive search by Zinnemann. Hemingway went with a second-unit camera crew to Talara, Peru, attempting to catch the largest marlin fish he could grab. The footage would be utilized in the final film.

Due to differences of opinion with producer Hayward and star Tracy, Zinnemann left the project and was replaced by John Sturges. The production was beset by problems and much of the filming took place in a water tank at Warner Bros. Studios. It lasted a total of six and a half months, including four months with Tracy and a crew of 100 in Cuba. An additional two weeks of filming two miles off the Kona Coast of Hawaii with Tracy and a crew of 50 were required to get the final exterior scenes for proper sea and sky effects.

Faithful to Hemingway to a fault, the film is perhaps the most literal word-for-word rendition of a written story ever filmed. It is essentially a one-character drama with voice-over narration and dialogue by Tracy. The camera stays with Tracy on the boat throughout his ordeal and personal triumph.

The universal story of man against the elements and his kinship with nature was difficult to transfer to film when most of the action is the inner thoughts of a man alone in a boat for days battling a fish. Critics were torn over the approach to the film, but most praised Tracy's acting efforts although they felt, good as he was, that he could not carry the film by himself. Tracy won an Academy Award nomination for Best Actor of 1958 as did James Wong Howe for Best Cinematography. The film won an Oscar for its music score by Dmitri Tiomkin.

Felipe Pazos was not invited to the Washington, D.C., premiere of the film in 1958, which was hosted by then Cuban ambassador Don Arroyo. Felipe's father had played a big role with Fidel Castro's revolutionaries before fleeing to the United States just a few months prior to the premiere. Arroyo represented the Batista regime.

One-Eyed Jacks (1961 Par)

D: Marlon Brando
S: Guy Trosper and Calder Willingham, based on the novel *The Authentic Death of Hendry Jones* by Charles Neider
P: Frank Rosenberg
Cast: Marlon Brando, Karl Malden, **Pina Pellicer**, **Katy Jurado**, Ben Johnson, **Larry Duran**, **Miriam Colon**, **Rodolfo Acosta**, Margarita Cordova

One of two bank robbers on the run in Mexico is deserted by his accomplice and spends five years in a Mexican prison. When he finally escapes with another prisoner, Johnny Rio (Brando) and his new accomplice, Modesto (Duran), join up with two other bandits and set out for California to rob a small-town bank. In Monterey, California, the four meet up with Rio's original partner in crime, Dad Longworth (Malden), who is now a respectable sheriff married to a Mexican woman, Maria (Jurado), with a stepdaughter Louisa (Pellicer). Rio strikes up a romance with Louisa as a way of getting to her stepfather. Later, Rio's group carries out the bank robbery without Rio. Longworth captures the innocent Rio and intends to execute him. Maria tells Longworth that Louisa is pregnant by Rio. Longworth lashes out at his wife, saying, "Is this the thanks I get for taking you out of the beanfields?"

The meaning of the film's title has to do with two sides of man's nature, one visible, the other (like the unseen reverse side of the one-eyed jack in a deck of cards) remaining in shadow. For the good man, the shadow side is evil.

This unusual revenge western, though overlong and somewhat slow, is highlighted by in-depth characterizations and beautiful color cinematography. Brando

Katy Jurado, Marlon Brando, Karl Malden,
and Pina Pellicer in *One-Eyed Jacks*.

points up the richness of the Mexican American culture of Monterey through the strong women characters played by Jurado and Pellicer. Larry Duran as Modesto, Rios's bandit friend, is allowed to be a human being instead of a stereotype. Lush romantic use is made of the Monterey location seascapes and the fiesta atmosphere. In the Mexico sequence Brando shows us a senorita and a whore (Colon), but as real characters, not stereotypes. Felipe Turich and Nacho Galindo have minor supporting roles in the film. The film is similar to *The Appaloosa*, a western Brando starred in several years later in 1966. Directed by Sidney J. Furie and much different in tone and style, *The Appaloosa* shares the loner-revenge motif in a Hispanic setting.

One from the Heart (1982 Zoetrope/Col)

   D: Francis Ford Coppola
   S: Francis Ford Coppola and Armyan Bernstein, based on a story by Bernstein
   P: Fred Roos, Gary Frederickson, and Armyan Bernstein
Cast: Frederic Forrest, Teri Garr, **Raul Julia**, Nastassia Kinski

Fantasy/musical acted out on a stylized studio set of Las Vegas with all the aplomb and dash that one would expect from a Coppola movie paying homage to the history of Latin-influenced Hollywood movies. Its importance is that the film took note of the definitive film images of the past. Raul Julia as a Latin lover type acknowledged the images and the fantasies that Hollywood created and that helped to shape our collective images.

During the course of a single day, Hank (Forrest) and Frannie (Garr) after many years of marriage have a tiff and take up with chance romantic partners, although they still love each other. Hank takes up with Leila (Kinski) and Frannie takes up with Ray (Julia), a tuxedoed Latin singer and piano player who turns out to be a waiter. At one point Frannie and Ray do the tango on a Hollywood South Seas island set. Later, they nuzzle while "The Carioca" (which Fred Astaire and Ginger Rogers danced in *Flying Down to Rio*) plays on the record player.

One Good Cop (1991 BV)

D: Heywood Gould
S: Heywood Gould
P: Laurence Mark
Cast: Michael Keaton, Rene Russo, Kevin Conway, **Benjamin Bratt, Tony Plana, Rachel Ticotin**

In this story of a moral dilemma, dedicated police detective Artie Lewis (Keaton) must choose between taking revenge on the punks who are indirectly responsible for his partner Diroma's (Anthony LaPaglia's) death and looking after Diroma's three young daughters, who are left in the care of Lewis and his wife. Putting the possible adoption of the children in jeopardy, Lewis, with the help of a streetwise undercover cop named Grace (Ticotin), who has managed to work her way into the drug lord's inner circle, sees a chance to steal a fortune from Latin drug lord Beniamino (Plana), who was one of those indirectly responsible for Diroma's death.

What should have been a much more interesting film is given the typical Hollywood "dumbing down" treatment, turning a possibly interesting moral dilemma into a morally questionable, violence-driven, cliched cops-and-robbers movie about (yet again!) Latin drug dealers. These images, however, are offset by police officers Felix (Bratt) and Grace (Ticotin).

100 Rifles (1969 TCF)

D: Tom Gries
S: Clair Huffaker and Tom Gries, based on the novel *The Californio* by Robert MacLeod
P: Marvin Schwartz
Cast: **Raquel Welch, Jim Brown, Burt Reynolds, Fernando Lamas**

An American lawman (Brown) crosses the border into Mexico in pursuit of Mexican outlaw Yaqui Joe (Reynolds), who has stolen rifles in order to arm the Indians against a Mexican general (Lamas) who is bent on annihilating them. Both are captured by the general and saved by a rebel Indian woman (Welch). They join forces in order to do away with the general. In the ensuing battle the Indian woman dies but the general and his forces are defeated. The lawman returns to the United States, and Yaqui Joe finds something he can believe in among the Indians.

Welch and Reynolds make believable Latins, Welch being of Bolivian background and Reynolds of part Native American heritage. Reynolds almost steals the film with his tough but fun bandido characterization, giving audiences a preview of the easygoing charm he would put to good use in his later starring films. The movie was filmed in Spain.

Burt Reynolds, Raquel Welch, and
Jim Brown engage in a shoot-out
with a Mexican general (portrayed by
Fernando Lamas, not shown) in *100 Rifles*.

One Way Street (1950 U)

  D: **Hugo Fregonese**
  S: Lawrence Kimble, based on his story "Death on a Side Street"
  P: Leonard Goldstein
Cast: James Mason, Marta Toren, Dan Duryea, **Rodolfo Acosta,**
      Margarito Luna, Tito Renaldo, **George J. Lewis,** Robert Espinoza,
      Jose Dominguez, Julia Montoya

A doctor (Mason) who treats gangsters in Los Angeles steals $200,000 from a gang-
ster and his girlfriend (Toren). He flees to Mexico, and en route his plane is forced
down near a small village, where he hides out and begins to find himself while
treating the natives and restoring their health. He lives with the fear of the inevitable day when he will be found by the gangsters.

    This routine crime melodrama, with an able cast and good direction by
Fregonese, who contrasted the dignity of the villagers with the ruthlessness of the
gangsters, was filmed partly on location in Mexico.

Typical Hollywood banana republic set for *Only Angels Have Wings*, a story about mail pilots who fly cargo over the Andes Mountains in Peru.

Only Angels Have Wings (1938 Col)

D: Howard Hawks
S: Jules Furthman, based on a story by Hawks
P: Howard Hawks
Cast: Cary Grant, Jean Arthur, **Rita Hayworth**, Melissa Sierra, Richard Barthelmess, Noah Beery, Jr.

Set in Barranca, Peru, the film tells the story of a group of mail-plane pilots in love with danger who battle storms and hardships to fly cargo over the Andes.

Geoff Carter (Grant) is the owner of the airplane firm, driving his fliers to undertake almost suicidal trips in decrepit planes in order to ensure a government subsidy that will put his business on a secure financial footing. Bonnie Lee (Jean Arthur), a showgirl who falls in love with Geoff and leaves her job to be with him, is attracted by his courage but repelled by his ruthlessness. Carter initially ignores her but gradually reveals the vulnerable side of his character. Judith (Hayworth) is Carter's old flame and is now married to Bat McPherson (Barthelmess). Melissa Sierra is Lily, a native girl who loves the young pilot Joe (Beery). Hayworth made an impression after years of toiling in B pictures.

Only Once in a Lifetime (1978 Movie Time Films)

D: Alejandro Grattan
S: Alejandro Grattan
P: **Moctezuma Esparza**
Cast: Miguel Robelo, Sheree North, Socorro Swan, Estrellita Lopez

Moctezuma Esparza produced this film about Dominguez (Robelo), a Chicano artist living in a Los Angeles barrio who has lost his desire to live. Dominguez is haunted by the memory of his dead wife and, though talented, limits his own artistic success by refusing to paint in a style that will attract buyers. He begins to be transformed when he meets a Chicana schoolteacher who helps him embrace life again.

In this technically proficient film, the sensitive realism of the barrio culture of the time is felt throughout. In an interview with Luis Reyes, Esparza recalled that "[making the film] was a satisfactory artistic experience, but an economic disaster. We previewed the film and got a warm reception from audiences and critics, but when we released it, nobody paid to see it."

Grattan is a Texas filmmaker, and Robelo has acted in theater and TV. *Only Once in a Lifetime* is one of the first feature films written, produced, directed, and cast by Spanish-surnamed people in Hollywood. The film is considered a Chicano film and was made on a $500,000 budget.

Our Man in Havana (1960 Col)

   D: Sir Carol Reed
   S: Graham Greene, based on his novel
   P: Sir Carol Reed
Cast: Alec Guinness, Maureen O'Hara, Ernie Kovacs, Ralph Richardson, Noel Coward

Mystery/comedy satire set in the period before the Castro revolution involves a British vacuum cleaner salesman (Guinness) turned British agent in Havana, in a fictional spy ring whose hilarious beginnings take on a dramatic aspect when Guinness's so-called phony agents begin to be killed by real agents in the Cuban capital. The film was critically acclaimed, but its sophisticated humor did not connect with American audiences, from whom the film met with a poor box-office reception.

Sir Carol Reed wanted to film in Cuba, but the overthrow of Batista in January 1959 left the possibility of filming there seriously in doubt. Amazingly, less than four months later, on April 13, 1959, cameras began rolling on the film after assurances from the new Cuban government under Castro that everything would go well. There was an advance agreement with Cuban labor unions that provided for 37 Cuban technicians to work on the film, an additional 21 persons to be employed in some facet of production, and over 1,000 paid extras. During the filming, American comic genius Ernie Kovacs, playing a Batista general, narrowly escaped death when he wandered off the set in uniform and was confronted by an armed Castro policeman, ready to shoot him, believing him to be a Batista supporter. After filming for five weeks in Cuba, the production moved on to London.

The Outrage (1964 MGM)

   D: Martin Ritt
   S: Michael Kanin
   P: A. Ronald Lubin
Cast: Paul Newman, Claire Bloom, Laurence Harvey, **Howard da Silva**

Indifferent remake of the Kurosawa film *Rashomon* in an Old West setting with an improbable blue-eyed all-American, Paul Newman, as darkened-up Mexican bandit Juan Carrasco. The story concerns the murder and rape of stagecoach passengers by a Mexican bandit as told from the points of view of the survivors.

"Paul Newman emerges as a sort of junior grade Leo Carrillo, spitting and spewing and wallowing in dialect and playing the villain, the lecher, the social outcast, the lover and the coward to the hilt for his own very private edification," Judith Crist, *New York Herald Tribune* (10/8/64).

"Mr. Newman . . . steams his way through the role of the supposed villain with notable effect," *New York Telegraph* (10/8/64).

The Ox-Bow Incident (1943 TCF)

  D: William Wellman
  S: Lamar Trotti, based on the novel by Walter Van Tilburg Clark
  P: Lamar Trotti
Cast: Henry Fonda, Dana Andrews, Mary Beth Hughes, **Anthony Quinn,** Francis Ford, **Chris-Pin Martin**

The story of three drifters (Andrews, Quinn, and Ford) who are summarily tried and hanged with no evidence for cattle rustling and murder. The film is a searing indictment of lynch-mob frontier justice and is considered by many to be one of the finest westerns ever made. In the end it is discovered that the hanged men did not commit the crime.

Anthony Quinn, billed as simply "Mexican," is lynched with his companions. At first he attempts to pass himself off as an ignorant Mexican, fulfilling the mob's stereotypical expectations with a series of "No Sabe" answers to the campfire interrogation. When he finally drops the ruse, he reveals himself as an articulate, intelligent, tough-talking hombre. The film was made at the insistence of star Henry Fonda and director William Wellman but proved too downbeat for audiences during World War II.

Panama Hattie (1942 MGM)

  D: Norman Z. McLeod
  S: Jack McGowan and Wilkie Mahoney, based on the play by Herbert Fields, B.G. De Sylva, and Cole Porter
  P: Arthur Freed
Cast: Ann Sothern, Red Skelton, Dan Dailey, Jr., Lena Horne

A showgirl in Panama (Sothern) helps to capture Nazi agents. The film introduced singing newcomer Lena Horne in a musical number.

Panama Sal (1957 Rep)

  D: William Witney
  S: Arnold Belgard
  P: Edward J. White
Cast: **Elena Verdugo,** Edward Kemmer, **Carlos Rivas,** **Jose Gonzalez-Gonzalez**

A wealthy American and his two buddies crashland a plane in Panama, where they find a sensational calypso singer at a nightclub whom they believe they can turn into a star back in the States.

This mildly amusing but conventional grade B romantic musical/comedy was one of the last Republic productions. It was a disappointing film return for Elena Verdugo after her success on television in the popular long-running series "Meet Millie."

Pan-Americana (1945 RKO)

  D: John H. Auer
  S: Lawrence Kimble, based on a story by Frederick Kohner and Auer
  P: John H. Auer
Cast: Phillip Terry, Audrey Long, Robert Benchley, Eve Arden, **Alma Beltran,** **Julian Rivero**

Film constructed to showcase the talents of various Latin American performers through the adventures of a group of American journalists who head south of the border to research a feature story. Along the way they stop off in such countries as Cuba, Mexico, and Brazil just long enough for a musical number in each. The film

Miguelito Valdes (center) is only one of many Latin performers featured in the musical extravaganza *Pan-Americana*.

is important in that it provides as a permanent film record of many Latin performers of the period at their musical best, such as Miguelito Valdes, Isabelita, Chuy Castillion, the Padilla Sisters, Chuy Reyes and his Orchestra, and Nestor Amaral and his Samba Band. Alma Beltran plays Miss Guatemala.

Pancho Villa (1972 Scotia Int.)

  D: Eugenio Martin
  S: Julian Halevy
  P: Bernard Gordon
Cast: Telly Savalas, Clint Walker, Anne Francis, Chuck Connors

Savalas makes an improbable bald-headed Pancho Villa in this badly made fictional recounting of the raid on Columbus, New Mexico, by Villa, filmed in Spain.

Passion (1954 RKO)

  D: Allan Dwan
  S: Beatrice Dresher, Joseph Leytes, and Howard Estabrook, based on a story by Dresher, Leytes, and Miguel Padilla
  P: Benedict Bogeaus
Cast: Cornel Wilde, Yvonne De Carlo, **Rodolfo Acosta, Alex Montoya, Rosa Turich**

Juan Obregon (Wilde) is a young rancher who seeks vengeance when his wife and friends are murdered by Mexicans disputing land rights. De Carlo plays two roles as the murdered wife, Tonya, and her younger sister, Rosa. This routine western in an early California setting is highlighted by location photography in the California Sierras.

Pat Garrett and Billy the Kid (1973 MGM)

D: **Sam Peckinpah**
S: Rudy Wurlitzer
P: Gordon Carroll
Cast: James Coburn, Kris Kristofferson, Jason Robards, R.G. Armstrong, Slim Pickens, **Katy Jurado, Emilio Fernandez**

In 1880s New Mexico, Pat Garrett (Coburn) warns young Billy the Kid (Kristofferson) that he must do his duty and capture Billy in spite of their former friendship. After Billy escapes, Garrett catches up with Billy and is forced to kill him.

Peckinpah's special talent for blending violence and a poetic vision of the Old West is very much in evidence in this, his last western. In killing Billy, Garrett not only seems to signal the end of the fierce idealism that had characterized the 1960s as well as the West of the 1880s as it gave way to more sedate, conservative civilization, he in effect also seals his own fate at the hands of the mainly faceless corporate types who hired him.

Katy Jurado is the wife of an old sheriff (Pickens) who goes to her husband's aid, shotgun in hand, to rid a hornet's nest of outlaws at Garrett's request. She weeps as the old sheriff, who has been shot during the outlaw confrontation, dies while he sits on a rock in the sunset. Emilio Fernandez plays a Mexican rancher who is attacked and left for dead by a rival gang of outlaws.

Billy's gang is seen bedding down some Mexican whores, and Maria, Billy's girl-friend, is played by Kris Kristofferson's then wife, Rita Coolidge, whom Billy also beds down. There are no virginal senoritas in Peckinpah's vision. Jorge Russek plays a nontraditional Mexican outlaw called Silva who wears a Stetson instead of a sombrero. Though the story takes place in New Mexico, it was filmed in Durango, Mexico.

The Pawnbroker (1965 AA)

D: Sidney Lumet
S: David Friedkin and Morton Fine, based on the novel by Edmund Lewis Wallant
P: Roger Lewis and Philip Langner
Cast: Rod Steiger, Geraldine Fitzgerald, **Jaime Sanchez**, Brock Peters

Jaime Sanchez (left) as Jesus, a young Puerto Rican apprentice to Sol Nazerman (played by Rod Steiger), wants to learn all he can about his boss's Spanish Harlem pawnshop in *The Pawnbroker*.

Classic character study of Sol Nazerman (Steiger), a Jewish man who owns and operates a pawnshop amid the urban squalor of New York's Spanish Harlem. The characters that inhabit his shop and the area in which he works have a sense of reality that has rarely been equaled in a mainstream movie. This was achieved in part by filming the movie in Spanish Harlem on and around 116th Street and Park Avenue as well as utilizing local actors. There is no sense of Hollywood here.

Nazerman's relationship with his young Puerto Rican apprentice, Jesus (Sanchez), slowly evolves as Jesus comes to discover the pawnbroker's struggle to survive the horrors of a Nazi concentration camp during World War II. The youth looks up to the pawnbroker as his teacher. "Teach me about gold, boss," he says to him, despite his negative attitude toward everyone. Jesus gives up his own life to save the man who, in a moment of despair, told him, "You mean nothing to me." The pawnbroker, who has cut himself off from all emotions, realizes too late his love for his assistant.

The Pearl (1948 RKO)

  D: **Emilio Fernandez**
  S: John Steinbeck, **Emilio Fernandez**, and Jack Wagner, based on the story by John Steinbeck. Spanish adaptation by **Emilio Fernandez** and Mauricio Magdaleno
  P: Oscar Dancingers
Cast: **Pedro Armendariz**, Maria Elena Marques, **Alfonso Bedoya**, Fernando Wagner

A struggling pearl diver, Kino (Armendariz), unable to support his family and needing money to pay for medical care for his baby Coyotito, finds the most mag-

Cinematographer Gabriel Figueroa (left), stars Maria Elena Marques and Pedro Armendariz, and (on end) director Emilio Fernandez pose for a picture on the set of *The Pearl*.

nificent pearl anyone has ever seen, but its beauty and power soon become a curse that threatens to destroy him, his wife, Juana (Marques), and their way of life.

Stunning night photography by the master Gabriel Figueroa and Acapulco seascapes support the inherent social and personal drama.

With John Steinbeck's active support, *The Pearl* was written for the screen and filmed in 1945, prior to the novel's publication in the States. The legend of Kino is based on an ancient Mexican legend. RKO shared financial responsibility for the $400,000 budget with RKO's Churubusco Studios and the Mexican government. Filmed in English and Spanish simultaneously, it grossed $2 million in its initial U.S. release. *The Pearl* won the International Prize at San Sebastian.

The Penitent (1988 New Century Vista Film Co.)

D: Cliff Osmond
S: Cliff Osmond
P: Michael Fitzgerald
Cast: **Raul Julia**, Armand Assante, Rona Freed, **Julie Carmen**

A romantic triangle melodrama set in a small present-day New Mexico town ruled by a Catholic sect of Flagellants who re-create the passion play, actually crucifying the participant playing Christ. This interesting but uneven story features high-powered performances from the leading performers. Though the story takes place in New Mexico, it was filmed in Mexico.

Pepe (1960 Col)

D: George Sidney
S: Dorothy Kingsley and Claude Binyon, based on a story by Leonard Spigelgass and Sonya Levien, from the play *Broadway Magic* by Ladislas Bush-Fekete
P: George Sidney
Cast: **Cantinflas**, Shirley Jones, Dan Dailey, **Carlos Montalban**

After his tremendous international success in *Around the World in 80 Days* (1956), Cantinflas settled on this three-hour star-studded extravaganza as a way of introducing himself to the American market as he stars in his own film, with the box-office insurance of Hollywood notables in cameo roles. Pepe (Cantinflas), who has taken care of a white stallion for years in Mexico, finds him one day sold to an American movie director (Dailey), so Pepe travels to the States to be with his horse.

The film, shot against Mexican backgrounds and Los Angeles, offered little, though a highlight was the tequila dance number with Debbie Reynolds and an animated sequence in which the real Cantinflas fights with a cartoon bull.

Philadelphia (1993 TS)

D: Jonathan Demme
S: Ron Nyswaner
P: Edward Saxon and Jonathan Demme
Cast: Tom Hanks, Denzel Washington, **Antonio Banderas**

Courtroom drama about a young lawyer, Andrew Beckett (Hanks), who is fired from a prestigious law firm when it is revealed he has AIDS. Determined to defend his professional reputation, Andrew hires a personal injury attorney (Washington) to represent him as he sues his former firm for wrongful termination. Antonio Banderas plays Miguel Alvares, Andrew's life partner and lover. It is the first major Hollywood film to present a humanistic portrayal of a gay Hispanic character.

Pirates of Monterey (1947 U)

    D: Alfred Werker
    S: Sam Hellman and Margaret Buell Wilder, based on a story by
       Edward T. Lowe and Bradford Ropes
    P: Paul Malvern
Cast: **Maria Montez**, Rod Cameron, Philip Reed, **Gilbert Roland**, George J. Lewis

A Technicolor action/adventure western about the Spanish Loyalist attempt to overthrow the Mexican regime just prior to California's entry into the United States, with sultry Maria Montez as Marguerita, a Spanish senorita. An American captain in 1840s California brings a shipment of new rifles to the Mexican presidio at Monterey in order to stop a possible attack by Spanish pirates. Gilbert Roland plays Major De Roja, commander of the garrison but a rebel leader in cahoots with the pirates. Chris-Pin Martin has a bit part in the film as a caretta man.

Plunder of the Sun (1953 WB)

    D: John Farrow
    S: Jonathan Latimer, based on the novel by David Dodge
    P: Robert Fellows
Cast: Glenn Ford, Diana Lynn, **Patricia Medina**, Sean McClory,
      Eduardo Noriega, Julio Villareal, Margarito Luna, Juan Garcia

Routine adventure/drama highlighted by Mexican location filming in Oaxaca amid the ancient ruins and a cast of Mexican supporting actors. American Al Colby (Ford) finds himself broke and stranded in Cuba, where he is hired by Ana Luz (Medina) to deliver a harmless-appearing packet to Oaxaca, Mexico. Ford's path is crossed by Julie Barnes (Lynn) and Jefferson (McClory). When Colby discovers that the package contains three sheets of old parchment covered with odd-looking writing that can lead him to the secret wealth of the ancient Aztecs, with the help of Navarro (Villareal), who can translate the manuscript, he strikes out with Ana Luz to solve the mystery of the Zapotec treasure.

According to director John Farrow in a Warner Bros. press item of the time, "The Mexican government is very pleased with our script because this will be the first picture ever made about Mexico and with Mexicans, where Americans are the villains and the Mexicans the heroes."

It was produced for Warner Bros. by the Wayne-Fellows company, owned by actor John Wayne, who also produced *Hondo* (1953) in Mexico the same year. Al Ybarra was the art director.

The Plunderers (1960 AA)

    D: Joseph Pevney
    S: Bob Barbash
    P: Joseph Pevney
Cast: Jeff Chandler, **John Saxon**

Four teenage saddle tramps ride into a small, lonely western town and cause a disturbance. Sam (Chandler), an embittered Civil War veteran who has lost the use of his arm, is riled into action against the hoodlums, who have killed the sheriff.

Juvenile delinquency out west is the theme of this downbeat western. One of the teenagers, a Mexican, Rondo, played by John Saxon, is only interested in the girl of the town. When he threatens to kill Sam with a knife, he is shot by the girl.

Abraham (Alan Arkin), a widower, orders his sons, Junior (Miguel Alejandro, rear) and Luis (Ruben Figueroa), to get into a skiff and take it out into the Gulf Stream in hopes that they may be rescued and then adopted by someone better able to care for them in *Popi*.

Popi (1969 UA)

   D: Arthur Hiller
   S: Tina and Lester Pine
   P: Herbert B. Leonard
Cast: Alan Arkin, **Rita Moreno**, Miguel Alejandro, Ruben E. Figueroa, Antonia Rey, Gladys Velez, **Santos Morales**, **Rene Enriquez**

Touching, funny story of a Puerto Rican widower, Abraham Rodriguez (Arkin), and his elaborate effort to rescue his sons from the dangers of New York barrio life by putting them in an open boat off the coast of Miami in the hopes of getting a new, state-assisted beginning.

As refugees from Castro's Cuba, they would be considered small heroes. Their daring actions would be well publicized and would lead to a probable adoption by someone who could provide all the material advantages Abraham cannot. In the end, his plan works all too well, but everyone realizes that love is more important than any material wealth, and father and sons are reunited.

Popi (meaning "father" in Puerto Rican Spanish) was a modest commercial success. It offered a rare glimpse into Puerto Rican life in New York and introduced to the screen two young actors who were discovered for the film, Ruben Figueroa and Miguel Alejandro.

Alan Arkin as Abraham touched all the right dramatic and comedic moments yet sported the weirdest-sounding Puerto Rican accent. Rita Moreno was featured as Lupe, a neighbor who is interested in Abraham and the kids.

The film was a departure from the Hollywood norm by presenting dignified Hispanic characters trying to overcome their harsh living situations in a humanistic manner. It also raised questions about how this country treats its Hispanic minorities. Refugees from Castro's Cuba sometimes have it better when they arrive here than Puerto Rican slum dwellers who are American citizens.

Portrait of Maria

See *Maria Candelaria*.

Posse (1993 Gramercy)

D: Mario Van Peebles
S: Sy Richardson and Dario Scardapone
P: Preston Holmes and Jim Steele
Cast: Mario Van Peebles, Tone Lōc, Billy Zane, Charles Lane, Blair Underwood

Story of a group of black soldiers in the U.S. Army fighting in Cuba during the 1898 Spanish-American War. Disillusioned with the racism and corruption of their commanding officer and having survived a suicide mission in which they best the Spanish soldiers, they find a cache of gold and desert back to the States to a black township out West called Freemanville, where they are forced to turn outlaw in order to protect themselves. The first 20 minutes of the film take place in Cuba. Director/star Mario Van Peebles makes a stylized, outrageously violent attempt to bring into focus the participation of black Americans in western history.

The Possession of Joel Delaney (1972 Par)

D: Waris Hussein
S: Matt Robinson and Grimes Grice, based on the novel by Ramona Stewart
P: Martin Poll
Cast: Shirley MacLaine, Perry King, **Miriam Colon**, Edmundo Rivera Alvarez

The spirit of Tonio Perez, a 17-year-old Puerto Rican murderer, invades the body of his best friend, Joel, who is living in Tonio's now-vacated apartment.

Joel is transformed into the ultimate Puerto Rican stereotype, complete with slicked-back hair, bad accent, black leather jacket, and switchblade. Norah (MacLaine), Joel's sister, who lives on the swank Upper East Side, can't understand why her brother wants to live with "those people." Joel continues Tonio's killing spree by first killing his girlfriend, then his psychiatrist, and attempting to murder his sister before a policeman's bullet finally stops him. But then the spirit of Tonio enters Norah's body, and the audience is left to ponder the possibilities.

Secondary roles were played by Miriam Colon as Norah's maid and Edmundo Rivera Alvarez as the conductor of a seance.

Gary Giddins in *The Hollywood Reporter* (5/17/72) summed up the film best: "The most remarkable thing about the film is that it is wildly anti–Puerto Rican, and in a country where xenophobia is often confused with patriotism, this cannot be passed over lightly. The inhabitants of the dreadful secretive barrios are always referred to as 'They' and 'They' are all believers in witchcraft."

Predator (1987 TCF)

    D: John McTiernan
    S: Jim Thomas and John Thomas
    P: Lawrence Gordon, Joel Silver, and John Davis
 Cast: Arnold Schwarzenegger, Carl Weathers, **Elpidia Carrillo**

Dutch (Schwarzenegger) leads a group of covert military troops on a mission to rescue American hostages held by guerrillas in a Central American jungle. In the jungle they encounter a strange alien being who hunts only armed humans for sport.

Exciting and unexpected, this is a well-made science fiction thriller. It is spoiled by a thankfully minor subplot of standard Reagan-era Contra politics, in which Latin guerrillas are put in their place by Americanos, which is quickly lost in the growing contest between Dutch and the alien.

The multiethnic U.S. fighting force features Carl Weathers as Dillon; Sonny Landham as Billy, a Native American; Richard Chaves as Pancho; and Bill Duke as Mac. Elpidia Carrillo appears in the role of Anna, a young native guerrilla operative. *Predator* was filmed near Puerto Vallarta, Mexico.

Predator 2 (1990 TCF)

    D: Stephen Hopkins
    S: James Thomas and John Thomas
    P: Joel Silver, Lawrence Gordon, and John Davis
 Cast: Danny Glover, Gary Busey, **Maria Conchita Alonso, Ruben Blades**

Set in 1997 in Los Angeles, where outgunned cops face hordes of Jamaican, Colombian, and other assorted drug dealers and criminal gangs who rule the streets. Suddenly something terrible and inexplicable begins to happen as, one by one, the gang leaders are killed by a mysterious and terrifying adversary who strikes with unbridled ferocity and cunning supernatural power. Harrigan (Glover) sets out to bring to justice those responsible for these brutal murders until he realizes that he and his squad are no longer the pursuers. The Predator is "on safari" in the streets of the city and has begun to hunt and kill the police, who have become his next big game.

The ethnically diverse cast is headed by Danny Glover as Detective Harrigan, Ruben Blades as his partner and childhood friend Danny Archuleta, and Maria Conchita Alonso as Detective Leona Cantrell.

The Pride and the Passion (1957 UA)

    D: Stanley Kramer
    S: Edward and Edna Anhalt, based on the novel *The Gun* by C.S. Forester
    P: Stanley Kramer
 Cast: Cary Grant, Sophia Loren, Frank Sinatra

During the Napoleonic Wars, Capt. Anthony Trumbull (Grant), a British naval officer, is sent to Spain to retrieve a huge cannon, abandoned by the Spanish army, so that the British can use it against Napoleon's army. Miguel (Sinatra), a Spanish guerrilla leader, wants to use the gun to attack a French garrison at Avila. Juana (Loren) is the beautiful camp follower. They move the gun across the Spanish countryside at a huge cost in human life in order to attack the city.

This spectacle has high-powered, somewhat miscast stars and a weak script that cannot sustain interest for its two-hour-plus running time. It was shot on location in Spain.

The Private Life of Don Juan (1934 UA)

D: Alexander Korda

S: Frederick Lonsdale, Lajos Biros, and Arthur Wimperis, based on the play by Henri Bataille

P: Alexander Korda

Cast: Douglas Fairbanks, Merle Oberon

Don Juan has retired to a quiet life in a Spanish village. Annoyed by the many books and plays about him, he returns to Seville for one last amorous adventure, but no one believes him to be Don Juan. An aging Douglas Fairbanks, in his last starring film, was not well received.

The Professionals (1966 Col)

D: **Richard Brooks**

S: **Richard Brooks**, based on the novel *A Mule for the Marquesa* by Frank O'Rourke

P: **Richard Brooks**

Cast: Burt Lancaster, Lee Marvin, Robert Ryan, Jack Palance, Woody Strode, Claudia Cardinale, Ralph Bellamy

During the Mexican Revolution of 1917, a group of American mercenaries (Lancaster, Marvin, Ryan, and Strode) are hired to rescue an American businessman's (Bellamy's) Mexican wife (Cardinale), who has been kidnapped by a Mexican revolutionary, Raza (Palance).

Jack Palance and Maria Gomez, as Chiquita (and an unidentified man), in *The Professionals*.

One of the mercenaries questions their being there: "What are Americans doing in a Mexican Revolution anyway?" Another answers, "Maybe there's only one revolution. The good guys against the bad guys. The only question is, which one are we?"

The film is full of images of mustachioed, scratching bandidos fiercely mowing down *rurales* (Mexican local police) and gringos besting the Mexicans. The image of Mexican women in this film is of the big-breasted, sexy spitfire type. As it turns out, good wife Cardinale is the childhood sweetheart of Palance's Mexican revolutionary and fled with him willingly. This rousing, well-written and -directed action/western by Richard Brooks features an all-star cast with some nice twists and turns. Among the many Hispanic performers featured are Maria Gomez as Chiquita, Carlos Romero, Jose Chavez, Rafael Bertrand, Daniel Nunez, Roberto Contreras, Dave Cadiente, Dolores Corral, Primo Lopez, and Tony Mirelez. It was filmed near Las Vegas, Nevada.

Pure Luck (1991 U)
- D: Nadia Tass
- S: Herschel Weingrod and Timothy Harris
- P: **Lance Hool** and Sean Daniel
- Cast: Martin Short, Danny Glover, **Pedro Armendariz, Jr.**

An accident-prone accountant, Eugene Proctor (Short), is sent on a mission to find a missing, accident-prone heiress. His partner is detective Ray Campanella (Glover), who does not at first believe in bad luck. This comedy/adventure was filmed in Acapulco and is a terribly weak version of the much funnier and more successful French original, *La Chèvre* (The Goat [1981]), starring Gérard Depardieu and Pierre Richard, which has the same Mexican setting.

Q [aka: *The Winged Serpent*] (1982 UFD)
- D: Larry Cohen
- S: Larry Cohen
- P: Larry Cohen
- Cast: David Carradine, Richard Roundtree, Michael Moriarty

A giant serpentlike bird monster, the spirit of the Aztec god Quetzalcoatl, comes to life in modern times. The bird comes to roost on a turret of the Chrysler Building in New York City, where it swoops down on its victims. Its lair is finally discovered, and there is a climactic attack with helicopters and planes. A poor man's flying *King Kong*, *Q* is a stupid horror movie with some good actors.

Q & A (1990 TS)
- D: Sidney Lumet
- S: Sidney Lumet
- P: Arnon Milchan and Burt Harris
- Cast: Nick Nolte, Timothy Hutton, Armand Assante, Jenny Lumet, **Luis Guzman**, Charles Dutton, **Gloria Irrizary**

In New York, young district attorney Riley (Hutton) is assigned to investigate the shooting of a Puerto Rican youth by the bigoted Irish cop Brennan (Nolte). He slowly uncovers within the police department a wide-reaching conspiracy involving the underworld and his own former lover, Nancy Bosch (Lumet), who is now the wife of a Puerto Rican dope dealer, Bobby Texador (Assante).

Director Sidney Lumet traveled this territory before in *Prince of the City* (1981), also an examination of the corruption and racism in the New York City Police Department and city politics.

Q & A is based on a book by New York Puerto Rican judge Edwin Torres. This vivid examination of the New York City Police Department and the justice system crackles with a reality that only a filmmaker who knows it intimately, like Lumet, could capture on film. It is a tough, fascinating, if in the end slightly flawed film, filled with unpleasant characters. Nolte's performance is a character study of a racist old-line cop. Hutton's character is an innocent who comes from a police family and has been a street cop for several years but is amazingly naive about the system. As an older lawyer friend tells him, "You suffer from the same disease I had: I thought I could make a difference."

Armand Assante makes a believable Puerto Rican as Bobby Texador, who is streetwise, cunning, and wants to get out and do right by Nancy, whom he loves. Assante also manages to bring some dignity to a role that might otherwise have been a caricature, equaling his Mafia counterparts. Luis Guzman brought an air of levity and reality to his role as Detective Valentin, making him a memorable and rounded character. Racist banter goes on at the station not only between Valentin and Chappy (Dutton) but among the other officers as well. In this microcosm of minorities and ethnic groups vying for power in New York, the criminals and the law enforcement officials are mirror images of each other in their corruption.

Jenny Lumet is excellent as a half-black, half–Puerto Rican woman who years before made Riley face his own prejudice upon revealing to him that her father is black. Paul Calderon gives a good performance as a homosexual informant. Gloria Irrizary plays Nancy's mother. Ruben Blades composed the score.

R.P.M. (1970 Col)

D: Stanley Kramer
S: Erich Segal
P: Stanley Kramer
Cast: **Anthony Quinn**, Ann-Margret

Quinn is "Paco" Perez, a 53-year-old Puerto Rican sociology professor who was raised in New York's Spanish Harlem (which wasn't Spanish when he would have been there as a growing boy). Because of his rapport with students he is appointed acting president of the university to facilitate negotiations with a group of militant students who have taken over a campus building. Eventually, however, he has to call in the police.

The inevitable violent clash between students and police occurs, and Perez questions his own values and moral stance. Inez Pedroza plays a Chicana student named Estella. This was one of a number of films based on campus unrest in the United States during the late 1960s. Quinn gives a good portrayal of a swinging sociology professor, who drives a motorcycle, wears no tie, and has a young co-ed as his mistress every semester (Ann-Margret, in this case).

Raices de Sangre (1979 Azteca)

D: **Jesus Trevino**
S: **Jesus Trevino**
P: CONACINE and **Jesus Trevino**
Cast: **Richard Yniguez**, Roxanna Bonilla-Gianini, **Pepe Serna**, Ernesto Gomez Cruz

The first Hispanic American, or Chicano, theatrical feature film, *Raices de Sangre* (Blood Roots) was written, produced, and directed by Jesus Salvador Trevino. Trevino had been active as an award-winning television producer and documentary filmmaker for Los Angeles public television station KCET since 1969. On an educational trip to Mexico, Trevino interested then-president of Mexico Luis Echevarria Alvarez in making a film dramatizing the problems of Chicanos in the United

States. The president had expressed an interest in the subject matter at a prior meeting with Trevino and other artists.

At the time, the Mexican film industry was controlled by the government and headed by the president's sister. The film was produced by the Corporación Nacional Cinematografica (CONACINE) in Mexico and became the first film to involve the combined talents of Chicano actors and filmmakers and Mexican actors and filmmakers.

The story takes place in one of the *maquilladorres*, the labor-intensive factories located in bordertowns all along the U.S.-Mexico border, and depicts the struggles of Mexican and Chicano workers on both sides of the border to create an international labor union. A complex, multilayered film, *Raices de Sangre* also deals with illegal aliens, drug trafficking, and Chicano pride.

The story centers on Carlos Rivera (Yniguez), a young lawyer fresh out of Harvard Law School who has established a practice in San Francisco. Back on the border to work for the community action group Barrios Unidos over a summer, Rivera is reluctantly drawn into the workers' struggle.

Yniguez stars in a cast that includes Roxanna Bonilla-Gianini as Lupe Carillo, a beautiful Chicana activist who slowly becomes the love interest of Carlos. She is politically aware, self-sufficient, and dedicated to the people of the barrio. She teaches Carlos about having to participate in all kinds of work for the cause, even making photocopies. She does not fall into the typical screen conventions of the dedicated secretary or camp follower but is one of the best representations and positive role models of a modern Mexican American woman. Also in the cast are Pepe Serna as an ill-fated labor organizer and Ernesto Gomez Cruz as a worker trying for a better life.

The film was shot in Spanish in 1976, and was released in Spanish-language theaters in the States and at art houses in an English-subtitled version in 1979. An original theme song was written for the film by actor/composer Daniel Valdez. *Raices de Sangre* received good reviews and did extremely well at the box office in Spanish-language theaters.

In an interview with Luis Reyes, Trevino remarked, "I was intrigued by the chance to write and direct the film in Mexico not only because of what it represented in terms of my own artistic growth, but also because of its importance within the context of the Latino experience. . . . I think it's quite significant that the first major motion picture on the Chicano and Latino experience was initiated by the Mexican film industry, and that it sought to explain much of the mutually shared reality of Mexicans to a U.S. audience."

The Raiders (1952 U)

   D: Lesley Selander
   S: Polly James and Lillie Hayward
   P: William Alland
Cast: Richard Conte, Viveca Lindfors, Barbara Britton, William Bishop, **Richard Martin, George J. Lewis**

Set in California during the Gold Rush days and early statehood. Jan Morrell (Conte) is a prospector whose claim is stolen and whose wife and brother are killed by outlaws working for a villainous land baron. Morrell, out for revenge, joins a group of California citizens who have lost their property, led by Felipe Ortega (Martin), a former wealthy landowner. Viveca Lindfors plays a California senorita, the daughter of a dispossessed landowner. There is plenty of action and gunplay in this Technicolor western. Richard Martin does well in a supporting role in his first film away from RKO, where he played Chito Rafferty, Tim Holt's sidekick, in a number of RKO B westerns.

Raiders of the Lost Ark (1981 Par)

  D: Steven Spielberg
  S: Lawrence Kasdan, based on a story by George Lucas and Philip Kaufman
  P: Frank Marshall
Cast: Harrison Ford, Karen Allen

In the prologue to this hit film, Indiana Jones (Ford), an adventurous American archaeologist, is chased by half-naked Indians in a South American rain forest after he steals a gold idol from a booby-trapped hidden temple.

The importance of the prologue lies in its reestablishing for a new generation of moviegoers the old racist caricatures of South America and themes of Americans in search of hidden treasure and adventure in exotic locales, clearly evident in the Saturday matinee serials to which the Indiana Jones films were paying homage. The scenes were actually shot on location on the island of Kauai in Hawaii.

Raiders of the Seven Seas (1953 UA)

  D: Sidney Salkow
  S: Sidney Salkow and John O'Dea
  P: Sidney Salkow
Cast: John Payne, Donna Reed, Gerald Mohr

Buccaneers led by Barbarossa (Payne) capture a Spanish galleon and a countess (Reed), with whom Barbarossa falls in love. Complications lead to an attack on the Spanish garrison at Havana harbor, Cuba.

Ramona (1916 Clune)

  D: Donald Crisp
  S: Lloyd Brown, based on the novel by Helen Hunt Jackson
  P: W.H. Clune
Cast: Adda Gleason, Monroe Salisbury, **Victor Vallejo**, Inez Gomez,
       Joe De La Cruz, Arthur Tovares

Silent. A massive film production for its time, offering direction by Donald Crisp, a member of D.W. Griffith's troupe. It was presented in seven reels divided into three parts, accompanied by a specially arranged musical score played live by a symphony orchestra.

Ramona (1928 UA)

  D: Edwin Carewe
  S: Finis Fox, based on the novel by Helen Hunt Jackson
  P: Edwin Carewe
Cast: **Dolores Del Rio**, Warner Baxter

Silent. Dolores Del Rio plays the raven-haired half-Indian girl who elopes with an Indian chief (Baxter) against the wishes of her stern guardian, a wealthy Spanish sheep rancher. Edwin Carewe, who discovered Del Rio, directed her in this popular-with-audiences, time-tested story, filmed in southern California locations.

Ramona (1936 TCF)

  D: Henry King
  S: Lamar Trotti, based on the novel by Helen Hunt Jackson
  P: Sol M. Wurtzel
Cast: Loretta Young, Don Ameche, Kent Taylor, **Pedro De Cordoba, J. Carroll Naish**

Romantic Old California is the setting of the tragic romance about the love of the beautiful "half-breed" Ramona (Young) and the Indian youth Allesandro (Ameche).

The story had been filmed twice before, in 1916 and 1928. Gilbert Roland and Rita Hayworth were originally scheduled to star in this version, but when Fox consolidated with Century Pictures, Young and Ameche were signed for the roles. Supporting players included Katherine DeMille as the jealous Margarita, Kent Taylor as an understanding *hacendado*, Pauline Frederick as his sternly aristocratic mother, Jane Darwell as a sympathetic settler from Tennessee, and Victor Kilian as a padre.

While filming on location in Mesa Grande near San Diego, California, Loretta Young saved the life of 2-year-old Ramon Lugo, narrowly escaping injury herself. Young and the child were acting in a scene beneath a gauze netting used for photographic effects; when the netting caught fire due to the hot Technicolor lights, she quickly removed the baby from its cradle. This was one of the first films to use the early two-strip Technicolor process.

Red River (1948 UA)

D: Howard Hawks
S: Borden Chase and Charles Schnee, based on the novel *The Chisholm Trail* by Chase
P: Howard Hawks
Cast: John Wayne, Montgomery Clift

In the opening sequence of *Red River*, Tom Dunson (Wayne) shoots one of Don Diego's outriders to prove that the grazing land north of the Rio Grande now belongs to him, visually and effectively illustrating the Manifest Destiny concept.

Red Sky at Morning (1971 U)

D: James Goldstone
S: Marguerite Roberts, based on the novel by Richard Bradford
P: Hal B. Wallis
Cast: Richard Thomas, **Desi Arnaz, Jr.**, Richard Crenna, Claire Bloom, **Victoria Racimo, Pepe Serna**, Mario Aniov, **Gregory Sierra**, Harry Guardino, **Alma Beltran**

Frank Arnold (Crenna) goes off to fight in World War II from a Gulf Coast port and relocates his wife, Ann (Bloom), and family to the small town of Sagrado, New Mexico. The focus is on Josh Arnold's (Thomas's) exposure to multiracial contemporaries in a school where whites are the minorities. Desi Arnaz, Jr., is Steenie Moreno, son of the town's Spanish American doctor and his Greek wife, who befriends Josh and guides him through the intricacies of the New Mexico social milieu, especially as it applies to Anglos, Indians, and Mexicans.

Characters are strictly formula types, including Nehemiah Persoff and Alma Beltran as faithful servants, and Spanish American gang toughs like Pepe Serna as Chango Lopez, the toughest of them all, and Mario Aniov as the cunning and dangerous Lindo Velarde. Victoria Racimo is Viola Lopez, the tragic schoolgirl. The sturdy sheriff is played by Gregory Sierra. It was filmed in New Mexico.

Repo Man (1984 U)

D: Alex Cox
S: Alex Cox
P: Jonathan Wacks and Peter McCarthy
Cast: **Emilio Estevez**, Harry Dean Stanton, Fox Harris, **Eddie Velez, Del Zamora**

A cult movie. Otto (Estevez), a young L.A. punker, becomes the protégé of Bud (Stanton), a crusty car repossessor. Otto soon comes to challenge his mentor for a $20,000 repo prize, a '64 Chevy Malibu driven by J. Frank Parnell (Harris), a lobotomized nuclear scientist. The Malibu is being pursued madly by ruthless gov-

Del Zamora (right) and Eddie Velez (left) as brothers Lagarto and Napa Rodriguez in *Repo Man*.

ernment agents, UFO cultists, and the infamous Rodriguez brothers, Lagarto (Zamora) and Napo (Velez). In the trunk is an unthinkable object that could change the course of civilization overnight. Then, of course, there is the climax with a "close encounter of the third kind."

You'll either like this film or loathe it.

Requiem for a Heavyweight (1962 Col)

    D: Ralph Nelson
    S: Rod Serling, based on his TV play
    P: David Susskind
 Cast: **Anthony Quinn**, Mickey Rooney, Jackie Gleason

Anthony Quinn plays the old heavyweight Mountain Rivera, whose winning streak has run out after 17 years of fighting, which has left him mentally dim and threatened with blindness. His manager, Maish Rennick (Gleason), is no worse than the other low lifes of his profession and might have preferred to see his man get some sort of peace and quiet in retirement. But Rennick has become deeply involved with strong-arm gamblers and is forced to try to squeeze some dollars out of his derelict hulk of a boxer to get himself out of a gambling debt.

Rivera was an Irish boxer in the television drama, but the role was changed to a Mexican American for the film version. Quinn drew on his own youth, when he boxed just to bring money in, and modeled the character, including his voice, partly on the great old boxer Primo Carnera. This is one of Quinn's greatest and most memorable portrayals.

In a letter in *Life* magazine (2/22/63), director Ralph Nelson said, "I differed with Anthony Quinn over his interpretation of the role. As written, the hero was a lonely, sensitive human being, a prizefighter who had worked out his hostilities in the ring. Quinn was afraid gentleness would reflect upon his image of masculinity, so [he] chose to play Sonny Liston [a well-known heavyweight boxer of the time] instead. I believe Palance's concept [Jack Palance starred as the boxer in the original TV version] was truer to the role and fulfilled the concept of the script more effectively than Quinn's attempts to dominate it."

Return of the Seven (1966 UA)

D: Burt Kennedy

S: Larry Cohen

P: Ted Richmond

Cast: Yul Brynner, Robert Fuller, Julian Mateos, Warren Oates, Claude Akins, **Emilio Fernandez, Rodolfo Acosta, Fernando Rey**

Yul Brynner as the gunfighter Chris was the only actor from the original *Magnificent Seven* to return to his role. This movie was directed by veteran western director Burt Kennedy, with Spain doubling for Mexico. Mexican actors Emilio Fernandez as the *hacendado* chieftain and Rodolfo Acosta as his aide bring authority and authenticity to their roles. Fernando Rey plays a priest. Castilian accents are noticeable in most of the Spanish actors playing Mexicans.

Revenge (1990 Col)

D: Tony Scott

S: Jim Harrison and Jeffrey Fiskin, based on a story by Jim Harrison

P: Hunt Lowry and Stanley Rubin

Cast: Kevin Costner, **Anthony Quinn, Madeleine Stowe, Tomas Milian, Joaquin Martinez**

Revenge is a lurid, violent tale with spectacular atmospheric Mexican location footage. A retired U.S. flyer, Cochran (Costner), falls in love with the young Miryea (Stowe), wife of his friend in Mexico, Tiburon Mendez (Quinn), a powerbroker with ties to the Mexican crime syndicate.

Quinn was good in the role but unfortunately about 25 years too old to make the relationship between himself and Costner believable. Based on a short story by cult novelist Jim Harrison, the film perpetuated the stereotypes of Mexican men as violent and menacing, Mexican women as whores, and peasants as people with a grudge against their patrons. We have seen this all before (but never quite this explicitly) in western dramas where the hero is left for dead and, like baby Moses, is found (in this case, in the middle of the desert) by noble peasants who nurse him back to health. He then returns to seek revenge. Good casting provided roles for Tomas Milian, Joaquin Martinez, Miguel Ferrer, John Leguizamo, Sally Kirkland, Joe Santos, and James Gammon. *Revenge* was filmed in Mexico on 50 separate locations on a 12-week schedule and features some of the country's most scenic areas including Durango, Puerto Vallarta, Cuernavaca, and Mexico City.

The Reward (1965 TCF)

D: Serge Bourguignon

S: Serge Bourguignon and Oscar Milland, based on the novel by Michael Barrett

P: Aaron Rosenberg

Cast: Max von Sydow, **Yvette Mimieux, Gilbert Roland**, Efrem Zimbalist, Jr., **Emilio Fernandez, Henry Silva, Rodolfo Acosta, Julian Rivero**

Offbeat, highly stylized contemporary western about an odd assortment of men seeking the $50,000 reward for the capture of an escaped American fugitive in a small Mexican desert town. Roland portrays an aristocratic police captain, and Fernandez portrays a brutal and cunning police sergeant in a small Mexican village. About a third of the film is spoken in Spanish, with English subtitles. Filmed in and around Old Tucson, Arizona, and Death Valley, this was the first and only American film by French director Serge Bourguignon, who directed *Sundays and Cybèle*, which won the Best Foreign Language Film Oscar in 1962. A promising story that backfires on itself, *The Reward* was a dismal failure at the box office.

Ride, Vaquero! (1953 MGM)
   D: John Farrow
   S: Frank Fenton
   P: Stephen Ames
Cast: Robert Taylor, Ava Gardner, Howard Keel, **Anthony Quinn,**
   Movita Castenada, Joe Dominguez

As Anglo settlers move in, outlaw Jose Esqueda (Quinn) and his gang's stranglehold on a frontier territory is threatened. Opposing him and his violent ways are settlers led by King Cameron (Keel), a rancher, and his wife, Cordelia (Gardner). Esqueda sends his half-brother Rio (Taylor) to scare them off. Rio is captured by the settlers and becomes drawn to Cordelia. Esqueda decides to take matters into his own hands, murders the town's sheriff, and has his men pillage the town. He almost kills Cameron, but Rio intervenes. Rio and Esqueda face each other in a gunfight, and they both die. Movita Castenada has a small role as a hussy.

This violent, downbeat western features Taylor in an uncharacteristic role as a vicious killer and bad guy. Quinn turns in an outrageous and vivid portrayal, almost as if he had set out to outdo Alfonso Bedoya in Mexican banditry portrayals. He broke all the rules with this vicious flesh-and-blood center-stage greaser portrayal. His gang is made up of Mexicans and Anglos.

Ride the Pink Horse (1947 U)
   D: Robert Montgomery
   S: Ben Hecht and Charles Lederer, based on the novel by Dorothy B. Hughes
   P: Joan Harrison
Cast: Robert Montgomery, Wanda Hendrix, **Thomas Gomez,** Rita Conde,
   Iris Flores, Tito Renaldo, **Martin Garralaga,** Maria Cortez

Half the characters are American gangsters, amateur and professional, who engage in an undercover but vicious fight for certain stakes at "San Pablo." The other half are inhabitants of San Pablo's predominantly Mexican community, and both they and the town itself reflect a certain realism of Hispanic New Mexico life. Thomas Gomez is Pancho, a hulking man with a proverbial heart of gold who runs a merry-go-round. Wanda Hendrix is Pila, a naive but purposeful Indian girl who follows Robert Montgomery after he pays for a carousel ride for her. Julian Rivero has a small role as a Mexican man. San Pablo is a composite of the Mexican districts of Santa Fe, Taos, and Albuquerque, New Mexico. Location scenes were filmed at Santa Fe's Hotel La Fonda and at the famous Fred Harvey winter resort, as well as at Santa Fe's cemetery and its business district.

Pasquale Martinez, real-life carousel operator of Taos, came to be known in Hollywood as the only wrangler (livestock handler) of wooden horses on record. A retired U.S. Forestry Service employee, he had a six-week paid vacation to Hollywood, for the Lions Club of Taos would not allow the actual carousel to be removed from Taos unless Martinez went along as custodian for the close-up process work at the studio.

Right Cross (1950 MGM)
   D: John Sturges
   S: Charles Schnee
   P: Armand Deutsch
Cast: **Ricardo Montalban,** June Allyson, Dick Powell

Johnny Monterez (Montalban) is a Mexican boxer with a chip on his shoulder about "gringos." While his prejudice is not the result of any direct bigotry on the part of anyone in the film, we do learn that it is due to the racial consciousness he developed growing up in Los Angeles. (If one knows the history of blatant dis-

Johnny Monterez (Ricardo Montalban, right) is a Mexican boxer in *Right Cross*, also starring (from left to right) Art Aragon, Dick Powell, and June Allyson. (The man in the hat is an unidentified player.)

crimination in Los Angeles toward its Mexican American citizenry, it is easy to sympathize with his feelings.)

He becomes U.S. middleweight champion and falls in love with Pat O'Malley (Allyson) and ultimately develops a more tolerant attitude toward the gringo. The action builds to a solid ring fight in which Monterez, contrary to usual film formula, goes down in defeat. He comes to realize that Pat loves him as a person and that the championship has nothing to do with it. Monterez at the fadeout wins Pat away from newspaperman Rick Gavery (Powell).

The promise of a happy life together through Anglo-Mexican integration was an important message for post–World War II audiences, especially when the Anglo girl was the all-American June Allyson.

By the last reel of earlier such films, the Mexican usually discovered that he was really an Anglo, deserted as a child and reared in some exotic land by locals. If it turned out he was really a native, he would die before the relationship with the Anglo woman was consummated. The experience of the war, however, led in the United States to a shift in values and perceptions of freedoms and civil rights. Hollywood filmmakers began to tackle more serious subjects, such as anti-Semitism and racial prejudice, in such films as *Gentleman's Agreement* (1947), *Home of the Brave* (1949), and *Pinky* (1949). The production code regarding miscegenation on screen began to loosen up. Also, as a result of the Good Neighbor Policy, Latin Americans had come to be considered white. In the case of this film, the protagonist is specifically an economically disadvantaged Mexican from the Los Angeles barrio, though the prejudice aspect is rather safely brought out as a psychological problem rather than something real that has to be dealt with.

The Ring (1952 UA)

 D: Kurt Neumann
 S: Irving Shulman, based on his novel
 P: Maurice, Herman, and Frank King
 Cast: **Lalo Rios**, Gerald Mohr, **Rita Moreno**, Martin Garralaga, Pepe Hern, **Victor Millan, Tony Martinez**

The Ring, starring Lalo Rios, deals with the social and economic pressures in 1952 Los Angeles that drive a disadvantaged Mexican American youth into the world of boxing.

The film was shot in the Boyle Heights section of East Los Angeles, where the producers, the King brothers, were raised. The Kings first produced "soundies," the forerunner of today's music videos. Soundies, short films that featured popular singers and orchestras, were designed to promote a song and talent. They were shown in specially constructed viewing boxes in record stores. Successful in this venture, the Kings went on to produce a number of low-budget pictures, of which *The Ring* was one.

The film's story line illustrates racial discrimination in scenes featuring tourists gazing at "those lazy Mexicans," Mexican boys being turned down for service by a waitress in a Beverly Hills restaurant, and a young couple being refused entry at a skating rink because it isn't "Mexican Night."

Lalo Rios (center) plays a disadvantaged Mexican American youth drawn into the world of boxing in *The Ring*. Also pictured here are Robert Osterloh (left) and Gerald Mohr (right).

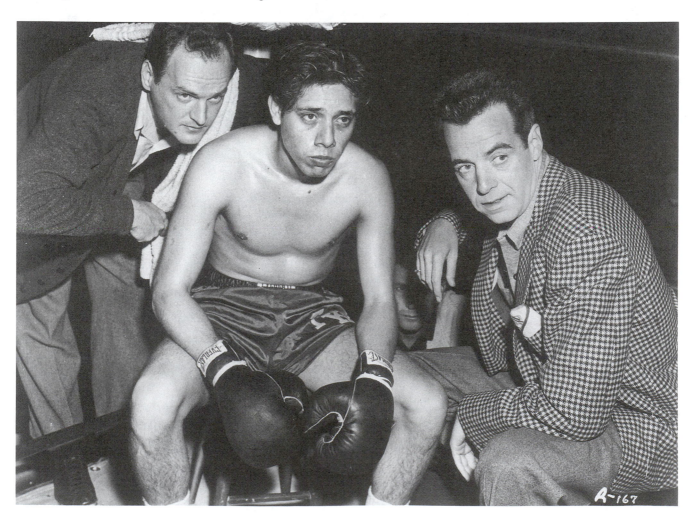

The Ring also recognizes the Mexican American as part of the American urban experience rather than presenting the more common rural depictions. It can also be said that the character played by Lalo Rios is a symbol of the Chicano Movement, which came into being in the 1960s and dealt specifically with Mexican Americans, their rights, history, and image within the American cultural context.

Both *The Ring* and *The Lawless* (1950), centering as they do on Mexican Americans, one urban, one rural, were filmed on low budgets and share the same leading actor (Rios), making them companion pieces among the American cinema's first statements on the Mexican American and/or Chicano consciousness.

Rio Bravo (1959 WB)

D: Howard Hawks
S: Jules Furthman and Leigh Brackett, based on a story by Barbara Hawks McCampbell
P: Howard Hawks
Cast: John Wayne, Dean Martin, Ricky Nelson, Angie Dickinson, Walter Brennan, John Russell, Claude Akins, Ward Bond, **Pedro Gonzalez-Gonzalez, Estelita Rodriguez**

John T. Chance (Wayne), sheriff of a Texas bordertown, has to keep a jailed killer in and his cohorts—who have surrounded the town—out, but he doesn't do it alone. During the course of these very human events, he is saved or protected by a reformed drunk, Dude (Martin); a gimp-legged old geezer, Stumpy (Brennan); a dance hall girl with a past (Dickinson); and a lone young gunfighter, Colorado (Nelson). They are aided by Carlos (Gonzalez-Gonzalez), a Mexican, and his wife, Consuela (Rodriguez), who own and run the town hotel. It was filmed on location in Old Tucson, Arizona.

Rio Conchos (1964 TCF)

D: Gordon Douglas
S: Joseph Landon and Clair Huffaker, based on the novel *Guns of the Rio Conchos* by Huffaker
P: David Weisbart
Cast: Richard Boone, Stuart Whitman, Jim Brown, Tony Franciosa, **Rodolfo Acosta**

Stereotypically violent, illogical, action-packed western in which four unsavory men head through Indian country in search of 2,000 rifles stolen from the U.S. cavalry. One of the four is Rodriguez, a Mexican bandit played by Tony Franciosa. Vito Scotti is featured as an older Mexican bandit with a mouthful of bad teeth. Rodolfo Acosta plays an Indian chief named Bloodshirt. Wende Wagner plays an Indian girl. It was filmed on location in Moab, Utah.

"En route they brawl and bicker, drink and debauch in a rugged old west that appears to be crawling with bandidos, prostitutes and sadistic savages," *Time* (10/20/64).

Rio Rita (1929 RKO)

D: Luther Reed
S: Luther Reed and Russell Mack, based on the musical by Guy Bolton and Fred Thompson
P: William LeBaron
Cast: Bert Wheeler, Robert Woolsey, Bebe Daniels, John Boles, Dorothy Lee, **Don Alvarado**, Georges Renavent

Rio Rita was an immensely popular 1927 Broadway musical that was made into an equally popular early sound musical film. The story concerns a Texas Ranger in an American bordertown who is after a notorious Mexican bandit, El Kinkajou. The show mixed romance, intrigue, music, and comedy with Bebe Daniels and John Boles the stars and Don Alvarado in a major supporting role. Georges Renavent played the bandit. The film and play relied more on the romantic dime novels and the conventions of the Broadway musical than on any reality or authenticity concerning the Southwest or Mexico. The film was remade by MGM in 1942 as a musical vehicle for Abbott and Costello.

Rio Rita (1942 MGM)

     D: S. Sylvan Simon
     S: Richard Connell, Gladys Lehman, and John Grant
     P: Pandro S. Berman
  Cast: Bud Abbott, Lou Costello

Abbott and Costello were borrowed from Universal to star in this musical remake.

The boys get fired from their job at a pet shop and decide to make their way to New York by hiding in the trunk of a car with New York license plates. Unfortunately, the driver, dreamy singer Ricardo Montera (John Carroll), is headed for a fiesta in a tiny southwest Texas town called Vista del Rio. After a long and exhausting ride, Bud and Lou find themselves mixed up in shenanigans involving Nazi spies, secret codes, old flames, and music. Julian Rivero has a small role as a Mexican gentleman.

The Ritz (1976 WB)

     D: Richard Lester
     S: Terrence McNally, based on his play
     P: Denis O'Dell
  Cast: **Rita Moreno**, Jack Weston

Rita Moreno won a Tony Award for her Broadway portrayal of Googie Gomez in Terrence McNally's zany comedy play *The Ritz*, which was written with her in mind. She re-created the role in the film version.

In a homosexual bathhouse in New York, Gomez is the star entertainer, a Puerto Rican waiting for her big break who mistakenly believes Jack Weston (also re-creating his Broadway role), who is hiding out from a murderous relative, is a Broadway producer. Jerry Stiller and Kaye Ballard also star.

"By playing Googie, I am thumbing my nose at all those Hollywood writers responsible for such lines like, 'You Yankee peeg, you rape my sister. I keel you!'" said Moreno in press notes for the film. *The Ritz*, for Moreno, was something of a rebirth. "*West Side Story*, my last big vehicle, was fifteen years ago," she said in an interview with Luis Reyes in 1977. Moreno said of her *Ritz* role, "Googie is the essence of all the Latin Spitfires I've ever played in bad movies. She would tear out the eye of the cyclops for the chance of hitting the big time. She is absolutely untalented and the only one in the film who comes out all right.

"In many ways, she's a bit like me. She perseveres—so do I. And Googie wasn't that difficult to get at, because she's based on a number of Latin women I've known. The accent comes from my mother."

The Road to Rio (1947 Par)

     D: Norman Z. McLeod
     S: Edmund Beloin and Jack Rose
     P: Daniel Dare
  Cast: Bob Hope, Bing Crosby, Dorothy Lamour, **Nestor Paiva**

Musicians Barton (Hope) and Sweeney (Crosby) accidentally set fire to a carnival where they are working and find it necessary, to escape arson charges, to stow away on a luxury liner bound for Rio. During the voyage the boys befriend a beautiful and mysterious young woman, Lucia De Andrade (Lamour), bound home for a marriage she does not want. Several days later they arrive in Rio and go searching for nightclub work. To improve their chances they befriend three talented but goofy Brazilian musicians (The Wiere Brothers) and are immediately hired by a nightclub owner (Paiva) who thinks they are all Americans.

Barton and Sweeney try to teach the Brazilian musicians American slang but to no avail, and they are quickly found out and fired. The boys learn that Lucia's wedding is about to take place and they decide to attend the affair disguised as a Caribbean pirate (Crosby) and a Carmen Miranda–like "Gootchy-gootchy" dancer (Hope), entertaining the guests by doing a hilarious Latin American routine. Abandoning their disguises, Hope and Crosby manage to obtain certain papers that enable Lucia to escape her unpleasant fate.

With a relatively traditional musical/comedy format, this "Road" film bristles with clever dialogue, situations, and songs. The opening titles are presented in animation where the names of the three principal players literally dance across the screen while a lively Latin American band plays the ever-popular samba song "Brasilia."

The Robin Hood of El Dorado (1936 MGM)

D: William Wellman
S: William Wellman, Melvin Levy, and **Joseph Calleia,** based on the novel by Walter Noble Burns
P: John W. Considine, Jr.
Cast: Warner Baxter, **Margo, Soledad Jimenez,** Bruce Cabot, Ann Loring, **J. Carroll Naish, George Regas, Carlos de Valdez, Nick De Ruiz,** Carlotta Monti

The central character is the legendary California bandit Joaquin Murieta. The facts are sketchy as to who he was but not to the events surrounding his life.

Murieta was a Mexican from Sonora who was attracted to the gold fields of California in the late 1840s. Many of the Mexican miners were subjected to racist attacks by Anglo Americans. Murieta gathered together a band of men and began in the early 1850s a series of raids, which the Mexicans regarded as justifiable retaliation. He is thought to have been captured by California Rangers in 1853, but his legend still had him alive well into the 1870s. He became a romantic revolutionary symbol for the Chicano movement of the 1960s and 1970s as a Mexican who fought against Anglo oppression and stood up for his rights in his own land.

Murieta here is a sympathetic avenger of his people. He suffers at the hands of American settlers, enduring the mistreatment of his blind mother and beloved bride, the loss of his land, and finally his public whipping while his brother is hanged. Warner Baxter plays Murieta in his Cisco Kid acting mode. The movie was filmed near Sonora, California.

Romancing the Stone (1984 TCF)

D: Robert Zemeckis
S: Diane Thomas
P: Michael Douglas
Cast: Michael Douglas, Kathleen Turner, Danny De Vito, **Alfonso Arau,** Manuel Ojeda

Joan Wilder (Turner) is a homebody writer of romantic adventure tales who begins to live the kinds of stories she writes when her sister is kidnapped in South America and Joan goes after her. Jack Colton (Douglas) is a rugged jungle hunter who reluctantly comes to her aid. Together they battle the dangers of the wild and the equally ferocious men who stand between them and a successful mission. The movie is filled with all the customary stereotypes, both Anglo and Latin, for this kind of tale, with Manuel Ojeda as a corrupt local detective and Alfonso Arau as a dope dealer who befriends our heroine and just happens to be one of her biggest fans.

This fast-paced and witty spoof of the action/adventure genre takes place in the jungles of Colombia, but it was filmed in Mexico in such locales as Vera Cruz, Jalapa, and Mexico City.

Romero (1989 Four Seasons Entertainment)

    D: John Duigan
    S: John Sacret Young
    P: Ellwood E. Kieser
Cast: **Raul Julia**, Richard Jordan, **Tony Plana**, **Ana Alicia**, **Eddie Velez**

The story of the assassination of Catholic archbishop Oscar Romero (Julia) in El Salvador in 1980 during the bloody political conflict in that country. Julia gives a moving performance of a mouselike, disinterested man who grows into the responsibility of his appointed position of archbishop when the events around him lead him to speak in favor of human rights and against the policies of the regime. The assassination of the gentle, once silent but ultimately outspoken man of god as he celebrated mass indelibly etched in the world's eyes the human tragedy of El Salvador.

During a press conference to promote the film, Julia stated, "One of the most important things about this film is that it is a true story about a Latin American character that takes place in Latin America. It is not about gringos in South America where Latins are background or supporting players." The Australian director John Duigan said, "I've always been fascinated with the politics of Central America, and I was familiar with the story of Oscar Romero. When I was offered the screenplay to direct, I found it a compelling piece of writing on a very important subject."

Richard Jordan portrays firebrand priest Rutilio Grande, a man whose own passionate efforts to aid his suffering flock would also mark him for death. Ana Alicia portrays a beautiful Salvadoran aristocrat whose husband, the minister of agriculture, mysteriously disappears.

Filmed on location, with Cuernavaca, Mexico, doubling for El Salvador, *Romero* represents the first mainstream theatrical feature ever produced by the Catholic Church. *Romero* received fairly wide distribution in the United States but managed to collect only $3 million at the nation's box offices. Critics were respectful but divided over the film but generally praised Julia's performance.

Rooftops (1989 New Century Vista)

    D: Robert Wise
    S: Terence Brennan
    P: Howard W. Koch, Jr.
Cast: Troy Beyer, Alexis Cruz, **Eddie Velez**, Jason Gedrick, **Luis Guzman**,
      Jay M. Boryea, Rafael Baez

In the streets of New York's "Alphabet City," the seamy section of Manhattan's Lower East Side, a group of multiethnic kids with no family to depend on create their own unique living spaces on the rooftops of abandoned tenement buildings. Squeak (Cruz), the artful dodger of the group, is famous for his colorful neighborhood murals. The menacing drug dealer Lobo (Velez), his henchmen, Willie (Boryea) and Raphael (Baez), and his beautiful cousin, Elena (Beyer), move into the neighborhood wreaking havoc on the lives of the rooftop dwellers.

Director Robert Wise tried to recapture the dance and excitement of his own *West Side Story* of nearly 30 years earlier but failed to do so with this thin material.

Rose of the Rancho (1936 Par)
- D: Marion Gering
- S: Frank Partos, Charles Brackett, Arthur Sheekman, Nat Perrin, Harlan Thompson, and Brian Hooker, based on the play by Richard Walton Tully and David Belasco
- P: William LeBaron
- Cast: Gladys Swarthout, John Boles, Willie Howard, **Don Alvarado,** Charles Bickford, H.B. Warner, **Pedro De Cordoba**

Based on Richard Walton Tully and David Belasco's 1906 play, filmed previously in 1914 by the Lasky Company and Cecil B. DeMille. In Old California, the queen of the fiesta moonlights as a masked bandit with a U.S. government agent in pursuit. The leads are fine, and plenty of operatic-style songs are included. Broadway comedy star Willie Howard is a Jewish cowboy.

Rosita (1923 UA)
- D: Ernst Lubitsch
- S: Edward Knoblock
- P: Mary Pickford Co.
- Cast: Mary Pickford, Holbrook Blinn, George Walsh

Silent. The king of Spain falls in love with Rosita, a Spanish streetsinger who in turn loves Don Diego, a penniless nobleman.

The Royal Hunt of the Sun (1969 NG)
- D: Irving Lerner
- S: Philip Yordan, based on the play by Peter Shaffer
- P: Eugene Frenke and Philip Yordan
- Cast: Christopher Plummer, Robert Shaw

Originally produced in 1964 by England's National Theatre, Peter Shaffer's *The Royal Hunt of the Sun* achieved considerable success in a subsequent Broadway staging and would seem to offer splendid possibilities to an imaginative filmmaker. Certainly, the conquest of Peru and the confrontation between Francisco Pizarro and Atahualpa, Inca sovereign and Sun God, provide both action of epic scope and characters of impressive strength. And there is philosophical drama in the rape of the centuries-old Inca nation by conquest-hungry, gold-obsessed Spanish Christian soldiers.

Yet, despite such promising material, this production, filmed in Spain and Peru, lacks impact and intelligence. The subject cries out for a visual expansion that the film never provides. *The Royal Hunt of the Sun* is infected by an oppressive, studio-bound claustrophobic screenplay. Yordan's most serious mistake, however, was in creating a superstitious, virtually barbaric Indian populace in place of the original play's concept of a sophisticated agrarian society that could shame the Spaniards. Without this sense of a powerful Inca nation awaiting both its sovereign's ransom and the opportunity for revenge, Pizarro's crucial dilemma over Atahualpa lacks reality, and the film's conclusion becomes gratuitous.

Christopher Plummer gave a Shakespearean, theatrical interpretation to the god-like Atahualpa, and Robert Shaw was good as Pizarro.

"The film is no more than an echo of J. Lee Thompson's *Kings of the Sun*. Its journey to Peru for authenticity yielding little more on screen values than Sam Katzman's old sex and sand quickies for Columbia," *Hollywood Reporter* (10/16/69).

"Christopher Plummer . . . wheezes, whispers, whines, struts, sings, and uses an accent that sounds sometimes like Charlie Chan and sometimes like Gonzalez-Gonzalez," Vincent Canby, *New York Times* (10/7/69).

Rumba (1935 Par)

D: Marion Gering

S: Howard Green, Harry Ruskin, and Frank Partos, based on a story by
Guy Endore and Seena Owen

P: William LeBaron

Cast: George Raft, Carole Lombard, **Margo**

Musical melodrama. Carmelita (Margo) and her dancing partner Joe Martin (Raft)
dance the rumba in Cuba, where they win a lottery with an heiress (Lombard)
who has her designs on Joe. A New York dance engagement where they will introduce the rumba is threatened by gangsters, and Carmelita refuses to dance with
Joe. The heiress takes her place, and Carmelita loses Joe.

Run for the Sun (1956 UA)

D: Roy Boulting

S: Dudley Nichols and Roy Boulting, based on the story "The Most
Dangerous Game" by Richard Connell

P: Harry Tatelman

Cast: Richard Widmark, Trevor Howard, Jane Greer, Peter Van Eyck,
Carlos Henning, Juan Garcia

Conventional adventure story about a journalist in the jungles of Mexico meeting
up with an ex-Nazi and forced to run for his life. This film features several Hispanic actors in small roles. One of many screen adaptations of Richard Connell's
story "The Most Dangerous Game," this one was filmed in Mexico, near Acapulco
and Cuernavaca.

Salsa (1988 Cannon)

D: Boaz Davidson

S: Boaz Davidson, Tomas Benitez, and Shepard Goldman

P: Menahem Golan

Cast: Robby Rosa, Rodney Harvey, **Magali Alvarado**, Moon Orona,
Miranda Garrison, Angela Alvarado, **Loyda Ramos**

A young man, Rico (Rosa), aspires to be king of the salsa dancers in a competition
at the club La Luna in Los Angeles. If he wins, he will go to the finals at the festival
of San Juan in Puerto Rico.

This film is the first to feature a Puerto Rican youth in a leading role. It is a low-
budget Hispanic American version of *Saturday Night Fever*.

Rico is a brown-skinned Puerto Rican, not an Anglo actor made up to look
brown- or light-skinned Hispanic. A cross-cultural relationship occurs between his
best friend, Ken (Harvey), and Rico's sister, Rita (Alvarado). Race is not a factor
here.

Rico works in a car repair shop and lives in a clean, lower-middle-class house
with his single working mother (Ramos) and his sister. The film is devoid of stereotypical ghetto trappings, and Rico is not alienated from U.S. culture. He is sure of
himself and his Latin identity. The first scenes of the film well delineate this as
Rico dances at his repair shop to a song titled "Mucho Money," with the American
flag draped overhead.

He is tempted by an older woman, La Luna (Garrison), the owner of the club, a
former Salsa Queen, to be her dance partner, thus virtually assuring a victory and a
last chance to regain her glory. Conflicts arise over his sister's growing affection for
Ken and with his own girlfriend Vicki (Angela Alvarado). In the end he wins the
dance contest and returns to his girlfriend, and Rita and Ken get together.

Robby Rosa as Rico does well in the dance sequences and acquits himself nicely
as an actor. (Rosa is a former member of the pop group Menudo.) What the film

lacks in its drama and story it makes up for in style and the energy and exuberance of the young performers. Kenny Ortega choreographed and staged the dance sequences imaginatively, though they look a lot like television soft-drink commercials, while Rosa's moves are reminiscent of Michael Jackson's. Celia Cruz, Tito Puente, and Willie Colon make cameo appearances.

Salt of the Earth (1954 IPC Distributors)

D: Herbert Biberman
S: Michael Wilson
P: Paul Jarrico
Cast: Juan Chacon, Rosaura Revueltas, Will Geer, Frank Talavera, Melvin Williams, Clinton Jencks, Virginia Jencks

Perhaps the most outstanding attempt to bring to the screen an honesty in the way Hispanic Americans were portrayed. The story behind the making of *Salt of the Earth* has been well documented in several books and one film documentary, so we'll only briefly summarize the origins here.

The film is based on an actual zinc miners' strike in New Mexico in the early 1950s and centers on the changing relationship and roles of a Mexican American worker and his wife through the progression of the strike.

The leading roles were played by Rosaura Revueltas, an actress from Mexico, and Juan Chacon, an actual zinc miner and union president. Blending professional actors with striking union members and their families, director Biberman rendered a blunt but honest critique of racial and economic inequality in America.

During production in New Mexico the film ran into trouble with threats and disruptions on the set from outsiders. Post-production on *Salt of the Earth* was completed under clandestine circumstances in Hollywood due to the Red Scare and Communist witch hunt.

Producer Paul Jarrico heard about the actual zinc miners' strike during a visit to New Mexico. He had recently formed an independent production company to develop progressive movies. Along with screenwriter Michael Wilson, who had just won an Academy Award for *A Place in the Sun* (1951), and director Herbert Biberman, Jarrico decided to tell this story as a fictionalized real-life drama.

Jarrico took a draft of his screenplay to the International Union of Mine, Mill, and Smelter Workers for their script approval. In the original script, the character Ramon Quintero, the married union leader, has an affair with the wife of a miner who is off fighting in Korea. The union felt that this reinforced the Latin lover stereotype, and it was stricken from the script. Another scene showed the wife at a party using her dress to wipe some spilled beer. That scene was deleted as well, for it was felt to be demeaning.

Despite many difficulties in production and post-production, the film was completed and was shown in limited independent release (no studio or distributor would touch the film because of its creators' alleged Communist affiliations). The projectionists' union refused to run the movie, and pressure from studios and Hollywood executives made it impossible for the film to achieve wide release. Newspapers even refused to run ads for the movie. *Salt of the Earth* was denounced as subversive and subsequently blacklisted because it was sponsored by the International Union of Mine, Mill, and Smelter Workers (which had been expelled from the CIO in 1950 for alleged Communist-dominated leadership). However, movie houses in the more progressive major cities like New York, San Francisco, and Los Angeles did show the film.

Biberman, one of the "Hollywood Ten," was convicted of contempt of Congress in 1950 when he was called before the House Un-American Activities Committee and refused to answer questions about his political affiliations. He served six months in jail. Paul Jarrico refused to deny or confirm Communist affiliations at the same hearings. Wilson clashed with the Committee and was blacklisted but managed to work by writing scripts under an assumed name.

In the years since, *Salt of the Earth* has become a cult classic and has been recognized as a pioneer film of women's liberation and the Mexican American civil rights movements. That it went so far against the grain of conventional movies of the time in the harsh political climate of the McCarthy era was monumental; even by 1990s standards, *Salt of the Earth* would be considered a daring, unconventional movie.

The heart of the movie is its harsh and powerful portrayal of human dignity in a social setting through the relationship of Esperanza and Ramon Quintero. Their struggle, personal growth, and role reversals in the face of the strike gave new dimensions to the portrayal and image of Mexican Americans in the United States.

Sadly, the film's ultimate effect on the industry was negligible because of its limited release, lack of star power, and controversial nature. Without the controversy it probably would have wound up a B movie on the second half of a double bill, much like *The Lawless* (1952) or *The Ring* (1952).

By comparison, Billy Wilder's major Paramount film *The Big Carnival* (1951), originally titled *Ace in the Hole,* a cynical look at a newspaper reporter during an actual news tragedy, was also based on a true-life event. It met with an indifferent response, though it starred Kirk Douglas, who was a major star at the time. Audiences preferred their heroes and institutions untainted.

Saludos Amigos (1942 BV)

     D: Bill Roberts, Jack Kinney, Hamilton Luske, and Wilfred Jackson
     S: Homer Brightman, Ralph Wright, Roy Williams, Harry Reeves, Dick Huemer, and Joe Grant
     P: Walt Disney
Cast: Aloysio Oliveira (narrator), Clarence Nash (Donald Duck), Aloysio Oliveira (Joe Carioca), Pinto Colvig (Goofy)

John Hay Whitney, the head of the Motion Picture Division for the Office of the Coordinator of Inter-American Affairs (CIAA), asked Walt Disney to make a goodwill tour of Latin America. The Disney films and characters were popular in South America, and CIAA officials were worried about the possible growth of pro-Axis sentiment there. Disney initially declined the offer but accepted after Whitney offered to underwrite $70,000 in tour expenses and advance up to $50,000 apiece for up to five films based on the tour. Disney, accompanied by an entourage of artists, animators, and film technicians, left for Latin America in August 1941, visiting Brazil, Argentina, Bolivia, and Chile.

Disney originally planned to make as many as twelve cartoons about Latin America and release them in packages of four. *Saludos Amigos* was the first installment, consisting of four films loosely strung together by travel footage of the Disney tour.

In "Lake Titicaca," Donald Duck plays a tourist who runs into trouble with a balky llama. In a variation of the 1930 Watty Piper story "The Little Engine That Could," "Pedro" is about a little mail plane struggling to fly over the Chilean Andes. Goofy wreaks some very funny havoc on the Pampas in "El Gaucho Goofy," and Donald returns to learn the samba from Joe Carioca, a jaunty parrot, in "Aquarela do Brazil" (Watercolor of Brazil).

Gilberto Souto, Alberto Soria, and Edmundo Santos were credited as foreign supervision associates. Backgrounds for "El Gaucho Goofy" were inspired by F. Molina Campos. *Saludos Amigos* opened to an enthusiastic response in Latin America and the States, and is generally regarded as a rough draft for the subsequent and more ambitious *The Three Caballeros* (1944).

James Woods portrays photojournalist Richard Boyle in *Salvador*, the story of violent political turmoil in El Salvador.

Salvador (1986 Hemdale)

D: Oliver Stone
S: Oliver Stone and Richard Boyle
P: Gerald Green and Oliver Stone
Cast: James Woods, James Belushi, Michael Murphy, **Elpidia Carrillo**, **Tony Plana**, **Juan Fernandez**

In 1980, two Americans, one the down-at-heels photojournalist Richard Boyle (Woods), the other the drug-crazed disc jockey Dr. Rock (Belushi), travel to war-torn El Salvador in Central America and are changed by their experiences.

The movie flings the viewer right into the events, and is unflinching in its depiction of the very human consequences of violent political action. Directing his second film on a low budget during a rigorous seven-week schedule in Mexico,

Stone was in frequent contention during production with the Mexican censors, who accused Stone of giving Mexico and Central America a negative image.

"The censor said we were making all of Latin America look like a pig sty, which of course is the reality of the situation," explained Stone in the *L.A. Times* (12/1/86). "So if I put in a ton of rubbish on the street, she [the censor] would take out half of it. Even when we asked for one thousand extras as dead bodies, she'd only let us use five hundred."

The film is based on the true story of Richard Boyle, a photojournalist who has covered wars in Vietnam, the Middle East, Northern Ireland, and Central America. Boyle gave a clue to his perceptions in the *L.A. Herald Examiner* (4/11/86): "Before the War, La Libertad used to be a great surfer hangout. I was into surfing. They'd come from all over the world. Good beer, beautiful women, cheap rent. What more do you want in life? I love the people in El Salvador. It's tragic that they're slaughtering each other." He continued, "None of this movie is fiction. Everything that happens is historically real."

This is clearly a North American view of the events, and many of the Latin women are made out to be sexual creatures easily available for the pleasure of men, both Anglo and Hispanic. In this case, perhaps, it is at least a truer reflection of the limited opportunities poor women have in oppressive, male-oriented cultures. The well-to-do Latinas, at least, are not presented this way. Cruel militaristic leaders, peasants struggling to survive, and opportunistic Americans are just some of the images presented. That the facts this time enforce the stereotypes is unfortunate. The film attempts fairly successfully to skewer covert efforts at American imperialism in Latin America, aided by poverty and cynical, brutal power plays by men seeking more and more power at the expense of their country.

Actor Belushi states in press notes on the movie's release, "My character is ignorant of Central American issues of which I feel most of the American general public is likewise, so I feel like I'm a touchstone for the audience at the beginning of the movie. My character discovers El Salvador as the audience does."

Tony Plana as the clever but brutal Major Max gives a chilling performance, as does Juan Fernandez as Lt. Smiling Death. Elpidia Carrillo does some fine work as the native girl Maria. James Woods was nominated for an Academy Award for his bravura and intensely multileveled performance as Boyle. The film moves at a frenetic pace with scenes of great power, such as whole towns being strafed and bombed, and the murder of Archbishop Romero (Jose Carlos Ruiz) during the celebration of mass.

One of the most shocking images depicting political atrocities is the sequence at El Playon, a huge garbage dump where hundreds of corpses lie visible as relatives search for missing loved ones who have been abducted from their homes and killed by death squads.

Boyle is slowly brought into events through his relationship with the native girl Maria. He finally abandons all hope of justice and fair play from a U.S. system in which he has stubbornly maintained a belief, despite previous confrontations in El Salvador with bigoted and politically cynical State Department officials and CIA "advisors" trying to maintain the brutal status quo for fear of a left-wing victory. The change in Boyle's attitude is completed when, after a harrowing journey to freedom and safety in the U.S., Maria is taken off the bus near Las Vegas, Nevada, by U.S. Immigration authorities and forcibly repatriated to El Salvador, where she will face almost certain torture and death.

Salvador was put into limited release by Hemdale when all the major distributors turned the film down because of its political content and was released before Stone's popular Academy Award–winning Vietnam War drama *Platoon* (1986).

Salvador earned two Oscar nominations, for Woods and for Best Original Screenplay for Boyle and Stone.

The Sandlot (1993 TCF)

D: David Mickey Evans
S: David Mickey Evans and Robert Gunter
P: Dale de la Torre and William S. Gilmore
Cast: Tom Guiry, **Mike Vitar**, Patrick Renna

Coming-of-age story about an awkward 12-year-old boy, Scott Smalls (Guiry), who moves to a San Fernando Valley, California, suburb in 1962 and tries to fit in with a loosely knit neighborhood baseball team made up of local misfits. The team leader is the athletically gifted Benny "the Jet" Rodriguez (Vitar). He befriends Smalls and instructs him in the game. Smalls learns to make new friends and conquer his own fears. Benny is Hispanic American and is presented without stereotypical cultural trappings within the cross-cultural context of the other kids. He is a leader, and at the end of the film it is revealed that he grows up to be a major league baseball player. He fulfills his promise as part of the American Dream.

Santiago (1956 WB)

D: Gordon Douglas
S: Martin Rackin and John Twist, based on Rackin's novel *The Great Courage*
P: Martin Rackin
Cast: Alan Ladd, Lloyd Nolan, Rossanna Podesta, Francisco Ruiz, Rico Alaniz

Rival gunrunners Cash Adams (Ladd) and Clay Pike (Nolan), en route by steamer to Cuba prior to the Spanish-American War of 1898, try to deliver guns to the people of Cuba, who are involved in a violent struggle to win independence from Spain. On board ship they meet Dona Isabella (Podesta), who is returning from a trip to the States to raise money for her people's struggle. The guns must be lugged overland, and Adams and Pike encounter Spanish troops in the jungle. They break through the Spanish blockade only to discover that the Cubans have suffered a costly defeat. Pike wants to turn around and sell the guns to the Spaniards, but Cash, now in love with Isabella, is determined his Cuban friends will have them.

The action is kept going by director Gordon Douglas, and some crackling dialogue between Nolan and Ladd makes for fun entertainment.

Saturday Night Fever (1977 Par)

D: John Badham
S: Norman Wexler
P: Robert Stigwood
Cast: John Travolta, Karen Lynn Gorney

Tony Manero (Travolta) is an Italian American working-class youth in Brooklyn, New York, with a dead-end job whose energies focus on a disco championship at the neighborhood disco club, 2001. The marginal Latin substory elements include a Puerto Rican couple who lose the disco championship to Tony and his girl, obviously only because they are not of the right ethnic background. In another scene Tony and his friends drive their car into a Puerto Rican gang's turf, which results in a fight that the Puerto Ricans lose.

Scandalous John (1971 BV)

D: Robert Butler
S: Bill Walsh and Don Da Gradi
P: Bill Walsh
Cast: Brian Keith, **Alfonso Arau**

A touching contemporary western comedy with a Don Quixote theme. A 79-year-old rancher, John McCanless (Keith), tilting against the windmill of progress, drives his last remaining cattle to market in an effort to save his ranch from developers. He sets off accompanied by Paco Martinez (Arau), his Mexican hired hand.

207

Al Pacino as the lead character in *Scarface*.

Scarface (1983 U)

D: Brian De Palma
S: Oliver Stone, based on the 1932 film script by Ben Hecht
P: Martin Bregman and Peter Saphier
Cast: Al Pacino, **Steven Bauer**, **Miriam Colon**, Mary Elizabeth Mastrantonio, Robert Loggia, **Pepe Serna**, Michelle Pfeiffer, **Victor Campos**, **Robert Contreras**, **Victor Millan**, **Santos Morales**

Brian De Palma directed this remake of the original 1932 gangster epic *Scarface*, directed by Howard Hawks and starring Paul Muni, updated to a Cuban American setting in 1980s Miami with the drug trade instead of Prohibition's liquor as the basis for Tony Montana's (Pacino) rise to power in the criminal underworld.

Pacino convincingly plays the ruthless and charming Cuban refugee who quickly learns his way around Miami. Through force of personality and a progression of criminal acts, he finds himself at the top of the criminal hierarchy. In an inspired classic finale, hundreds of Colombian hitmen pursue the cocaine-addicted Montana through his Florida mansion as he blasts away at them with an automatic weapon till he is felled and killed. Pacino spent time studying with Cubans in order to get the speech patterns and mannerisms right.

Scarface

The predominantly Hispanic cast introduced Steven Bauer as Montana's best friend and included Miriam Colon as his mother, Pepe Serna as his doomed refugee buddy who meets his demise at the end of a chainsaw, Angel Salazar as another friend of Montana's, and Arnaldo Santana as Ernie. Mary Elizabeth Mastrantonio is Montana's sister, of whom he is overprotective. The film was directed in grand style and tone by Brian De Palma from a script by Oliver Stone.

Scarface provided the movies with a new screen villain and Hispanic stereotype, the drug lord or kingpin. Previously, Hispanics had been seen as the victims of drugs, small-time hoodlums, or street dealers. Hispanics were now in control of the drug trade and every bit as clever and ruthless as their Italian Mafia screen counterparts.

Miami was re-created in an exaggerated art deco style similar to that of Michael Mann's later hit TV show "Miami Vice," and reintroduced as a new city of overheated ambiance and color, Cuban dominated, and peopled with Caribbean and South American types. Previous cinematic incarnations had pictured the city as a retirement beach resort community for middle-class Americans.

The film was a tremendous box-office hit but critics were divided over the film's excessive foul language, violence, and depiction of drugs. It should be pointed out, too, that De Palma and Stone take almost *3 hours* to achieve what Hawks did in 90 minutes!

Tony (Al Pacino), his mother (Miriam Colon, standing), and his sister, Gina (Mary Elizabeth Mastrantonio) in *Scarface*.

209

Second Chance (1953 RKO)

   D: Rudolph Mate
   S: Oscar Millard, Sydney Boehm, and D.M. Marshman, Jr., based on
      a story by Marshman
   P: Sam Wiesenthal
Cast: Robert Mitchum, Linda Darnell, Jack Palance, **Rudolfo Hoyos, Jr.,**
      Fortunio Bonanova, Abel Fernandez, Martin Garralaga

A south-of-the-border melodrama in which Russ Lambert (Mitchum), an American prizefighter, barnstorms through Mexico trying to assuage the guilt he feels for killing a man in the ring. There he meets Clare Shepard (Darnell), a gangster's moll, who is being stalked by a hit man (Palance) sent to kill her before a Senate crime committee can find her to testify against her ex-boyfriend.

The high point of the film is a fight atop a funicular railway between two Andean peaks (despite the fact that the film takes place in Mexico). Part of the film was shot in Cuernavaca and Taxco, Mexico. Cast members include Rudolfo Hoyos, Jr., Salvador Baguez, Maurice Jara, Fortunio Bonanova, Abel Fernandez, Martin Garralaga, Jose Dominguez, Tony Martinez, and Tina Menard.

Secret of the Incas (1954 Par)

   D: Jerry Hopper
   S: Ranald MacDougall and Sydney Boehm, based on the story "Legend of
      the Incas" by Boehm
   P: Mel Epstein
Cast: Charlton Heston, Robert Young, Thomas Mitchell, Yma Sumac [Amy Camus]

Routine action programmer highlighted by Technicolor and location photography in Machu Picchu, Peru. Two American soldiers of fortune are on the trail of the Inca Sunburst jewels. The film features Yma Sumac, Peruvian songbird of the Andes, in her film debut.

Martin Garralaga, Rudolfo Hoyos, Rosa Rey, and Carlos Rivero, among other Hispanic actors, have minor roles in the film.

Serenade (1956 WB)

   D: Anthony Mann
   S: Ivan Goff, Ben Roberts, and John Twist, based on the novel
      by James M. Cain
   P: Henry Blanke
Cast: Mario Lanza, Joan Fontaine, **Sarita Montiel, Joseph Calleia**

Lanza's comeback film after four years away from the cameras since 1952's *Because You're Mine*. Lanza, as Damon Vincente, is a potent personality with a rich singing voice that makes up for any acting inadequacies.

This is the tale of a California vineyard worker's rise to operatic eminence and the two women from different worlds, one Anglo, the other Mexican, who love him. Kendall Hale (Fontaine) is the wealthy society patroness who jilts him when something better comes along, and Juana Montes (Montiel) is the Mexican senorita who weds him at the finale. Mexican location scenes were filmed in San Miguel de Allende.

Serenade is based on the James M. Cain novel, extensively watered down in its adaptation for the movies. The novel dealt with male homosexuality, impotence, and prostitution in the shantytowns of Mexico. It also included a lot of inside stuff about singers and their problems, after which a doxy from below the Rio Grande stabs Fancy Dan in the course of a mock bullfight in a New York penthouse.

The film shared more parallels with *Blood and Sand* (1922 and 1941) than with its original source. The hero, a simple elemental man with a superb voice, is brought to the heights of success and then abandoned by a sensuous, sensation-hungry female aristocrat (Dona Sol in *Blood and Sand*). This proves to be more than he can handle. His breakdown is cured by the love of a good woman (Carmen Espinosa in *Blood and Sand*).

Hispanic actor Martin Garralaga plays Romero, a minor role, and Jose Torvay is a mariachi bandleader.

Seven Cities of Gold (1955 TCF)

D: Robert D. Webb

S: Richard L. Breen, John C. Higgins, and Joseph Petracca, based on a novel by Isabelle Gibson Ziegler

P: Robert D. Webb and Barbara McLean

Cast: Richard Egan, **Anthony Quinn**, Michael Rennie, Jeffrey Hunter, **Rita Moreno**, Eduardo Noriega, Victor Juncos, Miguel Inclan, Carlos Musquiz, Pedro Galvan

Quinn plays the hardened Spanish military explorer Gaspar de Portola, who, along with Father Junipero Serra (Rennie), explored northern Mexico and helped establish the missions of California in 1769.

Following many difficulties in the hostile lands, the expedition arrives at the present site of San Diego, California, where Portola sets up a garrison and leaves it in the care of Lieutenant Jose Mendoza (Egan) before continuing northward in search of the mythical Seven Cities of Cibola, where the streets are reportedly paved with gold.

Hostile Indians harass the settlement, but an understanding is reached when Serra saves the life of one of the chiefs. Mendoza seduces Ula (Moreno), a pretty Indian girl and sister of the chief. Portola returns, expecting a supply ship at the bay. Mendoza rejects Ula's proposal of marriage. Ashamed of herself and unable to return to her people with honor, Ula commits suicide by leaping from a cliff. Her brother, seeking revenge for his sister's death, demands that Mendoza be turned over to him. Portola and Serra refuse, but Mendoza finally surrenders himself to the Indians in order not to further endanger the garrison. The Indians cut out Mendoza's heart, and Serra brings back the body. The supply ship finally arrives and allows for the establishment of a mission at San Diego.

This film should have been called *The Father Serra Story* or *San Diego*. The title *Seven Cities of Gold* led audiences to expect an action spectacle about conquistadors in search of ill-gotten treasures from ancient Indian civilizations. Instead, audiences got this bare (production-wise) story that focuses on the standard Indians-versus-settlers conflicts.

It did address on a superficial level certain truths about the interactions and cross-purposes among the Catholic church, Spanish explorers, and Native Americans in the New World. Quinn as Portola comes off best because of his Latin quality, while Rennie as Father Serra is very British but supplies the dignity and authority the character demands. Egan comes off as hopelessly American. Rita Moreno is quite good as Ula, yet she was already growing tired of these native-girls-with-bare-feet depictions, which until then accounted for more than half her film roles.

Filmed on location in Mexico around the rugged deserts of Guadalajara and the beaches of Manzanillo, the production involved some of the top motion picture talent in Mexico, both in front of and behind the camera. Rene Cardona, Mexican film producer and director, served as co-director, while Sanchez Tello and Jaime Contreras were assistant directors. Jorje Stahl, whose father was one of the pioneers of the Mexican film industry, worked as camera operator. Among the cast were Eduardo Noriega, Fernando Wagner, Lucila Nieto, Jose Torvay, Carlos Musquiz, Pedro Galvan, Yerye Beirute, John Cusick, and Eduardo Pliego.

Short Eyes [aka: *The Slammer*] (1977 Film League)
     D: Robert M. Young
     S: **Miguel Pinero**, based on his play
     P: Lewis Harris
  Cast: Bruce Davison, **Jose Perez**, Tito Goya, **Miguel Pinero**

Searing and grueling slice-of-life prison drama actually filmed in the New York correctional institution known as "The Tombs." The Obie Award–winning play was written by Miguel Pinero, who also wrote the screenplay, based on his five-year experience as an inmate at Sing Sing Prison.

A child molester is brought into the cell block, where passions run high, not only among the black and Puerto Rican inmates but also among the guards. Juan, played by Jose Perez, is a rational and compassionate Puerto Rican inmate. Tito Goya plays Cupcakes, and Shawn Elliott plays a cynical Puerto Rican. Mexican American singer Freddy Fender makes a cameo appearance as an inmate.

A Show of Force (1990 Par)
     D: Bruno Barreto
     S: John Strong
     P: John Strong
  Cast: Amy Irving, Robert Duvall, **Erik Estrada**, **Andy Garcia**,
       Lou Diamond Phillips

This film is a misrepresentation of an actual incident that was uncovered by three Puerto Rican journalists who implicated the local police and the U.S. government in the murder of several radical students. The film combines the journalists into one Anglo female reporter who is the widow of a Puerto Rican activist (which conveniently provides her with a Hispanic last name).

Reporter Kate Melendez (Irving) tries to get to the bottom of the killing of two militant students by police at a remote broadcast tower in Cerro Maravilla, Puerto Rico. The island is presented as a cross between Miami and a Latin American country and features a tyrannical governor surrounded by goony, villainous police officials. Howard (Duvall), the television station news manager, doesn't seem to care about Melendez's story. Her father, a seemingly bigoted naval officer, tells her, "My biggest mistake was sending you to college. I had you leave Puerto Rico and what do you do, you come back with a Puerto Rican; not just any Puerto Rican—a radical leftist one." And she retorts, "He was a lawyer with a cause."

The problems of Puerto Rico and Puerto Ricans are seen here as internal ones, with Anglo-Americans not caring about whether justice is served, even though Puerto Ricans are also U.S. citizens.

There is no suspense in the film, which does not create any sympathy for the victims or involve the viewer in this miscarriage of justice or its implications. The causes of the dissatisfaction of these radicals and the politics are never explored. The final cop-out of the film is to place responsibility on an individual, not the system. Melendez seems to be the only one who has a nice family life or home. Puerto Ricans' homes and living conditions are represented as if Puerto Rico were a Third World country.

An interesting performance is given by Lou Diamond Phillips, and a fine cameo is provided by Andy Garcia as an opposition party lawyer. Another cameo features Erik Estrada as a police officer with a conscience. The movie was filmed entirely in Puerto Rico.

Sierra Baron (1958 TCF)

    D: James B. Clark
    S: Houston Brach
    P: Plato A. Skouras
Cast: Brian Keith, Rick Jason

Routine western shot in Mexico by Alex Phillips. A Spanish don's land grants in California are being threatened by encroaching Americanos.

The Slammer

See *Short Eyes*.

Sniper (1993 TS)

    D: **Luis Llosa**
    S: Michael Frost Beckner and Crash Leyland
    P: Robert L. Rosen
Cast: Tom Berenger, Billy Zane

A U.S. Marine sniper and an observer go on a mission into the jungles of Panama to take out a powerful rebel guerrilla leader and his financier, a Colombian drug lord. Filmed in Australia, doubling for Panama, by Peruvian filmmaker Luis Llosa in his American directorial debut.

Sol Madrid (1968 MGM)

    D: Brian G. Hutton
    S: David Karp, based on the novel *Fruit of the Poppy* by Robert Wilder
    P: Hall Bartlett
Cast: David McCallum, Stella Stevens, **Ricardo Montalban**, Rip Torn, **Perry Lopez, Abel Franco**, Joe Dominguez

Sol Madrid (McCallum), an undercover narcotics agent, is assigned the task of tracking down a gangster who is on the run from his Mafia cohorts. In the course of the investigation Sol comes across one of the main sources of heroin supply from Mexico to the States. All this is routinely played out against sunny Acapulco, Mexico, locations. Montalban plays Jalisco, a charismatic double-crossing Mexican agent.

Sombrero (1953 MGM)

    D: Norman Foster
    S: Norman Foster and Josefina Niggli, based on Niggli's novel *A Mexican Village*
    P: Jack Cummings
Cast: **Ricardo Montalban**, Pier Angeli, Vittorio Gassman, Cyd Charisse, Yvonne De Carlo, Rick Jason, **Jose Greco, Alfonso Bedoya**

A blending of three love stories based on Josefina Niggli's novel *A Mexican Village*, published in 1945. Born and raised in Monterey, Mexico, Niggli resided in North Carolina at the time of production. The book consisted of ten short stories, but only three were used in *Sombrero*. The film features three Latin leading men—Ricardo Montalban, Vittorio Gassman (the Italian neorealist film idol in his American film debut), and newcomer Rick Jason—and three leading ladies: Pier Angeli, Yvonne De Carlo, and Cyd Charisse, who performs a sensuous dance before an ancient Aztec idol. Spanish dancer Jose Greco plays a matador in his film debut.

    This well-intentioned, handsomely produced, but caricatured, episodic musical was filmed in Technicolor largely on location in Tepotzlan and Tetecala, Mexico, in the state of Morelos near Cuernavaca. Producer Cummings had filmed in Puebla,

Ricardo Montalban and Pier Angeli in *Sombrero,* a film combining three stories of love and romance in Mexico.

Mexico, six years previously on *Fiesta* for MGM. Foster was a top-flight director in Mexico City, where he lived for seven years before returning to Hollywood. The Mexican-born Montalban had become a star in Mexico under Foster's direction before coming to Hollywood. Rosaura Revueltas (*Salt of the Earth*) is featured as Tia Magdalena, and Alfonso Bedoya is Don Inocente. Alma Beltran and Pilar Del Rey have minor roles in the film.

"*Sombrero* is another of those musicals which are bright, gaudy and meaningless. All the fancy trappings . . . can't compensate for lack of conviction in plot," *Hollywood Citizen News* (4/14/53).

Sorcerer (1977 U/Par)

D: William Friedkin
S: Walon Green
P: William Friedkin
Cast: Roy Scheider, Ramon Bieri

Story of four men, each of whom has had to flee his native country, who end up in a poverty-stricken village in South America where they work on American oil pipelines. When an oil well some 200 miles from the village explodes, they are hired to drive six cases of nitroglycerin across treacherous mountains and jungle roads. In return they are promised $10,000 each and legal residence in the country without police harassment. Based on Georges Arnaud's novel *The Wages of Fear* and on the critically acclaimed 1955 French film of the same name, directed by Clouzot. Friedkin's film, though well made, met with indifference at the box office. It was filmed in central Mexico and the Dominican Republic.

Speedy Gonzalez (1955)

This cartoon short starred Speedy Gonzalez, a Mexican cartoon character created in 1953 at Warner Bros. Speedy Gonzalez won an Academy Award for this in 1955. The voice of Speedy Gonzalez was created and done by the versatile Mel Blanc. Billed as "the fastest and smartest mouse in all of Meheeco!," Speedy proved a popular addition to the Warner Bros. Looney Tunes characters, which included Bugs Bunny, Porky Pig, and Daffy Duck.

Stand and Deliver (1988 WB)

    D: **Ramon Menendez**
    S: **Ramon Menendez** and Tom Musca
    P: **Edward James Olmos, Ramon Menendez,** and Tom Musca
  E/P: Tom Musca
  Cast: **Edward James Olmos, Lou Diamond Phillips, Rosana De Soto,** Carmen Argenziano, Virginia Paris

Stand and Deliver is based on the true story of mathematics teacher Jaime Escalante and his success with a group of underachieving East Los Angeles high school students at Garfield High.

In 1982, 18 of his students took the Advanced Placement Test in calculus. The exam, which qualifies students for college credit, is so demanding that less than 2 percent of all high school students in the U.S. even attempt it. Through diligence and determination, all of Escalante's students received passing grades, six with perfect scores.

Actor Edward James Olmos (left) and real-life mathematics teacher Jaime Escalante discuss a key scene at Garfield High School in East Los Angeles, the location of the true drama depicted in the movie *Stand and Deliver*.

From the cast of *Stand and Deliver*, Edward James Olmos (back row, left) portrays inspiring high school teacher Jaime Escalante and Lou Diamond Phillips (right) is Angel, a school troublemaker harboring a secret desire to improve himself. Among Escalante's students are (back row, left to right) Ingrid Oliu as Lupe, Will Gotay as Pancho, Lydia Nicole as Rafaela; (front row, left to right) Vanessa Marquez as Ana, Patrick Baca as Javier, Karla Montana as Claudia, and Mark Eliot as Tito.

However, the initial triumph was short lived. After carefully examining the test papers, the Educational Testing Service concluded there was such a distinct pattern of incorrect answers among the Garfield students that they must have cheated. Their scores were invalidated and, despite the protests of Escalante, the students were given a choice: accept the Testing Service's verdict or retest. They chose to retest and again passed.

The controversial story was not lost on filmmakers Ramon Menendez and Tom Musca, who co-wrote the screenplay and produced the film with Edward James Olmos. They first learned of the story from a *Los Angeles Times* article. "The idea of being truly innocent and having to prove it seemed like an intriguing premise for a film," recalled Musca in an interview with Luis Reyes. "There was an enormous probability that the students' scores would never have been questioned had they not all come from Garfield High with predominantly Hispanic surnames. In other words, there was the distinct possibility of institutional racism."

After a discouraging response from the studios, Menendez and Musca turned to a prior relationship with Lindsay Law, the executive producer of the "American Playhouse" series. Menendez and Musca sent a synopsis of the Escalante story to Law, whose reaction was positive. Besides "American Playhouse," Musca received funding from organizations such as Arco, the National Science Foundation, the Corporation for Public Broadcasting, and the Ford Foundation.

When it came time to find an actor to portray Jaime Escalante, Menendez and Musca contacted Olmos, who was excited not only about the prospect of portraying Escalante, but also about joining them in a production capacity. "The concept of false accusation was a theme I had dealt with in my earlier film roles, both in

Zoot Suit [1981] as well as in *The Ballad of Gregorio Cortez* [1983]," remarked Olmos in an interview with Luis Reyes. Once committed, Olmos began preparations for the part of the Bolivian-born schoolteacher by studying the man. "Jaime and I spent extensive time together," recalled the actor. Olmos spent 18 hours a day for a month at the instructor's side. The actor concentrated on Escalante's physical characteristics. He had his hair thinned to resemble the teacher's pate and gained 40 pounds. Olmos reasoned, "Jaime's appearance, even his mannerisms, have a lot to do with the way his kids treat him. So I could not see myself playing the role in peak condition."

Lou Diamond Phillips, still relatively unknown since *La Bamba* (1987) had not yet been released, joined the cast as Angel, a youth who has to choose between education and the lure of street gang life.

Stand and Deliver was shot in and around East Los Angeles and on the actual Garfield High School site on a shoestring budget (by current standards) of $1 million, over a period of six weeks. After being screened by all the major studios, the film was picked up for theatrical distribution by Warner Bros. prior to its airing on PBS.

The movie struck a responsive chord with the American moviegoing public as well as with film critics, educators, and politicians, in what it had to say about the state of American education and the difference one teacher can make in the lives of students. At a time in American life when there is concern over the quality of education and the plight of teachers and students, the film was hailed for its inspirational message.

The critics hailed Olmos's sensitive portrayal of the math teacher. He was nominated for a Golden Globe Award and an Academy Award for Best Actor of 1988. The film introduced a number of young Hispanic performers to the screen and showcased the talents of many established performers such as Rosana De Soto, Virginia Paris, Carmen Argenziano, and Andy Garcia as an Educational Testing Service investigator.

Stand and Deliver departs from the usual Hollywood formula of a white teacher helping disadvantaged minority youth, implying racial superiority of the dominant culture and accepted U.S. middle-class values. Usually, minority teachers are relegated to the background of the story and are presented as ineffectual at best. This was demonstrated as early as *Blackboard Jungle* (1955) and as recently as *The Principal* (1987). *Stand and Deliver*, however, paved the way for another film about a minority teacher, in a predominantly black New Jersey inner-city school, *Lean on Me* (1989), a much less effective movie, which starred Morgan Freeman as real-life controversial black principal Joe Clark.

The creative forces behind *Stand and Deliver*, Menendez and Olmos, are Hispanic. Even though Menendez is Cuban and Olmos is Mexican American, *Stand and Deliver* is regarded as a Chicano film because of the overwhelming presence and involvement of Edward James Olmos, who helped to shape the final film as star and producer and helped to clarify its poignant subject matter.

Stars and Guitars

See *Brazil*.

Summer and Smoke (1961 Par)

D: Peter Glenville
S: James Poe and Meade Roberts, based on the play by Tennessee Williams
P: Hal Wallis
Cast: Laurence Harvey, Geraldine Page, **Rita Moreno, Thomas Gomez, Pepe Hern**

Set in a southern town in 1916, this is a typically torrid Tennessee Williams tale of Alma (Page), the inhibited daughter of a minister, and John (Harvey), the boy next door and hell-bent son of the town's respected doctor.

Although intrigued by Alma's shy gropings toward love, John takes up with Rosa (Moreno), the earthy daughter of a gambling casino owner (Gomez). John's father is accidentally killed by Rosa's father after a drunken party. After his father's death, John reforms but refuses Alma's love in favor of an adoring teenager. Alma is left alone to find love with whomever comes her way.

The Sun Also Rises (1957 TCF)

D: Henry King
S: Peter Viertel, based on the novel by Ernest Hemingway
P: Darryl F. Zanuck
Cast: Tyrone Power, Errol Flynn, Ava Gardner, **Mel Ferrer**, Eddie Albert

Set in Europe during the 1920s just following the end of World War I, *The Sun Also Rises* covers a few weeks in the lives and loves of a "Lost Generation" of people who lived as though they might die at any time.

Based on the novel by Ernest Hemingway (published in 1926), the film version concentrated on the tragic tale of the lives and loves of Jake Barnes (Power) and Lady Brett Ashley (Gardner). Traveling with friends from Paris to the bullfights in Spain, they meet Mike Campbell (Flynn). They become entangled with a bullfighter, Pedro Romero, played by then-unknown Robert Evans (who forsook an acting career to become a major producer).

This film is a well-acted, visually sweeping Technicolor production, though the actors were a little too old for the roles as written in the Hemingway novel. Censorship restrictions and a Hollywood-imposed happy ending marred the work's original intent.

Although the San Fermin fiesta in Pamplona, Spain, was filmed in its entirety, Pamplona had to be doubled by Morelia, Mexico, for the scenes with the principal actors because of the weather. Shooting also took place in Spain, France, and California. Morelia was last used as a filming location by Fox in 1946 for its production of *Captain from Castile* (1947), also directed by Henry King and starring Tyrone Power.

Ernest Hemingway told the *London Sunday Dispatch,* as reported in *Time* magazine (12/2/57), "I saw Darryl Zanuck's splashy Cook's tour of Europe's lost-generation bistros, bullfights, and more bistros. It's all pretty disappointing and that's being gracious. You're meant to be in Spain and all you see walking around are nothing but Mexicans. Pretty silly."

The Super (1991 TCF)

D: Rod Daniel
S: Sam Simon
P: Charles A. Gordon
Cast: Joe Pesci, Vincent Gardenia, Madolyn Smith Osborne, **Ruben Blades**

Comedy/drama about Louie Kritski (Pesci), a slumlord who is ordered by a judge to live in one of his own decrepit tenements in New York City as punishment for deliberately ignoring building code violations. While living in the tenement he gets to know its inhabitants and experiences their terrible living conditions. Ruben Blades plays Marlon, a crafty street hustler who keeps dreaming up new ways to scam Kritski, while gradually teaching him to feel compassion for his tenants. Other Hispanics featured in the cast are Steve Rodriguez, Eileen Galindo, Marina Durrell, Olga Merediz, Chris Herrera, and Juan Manual Aguero.

Sweet Charity (1969 U)
D: Bob Fosse
S: Peter Stone, based on the play by Neil Simon, Cy Coleman, and Dorothy Fields, adapted from the screenplay *Notti di Cabiria* by Federico Fellini, Tullio Ponelli, and Ennio Flaiano
P: Robert Arthur
Cast: Shirley MacLaine, **Chita Rivera, Ricardo Montalban**, Sammy Davis, Jr.

The first screen appearance of famed Broadway actress/dancer Chita Rivera, who created on stage many roles played by other actresses in the later film versions, including Anita (Rita Moreno) in *West Side Story* and Rosie (Janet Leigh) in *Bye, Bye Birdie.*

Rivera plays one of Charity's best girlfriends and demonstrates her unique singing and dancing ability to great effect. Ricardo Montalban gives a splendid caricature performance of a Latin lover leading man in this musical directed by Bob Fosse (making his feature film directorial debut).

Taggart (1964 U)
D: R.G. Springsteen
S: Robert Creighton Williams, based on a novel by Louis L'Amour
P: Gordon Kay
Cast: Tony Young, Dan Duryea, David Carradine, **Elsa Cardenas**

One of the last of Universal's modest-budget color programmers, which gave way to television movies, *Taggart* was based on a novel by famed western writer Louis L'Amour. The slaughter of a homestead family and the revenge sought by the surviving son, Taggart, are the thrust of the story. After obtaining revenge Taggart finds himself with a price on his own head. He vies for the love of a vivacious and treacherous Mexican, Consuela (Cardenas), and a good blonde girl. The blonde Anglo wins his love.

Tampico (1944 TCF)
D: Lothar Mendes
S: Kenneth Gamet, Fred Niblo, Jr., and Richard Macaulay, based on an original story by Ladislas Fodor
P: Robert Bassler
Cast: Edward G. Robinson, Lynn Bari, Victor McLaglen, Marc Lawrence, **Mona Maris**

Story of a tanker captain who loses his ship to a torpedo from a Nazi submarine shortly after the vessel has left the Mexican oil port from which the story takes its name. He seeks to avenge himself by discovering which of several persons who knew of his departure leaked the information to the enemy. The story becomes one of conflict and romance between the captain (Robinson) and a rescued passenger (Bari) and of the intrigue of wartime espionage in the Gulf city of Tampico. Antonio Moreno appears in a small role as a justice of the peace. Chris-Pin Martin, Nestor Paiva, and Martin Garralaga also have small roles. Grace Poggi, a Spanish-Italian California-born dancer, plays the dancer in a café sequence. Mexican musicians and composers Gilbert Ysais and Noel Desilva perform in the wedding sequence.

Tarzan and the Great River (1967 Par)
D: Robert Day
S: Bob Barbash
P: Sy Weintraub
Cast: Mike Henry, **Manuel Padilla, Jr.**, Rafer Johnson

Tarzan adventure set in South America along the Amazon River.

Terror in a Texas Town (1958 UA)

D: Joseph H. Lewis
S: Ben L. Perry [Dalton Trumbo]
P: Frank N. Seltzer
Cast: Sterling Hayden, Sebastian Cabot, **Victor Millan**, Ann Varela

Ed McNeil (Cabot), a Texas land baron, intimidates local farmers into giving up their land because, as the resident Mexican Jose Mirada (Millan) explains, "The ground she is filled with oil." George Hansen (Hayden), a Swedish American sailor, returns to his father's home in Texas and finds that his dad has been murdered. Upon his arrival, George is beaten up by McNeil's henchmen and is found and nursed back to health by Mirada, who tells Hansen the truth about his father's murder, which Mirada witnessed. Mirada is also killed, and Hansen faces down the henchmen with a whaling harpoon.

A combination poor man's *High Noon* and *Bad Day at Black Rock*, *Terror in a Texas Town* was filmed in 10 days for $80,000 and was written by blacklisted writer Dalton Trumbo. It has become a cult B movie favorite on campus and in art house theaters.

"Outdoor drama that examines fear and its consequences on men. Well made within modest framework," *Film Daily* (8/25/58).

That Night in Rio (1941 TCF)

D: Irving Cummings
S: George Seaton, Bess Meredyth, Hal Long, Samuel Hoffenstein, and Jessie Ernst, based on a play by Rudolph Lothar and Hans Adler
P: Fred Kohlmar
Cast: Alice Faye, Don Ameche, **Carmen Miranda, J. Carroll Naish, Maria Montez**

Don Ameche plays two roles in this Technicolor musical/comedy—Larry Martin, an American entertainer in Rio at the Cafe Samba, and Baron Duarte, a notorious Brazilian rake. Carmen Miranda plays an entertainer called Carmen in this, her second American film, in which she not only sings and dances but also acts. She firmly established her persona with rapid-fire dialogue, punctuated by her inspired brand of broken English, and with a variation of the Bahian-style costume of her native Brazil. The "Chica, Chica, Boom, Chica" opening production number was spectacularly staged by Hermes Pan.

No real attempt was made to depict Rio accurately except for some painted scenic backdrops. Through Miranda's personal intervention, a young Spanish dancer, a sloe-eyed Maria Montez, was given one of the key dance spots as Inez in the picture. The film features Carmen Miranda's orchestra, Banda de Lua. Also featured are Frank Puglia as Pedro, Fortunio Bonanova as Pereira the headwaiter, Alberto Morin as Eca the pilot, and the Flores Brothers, who also made musical contributions to *Down Argentine Way* (1940). Mack Gordon and Harry Warren, who wrote the music and lyrics but who had never been to South America, wrote some Spanish lyrics, not realizing that Portuguese is the language of Brazil. With the help of the Brazilian technical adviser, the song was translated from the Spanish "Buenas Noches" to the Portuguese "Boa Noite." The Brazilian embassy in Washington gave the film's script and music its approval.

They Met in Argentina (1941 RKO)

D: Leslie Goodwins and Jack Hively
S: Jerry Cady, based on a story by Brock and Harold Daniels
P: Lou Brock
Cast: Maureen O'Hara, James Ellison, Alberto Vila, Buddy Ebsen, Robert Barrat, Joseph Buloff, Diosa Costello, Victoria Cordova, **Antonio Moreno, Fortunio Bonanova**

Behind-the-scenes RKO power Nelson Rockefeller, holding the title of "Coordinator of Commercial and Cultural Relations Between the American Republics," was determined to see RKO join in the trend to produce films with Latin American themes and settings. Lou Brock, producer of the hit *Flying Down to Rio* (1933), was brought in to supervise the first of three productions. The result, *They Met in Argentina*, was a major flop in every way.

It started with the script, set against an Argentine background, in which the conflict is between a young man who doesn't want to fall in love and a young girl who is used to having her own way. Maureen O'Hara was miscast as a senorita. The songs and score by Rodgers and Hart never seemed to click. Spanish-speaking audiences were offended by the whole exercise, and U.S. audiences weren't interested.

¡Three Amigos! (1986 Or)

  D: John Landis
  S: Steve Martin, Lorne Michaels, and Randy Newman
  P: George Folsey, Jr., and Lorne Michaels
Cast: Steve Martin, Chevy Chase, Martin Short, **Patrice Martinez, Alfonso Arau, Tony Plana, Jorge Cervera, Loyda Ramos,** Joe Mantegna, **Santos Morales**

In Mexico in 1916, the poor village of Santa Poco is being terrorized and despoiled by the notorious bandit chieftain El Guapo (Arau), his henchman Jefe (Plana), and their army of ferocious outlaws. Carmen (Martinez), a beautiful young woman from the village, sends a desperate plea for help (Santos Morales is the telegrapher) to three men whom she has seen fighting oppression and conquering evil—those dashing stars of the silent screen, The Three Amigos!

On screen, Lucky Day (Martin), Dusty Bottoms (Chase), and Ned Nederlander (Short) are fearless romantic heroes. In real life they're innocent, bumbling guys sweetly sheltered by the luxuries of stardom. Those luxuries are suddenly stripped away when the fast-talking Lucky demands a new contract from movie mogul Harry Flugleman (Mantegna). Instead, Flugleman fires the trio.

The cable from Carmen comes just in time. Assuming they've been asked to make a personal appearance—at a whopping fee of 100,000 pesos—the trio takes off for Santa Poco. Once in the village, our heroes think the bandits are fellow actors and put on a performance that dumbfounds the outlaws. But Lucky, Dusty, and Ned soon discover that the bullets and bandits are real, and so is their chance to become true heroes. When El Guapo attacks Santa Poco and kidnaps Carmen, the Amigos cross the desert and infiltrate his fortress. They rescue Carmen and narrowly escape in a biplane. Then they rally the people of Santa Poco to fight for their freedom. After all, they are The Three Amigos!

A mildly amusing spoof of many westerns, in particular, *The Magnificent Seven*, the film is played entirely for laughs, and the actors have a field day in their bandido roles, brandishing their guns, flashing smiles with missing teeth, and sporting scars, hairpieces, and several days' growth on their faces. Alfonso Arau actually had a similar serious bad guy role in Peckinpah's *The Wild Bunch* (1969).

All the stereotypes are present, both Anglo and Hispanic. The three Anglo amigos are a not-too-bright lot who resemble the 1930s series western stars The Three Mesquiteers and a number of western characterizations. The virginal senorita (Martinez), the Latin spitfire (Ramos), the noble peasant villager (Abel Franco), and the bandit leader (Arau) are all here. The more familiar the viewer is with film history and westerns in particular, the more enjoyable the film is, as the targets of its spoofing become obvious.

The Three Caballeros (1944 RKO)

D: Norman Ferguson, Clyde Geronimi, Jack Kinney, Bill Roberts, and Harold Young

S: Homer Brightman, Ernest Terrazzas, Ted Sears, Bill Peet, Ralph Wright, Elmer Plymmer, Roy Williams, William Cottrell, Del Connell, and James Bodrero

P: Norman Ferguson

Cast: **Aurora Miranda,** Dora Luz, Carmen Molina, Nestor Amaral, and the voices of Sterling Holloway, Clarence Nash (Donald Duck), Jose Oliveira (Joe Carioca), and **Joaquin Garay** (Panchito)

Captivating music and a spectacular blend of animation and live action create a dazzling south-of-the-border adventure. In this classic Disney feature, Donald Duck celebrates his birthday with his friends Joe Carioca, the Brazilian parrot, and a Mexican rooster named Panchito. Donald opens a wondrous collection of gifts that evolve into musical journeys with a Latin American beat. The cartoon characters visit beautiful locations and interact with such human performers as Aurora Miranda of Brazil and Carmen Molina and Dora Luz of Mexico. The segments include a magical serape ride and the animated tales of "The Cold Blooded Penguin," "Baia," and "The Flying Gauchito."

This was one of the most successful American films to play in Latin America during the 1940s.

Three Godfathers (1948 MGM)

D: **John Ford**

S: Laurence Stallings and Frank Nugent, based on the story by Peter B. Kyne

P: **John Ford** and Merian C. Cooper

Cast: John Wayne, **Pedro Armendariz,** Harry Carey, Jr.

While running from the law, three bandits (Wayne, Armendariz, Carey) come upon a dying woman who is about to give birth in the desert. Two of them die trying to get the newborn child to town and safety.

This offbeat western with biblical parallels to the three wise men's journey to Jerusalem is highlighted by the performances of the three leads and stunning color photography. The story was filmed before: twice as *The Three Godfathers* (in 1916 and 1936,) as *Marked Men* (in 1919), and as *Hell's Heroes* (in 1929), but this is the only version in which one of the bandits was portrayed as a Mexican.

Armendariz is most able as the bilingual bandit Pete, who admits to the dying woman, after he has delivered her baby, that his actual name is Pedro Incarnacion Yrango y Roca Fuerte. Hightower (Wayne) keeps riding Pete about his speaking Spanish around the baby. "Cut out that Mex lingo around the kid, will you, Pete, first thing you know he'll be talking it. We got to raise him with good all-American habla, like his Ma." Pete is noticeably hurt and continues to speak Spanish.

Pete suffers a broken leg during the desert trek; knowing he cannot go on, he takes his own life with a pistol. This is an eerie foreshadowing of Armendariz's own death 15 years later when he shot himself with a pistol after he found out he had terminal cancer.

Ironically, at the end of the film, Hightower, the only surviving member of the trio, speaks his last words to the baby in Spanish, "Adios, compañero," before he is taken off to jail.

In *Three Godfathers,* Pedro Armendariz (center) portrays one of three happy but concerned bandits who care for a child when the mother dies in a desert wagon shortly after childbirth. John Wayne (left) and Harry Carey, Jr. (right) portray the other two bandits.

"Armendariz has done much better in the past, but only because his material has always been better. Here he's too close to being a caricature of a Mexican," Darr Smith, *L.A. Daily News* (2/9/49).

On the other hand, Edwin Schallert in the *L.A. Times* (2/9/49) said, "Armendariz combines comedy with effectiveness and discretion."

The Thrill of Brazil (1946 Col)

   D: S. Sylvan Simon
   S: Allen Rivkin, Harry Clork, and Devery Freeman
   P: Sidney Biddell
Cast: Evelyn Keyes, Keenan Wynn, Ann Miller, Allyn Joslyn, **Tito Guizar,** Veloz and Yolanda, Enric Madriguera and his Orchestra

Steve Farraugh (Wynn) is the manager and producer of a revue which is trying out at Hotel Carioca, in Rio, before going to Broadway. Linda Lorens (Miller) is his star. She is in love with him, but he is still in love with his ex-wife, Vickie Dean (Keyes), a famous director. At the same time, singer Tito Guizar (playing himself) loves Linda, but she doesn't return his love. Vickie arrives in Rio with a prospective

In a scene from the lavish Latin American musical *The Thrill of Brazil,* guitarist-singer Tito Guizar sings "She Doesn't Say Yes and She Doesn't Say No" in the Zamba Lele, a nightclub in the native quarter of Rio de Janeiro.

new husband to get Steve to sign the final divorce papers (Steve has already signed them once, but he has a habit of using disappearing ink). In the end, all is resolved when Vickie admits that she really loves Steve and came to Rio just to see him. Robert Conte, Nino Bellini, Martin Garralaga, Manuel Paris, Joe Dominguez, and Alex Montoya are featured.

The Tijuana Story (1957 Col)

   D: Leslie Kardos
   S: Lou Morheim
   P: Sam Katzman
Cast: **Rodolfo Acosta**, Robert Blake, James Darren, Joy Stoner

The assassination of real-life newspaperman Manuel Acosta Mesa in Tijuana inspired this weak teenage exploitation drama. Robert Blake plays the newspaperman's son, who, in the course of the screenplay, brings the leaders of a narcotics ring to justice after his crusading father falls victim to them. The best thing about the movie is Rodolfo Acosta as Acosta Mesa; unfortunately, he is given too little screen time.

Too Many Girls (1940 RKO)

    D: George Abbott
    S: John Twist, based on the stage play by George Marrion, Jr.
    P: Harry E. Edington
Cast: Lucille Ball, Ann Miller, Eddie Bracken, **Desi Arnaz**

Sexy (for its time) college football musical with a Latin twist, which was a success on the Broadway stage and was transferred to film by its stage director, George Abbott, with uneven results. Desi Arnaz, in his film debut, re-created his Broadway stage role as Manuelito, a Latin football player. While making the film, Desi met and fell in love with his soon-to-be-wife, Lucille Ball.

Topaz (1969 U)

    D: Alfred Hitchcock
    S: Samuel Taylor, based on the novel by Leon Uris
    P: Alfred Hitchcock
Cast: Frederick Stafford, Dany Robin, John Forsythe, Karin Dor, John Vernon, **Roberto Contreras, Carlos Rivas**

This Hitchcock thriller about Russian agents infiltrating the French government and betraying French security has a major subplot concerning missiles in Castro's Cuba. Juanita (Dor), a heroine of the Cuban Revolution and the mistress of French spy Devereaux (Stafford), is sent to Cuba to find evidence of Russian missiles for the U.S. government. John Vernon is Cuban revolutionary Rico Parra, who, though he is in love with her, must kill Juanita when he finds out she has betrayed the Revolution. Carlos Rivas plays Hernandez, a Cuban soldier, and Roberto Contreras plays Munoz.

    The laser disc release of the film includes two alternate endings that Hitchcock shot but decided not to use.

The Torch (1950 Eagle-Lion)

    D: **Emilio Fernandez**
    S: Adapted by Bert Granet, Inigo de Martino Noriega, and **Emilio Fernandez**
    P: Bert Granet
Cast: **Pedro Armendariz**, Paulette Goddard, **Gilbert Roland**

A Mexican revolutionary general falls in love with the daughter of a leading citizen of a town he takes over. Their courtship is a series of violent comic arguments, played against a background of firing squads, religious fervor, and a deadly flu epidemic. *The Torch* is a remake of a Spanish-language film made in Mexico in 1946 under the title *Enamorada*. Both films have the same leading man (Pedro Armendariz), director (Emilio Fernandez), and cameraman (Gabriel Figueroa). The only critical difference is that the Spanish-language version stars Maria Felix, and the English-language one, Paulette Goddard. There are minor variations in editing and the supporting players, and one scene was rewritten. Goddard had a Hollywood-style narration added at the beginning of the film.

    Goddard saw the original film on a trip to Mexico in 1947 and decided she wanted to do an English-language version and play the Maria Felix role. The film was shot a year later in the same Mexican location, the town of Cholula. Azteca Films, the Mexican national film distributor in the United States, released an English-subtitled version of the original a month after the English-language version was released. Director Emilio Fernandez later said it was a mistake to remake the film in another language. The rhythms are different and so are the circumstances that breathe life into a particular film; it is hard enough to make a film work once, let alone try to duplicate its success in other circumstances.

Torrid Zone (1940 WB)

    D: William Keighley
    S: Jerry Wald and Richard Macauley
    P: Mark Hellinger
 Cast: James Cagney, Ann Sheridan, Pat O'Brien, George Tobias

Original comedy/drama set on a Central American banana plantation and involving a love triangle among plantation boss Nick Butler (Cagney), manager Steve Case (O'Brien), and American showgirl Lee Donly (Sheridan). A local bad man, Rosario (Tobias), recruits a band of marauders from among the plantation workers, and Butler leads a posse against the insurrectionists. Hispanics in small roles include Paul Porcasi, Frank Puglia, George Humbert, Elvira Sanchez, George Regas, Joe Dominguez, and Manuel Lopez.

Tortilla Flat (1942 MGM)

    D: Victor Fleming
    S: John Lee Mahin and Benjamin Glaser, based on the novel by John Steinbeck
    P: Sam Zimbalist
 Cast: Spencer Tracy, John Garfield, Hedy Lamarr, Akim Tamiroff, Sheldon Leonard

Based on John Steinbeck's novel, set in the years after World War I, about Mexican farmers and fishermen who live in carefree poverty near Monterey, California.

Danny's (Garfield) inheritance of two houses brings him instant respectability and estranges him from Pilon (Tracy) and his other friends. Danny and Pilon vie for the affections of the Portuguese girl Dolores (Lamarr) and become enemies. But when one of Danny's houses burns down and Danny is hurt in a fight, Pilon comes to his aid, and all ends happily. Hispanic actors Roque Ybarra as Alfredo and Tito Renaldo as a boy have minor roles in the film. Mercedes Ruffino plays Mrs. Morales, the amorous widow. Nina Campana plays Senora Cortez, mother of a brood of children.

Not an easy tale to translate into a motion picture, it might have emerged as a leering study of vagrancy. Luckily, what emerged through the direction of Victor Fleming (*Gone with the Wind* [1939]) was a sensitive if sentimental character study.

Spencer Tracy, Hedy Lamarr, and John Garfield portray poor Mexican Americans in a California fishing village in the film adaptation of John Steinbeck's *Tortilla Flat*.

A poignantly funny scene involves a health department doctor asking the Mexican children, who seem healthy, what they eat. They naturally reply, "Tortillas and beans" to his every question. He exclaims in disbelief, "Don't you eat anything else?" The children reply, "What else is there?"

Touch and Go (1986 TS)

D: Robert Mandel
S: Alan Ormsby, Bob Sand, and Harry Colomby
P: Stephen Friedman
Cast: Michael Keaton, **Maria Conchita Alonso**, Ajay Naidu

Dramatic comedy about the romance between a professional hockey player, Bobby Barbato (Keaton), and a single Latina mother, Denise De Leon (Alonso), whose little street-savvy son, Louis, is played by Ajay Naidu.

Touch of Evil (1958 U)

D: Orson Welles and (uncredited) Harry Keller
S: Orson Welles, based on the novel *Badge of Evil* by Whit Masterson
P: Albert Zugsmith
Cast: Charlton Heston, Orson Welles, Janet Leigh, **Joseph Calleia**, Marlene Dietrich, Akim Tamiroff, Val De Vargas, **Victor Millan**, **Lalo Rios**

In the small, seedy town of Los Robles, situated on the U.S.-Mexican border, an inquest into the murder of prominent local politician Rudy Linneker develops into a war of wits between a ruthless American police captain, Hank Quinlan (Welles), and a top-ranking Mexican narcotics officer, Vargas (Heston). Though officially honeymooning with his wife, Susan (Leigh), Vargas finds himself increasingly embroiled in the criminal investigation.

Mistrustful of Quinlan's motives in arresting the suspect, Sanchez (Millan), the Mexican lover of Linneker's daughter, Marcia (Joanna Moore), Vargas becomes convinced that Quinlan is attempting to frame an innocent man.

Quinlan's service to justice has degenerated into a personal vendetta against Mexican Americans due to his wife's murder (for which no one was convicted due to lack of evidence) many years before.

Vargas previously has been working on exposing the Grandi gang, a pack of Mexican dope dealers headed by Joe Grandi (Tamiroff) who are active in Los Robles, and he becomes equally engaged in exposing the venal and unprincipled Quinlan. Vargas is beleaguered by an uncaring or positively antagonistic populace, and affected by the understated problem of being a Mexican in a racist society. He describes the bombing incident that killed Linneker as being bad for "us," ambiguously referring to both his country and his wife. Since the bomb was planted in Mexico, but went off in the United States, his jurisdiction is in question, making him an observer, an outsider. At one point, Vargas is framed against a billboard that reads: "Welcome Stranger to Picturesque Los Robles, Paris on the Border." As a Mexican he represents an alternate system of justice, and on the American side he has no authority. By the time his wife has been abducted by the Grandi gang, who intend to frame Vargas through his wife, he is acting as a husband, not as a police officer.

Menzies (Calleia), who is of Mexican heritage, is a lifelong friend of Quinlan's. He is the peon to this gringo master until Vargas crosses the border and frees Menzies from Quinlan's grip. Vargas helps Menzies find his own identity by helping him realize that Quinlan has been circumventing the law for years, abetted by Menzies, who has supported him out of friendship and fear. Menzies saves Vargas's life by killing Quinlan. Menzies loses his own life in the process, but not until he has found "salvation" through self-identity.

The film was directed by Welles at the insistence of star Charlton Heston. Heston's customary heroic look was toned down, and he was given a darker skin tone, a curl to his blackened hair, and a neat mustache. The famous, nearly four-minute tracking shot that runs under the credits is more than just a magnificent virtuoso effect; it brilliantly sets up what is to follow. It presents the milieu, the central characters, and the action that drives the plot, all with remarkable economy. It was filmed in Venice, California, on Main Street, which was transformed with the help of art directors into a bordertown. Universal took the film away from Welles and recut it. Some 30 years later the film was restored to its original length and is now considered a classic; one critic described it as perhaps the greatest B movie ever made.

Orson Welles (left) as corrupt cop Quinlan and Charlton Heston (right) as Mexican narcotics officer Vargas are at odds over a murder investigation in *Touch of Evil*. Victor Millan (center) portrays Sanchez, the Mexican lover of the murdered politician's daughter. Joseph Calleia (background) portrays Menzies, a lifelong friend of Quinlan's.

Trackdown (1976 UA)

   D: Richard T. Heffron
   S: Paul Edward
   P: Bernard Schwartz
Cast: Jim Mitchum, Karen Lamm, Ann Archer, **Erik Estrada**

The subject of teen runaways and inner-city crime is exploited to the fullest in this blatantly racist story of a young Anglo rancher's revenge for the brutalization of his runaway sister in the big city, who has been beaten and raped by a Chicano gang in East L.A. and sold into prostitution. She becomes a high-class hooker and is murdered by a sadistic client. Erik Estrada plays Chucho, a sensitive gang member who falls for the girl and who ends up helping her brother. Gilbert De la Pena and Rafael Lopez also play gang members.

A Tragedy in the Life of General Villa

See *The Life of Villa*.

The Treasure of Pancho Villa (1955 RKO)

D: George Sherman
S: Niven Busch, based on the story by J. Robert Bren and Gladys Atwater
P: Edmund Grainger
Cast: Rory Calhoun, Shelley Winters, **Gilbert Roland, Joseph Calleia,** Carlos Mosquiz, Tony Carvajal, Pasquel Pena

American soldier of fortune Tom Bryan (Calhoun) decides he would rather steal gold for himself than for the Mexican Revolution, despite the example set by dedicated Villa supporters Juan (Roland) and Ruth (Winters), who became a loyal supporter when her father was killed by Federales troops.

Filmed on location in Mexico, the movie is full of explosive action. Though Pancho Villa is in the title, he never appears in the film.

Villa supporter Juan (Gilbert Roland, right) faces off with American soldier of fortune Tom Bryan (Rory Calhoun, left) in *The Treasure of Pancho Villa*.

Treasure of the Golden Condor (1952 TCF)

   D: Delmer Daves
   S: Delmer Daves
   P: Jules Buck
Cast: Cornel Wilde, Constance Smith

Technicolor swashbuckler set among eighteenth-century French nobility. A young man, Jean Paul (Wilde), is deprived of his royal inheritance by an unscrupulous uncle who has made him a virtual bonded servant. Jean Paul meets a man who is in possession of a map to a fabulous Mayan treasure. Jean Paul takes off with him and his beautiful daughter to Guatemala to get the treasure. After it is found, he returns to France to reclaim his possessions. He then returns to Guatemala to join his friend and the daughter, with whom he has fallen in love.

This is a remake of the 1942 film *Son of Fury* with the locale switched from the Pacific to Central America. The background scenes filmed in Guatemala with the principal players showcase the ancient Mayan ruins and the city of Antigua.

The Treasure of the Sierra Madre (1948 WB)

   D: **John Huston**
   S: **John Huston**, based on the novel by B. Traven
   P: Henry Blanke
Cast: Humphrey Bogart, Walter Huston, Bruce Bennett, Tim Holt, **Alfonso Bedoya**, Bobby Blake, A. Soto Rangel, Manuel Donde, **Jose Torvay**, Margarito Luna, Jacqueline Dalya

This movie signaled the end of the Good Neighbor Policy with its reintroduction of the Mexican bandit while at the same time using Mexican landscapes and people. Mexicans in the film are depicted as either bloodthirsty bandits or as innocent, primitive natives.

Based on the novel by B. Traven, it is a story of a clash between three down-on-their-luck Americans (Bogart, Huston, Holt) in Tampico, Mexico, who make a last desperate attempt to find gold in the rugged Sierra Madres, where few white men have ever been. Hounded by Indians, a fortune-hunting Texan (Bennett), and cold-blooded bandidos, they must finally confront the most dangerous adversary of all, themselves.

Mexican actor Alfonso Bedoya created a permanent niche for himself in movie history as the bandit Gold Hat, with the following memorable line: "Badges, we don't need no stinkin' badges." Gold Hat is a dumb bandido who mistakes gold for sand and throws it away, machetes Dobbs (Bogart) to death, and is easily caught by the Federales (Mexican police), who make him dig his own grave before they shoot him. Also featured in minor roles are Julian Rivero as a barber and Martin Garralaga as a railroad conductor.

The film was not a box-office success, but today it is considered a classic. Huston wanted to shoot on the actual locations to bring to life this harsh story, of which the country is as much a part as are the leading characters. Other filming took place at Warner Bros. Studios in Burbank and in the mountains near Bakersfield, California. The reviews particularly noted the realism Huston achieved by filming on location and praised Bedoya's characterization. The film won three Academy Awards for the father-and-son team of Walter and John Huston—Walter for Best Supporting Actor and John for Best Director and Best Screenplay.

"John Huston's handling of the Indians is especially effective. Whether bandits, courteous mountain natives or townspeople, they have a compelling kind of dignity tempered by humor. A few among them address the Americans in pidgin English, but for the most part they speak their native tongue. A pleasant relief from the customary use of phony dialects," Virginia Wright, syndicated columnist (1/48).

"If there were no other reason to laud *The Treasure of the Sierra Madre* we'd find words of praise for the manner in which it presented the native people of Mexico in their contact with its Americans in the story," Lloyd Sloan, *Hollywood Citizen News* (1/15/48).

"In the background, John Huston has utilized richly Indian faces that were available in rural districts of Mexico. It is a measure of the difference between two of America's greatest directors that when they both sought Mexican villains, one, John Ford, used the Hollywood actor J. Carroll Naish [in *The Fugitive*] very effectively, while the other, John Huston, has exercised sheer genius in his choice

Alfonso Bedoya (left) as the Mexican bandit Gold Hat in *The Treasure of the Sierra Madre*, also starring Humphrey Bogart (right).

of that particular Mexican for the role. The two parts have much in common, actually Naish is as good as it is possible for an actor to be but the man John Huston uses, Alfonso Bedoya, is better than that. He is tremendous and very simple," Archer Winston, *New York Post* (1/26/48).

Trial (1955 MGM)

    D: Mark Robson
    S: Don Mankiewicz, based on his novel
    P: Charles Schnee
 Cast: Glenn Ford, Arthur Kennedy, **Katy Jurado, Rafael Campos,**
        Juano Hernandez

A high-powered, well-intentioned screen drama, full of the anti-Communist hysteria of McCarthyism. It manages to make its point about racism and bigotry in small-town America, while at the same time demonstrating an underlying and unswerving faith in American justice.

David Blake (Ford) comes to the town of San Juno to gain courtroom experience, and his first case, in association with Barney Castle (Kennedy), involves a young Mexican (Campos) who has been charged with the murder of a white girl (who, it is eventually revealed, was a rheumatic, and who died of a heart attack). Bigots in the town attempt to lynch the youth but are turned back by the arguments presented. Castle seeks to raise funds for the defense and does so in a flamboyant manner, following the Communist line and turning obscure victims of local injustice into symbols. (There are states and towns that have had their labor and race prejudice cases given this blowup technique.) As the trial progresses, Blake does everything in his power to save the youth from hanging, legally, and is successful. However, the prosecution's final courtroom address leads him to realize he's been duped by Castle and the Communists, who have used the case to further their own cause.

Rafael Campos as the defendant, Angel Chavez, and Katy Jurado as his mother give believable performances in the young-Mexican-boy-in-trouble and the suffering mamacita tradition. Puerto Rican actor Juano Hernandez, in an offbeat and provocative decision in keeping with the tone of the film, is cast as the black judge who presides over the case. To see a black judge in a 1955 film was, as in real life, extremely rare. Hernandez brings dignity and strength to the role, and is given sufficient screen time to create a three-dimensional character.

Tropic Holiday (1938 Par)

D: Theodore Reed
S: Arthur Hornbow, Jr.
P: Arthur Hornblow, Jr.
Cast: **Dorothy Lamour**, Ray Milland, Martha Raye, **Tito Guizar**

Musical/comedy set in Mexico about a local beauty romanced by a visiting scriptwriter. The title was originally *Ensenada,* but the studio changed it to capitalize on Dorothy Lamour's tropical image. Augustin Lara wrote six numbers for the film, and Jose Fernandez, a Latin dance director, worked with dance director Leroy Prinz.

Tropic Zone (1953 Par)

D: Lewis R. Foster
S: Lewis R. Foster, based on the novel *Gentleman of the Jungle* by Tom Gill
P: William H. Pine and William C. Thomas
Cast: Ronald Reagan, Rhonda Fleming, **Argentina Brunetti**, Rico Alaniz, Maurice Jara, **Pilar Del Rey, Estelita**

Adventure/drama filmed in Technicolor and set in the fictional Central American town of Puerto Barrancas, where an American man and woman are fighting to survive in a locale dominated by crooked politicians and a ruthless dictator. Estelita sings and dances in the role of a café entertainer. The story elements are cliched and stereotypical.

12 Angry Men (1957 UA)

D: Sidney Lumet
S: Reginald Rose, based on his teleplay
P: Henry Fonda and Reginald Rose
Cast: Henry Fonda, Lee J. Cobb, Jack Klugman

Reginald Rose wrote this script originally for television's "Playhouse 90." There are no Hispanics in this offbeat courtroom drama, which focuses almost exclusively on the jury room deliberations. The subject of the trial, however, is a 19-year-old Puerto Rican who purportedly killed his father with a switchblade. The film version indicates that the young man (John Savoca) is a slum youth. One of the jurors reveals himself as a prejudiced man who hates the "them" the defendant represents. The script was inspired by a real manslaughter case in which Reginald Rose was a juror.

Two Mules for Sister Sara (1970 U)

D: Don Siegel
S: Albert Maltz, based on a story by **Budd Boetticher**
P: Martin Rackin and Carroll Case
Cast: Clint Eastwood, Shirley MacLaine, **Alberto Morin**, Armando Silvestre

Popular action/western starring Clint Eastwood in a variation of the "Man with No Name" characterization that had made him a superstar three years earlier.

An American gunfighter, Hogan (Eastwood), rescues a nun, Sister Sara (MacLaine), from being raped by French troops in 1860s Mexico. The nun decides to tag along with Hogan, who is joining a band of Juaristas fighting against the French occupation of Mexico. A romance develops, and Hogan discovers Sister Sara is really a prostitute. Jose Torvay, among other Hispanics, has a small role in the film.

It was adapted from an original story by director/writer Budd Boetticher, who had hoped to direct it with John Wayne and Mexican actress Silvia Pinal. Boetticher sold the rights to the story years later, and Elizabeth Taylor was cast opposite Eastwood. Shortly before production was to begin, she dropped out and MacLaine replaced her.

It was filmed on location in Mexico with cinematography by Gabriel Figueroa with an intimate and grand feeling for the Mexican landscapes he knows so well. The opening credit sequence features Eastwood riding through the rugged terrain of northern Mexico at dawn. While the credits appear, the camera cuts back and forth between Eastwood and the animals that inhabit the desert. The assault on the garrison, beginning with a religious procession through the streets by the townsfolk at night, is spectacularly staged and lighted. Eastwood liked Figueroa's work so much he used him to photograph his next film, *Kelly's Heroes* (1970), in Yugoslavia.

Tycoon (1947 RKO)

D: Richard Wallace
S: Borden Chase and John Twist, based on the novel by C.E. Scoggins
P: Stephen Ames
Cast: John Wayne, Sir Cedric Hardwicke, Laraine Day, **Anthony Quinn**, Fernando Alvarado, **Martin Garralaga**, Judith Anderson

The story line of this film involves the feud between an obsessive engineer (Wayne) who is attempting to build a railroad through the Andes Mountains and his employer (Hardwicke), who objects to his methods and his romance with his daughter (Day).

Quinn plays an ill-defined character named Enrique "Ricky" Vargas, an engineer and troubleshooter. This overlong but action-filled story features Englishman Hardwicke, American Day, and Australian Judith Anderson playing South Americans.

It was filmed in Lone Pine, California, with the Sierra Nevadas subbing for the Andes. A complete side of a mountain was built for the film in order to simulate mine shafts and tunnels in the mountainsides, while an entire Andean village complete with llamas was constructed on 14 acres. Hundreds of Hispanic extras and supporting players were used. Some of the featured players include Argentina Brunetti, Fernando Alvarado, Martin Garralaga, Frank Leyva, Joe Dominguez, Alberto Morin, and Nacho Galindo.

Tony Aguilar (left) as a rebel general raises glasses with a Confederate colonel (Rock Hudson, right) and a Union colonel (John Wayne, center), who have fled the post–Civil War South, in an unlikely liaison in *The Undefeated*.

The Undefeated (1969 TCF)

D: Andrew V. McLaglen
S: James Lee Barrett, based on a story by Stanley L. Hough
P: Robert L. Jacks
Cast: John Wayne, Rock Hudson, **Tony Aguilar, Pedro Armendariz, Jr., Carlos Rivas**

A Confederate colonel (Hudson) sets fire to his plantation house at the end of the Civil War rather than let it fall into the hands of carpetbaggers. He sets off for Mexico with his family and a group of followers to set up a new home for themselves. They are saved from attacks by Mexican bandits by a former Union colonel (Wayne), who has decided to drive his herd of 3,000 horses into Mexico rather than be tricked by crooked army agents. The two former enemies join forces to fight off the soldiers of Emperor Maximilian and those of the rebel leader Juarez. When the rebels take the Confederate party prisoners, the Union men end up sacrificing their horses to free the southerners.

This good old-fashioned, leisurely John Wayne western, filmed in Durango, Mexico, with excellent production values, also features Pedro Armendariz, Jr., as a bandit, Carlos Rivas as an emissary of Maximilian, and Tony Aguilar as a no-nonsense rebel general.

Under a Texas Moon (1930 WB)

D: Michael Curtiz
S: Gordon Rigby, based on the story "Two Gun Man" by Stewart Edward White
P: Unknown
Cast: Frank Fay, **Raquel Torres**, Myrna Loy, **Armida**, Noah Beery, Inez Gomez, **Mona Maris**

This film is distinguished as the first sound western shot in Technicolor. Director Curtiz juggled color, music, dialogue, and a temperamental lead from vaudeville, Frank Fay, who had played the master of ceremonies in the revue film *Show of Shows* (1929). An atypical western, *Under a Texas Moon* is set in Mexico and Texas, and is full of fiestas and beautiful ladies fighting over its singing desperado hero, Don Carlos (Fay), who renders the title song frequently.

Under Fire (1983 Or)

D: Roger Spottiswoode
S: Ron Shelton and Clayton Frohman
P: Jonathan Taplin
Cast: Gene Hackman, Nick Nolte, Joanna Cassidy, **Alma Martinez**, Jean-Louis Trintignant, **Rene Enriquez**, Ed Harris

Three longtime journalist friends find themselves in Managua, Nicaragua, in 1979 on the eve of the Sandinista revolution. Russell Price (Nolte) is a photojournalist; Claire Snyder (Cassidy) is a radio correspondent who is about to split up with her husband, Alex (Hackman), a newspaper correspondent who decides to leave war-torn Nicaragua to work as a television reporter in the States. Perhaps Gene Hackman expressed it best in the movie: "Two guys in love with the same dame in an exotic country with bullets flying."

The film features a multidimensional, humanistic view of the events surrounding the fall of the Somoza regime and the struggle of the Sandinista rebels as seen through the eyes of American journalists.

The attractive translator at the hotel, Isela Cruz (Martinez), turns out to be a rebel. At one point, Russell, the photographer, cries out in anguish, "Christ, what are we doing here?" He meets up with an old acquaintance, Hobbs (Harris), an American mercenary who in Africa had confided to Russell that he couldn't stand "too many spooks," and now in Nicaragua, "a shit load of greasers." Hobbs is a cold-blooded killer who hires himself out to whichever side pays him the most, in this case the CIA and the Somoza regime.

Russell and Claire help the rebels convince the world that the charismatic leader Rafael is not dead, as had been announced by the government, by showing photos that make him appear to be still alive. This unethical act helps bring down the Somoza regime but also brings Alex back to Nicaragua and leads to his eventual death by Somoza soldiers at a roadblock. Hackman's casual, unprovoked murder in front of the journalists is one of the movie's most startling moments. Seeing Claire mourning over Alex, a Nicaraguan woman asks, "You knew the dead journalist?" She answers yes in a flood of tears. Unmoved, the woman says, "Fifty thousand Nicaraguans have died and now one Yankee. Perhaps now America will be afraid of what is happening here. We should have killed an American journalist 50 years ago."

Russell, who finally crosses the line from observer to participant in the trick he pulls with Rafael's picture, is shocked to find out why he was allowed to visit the rebel camp unmolested by the authorities: his photos are being used to track down and murder insurgents who appear in them.

A powerful, if flawed, movie that opts for perhaps too much sentimentality in its portrayal of a very unpopular left-wing revolution, this is one of the best portrayals of journalists in action, along with *Salvador* (1986) and *All the President's Men* (1976).

Under the Pampas Moon (1935 Fox)

D: James Tinling
S: Ernest Pascal, Bradley King, and Henry Jackson, based on the original story by Gordon Morris
P: B.G. De Sylva
Cast: Warner Baxter, Ketti Gallian, **J. Carroll Naish**, John Miljan, **Soledad Jimenez, Armida**

A passenger plane makes a forced landing, and Cesar Campo (Baxter) takes the passengers to a ranch where he is one of the gauchos. They stay overnight to see a race in which Campo's rival cuts the horses' cinches to the saddle, but despite such cheating Campo manages to win the race. The prized horse is stolen, and

Campo goes to Buenos Aires to retrieve it. Armida appears only in the beginning sequence, and Baxter offers a variation of his Cisco Kid portrayal. Tito Guizar is seen briefly as a singer in the café; two years later he achieved international popularity. Many Latin players and extras worked on this film, including Rita Cansino (who later became Rita Hayworth), the popular dance team of [Frank] Veloz and [Miss] Yolanda, Chris-Pin Martin, George J. Lewis, Paul Porcasi, Joe Dominguez, and Martin Garralaga.

Under the Volcano (1984 U)

D: **John Huston**
S: Guy Gallo, based on the novel by Malcolm Lowry
P: Michael Fitzgerald
Cast: Albert Finney, Jacqueline Bisset, **Katy Jurado, Emilio Fernandez**

Directed by John Huston and based on the celebrated novel by Malcolm Lowry, *Under the Volcano* is the story of an alcoholic British consul during his last days before leaving his post in Mexico at the beginning of World War II.

Albert Finney, in an extraordinary performance, plays the consul Fermin, who descends into hell against an exotic and primitive Mexican background, filled with the symbolism of death during the Day of the Dead religious festival in 1939. Finney's Fermin, like Bogart's Fred C. Dobbs in Huston's *Treasure of the Sierra Madre* (1948), virtually disintegrates on screen. The film was photographed in color on location in Cuernavaca, Mexico, by noted Mexican cinematographer Gabriel Figueroa, who had worked previously with Huston on *The Night of the Iguana* (1964). Acclaimed Mexican artist Gunther Gerzo was the art director. Emilio Fernandez as a cantina patron and Katy Jurado as an old friend of Fermin's were featured in the film.

The movie perpetuated the image of Mexican women as whores and Mexican men as violent and treacherous. The climactic sequences in the El Farolito brothel are harrowing.

Under the Volcano is an adult and dark work from a master filmmaker. The $4 million production was co-produced by the Mexican government, along with Twentieth Century–Fox and Universal, in an attempt to break into the international filmmaking arena after years of artistic slump. Figueroa's cinematography and Finney's performance were nominated for Academy Awards.

Underwater! (1955 RKO)

D: John Sturges
S: Walter Newman
P: Harry Tatelman
Cast: Jane Russell, **Gilbert Roland**, Richard Egan, **Joseph Calleia, Eugene Iglesias**

Theresa (Russell) is a shapely Cuban treasure hunter who is joined by her husband, Johnny (Egan), and an adventurer, Dominic (Roland), in the search for a long-lost Spanish galleon that sank laden with gold and silver bullion while en route from the Caribbean to the Old World. Accompanied on screen by Perez Prado and his Orchestra, Russell dances the mambo.

Up in Smoke (1978 Par)

D: Lou Adler
S: **Cheech Marin** and Tommy Chong
P: Lou Adler and Lou Lombardo
Cast: **Cheech Marin**, Tommy Chong

This funny and vulgar drug counterculture–inspired comedy stars Cheech and Chong, a Mexican/Chinese American comedy team who achieved success through recordings and concert appearances.

The film casts Cheech Marin as a character of his own creation, a lowriding, dope-smoking, ignorant Mexican American from East Los Angeles. This is one of the first film appearances of the lowrider car associated with the contemporary urban Mexican American culture. The enormous $28 million gross of this low-budget entry spawned four more films starring this comedy team: *Cheech and Chong's Next Movie* (1980); *Cheech and Chong's Nice Dreams* (1981); *Things Are Tough All Over* (1982); and *Cheech and Chong: Still Smoking* (1983).

Up the Down Staircase (1967 WB)
   D: Robert Mulligan
   S: Tad Mosel, based on the novel by Bel Kaufman
   P: Alan J. Pakula
Cast: Sandy Dennis, Patrick Bedford, Eileen Heckart

Based on the best-selling novel by Bel Kaufman, the film dramatizes the first-year frustrations of metropolitan high school teacher Sylvia Barrett (Dennis).

The story is set in a rundown school in the fictional Calvin Coolidge High School in New York's Spanish Harlem. Many of the students are hostile blacks and Puerto Ricans with no inclination toward the joys of English literature, and Barrett is discouraged by her inability to get through to them. It was actually filmed at several high schools in New York, which added to the feeling of realism, and many ethnic teenagers with no prior acting experience were cast to play a variation of themselves for the film.

Jose Rodriguez, from the New York School of Printing, was cast as a withdrawn Puerto Rican student who bursts to life as a tough-minded judge in a classroom trial. The Italian kid Joe Ferone, played by Jeff Howard, is the knife-wielding gang tough.

In the tradition of *Blackboard Jungle* (1955), but with a woman teacher instead of a man, this film is a deeply moving exposé of the deficiencies of the urban public school system. The film touches on the problems of delinquency, racial discrimination, and drug addiction present in many inner-city American schools.

Valdez Is Coming (1971 UA)
   D: Edwin Sherin
   S: Roland Kibbee and David Rayfiel, based on the novel
      by Elmore Leonard
   P: Ira Steiner
Cast: Burt Lancaster, **Frank Silvera**, Jon Cypher, Susan Clark,
      Hector Elizondo

Valdez Is Coming is a hard, violent western about a solitary ex-cavalry man, Bob Valdez (Lancaster), of Mexican heritage who wages a private war to raise $200 for a widowed Apache woman, the squaw of a black man, also a former soldier, whom he has helped to kill.

The film, under the guise of a western, speaks out against racial prejudice and the oppression of the weak by the strong. Lancaster acquits himself well in a believable portrayal as the Mexican American constable Valdez. Frank Silvera in his last film appearance gives a gritty performance as Valdez's Mexican compadre, Diego. Hector Elizondo plays one of the bandidos. Filmed in Spain, it owes much in style to the "spaghetti westerns" of the time.

Vera Cruz (1954 UA)

D: **Robert Aldrich**
S: James R. Webb and Roland Kibbee, based on the story by Borden Chase
P: James Hill
Cast: Burt Lancaster, Gary Cooper, **Sarita Montiel, Cesar Romero**

Devastated by the South's defeat in the Civil War and suppressing his idealism, Col. Ben Trane (Cooper) travels to Mexico as a soldier of fortune. There he meets a flamboyant, unscrupulous counterpart, Joe Erin (Lancaster). The two professionally hire out their guns to Emperor Maximilian while being courted by the Juaristas and planning to double-cross each other as they escort, through rebel territory, a countess who is making a trip to Vera Cruz. The trip is a cover-up for the shipment of a fortune in gold.

This is a fast-moving, colorful, action-filled, and often humorous western, directed by Robert Aldrich in a robust manner, with Cooper and Lancaster at their best in roles suited to their screen personas. This was Cooper's third film in Mexico, following *Blowing Wild* (1953) and *Garden of Evil* (1954). The supporting cast includes Cesar Romero as the military Marquis de Labordere, Denise Darcel as the unprincipled Countess Marie Duvarre, and Sarita Montiel as the young Mexican Nina, with whom Trane is smitten. George Macready is Emperor Maximilian, Ernest Borgnine is Donnegan, Morris Ankrum is the Juarista general, and a young actor named Charles Buchinsky, later to be better known as Charles Bronson, is Pittsburgh.

Vera Cruz etched an indelible south-of-the-border escapist western fantasyland. Mexico is a last untamed refuge for those seeking new adventures, beautiful senoritas, and gold. In this fantasy Mexico, men could be spiritually renewed by upholding American values, such as the pursuit of happiness, through fighting for freedom or lusting after gold. In fact, Mexico attracted many Americans after the Civil War to fight for either Maximilian or the Juaristas. Others came as businessmen and opportunists or to establish religious communities.

It was filmed in Mexico utilizing such national landmarks as Chapultepec Castle, the Pyramids outside of Mexico City, Cuernavaca, and Churubusco Studios for some interiors.

Vibes (1988 Col)

D: Ken Kwapis
S: Lowell Ganz and Babaloo Mandel, based on a story by Deborah Blum, Ganz, and Mandel
P: Deborah Blum and Tony Ganz
Cast: Jeff Goldblum, Peter Falk, Cyndi Lauper, **Elizabeth Pena**, Ramon Bieri

Sylvia (Lauper) and Nick (Goldblum) help Harry (Falk) by using their extraordinary psychic powers to find a room of gold hidden in a lost Ecuadorian city. Pena plays Consuelo, a spitfire who tries to seduce and kill Nick. Dreadful.

Victory (1981 Par)

D: **John Huston**
S: Evan Jones and Yabo Yablonsky, based on a story by Yablonsky, Djordje Milicevic, and Jeff Maguire
P: Freddie Fields
Cast: Sylvester Stallone, Michael Caine, Max von Sydow, **Pele**

An ill-prepared group of Allied prisoners of war form a soccer team and are forced to play a crack Nazi team in a life or death match. Pele, a world-renowned Brazilian soccer star, is featured as Luis Hernandez, a soldier from British Trinidad captured by the Germans early in the war, who joins the Allied prisoner team.

Villa! (1958 TCF)

    D: James B. Clark
    S: Louis Vittes
    P: Plato A. Skouras
  Cast: **Rudolfo Hoyos, Jr.**, Brian Keith, **Cesar Romero**

Villa! is somewhat episodic, and the motivations are not clear in the script, which introduces Villa as a small-time bandit and follows his rise to national prominence when he meets Madero and is inspired to fight for the Revolution.

Hoyos is adequate as Villa but fails to infuse the character with the larger-than-life fire needed to pull off a memorable and real characterization, not that he gets much help from the script. The film is similar in concept in many ways to *Villa Rides* (1968) except that the latter has a grounded performance by the charismatic Yul Brynner and a sweeping historical atmosphere that *Villa!* totally lacks. Brian Keith is the Yankee adventurer who asks Villa to let him join his army, just as Mitchum does in *Villa Rides*. Cesar Romero and Carlos Musquiz are Villa's aides. Mexican actress Rosenda Monteros has a small role. Well photographed by Mexican cinematographer Alex Phillips on location in Mexico, the movie looks and plays like an above average B western, which, in truth, it is.

Villa Rides (1968 Par)

    D: Buzz Kulik
    S: **Sam Peckinpah** and Robert Towne, based on the book *Pancho Villa* by William Douglas Lansford
    P: Ted Richmond
  Cast: Yul Brynner, Robert Mitchum, Charles Bronson, Grazia Buccella, Robert Viharo, **Robert Carricart**, **Fernando Rey**

This routine film, with grand, sweeping action sequences, is sadly lacking in impact, considering the subject matter. Yul Brynner's charismatic star presence gives his bewigged Villa star quality. Robert Mitchum plays Lee, an American soldier of fortune, a flyer who becomes mixed up with Villa after running guns to his enemies. Charles Bronson plays the cold-blooded killer Fierro, aide to Villa.

Bewigged Yul Brynner (right) as Pancho Villa and Charles Bronson as cold-blooded killer and Villa aide Fierro in *Villa Rides*.

As directed by Buzz Kulik, in Panavision and Technicolor, the film takes Villa and his cohorts from his attack on the city of Parral, captured by a ruse without a shot, through his subordination to the power-hungry Gen. Huerta, his arrest, and his final escape from prison, when he embarked on the raising of a new army.

Produced by Ted Richmond, the picture took some 14 weeks to film on location in Spain and involved thousands of horses and extras, trains, 3 antique aircraft, over 10 separate locations, and a crew of 150 persons behind the camera. The film was made in Spain mainly for financial reasons, and because the Spanish countryside offers much of the same terrain, architecture, and backgrounds as the real Mexico. The producers also doubted that the Mexican government would have given approval for *Villa Rides* to film in Mexico.

Viva Max! (1969 Commonwealth United Release)

D: Jerry Paris
S: Elliot Baker, based on the novel by James Lehrer
P: Mark Carliner
Cast: Peter Ustinov, Jonathan Winters, John Astin, Keenan Wynn

Contemporary comedy about Mexican soldiers taking back the Alamo. A present-day second-rate general in the Mexican army, Gen. Maximilian (Ustinov), mounted on a white horse, leads 87 soldiers across the border to Laredo and on to San Antonio. Maximilian's occupation of the Alamo brings out the national guard and an uptight conservative militia faction.

This uneven, spirited comedy features a buffoonish but dignified portrayal by Ustinov, whose accent sounds more Spanish than Mexican. There are a few zany and comic bits, including some by John Astin as Sgt. Valdez, who is forever protecting his commanding officer.

The film elicited complaints from Mexican American civil rights groups regarding the Mexican portrayals by non-Mexicans, and from the Daughters of the Republic of Texas, who felt the film was insulting to the memory of those who died at the Alamo and would not allow the company to film there. After several weeks of location filming in San Antonio and just outside the Alamo shrine, the production left for Italy, where the interiors of the Alamo were built on a soundstage and the film was completed.

Viva Villa! (1934 MGM)

D: Jack Conway and (uncredited) Howard Hawks
S: Ben Hecht, based on the book by Edgcumb Pichon and O.B. Stade
P: David O. Selznick
Cast: Wallace Beery, **Leo Carrillo**, Stuart Erwin, Fay Wray, Frank Puglia, Katherine DeMille, **Pedro Regas, George Regas**

Wallace Beery plays the historical Mexican figure as a likable overgrown child who has great difficulty understanding why people try to dissuade him from slaughtering his defeated adversaries. Leo Carrillo is excellent as his aide Fierro, as is Stuart Erwin as the newspaper reporter who follows Villa's campaign. Providing feminine interest are Fay Wray and Katherine DeMille. Julian Rivero and Chris-Pin Martin are featured in minor roles.

Filmed largely in Mexico, near San Marcos, frequently despite obstacles that seemed insurmountable, director Howard Hawks walked off the picture and Jack Conway took over halfway through filming in Mexico. The Hollywood troupe was thrown out of Mexico when, in a state of intoxication, actor Lee Tracy urinated from his hotel balcony on a passing parade of soldiers. MGM president Louis B. Mayer sent a telegram to Mexican president Abelardo Rodriguez apologizing for the deplorable conduct of Tracy, which, he said, "shocked his company as deeply as it did Mexico." As a result, MGM dismissed Tracy and canceled his contract, and he was replaced in the film by Erwin.

The film was completed at MGM Studios and at a San Fernando Valley ranch location in California. *Viva Villa!* is presented as a fictional recording of Villa's achievements in freeing the poor, dethroning the tyrants, and restoring peace to Mexico. Thousands of extras were used in the battle scenes. Beery's performance and the powerful visual experience are among the reasons this version of the story is remembered more than any other.

Viva Zapata! (1952 TCF)

  D: Elia Kazan
  S: John Steinbeck, based on the novel *Zapata the Unconquered* by
     Edgcumb Pichon
  P: Darryl F. Zanuck
Cast: Marlon Brando, **Anthony Quinn**, Jean Peters, Joseph Wiseman,
     Alan Reed, **Frank Silvera**, **Margo**, **Henry Silva**

With the success of *The Pearl* (1948) and *The Red Pony* (1949), to whose screenplays John Steinbeck made contributions, Steinbeck began working on a script about the legendary Mexican Indian revolutionary leader Emiliano Zapata, spending considerable time in Mexico over the years gathering much information.

Director Elia Kazan also had been making notes for a possible film about Zapata since 1944, and his success with several films at Twentieth Century–Fox, including an Academy Award for *Gentlemen's Agreement* (1947), made *Viva Zapata!* possible.

Kazan claims that he and Steinbeck collaborated on the final script, although Steinbeck received sole screen credit.

Kazan and Steinbeck had hoped to film in Mexico, but the head of the Mexican film industry did not approve of the script or the idea of gringos making a film about their revolutionary hero.

Kazan and cinematographer Joe MacDonald tried to re-create the Mexican Revolution by poring through hundreds of photographs of the Revolution and capturing the look and feel of the towns and terrain they were working in as well as the faces of the Mexican populace. Several moments in the film are almost exact reproductions of some of those photographs.

The film was shot in 1951 along the Texas-Mexico border near Del Rio, McAllen, and Roma. Some scenes were shot at the Fox ranch near Malibu, just outside Los Angeles. Interiors at the studio ranged from squalid mud huts to a re-creation of the ornate national palace in Mexico City. Kazan used Mexican American locals as extras wherever he could.

The story follows Zapata's life, beginning with his early years as the leader of a delegation to Mexico City to protest the stealing of land from his people. It follows his being outlawed, to his leading role in the Revolution that overthrew the Diaz regime, to his assassination by political rivals.

Marlon Brando was cast as Emiliano Zapata over the protest of Fox chief Darryl F. Zanuck, who favored Tyrone Power or Anthony Quinn. Zanuck was quoted as saying of Brando, "How are you going to make that Illinois farm boy a Mexican?"

Marlon Brando (seated) portrays the legendary Mexican Indian revolutionary leader Emiliano Zapata, and Anthony Quinn (left) portrays Zapata's brother, in *Viva Zapata!*

For the role, Brando studied every book written on Zapata and the Mexican Revolution. He lived among Mexicans for weeks at a time. Brando suggested to the makeup artists that they flare out his nostrils with plastic rings or bands and glue up his eyelids to enhance his resemblance to Zapata.

Anthony Quinn was cast as his troubled brother, Eufemio. Both Brando and Quinn had been directed by Kazan in the stage production of *A Streetcar Named Desire*, in which Brando had made his name on Broadway (the film version had not been released at the time of *Viva Zapata!*) as Stanley Kowalski. Quinn followed him in the role in a national tour.

Kazan used his stage rehearsal techniques during location filming. While technicians lit the set, he rehearsed his actors. The director credits Quinn for his inventiveness during the sequence when Emiliano (Brando) is captured by Federales troops. Eufemio (Quinn), while observing the capture, begins to tap two small rocks together and is joined by the townspeople, who mimic his action in a show of solidarity.

Quinn's surly portrayal of a man who has both an attractive appetite for life and a violent destructiveness had an inspired credibility. Quinn had only to look to his own origins, for he was born in Mexico at the height of the Revolution and his parents fought for Villa before they immigrated to the United States. In an interview with Luis Reyes, Quinn credited Kazan's intense direction for much of his successful performance: "I learned a lot from Kazan . . . a whole new style of acting. Kazan was able to create the atmosphere for you. Kazan works from a terribly personal point of view . . . sometimes so personal it's painful."

Quinn referred to the explosive confrontation scene between the brothers in which Quinn shows his disgust for Emiliano's selfishness, defies his authority, and tells him he will take what he wants: "It took Brando and me three days to recover from that confrontation scene. Kazan had really worked us up, making us hate and love each other. Kazan insults you, tells you Brando hates your guts, anything!"

The cast includes many of Kazan's Group Theater actors, among them Harold Gordon, Lou Gilbert, Joseph Wiseman, and Alan Reid as Pancho Villa; their New York accents sometimes clashed with the Mexican accents on the dialogue tracks. Among the Hispanic actors cast are Frank Silvera, Nina Varela, Margo, and Henry Silva in his film debut. Nestor Paiva also has a small role.

The events of this complicated Revolution are simplified for easier storytelling.

Chicano activists of the 1960s criticized the film for casting Anglos in Mexican roles and questioned whether Kazan had a basic psychological understanding of the Latin male because of a scene in which, on the wedding night, Zapata would rather learn to read than make love to his bride, Josefa (Peters).

Before *Viva Zapata!*, very few Hollywood movies had told a story totally from a Mexican character's perspective. There is no gringo lead or any gringo supporting characters, as in other Hollywood Latin films. For example, in *Viva Villa!* (1934), the story is told through the eyes of a gringo reporter.

The studio was unsure how to market this story about an unknown-to-most-Americans Mexican hero and his country's struggle. Zanuck thought of the film as a western. Zanuck insisted that Zapata ride a white horse and suggested the final fadeout, where the horse symbolically runs free in the mountains after Zapata's death. At first Kazan thought the idea corny, but it worked surprisingly well in the final film.

Even though the film won several Academy Award nominations and received generally good reviews, it became a victim of the McCarthy era. In 1952, Kazan freely discussed his brief association with the Communist Party in the 1930s and named several Hollywood colleagues, which caused dissension among his Hollywood and New York associates. Given the pervasive political climate, the studio just gave up on the film after its initial openings.

This remains Kazan's most visual movie, with striking black-and-white photography, while the editing helps the film's sweeping episodic structure, cutting on sound and image transitions. An example: Tricked into entering a deserted fort in search of munitions, Zapata finds himself alone but for his old white horse, which he had thought lost. An entire Mexican regiment encircles him from the battlements above and opens fire, emptying round after round of ammunition into his bleeding and mutilated body. A very similar ending was used over 20 years later by George Roy Hill in *Butch Cassidy and the Sundance Kid* (1969). Kazan went further, however. Zapata's body is flung down with a dull thud in the plaza of a tiny village and is administered to by silent, shrouded Mexican women.

Brando was nominated for Best Actor for his brooding, passionate portrayal. Anthony Quinn won the Best Supporting Actor Oscar for his work as the lustful, swaggering, weak-willed Eufemio.

Voyage of the Damned (1976 Avco Embassy)

D: Stuart Rosenberg
S: Steve Shagan and David Butler, based on the book by Max Morgan-Witts and Gordon Thomas
P: Robert Fryer
Cast: James Mason, Faye Dunaway, Max von Sydow, Oskar Werner, Malcolm McDowell, Orson Welles, **Jose Ferrer, Fernando Rey**

The shameful true story of 900 German Jewish refugees trapped on an ocean liner on the high seas. In 1939, the Nazis allowed a select group of German Jews of every social class and background to leave Europe on board the German ocean liner *St. Louis*, bound for Cuba. The Nazis then conspired with the Cuban government to have the Jews' entry permits to Cuba canceled. The entry permits were invalidated eight days before the ship sailed, but no one on board ship knew this. The ship sat in Havana harbor for five days and then set sail toward the United States, where it was denied entry.

The Nazis allowed the ship to leave in response to worldwide pressure over their treatment of the Jews, using the incident as a propaganda tool to test the willingness of other countries to receive them. Not even the United States would allow the refugees entry.

James Mason plays the Cuban minister of state, Dr. Juan Remos, who unsuccessfully tries to persuade President Bru (Rey) to accept the large group of immigrants. Orson Welles plays Raul Estedes, an aristocratic Cuban industrialist. Jose Ferrer plays the corrupt official Manuel Benitez. It was filmed in Barcelona, Spain, near the waterfront, which was transformed into Havana harbor and its environs.

Walk Proud [aka: *Gang*] (1979 U)

D: Robert Collins
S: Evan Hunter
P: Lawrence Turman and David Foster
Cast: Robby Benson, Sarah Holcomb, **Pepe Serna, Trinidad Silva, Domingo Ambriz, Henry Darrow**

Story of barrio youth gang rivalry set against the backdrop of Venice, California, starring Robby Benson as Emilio Mendez, a young Chicano gang member who wants to leave the gang life behind him when he finds true love at school with an Anglo girl from the ritzy side of town.

The movie resembles the 1950s gang movies in spirit, style, and execution, and was scripted by Evan Hunter, who wrote the original novel on which the film *Blackboard Jungle* (1955) was based.

This well-acted drama, directed by Robert Collins, is a bit conventional and formulaic. It features a number of talented young Hispanic actors in major sup-

Chicano youth gang members show their solidarity in *Walk Proud*. Standing from left to right: Gary Cervantes, Pepe Serna, Robby Benson as Emilio Mendez, Luis Reyes, and Tony Alvaranga. Seated are Trinidad Silva and Angel Salazar.

porting roles, including Pepe Serna, Trinidad Silva, Domingo Ambriz, Irene Du Bari, Rose Portillo, Gary Cervantes, Angel Salazar, Panchito Gomez, Luis Reyes, and Tony Alvaranga. Henry Darrow plays a youth gang counselor. Felipe Turich plays a priest.

The Mexican American community protested the casting of Robby Benson (of Jewish American ancestry) as a Chicano youth. Actor A Martinez, who had done several films and television shows at Universal, would have been a good choice for the role, for example. The studio's argument was that the film needed a recognizable name for the film to be a successful commercial venture at the box office, but there were no Hispanic leading actors. By 1978, *Rocky* (1976) and other low-budget films that had gone on to enormous success had proved otherwise. A star in a film did not always ensure financial success, and in the latter case, *Rocky* starred the then-unknown Sylvester Stallone, in a role that catapulted him to stardom.

With a wave of films and television shows focusing on youth gangs, the Screen Extras Guild in 1978 found itself with few or no Hispanic teenagers in its ranks. The production of *Walk Proud* made it possible for a dozen young adults to enter the guild and pay for their college educations and homes by playing gang members in films and television shows for a number of years.

Walker (1987 U)

D: Alex Cox
S: Rudy Wurlitzer
P: Lorenzo O'Brien and Angel Flores Marini
Cast: Ed Harris, Marlee Matlin, Blanca Guerra, **Alfonso Arau, Pedro Armendariz, Jr.**

Alex Cox's (*Sid and Nancy*, *Repo Man*) black, broad, comic approach can be an alienating, crazy, unsettling film experience. This film is ultimately a failed attempt at re-creating on the screen South American literature's Magic Realism and the surrealism of Bunuel by juxtaposing a historical story with modern artifacts.

Walker is the incredible saga of William Walker (Harris), an American freebooter who invaded Nicaragua in 1855 with 56 men, became president of the country, and died in front of a Honduran firing squad in 1860 at age 36.

Cox fills the movie with anachronisms that are as funny as they are glaring. The characters read about Walker in *People* magazine, for example. Walker sees himself on the cover of *Time*, and modern vehicles swoop across the screen. At the climax, the U.S. State Department sends a helicopter gunship to evacuate American citizens as the country teeters on the edge of collapse. As president of Nicaragua, Walker doesn't qualify for the airlift and is left behind to be executed. Ed Harris turns in a fine portrayal of the deranged Yankee imperialist. Asked about the turmoil he's inflicted on Nicaragua, he replies: "The ends justify the means." "What are the ends?" someone asks. "I forget," he replies.

Filmed on location in Nicaragua with the financial cooperation of the Sandinista government, the film paralleled and attacked the history of American involvement in Nicaragua from Walker to the present. The film engendered controversy because of its style and its statement against U.S. policy in Central America, which supported the Nicaraguan rebels, the Contras.

The Warriors (1979 Par)

D: Walter Hill
S: David Shaber and Walter Hill, based on the novel by Sol Yurick
P: Lawrence Gordon
Cast: Michael Beck, Deborah Van Valkenburgh, Marcelino Sanchez

A multiethnic urban gang, the Warriors, fights its way through the dark urban landscape of enemy gang territory back home to Coney Island from a Manhattan gang conference, where they had been falsely accused of slaying a gang leader. This fantasy about urban street gangs with outlandish wardrobes and stylized violence was shot in a cartoonish, pop art manner. This visually exciting film makes great use of color and has a sense of urban grittiness. Deborah Van Valkenburgh plays a supposed Hispanic street girl named Mercy. Marcelino Sanchez, a young Puerto Rico–born actor raised in the Williamsburg section of Brooklyn, is a quick-witted graffiti artist named Rembrandt.

The Waterdance (1992 Samuel Goldwyn)

D: **Neal Jimenez** and Michael Steinberg
S: **Neal Jimenez**
P: Gale Ann Hurd and Marie Cantin
Cast: Eric Stoltz, Wesley Snipes, William Forsythe, Helen Hunt, **Elizabeth Pena**

This film was inspired by the personal experience of screenwriter/co-director Neal Jimenez, who drew upon his rehabilitation from a paralyzing accident that left him a wheelchair-bound paraplegic.

Writer Joel Garcia (Stoltz) falls off a cliff while hiking and breaks his neck. When he awakens he is rolling on a hospital gurney and is told he will be paralyzed for life. Later he learns to deal with the tough world of the rehabilitation facility through his wardmates, who face the same challenges and fears, but are from disparate backgrounds. The task at hand is to work through the conflicts, jealousies, and prejudices that divide them, to find their personal roads to survival. This is an unflinching, straightforward, honest film, told with humor, compassion, and humanity.

Way of a Gaucho (1952 TCF)

D: Jacques Tourneur
S: Philip Dunne, based on the novel by Herbert Childs
P: Philip Dunne
Cast: Rory Calhoun, Gene Tierney, Richard Boone, Hugh Marlowe

Formula western whose unusual Argentine background is just different enough to make it interesting.

The soap opera story concerns one of the wild horsemen who once roamed the great plains of Argentina. A sometime worker and full-time bandit before law and order fenced him in, the Gaucho (Calhoun) meets a girl (Tierney) and tries to make a go of things.

The company traveled over 1,800 miles of Argentine plains and mountains from Mendoza in the Andean foothills and through San Luis, Cordova, and Entre Rios. Some delays occurred before shooting could begin. The ship carrying the camera and other equipment arrived on the morning of the short-lived September 28 revolution. The equipment didn't get unloaded or go through customs for over a week. There were a few delays with the clearing of the script by the Argentine government, but Raul Apold, head of the Secretariat of Information, gave his wholehearted approval. Most enthusiastic of all were the members of the Sixteenth Mountain Brigade, who not only acted as extras but helped as prop men and laborers when needed.

Argentine actors including Mario Abdah, Douglas Poole, C. Spindola, Claudio Torres, and Lia Centeno were hired to play small roles. When actress Gene Tierney became ill and the company was forced to shoot around her for a week, President Juan Peron intervened, sending his personal physician to treat the actress.

Writer and producer Philip Dunne said in a *New York Times* interview (1/13/52), "We believe we've got a good picture. The scenery has been magnificent and Darryl F. Zanuck gave me some of his best people to work with. We've made everything authentic for the period. Whenever our Argentine technical advisor told us something wasn't right, we changed it."

Star Rory Calhoun recalled in a *Saturday Evening Post* interview (10/10/53), "I still rate this experience and my role as Martin, the Gaucho, as tops." *Way of a Gaucho* was really a Latin film, and although it did moderately well in the United States, it hit its peak of popularity south of the border.

We Were Strangers (1949 Col)

D: **John Huston**
S: **John Huston** and Peter Viertel, based on the novel *Rough Sketch* by Robert Sylvester
P: Sam Spiegel
Cast: John Garfield, Jennifer Jones, **Pedro Armendariz, Gilbert Roland, Ramon Novarro, Jose Perez**

Story of a Cuban-born American (Garfield) who returns to Cuba during the 1933 Machado revolution and is involved in a plot to dig a tunnel in order to plant and explode a bomb underneath a cemetery where a state funeral will take place. The plan goes wrong when the family of the dead official makes a last-minute change in the arrangements. Garfield dies, but the revolution goes on.

Though the film is slow-moving, ponderous, and talky, Pedro Armendariz as a police captain, Gilbert Roland as a Cuban revolutionary, and Ramon Novarro as a rebel chief all come off well. Argentina Brunetti, Felipe Turich, Julian Rivero, and Tina Menard have minor roles in the film.

Weekend in Havana (1941 TCF)

D: Walter Lang
S: Karl Tunberg and Darrell Ware
P: William LeBaron
Cast: Alice Faye, **Carmen Miranda, Cesar Romero,** John Payne, Cobina Wright, Jr., Billy Gilbert, Sheldon Leonard

Nan Spencer (Faye), a salesgirl at Macy's New York department store, at first refuses to sign a waiver when the boat on which she is sailing to Havana hits a reef, but then agrees to do so if her trip to Havana, paid for by the steamship company, is satisfactory.

Jay Williams (Payne), company vice president, who is to marry Terry (Wright), goes with Spencer to keep her happy. But she craves romance and finally gets it with Monte Blanca (Romero), the manager of entertainer Rosita Rivas (Miranda). Blanca, however, turns out to be a heel who is after the money he thinks Spencer has.

Williams pays Blanca to make love to Spencer, and he takes over the management of Rosita to keep her away from Blanca. But the plan doesn't succeed. Williams discovers he loves Spencer, and vice versa. Terry, however, arrives and gets Spencer to sign the waiver through trickery. Williams learns the truth, ditches Terry, and returns to Spencer.

This pleasant, colorful musical is similar in content to other musicals set in South America, and showcases Carmen Miranda at her best.

Swank hotels, beautiful nightclubs, and a spectacular gambling casino in Havana were designed by Richard Day and Joseph Wright. Before Romero began work on the picture in Hollywood, Twentieth Century–Fox sent a Technicolor crew to Havana to film backgrounds for the picture. Romero's debutante cousins appeared as background models but did not learn that he was to star in the picture until after they wrote his mother in New York, mentioning that they had appeared in an American film called *Weekend in Havana*.

One of the musical high points is a production number with 200 gorgeous female zombies and Carmen Miranda in a voodoo jive called "Nango." Chris-Pin Martin and Alberto Morin are featured.

"A Technicolor Havana that the Cubans would be last to recognize," Nelson B. Bell, *Washington Post* (11/7/41).

West Side Story (1961 UA)

D: Robert Wise and Jerome Robbins
S: Ernest Lehman, based on the stage play by Arthur Laurents, Leonard Bernstein, and Stephen Sondheim
P: Robert Wise
Cast: Richard Beymer, Natalie Wood, George Chakiris, **Rita Moreno**

Winner of 10 Academy Awards, *West Side Story,* based loosely on Shakespeare's *Romeo and Juliet,* was one of the most popular films of its time. Rival teenage gangs, one Puerto Rican, the other a mixture of Italian, Irish, and Polish American youths, fight in the streets of New York. The story centers around Maria (Wood), a Puerto Rican girl, who falls in love with an Italian boy, Tony (Beymer), and the tragic consequences of their love for each other.

West Side Story depicted the then very real problem of juvenile delinquency and gang warfare in New York City. It was filmed partly on the Upper West Side of Manhattan (the site where Lincoln Center for the Performing Arts stands today), where actual gangs roamed. The film exposed the plight and concerns of Puerto Ricans to a worldwide audience in a superficial way.

West Side Story was first presented as a hit Broadway stage musical in 1959 with landmark choreography by Jerome Robbins and a timeless musical score by Leonard Bernstein. For the motion picture version, Robbins's choreography and the direction by Robbins and Robert Wise achieved a delicate balance in their integration of the musical numbers within the story.

Rita Moreno won an Academy Award for Best Supporting Actress for her role as the strong and fiery Anita. The award cemented her image as a Latin spitfire, and for years all the roles offered to her were in that vein. However, she refused to accept roles that she felt limited her and that were demeaning, so she chose not to work in films for over seven years. She appeared instead in several stage productions in roles that she felt were challenging.

Among the Puerto Ricans in the cast are Jaime Rogers, Rudy Del Campo, Yvonne Othon, and Jose De Vega, who is part Filipino. George Chakiris, a Greek American, won an Oscar as Best Supporting Actor for the role of the tough Puerto Rican gang leader, Bernardo.

The film's social commentary is particularly well expressed in Stephen Sondheim's lyrics for the song "America." It talks about how much easier it is for the women to adapt to life in the United States because of the various conveniences, whereas the men point out the realities of not being white in America.

West Side Story won 10 Academy Awards; in addition to those for Moreno and Chakiris, its Oscars included Best Picture and Best Director (Robbins and Wise).

What Happened to Santiago (1989 Manley Prod.)
D: **Jacobo Morales**
S: **Jacobo Morales**
P: Pedro Muniz
Cast: Tommy Muniz, Gladys Rodriguez, Johanna Rosaly, Rene Monclova

A charming love story about a retired accountant, Santiago Rodriguez (Muniz), and a mysterious younger woman in modern-day Puerto Rico.

Made on a budget of $480,000, the film was nominated for an Academy Award for Best Foreign Language Film (Puerto Rico). Filmmaker Morales is a 40-year veteran of the Puerto Rican entertainment industry and has appeared in such American films as *Bananas* (1971) and *Up the Sandbox* (1972) and directed *Dios los Cria* (1980) and *Nicolas y los Demas* (1985).

Which Way Is Up? (1977 U)
D: Michael Schultz
S: Carl Gottlieb and Cecil Brown, based on the film script *The Seduction of Mimi* by Lina Wertmuller
P: Steve Krantz
Cast: Richard Pryor, Lonette McKee, **Luis Valdez, Daniel Valdez**

Unsuccessful reworking of Lina Wertmuller's 1974 Italian comedy *The Seduction of Mimi*, in an American setting. Driven out of the groves by the boss when he accidentally becomes a union hero, an orange picker (Pryor) eventually goes to work for the company, turning his back on friends and family.

This was the first feature film appearance of actor/director/writer Luis Valdez and his brother, actor/composer/singer Daniel Valdez, and other members of the internationally acclaimed El Teatro Campesino (Farm Workers Theater). The Teatro's main contribution, aside from providing actors for the film, was in reshaping portions of the script dealing with the Chicano characters. Daniel plays Chuy Estrada, an energetic, fun-loving fruit picker with a serious streak, and Luis plays Ramon Juarez, a Cesar Chavez–like labor organizer. Director Michael Schultz had seen several of their stage presentations and sought out Luis and Daniel to work in the film.

White Men Can't Jump (1992 TCF)
D: Ron Shelton
S: Ron Shelton
P: Dan Miller and David Lester
Cast: Woody Harrelson, Wesley Snipes, **Rosie Perez**

Two street basketball hustlers, one black, Sid (Snipes), the other white, Billy (Harrelson), outwit each other and then decide to join forces and become partners in order to pull off a series of scams.

Billy shares a cramped motel room with his Puerto Rican girlfriend, Gloria (Perez), in this, the first Hollywood film to have a Puerto Rican lead female character played by a Puerto Rican. Perez's eccentric portrayal is cute, comical, sexy, and endearing. The Puerto Rican–Anglo-American Gloria-Billy love relationship is another breakthrough in American cinema, as the characters are on equal standing in their sexual and psychological relationships. Gloria is obviously a "New Yor-ican" (a Puerto Rican born and raised in New York), so even though she is Latin she has no accent and is fully American, not a stereotyped Spanish-accented "Rosita" character.

Though the story takes place in an inner-city Los Angeles environment, it is free from the typical barrio trappings. Gloria sings a Puerto Rican song, "Que Bonita Bandera" (What a Beautiful Flag), while in the shower with Billy, indicating her cultural roots. She spends her days accumulating useless information, for she dreams of going on the popular television game show "Jeopardy" and winning a fortune, which she eventually does.

Why Worry? (1923 Pathé)

    D: Fred Neumeyer and Sam Taylor
    S: Sam Taylor
    P: Hal Roach
 Cast: Harold Lloyd

Silent. This Harold Lloyd comedy has the popular comedian caught in a South American revolution. It turns into a burlesque comedy filled with hilarious sight gags and with shallow stereotypes.

Harold Van Pelham (Lloyd) is a rich young man who is mistaken for a world banking executive when he arrives in Paradiso, a tiny island country off the west coast of Chile in which an American renegade has gathered together a band of outlaws to overthrow the government.

The Wild Bunch (1969 WB)

    D: **Sam Peckinpah**
    S: Walon Green and **Sam Peckinpah**, based on a story by Green and
          Roy N. Sickner
    P: Phil Feldman
 Cast: William Holden, Robert Ryan, Ernest Borgnine, Edmond O'Brien,
        Warren Oates, Ben Johnson, **Jaime Sanchez, Emilio Fernandez,**
        Alfonso Arau

A classic western remembered more for its choreographed, slow-motion bloodbaths and less for its textured acting and feeling of authenticity. *The Wild Bunch* best illustrates the quintessential American view of Mexico as a place where gringos can play out their fantasies, a never-never land of sex, violence, and ultra machismo.

In this brutal drama of violent men who have outlived their times, Holden as Pike, Borgnine as Dutch, Oates as Lyle Gorch, and Johnson as Tector Gorch fully realize the conflicting strains of their harsh yet humane characters.

After a violent bank robbery in a U.S. bordertown, the Bunch crosses the Rio Grande into Mexico, where they are cleansed and given a rebirth. The film then takes on a sudden tranquility in a brief pastoral interlude when they enter the village of the Bunch's only Mexican member, Angel (Sanchez).

In 1913 Mexico, Villa is fighting a repressive Huerta government. Mexican women are seen slung with bandoliers, breast-feeding their babies, and making tacos in General Mapache's (Fernandez) encampment while German military advisers stand by and watch. To Pike, Mexico is a last frontier, but the reality is that it has always been in a state of upheaval, exemplified by the contrast between Angel's village and Mapache's encampment.

Where the others in the Bunch are indifferent (a condition of their situation as well as the western tradition), one part of Angel at least is committed to the still unsettled cause of his people. The others do not understand it but are affected by Angel's positive force. In the end, Pike urges the others to protect Angel from General Mapache, and even Dutch sympathizes as far as he can with Angel's cause. It is Angel's inability to accept the brotherhood ethic in an American context that propels the Bunch into their final conflict. It is his sense of Latin machismo that leads him to shoot his former girlfriend, who has become one of Mapache's whores, an act that introduces a deadly disequilibrium into the relations of the Bunch and the Mexicans after they have managed to achieve a fragile détente. Mapache treats Angel like a peon. After this, a confrontation can be postponed but not avoided. The Bunch never kill or commit a crime in Mexico except for the final showdown. Instead, they cross back north of the border to rob a train.

Ernest Borgnine as Dutch and
William Holden as Pike depart a Mexican
village in a scene from *The Wild Bunch,* a
classic western directed by Sam Peckinpah.

Peckinpah does not portray Mexico as a complete paradise for the Bunch. Mapache represents an early form of twentieth-century petty tyrant. He is evil incarnate, possessed of all the trappings of the industrial world. Before meeting Mapache, the Bunch has never seen an automobile. Later, that car will be used to drag around the body of the tortured Angel. The machine gun, which becomes the chief instrument of the Bunch's and Mapache's demise, is another modern-day weapon. Surrounded by adoring children, German military advisers, whores, and sadistic killers, Mapache delights in the destructive power of a machine gun.

Four Americans, killing hundreds of Mexicans before meeting their own demise, could be interpreted as a symbol of American superiority, a remnant of the Alamo ethic and the white man saving the poor "little brown brothers" from themselves attitude of the Teddy Roosevelt era. The introduction of the machine gun, however, makes that an uncomfortable interpretation to maintain.

Peckinpah's vision of a whole Mexican village lining up to bid farewell to the Americanos can be regarded as a projection of white benign imperialism. The villagers, as it turns out, do not need the protection of the Bunch; they are using the Americanos to preserve their revolution but are perfectly capable of careful planning and execution. This is illustrated by their swift action in retrieving the rifles promised to them by Angel. The villagers do not ask the Bunch (as in *The Magnifi-*

cent Seven) to do their fighting for them; all they want is guns. The elder says, "In Mexico, Senor, these are the years of sadness, but if we had rifles like these . . .?!"

Poor Mexican women in the film are seen exclusively as whores. Angel screams "puta" (whore) and shoots his former girlfriend in the heart when he sees her with General Mapache, the man responsible for his parents' death. Mapache quickly replaces her with another woman. The Bunch seek comfort with the whores. Sex and death are irretrievably linked for the Bunch; Pike is shot dead in the back by a whore at the finale. The women in Angel's village, though not whores, seem to be easily available to the Americanos. Since Angel's girlfriend came from that village, the implication is clear, especially when she tells Angel it is better to have status as Mapache's woman than to starve to death in her own village. It is ironic that Emilio Fernandez, who as a director contributed with cameraman Gabriel Figueroa some of the most beautiful images of Mexico and its people and a national identity through its cinema, would in later life play some of the most despicable and memorable Mexican bandido characters in American films. Fernandez's larger-than-life personality, forged on drunken brawls, shoot-outs, and run-ins with Mexican government officials, eventually became a caricature both on screen and off.

The movie was filmed in Parras, Coahuila, Mexico. The final shoot-out was filmed at La Cieniga de San Carmen, a 300-year-old winery that served as the military headquarters of Mapache. The screenplay, by director Sam Peckinpah and Walon Green, is based on an original story by Green and Roy Sickner inspired by an actual border incident in 1913 when a gang of American outlaws posing as U.S. soldiers hijacked a munitions train on its way to Pancho Villa. *The Wild Bunch* touches on one of Peckinpah's favorite themes: the changing West and its impact on the unchanging loner in a frontier being replaced by civilization.

Jaime Sanchez, a Puerto Rican–born actor, plays Angel, the only Mexican member of the outlaw gang. The Mexican performers constitute a gathering of some of Mexico's most talented actors, including Chano Urrueta as the village headman, Sonia Amalio as William Holden's lover, Alfonso Arau as one of Mapache's military aides (he played a comic version of this character in the later movie spoof *¡Three Amigos!*), Fernando Wagner as a German military aide, and Jorge Russek as Lt. Zamora, a military aide and bodyguard.

Charles Champlin in the *L.A. Times* (6/15/69) said, "It is all framed within the comfortably familiar conventions of the classic western, including, I would say, the characterizing of Mexicans as childlike and simple, whether good (poor exploited but rebellious), bad (bandidos or army), or indifferent (fun loving senoritas)."

The Winged Serpent

See *Q.*

Wings of the Hawk (1953 U)

D: **Budd Boetticher**
S: James E. Moser and Kay Leonard, based on the novel by Gerald Drayson Adams
P: Aaron Rosenberg
Cast: Van Heflin, Julia Adams, **Rodolfo Acosta**, Abbe Lane, **Antonio Moreno**, **Pedro Gonzalez-Gonzalez**

Heflin plays Irish Gallager, a Yankee prospector in Mexico who finds himself at odds with government troops under the command of Col. Ruiz (George Dolenz) and sides with a revolutionary army led by the beautiful Lt. Raquel (Adams) and Arturo (Acosta). Raquel's parents have been killed by Presidente Diaz's troops, and her sister Elena (Lane) is in league with the colonel. Gallager becomes the insur-rectionist leader after deposing Arturo, who later betrays the insurrectionists. Gallager's feats range from slaughtering endless numbers of Presidente Diaz's troops to blowing up a gold mine.

This action/adventure yarn with a gringo in Mexico is well directed with strong character flair by Boetticher in Technicolor. Pedro Gonzalez-Gonzalez scores in a comedic role. Also in the cast are Paul Fierro, Felipe Turich, Joe Dominguez, Rocky Ybarra, and Ruben Padilla.

The Wonderful Country (1959 UA)
      D: Robert Parrish
      S: Robert Ardrey, based on the novel by Tom Lea
      P: Charles Erskine
   Cast: Robert Mitchum, **Pedro Armendariz**, Victor Mendoza

"Half-breed" Martin Brady (Mitchum) is a Mexican hired gun for the powerful Castro brothers (Armendariz and Mendoza), one a petty dictator and the other an army leader. Brady symbolically lays down his gun by his dead horse Lagrimas (Tears), crosses the Rio Grande, and returns to his lover, reclaiming his heritage. "Why don't you start your life all over again this side of the border?" suggests an American to Brady. The prejudice he faces is not from the Anglos who resent his Mexican ancestry but from the Castro brothers, who label him a gringo because "it is not easy to wipe out the heritage in the blood."

Mitchum, who also functioned as a producer, works somewhat uncharacteris-tically with a Mexican accent and the mannerisms of a Mexican peon. The movie was shot on location in Mexico.

The Wrath of God (1972 MGM)
      D: Ralph Nelson
      S: Ralph Nelson, based on the novel by James Graham
      P: Ralph Nelson
   Cast: Robert Mitchum, **Rita Hayworth**, Frank Langella, Victor Buono

Mitchum is a drunken American priest running guns in a fictional South Ameri-can country. Rita Hayworth, in her last film appearance, is the mother of a deranged counter-revolutionary (Langella). Gregory Sierra plays Jurado, a one-eyed rebel. It was filmed in Mexico and includes the usual assortment of stereo-types.

Wrestling Ernest Hemingway (1993 WB)
      D: Randa Haines
      S: Steve Conrad
      P: Todd Black and Joe Wizan
   Cast: Robert Duvall, Richard Harris, Shirley MacLaine, Piper Laurie,
          Sandra Bullock

Walter (Duvall), a circumspect Cuban immigrant always practicing for tomorrow's triumphs, and Frank (Harris), a salty Irish ex–sea captain, are two very different 75-year-old men who meet in the park of a sleepy southern Florida town and who begin a shaky relationship that breathes new life into each of them.

You Were Never Lovelier (1942 Col)
D: William A. Seiter
S: Michael Fessier, Ernest Pagano, and Delmer Daves, based on
the story and screenplay "The Gay Senorita" by Carlos Olivari
and Sixto Pondal Rios
P: Louis F. Edelman
Cast: Fred Astaire, **Rita Hayworth**, Adolphe Menjou, **Adele Mara**,
Leslie Brooks, **Xavier Cugat**, **Lina Romay**

Set in Buenos Aires, *You Were Never Lovelier* is an enchanting musical bringing together Hayworth and Astaire at the top of their form for the second and last time. They were previously teamed in *You'll Never Get Rich* (1941).

A New York nightclub dancer (Astaire) with a passion for horse racing meets the daughter (Hayworth) of a wealthy Latin American hotelier (Menjou).

Xavier Cugat and his Orchestra, accompanied by singer/actress Lina Romay, are on hand to provide the Latin flavor in a film shot totally in Hollywood.

Young Guns (1988 TCF)
D: Christopher Cain
S: John Fusco
P: Joe Roth and Christopher Cain
Cast: **Emilio Estevez**, Kiefer Sutherland, **Lou Diamond Phillips**,
Charlie Sheen, Casey Siemaszko, Dermot Mulroney, Jack Palance,
Terence Stamp

The year is 1878, the place, Lincoln County, New Mexico. John Tunstall (Stamp), a British rancher, hires six rebellious boys as "regulators" (gunfighters) to protect his ranch against a ring of ruthless cattle ranchers. When Tunstall is killed in an ambush, the regulators, led by Billy the Kid (Estevez), declare war on the cattle ranchers, and their vendetta turns into a bloody rampage. Lou Diamond Phillips plays a knife-wielding gunslinger called Chavez y Chavez, referred to as a "half-breed," who is part of Billy's gang.

Young Guns II (1990 TCF)
D: Geoff Murphy
S: John Fusco
P: Paul Schiff and Irby Smith
Cast: **Emilio Estevez**, Kiefer Sutherland, Christian Slater, William Petersen,
Lou Diamond Phillips, James Coburn

An old man on a deserted New Mexico highway circa 1940 agrees to meet a journalist and tells him the true story of Billy the Kid (Estevez) and Pat Garrett (Petersen). As he tells the story, the events unfold in flashback, bringing the viewer to the slow realization that Billy did not meet his end at the hands of Garrett, as was documented, but that Garrett staged Billy's death so he could get on with his life and turn over a new leaf. The old man turns out to be Billy the Kid.

This effective, action-filled western stars many of the young stars of the day. It is one of the few sequels that is as good as, if not better than, its original, *Young Guns* (1988). Lou Diamond Phillips reprised his role as Chavez y Chavez.

The Young Land (1959 Col)
D: Ted Tetzlaff
S: Norman Shannon Hall, based on the story "Frontier Frenzy" by John Reese
P: Patrick Ford
Cast: Patrick Wayne, Yvonne Craig, Dennis Hopper

The story of a town in post–Mexican War 1848 California that is acquired by the United States, and of the town's sheriff, Jim Ellison (Wayne).

A reckless Anglo gunman, Hatfield Carnes (Hopper), goads a respected Mexican into an obviously one-sided gun duel. This leads to the first murder trial involving an American accused of killing a Mexican, and in the eyes of the Mexicans, "American justice is on trial." Following the jury's verdict of guilty, the federal judge on the case faces the difficult task of sentencing the criminal, whose henchmen are preparing to save him while a group of Mexican *vaqueros* are planning to lynch him. The judge, stating that the laws of California have not been established, sets aside a 20-years-to-life sentence and sentences Carnes instead to a life without the privilege of carrying a gun. This infuriates Carnes to the point of snatching a gun from a deputy's holster and inviting Ellison (Wayne) to a duel outside the courtroom. Ellison kills Carnes in the showdown. The film ends with Ellison's betrothal to Elena de la Madrid (Craig), the daughter of a wealthy Mexican patron of the region.

The cast also includes Roberto de la Madrid, Pedro Gonzalez-Gonzalez, John Quijada, Miguel Camacho, Carlos Romero, and the mariachi band Los Reyes de Chapala. It was filmed in Mexico.

The Young Savages (1961 UA)

D: John Frankenheimer
S: Edward Anhalt and J.P. Miller, based on the novel *A Matter of Conviction* by Evan Hunter
P: Pat Duggan
Cast: Burt Lancaster, Dina Merrill, Edward Andrews, Shelley Winters, Jose Perez

American social melodrama that addresses several important issues of the time—juvenile delinquency, racial prejudice, the death penalty, drugs, and gangs.

In the late 1950s, the Spanish Harlem section of New York is controlled by teenage gangs. Two such gangs are the Thunderbirds, from an Italian neighborhood, and the Horsemen, from a Puerto Rican neighborhood. Three members of the Thunderbirds stab and kill a blind Puerto Rican boy. The three youths are caught by the police, and the case is turned over to Hank Bell (Lancaster) of the D.A.'s office.

Bell's investigation takes him to the two neighborhoods, where he talks to the witnesses and the various gang members. It is revealed that the "innocent" Puerto Rican boy was, in fact, a gang member and a pimp for his sister. The boys are convicted of murder in varying degrees and are sentenced.

The film, based on a book by Evan Hunter of *Blackboard Jungle* fame, has the familiar ring of the white-man-saving-the-poor-minorities-from-themselves theme, except that the "white man" in this film is a minority himself.

Hank Bell is actually Italian American Henry Bellini, who is trying to move up the social scale and forget his past, which he can never really escape. This well-intentioned film unfortunately further embellishes the stereotypes of Puerto Rican city dwellers as gang members, suffering mothers, and easy women. Vivian Nathan plays Mrs. Escalante, the suffering mother of the blind boy (Rafael Lopez) and his sister Louisa (Pilar Seurat). Luis Arroyo plays the gang leader Zorro, and Jose Perez plays Roberto Escalante. The movie was filmed on location in Spanish Harlem in New York City, where Lancaster grew up. It was a predominantly Italian area during Lancaster's youth, but by the time of the film, the area around First and Pleasant avenues was all that was left of the Italian area, and Puerto Ricans inhabited the area from Second to Fifth avenues.

Zandy's Bride (1974 WB)

    D: Jan Troell
    S: Marc Norman, based on the novel *The Stranger* by Lillian Bos Ross
    P: Harvey Matofsky
  Cast: Gene Hackman, Liv Ullmann, Susan Tyrrell, **Joe Santos**,
       Fabian Gregory Cordova

Zandy (Hackman) is a frontiersman who sends for a mail-order bride, Hannah (Ullmann). The movie is the story of two very different people struggling to make a life together in the harsh western environment of Monterey, California, in the 1860s. Zandy has a fling at a barbecue when he is seduced by the jealous, hot-blooded Maria Cordova (Tyrrell). Joe Santos plays a Spanish cattle rancher named Frank Gallo. The film was directed by Swedish filmmaker Jan Troell, who won acclaim for The Emigrant Saga, including *The Emigrants* (1971) and its sequel, *The New Land* (1972).

"Susan Tyrrell makes a fiery Maria Cordova, an aggressive girl spurned by Zandy, but one can't help but wonder why [Maria] wasn't played by a Chicana actress," Kevin Thomas, *L.A. Times* (6/26/74).

Zoot Suit (1981 U)

    D: **Luis Valdez**
    S: **Luis Valdez**, based on his play
    P: Peter Burrell, Kenneth Brecher, and William P. Wingate
  Cast: **Edward James Olmos, Daniel Valdez, Rose Portillo, Lupe Ontiveros, Abel Franco**, Tyne Daly, Charles Aidman, John Anderson, **Mike Gomez, Alma Beltran, Sal Lopez, Robert Beltran, Alma Rosa Martinez**

Luis Valdez became the first Mexican American or Chicano to write and direct a major studio-backed feature film with the screen adaptation of his hit play *Zoot Suit*.

The musical/drama about Los Angeles in the 1940s opened in 1978 at the Mark Taper Forum in Los Angeles to overwhelming critical and audience reception, breaking box-office records. The run was extended and the production moved to the Aquarius Theatre in Hollywood, where it continued to break attendance records. With *Zoot Suit*, Valdez became the first Chicano playwright to have his work performed on the Broadway stage when the production opened at New York City's Winter Garden Theatre.

Zoot Suit is the story of a group of Mexican American boys who are falsely accused of murdering another boy at a party in Los Angeles during the 1940s. Based on fact, it retells the events of the Sleepy Lagoon murder and the Zoot Suit riots that took place in 1942 and 1943. Zoot suits were a style of clothing popularized stateside by Mexican American and black youths during World War II. The Sleepy Lagoon murder case is a landmark in American legal annals, for it established a precedent against mass trials. The trial was a mockery of justice, presided over by an obviously biased judge who sentenced 12 of the defendants to San Quentin Prison for life even though there were no eyewitnesses to the killing. Fueled by racism, yellow journalism, and wartime hysteria, Anglo G.I.'s stationed in Los Angeles invaded the downtown barrios, beating up any Mexican wearing a zoot suit. Police were either unable or unwilling to stop the rioting, which spread to other communities and lasted five days.

In 1981, Universal Pictures agreed to film the play over a period of 14 days on the stage of the Aquarius Theatre, using most of the original stage cast. The budget was $2.5 million.

Edward James Olmos re-created his award-winning (Los Angeles Drama Critics Circle Award and a Tony Award nomination), critically acclaimed portrayal of El Pachuco for the screen. El Pachuco, giant switchblade in hand, cuts through blown-

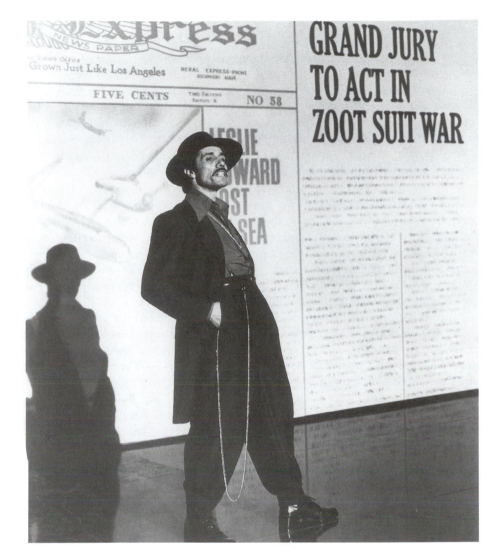

Edward James Olmos as the zoot-suited El Pachuco in Luis Valdez's *Zoot Suit,* the first major studio-backed feature film written and directed by a Mexican American.

up newspaper headlines, in effect cutting through the stereotype by using one of its more potent images. Olmos swaggers and struts with an economical grace as the ultimate zoot suiter who symbolizes Chicano pride and a darker foreboding element. With the snap of his fingers, El Pachuco moves the film from one event to another, offering sly, witty, and insightful commentary on the plight of the Mexican American.

The action centers around Henry Reyna (played by Daniel Valdez), the leader of the youths, his family, his followers and their girls, and the people they come into contact with during their arrest and trial. The drama is bathed in the sights and sounds of World War II Americana, such as the big band sounds of Glenn Miller and Harry James, patriotic flag waving, jitterbug swing dancing, and men in uniforms.

Zoot Suit skillfully combines cinematic theatrical techniques, cutting on movement and sound, making a radical and innovative film record of the stage play that sometimes works well and sometimes doesn't. Through the story of the four Chicano boys, it recounts the racial tension and rioting that plagued Los Angeles during World War II. Being a musical, however, it mixes these somber events with an uplifting and celebratory spirit. It was during the zoot suit era that Mexican Americans first recognized their cultural heritage and established a pride in their identity. Some of the music and songs in the play and film were contributed by Daniel Valdez and Lalo Guerrero.

In an interview with Luis Reyes, Valdez explained the development of *Zoot Suit*: "*Zoot Suit* is [an] extremely spiritual, political play and it was never understood. People thought it was about juvenile delinquents and that I was putting the Pachuco on the stage just to be snide. But the young man, Henry Reyna, achieves his liberation by coming into contact with this internal authority. The Pachuco is the Jungian self-image, the superego if you will, the power inside every individual greater than any institution. The Pachuco says, 'It'll take more than the U.S. Navy to beat me down [referring to the sailors and Marines stripping zoot suiters in the 1940s], I don't give a fuck what you do to me, you . . . take [that] . . . guise from me, and I reassert myself in this guise.'

"The fact that the critics couldn't accept that guise was too bad, but it doesn't change the nature of what the play's about. It deals with self-salvation. And you can follow the playwright through the story. I was also those two dudes. With *Zoot Suit* I was finally able to transcend social conditions and the way I did it on stage was to give the Pachuco absolute power, as the master of ceremonies. He could snap his fingers and stop the action. It was a Brechtian device that allowed the plot to move forward, but psychically and symbolically, in the right way. Chicanos got off on it. That's why half a million people came to see it in L.A., because I had given a disenfranchised people their religion back. I dressed the Pachuco in the colors of Testatipoka, the Aztec god of education, the dean of the school of hard knocks. There's another god of culture, Quetzalcoatl, the feathered serpent, who's much kinder. He surfaces in *La Bamba* as the figure of Ritchie Valens. He's an artist and poet and is gentle and not at all fearful. When audiences see *La Bamba*, they like the positive spirit. The Pachuco's a little harder to take. But these are evolutions."

"Enlightening and challenging musical drama that runs the gamut from Greek Tragedy to *West Side Story*," Mark Kane, *Film Journal* (1/16/82).

INTRODUCTION

At first glance it seems that there have been as few Hispanics as blacks and other minorities on network television. Character names like Ricky Ricardo, the Cisco Kid, Zorro, and Jose Jimenez easily come to mind, but it's hard to come up with other names or role models. This is a deceptive conclusion, however, because more Hispanics have entered our homes and our lives through the television set than perhaps we realize.

For example, there were Henry Darrow and Linda Cristal on "The High Chaparral," and Elena Verdugo on "Marcus Welby, M.D." in the late 1960s and early 1970s , and, though not an overwhelmingly positive Hispanic image, Freddie Prinze on "Chico and the Man." More recently, comedian Paul Rodriguez, despite several ill-fated network series attempts, has had huge success with Fox and HBO comedy specials.

As is the case with black Americans, many early Hispanic successes focused on comedy images within an American framework. Only with such recent shows as "Miami Vice" and "L.A. Law" has there been any success within the dramatic format, and then only in supporting roles such as Edward James Olmos's senior policeman Lt. Castillo; Jimmy Smits's high-powered L.A. lawyer Victor Sifuentes; and to a lesser degree, Rene Enriquez's beleaguered second-in-command station cop Lt. Ray Calletano on the gritty inner-city cop show "Hill Street Blues." "CHiPs," starring Erik Estrada as a California Highway Patrol officer, was an exception in that, with its breezy southern California action style, it fit neither the comedy nor drama category comfortably.

On close inspection, one finds that a surprising amount of Hispanic American talent has been working constantly in American television, both in front of and behind the camera. Yet, although Hispanics have been featured on series since TV started, there have been few Hispanic star- or character-driven vehicles. Many of the shows that featured Hispanic characters were short-lived or the character portrayals were limited or unpopular with the public.

The first important Hispanic presence, of course, was Desi Arnaz as Ricky Ricardo on the "I Love Lucy" show (1951–1957). Even though "The Cisco Kid" (1950–1955) was on the air prior to "I Love Lucy," it came to television via its film success as one of the first Saturday matinee westerns transferred to the new medium. "I Love Lucy" with Arnaz as Lucy's husband was a unique, contemporary, and untried concept. Arnaz was not only a performer but also a producer, and his influence is still felt almost 50 years later. For example, he pioneered a three-camera technique for filming situation comedies that is still in use today. By filming "I Love Lucy" and retaining ownership of the filmed shows, he created the industry stan-

Lucille Ball and Desi Arnaz on "I Love Lucy."

dard for syndicated reruns. Through his and his wife Lucille Ball's Desilu production company he oversaw the development of such memorable television series as "The Untouchables" and "Star Trek," and many shows of the time used the Desilu Studios facilities.

The funny-talking musician known rather patronizingly as "Cuban Pete" proved to be not only a capable performer but a shrewd businessman. Arnaz followed the original "I Love Lucy" series with "The Lucy-Desi Comedy Hour" (1957–1960), which ceased production the same year that Castro came to power in Cuba and Lucy and Desi, America's favorite couple, filed for divorce. Two years later Castro declared his Communist ties. Suddenly the image of the funny, friendly, romantic Cuban turned into the fierce, bearded, cigar-chomping Communist revolutionary Fidel Castro. Almost overnight, the image of the Hispanic on television was transformed by the evening news. The American media bombarded the airwaves with images of Castro and his armed America-hating revolutionaries and the debacle of the Bay of Pigs affair. The public became terrified by the prospect of a nuclear World War III during the Cuban Missile Crisis.

Latin banana republics with revolutionaries or military dictators, most sporting Castro-like beards and military fatigues or spit-and-polish *generalisimo* images, became a staple of episodic action shows. From "The Twilight Zone" to "I Spy" and

"Hart to Hart" to "The A-Team" to "MacGyver," the amusing, funny-talking south-of-the-border clown turned deadly.

Duncan Renaldo as the Cisco Kid and Leo Carrillo as his sidekick Pancho followed in the traditional western hero mold. Some 156 half-hour episodes were filmed in color between 1950 and 1955. Making thousands of personal appearances in costume, Renaldo and Carrillo brought the magic of the Latin cowboy hero to small-town and big-city America alike. In the late 1960s, Chicano activists found fault with Carrillo's buffoonish portrayal of Pancho on the show, and the series was pulled from syndication for many years, primarily in the southwestern United States.

In the late 1950s, when there was a preponderance of western cowboy series like "Wagon Train," "Gunsmoke," "Maverick," "Cheyenne," and "Bonanza," Hispanics were portrayed in stock bandido, spitfire, or peon roles whether they were played by Hispanic actors or not. When the major movie studios began to let many of their stars and contract players go during the 1950s, television was a way of escaping the rigid typecasting they had been subject to while under contract. Ricardo Montalban, Fernando Lamas, and Rita Moreno worked regularly in television during the 1950s in a wider variety of roles than they had found in films. In a *TV Guide* interview in the issue of January 24, 1970, Montalban said, "It is to TV that I owe my freedom from the bondage of the Latin Lover image. Television came along and gave me parts to chew on. It gave me wings as an actor." His TV credits include varied parts in such vintage series as "Playhouse 90," "Climax," "Wagon Train," "Ben Casey," "Star Trek," and "Fantasy Island."

Hispanic women have usually been relegated to the overweight mamacita, the spitfire, and the suffering mother or girlfriend. The image of the strong, self-reliant, attractive Latin woman was first memorably portrayed in two TV series, by Linda Cristal as Victoria Cannon in "The High Chaparral" and Elena Verdugo as Nurse Consuelo in "Marcus Welby, M.D."

Even though both these characters were subservient to Anglo men (Victoria was married to John Cannon and Consuelo worked for Dr. Welby), this had as much to do with the portrayal of women generally on TV as it did with what TV producers thought the public would "accept." These two female characters were sufficiently developed through the course of the series to give them dimension and control over events in many of the story lines. One might laugh at their fiery tempers on occasion as they broke into rapid-fire cursing in Spanish (pretty much as Ricky Ricardo used to do when exasperated by Lucy's antics a decade earlier), but they were also portrayed with dignity and a generally implied acceptance of equality, both in terms of their gender and their racial origin, which was refreshing. They were, in other words, as good as the white males featured in the shows, and this was a reflection of the successful impact of the civil rights and women's rights movements of the 1960s and 1970s.

Beginning with the police series "Dragnet," Hispanics came to be recognized as part of the modern urban population. One of Jack Webb's (Sgt. Joe Friday's) detective partners was a Mexican American. "Naked City," a police series filmed on location in New York City, and "East Side/West Side," about social workers and also filmed in New York, featured a few episodes that dealt with Puerto Ricans.

However, another image was beginning to take shape in much later series like "Baretta," "Kojak," "Starsky and Hutch," "Police Story," and more recently "Hill Street Blues," "T.J. Hooker," and "Hunter." This image was that Hispanics are low-class, poverty-stricken ghetto dwellers, unable and unwilling to communicate in proper English, whose lives are filled with drugs, gang violence, and extreme family crisis. A virtual parade of maids, hookers, hoods, gang members, and their suffering mamacitas and girfriends has been the overriding contemporary image of Hispanics as presented on American television.

Introduction

In 1969, Nosotros, a Hispanic American actors organization dedicated to improving the image of Hispanic Americans and Spanish-speaking peoples in the media, was formed (*See* Movie Introduction, pp. 24–25). The outcry from the community put national focus on the preponderance of negative stereotypical images of Hispanics in the media, and small but significant changes began to take place.

Movies made for television that deal with Hispanic characters have been relatively few compared with the total number made each year. Now well into its twentieth year, the television movie has become a staple of network programming. All three networks combined produce about 75 TV movies a year. The most noteworthy TV movies featuring Hispanics have been produced by Hispanic producer Antonio Calderon for NBC, including *The Deadly Tower* and *Three Hundred Miles for Stephanie*. Except for the two *Drug Wars* miniseries, there has not been even one miniseries devoted exclusively to the Hispanic American experience. On the other hand, there have been several black-oriented miniseries (e.g., *Roots, The Autobiography of Miss Jane Pittman*) and a number of Movies of the Week on the Asian American experience (e.g., *Farewell to Manzanar, Kung Fu, Kung Fu: The Legend Continues*).

There have been Hispanics working in roles not perceived to be Hispanic, such as Joe Santos as PI Jim Rockford's cop buddy in "The Rockford Files" opposite James Garner, Lynda Carter in "Wonder Woman," Catherine Bach as Daisy on "The Dukes of Hazzard," and Martin Sheen in most of his TV roles. Ricardo Montalban played a man of unspecified origin, the mysterious Mr. Roarke, on "Fantasy Island" from 1978 through 1984. Montalban contributed to the TV image of Hispanics as glamorous with his style and demeanor. He also played multimillionaire playboy Zach Powers on "The Colbys," a spin-off of "Dynasty." Montalban won an Emmy Award for his portrayal of a Native American Cheyenne chief in the miniseries *How the West Was Won*. He also directed several episodes of the "Fantasy Island" series. Rita Moreno won an Emmy Award for her portrayal of a Polish hooker on an episode of "The Rockford Files." Child actor Brandon Cruz played the role of Eddie in the popular but short-lived series "The Courtship of Eddie's Father," opposite Bill Bixby as a single father. Alfonso Ribeiro, who came to television from Broadway as a child dance star, is a Dominican American and has played black characters in such series as "Silver Spoons" and "Fresh Prince of Bel Air." Enrique Castillo, a young Mexican American actor, guest starred on an episode of "The Waltons" as World War II hero Sgt. Eddie Ramirez, who has a brief affair with Mary Ellen when he brings home her deceased husband's Medal of Valor. "Tour of Duty," through the character of New York Puerto Rican Ruiz, is the only show to consistently recognize Hispanic American involvement in the nation's armed conflicts, in this case, Vietnam.

As mentioned earlier, Hispanic actors had guest spots on shows that briefly mentioned Hispanic American participation, from the World War II shows "Combat" and "The Gallant Men," to the Korean War setting of "M*A*S*H," to the Vietnam-era "China Beach."

On daytime TV, A Martinez drew a huge following as Cruz Castillo during an eight-year run, beginning in 1984, on the soap opera "Santa Barbara." He won a 1990 Daytime Emmy Award as Best Actor in a Drama Series. Henry Darrow won a Daytime Emmy Award for Best Supporting Actor in his role as Castillo's father.

Notable behind-the-scenes people who are Hispanic American include Claudio Guzman, best known as the producer and director of the "I Dream of Jeannie" comedy series; Lalo Schifrin, the jazz pianist and composer of, among many other themes, the "Mission: Impossible" series' music; Jaime Rogers, choreographer/director of many musical specials and episodes of the series "Fame"; and Vincent Gutierrez, a writer on Michael Landon's "Little House on the Prairie" and "Highway to Heaven" series. One of the most interesting episodes of "Highway to Heaven," titled "The People Next Door," was written by Gutierrez. It centered around a Hispanic doctor who passes himself off as an Anglo in order to get ahead, and the consequences for those closest to him of his living a lie.

"The Cosby Show" introduced many Hispanic characters in a variety of roles including doctors, nurses, social service assistants, an estranged father, and students. Some of these characters were played by such well-known actors as Sonia Braga, Tony Orlando, and Anthony Quinn. An episode with Tony Orlando as a community worker was intended as a series pilot, but the series was not picked up by the network. Tito Puente is heard on the soundtrack of the first several seasons, playing the show's opening theme music. The sitcom series "227" and the hour family drama "Life Goes On" tried unsuccessfully to introduce Hispanic families to their established series formats. Playwright Jose Rivera co-created the one-season series "Eerie, Indiana" (1991–1992).

Geraldo Rivera, an award-winning, high-profile broadcast journalist, national TV talk show host, and producer, has for over 20 years contributed to a positive image of Hispanics in the U.S. media.

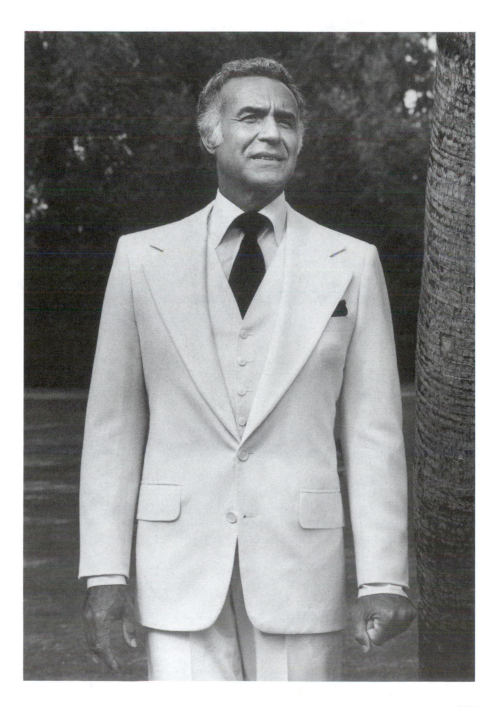

Ricardo Montalban as the elusive Mr. Roarke on "Fantasy Island."

Rita Moreno in an Emmy Award–winning performance appeared as a guest star opposite James Garner in the episode "Rosendahl and Gilda Stern Are Dead" of the TV series "The Rockford Files."

Tony Orlando starred in a musical variety show on CBS in the 1970s, and Jose Feliciano starred in several musical specials on NBC at the height of his popularity in the late 1960s and early 1970s. Feliciano also performed the theme song for the series "Chico and the Man." Dolores Del Rio and Cesar Romero co-hosted a special on Mexico in the mid-1960s, as did Ricardo Montalban, Gilbert Roland, and Janet Blair on the "Mexican Fiesta" special on "The Chevy Show" in 1960. Episodes of the popular series "Columbo" and "Madigan" were filmed in Mexico City in the early 1970s with predominantly Latin casts.

For years, episodic television series always seemed to have at least one episode that featured the Anglo series protagonists in a Latin environment, either in the United States or outside of it. "The Fugitive" once had Dr. Kimble hide out with some Mexican farmworkers. In an episode of the western series "The Rifleman," a Mexican gunman and his gang took over a town. An episode of "Ironside" reflected 1970s Chicano student activist unrest in the barrios; Buddy Ebsen in "Barnaby Jones" helped an aging Chicano cop involved in illegal activities who is determined to seek revenge on his son's murderer. On "Medical Center," the doctors faced a Mexican medicine man played by Gilbert Roland. Most recently, "Beverly Hills, 90210" featured an episode in which a Mexican American teenager shows up at Beverly Hills High. As it turns out, she has left the confines of her Pomona home for East L.A. because she is in a witness protection program. She attracts the amorous attention of one of the Anglo boys in a mature and sensitively written cross-cultural love affair.

Yet, even though Desi Arnaz hit the airwaves in 1951, nearly 50 years later there is still not one regular network series featuring a Hispanic American leading character or one revolving around a Hispanic family at a time when the Hispanic population in the United States is estimated to be over 20 million and growing.

In the following section, entries are listed alphabetically, with general credits and information for only those shows from "I Love Lucy" to the present that could be considered major Hispanic-oriented prime-time network television. Also included are comments, credits, and information on prime-time network miniseries, made-for-TV movies, and specials that reflect the Hispanic experience. Hispanic performers have played non-Hispanic roles on episodic series television, but they are not listed. However, some have been mentioned already in this introduction (e.g., Lynda Carter in "Wonder Woman," Martin Sheen's several portrayals of John F. Kennedy and other roles, and Catherine Bach on "The Dukes of Hazzard"). There are also no listings for individual episodes of series that from time to time featured Hispanic-themed story lines or guest characters.

HISPANIC AMERICANS ON AMERICAN NETWORK TELEVISION

This section focuses on Hispanic American images and talent as presented on the three major American television networks from 1951 through 1993: the American Broadcasting Company (ABC), the Columbia Broadcasting System (CBS), and the National Broadcasting Company (NBC). From 1949 to 1956 there was a fourth, small-scale national TV network in operation called the Dumont Network, and more recently a new national network, Fox. Programming from cable television is also presented, including HBO, TNT, and Showtime, as well as from the non-commercial Public Broadcasting System (PBS). **Boldface** type indicates individuals included in the Biographies section.

SERIES

"A.E.S. Hudson Street" (1978 ABC)
Cast: **Gregory Sierra, Rosana De Soto**

In this short-lived half-hour situation comedy, Sierra played Dr. Ralph Menzies, who works in an emergency ward in a Lower East Side New York hospital.

"A.K.A. Pablo" (1984 ABC)
Cast: **Paul Rodriguez, Katy Jurado, Hector Elizondo, Maria Richwine**

In this series, a struggling young comedian's chance to star in his own series thrills his large Mexican American family but provokes a dramatic confrontation with his proud father, who disapproves of his son's lifestyle.

This half-hour situation comedy created by Norman Lear and Rick Mitz reflected every stereotype in the book with its story of a 13-member Hispanic family in a single household. The show was created to showcase stand-up comedian Paul Rodriguez, who was discovered by Lear. It was short-lived but did showcase many Hispanic performers. Actor Hector Elizondo made his television directorial debut with an episode of the series.

"Acapulco" (1961 NBC)
Cast: Ralph Taeger, James Coburn, Telly Savalas

Half-hour action/adventure series set in sunny Acapulco about two former Korean War buddies who take on a job protecting from former enemies a crime-busting lawyer who resides in Mexico. The show lasted only four weeks. In a funny way, it was a precursor of "Magnum, P.I."

"The Addams Family" (1964–1966 ABC)
Cast: Carolyn Jones, John Astin, Jackie Coogan

Based on the wickedly dark-humored Charles Addams cartoons for *The New Yorker* magazine, the show was fashioned by creator/executive producer David Levy into a bizarrely outlandish but lovable family sitcom. Gomez Addams, who presumably had Spanish blood and was a bit of a romantic swashbuckler, was played by John Astin. In 1991, the characters were reworked into a hit theatrical movie, *The Addams Family,* with Raul Julia as Gomez (*see* Movie listings).

"The Adventures of Kit Carson" (1951–1955 syndicated)
Cast: Bill Williams, **Don "El Toro" ("The Bull") Diamond**

Kit's Mexican sidekick was played by Brooklyn-born Don Diamond.

"All in the Family" (1971–1989 CBS)
Cast: Carroll O'Connor, Jean Stapleton, Rob Reiner, Sally Struthers

"All in the Family," developed by Norman Lear from scriptwriter Johnny Speight's successful British comedy "'Til Death Do Us Part," changed the course of television history with a harsh, no-nonsense look at a working-class bigot called Archie Bunker (O'Connor). Archie derided every minority group and said aloud what most other bigots only thought about negative ethnic stereotypes. In the 1976–1977 season Archie was temporarily laid off from his job, and the Bunkers were forced to take in a Puerto Rican live-in, Teresa Betancourt, played by Liz Torres. When the show changed format to "Archie Bunker's Place" in 1979–1980, following the departure of Archie's long-suffering wife, Edith (Stapleton), Abraham Alvarez joined the cast as the Puerto Rican busboy Jose.

"Amigo" (1959 MGM-TV)
Cast: **Gilbert Roland**

This pilot film starred Gilbert Roland as police detective Johnny Domingo, who fights crime in the El Paso–Juarez border area.

"The A-Team" (1983–1987 NBC)
Cast: George Peppard, Dirk Benedict, Mr. T., Dwight Schultz

A one-hour action/adventure series, created by Frank Lupo and Stephen J. Cannell, in which Hannibal Smith and three of his buddies have all escaped from a military prison shortly before the end of the Vietnam War. Now back in the U.S. under assumed identities, they have formed the A-Team and will take on any mission, anywhere, for a price. In its last season, Eddie Velez joined the cast as Frankie Santana, a demolitions expert.

"At Ease" (1983 ABC)
Cast: David Naughton, Jimmie Walker, **John Vargas**

This peacetime stateside Army service comedy in which John Vargas played Cardinel, was on for only a few months.

"B.L. Stryker" (1989–1990 ABC)
Cast: **Burt Reynolds, Rita Moreno**, Ossie Davis

This two-hour-per-episode series featured a retired New Orleans cop who becomes a private eye and lives on a houseboat in Palm Beach, Florida. Rita Moreno portrayed Stryker's outrageous ex-wife, Kimberly Baskin.

"Bakersfield P.D." (1993 Fox)
Cast: Giancarlo Esposito, Brian Doyle-Murray, **Tony Plana**, Jack Hallet, Chris Mulkey, Ron Eldard

This series revolves around the members of the Bakersfield, California, Police Department and features Tony Plana as Officer Luke Ramirez.

"Barney Miller" (1975–1982 ABC)

Cast: Hal Linden, Jack Soo, Ron Glass, Abe Vigoda

Linden played Barney Miller, the precinct captain, in this long-running half-hour ensemble situation comedy set in a New York City police station. Gregory Sierra played Chamo, a Puerto Rican detective. The series was created by Danny Arnold and Theodore J. Flicker.

"Bay City Blues" (1983 NBC)

Cast: Michael Nouri, Bernie Casey, Dennis Franz

This one-hour series from Steven Bochco, the creator of "Hill Street Blues," was about the ups and downs of a minor league baseball team. It aired for only two months (October and November) before it was canceled, and featured Marco Rodriguez and Eddie Velez as members of the team.

"Berenger's" (1985 NBC)

Cast: Sam Wanamaker, Ben Murphy

Eddie Velez played Julio Morales, a clothing designer, on the ensemble series, which was set in a big-city department store.

"The Bill Dana Show" (1963–1965 NBC)

Cast: Bill Dana

Bill Dana's comedic characterization of Jose Jimenez was a cross between Chaplin and Cantinflas, an immigrant in search of the American Dream. In this series he was a bellhop at a luxury hotel.

Jose Jimenez was born out of a joke on a skit Bill Dana wrote for "The Steve Allen Show." He chose the name Jose Jimenez because the "J" sound would emphasize a joke in the skit, in which a Latin American is teaching a class at a school for Santa Clauses and mistakes the "Ho, Ho, Ho," for "Jo, Jo, Jo," as it would be said in Spanish. Dana had a good ear for dialect and was asked to play the character himself. The reaction to the character as played by Dana was phenomenal. Since Dana was a writer who had not been seen before on television, many thought he really was Jose Jimenez.

According to Bill Dana in a 1992 interview with Luis Reyes, "There were two Jose Jimenez characterizations that evolved. The first one is the Walter Mitty–like character who was the astronaut in the album recordings that sold over a million copies, both album and single. The second is the character on 'The Danny Thomas Show' who was the bumbling doorman and elevator operator who was more a real person. A sweet guy trying to assimilate into American society.

"He was a unique nonstereotypical Latin portrayal, for up to that time Hispanics were portrayed as a Cha Cha, a bandido, or a switchblade-wielding youth."

Jose Jimenez is a Latin American, but he was purposely never identified with a particular nationality. Hispanic Americans assumed he was Puerto Rican, Cuban, or Mexican American, and everyone thought of him as one of their own.

After "The Danny Thomas Show," Jose Jimenez was given his own show, called "The Bill Dana Show," of which 42 episodes were produced. The series ran for a year and a half beginning in the fall of 1963. Jose Jimenez also headlined several TV specials. The character was caught in the political crossfire of the civil rights movement in the mid-1960s, during which Latino political activists found the character offensive in light of the political realities of the times and the more positive assimilated vein in which they wished to be perceived. Advertisers shied away

Bill Dana in his memorable comedic characterization as Jose Jimenez on "The Bill Dana Show."

from Dana's Jose Jimenez character, and Dana went on to write and produce the TV series "Get Smart." The character still remains a favorite of audiences to this day, and Dana occasionally brings him back for nightclub engagements and on award and variety shows.

"CPO Sharkey" (1976–1978 NBC)

Cast: Don Rickles, Harrison Page

This half-hour comedy series starred Don Rickles as Naval Chief Petty Officer Sharkey. Richard Beauchamp played Rodriguez.

"Cade's County" (1971–1972 CBS)

Cast: Glenn Ford, **Victor Campos**

This series featured Ford as contemporary New Mexico sheriff Sam Cade and Victor Campos as his deputy, Rudy Davillo.

"Carrascolendas" (1972–1977 PBS)

Cast: **Mike Gomez**, Pete Leal

This bilingual series was aimed at Spanish-speaking children, grades K–2, to help them develop an increased pride in their Spanish heritage and foster a better understanding of the English language.

"Cassie and Company" (1982 NBC)

Cast: Angie Dickinson

Angie Dickinson starred as Cassie Holland, a private investigator who takes over an existing detective agency. A Martinez played Benny Silva, a streetwise fellow who runs a gym. The series ran from January until August.

"Checking In" (1981 CBS)

Cast: Marla Gibbs

In this half-hour situation comedy, Marla Gibbs starred in her popular role as Florence Johnston. In this spin-off from "The Jeffersons" (itself a spin-off from "All in the Family"), Gibbs played the executive housekeeper at a posh New York hotel. Liz Torres played her efficient assistant Elena, who is happy to remain an assistant as long as the job leaves her free to attend to the needs of her little son. The show aired for only three weeks before it was canceled.

"The Cheech Show" (1988 NBC)

Cast: **Cheech Marin**, Jackée

Marin developed and starred in this pilot, which did not make it to series but aired as a one-time comedy/variety special.

"Chico and the Man" (1974–1978 NBC)

Cast: Freddie Prinze, Jack Albertson, Scatman Crothers

This half-hour situation comedy created by James Komack starred Freddie Prinze and Jack Albertson and was a variation of the Archie Bunker–type sitcom. A Chicano street kid in East Los Angeles finds employment working in a garage run by a bigoted old Anglo man. The comedy revolved around the American people's stereotyped impressions of the many ethnic groups that make up the United States. Being half–Puerto Rican and half-Hungarian, Prinze made it a focus of his routines. Albertson, a well-known stage actor and vaudevillian, made a perfect match for the spunky streetwise kid as the salty old garage owner Ed. The mixing of the old and the new comedy styles proved so popular that the show was an immediate hit.

Prinze was most definitely a Hispanic American figure. He was not an immigrant and did not speak Spanish with an accent, except as an exaggeration to make a point. He was an American, and he made Americans laugh at themselves.

There was a small backlash to the series when Chicano or Mexican American groups protested Prinze's portrayal of a Chicano. Prinze's character was that of a Mexican American raised in Los Angeles, but he came across as a New York Puerto Rican, which in fact he was. He was not yet a skilled enough actor or performer to put over the subtleties of characterization needed to make Chico a believable, ethnically correct portrayal. Audiences didn't seem to mind or know any better, but the Chicano groups felt they were being misrepresented. This controversy made not only the network but the country take a look at an insensitivity to the rich cultural diversity of Hispanic Americans.

Prinze's meteoric rise as a superstar ended tragically in suicide in 1977. After his death the show continued with a young street urchin played by Gabriel Melgar, who replaced Prinze, but the memory of Prinze was too big a void to fill. Several Hispanic American character actors were featured on the show, including Danny Nunez, Alma Beltran, Danny Mora, and Tina Menard, and Charo in the final season.

"CHiPs" (1977–1983 NBC)

Cast: **Erik Estrada**, Larry Wilcox

This series followed the adventures of two young California Highway Patrol motorcycle officers who patrolled the southern California highways. Estrada's cocky streetwise portrayal of Frank "Ponch" Poncherello was one of the best and most positive portrayals of Hispanic Americans on television to that time.

Ponch is in the mainstream of American society and life. He is young, good looking, and very American. Very little mention is made of his Hispanic heritage. He is a fantasy character surrounded by fast vehicles, adventure, and beautiful women. He is also a law enforcement officer dedicated to helping people and as such a positive role model.

Erik Estrada and Larry Wilcox in "CHiPs."

On August 6, 1979, Estrada suffered injuries in a motorcycle accident during the filming of the show's 1979–1980 third season premiere episode. Because eight episodes had already been filmed, Estrada was given weeks of lead time in which to recuperate. His condition was used on the show, and a stuntman re-created the motorcycle accident for the cameras. Rick Rosner created the popular MGM-TV series.

"The Cisco Kid" (1950–1956 syndicated)
See "Zorro & The Cisco Kid" listings.

"CITY" (1990 CBS)
Cast: Valerie Harper

In this short-lived half-hour situation comedy, an energetic city manager (Harper) juggles the chaos of City Hall with her life as a single mother. Liz Torres and LuAnne Ponce were series regulars.

"Condo" (1983 ABC)
Cast: **Luis Avalos**, McLean Stevenson, Yvonne Wilder, **Julie Carmen, James Victor**

This half-hour situation comedy concerned an upwardly mobile Hispanic American family living next door to a WASP family in a new condominium complex. There were constant comedic clashes based on racial prejudice and cultural differences between the two families. The head of the Hispanic family was Jesse Rodriguez (Avalos) and the head of the WASP family was James Kirkridge (Stevenson). Yvonne Wilder, who plays Mrs. Rodriguez, was one of the dancers in the film version of *West Side Story*, under the name Yvonne Othon. With the aid of makeup, 43-year-old actor James Victor memorably and effectively played a 70-year-old grandfather. John Rich directed the teleplay, which was created and written by Sheldon Bull.

"The Cowboys" (1974 ABC)
Cast: Jim Davis, Diana Douglas

Based on the hit John Wayne film of the same name, this show featured many of the film's young actors, including Clay O'Brian, Robert Carradine, and A Martinez as Cimarron, a Mexican American youth. Seven homeless boys go to work on a ranch run by a widower.

"Crime and Punishment" (1993 NBC)
Cast: **Rachel Ticotin**, Jon Tenney

A one-hour limited-run series focusing on the professional and personal lives of L.A. police detectives Ken O'Donnell (Tenney) and Annette Rey (Ticotin). Rey is a single parent raising a teenage daughter. This pairing of an Anglo man and a Hispanic woman on a series as equals and showing them as positive law enforcement characters was a major step toward more varied and rounded portrayals of Hispanics on television.

"The D.A." (1971–1972 NBC)
Cast: Robert Conrad, Harry Morgan, **Ned Romero**

This short-lived half-hour courtroom drama series featured Ned Romero as investigator Bob Ramirez.

"DEA—Drug Enforcement Agency" (1991 Fox)

Cast: **Jenny Gago**, Tom Mason, Byron Keith Minns, Chris Stanley, David Wohl

Jenny Gago played Teresa Robles, one of five U.S. Drug Enforcement Agency officers in the war against drugs, in this violent, reality-inspired, short-lived one-hour action series set in the United States and South America, created by Richard Dilello. Pepe Serna had a recurring role as a bodyguard to the daughter of a drug kingpin. John Vargas, Miguel Sandoval, and Ron Henriquez were also featured.

"Dallas" (1978–1991 CBS)

Cast: Larry Hagman, Patrick Duffy, **Victoria Principal**, Linda Gray, Barbara Bel Geddes, Charlene Tilton, Jim Davis

The long-running dramatic series "Dallas" premiered on April 2, 1978, and evolved into an American institution, chronicling the personal and professional lives of the wealthy Ewing family of South Fork ranch in Texas, centering on the battles between the notorious J.R. Ewing (Hagman) and his brother, the beloved Bobby Ewing (Duffy). Victoria Principal in a non-Hispanic role played Pamela Ewing, an outsider and the straightlaced, loving wife of Bobby. The popularity of "Dallas" transcended domestic appeal; the show was an international sensation in the more than 56 countries in which it aired. The show brought international recognition, fame, and wealth to all the regular cast members. After 13 seasons and a total of 356 filmed episodes, its run ended in 1991. Well-known Hispanic guest stars who appeared on the show over the course of its run include Barbara Carrera, Mel Ferrer, and Henry Darrow.

"Dan August" (1970–1971 ABC)

Cast: **Burt Reynolds, Ned Romero**

This Quinn Martin–produced, hour-long police action show set in the fictional city of Santa Luisa, California, starred Burt Reynolds as police detective Dan August and Ned Romero as his partner, Detective Sgt. Joe Rivera.

"The Danny Thomas Show" (1953–1957 ABC; 1957–1964 CBS)

Cast: Danny Thomas, Marjorie Lord

In 1960, Bill Dana's character Jose Jimenez, introduced in 1959 on "The Steve Allen Show," was further expanded and joined the cast of "The Danny Thomas Show" (originally known as "Make Room for Daddy") as a bumbling doorman and elevator operator. Jimenez was a Latin American who spoke very little English and always met any situation coolly with the now legendary line, "My name, Jose Jimenez." This character was so popular that the Jose Jimenez character was spun off into his own series ("The Bill Dana Show") and television specials.

"Disney Presents the 100 Lives of Black Jack Savage" (1991 NBC)

Cast: Daniel Hugh-Kelly, Steven Williams, **Bert Rosario**

In this hour-long fantasy/adventure/comedy series, Wall Street wizard Barry Tarberry (Hugh-Kelly), a fugitive billionaire, flees to the Caribbean island of San Pietro and sublets an ancient castle. He gets a ghostly roommate in the bargain: Black Jack Savage, a dastardly seventeenth-century pirate who haunts the castle. Bert Rosario played the corrupt island governor Gen. Abe Vasquez.

"Doctors' Hospital" (1975–1976 NBC)

Cast: George Peppard

In this hour-long medical series, George Peppard was featured as a neurosurgeon and Victor Campos was one of the doctors.

"Dudley" (1993 CBS)

Cast: Dudley Moore, **Lupe Ontiveros**

This six-episode half-hour situation comedy series starred Dudley Moore as a much-sought-after piano-playing composer in New York City. Lupe Ontiveros played Marta, his Spanish-speaking housekeeper.

"E/R" (1984–1985 CBS)

Cast: Elliott Gould

This half-hour sitcom about the staff and patients of a Chicago hospital emergency room featured Luis Avalos as Dr. Thomas Esquivel.

"Eisenhower and Lutz" (1988 CBS)

Cast: Scott Bakula, Henderson Forsythe, DeLane Matthews

An ambitious young attorney runs a law firm in Palm Springs. Rose Portillo played Millie Zamora, a harried secretary, in the short-lived half-hour situation comedy series created by eight-time Emmy Award winner Allan Burns.

"The Electric Company" (1971–1985 PBS)

Cast: Bill Cosby, **Rita Moreno, Irene Cara**, Morgan Freeman

The Children's Television Workshop designed this series to teach reading skills to children seven to ten years old. It included fast-moving comedy, song, and animation sequences, many involving state-of-the-art means of putting print on the screen. The seasons 1971 through 1977 presented original productions, and for the following eight seasons it was seen in repeats. It won six Emmys and a Grammy as well as other major awards.

"Empire" (1962–1963 NBC; 1964 ABC)

Cast: Richard Egan

This modern western series set in New Mexico starred Richard Egan as Jim Redigo, foreman of a huge cattle ranch. During the 1963 run of the show, Charles Bronson joined the cast as Paul Moreno, a Mexican American ranch hand.

"Falcon Crest" (1981–1990 CBS)

Cast: Jane Wyman, **Lorenzo Lamas, Ana Alicia**

Created by Earl Hamner, who also created "The Waltons" for Lorimar Productions, "Falcon Crest" was the story of a wealthy wine-growing family headed by matriarch Angela Channing (Wyman) in the fictional Tuscany Valley of California. A Hispanic family of caretakers headed by Gus Nunouz, played by Nick Ramus, was dropped after the first season. Through the years the show featured Hispanic performers in both Hispanic and non-Hispanic roles. The show made stars out of series regulars Lorenzo Lamas (son of movie star Fernando Lamas) as Angela's grandson, Lance Cumson, and Ana Alicia as the daughter of a rival wine-growing family, Melissa Agretti. Corene Powers was played by Victoria Racimo; Apollonia played a character called Apollonia; Cesar Romero played Greek tycoon Peter Stavros; and Julie Carmen played Romero's daughter Sofia.

During the 1988–1989 season a Hispanic vineyard foreman and his family were reintroduced into the story line. Pilar Ortega (Kristian Alfonso), the foreman's daughter, a powerful bank executive, returns home after many years away and finds herself in direct conflict with Angela Channing. The Hispanic family was headed by Castulo Guerra as Cesar, Dan Ferro as his son Tommy, and Danny Nucci as his other son, Gabriel.

"Fame" (1982–1983 NBC; 1983–1987 syndicated)
Cast: Debbie Allen, Gene Anthony Ray

Based on the hit movie of the same name, the series first aired for one season on NBC and then was picked up for advertiser-supported first-run syndication in 1983. The hour-long dramatic musical series revolved around multi-ethnic students at New York City's High School of the Performing Arts. Coco Hernandez, a talented dance student, was played by Erica Gimpel. Later, Jesse Borrego played the Mexican American dancer Jesse Velasquez, from 1984 to 1987. These characters were an integral part of the story lines, which tried, though sometimes rather unsuccessfully, to reflect their ethnicity. Jaime Rogers choreographed and directed a few episodes.

"The Family Martinez" (1986 CBS)
Cast: **Robert Beltran**, Daniel Faraldo, Anne Betancourt, Karla Montana

This domestic half-hour comedy show, directed by Oz Scott and produced and written by Tommy Chong (of Cheech and Chong fame), about a contemporary Hispanic family, did not make it onto the network schedule as a series, but its pilot was broadcast as a special. The story involves Hector Martinez (Beltran), a former gang member, now a law school graduate, who moves back home to live with his family.

"Fantasy Island" (1978–1983 ABC)
Cast: **Ricardo Montalban**, Herve Villechaize

In this one-hour anthology drama series, guests arrived at the tropical island paradise of the mysterious Mr. Roarke (Montalban) and his midget associate Tattoo (Villechaize) seeking to realize their fantasies.

The series began as a two-hour TV movie that drew incredibly high viewer ratings in 1977. Then, another two-hour movie, *Return to Fantasy Island,* earned high ratings as well in January 1978. It then went into its series run on January 28, 1978.

In an immaculate pressed white suit, Montalban as Roarke ushered the guests in and out of Fantasy Island, delivering expository speeches between the stories. Roarke had power over life and death on the island, and many times the fantasy did not quite turn out as requested. Montalban as Roarke embodied elegance and class, playing a man of unspecified origin. The formal figure of Roarke and the lusty, outspoken midget Tattoo were an odd team that nevertheless worked within the concept of the series.

The network originally wanted Orson Welles for the Mr. Roarke role, but when he was reluctant or unable to commit, producer Aaron Spelling called on Montalban, who was perfectly suited to play the enigmatic Roarke.

"Father Knows Best" (1954–1955 CBS; 1955–1958 NBC; 1958–1962 CBS; 1962–1963 ABC)

Cast: Robert Young, Jane Wyatt

Natividad Vacio occasionally appeared as Frank Smith, the Mexican gardner, on this family show in which Young played insurance salesman Jim Anderson.

"Flamingo Road" (1981–1982 NBC)

Cast: Howard Duff, Morgan Fairchild, Mark Harmon

This one-hour series was loosely based on the 1949 Joan Crawford movie of the same name and took place in the steamy fictional Florida city of Truro. The series concerned the pursuit of power and pleasure among wealthy and working-class citizens. There were subsidiary Hispanic characters in the form of Cuban refugees played by Fernando Allende as Julio Sanchez and Gina Gallego as his sister Alicia in plotlines that dealt with the Cuban barrio of the city.

"The Flying Nun" (1967–1970 ABC)

Cast: Sally Field, **Alejandro Rey**

This comedy series, which took place in the fictional Convent San Tanco in the hills above San Juan, Puerto Rico, starred Sally Field as Sister Bertrille and Alejandro Rey as swinging playboy Carlos Ramirez, who was constantly befuddled by Bertrille's antics. It was based on the book *The Fifteenth Pelican* by Tere Rios. Shelley Morrison played Sister Sixto, a nun who mangles the English language to comic effect.

"Foley Square" (1986 CBS)

Cast: **Hector Elizondo**

Elizondo, in a refreshing bit of casting in a non-Hispanic role, played a Jewish deputy district attorney in New York City.

"For Love and Honor" (1983 NBC)

Cast: Cliff Potts, Yaphet Kotto

This hour-long drama series ran from September through December and focused on the personal and professional lives of Naval Air recruits. Rachel Ticotin portrayed Corporal Grace Pavlik.

"Fort Figueroa" (1988 CBS)

Cast: **Pepe Serna**, Charly Heard, **Evelyn Guerrero**

Luis Valdez directed this pilot for Warner Bros. Television. It was an hour-long comedy/drama about a WASP family from the Midwest who lose their farm and move to Los Angeles to live in a building that has been left to them by a deceased relative. When they arrive in L.A. they discover that the building is a dilapidated apartment building in the heart of the inner city. The tenants of the building are a Hispanic family and a Vietnamese family. The WASP family take the empty apartment and must face the trials and tribulations of learning to live in a multi-ethnic inner-city community.

"Frannie's Turn" (1992 CBS)

Cast: Miriam Margolyes, **Tomas Milian**

This short-lived half-hour situation comedy was about a middle-aged Brooklyn woman. Tomas Milian played her Cuban-born husband, Joseph Escobar.

"Freebie and the Bean" (1980–1981 CBS)

Cast: **Hector Elizondo**, Tom Mason

This one-hour crime/comedy/drama derived from the motion picture of the same name. The series starred Elizondo as Dan "The Bean" Delgado and Mason as Tim "Freebie" Walker.

"From Here to Eternity" (1979–1980 NBC)

Cast: Barbara Hershey, William Devane, Will Sampson

This hour-long short-lived series began as a successful television miniseries, which was based on the classic 1953 Columbia Pictures movie of the James Jones novel about the peacetime Army in Hawaii in the days before the attack on Pearl Harbor. Rocky Echevarria, who later changed his name to Steven Bauer, played Pfc. Ignacio Carmona on the series.

"Gavilan" (1982–1983 NBC)

Cast: Robert Urich, **Fernando Lamas**

This hour-long action/adventure series featured Fernando Lamas playing the role of Caesar de Portago in the first episodes. Lamas took ill and died soon after the series production began, and Patrick Macnee took over in a similar role.

"Going to Extremes" (1992–1993 ABC)

Cast: Erika Alexander, June Chadwick, Roy Dotrice, Camilo Gallardo

This one-hour drama series was about young Americans determined to become doctors, who attend a medical school on a fictional West Indian island. Camilo Gallardo played medical student Kim Selby, who came from an old and prominent Chilean family, though he was born in Miami.

"The Golden Palace" (1992–1993 CBS)

Cast: Betty White, Rue McClanahan, Estelle Getty, **Cheech Marin**

America's favorite Golden Girls—Rose Nylund (White), Blanche Devereaux (McClanahan), and Sophia Petrillo (Getty)—set up housekeeping in an art deco Miami hotel they've purchased, continuing the characters they portrayed on the seven-year hit "The Golden Girls," and for which they each won Emmy Awards. Cheech Marin played Chuy Castillos, a recently divorced chef from East L.A. who worked at the Golden Palace and found himself at the mercy of Sophia.

"Grand Slam" (1990 CBS)

Cast: John Schneider, **Paul Rodriguez**

An hour-long action/adventure series that concerned two rival bounty hunters in San Diego who decide to make a go of it together. It premiered after the Super Bowl, but the ratings quickly plummeted.

"Hangin' with Mr. Cooper" (1992– ABC)

Cast: Mark Curry, Dawnn Lewis, Holly Robinson

Mark Cooper (Curry) is a teacher at a local high school who shares a house with two young women in this half-hour situation comedy created by Jeff Franklin. Luis Avalos has a recurring role as Rivera, the school principal.

"Harry O" (1974–1976 ABC)

Cast: David Janssen, **Henry Darrow**

This hour-long detective series created by Howard Rodman and executive produced by Jerry Thorpe starred David Janssen as a former police detective who has left the force and become a private eye. Henry Darrow co-starred as Lt. Manny Quinlan in the first season of the show, when it was set in San Diego. He was killed off when the show switched its locale to Los Angeles.

"The Hat Squad" (1992 ABC)

Cast: Nestor Serrano

In this series Nestor Serrano played Rafael Martinez, the Latino end of a special crime unit consisting of three young men and their foster father, who is also their commanding officer. All the boys have lost their parents to violence and have vowed to fight crime.

"Head of the Class" (1986–1991 ABC)

Cast: Howard Hesseman

In this half-hour situation comedy, created by Michael Elias and Rich Eustis, Charlie Moore (Hesseman) is a substitute teacher at a New York City high school who has to deal with and motivate brainy but underachieving students. Leslie Bega played the grade-obsessed student Maria Borges from 1986 through 1989, and Michael De Lorenzo played student Alex Torres from 1989 through 1991.

"Hearts of the West" (1993– CBS)

Cast: Beau Bridges, Lloyd Bridges

A contemporary hour-long series about a man with a mid-life crisis who moves his family from the East to settle on a ranch near a small town in Nevada. Talisa Soto is a series regular as a Native American girl.

"Hernandez, Houston P.D." (1973 NBC)

Cast: **Henry Darrow**

Darrow starred in this 60-minute pilot episode for a possible series. He played Juan Hernandez, a detective with the Houston Police Department.

"The High Chaparral" (1967–1971 NBC)

Cast: Leif Ericson, Cameron Mitchell, **Linda Cristal, Frank Silvera, Henry Darrow**

This western/adventure series, set in the Arizona Territory of the 1870s, prominently featured a Hispanic family alongside an Anglo family. It was created by David Dortort ("Bonanza"). Frank Silvera played the Mexican cattle baron Don Sebastian Montoya with grace, dignity, and ruthlessness that were every bit the equal of his Anglo counterpart, John Cannon (Ericson). Henry Darrow, as Montoya's son, Manolito, was a slightly soiled, less-than-heroic dashing caballero. He captured the TV public's imagination with a spirited portrayal that brought him stardom and international recognition. Linda Cristal, already an established film actress, played Victoria Cannon, Montoya's daughter, who becomes the young wife of John Cannon. The uneasy alliance of the two families seemed symbolically to characterize U.S.-Mexican relations. Several Hispanic actors were featured on the

Henry Darrow as Manolito
on "The High Chaparral."

show in regular roles including Rodolfo Acosta and Roberto Contreras. In its final year Rudy Ramos joined the show as a half-breed, and Gilbert Roland took the role of Montoya's brother when Frank Silvera unexpectedly passed away.

"High Mountain Rangers" (1988 CBS)
 Cast: Robert Conrad

An hour-long action/adventure series that concerned an elite rescue squad of young men and women in California's High Sierras led by veteran ranger Jesse Hawks (Conrad). Tony Acierto played Ranger Frank Avila.

"Highcliffe Manor" (1979 NBC)
 Cast: Shelley Fabares

This comic send-up of horror movies featured Luis Avalos as Dr. Sanchez, an evil scientist.

Rene Enriquez (left) as Lt. Calletano and
Daniel J. Travanti as Captain Frank Furillo
in "Hill Street Blues."

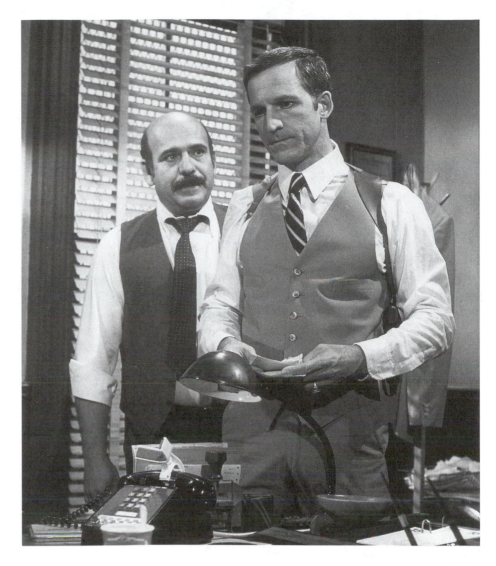

"Hill Street Blues" (1981–1987 NBC)

Cast: Daniel J. Travanti, Bruce Weitz, Michael Conrad, Veronica Hamel,
Michael Warren, Betty Thomas, **Rene Enriquez**, Kiel Martin,
Barbara Bosson

This much-acclaimed, Emmy Award–winning, long-running hour-long drama series, created by Steven Bochco and Michael Kozoll, about the grim, realistic, and often humorous sides of police work in a decaying section of a large U.S. city had one Hispanic officer, Lt. Ray Calletano, played by Rene Enriquez, among its large ensemble cast of regulars. His participation as a major character in the show was diffused by the story lines, which gave him little to do, and played off the image of Hispanics as the victims or perpetrators of the many crimes.

One episode did revolve around Lt. Calletano having to deal with prejudice when he finds himself the only Hispanic at a dinner in his honor. Through the seven-year run of the series there was a recurring character of a gang leader called Jesus, played by Trinidad Silva, who by the end of the series had become a social worker and a lawyer. Another recurring character was a troubled youth, Hector Ruiz, played by Panchito Gomez, who was finally jailed after a robbery turned into a hostage situation. Future star Andy Garcia played a small role in the series' premiere episode.

"Home Free" (1988 NBC)
Cast: Michael Warren, **Trinidad Silva**

This hour-long dramatic pilot featured a social worker who ran a home for troubled youth. He was assisted by his Mexican American cook, Benny, played by Trinidad Silva.

"Hot L Baltimore" (1975 NBC)
Cast: James Cromwell, Richard Masur, Al Freeman, Jr.

This half-hour comedy series was based on the hit off-Broadway play of the 1970s. Jeannie Linero was one of the cast members.

"Houston Knights" (1987–1988 CBS)
Cast: Michael Pare, Michael Beck

This hour-long crime/drama concerned two police detectives, one from Texas and one from Chicago, who are partnered in Houston, Texas. Efrain Figueroa played Lt. Esteban Gutierrez. The series lasted for only one season.

"Hunter" (1984–1991 NBC)
Cast: Fred Dryer, Stepfanie Kramer

In the 1987 season of this police action/drama, created by Frank Lupo, Erik Estrada guest starred on a three-part episode, "City of Passion," as Detective Brad Navarro, who joins series lead characters Hunter and McCall in tracking down a serial rapist. Also in the 1987–1988 season, Rudy Ramos played a recurring character named Reuben Garcia.

"I Had Three Wives" (1985 CBS)
Cast: Victor Garber

This hour-long comedy/adventure featured a charming private detective who was aided by his three ex-wives. Luis Avalos was Lt. Gomez.

"I Love Lucy" (1951–1957 CBS)
Cast: Lucille Ball, **Desi Arnaz**, William Frawley, Vivian Vance

The first important Hispanic presence on television was Desi Arnaz as Ricky Ricardo on the "I Love Lucy" show. The phenomenal, long-running classic series was initially turned down by CBS, even though Lucille Ball had been successful in both movies and radio. She had a hit CBS Radio series called "My Favorite Husband," which the network wanted to transfer to television. But Ball was interested in starting a family and keeping her marriage together and wanted her real-life husband, Desi Arnaz, to star in the series with her. CBS felt the concept of a red-headed all-American housewife married to an excitable Cuban bandleader would not reach a wide enough segment of the American public. Desi and Lucy took their series concept and worked out an act with the help of comedian Buster Keaton and clown Pepito Perez. The couple performed before live audiences around the country, and the enthusiastic responses proved they were accepted as a show-business husband-and-wife team. Arnaz and Ball financed the pilot episode of the TV show themselves. It was produced in March 1951, with Lucy and Desi playing the characters Lucy and Desi Lopez.

Later, their neighbors, the Mertzes, were added to the show, and the characters were renamed Lucy and Ricky Ricardo. The network and sponsors approved the show, and the first episode aired on October 15, 1951. It was filmed before a live studio audience with three 35mm film cameras capturing the action simultaneously from different angles. The show was then edited together like a film. "I Love Lucy" was an immediate hit and turned TV watching into a pop cultural event. Over the course of its six years of original episodes, the show rarely ranked lower than third in the ratings. Arnaz's portrayal of the good-looking, excitable, short-tempered Cuban bandleader who spoke with an accent and rattled off expletives in Spanish was so well etched that he created an image of the Hispanic American that could almost be regarded as archetypal. The character of Ricky was an exaggerated comedic characterization that grew to a certain extent over the life of the series. In comparison to similar shows and formats of the same era, "I Love Lucy" was somewhat realistic. (On "The Adventures of Ozzie and Harriet," for example, Ozzie was never seen going to work, and the family never had trouble making financial ends meet.) During a 1990 television interview, Lucille Ball said, "We wanted to focus on all the trials and tribulations that most people experience. We didn't want to be a Hollywood couple that no one could relate to."

Television audiences of the 1950s readily related to the Ricardos' all-too-human circumstances. Hispanics saw a bit of themselves in Arnaz's portrayal of the hardworking husband and father trying to make it in American society. The Span-

Lucille Ball and Desi Arnaz.

ish and Cuban music that alternated with American popular music on the show brought an understanding and cultural awareness, no matter how superficial, to millions of TV viewers. Ricky's difficulty with the English language and his speaking Spanish on the show were for many a source of amusement, but Hispanic Americans well appreciated what became a real, honest, and personal bond to them. From time to time, relatives from Cuba and other Spanish-speaking characters appeared on the show.

Arnaz and Ball were introduced living in a New York apartment. They then had a baby and moved to the suburbs, and Ricky eventually came to own the nightclub at which he worked. The couple became the incarnation of the 1950s post–World War II American Dream fulfilled for millions of TV viewers.

Behind the scenes, Arnaz was responsible for the development of the multicamera techniques still used today in most filmed or taped situation comedies. Since "I Love Lucy" was filmed, and Arnaz and Ball retained ownership of the programs after the initial CBS runs, they created an industry standard for syndicated reruns. The couple purchased RKO Studios, which then became Desilu Studios. It was turned into a rental facility and also produced many filmed TV series including "The Untouchables" and the original "Star Trek" series. In a 1984 television interview Arnaz said, "'I Love Lucy' is something that happens only once in a lifetime, if you're lucky enough to have it happen at all."

Lucy and Desi are part of American popular culture and a part of our lives, and more than 40 years later these shows are still being seen in reruns worldwide and have become fodder for fiction in such books and movies as *The Mambo Kings*.

"I Married Dora" (1987–1988 ABC)
Cast: **Elizabeth Pena**, Daniel Hugh-Kelly

This half-hour sitcom was about a widowed architect with two children who marries his Central American housekeeper so that she won't be deported as an illegal alien.

"The John Larroquette Show" (1993– NBC)
Cast: John Larroquette, **Liz Torres**

Torres portrays Mahalia Sanchez, urban bus station manager John Hemingway's (Larroquette's) closest ally. As his streetwise, no-nonsense assistant, she's tough and sarcastic, but her years of experience at the station make her invaluable to Hemingway.

"Juarez" (1987 ABC)
Cast: **Benjamin Bratt Banda**, Ada Maris

This one-hour pilot for a series about an El Paso police detective starred newcomer Benjamin Bratt Banda. The stories were to concern the border area around El Paso and Juarez, Mexico. The series had an initial six-episode order as a mid-season replacement, but only two episodes were shot. "Juarez" was canceled before it was aired due to creative differences between the producers and the network. No Hispanic writers, producers, or directors were part of the show's creative team, and the scripts prominently featured border stereotypes. The pilot did eventually air as a one-hour special.

"Kay O'Brien" (1986 CBS)
Cast: Patricia Kalember, Lane Smith

This hour-long hospital drama focused on a 28-year-old female second-year surgical resident at a New York City hospital trying to excel in the male-dominated world of surgery. Priscilla Lopez played nurse Rosa Villanueva.

"Knight & Daye" (1989 NBC)

Cast: Jack Warden

This half-hour four-week summer replacement series featured a Hispanic family, the Escobars, played mostly by non-Hispanics.

"Knightwatch" (1988–1989 ABC)

Cast: **Benjamin Bratt**, Don Franklin, Ava Haddad, Joshua Cadman

This hour-long series was about a dedicated group of young inner-city people, men and women, black and white, who voluntarily band together to battle the crime that has swept over their city. They were the Knights, and Knightwatch was led by its founder, Tony Maldonado (Bratt).

"L.A. Law" (1986– NBC)

Cast: Corbin Bernsen, Jill Eikenberry, Richard Dysart, Susan Dey, Susan Ruttan, Michael Tucker, Larry Drake, **Jimmy Smits**, Blair Underwood, Harry Hamlin

This hour-long drama series about a law firm, created by Steven Bochco and Terry Louise Fisher, won 14 Emmy Awards in its first five years, including Outstanding

Jimmy Smits and Harry Hamlin
in "L.A. Law."

Drama Series in 1987, 1989, 1990, and 1991. Located in a downtown L.A. high-rise building, the partners and associates of McKenzie, Brackman, Chaney, and Kuzak constitute a full-service, if chaotic, law firm that usually wrangles with the mounting contradictions of the contemporary legal system.

The series provided an important Hispanic American character in lawyer Victor Sifuentes, played by Jimmy Smits. Sifuentes was a Mexican American who was every bit an equal of the Anglo members of the law firm. He was part of the American mainstream of good education, hard work, and perseverance and was socially responsible. Many of the episodes centered around Sifuentes, his court battles, and his personal life.

Tomas Milian and Miriam Colon played Sifuentes's parents in one episode, and such actors as Tony Plana and Joaquin Martinez have guest starred on the show. Jimmy Smits left the series in May 1991 to pursue a career in motion pictures, following his leading role in *Old Gringo,* opposite Jane Fonda, filmed in Mexico while "L.A. Law" was still in production. Smits had a grueling schedule, working simultaneously on "L.A. Law" and *Old Gringo,* flying back and forth every three weeks between L.A. and Mexico.

Smits won an Emmy Award as Outstanding Supporting Actor in a Continuing Series in 1990 for his work on the series during the 1989–1990 season.

In 1992, A Martinez joined the cast as the eagle-eyed single-parent litigator David Morales.

"The Lucie Arnaz Show" (1985 CBS)
Cast: **Lucie Arnaz**

Arnaz (daughter of Desi Arnaz and Lucille Ball) starred in her own half-hour sitcom as Jane Lucas, a psychologist who co-hosted a popular radio talk show in New York.

"The Lucille Ball–Desi Arnaz Show" [aka: "The Lucy-Desi Comedy Hour"] (1957–1960 CBS)
Cast: **Lucille Ball, Desi Arnaz**

Thirteen one-hour episodes were produced for this series, which was a continuation of their Lucy and Desi characterizations. Desi Arnaz directed several of the episodes.

"Mama Malone" (1984 CBS)
Cast: **Lila Kaye**

This offbeat half-hour comedy series about a cooking show host featured Richard Yniguez as Father Jose Silva, a regular character.

"The Man and the City" (1971–1972 ABC)
Cast: **Anthony Quinn**

Anthony Quinn as Thomas Jefferson Alcala, in his first foray into series television, starred as the socially conscious Mexican American mayor of a southwestern metropolis. The hour-long drama series lasted for only half a season after the initial television movie presentation.

"Marblehead Manor" (1987–1988 syndicated)

Cast: Paxton Whitehead, Linda Thorson, Phillip Morris, **Dyana Ortelli**

Dyana Ortelli played the wacky maid Lupe in this syndicated situation comedy series, which also featured her son Humberto Ortiz as Elvis. It was syndicated in the United States and also aired in England, France, Israel, and Spain, where it was known as "Casa de Locos." Rob Dames and Bob Fraser were the creators, writers, and producers of the series.

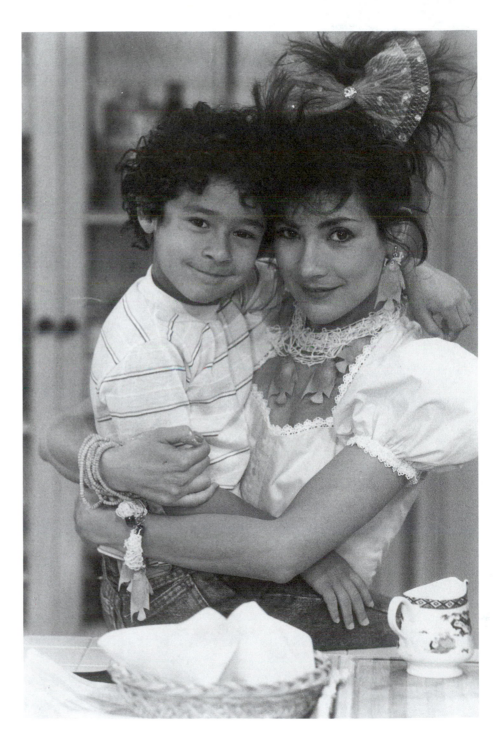

Dyana Ortelli and Humberto Ortiz as Lupe and Elvis on "Marblehead Manor."

Robert Young, Elena Verdugo as
Nurse Consuelo, and James Brolin
in the TV series "Marcus Welby, M.D."

"Marcus Welby, M.D." (1969–1976 ABC)

Cast: Robert Young, James Brolin, **Elena Verdugo**

In this medical series Elena Verdugo was the all-knowing, wise-cracking Nurse Consuelo Lopez who worked for Dr. Welby (Young). Entire scripts were written to match Verdugo's comedic and dramatic talent. Dolores Del Rio played her mother in an episode in which Del Rio was dying of cancer. A love story featured Verdugo and guest actor Joseph Campanella, who was suffering from a back ailment. She was twice nominated for an Emmy as Best Supporting Actress in a Continuing Drama Series.

"Meet Millie" (1952–1956 CBS)

Cast: **Elena Verdugo**

In this half-hour comedy series, Elena Verdugo starred as an all-American girl, Millie Bronson, who lived and worked as a secretary in Manhattan.

"Miami Vice" (1984–1989 NBC)

Cast: Don Johnson, Phillip Michael Thomas, **Edward James Olmos**, Saundra Santiago

Created by Anthony Yerkovich and with a creative team headed by executive producer Michael Mann, this was an innovative police action/drama set in Miami with a 1980s art deco style, integrating MTV-like visuals and rock video editing and music and a multiracial cast. Detective Sonny Crockett (Johnson) and Detective Ricardo Tubbs (Thomas) are two flashy vice cops who work in the bustling new city of the Americas, Miami, battling drug dealers from the city's fast-paced boulevards and dimly lit back alleys to art deco hotels, mansions, and open waterways. The show won four Emmys in 1984–1985, its first season. "Miami Vice" was characterized by the *New York Times* as "aggressively contemporary," hailed by *Newsweek* for its "visual style and audio tone" and "impressionistic fast cut cinematography," and by *USA Today* as a "pop palette, full of visions lovely, complex, surreal."

The show had positive role models, but it overwhelmingly paraded blacks and Hispanics as drug dealers, pimps, and prostitutes in an exotic, crime-filled city. It did cast many Hispanic actors over the length of its run, including Tito Goya, Miguel Pinero, Esai Morales, Pepe Serna, Luis Guzman, Rosana De Soto, Lou Diamond Phillips, Daniel Lugo, Francesco Quinn, and Alfonso Arau.

Edward James Olmos created the role of the sullen, no-nonsense Lt. Martin Castillo. He won an Emmy Award as Best Supporting Actor in a Drama Series as well as a Hollywood Foreign Press Association Golden Globe Award. Olmos directed an episode of the series called "Bushido," which was one of the highest-rated episodes of the series. Saundra Santiago played Detective Gina Calabrese, an undercover police officer. Gregory Sierra portrayed Lt. Lou Rodriguez in the pilot and initial episodes, but his character was killed off and replaced by Olmos's Lt. Castillo.

"Nasty Boys" (1990 NBC)

Cast: Dennis Franz, **Benjamin Bratt**, Don Franklin

This hour-long action/adventure series was inspired by the real-life North Las Vegas Nasty Boys, a crime-fighting unit whose members protect their anonymity by wearing black ninja-style hoods. Bratt played Cruz, a maverick undercover cop.

"The New Dick Van Dyke Show" (1971–1974 CBS)

Cast: Dick Van Dyke

In its third and final season the show changed locale to Los Angeles from Phoenix. The season co-starred Chita Rivera as next-door neighbor Connie Richards, Henry Darrow as Alex the stage manager, and Carmen Zapata as the maid.

"The New Odd Couple" (1982–1983 ABC)

Cast: Ron Glass, Demond Wilson

In this black version of the popular Neil Simon play, film, and series *The Odd Couple*, Liz Torres played the role of Maria.

"Nightingales" (1989 NBC)

Cast: Suzanne Pleshette

Roxann Biggs played a Hispanic nurse, Yolanda Puente, in this short-lived, controversial series about the professional and personal lives of young student nurses.

"The Nine Lives of Elfeco Baca" (1958–1960 NBC)

Cast: Robert Loggia, Robert F. Simon, **Nestor Paiva**, Rico Alaniz

Walt Disney produced a series of 10 color episodes detailing the story of Elfeco Baca, a Spanish American sheriff turned lawyer in the New Mexico Territory of the Old West. Robert Loggia played Elfeco Baca, and the series was directed by Norman Foster, based on his teleplay. James Pratt was the producer.

The show relied on formula western adventures and was condescending toward its protagonist, with Anglo characters spouting lines like, "You're not going to like this job; you're going after one of your own countrymen," to which Elfeco would respond, "A man like that gives our people a bad name."

"9 to 5" (1982–1983 ABC)

Cast: **Rita Moreno**, Valerie Curtin, Rachel Dennison

Rita Moreno co-starred as Violet, an office worker, in this half-hour comedy series. She represented a modern Hispanic woman with no accent, a positive role model who was part of the mainstream. Violet was an integral part of the story lines, which revolved around herself and her two co-workers in and out of the office. She was also a single mother with a young son. The series presented a refreshing image change. The show was based on the hit movie of the same name, in which Violet's character was originally non-Hispanic and played by Lily Tomlin. Moreno asked that the character Violet use the maiden name of Fernandez instead of Newstead on the series, since her husband was deceased.

"Nurses" (1991– NBC)

Cast: Stephanie Hodge, Arnetia Walker, Mary Jo Keenen, Markus Flanagan, **Ada Maris**

Susan Harris ("Soap") created this ensemble situation comedy, which features five nurses—four women and a man—who face their professional lives with lighthearted camaraderie, though they're overworked, underpaid, and often unappreciated. It features Gina Cuevas (Maris), the ethical young Central American immigrant who is zealously studying to become an American citizen, and Paco Ortiz (Carlos LaCamara), the orderly with his finger on the pulse of life at the hospital.

"Ohara" (1987–1988 ABC)

Cast: Pat Morita, Kevin Conroy, Madge Sinclair

Pat Morita in this one-hour crime series was featured as an offbeat Asian American police detective in Los Angeles. The first season featured Richard Yniguez as police detective Jesse Guerrera in a regular supporting role. In its second season, Rachel Ticotin was featured as Assistant D.A. Teresa Storm.

"On the Rocks" (1975–1976 ABC)

Cast: **Jose Perez**, Buddy Sandler, Hal Williams

This half-hour situation comedy was set in a Southwest prison and aired for one season.

"100 Centre Street" (1984 ABC)

Cast: Len Cariou, Dee Wallace, J.A. Preston, Lela Ivey, **Henry Darrow**

This half-hour comedy pilot was about life in the judge's chambers, which isn't all law and order: Supervising Judge Charles Felt wishes his colleagues would stick to the law and stop complaining about their assignments. His own life becomes disordered when his wife files for divorce. Henry Darrow starred as Judge Ramon Robledo.

"One of the Boys" (1989 NBC)

Cast: **Maria Conchita Alonso**, Robert Clohessy

Alonso made her American TV debut in this half-hour situation comedy. She starred as Maria, a vivacious Venezuelan immigrant who hopes to gain her share of the American Dream by working as a bookkeeper in an otherwise all-male construction firm. The series lasted for only a few episodes.

"Oye Willie" (1979 PBS)

Cast: Fernando Lopez, **Alfonso Ribeiro**

This seven-part half-hour dramatic series was about a 12-year-old Puerto Rican boy, Willie, and his adventures growing up in New York's Spanish Harlem. The series was filmed on location, and it offered the largest concentration, up to that time, of Hispanics, both in front of and behind the camera. Olivia Perez directed three segments, as did Luis Soto. The executive producer and creator was Lou de Lemos.

"Passport to Danger" (1954–1956 syndicated)

Cast: **Cesar Romero**

Romero starred in 39 episodes of this weekly half-hour adventure series in which he played Steve McQuinn, a diplomatic courier sent on assignment to different countries.

"Phyllis" (1975–1977 CBS)

Cast: Cloris Leachman

Leachman played Phyllis and Liz Torres played Julie Erskine, a photographer, on this series spin-off from "The Mary Tyler Moore Show."

"Popi" (1976 CBS)

Cast: **Hector Elizondo**, **Edith Diaz**, Anthony Perez, Dennis Vasquez

This short-lived series about a Puerto Rican widower (Elizondo) and his two sons living in New York's Spanish Harlem was based on the 1969 motion picture of the same name written by Tina and Lester Pine (*see* Movie listings). The pilot episode was shown on CBS in May 1975, but the series did not air until January 1976.

"Que Pasa, U.S.A.?" (1978 PBS)

Cast: Velia Martinez, Luis Oquendo, Ana Margarita Menendez, **Rocky Echevarria [Steven Bauer]**, Manolo Villaverde

Set in Little Havana, Miami's Cuban exile community, the program traces the lives of Cuban Americans trying to make it in their new homeland. Three generations—grandparents, parents, and teenagers—each with their own special needs and desires, form the central core of the story lines. A host of supporting characters of various races and nationalities blend to create unique situations fraught with both comic and serious consequences.

The show was the first national Hispanic situation comedy/drama series written, directed, and produced by, and starring Cuban Americans. It was originated and taped at WPBT, the Miami public television station. Rocky Echevarria went on to achieve stardom when he landed the role of Manny in *Scarface* opposite Al Pacino and changed his name to Steven Bauer.

"Rawhide" (1959–1966 CBS)

Cast: Eric Fleming, Clint Eastwood

This western series was created by Charles Marquis Warren and dealt with the adventures of cowboys on the long cattle drives between Texas and Kansas. One of the cowboys was a Mexican called Hey Soos, more than likely a supposed comic takeoff on the Spanish name Jesus. He was played by Robert Cabal from 1961 through 1964.

"The Real McCoys" (1957–1962 ABC; 1962–1963 CBS)

Cast: Walter Brennan, Richard Crenna

This half-hour rural comedy series about a contemporary California farm family starred Walter Brennan and Richard Crenna. It featured the supporting character Pepino Garcia, a musically inclined farmhand, memorably played by Tony Martinez. A largely one-dimensional character, Pepino was a live-in Mexican farmworker who spoke broken English in an exaggerated manner.

"Realidades" (1975–1976 PBS)

This magazine format show was produced locally at WNET-TV 13 in New York in 1973–1974 with a dominant Puerto Rican focus. It was nationally broadcast with a focus on Hispanic issues and culture in the United States in 1975 and 1976. It was the first national Hispanic bilingual show in the history of U.S. television, a breakthrough for U.S. Hispanics in the media. "Realidades" featured everything from drama (film and videotaped segments and entire shows) to documentary to news features. It was one of the first shows to present Luis Valdez's El Teatro Campesino and many other prominent Hispanic arts groups and performing artists. Jesus Trevino and Jose Luis Ruiz were segment producers for a number of episodes concerning Chicanos in the Southwest. Willie Colon was musical director for the series. The executive producer was Humberto Cintron and the series producer was Lou de Lemos.

"The Redd Foxx Show" (1986 ABC)

Cast: Redd Foxx, **Rosana De Soto**, Pamela Segall

In this half-hour comedy created by Rick Kellard and Bob Comfort, Foxx played Al Hughes, owner of a combination newsstand and coffee shop in the heart of New York City. The comedy was accented by Diana Olmos (De Soto), Al's flippant, sexy Puerto Rican cook-waitress, who served up as many wisecracks as she did short orders.

"Rhoda" (1974–1978 CBS)

Cast: Valerie Harper

"Rhoda" was a spin-off of "The Mary Tyler Moore Show," where Rhoda was first introduced as a supporting character. In this series she returned from Minnesota to live in New York. During the 1977–1978 season Rhoda was given a new job with a theatrical costume company. One of the regulars during that season was Ramon Diaz, played by Rafael Campos, a happy-go-lucky Hispanic worker. The half-hour comedy series was created by James L. Brooks and Allan Burns.

"The Rita Moreno Show" (1976 ABC)

Cast: **Rita Moreno**

This half-hour comedy pilot film starred Tony winner Rita Moreno as Googie Gomez, the zany character she created in the Broadway play and movie *The Ritz* (*see* Movie listings).

"Roseanne" (1988– ABC)

Cast: Roseanne Arnold, John Goodman

Evelina Fernandez played a small role as Juanita Herrera, a factory co-worker of Roseanne's, in the first seven episodes of the first season of this half-hour situation comedy about a blue-collar family barely making ends meet.

"Sanchez of Bel Air" (1986 USA Cable)

Cast: **Reni Santoni**, Marcia Del Mar, Richard Coca, Alitzah Wiener, **Alma Beltran**

This 13-episode situation comedy series was executive produced and created by April Kelly and Dave Hackel. Ricardo Sanchez's (Santoni's) clothing business has finally taken off after 20 years of struggling, and the family is able to move to Beverly Hills from their East L.A. barrio. However, the move causes crises for all members of the family, as they adapt to life in well-to-do Beverly Hills.

This series was essentially "The Beverly Hillbillies" and "The Jeffersons" by another name, and reworked for Latinos. The two non-Hispanic writers, who had limited knowledge of U.S. Latino life and culture, were never able to convey a comedic cultural identity; thus the show rang false with audiences. Latino actors played all three generations of the Sanchez family; the only non-Hispanic regular character on the series was next-door neighbor Frankie Rondell, played by Bobby Sherman.

"Sanford and Son" (1972–1977 NBC)

Cast: Redd Foxx, Demond Wilson

Another half-hour situation comedy developed from a successful British comedy series ("Steptoe and Son," by Ray Galton and Alan Simpson), "Sanford and Son" starred Redd Foxx as cantankerous old Fred Sanford and Demond Wilson as his 30-year-old bachelor son Lamont, who ran a junk business out of their home in south central Los Angeles. Gregory Sierra became a semiregular in the role of Julio Fuentes, the Puerto Rican next-door neighbor whose ethnicity was the brunt of many jokes, exposing in the process the ugly face of prejudice among minorities themselves. Sierra created a very human and charismatic character.

"Santa Barbara" (1984–1993 NBC)

Cast: Dame Judith Anderson, Marcy Walker, Lane Davies, Todd McKee, **A Martinez**

The lush, progressive beach community of Santa Barbara, California, was the setting for this NBC-TV continuing daytime drama, created by Jerome and Bridget Dobson, focusing on the lives and loves of four resident families—the Lockridges, Perkinses, Andrades, and Capwells.

The Andrades were a Mexican American family struggling to attain the American Dream. Strong-willed daughter Santana (Ava Lazar) was determined to rise above her parents' lot and find the baby she was forced to give up for adoption years before. The family members were played by Ismael East Carlo, Margarita Cordova, and Rupert Ravens.

"Santa Barbara" was the first daytime drama series to prominently feature a Mexican American family and major Hispanic characters and the first to feature a relationship between a Mexican American and an Anglo.

Over the course of the first five seasons, the series focused almost exclusively on the lives and loves of the Capwell family. A Martinez was one of the original cast members. His character, Cruz Castillo, was a strong leading man who interacted with nearly all the show's other characters. Cruz went on to marry the series' heroine, Eden Capwell, culminating a four-year romance; their wedding was one of daytime television's most eagerly anticipated events.

Due to the show's syndication outside the United States, Martinez developed passionately devoted fans in over 30 countries. When "Santa Barbara" went on location to Paris, France, to shoot a few segments, Martinez and other cast members were mobbed wherever they went. Martinez won a Daytime Emmy as Outstanding Lead Actor in a Drama Series for his role as Castillo. Henry Darrow played Cruz Castillo's father, Rafael, on the series and won a Daytime Emmy for Outstanding Supporting Actor in a Drama Series. The series ended its run on January 15, 1993.

"Saved by the Bell" (1989–1993 NBC)
Cast: Mario Lopez

Mario Lopez, born in California of Mexican descent, is featured as muscleman Slater in this Saturday morning situation comedy series about a group of high school students. It was produced by Peter Engel.

"Saved by the Bell: The College Years" (1993– NBC)
Cast: Mario Lopez, Mark-Paul Gosselaar, Tiffani-Amber Thiessen

Mario Lopez reprises his role of Slater from the highly successful Saturday morning series "Saved by the Bell" in this prime-time series, which finds his character having to be a freshman all over again, this time on a wrestling scholarship at California University, where life away from home isn't as easy as he had anticipated.

"Saved by the Bell: The New Class" (1993– NBC)
Cast: Jonathan Angel

This Saturday morning continuation of "Saved by the Bell" with a new class of students features Hispanic student Tommy DeLucca (Angel).

"seaQuest DSV" (1993– NBC)
Cast: Roy Scheider, Stephanie Beacham, Don Franklin, Marco Sanchez

This futuristic action/adventure series set in the year 2018 is about a spectacular submarine and its multinational crew, who serve to explore and oversee the expanding oceanic frontier. Marco Sanchez plays Mundo Ortiz, a naval crewman responsible for the submarine's high-tech information systems—an exemplary role showing a Hispanic as responsible and intelligent.

"Second Chances" (1993– CBS)
Cast: Connie Sellecca, Matt Salinger, Jennifer Lopez, Ronnie Cox,
      Megan Follows, Michelle Phillips, **Pepe Serna**

This hour-long drama series follows a group of characters whose lives are tied together by a murder investigation. Pepe Serna plays Sal Lopez, a proud, middle-class Chicano parole officer whose daughter Melinda (Jennifer Lopez), a beautiful co-ed, is to be wed to the son of a blue-blood Anglo family.

"The Second Half" (1993– NBC)

Cast: **John Mendoza**, Wayne Knight

This situation comedy stars stand-up comedian John Mendoza as a recently divorced sportswriter who is raising two young daughters and facing a mid-life crisis.

"Sesame Street" (1969– PBS)

A creation of the Children's Television Workshop, "Sesame Street" is in its twenty-fifth season and has won a record 50 Emmy Awards. For over two decades Maria (Sonia Manzano) and Luis (Emilio Delgado) have been a vital Latino (Puerto Rican and Mexican) presence on the national children's show, which features an array of live performers, music, song and dance, filmed segments, animation, and puppets to teach young children. Many of the segments are bilingual and bicultural, introducing children to Spanish culture in the United States. It also introduced Big Bird and Jim Henson's world famous Muppet characters, including Kermit the Frog. Manzano is a Puerto Rican who grew up in the South Bronx section of New York City. Emilio Delgado was born in Calexico, California, and studied in Los Angeles before moving to New York.

"Shannon's Deal" (1990–1991 NBC)

Cast: **Jamey Sheridan**, **Elizabeth Pena**

This hour-long drama series was created by independent filmmaker writer/director John Sayles. It concerned a Philadelphia lawyer with heavy gambling debts

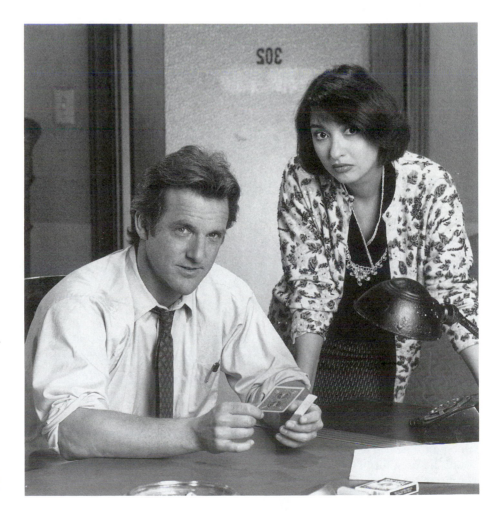

Elizabeth Pena as Lucy Acosta stars with Jamey Sheridan in "Shannon's Deal."

297

whose former addictive gambling has cost him his family and a lucrative partnership in a prestigious corporate law firm. Returning to his roots to start over, Shannon is eking out a living in solo practice. Elizabeth Pena co-starred as his loyal secretary, Lucy Acosta, in a nonstereotypical portrayal. The music was by jazz trumpeter Wynton Marsalis.

"Slattery's People" (1964–1965 CBS)
Cast: Richard Crenna, Ed Asner

This series concerned the professional and personal conflicts of an idealistic state representative (Crenna) interested in government reform and involved in causes and legislation to help his constituency. During the first season Paul Geary played the politician's aide, Johnny Ramos. Geary was replaced in the second season by Alejandro Rey, who played Mike Valera.

"The Steve Allen Show" (1956–1960 NBC; 1961 ABC)
Cast: Steve Allen

In 1959, this variety show introduced Bill Dana as the character of Mexican immigrant Jose Jimenez.

"Sword of Justice" (1978–1979 NBC)
Cast: Dack Rambo, **Bert Rosario**

An ex-con goes after lawbreakers with the help of his former cellmate, Hector Ramirez (Rosario), in this hour-long adventure series.

"T.H.E. Cat" (1966–1967 NBC)
Cast: Robert Loggia, **Robert Carricart**

This half-hour series was about a former circus aerialist and cat burglar who fights crime as a personal bodyguard. He is aided by a Spanish Gypsy named Pepe (Carricart) who runs a nightclub, the Casa Del Gato, where he maintains an office.

"Tarzan" (1966–1969 NBC)
Cast: Ron Ely, **Manuel Padilla, Jr.**

This hour-long "Tarzan" series was filmed entirely in Mexico though it was purportedly set in Africa. It had a decidedly Latin flavor in its atmosphere, and featured Manuel Padilla, Jr., as Jai, Tarzan's young native companion.

"Tony Orlando and Dawn" (1974–1976 CBS)
Cast: **Tony Orlando**

This one-hour musical variety show started as a four-week summer replacement and was continued when it met with good audience response and ratings.

"Tough Cookies" (1986 CBS)
Cast: Robby Benson, Lainie Kazan

In this half-hour police drama Robby Benson starred as Cliff Brady, a young Chicago police detective who lives and works in the tough Chicago neighborhood in which he grew up. Elizabeth Pena, in her first TV series, was Connie Rivera, a young undercover policewoman.

"Tour of Duty" (1987–1990 CBS)

Cast: Terence Knox, Stephen Caffrey, Joshua Maurer, **Ramon Franco**

This story of the American soldiers of Firebase Ladybird who forged friendships under fire in Vietnam in 1967 was created by L. Travis Clark and Steve Duncan. Ruiz, played by Ramon Franco, was a Puerto Rican recruit from the streets of New York. The subtleties of the character's New York Puerto Rican background were successfully conveyed by the writers and by actor Franco.

Miguel Nunez also played a recruit, but he didn't portray a Hispanic. "Tour of Duty" is the only television show to have recognized Hispanic American involvement in the nation's armed conflicts, through the character of Ruiz. From "Combat" through "M*A*S*H" to "China Beach," Hispanics had never been acknowledged in the form of leading characters.

"Trial and Error" (1988 CBS)

Cast: **Eddie Velez, Paul Rodriguez**

A young lawyer, John Hernandez (Velez), and a T-shirt seller, Tony Rivera (Rodriguez), were roommates in Los Angeles in this short-lived half-hour situation comedy.

"The Untouchables" (1959–1963 ABC)

Cast: Robert Stack, Paul Picerni, Nicholas Georgiade, **Abel Fernandez**

In 1959, this show originally aired as a two-part "Desilu Playhouse" drama with a strong filmic style. It was such a ratings hit that ABC with Desilu developed it into a weekly series. Abel Fernandez played Bill Youngfellow, one of The Untouchables on the popular series, which was based on the real-life exploits of Eliot Ness and his squad of incorruptible Treasury agents who fought Al Capone and other gangland figures during Prohibition in 1920s Chicago.

"Villa Alegre" (1974–1981 PBS)

Cast: Gilbert Duron, Julio Medina, **Carmen Zapata**

This bilingual (Spanish/English) series was geared toward 4- to 10-year-olds to teach them about human relations, the natural environment, communication, energy, and man-made objects. Claudio Guzman was the executive producer.

"Viva Valdez!" (1976 ABC)

Cast: **Carmen Zapata, Rodolfo Hoyos, James Victor, Jorge Cervera, Jr.**

This series about a Mexican American family in Los Angeles was neither well received nor well conceived. It ran from May until September. The show was noteworthy in that it was an attempt to produce a Hispanic family series and in that it showcased a number of talented Hispanic performers.

"Welcome Back, Kotter" (1975–1979 ABC)

Cast: Gabriel Kaplan, Marcia Strassman, John Sylvester White, John Travolta, Robert Hegyes, Lawrence-Hilton Jacobs

This half-hour comedy concerned a young teacher, Gabe Kotter (Kaplan), who returns to the city high school from which he graduated and attempts to teach a remedial academics class. The class members, reluctantly enrolled in school, were affectionately known as "The Sweathogs." Robert Hegyes played Juan Epstein, a half-Hispanic, half-Jewish student. The series was created by Gabriel Kaplan and Alan Sacks.

"What a Country" (1986–1987 syndicated)

Cast: Garrett M. Brown, Yakov Smirnoff, Gail Strickland, George Murdock, **Ada Maris, Julian Reyes**, Leila Hee Olsen

This was a first-run syndicated comedy series about the humorous adventures of an American citizenship class taught by a rather reluctant but dedicated night school teacher. Ada Maris portrayed Maria Conchita Lopez, a sexy Mexican girl working as a maid for a wealthy Beverly Hills couple who thinks she has found the promised land on Rodeo Drive. Julian Reyes played Victor Ortega, a macho street kid who has the same dreams and insecurities as many immigrants.

"The White Shadow" (1978–1981 CBS)

Cast: Ken Howard, Kevin Hooks, Thomas Carter

This hour-long series about a white basketball coach in a racially mixed L.A. high school featured Ira Angustain as Hispanic team member Ricardo Gomez. Several episodes revolved around him.

"Wichita Town" (1959–1960 NBC)

Cast: Joel McCrea, Jody McCrea, **Carlos Romero**

Marshall Mike Dunbar (Joel McCrea) maintained law and order in Wichita, Kansas, in the years following the Civil War in this 26-episode, half-hour western series. Carlos Romero played a regular supporting role as Rico Rodriguez.

"Wiseguy" (1986–1990 CBS)

Cast: **Steven Bauer**

In its fourth and last season, this critically acclaimed one-hour drama series/serial from Stephen J. Cannell introduced a new leading actor, Steven Bauer, following the departure of its original star, Ken Wahl. Bauer played disbarred federal prosecutor Michael Santana, who joins forces with the FBI's Organized Crime Bureau in order to infiltrate the ranks of powerful criminal organizations. This six-hour (five-episode) first arc of the 1990–1991 season was filmed on location in Miami. It involved an investigation by Santana into the murder of undercover agent Vinnie Terranova (Wahl's character) by a Latin American death squad.

The story guest starred Academy Award winner Maximilian Schell as Cuban Amado Guzman, pop recording artist Martika, and Manolo Villaverde. This reincarnated "Wiseguy" gave us a Miami where two of the main characters were veterans of the Bay of Pigs invasion; where the hero's father was a prisoner in a Castro jail; and where the love interest was a Cuban American singer. It brought a recognition of the contributions made to American culture, history, politics, and crime, particularly in Miami and southern Florida, by Cuban Americans over the last 30 years in a realistic manner with Cuban-born, Miami-reared central characters. The Nielsen viewers did not accept this new incarnation of "Wiseguy," and the series ended its run after the Miami episodes.

"The Xavier Cugat Show" (1957 NBC)

Cast: **Xavier Cugat**

This musical variety show, only 15 minutes long, was paired with the 15-minute NBC nightly news. The show lasted from February to May and starred Cugat and his then wife, singer Abbe Lane.

"The Yellow Rose" (1983–1984 NBC)
Cast: Sam Elliott, Cybill Shepherd, Susan Anspach, David Soul

This hour-long drama series centered around a contemporary Anglo Texas ranch family as they struggled to maintain values and traditions established a century earlier. One of the sons, a half-Mexican lawyer named Quisto Champion, was played by Edward Albert, who is half-Hispanic himself. Several of the story lines dealt with border smuggling and exploitation of Latino undocumented workers.

"You Again" (1986–1987 NBC)
Cast: Jack Klugman

A middle-aged divorcé is surprised when his 17-year-old son enters his life again. Luis Avalos played the character of Luis Robles.

"Zorro" (1957–1959 ABC)
See "Zorro & The Cisco Kid" listings.

"Zorro and Son" (1983 CBS)
See "Zorro & The Cisco Kid" listings.

MOVIES AND MINISERIES

Alambrista
See Movie listings.

The Alamo: 13 Days to Glory (1987 NBC)
D: Burt Kennedy
Te: Clyde Ware and Norman Mcleod Morrill
P: Bill Finnegan, Pat Finnegan, and Sheldon Pinchuk
Cast: James Arness, Brian Keith, **Raul Julia**, Alec Baldwin, **Isela Vega, Fernando Allende**

This is a routine version of the Alamo story, which tried minimally to show the participation of the Mexican defenders at the Battle of the Alamo, including Juan Seguin and Gregorio Esparza as well as the Hispanic women. It gave insight into the character of Gen. Santa Anna, as played by Raul Julia. Among the other Hispanic actors featured were Eloy Casados, Laura Martinez Herring, Loyda Ramos, Laura Fabian, Sol Castillo, and Bel Sandre.

All Star Fiesta at Ford's (1992 ABC)
Cast: **Ricardo Montalban**

This two-hour taped gala evening at Ford's Theater in Washington, D.C., featured President and Mrs. George Bush in a salute to Hispanic heritage and the achievements of the National Hispanic Scholarship Fund. It also starred Paul Rodriguez, Rita Moreno, Tito Puente, Vikki Carr, and many other celebrities.

Antonio and the Mayor (1976 CBS)
    D: Jerry Thorpe
    Te: Howard Rodman
    P: Jerry Thorpe
  Cast: **Gregory Sierra**

This story of a young Mexican boy who defies the authority of the town's mayor was filmed in Mexico.

The Ballad of Gregorio Cortez
See Movie listings.

The Boy and the Turtle (1971 PBS)
    Te: Eugene Poinc
    P: Earl Miller
  Cast: **Manuel Padilla, Jr., Gilbert Roland, Katy Jurado**, Henry Calvin,
      Enrique Lucero

This drama, written especially for WNET's Children's Special and filmed on the Yucatan Peninsula, concerns a 12-year-old Mexican youth who discovers a Mayan relic and a huge friendly turtle.

Break of Dawn
See Movie listings.

Brotherhood of the Gun (1992 CBS)
    D: Vern Gillum
    Te: Robert Ward
    P: Robert Ward
  Cast: Brian Blessed, **Jorge Cervera, Jr.**

Jorge Cervera, Jr., plays Sheriff Charlie Sanchez, who looks like a stereotype but who is tough, smart, and self-sufficient. Sanchez is overweight, wears a large, wide-brimmed Mexican hat, and eats tamales as he chases bad guys. He also helps the film's hero out of a tough situation.

Burden of Proof (1992 ABC)
    D: Mike Robe
    Te: John Gay
    P: John Perrin Flynn
  Cast: **Hector Elizondo**, Brian Dennehy, Stephanie Powers, **Victoria Principal**,
      Mel Harris

Elizondo plays Sandy Stern (the character Raul Julia played in the 1990 theatrical feature *Presumed Innocent*), a middle-aged Jewish criminal attorney of Argentine-German descent who finds his ordered world turned upside down after his wife commits suicide. Elizondo was the best thing about this otherwise overlong, rather weak mystery/thriller, aired in two parts.

Can You Hear the Laughter? The Story of Freddie Prinze (1979 CBS)
    D: Burt Brinckerhoff
    Te: Dalene Young
    P: Roger Gimbel
  Cast: **Ira Angustain**, Kevin Hooks, **Julie Carmen**

Ira Angustain was selected to portray the brilliant but tragic young comedian Freddie Prinze in this TV movie dealing with Prinze's life and death by suicide in 1977.

Centennial (1978–1979 NBC)

    D: Paul Krasny, Virgil W. Vogel, Harry Falk, and Bernard McEveety

  Te: John Wilder

    P: John Wilder

Cast: Robert Conrad, Richard Chamberlain, **Barbara Carrera**, Dennis Weaver, David Janssen, **Karmin Murcelo, A Martinez, Rafael Campos**

The Mexican American cultural influence in the winning of the American West was significantly portrayed in the epic 26-hour miniseries *Centennial*, based on the novel by James A. Michener. It traces the lives of those who founded the fictional town of Centennial, Colorado, and their descendants from the time of the Native American to the present.

The miniseries featured a number of Hispanic actors in important roles. In the early episodes involving the trappers and Indians, beautiful Barbara Carrera portrayed the Native American woman Clay Basket. Trail cook Nacho Gomez, who

A Martinez holds a wounded Rafael Campos in the miniseries *Centennial.*

helped on the great cattle drives from Texas to Colorado during the 1870s, was played by Rafael Campos. The political unrest of turn-of-the-century Mexico, along with the beginnings of the exploitation of migratory workers, was brought into play in the story of Tranquilino Marquez, played by A Martinez. The racism and injustice that Tranquilino's descendants encountered and their struggle to make a life for themselves as Americans was touched upon. An Anglo-Chicano marriage in the contemporary final episode between Flor Marquez (Murcelo) and Paul Garrett (Janssen) represented a further bridging of peoples. Julio Medina, Silvana Gallardo, Henry Darrow, Rene Enriquez, Alex Colon, and David Yanez were also in the cast.

Choices of the Heart [aka: *In December the Roses Will Bloom Again*] (1983 NBC)

- D: Joseph Sargent
- Te: John Pielmeier
- P: Joseph Sargent and David W. Rintels
- Cast: Melissa Gilbert, **Martin Sheen**, Mike Farrell, **Rene Enriquez**, Pamela Bellwood

This fact-based movie concerns the life of Jean Donovan, the 27-year-old missionary slain with three American nuns in El Salvador in 1980. Gilbert plays Donovan and Sheen plays Father Corcoran, an Irish priest who was an inspiration to Donovan. Enriquez portrays Archbishop Romero, the martyred Salvadoran church leader.

Copacabana (1986 ABC)

- D: Waris Hussein
- Te: James Lipton
- P: Dick Clark
- Cast: Barry Manilow, Annette O'Toole, Joseph Bologna

A musical drama based on the popular hit song by Barry Manilow, this film focuses on the characters who work and inhabit the legendary Copacabana Latin nightclub in 1940s New York. All the lead characters are WASP or Italian, and the Latin characters are minor. Silvana Gallardo played an aging nightclub headliner, and Dyana Ortelli played a showgirl.

Corridos! Tales of Passion and Revolution (1987 PBS)

- D: **Luis Valdez**
- Te: **Luis Valdez**
- P: Janis Blackschleger
- Cast: Clancy Brown, Evelyn Cisneros, George Galvan, **Sal Lopez**, **Alma Martinez**, Linda Ronstadt, **Daniel Valdez**, **Luis Valdez** (as El Maestro)

This KQED/San Francisco one-hour videotaped entertainment special was produced in association with El Teatro Campesino. Written, directed, and starring El Teatro Campesino founder Luis Valdez, the production realizes the dramatic potential of the most famous and tuneful Mexican American folk ballads, or *corridos*. Brought to life through a rich combination of drama, music, dance, and imaginative art direction, these ballads carry the viewer from Mexico in the late 1800s to 1920s America. It was adapted for television from the acclaimed El Teatro Campesino stage production featuring members of the original cast. A bilingual production with songs in Spanish and dialogue in English, the special featured the talents of 15 musicians, including Los Camperos, America's premier Mariachi group, all under the musical direction of Daniel Valdez.

Crazy from the Heart (1991 TNT)

D: Thomas Schlamme
Te: Linda Voorhees
P: R.J. Louis
Cast: Christine Lahti, **Ruben Blades**, William Russ, Tommy Muniz, **Kamala Lopez**

In this charming tale of unexpected love that defies logic and small-town prejudice, an uptight southern Texas high school principal falls in love with a Mexican American janitor.

For seven years, Charlotte Bain (Lahti) has been content with her career and the noncommittal relationship she's had with Coach Dewey Whitcomb. The bubble bursts when she learns that her best friend since grade school is going to be a grandmother, a revelation that reminds Charlotte her own biological clock is ticking.

Wanting more from her life, she gives Dewey a wedding ultimatum, and their relationship buckles under the pressure. On the rebound, she meets Ernesto Ontiveros (Blades), a down-on-his-luck Mexican American farmer who is working as a janitor at her high school to save his ranch from foreclosure. Ernesto asks Charlotte for a date, and, despite herself, she accepts. Love is not far behind.

Tommy Muniz plays Tomas, Ernesto's father, and Kamala Lopez portrays Ernesto's strong-willed daughter, Alcira, who is a lawyer determined to carve her own niche in town. Ruben Blades was nominated for an Emmy in 1992 for his role in this comedy/drama.

Curacao (1993 Showtime)

D: Carl Schultz
Te: James David Buchanon
P: Art Levinson
Cast: George C. Scott, William Petersen, **Julie Carmen**

Two loners have washed up on Curacao, a Caribbean island located in the Netherland Antilles, off the coast of Venezuela, during Carnival time. Julia Fernandez (Carmen), the Caribbean station chief for an American intelligence agency, adds an element of intrigue and romance to the mix when she is sent to Curacao from Puerto Rico to investigate the two men.

Dead Man Out (1989 HBO)

D: Richard Pearce
Te: Ron Hutchinson
P: Forrest Murray
Cast: Danny Glover, **Ruben Blades**, Tom Atkins

Psychiatrist Alex Marsh (Glover) is hired to "cure" an insane convict, Ben (Blades), so that the state can execute him. This is a gritty drama about the battle of wits that erupts between the psychiatrist and the death-row inmate when they confront each other without the protection of prison bars.

The Deadly Tower (1975 NBC)

D: Jerry Jameson
Te: William D. Lansford
P: Antonio Calderon
Cast: Kurt Russell, **Richard Yniguez**

This film re-creates the Texas tower massacre of August 4, 1966, during which a

Richard Yniguez (lower right) stars with Kurt Russell (upper left) in *The Deadly Tower*.

disturbed student, Charles Whitman (Russell), at the University of Texas began firing on students. A Texas officer, Ramiro Martinez (Yniguez), brought him down.

The Desperate Mission (1971 NBC)

   D: Earl Bellamy
   Te: Jack Guss
   P: David Silver
   Cast: **Ricardo Montalban,** Roosevelt Grier, Slim Pickens, Ina Balin, **Miriam Colon**

This is a fictionalized story of the legendary bandit Joaquin Murieta (Montalban) and how he comes to the aid of some pioneers.

Double Crossed (1991 HBO)

- D: Roger Young
- Te: Roger Young
- P: Albert J. Salzer
- Cast: Dennis Hopper, Robert Carradine, Adrienne Barbeau

This film is loosely based on the real-life story of drug dealer Barry Seal (Hopper). When Seal piloted his plane to deliver illicit cargo from South America into eager American hands, he flew with a sense of adventure. However, when Seal switched allegiances, identifying the pivotal drug kingpins he smuggled for and at the same time accumulating evidence for the federal government at great risk to his life while continuing his smuggling operation, this new twist made the game even more tantalizing.

But then the government double crossed him, leaving him out in the cold, and Barry Seal became easy prey for the drug dealers he had betrayed. He was gunned down in Baton Rouge, Louisiana, on February 19, 1986, after the IRS had confiscated all his money and assets for back taxes owed on the money he had made smuggling. His widow and children were left homeless and penniless. It was filmed partly in Louisiana and Puerto Rico.

Drug Wars: The Camarena Story (1989 NBC)

- D: Brian Gibson
- Te: Christopher Canaan, Mel Frohman, Ann Powell, and Rose Schacht
- P: Branko Lustig
- Cast: **Steven Bauer, Elizabeth Pena**, Craig T. Nelson, Treat Williams, **Miguel Ferrer**

This is a powerful miniseries about United States Drug Enforcement Administration agent "Kiki" Camarena, who in 1985 was tortured and killed in Mexico because his investigations threatened major drug lords allegedly connected to senior members of the Mexican government. His fellow agents and his wife, Mika, determined to identify and expose the murderers, fought against corrupt Mexican officials, American diplomatic inaction, and personal frustration in their struggle to bring those responsible to justice. This straightforward drama was based on *Desperados*, a book by *Time* reporter Elaine Shannon, which exposes the greed and corruption extending from those behind the drug cartels to high government officials. Michael Mann ("Miami Vice") was the executive producer of the miniseries. It also featured Hispanic actors Pepe Serna, Tony Plana, Benicio del Toro, Tomas Goros, Eddie Velez, Mike Moroff, Jacob Vargas, Joaquin Martinez, Geoffrey Rivas, and Tomas Milian. It was filmed in Los Angeles and in Spain because the Mexican government would not allow the company to film in Mexico, as the movie put the Mexican government in an unfavorable light due to the political controversy that still lingers over the murder of Camarena.

Drug Wars: The Cocaine Cartel (1992 NBC)

- D: Paul Krasny
- Te: Gordon Greisman and Gail Morgan Hickman
- P: Richard Brams and Gordon Greisman
- Cast: Alex McArthur, Dennis Farina, **Julie Carmen**, John Glover

This dramatic retelling of the fight to bring down two powerful drug lords in Medellín, Colombia, and the inside story of the DEA's courageous infiltration into the empire of billionaire narco-terrorists, was filmed in Miami and Spain.

El Baquine de Angelitos Negros (1977 PBS)
    D: Mike Cuesta
    Te: Lou de Lemos
    P: Lou de Lemos and Livia Perez
    Cast: Brunilda Ruiz, **Hector Mercado**, Beatriz Rodriguez

The first all-Latino dance production ever to be produced exclusively for national television distribution, this was part of the "Realidades" television series. Salsa bandleader Willie Colon composed the entire musical ballet expressly for this film program. It is a modern-day updating of Latin American folklore set in New York's Puerto Rican community of Spanish Harlem.

When a black Puerto Rican child died on the island, a festival was held to celebrate the passage of the innocent child's soul to heaven, where it was welcomed by God and immediately transformed into an angel. Friends and family would dance late into the night to assure the ascent of the child's spirit. This joyous celebration is called a Baquine. Brunilda Ruiz was a principal dancer with the Harkness Ballet. Hector Mercado was a dancer with the Alvin Ailey company and went on to perform on Broadway and in feature films.

El Corrido: La Gran Carpa de los Rasquachis (1976 PBS)
    D: Kirk Browning
    Te: **Luis Valdez**
    P: Barbara Schultz
    Cast: Felix Alvarez, Lily Alvarez, Socorro Cruz, Jose Delgado, Phil Esparza, Andres Gutierrez, Diane Rodriguez, **Daniel Valdez**

This 70-minute videotaped broadcast production was presented as part of the "Visions" series. Written and staged by Luis Valdez, it evolved out of the skits performed by members of the theater group El Teatro Campesino during the early days of the farmworkers' strikes. This work centers on the adventures of a fictional farm laborer, Kose Pelado Rasguachi, a character in the tradition of Mexican comedic actor Cantinflas.

El Diablo (1990 HBO)
    D: Peter Markle
    Te: Tommy Lee Wallace, John Carpenter, and Bill Phillips
    P: Mickey Borofsky and Todd Black
    Cast: Anthony Edwards, Lou Gossett, Jr., **Robert Beltran**

Comic western with a twist. When a Mexican bandit, El Diablo (Beltran), rides into town with his band of armed men, robs the bank, and kidnaps a sweet-faced frontier student, a mild-mannered tenderfoot schoolteacher, Billy Ray (Edwards), takes a crash course in Wild West gunslinging and more from the grizzled veteran Van Leek (Gossett) in order to rescue the girl from El Diablo.

Evita Peron (1981 NBC)
    D: Marvin J. Chomsky
    Te: Ronald Harwood
    P: Marvin J. Chomsky
    Cast: Faye Dunaway, James Farentino, **Rita Moreno, Jose Ferrer, Pedro Armendariz, Jr.**, Michael Constantine, **Katy Jurado**

Argentina's charismatic famed First Lady, Evita Peron (Dunaway), rises from the slums of Buenos Aires to become a film actress and win the heart of dictator Juan Peron and the people. This miniseries was filmed in Mexico.

Finding the Way Home (1991 ABC)

 D: Rod Holcomb
Te: Scott Swanton
 P: Peter K. Duchow and Rob Holcomb
Cast: George C. Scott, **Hector Elizondo, Julie Carmen**, Beverly Garland

An elderly hardware store owner finds himself and redemption among some Latino farmworkers in the Southwest.

Florida Straits (1986 HBO)

 D: Mike Hodges
Te: Roderick Taylor
 P: Stuart B. Rekant
Cast: **Raul Julia**, Fred Ward, Daniel Jenkins

A trio of adventurers brave the treacherous Cuban jungle to search for a fortune in buried gold. Carlos (Julia) has just been released after 20 years in a Cuban jail for the part he played in the Bay of Pigs invasion. During the invasion, Carlos piloted a plane loaded with $2 million in gold for the U.S. government. When the plane crashed in the Cuban jungle, Carlos went to jail, and the gold stayed in the wilderness. Now he wants to go back and get it. Carlos hires the boat *White Witch,* and fast-talks its crew, Lucky (Ward) and Mac (Jenkins), into joining him in his long-held dream of retrieving the $2 million treasure.

For the Love of My Child: The Anissa Ayala Story (1993 NBC)

 D: Waris Hussein
Te: Anna Sandor
 P: Michelle Maxwell MacLaren
Cast: **Priscilla Lopez**, Teresa DiSpina, Tony Perez, Danny Nucci

In 1990, leukemia patient Anissa Ayala made national headlines when her parents conceived a child in the hope of achieving a successful bone marrow match and saving Anissa's life. The events that led up to that decision and the national controversy that followed are dramatized in this telefilm. Miraculously, the Ayalas' new daughter turns out to be a perfect bone marrow match, and Anissa courageously triumphs over leukemia. Tony Award–winner Priscilla Lopez stars as the mother in a TV movie that presents a middle-class Hispanic American family without stereotypical trappings. The cast was made up of experienced but not well-known Hispanic actors, which contributed to the credibility of the film.

Gangs (1988 CBS)

 D: Jesus Trevino
Te: Paul Cooper
 P: Howard Metzer and Eli Johnson
Cast: David Labiosa, Gabriel Gonzales, Raymond Cruz, Will Gotay, **Kamala Lopez, Panchito Gomez**

A former gang member returns to his East L.A. home from the Army to find his younger brother involved in his former gang. Director Jesus Trevino won a Directors Guild of America Award for Best Direction of a Daytime TV Drama for this movie. It is sensitively written and directed and offers no easy answers to the serious problems of drugs and gang violence that confront families in the barrio.

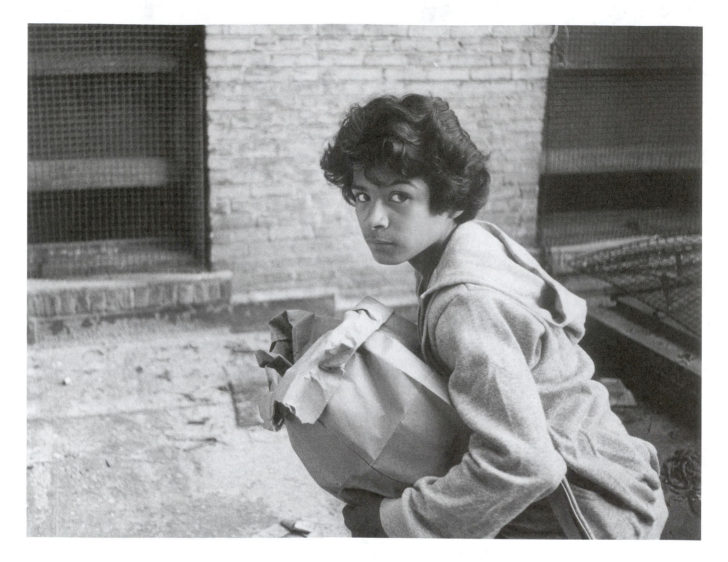

Panchito Gomez plays the lead in the
ABC Afterschool Special *Gaucho*.

Gaucho (1978 ABC)

 D: Rob Lieberman
 Te: Arthur Heinemann
 P: Martin Tahse
Cast: **Panchito Gomez, Alma Beltran**

A 14-year-old Puerto Rican boy, Gaucho, moves to New York City with his mother
and older brother and must deal with conflicting values in his new environment.
His older brother, Angel, marries an Anglo girl whose brother is a policeman. Angel
also forgets about his promise to take his mother back to Puerto Rico, and Gaucho
is determined to earn money any way he can to take his mother home. The movie
was based on the book *Gaucho* by Gloria Gonzalez.

Glitz (1988 NBC)

 D: Sandor Stern
 Te: Alan Trustman and Steve Zito
 P: Steve McGlothen
Cast: **Jimmy Smits**, Markie Post, John Diehl, **Geno Silva**

In this adaptation of Elmore Leonard's best-selling detective novel about a Miami-
based police officer, Vincent Mora (Smits) tracks down the killer of a call girl through
the casinos of Atlantic City and Puerto Rico, unaware that he is the real target of
the killer.

Gore Vidal's Billy the Kid (1989 TNT)

- D: William A. Graham
- Te: Gore Vidal
- P: Frank Von Zerneck and Robert M. Sertner
- Cast: Val Kilmer, Duncan Regehr, **Julie Carmen**, Wilford Brimley

This two-hour film about Billy the Kid, the legendary outlaw of the New Mexico Territory of the 1870s, has a script by Gore Vidal, one of America's most prolific and respected writers. Julie Carmen plays Celsa, Billy's romantic interest. An earlier Vidal teleplay, *The Death of Billy the Kid,* was adapted as a feature-length film in 1958, *The Left-Handed Gun* (*see* Movie listings).

Gryphon (1988 PBS)

- D: Mark Cullingham
- Te: Manuel Arce and Carl Haber
- P: Manuel Arce and Carl Haber
- Cast: Amanda Plummer, Sully Diaz, Alexis Cruz

Based on a short story by Charles Baxter, this is a tale of a tough Hispanic boy whose life is changed by a magical substitute teacher. A presentation of the "WonderWorks" series.

HBO Comedy Hour: John Leguizamo's Spic-O-Rama (1993 HBO)

- D: Peter Askin
- Te: **John Leguizamo**
- P: Jeff Ross
- Cast: **John Leguizamo**

In his second HBO Comedy Hour special based on his own stage production, acclaimed talent John Leguizamo portrays five members of a dysfunctional New York Latino family, from a 9-year-old self-proclaimed genius to a troubled Desert Storm vet to a cynical mom, in a one-man tour-de-force performance filmed in front of a live audience at New York's American Place Theatre. *Spic-O-Rama* premiered at the Goodman Theatre in Chicago, moving to the West Side Arts Theatre in New York for a sold-out three-month run. *Time* magazine called it one of the best plays of 1992, hailing Leguizamo for "hilarious monologues that moved beyond performance art to become a true and deeply moving play."

HBO Comedy Hour: Mambo Mouth (1991 HBO)

- D: Thomas Schlamme
- Te: **John Leguizamo**
- P: Jeff Ross
- Cast: **John Leguizamo**

A tour-de-force performance adapted from the actor/writer's acclaimed Off-Broadway one-man show, *Mambo Mouth* was inspired by characters Leguizamo encountered growing up in Jackson Heights, Queens. A response to the media's negative image of Latinos, the show is Leguizamo's declaration that "Latinos can be funny and strong in the face of adversity." The original stage presentation at the American Place Theatre in New York in 1990 won an Obie and an Outer Critics Circle Award.

Erik Estrada and Morgan Fairchild in *Honeyboy*.

Honeyboy (1982 NBC)

 D: John Berry
 Te: John Berry and Lee Gold
 P: **Erik Estrada** and John Berry
Cast: **Erik Estrada**, Morgan Fairchild, **Hector Elizondo**

Erik Estrada produced this television film about the rise and fall of Rico "Honeyboy" Ramirez, a tough boxer from the streets of New York's Spanish Harlem, in the classic melodramatic John Garfield Warner Bros. tradition.

The House of Ramon Iglesias (1986 PBS)

 D: **Luis Soto**
 Te: **Jose Rivera**
 P: Laura Mola
Cast: **Jaime Sanchez**, Robert Badillo, Annie Golden, Nick Corri, Marina Durell

Adapted by Rivera from his own stage play, this is the story of a Puerto Rican family in New York who, after 19 years, decides to move back to Puerto Rico. The oldest son objects to the move, and the resulting conflict highlights the themes of assimilation and returning to one's homeland. The movie aired on the "American Playhouse" series in April 1986.

Jacobo Timerman: Prisoner Without a Name, Cell Without a Number (1983 CBS)

D: Linda Yellen
Te: Linda Yellen, Jonathan Platnick, and Oliver Drexell, Jr.
P: Terry Ellis and Richard Dorso
Cast: Roy Scheider, Liv Ullmann, Sam Robards

Set in Argentina, this political thriller is based on the true story of outspoken newspaper publisher Timerman (Scheider), who was imprisoned and tortured by a repressive political regime. No Latin actors are featured in leading roles in this film, shot in New Jersey.

La Carpa (1993 PBS)

D: Carlos Avila
Te: Carlos Avila and Edit Villareal
P: Michael Zapanta and Carlos Villareal
Cast: Jaime Gomez, Nicolas Coster, **E.J. Castillo**, **Bel Sandre**, Karla Montana

In 1938 in Florencia, California, a farmworker witnesses the accidental shooting of his friend by the local sheriff in a dark alley. Disturbed by his friend's death and everyone's complacent attitude toward the shooting, he raises the ire of local authorities, both Mexican and Anglo, by his blatant outrage and constant questions. He finds employment and spiritual renewal with La Carpa, a traveling sideshow of performers that entertains Mexican farmworkers. Through a chance encounter in the same dark alley where his friend met his death, the farmworker and the sheriff find mutual understanding and truth. The film aired on the "American Playhouse" series in June 1993.

La Pastorela (1991 PBS)

D: **Luis Valdez**
Te: **Luis Valdez**
P: **Richard Soto**
Cast: **Paul Rodriguez, Cheech Marin**, Linda Ronstadt, Karla Montana

Presented on the Public Broadcasting Service as part of the "Great Performances" series, this contemporary one-hour film adaptation of a traditional holiday play, performed by Luis Valdez's El Teatro Campesino at San Juan Bautista Mission, California, featured music by Los Lobos and Lalo Guerrero. *La Pastorela* is a musical retelling of the shepherd's journey to Bethlehem to see the Christ child. Valdez opens up the pageant for television, taking it outdoors and adding more comedy, music, and special effects. The play is seen through the eyes of a young Chicana accidentally knocked unconscious during a rather raucous performance. In her surrealistic dream, she repeats the journey through her own contemporary frame of reference.

The Last Prostitute (1991 Lifetime)

D: Lou Antonio
Te: Carmen Culver
P: Peter Bogart
Cast: Wil Wheaton, **Sonia Braga**, David Kaufman, Cotter Smith

Young boys leave home and go in search of an infamous prostitute they read about in their late grandfather's diary, in order to lose their virginity. They find a not-so-beautiful middle-aged woman living alone on a ranch, where they learn lessons in life.

Lucy and Desi: Before the Laughter (1991 CBS)

D: Charles Jarrott
Te: William Luce and Cynthia Cherback
P: John Lenox
Cast: Frances Fisher, Maurice Benard

This movie tells of the intimate, often stormy, private life of Lucille Ball and Desi Arnaz. Beginning on the eve of their unprecedented career success, the night the first episode of "I Love Lucy" is to be filmed before a live audience, their story unfolds through a series of flashbacks and recounts their relationship from 1940 to 1951. Credible performances are turned in by Fisher and Benard as Lucy and Desi.

Manhunt: Search for the Night Stalker (1989 NBC)

D: Bruce Seth Green
Te: Joe Gunn
P: Ron Gilbert
Cast: **A Martinez**, Richard Jordan, **Julie Carmen**

In this fact-based drama, Los Angeles detectives Gil Carrillo (Martinez) and Frank Salerno (Jordan) are assigned to head the investigation into a string of brutal murders, which leads to the arrest of Richard Ramirez, a serial killer who terrorized the state of California during the summer of 1985.

Maricela (1984 PBS)

D: Christine Burrell
Te: Nancy Audley
P: **Richard Soto**
Cast: Linda Lavin, Carlina Cruz, Irene De Bar

A young El Salvadoran girl struggles to find her place in America when she and her mother come to work for a wealthy Malibu, California, family. This presentation was part of the "WonderWorks" series.

Mrs. Cage (1992 PBS)

D: Robert Allan Ackerman
Te: Nancy Barr
P: Dan Lupovitz
Cast: Anne Bancroft, **Hector Elizondo**

This powerful, essentially two-character drama was adapted from Barr's stage play about the interrogation of a housewife who, for reasons unknown, has murdered a woman in the parking lot of a local supermarket. She is interrogated by Police Lieutenant Ruben Angel, played by Elizondo. The movie aired on the "American Playhouse" series in May 1992.

Ned Blessing: The Story of My Life and Times (1993 CBS)
    D: Jack Bender
    Te: William D. Wittliff
    P: William D. Wittliff
Cast: Brad Johnson, Wes Studi, **Luis Avalos**

This two-hour movie and four-episode limited series about a western outlaw turned sheriff, Ned Blessing (Johnson), and his sidekick, Crecencio (Avalos), in Plum Creek, Texas, was created and written by William D. Wittliff.

The Old Man and the Sea (1990 NBC)
    D: Jud Taylor
    Te: Roger O. Hirson
    P: Bill Storke and Robert Fuisz
Cast: **Anthony Quinn**, Gary Cole, Patricia Clarkson, Francesco Quinn, Valentina Quinn

Anthony Quinn gives a powerful performance as Santiago in Ernest Hemingway's *The Old Man and the Sea*, based on the classic novella about an old Cuban fisherman's battle with a giant marlin in the Gulf Stream. It was filmed on Tortola in the Virgin Islands and is the second movie version of the Pulitzer Prize–winning book to be produced, following the 1958 theatrical original, in which Spencer Tracy played Santiago.

One Man's War (1991 HBO)
    D: Sergio Toledo
    Te: Mike Carter and Sergio Toledo
    P: Ann Skinner
Cast: Anthony Hopkins, **Norma Aleandro**, **Ruben Blades**

When the authorities brutalize Dr. Joel Filartaga's (Hopkins) fellow citizens, he courageously speaks out against the injustice of repression. But when the secret police kidnap, torture, and murder his teenage son, he declares war.

Based on a real-life case, *One Man's War* is the shocking story of a South American family resisting a brutal dictatorship in Paraguay. The Filartagas enlisted a celebrated criminal lawyer, Perrone (Blades), to aid them. The family subsequently carried their struggle to the United States, where, working with the Center for Constitutional Rights, they filed a civil suit in federal court. The result was a landmark victory for international human rights which set a legal precedent that continues to this day.

Prison Stories: Women on the Inside—"Esperanza" (1991 HBO)
    D: Donna Deitch
    Te: Martin Jones
    P: Gerald T. Olson
Cast: **Rachel Ticotin**, **Talisa Soto**, Francesca Roberts

Prison Stories is a feature-length dramatic trilogy that takes a gritty look at the struggles of women in prison, portraying the family tragedy when a mother is jailed. "Esperanza" is the story of a child who follows in his mother's criminal footsteps. Iris Martinez (Ticotin), doing hard time for a drug deal engineered by her husband, must leave her son Mico in the care of her sister Rosina (Soto) for the duration of her prison term. Despite his aunt's efforts, Mico continues his family's crime cycle by selling crack and ends up being arrested and sentenced to juvenile detention.

Return of the Gunfighter (1967 ABC)

D: James Neilson
Te: Robert Buckner
P: Frank King and Maurice King
Cast: Robert Taylor, Chad Everett, **Rudolfo Hoyos, Jr.**, Ana Martin

An aging gunfighter and a wounded saddle tramp team up to help a Mexican girl avenge the death of her parents, murdered for their land.

Rita Hayworth: The Love Goddess (1983 CBS)

D: James Goldstone
Te: E. Arthur Kean
P: Andrew Susskind
Cast: **Lynda Carter**, Michael Lerner, **Alejandro Rey**

This television movie dramatizes the remarkable story of the legendary actress from her early career as a dancer through her evolution into one of Hollywood's most popular stars.

River of Promises (1977 NBC)

D: Lee Katzin
Te: Michael Mann
P: David Gerber
Cast: **Richard Yniguez, Joe Santos**, Julio Medina, **Jaime Sanchez, Rose Portillo, Gregory Sierra, Edward James Olmos**

This two-hour special "Police Story" episode starred Richard Yniguez as Ratazza, a policeman who goes undercover to expose a ring smuggling illegal aliens into East Los Angeles. This sensitively written drama was acted by a top-notch, predominantly Hispanic cast.

The Sacketts (1979 CBS)

D: Robert Totten
Te: Jim Byrnes, based on the novels *The Day Breakers* and *Sackett* by Louis L'Amour
P: Douglas Netter and Jim Byrnes
Cast: Sam Elliott, Tom Selleck, Jeff Osterhage, Glenn Ford, Ben Johnson, **Gilbert Roland, Ana Alicia**

This four-hour, two-part miniseries was based on a story by famed western writer Louis L'Amour about the adventures of the three Sackett brothers in the New Mexico Territory after the Civil War. Gilbert Roland plays Don Luis Alvarado, a terminally ill rancher who is anxious to preserve the lands of the New Mexico Territory from the marauding Anglos who would drive out all Spanish-speaking people from the area. His granddaughter, Drusilla Alvarado, played by Ana Alicia, falls in love with the youngest of the Sackett brothers, Tyrell (Osterhage), who is recruited to the Alvarado cause by Don Luis.

Santiago's America (1973 ABC)

D: Albert Waller
Te: Albert Waller
P: Albert Waller
Cast: Ruben Figueroa, **Alex Colon, Rene Enriquez, Miriam Colon**

This one-hour color film, a sequel to the higly successful *Santiago's Ark* (see below), was designed as a series pilot but was never picked up. It concerned the further adventures of young Santiago, who, with a New York City junk man, sets off in a battered taxicab to discover America.

Both *Santiago's Ark* and *Santiago's America* were packaged by writer/producer/ director Albert Waller based on original story ideas by Waller, who saw Santiago as "a modern-day Hispanic Huckleberry Finn." Waller went on to write, direct, and produce "La Raza," a series of three one-hour documentaries that were broadcast on television nationwide. Narrated by Ricardo Montalban, they traced the history of Mexican Americans in the United States.

Santiago's Ark (1972 ABC)

D: Albert Waller
Te: Albert Waller
P: Albert Waller
Cast: Ruben Figueroa, **Alex Colon, Rene Enriquez**

Santiago's Ark was the one-hour color dramatic film that launched the ABC Afterschool Specials, under the auspices of executive producers Michael Eisner (now the Chief Executive Officer of the Walt Disney Company) and Brandon Stoddard.

It is the story of a boy from Spanish Harlem in New York who dreams of building a boat out of scraps of lumber on the roof of his East Side tenement building. The ark becomes a symbol of the hopes and dreams of the entire neighborhood.

The film starred Ruben Figueroa, who was known for his work in the film *Popi* starring Alan Arkin, and his father was played by Rene Enriquez, who a decade later became famous as Lt. Calletano on "Hill Street Blues."

The *New York Times* listed *Santiago's Ark* as one of the 10 best TV shows of the year. It won numerous awards including the Gabriel Award, the Christopher Award, the Peabody Award, and a Golden Gate Award from the San Francisco International Film Festival.

Seguin (1982 PBS)

D: **Jesus Trevino**
Te: **Jesus Trevino**
P: **Severo Perez**
Cast: **A Martinez, Henry Darrow, Rose Portillo, Pepe Serna, Danny De La Paz, Enrique Castillo, Lupe Ontiveros, Edward James Olmos**

Seguin is the story of Juan Seguin, an unsung hero of the Texas Wars for Independence and one of the Mexican defenders of the Alamo. Don Erasmo Seguin, along with Stephen Austin, brought the first Anglo settlers to help develop the Mexican state of Texas. His son Juan came into conflict with his father because he sympathized with both Mexico and the American colonists' struggle for possession of Texas.

This sensitive film features evocative color cinematography and a good central performance by A Martinez and a cast including many of the most prominent young Hispanic American actors of their generation. Edward James Olmos plays a snarling and vicious Gen. Santa Anna.

Filmed as part of a proposed PBS series called "La Historia," which never received additional funding, *Seguin* was shown at film festivals around the United States and in Spain. It was broadcast as part of the PBS "American Playhouse" series. It was filmed in 16mm on a 21-day schedule at a cost of $500,000 in Brackettville, Texas, on the sets John Wayne had used to film *The Alamo* (1960).

Stand and Deliver
See Movie listings.

Steambath (1973 PBS)
  D: Burt Brinckerhoff
  Te: Bruce Jay Friedman, based on his play
  P: Norman Lloyd
Cast: Bill Bixby, **Jose Perez**, Valerie Perrine

A videotaped production aired on KCET's "Hollywood Television Playhouse" series, this show was controversial due to its language and partial nudity. Bruce Jay Friedman adapted his bizarre and inventive off-Broadway play about recently deceased people trapped in a steambath who discover it to be a purgatory in which the Puerto Rican steambath attendant is God.

Stones for Ibarra (1988 NBC)
  D: Jack Gold
  Te: Ernest Kinoy
  P: Bruce Pustin
Cast: Glenn Close, Keith Carradine, **Alfonso Arau, Jorge Cervera, Jr.,**
    Ron Joseph, **Lupe Ontiveros, Trinidad Silva**

This "Hallmark Hall of Fame" contemporary drama concerns an American couple who move to a small Mexican village and adapt to the different values and perceptions of life and death. The film portrays Mexicans as simple, superstitious, and emotionally volatile. Except for the two leads, nearly the entire cast is Hispanic.

The Streets of L.A. (1979 CBS)
  D: Jerrold Freedman
  Te: Marvin A. Gluck
  P: George Englund
Cast: Joanne Woodward, **Fernando Allende, Pepe Serna, Isela Vega**

A middle-class white woman (Woodward) goes off in lone pursuit of three teenage hoods in the L.A. barrio after becoming incensed by their malicious slashing of the tires of parked cars, including hers. Spanish-language film star Fernando Allende made his American television debut as the lead tough. He was joined by Mexican actress Isela Vega in a fine performance as his mother. The film shows Mexicans and Mexican Americans in the usual stereotyped urban violence image.

Sweet 15 (1990 PBS)
  D: Victoria Hochberg
  Te: Sharon Weil
  P: **Richard Soto**
Cast: Karla Montana, **Jenny Gago**, Susan Ruttan, **Tony Plana,**
    Panchito Gomez, Liz Torres

Marta, a 14-year-old Mexican American, has never taken the plight of undocumented immigrants seriously. She selfishly looks forward to her "Quinceanera" (Sweet 15) celebration. In preparation, she must perform some kind of community service, which consequently finds her working at the church's amnesty office, leading her to the shocking discovery that her own father is an illegal. Another presentation from the "WonderWorks" series, *Sweet 15* was an Emmy Award winner.

Three Hundred Miles for Stephanie (1981 NBC)

D: Clyde Ware
Te: Clyde Ware
P: Antonio Calderon
Cast: **Tony Orlando, Julie Carmen, Edward James Olmos, Pepe Serna, Gregory Sierra**

This film was based on the true story of a San Antonio, Texas, police officer (Orlando) who vowed to run more than 300 miles as a grueling act of faith for his critically ill, brain-damaged daughter. This film showed sensitivity in portraying Mexican Americans in the mainstream of society with the subtleties of their Latin backgrounds. This was Orlando's dramatic acting debut.

Victims for Victims: The Theresa Saldana Story (1984 NBC)

D: Karen Arthur
Te: Arthur Heinemann
P: Harry R. Sherman
Cast: **Theresa Saldana**, Adrian Zmed

This is a fact-based account of one woman's struggle to survive both physically and mentally after a near-fatal attack on her life by a deranged fan, who stabbed her repeatedly. Actress Theresa Saldana played herself in this TV movie. In the aftermath of her long, painful recovery, she went on to form an organization (Victims for Victims) devoted to helping victims of violent crime deal with their pain and anger.

Wanted: The Sundance Woman (1976 ABC)

D: Lee Philips
Te: Richard Fielder
P: Stan Hough
Cast: Katharine Ross, Steve Forrest, **Hector Elizondo**

After Butch Cassidy and the Sundance Kid are reportedly killed in Bolivia, Etta Place (Ross) roams around the Southwest pursued by Charlie Siringo (Forrest) and winds up in Mexico with Pancho Villa, played by Hector Elizondo.

The Young Indiana Jones Chronicles: Young Indiana Jones and the Curse of the Jackal (1992 ABC)

D: Carl Schultz
Te: Jonathan Hale
P: Rick McCallum
Cast: Sean Patrick Flanery, **Mike Moroff**, Francesco Quinn

The second half of this two-hour movie, which begins in Egypt on an archeological dig for Tutankhamen's tomb, takes 16-year-old Indiana Jones to 1916 Mexico, where he meets and joins Pancho Villa. The general and his men are on the run from Gen. John Pershing and his American troops, led by young George Patton, who is already displaying his rugged individualistic command style. This is a well-done, nicely balanced, insightful, and stereotype-free episode, with a strong performance from Moroff as Villa and featuring Quinn as one of his men. Filmed in Spain, the movie was executive produced by George Lucas, who was responsible for the theatrical *Indiana Jones* trilogy starring Harrison Ford.

ZORRO & THE CISCO KID

HISPANIC AMERICAN CINEMA HEROES

Despite overwhelmingly negative images and stereotypes, two Hispanic American heroes have managed to make it into popular American culture—Zorro and the Cisco Kid.

ZORRO

Zorro means fox in Spanish and first appeared in an original story "The Curse of Capistrano" by Johnston McCulley, published in 1919 in the pulp magazine *All Story*. Though based on California history and the romanticism surrounding the Spanish/Mexican period, Zorro is a purely fictional character whose story is the amalgam of two different historical periods (the Mission and the Rancho periods existed at their height many years apart) and facts set around the period of 1820 when California was still a borderland territorial possession of Spain.

Even though the story takes place in the pueblo of Los Angeles, McCulley used the Capistrano title for its alliteration and had only a cursory knowledge of California history. He also must have been influenced by another literary character *The Scarlet Pimpernel*, written in 1905.

Zorro and his alter ego, Don Diego de la Vega, the seemingly spoiled son of Spanish aristocrats, is one of the best-known characters of popular fiction. When confronted with injustice, Don Diego transforms himself into Zorro, a Robin Hood defender of his countrymen. Zorro identifies himself to villains with his bullwhip, black mask, cape, and his signature, using his foil to make the sign of the "Z" at the site of the deed. Zorro's popularity, fed by a continuous stream of magazine stories, books, comic books, motion pictures, and television, has remained high through the years. Zorro stories have been published in 26 languages. He is the most popular fictional character in many of the Spanish-speaking countries. During the 1960s and 1970s, a number of low-budget Zorro adventure films were made by Italian, Spanish, and Mexican production companies; most bear little resemblance to the original concept or character except for the black outfit and mask. Frank Latimore, an American-born actor, plays Zorro in several Italian movies; Sean Flynn (Errol Flynn's son, who became a war photographer in Vietnam and who is missing in action) plays Zorro in *Mark of Zorro* (1963). Gordon Scott (a former Tarzan) became Zorro in *Zorro and The Three Musketeers*, set in seventeenth-century Spain and France, where Zorro and The Three Musketeers fight the men of Cardinal Richelieu and defend Isabella, duchess of Seville. In 1990, on a nationally syndicated talk show, cartoonist Bob Kane revealed that Zorro had been the inspiration for Kane's modern-day crime-fighting hero, Batman.

ZORRO MOVIES

The movies and TV listings below appear in chronological order, tracing the development of the character's popularity.

The Mark of Zorro (1920 UA)

D: Fred Niblo
S: Elton Thomas [Douglas Fairbanks], based on the story "The Curse of Capistrano" by Johnston McCulley
P: Douglas Fairbanks
Cast: Douglas Fairbanks

Silent. Douglas Fairbanks was the first to recognize the cinematic potential in Zorro. He purchased the screen rights in 1920 and promptly made the film.

One of United Artists' (the company Fairbanks founded in 1919 with Mary Pickford, Charlie Chaplin, and D.W. Griffith) first feature films, *The Mark of Zorro*

Douglas Fairbanks in *The Mark of Zorro*.
Photo: The Museum of Modern Art/Film Stills Archive.

provided a new type of role for Fairbanks, and the overwhelming success of the movie launched him as a swashbuckling screen hero in adventure dramas until 1934, when the aging star was no longer accepted by the public in this kind of role. He was succeeded in these roles by Errol Flynn, Tyrone Power, and his son, Douglas Fairbanks, Jr.

Fairbanks brought his athletic ability to the part of Zorro and his well-known comic skill to the role of the fop Don Diego. All of the props and sets were made to glorify Fairbanks's athletic abilities. The emphasis of the film is on action: There are several exciting duel sequences and a chase in which Zorro eludes his pursuers through an amazing series of acrobatic stunts.

Many of the characters in the photoplay are stereotypes, present merely to move the action along.

Fairbanks established the classic model after which all later interpretations of Zorro were to be patterned. The film's story, too, set the style for most of the screenplays to follow.

The aristocratic Don Diego, returning from Spain, where he has been educated, is horrified at the tyranny prevailing in Spanish California. As El Zorro, Diego wages a one-man war against the villainous Captain Ramon (Robert McKim), who is in cahoots with the corrupt governor. In order to divert suspicions from himself, Diego assumes the guise of an empty-headed, handkerchief-flourishing dandy, fooling everyone including his father and lady love, Lolita. The basic plot is the same as that of any number of nineteenth-century American morality plays in which the hero saves a family from ruination and thereby wins the daughter. Both Fairbanks and his director, Fred Niblo (a former actor), came to films from the stage.

The Mark of Zorro inaugurated a series of historical costume dramas that Fairbanks would star in and produce for United Artists.

Don Q, Son of Zorro (1925 UA)

D: Donald Crisp
S: Jack Cunningham, based on "Don Q's Love Story" by Hesketh Prichard and Kate Prichard
P: Douglas Fairbanks
Cast: Douglas Fairbanks, Mary Astor, Jack MacDonald, **Enrique Acosta**

Silent. This sequel to *The Mark of Zorro* repeats the success of the original. As Valentino did in *Son of the Sheik* (1926), Fairbanks plays a dual role as the son as well as the father, who comes to the aid of his offspring in Spain. Enrique Acosta plays Ramon.

Bold Caballero (1936 Rep)

D: Wells Root
S: Wells Root
P: Nat Levine
Cast: Robert Livingston, Heather Angel, Ferdinand Munier, **Chris-Pin Martin, Carlos de Valdez**

Zorro did not appear again on screen until this 1936 Republic feature film. The star was Robert Livingston, a popular western serial star at Republic.

The story line is that Diego, incensed by the cruelty and taxation being imposed upon the Indians of Santa Cruz (the original Zorro story was based in the pueblos of Los Angeles) by the commandante of the local garrison, decides to correct the situation. When a governor appointed by the king of Spain arrives in California to take over the province, the commandante kills him and blames it on Zorro.

The Phantom of Santa Fe (1937 Burroughs-Tarzan Pictures)
D: Jacques Jaccard
S: Charles Royal
P: Ashton Dearholt
Cast: Norman Kerry, Frank Mayo

A pseudo-Zorro movie actually filmed six years previously, in 1931, as *The Hawk*.

This feature was originally put on the shelf due to technical difficulties, not the least of which was star Norman Kerry's bad speaking voice. A leading man of the silents, Kerry found his poor vocal abilities to be his downfall in the talkies.

Ashton Dearholt, a former actor turned producer and one of the partners in the Burroughs-Tarzan company, became interested in the footage in 1936 and managed to turn it into a salable property.

Reedited and with a completely dubbed voice track plus musical score, the resulting effort was titled *The Phantom of Santa Fe* and was sold as a brand new film. While not an exact imitation of *Zorro* in that the hero did not wear a mask, the screenplay did follow the classic story line laid down by McCulley. Kerry employed the lazy, sleepy fop persona as a disguise and became the mysterious Hawk to avenge the wrongs perpetrated by the villain (Mayo) and his band of renegades.

Zorro Rides Again (1937 Rep)
D: William Witney and John English
S: Barry Shipman, John Rathmell, Franklyn Adreon [alternate spelling: Franklin], Ronald Davidson, and Morgan Cox
P: Sol C. Siegel
Cast: John Carroll, **Duncan Renaldo**, Noah Beery, Dick Alexander

Republic followed *Bold Caballero* (1936) with a 12-chapter serial. These serials were 30-minute or so shorts that played in theaters to accompany the main film. Directed toward younger audiences, they were usually full of action with cliffhanger endings to keep the audience returning week after week.

Zorro Rides Again was a contemporary western in which Zorro was no longer Don Diego but was instead his great-grandson, James Vega (Carroll). The plot centers around attempts to sabotage the building of the California-Yucatan Railroad. Yakima Canutt did all the double and stunt work for Carroll.

Zorro's Fighting Legion (1939 Rep)
D: William Witney and John English
S: Ronald Davidson, Franklyn Adreon [alternate spelling: Franklin], Morgan Cox, Sol Shor, and Barney A. Sarecky
P: Hiram S. Brown, Jr.
Cast: Reed Hadley

This next 12-chapter serial was the first of the Zorro adventures to take place in Mexico rather than California. The story was also set almost 40 years after the original. In the film, the Legion is organized to combat the activities of a false Yaqui Indian idol who is stealing much-needed gold that was to be used to help Benito Juarez.

Tyrone Power in the classic
The Mark of Zorro.

The Mark of Zorro (1940 TCF)

D: Rouben Mamoulian
S: John Taintor Foote, Garrett Fort, and Bess Meredyth
P: Raymond Griffith
Cast: Tyrone Power, Basil Rathbone, Linda Darnell, Gale Sondergaard, Eugene Pallette, **Chris-Pin Martin**, **George Regas**, Frank Puglia, **Pedro De Cordoba**

In November 1940, Twentieth Century–Fox released the first official remake bearing the original title. Directed by noted stylist Rouben Mamoulian, the film stars Tyrone Power, Basil Rathbone, and Linda Darnell.

Power's performance as Zorro was thought by many critics to suffer in comparison to that of Fairbanks. A good actor, Power was not an athlete in the way Fairbanks and Flynn were; he was, however, handsome, romantic, and dashing. The new film proved successful and popular with audiences, and made Power an idol in South America. A rousing finale in the form of an action-filled duel between the unmasked Zorro (Power) and the villainous Captain Esteban (Rathbone) remains one of the memorable examples of swordplay on screen. In addition to the Hispanics in the cast list above, Fortunio Bonanova has a small role in the film.

The Mark of Zorro

Rathbone was a classically trained British actor and an accomplished fencer and athlete. He also played the villainous Sir Guy of Gisbourne in *The Adventures of Robin Hood* (1938), in which he gave another memorable screen display of swordsmanship, this time against Errol Flynn. The dueling scenes were created by Albert Cavens, who also instructed Douglas Fairbanks.

Mamoulian chose his extras as if they were playing leads. He insisted that the extras all be either Spaniards or Mexicans. When Mamoulian started drawing up plans for the film, he discovered through the studio's research department that the Los Angeles of 1820 was a hot and dusty place, a squat adobe settlement inhabited by Indians, Spaniards, and one American. Street brawls were an everyday affair, and the people mostly used hides as a medium of exchange. The director decided that such a primitive, dirty outpost would never do.

At the Fox Ranch in Agoura, California, he had a town constructed that glistened in its whiteness, pleased the eye with its greenness, and boasted a preponderance of dashing caballeros, gentlemen adventurers, and beautiful senoritas—a classic example of Hollywood never letting the facts interfere with a good story. History was followed closely, though, in re-creating the town plaza and church.

A Franciscan monk donated original music from the period to be used in the film, which was scored by Alfred Newman. Power and Darnell practiced a dance sequence for weeks. Ernesto A. Romero, former vice consul of Mexico in Los Angeles, was the technical adviser, hired at the insistence of Fox chief Darryl F. Zanuck.

Zorro's Black Whip (1944 Rep)
    D: Spencer Bennet and Wallace Grisell
    S: Basil Dickey, Jesse Duffey, Grant Nelson, and Joseph Poland
    P: Ronald Davidson
Cast: **George J. Lewis**, Linda Sterling

This 12-chapter serial utilizes the name Zorro but has no other connection to the character. A girl hero clad in a black outfit uses a whip.

Son of Zorro (1947 Rep)
    D: Spencer Bennet and Fred C. Bannon
    S: Franklyn Adreon [alternate spelling: Franklin], Basil Dickey, Jesse Duffy, and Sol Shor
    P: Ronald Davidson
Cast: George Turner, Peggy Stewart

Turner is a descendant of Zorro, assuming the name to fight injustice in the West following the Civil War.

Ghost of Zorro (1949 Rep)
    D: Fred C. Bannon
    S: Royal Cole, William Lively, and Sol Shor
    P: Franklyn Adreon [alternate spelling: Franklin]
Cast: Clayton Moore, Pamela Blake

A 12-chapter serial starring Clayton Moore, who became famous as the Lone Ranger on television a few years later. A reedited version of this serial was released in 1959.

Moore plays the grandson of the original Zorro, who fights a gang out to stop the extension of telegraph lines from St. Joseph to Twin Bluffs, California. Alex Montoya has a small role as Yellow Hawk.

off326

Don Daredevil Rides Again (1951 Rep)

D: Fred C. Bannon
S: Royal Davidson
AP: Franklyn Adreon [alternate spelling: Franklin]
Cast: Ken Curtis

In this 12-chapter serial, Ken Curtis plays the masked hero, who is dressed to utilize stock film footage from the old Zorro serials.

Curtis had a long association with director John Ford, appearing in several of his westerns; he is best known as the character of Festus on the long-running "Gunsmoke" television series in the 1960s and 1970s.

The Man with a Steel Whip (1954 Rep)

D: Franklin Adreon
S: Donald Davidson
AP: Franklin Adreon [alternate spelling: Franklyn]
Cast: Richard Simmons

Dressed in a costume identical to that worn by Zorro, Simmons was called El Latigo. Old film footage was again utilized in this last western serial to be produced by Republic.

The Sign of Zorro (1960 BV)

D: Norman Foster and Lewis R. Foster
S: Norman Foster, Lowell S. Hawley, Bob Wehling, and John Meredyth Lucas
P: Walt Disney and William H. Anderson
Cast: **Guy Williams**, Henry Calvin, Gene Sheldon, Britt Lomond, **George J. Lewis**, **Romney Brent**

Two theatrical feature films were released that drew heavily from footage from the first year of the Walt Disney "Zorro" television series. *The Sign of Zorro*, from episodes 1 through 13, was released worldwide in June 1960.

Don Diego returns home from his schooling in Spain to find injustices being inflicted on the people of the pueblo of Los Angeles. As Zorro, he fights to defeat the corrupt rule of Capt. Monastario (Lomond). Aided by his mute manservant (Sheldon) and astride his remarkable horse, Tornado, Zorro thwarts and finally defeats the evil official and his men in a series of escapades and thrilling encounters of swordplay and feats of horsemanship.

Zorro, the Avenger (1961 BV)

D: Charles Barton
S: Lowell S. Hawley and Bob Wehling
P: William H. Anderson
Cast: **Guy Williams**

Culled from the Walt Disney television series "Zorro," episodes 27 through 39, *Zorro, the Avenger* was released worldwide in April 1961. The story pits Zorro against The Eagle, portrayed by Charles Korvin. The Eagle is a Spanish renegade of the 1820s who plots to overthrow Spanish rule and turn California over to the highest bidder from overseas.

Zorro (1975)

    D: Duccio Tessari
    S: Unknown
    P: Unknown
Cast: Alain Delon, Stanley Baker

This film was never released in U.S. theaters but is shown quite often on American television, primarily because it was shot in color. Alain Delon, a leading French actor and international star, plays Zorro in a story curiously set in Latin America. This "spaghetti Zorro" from Spain is fun on its own terms.

Zorro, the Gay Blade (1981 TCF)

    D: Peter Medak
    S: Hal Dresner
    P: George Hamilton and C.O. Erickson
Cast: George Hamilton, Brenda Vaccaro, Ron Leibman

Zorro's son, Don Diego, returns to California only to find his father mysteriously dead and his onetime friend Esteban (Leibman) the ruthless new *alcalde* (mayor). The father has one last wish—that the legend of Zorro be carried on by either Don Diego or his long-lost twin brother, Ramon. Diego accepts his calling and assumes his father's trademark cape and mask.

George Hamilton stars in the swashbuckling adventure/comedy *Zorro, the Gay Blade* as the son of the legendary hero of Old California who crosses swords with the enemies of the oppressed.

All goes well for the new Zorro until he breaks his foot in a fall and is forced to retire. In his absence the peasants suffer, but just as the outlook becomes hopelessly grim, his brother Ramon shows up. In the years since, he has become a prissy aesthete, quite the stereotypical Flaming Queen. Diego tells Ramon (who has changed his name to Bunny Wigglesworth) that he must fulfill their father's wish and take over the job of Zorro, an idea which doesn't really thrill Bunny. However, he sees it as a chance to spruce up Zorro's rustic image. Dressed in mauve silk and with bullwhip, Bunny goes out into the night and fights for the people. Two women who have been vying for Zorro's attention get the two Zorros confused, with predictable humorous results.

George Hamilton plays Zorro in this spoof, which was not popular with audiences. It is debatable who overacted more, Leibman or Hamilton. Hamilton's portrayal of a "gay" (in more ways than one) caballero is sophomoric and offensive, and he was not as successful spoofing Zorro and the swashbuckling genre as he was spoofing Dracula in *Love at First Bite* (1979). *Zorro, the Gay Blade* was handsomely produced and filmed on location with Cuernavaca, Mexico, doubling for early Los Angeles, California. The cinematographer was John Alonzo. The film was affectionately dedicated to the director of the 1940 *The Mark of Zorro*, Rouben Mamoulian.

ZORRO TELEVISION SERIES

"Zorro" (1957–1959 ABC)

Cast: Guy Williams

The "Zorro" television series starring Guy Williams started on ABC in the fall of 1957 and ran for two seasons of 39 episodes each. It completed the second season with a 26.6 average Nielsen rating. It proved so popular that Walt Disney produced four one-hour specials—"Adios El Cuchillo," "Auld Acquaintances," "El Bandido," and "The Postponed Wedding"—after the series run for the Walt Disney program. A legal dispute arose when Walt Disney wanted to move the show from ABC to NBC. It was not settled until two years later, which put an end to the show.

Guy Williams, a handsome six-foot, three-inch Italian American actor from New York whose real name was Armando Catalano, scored a personal triumph with the role of Zorro. His magnetic personality, good looks, and acting and physical abilities made him an instant star. He was still closely associated with the role when he died at age 65 in 1989.

Williams was a struggling New York actor when he made a screen test at Walt Disney Studios in April 1957. A few months later he debuted on television as Zorro, the legendary masked hero of Spanish California. Henry Calvin co-starred as Sgt. Garcia, the robust, bumbling comic villain, and Gene Sheldon co-starred as Bernardo, Zorro's mute servant and sidekick. George J. Lewis played Zorro's father, Don Alejandro de la Vega, and Britt Lomond played Monastario, the arch villain governor of El Pueblo de Los Angeles. Many Hispanic actors found work on the series, and both Gilbert Roland and Cesar Romero guest starred on the show. "Zorro" as a television series went far beyond the story confines of the earlier motion pictures, though it followed the classic formula.

Tornado could not be portrayed by a single horse because no one animal could perform all the feats required of Tornado. Three horses portrayed Tornado, Zorro's talented black stallion. One reared magnificently before the cameras, another worked uninhibitedly with other horses during fight sequences, and a third was used for the long, treacherous runs over hills.

Guy Williams as the swashbuckling swordsman Zorro, in Walt Disney's *The Sign of Zorro*, a 1960 feature that drew heavily from the opening episodes of the acclaimed TV series.

Zorro became a phenomenon that was accorded one of the largest merchandising campaigns of its time. The series spawned a Zorro craze among the youth of the nation. Kids were writing Z's on their homework assignments and carrying Zorro lunchboxes to school. Toy stores were selling Zorro capes, hats, masks, and swords. Twentieth Century–Fox re-released the Tyrone Power version of *The Mark of Zorro* and Republic re-released its "Zorro" serials to cash in on the high level of interest the TV show created.

The Disney story begins with Don Diego de la Vega (Williams) en route from Spain to his home in the pueblo of Los Angeles. He learns of the unjust military dictatorship imposed on the city by the villainous Monastario (Lomond) and vows to fight his evil regime.

Posing as a foppish intellectual, Don Diego and his manservant Bernardo (Sheldon) arrive in time to witness Monastario's hatred for the de la Vega family when Monastario's men unjustly accuse a neighbor, Torres, of treason and throw him into jail. Convinced that open resistance to the tyranny would be fatal, Diego transforms himself into El Zorro, "The Fox," a black-clad, masked avenger who will fight tyranny with a flashing sword, superior horsemanship, and daring bravery. Bernardo, who is mute, pretends also to be deaf, and serves as Diego's listening post.

Don Diego is careful to keep his identity secret from his father and at the rancho constructs a secret passageway that leads from the main house to an underground cavern where he keeps his horse, Tornado, and his Zorro disguise. This cavern leads out to a brush-covered hillside cave entrance not far from the main road into and out of Los Angeles.

Norman Foster, who had directed the phenomenally successful "Davy Crockett" television films starring Fess Parker for Disney, directed the "Zorro" series. A former actor, Foster first made a name for himself directing the *Charlie Chan* and *Mr. Moto* film series for Twentieth Century–Fox. He then joined Orson Welles's Mercury Theater and co-directed and co-wrote *Journey into Fear* (1942) for RKO. He went to Mexico for several years, where he directed a number of Mexican films before returning to the States, where he directed films until assignments at Disney Studios, beginning with Davy Crockett, brought him into the forefront of television film directors. Having lived and worked in Mexico, Foster had an understanding of Latin culture and style that served the "Zorro" series well.

The main exterior "Zorro" set covered several acres of the Disney backlot in Burbank, California. It included the governor's fortress, the barracks, an inner courtyard, stables, Don Diego's hacienda, and the plaza and church. Considerable attention was given to authenticity and detail in the set design and construction to give the entire pueblo an aged and weathered adobe and wood appearance. Location scenes were shot at the Disney Ranch and at Mission San Luis Rey near Oceanside, California, where a special archway was constructed and added to the existing historical structure, which is still standing over 30 years later.

Albert Cavens, the fencing master who had coached both Douglas Fairbanks and Tyrone Power, was brought in to work with Williams, who was an accomplished fencer, as was Dave Sharpe, who had worked as a stuntman in Republic serials, to stage the exciting screen swordplay. William Lava provided the music and director Foster provided the lyrics to the "Zorro" theme song, which became a best-selling record.

"The Mark of Zorro" (1974 TCF)

    D: Don McDougall
    S: Brian Taggert
    P: Robert C. Thompson and Rodrick Paul
Cast: Frank Langella, **Ricardo Montalban, Gilbert Roland**

Frank Langella took up the Zorro mantle in an inferior Twentieth Century–Fox television film remake, which went so far as to borrow the stirring music score by Alfred Newman from the 1940 version. Ricardo Montalban played the evil Captain Esteban, and Gilbert Roland played Zorro's father.

"Zorro and Son" (1983 CBS)

    D: Various
Cast: **Henry Darrow**, Paul Regina, Bill Dana, **Gregory Sierra**

Henry Darrow of TV's "The High Chaparral" fame became the first Hispanic American or Latin to play Zorro in this short-lived comedy series produced by Walt Disney Studios. Paul Regina played the youthful son who wants to follow in his father's footsteps.

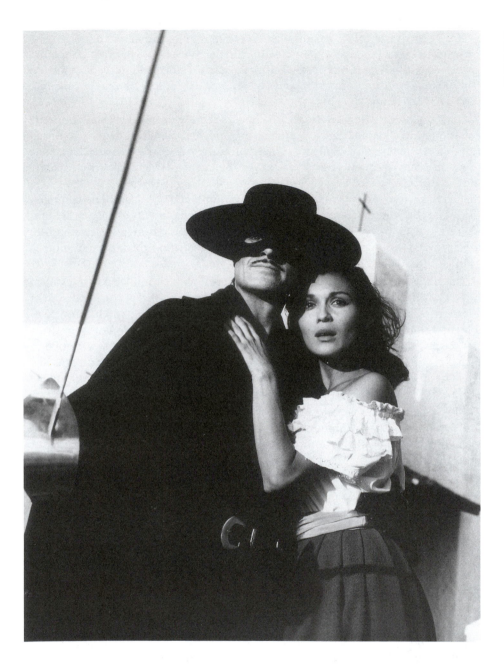

Duncan Regehr as Zorro, the swashbuckling defender of Old Spanish California, brandishes his sword to defend his beauteous senorita, Victoria Escalante (Patrice Camhi), in the TV series "Zorro."

"Zorro, the Legend Continues" (1990 New World Television)

D: Various

Cast: Duncan Regehr, **Henry Darrow, Patrice Camhi [aka: Patrice Martinez]**

In 1990, New World Television began production in Spain on 22 episodes of a "Zorro" series for international syndication. The first major "Zorro" TV series commitment in over 30 years and the first series to be filmed in color, the series brought the classic spirit of the masked crusader to a new generation. Don Diego is portrayed not as a fop and dandy but as an educated man, well versed in both the arts and sciences, who uses his knowledge to solve the problems he faces in his adventures.

The series starred Duncan Regehr (who had previously portrayed another swashbuckler, Errol Flynn, in a TV movie based on his life), whose distinctive style and personality enhanced the role. Regehr is a native of Canada and was once an Olympic boxing contender and a champion figure skater; in addition, he has classical Shakespearean stage training. Veteran stunt coordinator and fencing master Peter Diamond tutored Regehr and handled the exciting swordplay, chases on horseback, and leaps from balconies and garrison walls. Diamond, who made his name as a stunt director for British television, lists among his credits the spectacular laser light swordfights in the *Star Wars* trilogy and the more traditional swashbuckling of *The Princess Bride.*

In contrast to the Walt Disney series, the Zorro character was given a continuing love interest, Victoria Escalante (portrayed by Patrice Camhi), a beautiful senorita who is attracted to the dashing Zorro but not to Don Diego in a variation on the Lois Lane and Superman/Clark Kent affair. Also in the cast were James Victor as the bumbling Sgt. Mendoza and Efrem Zimbalist, Jr., as Zorro's father. In the second season, Zimbalist was replaced by Henry Darrow in the role of the father. Darrow, coincidentally, is the only Hispanic to date to have played Zorro (in the short-lived "Zorro and Son" series), and he also provided the voice of Zorro for a syndicated 13-episode animated series.

"Zorro, the Legend Continues" was produced over a four-year period for a total of 88 episodes, four of which were culled into a two-hour TV movie. It is shown on the cable Family Channel in the States and is in syndication throughout the world. On April 23, 1991, a story in *The Hollywood Reporter* announced that Steven Spielberg would produce and direct a big-budget screen version of *Zorro* for TriStar Pictures. At the time of the announcement, Spielberg was directing *Hook* and then went on to direct *Jurassic Park* and *Schindler's List.* As of early 1994, the project was still in development.

THE CISCO KID

O. Henry's Robin Hood of the Old West first came to life in a short story called "The Caballero's Way," originally published in the collection *Heart of the West* in 1904, and then three years later in *Everybody's* magazine.

O. Henry's character is a rather unlovable Anglo gunfighter who kills "for the love of it—because he was quick tempered, to avoid arrest, for his own amusement, any reason that came to mind would suffice." In the story, the Cisco Kid tricks a Texas Ranger into shooting the Kid's unfaithful girlfriend and then disappears into the chaparral.

No one is quite sure where O. Henry discovered the Cisco Kid. O. Henry (William Sidney Porter) had spent much of his life as a gambler, working odd jobs and wandering around New Orleans, Texas, and Central America. He began writing short stories while serving time in prison near Cisco, Texas. The character is thought to be a combination of the legend of Billy the Kid and the Mexican gunfighter Blas. The development of the Cisco Kid into the character we know today is largely the work of many different people over a 90-year period of film, comics, radio, and television.

Again, we list the screen career in chronological order.

THE CISCO KID MOVIES

The Cisco Kid (1914–1916 Eclair Films)
Cast: Herbert Stanley Dunn

Silent. When the Cisco Kid was first brought to the screen, the O. Henry image remained intact. Eclair Films, a French company, produced numerous one-reelers during the silent era portraying a bittersweet individual who was neither all bad nor all good. Stan Dunn was the first actor to play the Cisco Kid.

Herbert Stanley Dunn, the original Cisco Kid, subdues his adversaries in this scene from *The Caballero's Way,* the first Cisco Kid movie, filmed in 1914 by Eclair Film Co., in Tucson, Arizona. It has been claimed that Dunn was the first Western film star to feature two six-guns, which is evidenced in this picture. The heavy leather gloves were cumbersome and Dunn couldn't fire the trigger until he cut a hole for his index finger. The tight leather costume was ordered from El Paso, Texas. Dunn once remarked that it was so tight "I had to get into it with a shoehorn."

(Courtesy Gene Autry Western Heritage Museum)

In Old Arizona (1929 Fox)

D: **Raoul Walsh** and Irving Cummings
S: Tom Barry, based on O. Henry's short story
P: William Fox
Cast: Warner Baxter, Edmund Lowe, Dorothy Burgess

A landmark 1929 film, filmed near Zion National Park in Utah, this was the first outdoor talkie western. As such, it made an impact on the public, as did Warner Baxter's Academy Award–winning performance as the Cisco Kid.

Baxter and director Raoul Walsh took liberties with O. Henry's character, in particular removing much of the viciousness from O. Henry's original character. Baxter immersed himself in Latin culture. (This was the era of Latin leading actors in Hollywood.)

Walsh, a former cowboy, had wanted to play the role himself, but he lost an eye in an accident on location when a jackrabbit jumped through the windshield of his car and shattered the glass. During Walsh's absence from the film, Irving Cummings took over as director and Warner Baxter was signed to play the Cisco Kid. Duncan Renaldo, a later Cisco, was also considered for the role, but he was in Africa filming *Trader Horn* (1931).

A great deal of the early footage was still usable, and Walsh returned in time to complete the picture. Microphones were concealed under prairie shrub, hung from the foliage, and hidden behind rocks. The sounds of bacon sizzling, six-guns shooting, horses' hooves, and cowboy ballads made the difference for audiences.

The time of the film is the late 1890s, and the beautiful half-breed girl Tonia Maria (Burgess), a temperamental flirt, lives in a little adobe house in a Mexican settlement near Wolf Crossing, a town close to the Grand Canyon. She is adored by the notorious Cisco Kid (Baxter), a charming, daring, and often eccentric bandit. He is a murderer but also a lover, and he has a $5,000 price on his head. The Cisco Kid has such a reputation that, in order to obtain a Wells Fargo strongbox, he merely fires two warning shots and the stagecoach drivers readily hand it over.

Sergeant Mickey Dunn (Lowe), an Irishman from Brooklyn who is attached to the 17th Cavalry, is dispatched to capture the Cisco Kid. Dunn is no less a ladies' man than the Kid, and he romances Tonia Maria, offering her a cash reward for her betrayal of the Kid, then waiting in her home to take in the outlaw.

The Cisco Kid, meanwhile, has been involved with cattle rustlers in Guadalupe. When he returns to Wolf Crossing, he finds Tonia Maria in the arms of Dunn. The Kid then sings a song, which begins: "Don't you monkey with my lulu girl, or I'll tell you what I'll do."

Warner Baxter as the Cisco Kid, Dorothy Burgess, and Edmund Lowe in *In Old Arizona*.

He overhears the two plotting to kill him and determines to settle matters with his faithless lover and the man who stole her from him. Tonia Maria sends Dunn a note asking him to go back to her shack; the Kid gets hold of it and forges an addition to it, saying that the outlaw will be there dressed as a woman. Dunn arrives and accidentally kills Tonia Maria. The Kid then escapes.

Unlike most cinematic lawbreakers, he is neither caught nor killed at the finale. It is generally thought that Warner Baxter made five Cisco Kid films, though, in fact, he made only four theatrical features and a short subject in which he appeared as the character of Cisco. *Romance of the Rio Grande* (1929 Fox) is mistakenly listed as a Cisco Kid film and appears in many books and film listings as such because Baxter played a Latin character and it was made during the same period as the other films. It was directed by Alfred Santell, who directed the Baxter Cisco feature *The Arizona Kid* (1930). *Romance of the Rio Grande* was also used as the title of a Cesar Romero Cisco film in 1941, so many film historians supposed that it was a remake of the 1929 film.

Baxter recalled in a 1948 *Saturday Evening Post* article, "I must admit that I rate the Kid's first film, *In Old Arizona*, as my top favorite. I like the role because of its warmth and color. I enjoyed trying out the lingo of a Mexican and I thought the mixture of comedy and drama in the story was fine. . . . Then, too, the fact that I got an Oscar for the job caused me no pain."

Soledad Jimenez plays the cook.

The Arizona Kid (1930 Fox)
D: Alfred Santell
S: Ralph Block
Cast: Warner Baxter, **Mona Maris**, Carole Lombard

The Cisco Kid has a secret gold mine in Utah that is his main source of revenue. Nick Hoyt (Theodore Von Eltz) robs the gold mine and attempts to turn the Kid in to the local sheriff.

Cisco Kid (1931 Fox)
D: Irving Cummings
S: Alfred Cohn, based on a story by O. Henry
Cast: Warner Baxter, Edmund Lowe, **Conchita Montenegro**, Nora Lane

The Cisco Kid robs a bank to save a widow's ranch, which sends Sgt. Mickey Dunn (Lowe) in pursuit. This film reunited Baxter and Lowe in a rather poor sequel of sorts to *In Old Arizona* (1929).

The Stolen Jools (1931 Fox)
D: Victor Heerman, William McGann, and others
S: Unknown
P: National Variety Artists
Cast: Warner Baxter, Edmund Lowe, Richard Barthelmess, Wallace Beery, Gary Cooper, Fay Wray, Joan Crawford

Warner Baxter appeared as the Cisco Kid and Edmund Lowe was Sgt. Dunn in this two-reeler short subject, which was produced for the National Vaudeville Association's benevolent fund. Fifty-five major stars of the era, representing every film studio, made cameo appearances.

The film is an amusing piece in which actress Norma Shearer's jewels are supposed to have been stolen and a police inspector in various disguises visits the different screen players, who are supposed to have been at a dance where the jewels were last seen.

The Cisco Kid and the Lady (1939 TCF)

  D: Herbert I. Leeds
  S: Frances Hyland
  P: John Stone
Cast: **Cesar Romero**, Marjorie Weaver, **Chris-Pin Martin**

This is Cesar Romero's first film as the Cisco Kid with Chris-Pin Martin as his side-kick, Gordito. Cisco battles bandits out to steal a gold mine owned by an orphan whose father has been shot by the bandit leader.

When Romero, a Twentieth Century–Fox contract player, replaced Warner Baxter in the role, the Cisco Kid became decidedly more Latin. A Cuban American with a Broadway stage background, Romero added his own debonair flavor to the role.

The State Department asked Darryl F. Zanuck, the head of Twentieth Century–Fox, to either change the format or stop production on the pictures because some Latin countries were having problems with the "greaser" portrayal of Gordito by Chris-Pin Martin. Zanuck decided to abandon the films (which were shot near Lone Pine, California) and sold the rights to Monogram Studios.

Cesar Romero as the Cisco Kid in the Twentieth Century–Fox film series.

The Return of the Cisco Kid (1939 TCF)

D: Herbert I. Leeds
S: Milton Sperling
P: Kenneth MacGowan
Cast: Warner Baxter, Lynn Bari, **Cesar Romero, Chris-Pin Martin**

The Cisco Kid (Baxter) helps a young woman hold onto her ranch in this, the final film in which Baxter would reprise the role. The next actor to play Cisco, Cesar Romero, has a supporting role in this film as Lopez.

The Gay Caballero (1940 TCF)

D: Otto Brower
S: Albert Duffy and John Larkin, based on a story by Walter Bullock, Duffy, and characters created by O. Henry
P: Walter Morosco and Ralph Dietrich
Cast: **Cesar Romero, Chris-Pin Martin**

Cisco seeks to clear himself after a series of crimes have been committed using his name.

Lucky Cisco Kid (1940 TCF)

D: H. Bruce Humberstone
S: Robert Ellis and Helen Logan, based on a story by Julian Johnson
P: Sol M. Wurtzel
Cast: **Cesar Romero, Chris-Pin Martin**

The Cisco Kid fights a gang of crooks led by a dishonest judge.

Viva Cisco Kid (1940 TCF)

D: Norman Foster
S: Samuel G. Engel and Hal Long
P: Sol M. Wurtzel
Cast: **Cesar Romero**, Jean Rogers, **Chris-Pin Martin**

The Cisco Kid rescues a stagecoach from a robbery attempt and falls for one of the lovely passengers, whose father is involved in crimes with a vicious partner.

Ride On, Vaquero (1941 TCF)

D: Herbert I. Leeds
S: Samuel G. Engel
P: Sol M. Wurtzel
Cast: **Cesar Romero**, Mary Beth Hughes, **Chris-Pin Martin**

The Cisco Kid works with the law in order to trap a gang of kidnappers.

Romance of the Rio Grande (1941 TCF)

D: Herbert I. Leeds
S: Harold Buchman and Samuel G. Engel, based on the novel *Conquistador* by Katherine Fullerton Gerould
P: Sol M. Wurtzel
Cast: **Cesar Romero**, Patricia Morison, **Ricardo Cortez, Chris-Pin Martin, Pedro De Cordoba**, Inez Palange

An aging cattle baron sends for his grandson to help him with the ranch. The grandson is shot en route, and the Cisco Kid takes his place so he can discover who did it.

The Cisco Kid Returns (1945 Mon)

D: John P. McCarthy
S: Betty Burbridge
P: Philip N. Krasne
Cast: **Duncan Renaldo, Martin Garralaga**

The Cisco Kid finds himself a guardian to a four-year-old girl whose father has been shot to death.

While the Cisco Kid film rights were changing hands from Fox to Monogram, there was a rising consciousness in Latin America over the portrayal of Latins in Hollywood films. The Cisco Kid films were not offenders in this regard (having made Cisco a hero and using many Latin supporting actors in the features), but the new producer and star, Duncan Renaldo, wanted to make sure that his portrayal was fair and acceptable, avoiding the offensive elements in the Romero Cisco film series.

After many meetings and discussions in Washington, D.C., Mexico City, and Hollywood, Renaldo hit upon the idea of adapting O. Henry's original character by basing him more on Cervantes's classic Spanish hero Don Quixote. He therefore created the character of Pancho from Sancho Panza, and the Mexican opera singer Martin Garralaga was chosen for this supporting role. Their first three films were immensely successful in the States and Latin America, and were shot with the kind of speed we associate with TV shows today.

In Old New Mexico (1945 Mon)

D: Phil Rosen
S: Betty Burbridge
P: Philip N. Krasne
Cast: **Duncan Renaldo, Martin Garralaga, Pedro De Cordoba**

The Cisco Kid comes to the aid of a pretty young nurse who has been falsely accused of murder.

South of the Rio Grande (1945 Mon)

D: Lambert Hillyer
S: Victor Hammond and Ralph Bettinson
P: Philip N. Krasne
Cast: **Duncan Renaldo, Martin Garralaga, George J. Lewis, Armida,** Lillian Molieri, **Pedro Regas, Soledad Jimenez,** Tito Renaldo

The Cisco Kid goes after a dishonest Mexican official.

Beauty and the Bandit (1946 Mon)

D: William Nigh
S: Charles S. Belden
P: Scott R. Dunlap
Cast: **Gilbert Roland, Martin Garralaga, Ramsay Ames, Felipe Turich, Alex Montoya,** Frank Yaconelli

The Cisco Kid meets a female bandit (Ames) and brings out the best in her.

The Gay Cavalier (1946 Mon)

D: William Nigh
S: Charles S. Belden
P: Scott R. Dunlap
Cast: **Gilbert Roland, Martin Garralaga**

The Cisco Kid has two prime goals: to rescue a maiden who is about to marry a supposedly wealthy suitor in order to save the family hacienda, and to capture the outlaws who held up a stagecoach bearing gold for a mission.

Gilbert Roland took over the role temporarily when Duncan Renaldo went back to work in the war effort, which was just winding down. Roland, a Mexican American who was raised in El Paso, Texas, had his own ideas about the character of the Cisco Kid and freely incorporated them in his portrayal. Over the course of the next few films, he downplayed Pancho. Martin Garralaga soon left the role after the first picture with Roland, because of an allergy to horses. But Garralaga managed to stay in the series, usually playing an assortment of Spanish aristocrats usually in interior scenes away from horses. Then Frank Yaconelli replaced him as a Pancho-like character called Baby, followed by the return of Chris-Pin Martin as Pancho.

There was no Pancho in the original O. Henry short story; Cisco was alone. Drawing upon the standard Hollywood convention that every Western hero needed a sidekick, a saddle partner named "Gordito" was introduced in the prior Cesar Romero series.

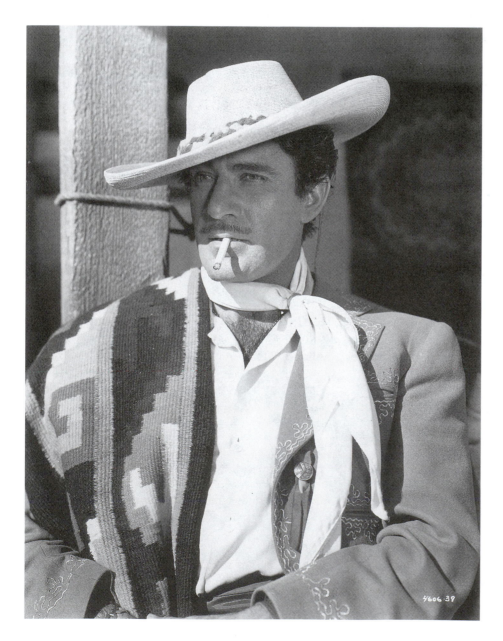

Gilbert Roland as the Cisco Kid.

Roland's interpretation also heightened the Robin Hood aspect and made his Cisco cocksure with the ladies.

Gilbert Roland said, "My Cisco Kid may have been a bandit, but he fought for the poor and was a civilized man in the true sense of the word." He also described an instance on the set: "Once I insisted on a piece of dialogue which as a result showed Cisco reading Shakespeare by a river bank. I wanted to be sure the Mexicano was not portrayed as an unwashed, uneducated, savage clown."

Riding the California Trail (1947 Mon)
D: William Nigh
S: Clarence Upton Young
P: Scott R. Dunlap
Cast: **Gilbert Roland, Martin Garralaga**, Inez Cooper, **Alex Montoya, Rosa Turich**, Gerald Echeverria, Frank Yaconelli

The Cisco Kid aids a young woman who is tricked out of an inheritance by a scheming uncle.

Robin Hood of Monterey (1947 Mon)
D: Christy Cabanne
S: Bennett Cohen
P: Jeffrey Bernerd
Cast: **Gilbert Roland, Chris-Pin Martin, Pedro De Cordoba, Nestor Paiva, Julian Rivero**

The Cisco Kid steps in when a woman kills her husband and frames her stepson for the crime.

South of Monterey (1947 Mon)
D: William Nigh
S: Charles S. Belden
P: Scott R. Dunlap
Cast: **Gilbert Roland, Martin Garralaga**, Frank Yaconelli

The Cisco Kid sets out to stop a land-swindling scheme involving a police captain and a tax collector in a small western town.

King of the Bandits (1948 Mon)
D: Christy Cabanne
S: Bennett R. Cohen, based on an original story by Cabanne. Additional dialogue by Gilbert Roland
P: Jeffrey Bernerd
Cast: **Gilbert Roland, Chris-Pin Martin**

The Cisco Kid pursues a stagecoach robber who has been impersonating him.

The Valiant Hombre (1948 UA)
D: Wallace Fox
S: Adele Buffington
AP: **Duncan Renaldo**
P: Philip N. Krasne
Cast: **Duncan Renaldo, Leo Carrillo**

When John James, who has just discovered gold, disappears and his partners are murdered, Cisco and Pancho set out to right things.

Barbara Billingsley, who plays the damsel in distress, went on to find success as June Cleaver, mother of the Beaver, on the "Leave It to Beaver" television series in the late 1950s and the early 1960s.

In 1948, Duncan Renaldo returned to the role and, in a brief period of time, became the most famous Cisco Kid of them all. With his friend Leo Carrillo as Pancho, he did five feature films between 1948 and 1950 for United Artists and producer Philip Krasne. Renaldo took an active part as associate producer and in the further development of the character.

The Cisco Kid changed dramatically when Renaldo returned to the role. "I came up with the idea of making Cisco a Don Quixote, only more reasonable and fighting the windmills of the troubles of humanity: also making Pancho a real compassionate, kind-hearted human being who thus inadvertently gets his partner into trouble," remarked Renaldo during an interview with Luis Reyes in 1979.

Cisco's costume changed, and Renaldo lost the mustache. The new costume reflected something from several Latin countries in style and dress. Cisco's hat is from early California, the boots and belt are from the Argentinian gaucho, and the shirt is from Mexico with a French-influenced fleur-de-lis design. Diablo was the name of the Cisco Kid's horse.

Garralaga did not return to the role of Pancho. Veteran character actor Leo Carrillo better complemented Renaldo as Pancho, in that he was not merely a sidekick but was a strong personality himself. Renaldo claims to have cautioned Carrillo about his comedic overplaying of Pancho with the accent, but Carrillo just went with the characterization, and children loved it.

The Daring Caballero (1949 UA)
   D: Wallace Fox
   S: Betty Burbridge
   P: Philip N. Krasne
Cast: **Duncan Renaldo, Leo Carrillo**, Kipper Valez, **Pedro De Cordoba**

Cisco and Pancho's task is to clear the name of the father of a little boy who is wrongly accused of murder and embezzlement and who is being hidden by a mission padre.

The Gay Amigo (1949 UA)
   D: Wallace Fox
   S: Doris Schroeder
   P: Philip N. Krasne
Cast: **Duncan Renaldo, Leo Carrillo, Armida**

A series of stagecoach holdups, ranch raids, and murders are terrorizing a western community. Cisco and Pancho are suspected of the banditry by the commander of an Army post, and they go about clearing their names by capturing the real outlaws.

Satan's Cradle (1949 UA)
   D: Ford Beebe
   S: Jack Benton
   P: Philip N. Krasne
Cast: **Duncan Renaldo, Leo Carrillo**

Cisco and Pancho come to the defense of a preacher who was roughed up by a gang of crooks running the town.

The Girl from San Lorenzo (1950 UA)

    D: Derwin Abrahams
    S: Ford Beebe
    P: Philip N. Krasne
 Cast: **Duncan Renaldo, Leo Carrillo**

Cisco and Pancho are accused of various crimes which are being committed by a duo impersonating them.

The Cisco Kid (1994 TNT)

    D: **Luis Valdez**
   Te: Michael Kane and **Luis Valdez**
    P: Moctezuma Esparza and Robert Katz
 Cast: **Jimmy Smits, Cheech Marin,** Sadie Frost, Bruce Payne, Ron Perlman, Tim Thomerson, **Pedro Armendariz, Jr.,** Yareli Arizmendi

A reinterpretation of the classic Hollywood film hero, filmed on actual locations in Mexico, starring Jimmy Smits ("L.A. Law") as Cisco and Cheech Marin (*Born in East L.A.*) as Pancho. Directed and co-scripted by Luis Valdez (*La Bamba, Zoot Suit*),

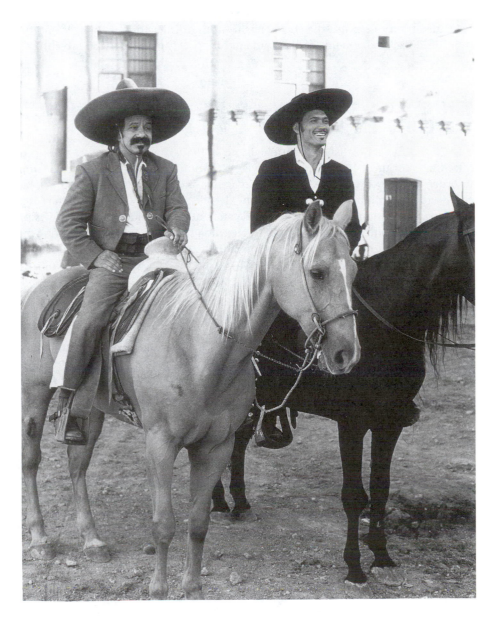

Cheech Marin as Pancho and Jimmy Smits as the Cisco Kid in the 1994 TNT production.

the story takes place during the French occupation of Mexico in 1867. Cisco smuggles guns across the border to help the Juaristas and finds a cause and a friend to believe in.

The Cisco Kid is a tongue-in-cheek action/western filled with fast gunplay, narrow escapes, wild rides, battling armies, and romance. It is also a funny and off-beat character study of the beginnings of a remarkable friendship that develops between Cisco and Pancho in this two-hour TV film, the first Cisco Kid film to be produced in 38 years.

In this version Cisco is a Californian, born in Los Angeles in 1836 when it was still a part of Mexico. He lives through California statehood in 1850 and all the dramatic, sweeping changes that occurred.

Cisco is a man in search of his own identity. Pancho is a Juarista and a family man whose cause is to free Mexico from the French. Cisco and Pancho are equal partners in this adventure, unlike the way they have been portrayed previously. Although Pancho acts as a catalyst for Cisco's involvement, he is still funny; the humor comes out of the situation.

Director Luis Valdez remarked in an interview with Luis Reyes, "I wanted to get away from the bandido stereotype, so I made Cisco independently wealthy like Batman so he could be free to roam the western landscape in search of his own identity and help fight injustice wherever he encountered it." The director added, "I've also tried to ground the characters in a historical setting without losing the fun, romance, and appeal of what audiences expect from a Cisco Kid adventure."

THE CISCO KID TELEVISION SERIES

The Cisco Kid was transferred to television in 1950, and 156 episodes were produced in color until 1955. The shows were shown in black and white at that time in order to save costs, since color broadcasting and color televisions did not become widely available until the end of the decade. Seemingly overnight, the Cisco Kid became a major pop figure alongside such other popular film and television heroes as the Lone Ranger, Roy Rogers, Hopalong Cassidy, and Gene Autry, who also made the jump to television in its formative years.

Renaldo and Carrillo made over 100 personal appearances a year at rodeos, county fairs, hospitals, and market openings. While the television program was being shown around the world, a radio program was running weekly. A series of Dell comics appeared; a superbly drawn comic strip by Jose Luis Salinas was widely featured in the daily newspapers. Children carried Cisco Kid lunchboxes and coloring books to school and wore Cisco Kid gun belts. Renaldo, who felt that television played an important role in forming character, was an early opponent of unnecessary violence on television, and campaigned against it. Renaldo's popularity was such that he still toured actively until 1965, ten years after the last television episode was filmed.

Set in the Old West, the Cisco Kid represents the epic qualities of the classic hero combined with Latin gentility. Duncan Renaldo, an orphan who had no country but his adopted one, saw Cisco as a modern knight, "a man of generosity and a friend to a better world." Gilbert Roland's Cisco was a "friend to the poor" and a dashing lover, while Warner Baxter and Cesar Romero gave him his devil-may-care attitude and his debonair suavity.

The television show has never really gone away. Through cable channels and videos, the Cisco Kid is still breaking senoritas' hearts, fighting injustice, laughing in the face of danger, and riding off into endless sunsets.

In the late 1970s, MGM announced a new Cisco Kid feature film to star then-popular television actor Erik Estrada, but the film was never produced.

Duncan Renaldo as the Cisco Kid and
Leo Carrillo as his sidekick Pancho
in the TV series "The Cisco Kid."

BIOGRAPHIES

The following is a listing of Hispanic American actors, actresses, and behind-the-camera personnel. Biographies are also included for a number of non-Hispanic individuals who are nevertheless identified in the public mind as Hispanic, on the basis of the roles they played or their Hispanic-sounding names. Also included, following the main biographical section, are additional profiles of selected non-Hispanic filmmakers who have contributed substantially to shaping the cinematic image of Hispanic Americans through the classic films they made. Birth and death dates are given when available, followed by a brief biography and, in some cases, selected film and television credits. Information has been difficult to obtain on less prominent artists. If there are no birth and death dates, it is because they were not available despite research in the *Motion Picture and Television Almanacs*, the *Daily Variety* obituaries, *Theater Worlds*, *Screen Worlds*, several screen *Who's Who*'s, newspaper and magazine articles, and studio biographies or through personal interviews with the subjects whenever possible. The Screen Actors Guild, agents, and personal managers were also contacted for information on their clients' histories but were forthcoming with only limited information for a number of reasons.

Enrique Acosta

B: 1870
D: 5/1948

This actor was born in Mexico City but left Mexico for the United States at the time of the revolution. He drifted to Los Angeles and found work as a bit player in Hollywood silent films such as *Don Q, Son of Zorro* (1925).

With the advent of talking pictures he began getting work in Spanish-language versions of Hollywood films as well as in original Hollywood Spanish-language productions of the early 1930s. With Laurel and Hardy, Acosta's credits include *Ladrones (Night Owls)* (1929), *Tiembla y Titubea (Below Zero)* (1930), *De Bote en Bote (Pardon Us)* (1931), *Politiquerias (Chickens Come Home)* (1931).

Rodolfo Acosta [alternate spellings: Rodolpho, Rudolpho, Rodolfa]

B: 7/29/1921
D: 11/7/1974

Acosta was a character actor with Mexican Indian features, a burly frame, and lightning quick changes of expression that usually condemned him almost exclusively to playing bandidos and Indians in American western dramas. He was born near El Paso, Texas, in the then U.S. community of Chamizac, midway between El Paso and Juarez, Mexico, which has since been ceded back to Mexico. When he

347

was three years old, his family moved to California, where he attended Los Angeles City College and UCLA. He was fascinated by acting, studying it at school as well as at the Pasadena Playhouse. His success in dramatic studies reached a peak at age 19 when he accepted a prize scholarship from the Palacio de Bellas Artes in Mexico City, where he stayed for three years. When World War II came, Acosta joined the U.S. Navy, where he was assigned to Naval Intelligence. Following the war, director John Ford saw him in a stage production and offered him a featured role in *The Fugitive* (1947). Following this, in 1948, the famous Mexican actor/director Emilio Fernandez wrote for him the role of Paco, a gigolo, in the Mexican film classic *Salón México* (1948). The part won Acosta Mexico's highest acting award, the Ariel. He was immediately signed by Hugo Fregonese to co-star with James Mason in the 1950 production *One Way Street,* which led to a Universal contract. He acted with a gallery of top box-office stars, including John Wayne, Robert Mitchum, Marlon Brando, and Dean Martin and appeared on many western television series, including "Have Gun Will Travel," "The Big Valley," and "The High Chaparral." Other credits include *Pancho Villa Returns* (1950), *Hondo* (1953), *Wings of the Hawk* (1953), *A Life in the Balance* (1955), *The Littlest Outlaw* (1955), *Bandido* (1956),*The Proud Ones* (1956), *The Tijuana Story* (1957), *One-Eyed Jacks* (1961), *How the West Was Won* (1962), *The Sons of Katie Elder* (1965), *Return of the Seven* (1966), and *Pat Garrett and Billy the Kid* (1973).

Tony Aguilar
B: 6/13/1922

A popular *charro* (Mexican cowboy) singing film star, Aguilar's only Hollywood film appearance was as the Juarista general Rojas in *The Undefeated* (1969), starring John Wayne.

Edward Albert
B: 2/20/1951

The son of Margo and Eddie Albert, Edward Albert made his motion picture debut in *Butterflies Are Free* (1972). He has also made numerous television guest star appearances (notably a recurring role in "Beauty and the Beast") and has starred in several movies.

Felix Enriquez Alcala

A director of photography, Alcala has worked on such recent, critically acclaimed television drama series as "I'll Fly Away" (1993), "Going to Extremes" (1992), "Homefront" (1992), and "Equal Justice" (1992). He has also directed episodes of "I'll Fly Away," "Homefront," and "South Beach."

Norma Aleandro
B: 1941

An Argentine actress, Aleandro won critical plaudits, including a New York Film Critics Award for Best Actress, for her role in the Argentinian film *The Official Story,* which won the Best Foreign Language Film Oscar in 1985. She played a Mexican Indian maid in *Gaby—A True Story* (1987), for which she was nominated for an Academy Award for Best Supporting Actress. She co-starred as Edie Costello in *Cousins* (1989) and in *Vital Signs* (1990).

Norma Aleandro as Edie Costello in the romantic comedy *Cousins*.

Ana Alicia

B: 1957

Born in Mexico City, Alicia attended high school in El Paso, Texas, and graduated with a degree in drama from the University of Texas. She moved to New York and landed a role on a soap opera and then went to Los Angeles, where she was signed as a contract player for Universal Television, appearing on many shows. In 1980 she landed the role of Melissa Cumson, starring with, among others, Jane Wyman and Lorenzo Lamas on the hit television series "Falcon Crest." Her only feature film appearance to date is in the 1989 film *Romero* opposite Raul Julia, in which she played the wife of an aristocrat.

Fernando Allende

B: 11/10/1954

A Cuban-born, Mexican-raised leading man, Allende had a strong run of success-ful films in Mexico in the late 1970s and 1980s. He made an unsuccessful bid for stardom in the States in the independent feature film *Heartbreaker* (1983), after having played opposite Joanne Woodward as a young gang tough in the television film *The Streets of L.A.* (1979). He has continued to work, guest starring in U.S. television and international productions.

Laurindo Almeida

B: 1917

A Brazilian-born master guitarist and composer, Almeida immigrated to the United States in 1947 after achieving tremendous success in his native country. With a recording career of 50 years, 5 Grammy Awards, 16 Grammy nominations, and several hundred films on his resumé, Almeida has contributed to the scores of many motion pictures, including *A Song Is Born* (1948), *The Old Man and the Sea* (1958), *Camelot* (1967), *The Adventurers* (1970), and the 1992 Academy Award–winning Best Picture, *Unforgiven,* in which his solo guitar work is prominently featured.

Nestor Almendros

B: 10/30/1930
D: 3/4/1992

A Spanish-born, Cuban-raised cinematographer, Almendros won an Academy Award for Best Cinematography for *Days of Heaven* (1978). He was nominated four more times for Best Cinematography, for the films *Kramer vs. Kramer* (1979), *The Blue Lagoon* (1980), *Sophie's Choice* (1982), and *Places in the Heart* (1984). *Madame Rosa* (1977), for which he was the director of photography, won the Academy Award as Best Foreign Language Film. Almendros was director of photography on eight films for French director François Truffaut. His other films include *Goin' South* (1978), *Nadine* (1987), and *Billy Bathgate* (1991). He died of lymphoma in 1992.

Chelo Alonso

B: 1938

A Cuban-born actress, Alonso went to Italy and starred in a number of Italian sand-and-spear spectacles of the 1960s that were dubbed into English and released in the States. Her credits include *Goliath and the Barbarians* (1960) opposite Steve Reeves, *Sign of the Gladiators* (1960), and a small part in Sergio Leone's "spaghetti western" *The Good, the Bad, and the Ugly* (1967).

Maria Conchita Alonso

B: 5/13/1957

The strikingly beautiful Alonso made a memorable film debut as the Italian immigrant salesgirl who gives sanctuary to a Russian defector (played by Robin Williams) and then becomes his lover in Paul Mazursky's *Moscow on the Hudson* (1984). She has since appeared in *Touch and Go* (1986), in which she played the mother of an 11-year-old who involves her with a hockey player; *A Fine Mess* (1986), as the Chilean wife of a gangster; and the sci-fi Arnold Schwarzenegger thriller *The Running Man* (1987), as a girl on the run with him. She plays a Mexican cantina singer in *Extreme Prejudice* (1987), a Chicana in *Colors* (1988), and a Latina cop in *Predator 2* (1990). Alonso has the distinction of having worked opposite some of the most important contemporary stars, including Robin Williams, Robert Duvall, Sean Penn, Michael Keaton, Danny Glover, Gary Busey, and Arnold Schwarzenegger.

Born in Havana shortly before Castro came to power, Alonso immigrated with her family to Venezuela at age five and settled in the capital city of Caracas. At age 15, she won the title of Miss Teenager of the World; she was later crowned Miss Venezuela and began a modeling career that led to television commercials, frequent appearances on variety shows, a two-year stint as the star of a soap opera, and a singing career that produced several albums.

Although successful in South America, Alonso was not fully satisfied in her career. She was fascinated with the idea of returning to the States (she had spent a year at a Catholic high school in Spokane, Washington, years earlier), even though it would mean starting all over again. In 1982 she settled in Miami and later moved to New York City. By the end of her first year there, after enduring a seemingly endless string of auditions, she began landing the small television roles that led to her cinematic bow in *Moscow on the Hudson*. Other films to her credit include *Vampire's Kiss* (1989) and *McBain* (1991).

John Alonzo

B: 1/3/1934

Cinematographer Alonzo was nominated for an Academy Award for his work on *Chinatown* (1974). He began his career as an actor in *The Magnificent Seven* (1960), in which he plays one of Calvera's bandidos.

Alonzo was born to Mexican parents in Dallas, Texas. He worked as a cameraman at a local television station before moving to Los Angeles in 1957. There he found work doing bit parts in movies and TV, usually as a Mexican bandido. Alonzo worked with some of the great old cameramen, including Joe MacDonald, who shot *Invitation to a Gunfighter* (1964), in which Alonzo worked as an actor. It was McDonald who encouraged the young Alonzo to pursue a career as a cinematographer. Alonzo shot a few short subjects and documentaries, but his big break came when he assisted cameraman James Wong Howe and director John Frankenheimer on the film *Seconds* (1966). Impressed with his work, Howe and Frankenheimer made it possible for Alonzo to join the cameramen's union. Frankenheimer later hired Alonzo to be his cameraman on *Black Sunday* (1977). His other films include *Harold and Maude* (1971), *Lady Sings the Blues* (1972), *Sounder* (1972), *Norma Rae* (1979), *Blue Thunder* (1983), *Scarface* (1983), *Runaway Train* (1985), and *Steel Magnolias* (1989).

Carlos Alvarado [born: Carlos Page]

B: 6/22/1901
D: 6/22/1983

The brother of actor Don Alvarado, Carlos became a noted agent of Latino talent in Hollywood, founding his own agency in 1943. He was born and raised in New Mexico under his real name of Page.

Don Alvarado [born: Don Page]

B: 1905
D: 1967

A native of Albuquerque, New Mexico, Alvarado came to Hollywood as a youngster. He began his career as an extra in 1924 and became a leading man in the early 1930s, appearing in such films as *The Loves of Carmen* (1927) with Dolores Del Rio, *Breakfast at Sunrise* (1927) with Constance Talmadge, *The Bridge of San Luis Rey* (1929), *Captain Thunder* (1931), and *Black Beauty* (1933). He changed his name to Alvarado (taken from a street in Los Angeles) when Latin leading men were in vogue.

He survived the transition from silent to sound movies, but his career never gained momentum. Alvarado appeared as a gigolo opposite Katharine Hepburn

Don Alvarado.

in *Morning Glory* (1933) and had a role in *La Cucaracha* (1934), the first Technicolor short subject. In the 1940s he appeared in films intermittently and became an assistant director at Warner Bros., managing a ranch for the Warner family under his real name.

His credits as an assistant director under the name Don Page include *Rebel Without a Cause* (1955), *The Old Man and the Sea* (1958), and *Auntie Mame* (1958). His ex-wife, Ann Page, later married studio chief Jack L. Warner. With Ann, Alvarado had a daughter, Joy, who also became an actress. Alvarado's brother, Carlos, became the first Hispanic talent agent in Hollywood to handle Hispanic talent exclusively.

Fernando Alvarado

A Mexican American child actor, Alvarado appeared in a number of films during the mid-1940s in a variety of ethnic roles. His credits include *A Medal for Benny* (1945), *Without Reservations* (1946), *Tycoon* (1947), and *Wake of the Red Witch* (1948).

Magali Alvarado

Born in Puerto Rico and raised in New Jersey, Alvarado made her motion picture debut in *Salsa* (1988), followed by Allison Anders's *Mi Vida Loca* (1994).

Trini Alvarado

B: 1967

Alvarado co-starred with Bette Midler and John Goodman in *Stella* (1989) and co-starred with Goodman in *The Babe* (1991), as Ruth's first wife.

A professional actress and dancer since childhood, she had early starring roles in Joseph Papp's Broadway production of *Runaways* (1978) and the part of Anne Frank in *Yours, Anne* (1989).

Born into a show business family in New York, Alvarado began performing at age seven as a flamenco dancer with her parents' dance troupe. After graduating from the Professional Children's School in New York, she enrolled at Fordham University.

Alvarado made her film debut at age 11 in Robert M. Young's *Rich Kids* (1979) and subsequently played Diane Keaton's daughter in *Mrs. Soffel* (1984). She later had leading roles in *Times Square* (1980), *Sweet Lorraine* (1987), *The Chair* (1987), *Satisfaction* (1989), and *American Blue Note* (1991).

Domingo Ambriz

B: 2/29/1948

A Texas-born Mexican American actor, Ambriz starred as the illegal Mexican immigrant in the film *Alambrista!* (1978). *Walk Proud* (1979), *Green Ice* (1981), *Young Guns II* (1990), and *American Me* (1992) are among his other motion picture credits.

Ramsay Ames [born: Rosemary Phillips]

B: 3/30/1924

Born in New York of a Spanish mother and an English father, Ames came to Hollywood's attention as a nightclub entertainer with her hazel-blue eyes, auburn

Ramsay Ames.

hair, and tawny complexion. She was a singer and leader of her own rumba orchestra and made her film debut in a small role in *Two Senoritas from Chicago* (1943). She also appeared as a harem beauty in *Ali Baba and the Forty Thieves* (1944) and in three serials, *Black Widow* (1954) and *G-Men Never Forget* (1948) at Republic and *The Vigilante* (1947) at Columbia. Ames also was in Monogram's *Beauty and the Bandit* (1946) and, much later, *Alexander the Great* (1956).

Ira Angustain
B: 8/6/1958

Born in Glendale, California, Angustain is best known for his portrayal of Gomez on the CBS television series "The White Shadow." He also portrayed comedian Freddie Prinze in the TV movie *Can You Hear the Laughter?* (1979). His acting career began at age three with an appearance in the television series "Pete and Gladys." He was active as a child actor until age 11, appearing in such shows as "Dan August," "Ironside," and "Lancer."

Apollonia
See Apollonia Kotero.

Alfonso Arau
B: 1932

A Mexican actor and director, Arau played a South American drug dealer in *Romancing the Stone* (1984), a Mexican army officer in *The Wild Bunch* (1969), a maniacal used car salesman in *Used Cars* (1980), a bandido in *El Topo* (1971), and the bandit chieftain El Guapo in *¡Three Amigos!* (1986). His other films include *Posse* (1975), *Scandalous John* (1971), and over 25 Mexican films. Arau also directed the highly acclaimed Mexican art film *Like Water for Chocolate*, which was released in the States in 1993.

Yareli Arizmendi

The co-star of the hit Mexican art film *Like Water for Chocalate* (1993), Arizmendi plays the gaseous older sister Rosaura. In the Turner Network Television film *The Cisco Kid* (1994), she plays Rosa, Pancho's independent, strong-willed, and loving wife. Arizmendi has a role as a Latin mother in *Beverly Hills Cop III* (1994) opposite Eddie Murphy. Born in Mexico, she attended schools in the States and now resides near San Diego, where she teaches drama at San Marcos College.

Pedro Armendariz
B: 5/12/1912
D: 6/18/1963

One of Mexico's most popular dramatic film stars, through his long career, Armendariz came to symbolize the heart and soul of the Mexican nation and its manhood in much the same way his good friend John Wayne symbolized America. Like Wayne, Armendariz made some of his best-known American films under the direction of John Ford. These included his roles as the police lieutenant who stalks Henry Fonda in *The Fugitive* (1947), a Mexican bandit in *Three Godfathers* (1948), and a southern-born cavalry sergeant in *Fort Apache* (1948). Armendariz was able to escape the rigid typecasting of the period and played a diverse selection of roles because he did not possess classic Latin lover good looks and spoke English without an accent. However, he was a supporting actor in American films and never played leading roles such as those he had in Mexican films.

Pedro Armendariz.

He was a descendant, through his father, Pedro Armendariz, Sr., of one of Mexico City's oldest families, though his mother, Della Hastings, was an American. Armendariz was born in Mexico City and was educated in San Antonio, Texas, and at California Polytechnic, where he majored in engineering.

The young actor began his career on the stage in Mexico City, entering films in 1935. Armendariz was an immediate success and rose from obscurity to stardom within the space of a few pictures. From *Maria Lena* in 1935 to *Maria Candelaria* in 1946, he made 42 Spanish-language films and established himself as one of Latin America's greatest actors and a leading figure in the development of the Mexican film industry. Director Emilio Fernandez and cinematographer Gabriel Figueroa frequently co-starred Armendariz with Dolores Del Rio in a series of films that were instrumental in creating a national cinema that came to be recognized on an international level.

He ventured to Hollywood in 1947 under contract to Argosy Pictures and made his Hollywood debut in John Ford's *The Fugitive* for RKO. Armendariz starred as a peasant fisherman in John Steinbeck's *The Pearl* (1948), directed by Emilio Fernandez and brilliantly photographed by Gabriel Figueroa on location in Mexico. The actor played a Cuban police officer in *We Were Strangers* (1949), an American Indian in *Tulsa* (1949), a Mexican general in *Border River* (1954), and a Mongol warrior in *The Conqueror* (1956).

An international star, Armendariz worked in films all over the world. His final film was the James Bond adventure *From Russia with Love* (1963), in which he portrayed agent Kerim Bey opposite Sean Connery. While shooting the film, he was seriously ill with advanced cancer of the lymph gland. Upon receiving the news that he had only a year to live, Armendariz shot and killed himself in his hospital room in Los Angeles.

His other films (English-language films only) include *The Torch* (1950), *Lucrece Borgia* (1953), *Diane* (1955), *The Littlest Outlaw* (1955), *The Big Boodle* (1957), *Stowaway Girl* (1957), *The Little Savage* (1959), *The Wonderful Country* (1959), *Francis of Assisi* (1961), *Captain Sinbad* (1963), and *My Son, the Hero* (1963).

Pedro Armendariz, Jr.

B: 1941

Son of the late international Mexican screen idol, Armendariz, Jr., has forged a career for himself in over 130 Mexican and Hollywood films. Among his many motion picture credits are *The Undefeated* (1969), *Earthquake* (1974), *Walker* (1987), *Licence to Kill* (1989), and *Old Gringo* (1989). In addition, Armendariz has guest starred on many U.S. television programs, including "The High Chaparral," "Columbo," "Knight Rider," "The Love Boat," and "Murder, She Wrote."

Armida

B: 5/29/1913

Born in Sonora, Mexico, Armida moved to and was raised in Arizona. She is the

Armida in *Always in My Heart* (1942).

daughter of Joaquin Venrell, a well-known stage actor of the early 1920s. At age 16, while performing in a dance act with her two sisters, she was seen by vaude-ville producer/songwriter Gus Edwards, who put her on the Orpheum circuit. She appeared in several short films before coming to the attention of actor/director/producer John Barrymore, who signed her for a part in his picture *General Crack* in 1929. She appeared in many films throughout the 1930s, usually as a jungle prin-cess, an island beauty, or a cantina girl. Her credits include RKO's *Border Romance* (1930), *On the Border* (1930), *Under a Texas Moon* (1930), *Border Cafe* (1937), *La Conga Nights* (1940), *Always in My Heart* (1942), *The Girl from Monterey* (1943), *Machine Gun Mama* (1944), *Jungle Goddess* (1948), and *Rhythm Inn* (1951).

Desi Arnaz
B: 5/17/1912
D: 12/2/1986

He was called "Cuban Pete" and "Mr. Babalu," but Desi Arnaz will always be remembered as Ricky Ricardo, the excitable Cuban bandleader husband of that crazy American redhead Lucille Ball on the popular television series "I Love Lucy."

The multitalented Arnaz assumed many roles in his show business career, in-cluding musician, singer, actor, bandleader, showman, producer, director, and studio chief. During the late 1930s and 1940s, along with Xavier Cugat and other musicians, he popularized Latin American and Afro-Caribbean music in the United States. On the "I Love Lucy" show he pioneered the three-camera film technique for situation comedy performed in front of a live audience that set the standard still in use today. By producing the shows on film for a licensing fee from the networks and retaining ownership, he led the way for the syndicated rerun. As producer and studio head of Desilu (which occupied the former RKO Studios), he was responsible for the development and production of numerous filmed televi-sion shows including "The Untouchables," "Make Room for Daddy," "Star Trek," and "The Mothers-in-Law."

Born in Santiago, Cuba, where his father was the town mayor, Desi and his family fled the 1933 Cuban revolution and settled in Miami. Desi worked at odd jobs until his musical training landed him a job as a guitarist in a rumba band, and eventually he went to New York and joined Xavier Cugat's band.

Arnaz started the first conga dance line in America, taken from dances per-formed at Afro-Cuban religious festivals. The conga dance craze soon swept through the States. His popularity led him to Broadway, where he had a featured role in George Abbott's *Too Many Girls* (1940) as Manuelito, a South American football player. Arnaz was brought to Hollywood in 1940 to re-create the role for the film version of the musical. He met Lucille Ball at RKO, where *Too Many Girls* was being filmed, and they married in November of that year. He then landed a role in *Father Takes a Wife* (1941), and at MGM he portrayed one of the Mexican American defenders in *Bataan* (1943) with Robert Taylor. Road tours with his orchestra, movie roles, and his marriage to Lucille Ball kept him busy throughout the 1940s.

Arnaz was the first Hispanic American presence on network television. When CBS proposed bringing Lucille Ball's popular radio series, "My Favorite Husband," to television, Ball requested that Arnaz be cast as her husband. CBS doubted that viewers would accept Arnaz as the mate of an average American female. But after the two performed together on a band tour across the country to enthusiastic au-dience response, proving that they would be accepted publicly as a couple, CBS finally agreed. Arnaz and Ball formed Desilu Productions and "I Love Lucy" de-buted on October 15, 1951, and ran through the 1956–1957 season.

Desi, in his Ricky Ricardo character, drew on his Latin background, making Ricky a struggling, not a successful bandleader. Arnaz and Ball capitalized on their TV success in two theatrical features, *The Long, Long Trailer* (1954) and *Forever Darling* (1956).

Desi Arnaz in 1940.

With the success of "I Love Lucy," Desi and Lucy created their own production company and purchased the facilities of the bankrupt RKO Studios. Desilu soon became one of the most important suppliers of filmed television programs.

Arnaz and Ball divorced in 1960. In 1962, Arnaz sold his holdings in Desilu to Ball. He appeared as a guest star on several TV series through the years and was a producer of "The Mothers-in-Law" series. His last film appearance was in Francis Ford Coppola's *The Escape Artist* (1982). Arnaz died of cancer in December 1986 at his home in Del Mar, California. His other film credits include *Four Jacks and a Jill* (1941), *The Navy Comes Through* (1942), and *Cuban Pete* (1946).

Desi Arnaz, Jr.

B: 1/19/1953

The son of Lucille Ball and Desi Arnaz, Desi, Jr., first made appearances on the "Here's Lucy" series with his mother and sister, Lucie. He formed a rock 'n' roll band called Dino, Desi, and Billy in the late 1960s. He made his motion picture debut in *Red Sky at Morning* (1971), for which he received wide critical acclaim, and followed it with a starring role in a western filmed in Israel, *Billy Two Hats* (1973), which starred Gregory Peck. He starred in the stage musical *Marco Polo* with Zero Mostel. On television in 1983–1984, he starred in his own series, "Automan." Alcohol- and drug-related problems kept him off the screen for many years, but after making a complete recovery, he entered Christian ministry. He has starred in summer stock productions of *Sunday in New York, Grease*, and *Promises, Promises* at the Melody Top Theatre and at the Sacramento Music Circus. He made a cameo appearance playing his father, Desi Arnaz, in the feature film *The Mambo Kings* in 1992.

Lucie Arnaz
B: 7/17/1951

The daughter of Lucille Ball and Desi Arnaz, Lucie began her show business career on the "Here's Lucy" TV show. Among her film credits are *The Jazz Singer* (1980), a remake with Neil Diamond, and *Second Thoughts* (1983). She was featured in a short-lived TV series in 1985, "The Lucie Arnaz Show," and in "Sons and Daughters" (1991). On Broadway, she starred in the Neil Simon–Marvin Hamlisch–Carole Bayer Sager musical *They're Playing Our Song* (1978) and took over the leading role during the run of Simon's *Lost in Yonkers*.

Isaac Artenstein
B: 12/5/1954

Artenstein served as a director, writer, and producer on the independent feature dramatic film *Break of Dawn* (1989), which was based on the television documentary *Ballad of an Unsung Hero*. Artenstein directed and edited *Ballad*, which was based on the life of Pedro J. Gonzalez, the first Spanish-language radio personality in southern California. *Ballad of an Unsung Hero* aired nationally in 1983 on PBS and won numerous awards and honors including an Emmy. Artenstein was born in San Diego and grew up in Tijuana. He studied in the Fine Arts Department at UCLA and received his BFA in film/video from the California Institute of the Arts in 1977.

Joe Aubel
B: 11/10/1939

The art director on *Dead and Buried* (1981) and *The Milagro Beanfield War* (1988) and production designer on *American Me* (1992), Aubel was born in East Los Angeles. He grew up speaking Spanish and claims that he learned English by watching Hollywood movies. Attempting to link his artistic leanings with a practical career, Aubel set out to be an architect, studying at a local junior college and interning at an architectural firm. One of his employers there suggested that his talents could be better utilized in movies and TV. In 1964, he got his first television work as a junior set designer on "The Adventures of Ozzie and Harriet." Over the next six years, he worked as an assistant set designer on such television programs as "The Danny Thomas Hour," "The Fugitive," and "The Mod Squad," and on such prestigious feature films as *The Chase* (1966), *Camelot* (1967), *Cool Hand Luke* (1967), and *The Wild Bunch* (1969). His other film credits include *Viva Max!* (1969), *Close Encounters of the Third Kind* (1977), and *Star Trek IV: The Voyage Home* (1986).

Luis Avalos
B: 9/2/1946

A Cuban-born character actor, Avalos has appeared in numerous films and television shows. His first film role was as a junkie in *Badge 373* (1973), followed by a major role in the comedy caper *Hot Stuff* (1979). His other film credits include *Love Child* (1982), *The Hunter* (1980), *The Butcher's Wife* (1991), and *Fires Within* (1991).

Luis Avalos co-stars as a Cuban-born, Miami-raised police detective who helps open a spurious swap shop—where criminals sell their stolen goods—in *Hot Stuff*.

He directed two films in Mexico and a television pilot in Venezuela. On television he has guest starred on many episodic series and starred in the series "Condo." He was a regular on "Hangin' with Mr. Cooper" and was then featured in "Ned Blessing."

Carlos Avila

B: 6/26/1961

The award-winning writer/director of the 1993 PBS "American Playhouse" television presentation *La Carpa*, Avila was born in Lima, Peru, but moved to the Echo Park area of Los Angeles at an early age. His work has been presented internationally at film festivals and museums. His short film *Distant Water* won the Grand Prize at the first Film Festival of International Cinema Students in Tokyo, Japan. He holds a master of fine arts degree from UCLA's School of Film and Television.

Angel Aviles

Among the young actress's film credits are Alan Rudolph's *Equinox* (1993) and *Mi Vida Loca* (1994).

Rick Aviles

An actor/comedian, Aviles was featured in the film *Ghost* (1990) as Patrick Swayze's murderer and in *The Saint of Fort Washington* (1993). Aviles made his screen debut in *The Cannonball Run* in 1981.

Hector Babenco

B: 2/7/1946

An acclaimed director, Babenco gained the attention of international audiences in 1981 with his film *Pixote,* in which an abandoned young boy is forced into a life of crime in the slums of São Paulo. In *Kiss of the Spider Woman* (1985), Babenco told the story of an emerging friendship between a political revolutionary and a homosexual child molester imprisoned in a South American jail. In *Ironweed* (1987), Babenco's first major Hollywood production, he directed Jack Nicholson and Meryl Streep in the screen version of William Kennedy's Pulitzer-Prize–winning novel set in Depression-era America about a man who spends 22 years of his life as an alcoholic street bum. In 1991, Babenco directed *At Play in the Fields of the Lord,* the story of a group of missionaries in the Amazon jungle, which featured an all-star cast.

Babenco was born in Buenos Aires, Argentina. His father was a tailor and embroiderer for the opera and died when his son was one year old. Babenco's mother, who had had a classical education, introduced him to music and books, and reading remains one of his strongest habits. As a youth he read all the classics, both Latin and American. Buenos Aires, one of South America's most European cities, also provided Babenco with the opportunity to see the films of all the great filmmakers of the period.

As he grew older, Babenco became aware of the immense threat that the military posed to democracy in his native country. At age 18, he refused army service and spent five years in Spain, working at various menial jobs before taking work in low-budget "spaghetti westerns." Facing a long prison sentence because he avoided army service, Babenco was unable to return to Argentina, and finally settled in Brazil in the early 1970s.

Babenco's first film was a documentary made in 1972 with money borrowed from friends. *The King of the Night* (1975) was his first feature. *Lucio Flavio* (1977), Babenco's next feature, was extremely well received. Based on actual evidence, it was the first film in Brazil to expose the full apparatus of death squads and the relationship between paramilitary and official police involved in drug dealing and prostitution. His next film, *Pixote* (1981), grew out of Babenco's deep involvement with juvenile delinquents. He worked with nearly 500 street youths, none of whom were professional actors, shooting over a period of five difficult months during 1979 and 1980. Critics have named *Pixote,* Bunuel's *Los Olvidados* (1950), and Truffaut's *The 400 Blows* (1959) as the three most important movies ever made about dispossessed children. *Pixote* was chosen by the New York and Los Angeles film critics societies as the best foreign film of the year.

Unable to raise money for it in the United States, he made *Kiss of the Spider Woman* (1985), his first film in English, on a $1.2 million budget with funds raised in Brazil. The film, starring William Hurt and Raul Julia, received four Academy Award nominations: Best Director, Best Film, Best Screenplay, and Best Actor for William Hurt, who won the award.

Catherine Bach

B: 3/1/1954

An actress of German-Mexican heritage, Bach co-starred as Daisy on the popular television series "The Dukes of Hazzard." Among her film credits are *The Midnight Man* (1974), *Thunderbolt and Lightfoot* (1974), *Hustle* (1975), and *Cannonball Run II* (1984).

Antonio Banderas

    B: 1960

A Spanish-born leading actor, Banderas made his international reputation in a series of films with Spanish writer/director Pedro Almodovar. He made his U.S. film debut in Madonna's documentary *Truth or Dare* (1991), followed by leading roles in *The Mambo Kings* (1992), *Philadelphia* (1993), and *The House of the Spirits* (1994).

Lita Baron [aka: Isabelita; born: Isabel Beth Castro]

    B: 8/11/1929

Born in Almaria, Spain, Baron came to the United States with her family when she was four years old. At first she adopted a single name, following a precedent set by the Mexican actress Margo. It was while singing with Xavier Cugat's band at the Trocadero in Hollywood that she was signed for her first film, an RKO musical titled *Pan-Americana* (1945). She appeared in a number of Paramount Technicolor musical short subjects, one of which, *Champagne for Two* (1947), was nominated for an Academy Award. She also appeared in six features, *That's My Baby* (1944), *A Medal for Benny* (1945), *Club Havana* (1946), *The Gay Senorita* (1946), *Slightly Scandalous* (1946), and *Border Incident* (1949).

Steven Bauer [aka and born: Rocky Echevarria]

    B: 12/2/1956

A Havana-born leading man, Bauer's big-screen break came when director Brian De Palma cast him as Al Pacino's Cuban gangster buddy, Manny Rivera, in the

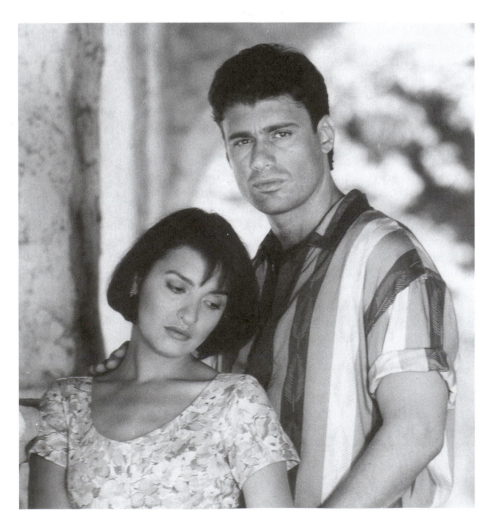

Steven Bauer and Elizabeth Pena
in *Drug Wars: The Camerena Story*.

362

remake of *Scarface* (1983). He followed with the lead role in *Thief of Hearts* (1984) and appeared in *Running Scared* (1986), *Two Moon Junction* (1988), and the TV movie *Drug Wars: The Camarena Story* (1989).

Bauer's family fled Castro's regime in 1959, moving to Miami, where he was raised. He attended the University of Miami for two years before moving to Los Angeles. Bauer made his acting debut on the Miami-based PBS TV series "Que Pasa, U.S.A.?" under his real name of Rocky Echevarria. In Los Angeles he signed a short-term contract with Columbia Television and appeared on several series such as "The Rockford Files," "Hill Street Blues," "From Here to Eternity," and "Wiseguy." He changed his name just before starring in *Scarface*. Bauer portrayed an Afghan rebel chief in *The Beast* (1988) and a detective in *Gleaming the Cube* (1989).

Alfonso Bedoya

B: 1904
D: 1957

Bedoya established a permanent niche in American movie history with only one role, that of Goldhat, the absurd menacing bandit in *The Treasure of the Sierra Madre* (1948), when he spoke the memorable line to Bogart, "Badges? We don't need no stinkin' badges."

Director John Huston met Bedoya while on location in Mexico and cast him in the film. Bedoya appeared in many American films over the next decade, mostly westerns, usually as a Mexican bandit. Bedoya had no formal training as an actor but appeared in 70 Mexican films, most notably in a comedic characterization in *Las Abandonados* (1944). His other films include *The Pearl* (1948), *Streets of Laredo* (1949), *The Black Rose* (1950), *California Conquest* (1952), *Border River* (1954), *Ten Wanted Men* (1955), and *The Big Country* (1958).

Alma Beltran

B: 1927

A veteran character actress, Beltran is best known for her role as the maid in the 1980 film *Oh God! Book II,* starring George Burns. She has also appeared in such films as *Red Sky at Morning* (1971), *Blue* (1968), *Herbie Goes Bananas* (1988), and *Zoot Suit* (1981). She has worked extensively in Los Angeles theater and in Spanish-language radio. She co-starred in the cable television series "Sanchez of Bel Air," and played Freddie Prinze's aunt on "Chico and the Man" and Julio Fuentes's mother on "Sanford and Son." Beltran was born in Mexico and raised in California and Arizona.

Robert Beltran

B: 11/19/1953

Having made his film debut with a small role in *Zoot Suit* (1981), Beltran is best known for his role as Raoul in the 1982 cult film *Eating Raoul.* A handsome leading actor type, he has co-starred in such films as *Lone Wolf McQuade* (1983), *Latino* (1985), and *Scenes from the Class Struggle in Beverly Hills* (1989).

Gabriel Beristain

Honored with the Silver Bear for Cinematography at the 1987 Berlin Film Festival for his work in *Caravaggio,* directed by Derek Jarman, Beristain has numerous other film credits in Latin America, Europe, and the United States. Born in Mexico, he grew up in a theatrical family; his father, Luis Beristain, was a successful Mexican actor (his last film was *The Exterminating Angel,* Luis Bunuel's masterpiece). Beristain's American films are *Waiting for the Light* (1990), starring Shirley MacLaine; Jonathan Lynn's *The Distinguished Gentleman* (1992), with Eddie Murphy; and Taylor Hackford's *Bound by Honor* (1993).

Ruben Blades

B: 7/6/1948

Born and raised in Panama City, Panama, Blades grew up listening to a melange of Latin music, American rock, and calypso from the West Indies. While performing with a number of Latin bands, he studied law at the University of Panama. He lived in New York City for a brief time and made some recordings. He went back to Panama, got his law degree, and returned to New York, where he began performing with various salsa bands.

Salsa music singer/songwriter turned actor, Blades made his film debut starring in Leon Ichaso's *Crossover Dreams* (1985) as a Latin star who abandons his salsa roots in an ill-fated bid for Top 40 stardom. Vincent Canby in his *New York Times* review called Blades "a fine new film performer who's also a screen natural."

Blades went on to co-star opposite Richard Pryor as a crazy orderly in *Critical Condition* (1986) and opposite Whoopi Goldberg as a cop in *Fatal Beauty* (1987). His most important role to date was as Sheriff Bernabe in *The Milagro Beanfield War* (1988). He was a hood in *Disorganized Crime* (1989). He played Jewish gangster Mickey Nice opposite Jack Nicholson in *The Two Jakes* (1990), and a police detective in *Predator 2* (1990). Blades appeared in a cameo role as a numbers runner in Spike Lee's *Mo' Better Blues* (1990). He also wrote and performed the music score for the film *Q & A* (1990).

Ruben Blades in *The Milagro Beanfield War.*

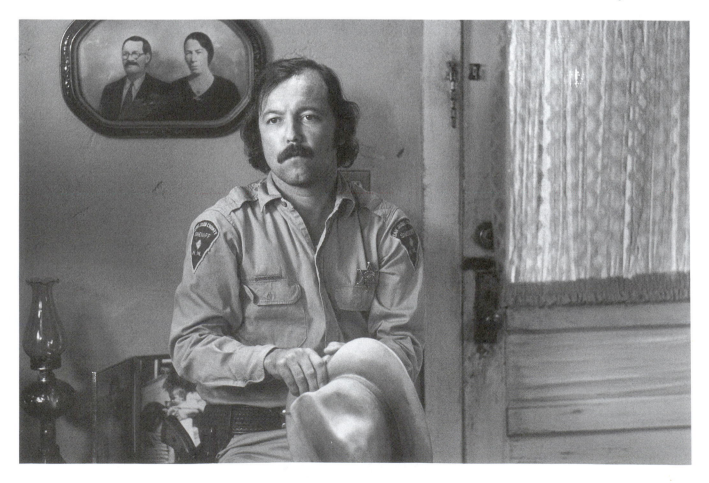

On cable television, Blades won an ACE Award as Best Actor for his portrayal of a death row inmate in HBO's *Dead Man Out* (1989) and played an Italian count in HBO's *The Josephine Baker Story* (1990). He was nominated for an Emmy Award for his role as a janitor in the Turner Network Television film *Crazy from the Heart* (1991).

Vicente Blasco Ibanez
B: 1867
D: 1928

The novels of this Spanish writer were very much in vogue during the 1920s, and inevitably several of them found their way to the screen, including *The Four Horsemen of the Apocalypse, Blood and Sand,* and *Mare Nostrum.* Greta Garbo's first two American films, *The Torrent* and *The Temptress,* were also adapted from Blasco Ibanez novels. He had been writing since early in the century, but his international reputation began with *The Four Horsemen of the Apocalypse* (1916; published in English in 1918), which became a record-breaking best-seller. *Sangre y Arena* (1908) had been published in English in 1911 as *Blood in the Arena,* but in 1919 was reissued as *Blood and Sand.*

Fortunio Bonanova
B: 1895
D: 1969

A character actor in American films, Bonanova is best known for his roles in *Citizen Kane* (1941), as the singing teacher who tries to teach Kane's talentless wife; *For Whom the Bell Tolls* (1943), as the Spanish mountain guerrilla fighter; and *Kiss Me Deadly* (1955), as an opera lover whose rare, vintage record is snapped in two before his eyes by private eye Mike Hammer.

The actor and opera star was born in Palma de Mallorca, Spain, the son of Nicolas Bonanova, an attorney. Bonanova studied at the Barcelona Institute, the University of Madrid Law School, the Real Conservatory of Madrid, with private music teachers in Milan, Italy, and at the Paris Conservatoire. At age 17, the young baritone was singing solo with the Royal Chapel group in Madrid when the great Feodor Chaliapin heard him and encouraged him in his musical ambitions. Bonanova made his operatic debut in Paris as the toreador in *Carmen* and later sang in opera companies internationally.

At age 19 he wrote, produced, directed, and starred in the first screen version of *Don Juan* in his native Spain. He wrote plays, operettas, and novels and toured with his own repertory company throughout Latin America. He performed in the American theater opposite actress Katharine Cornell on Broadway. In 1927 he made his American film debut in *The Love of Sunya* with Gloria Swanson. He was the star, writer, producer, and director of 12 Spanish-language shorts made at the Fort Lee Studios in New Jersey.

From 1932 to 1935 Bonanova starred in many Spanish-language films made in Spain, Mexico, and South America. In 1935, he began appearing in Hollywood films, starring in numerous Spanish versions of English films and playing roles in many English-language Hollywood productions as well. When *La Immaculada* was made in 1939, Bonanova adapted the story, wrote the music, produced, directed, and starred. His other films include *Bulldog Drummond in Africa* (1938), *Romance in the Dark* (1938), *Tropic Holiday* (1938), *Blood and Sand* (1941), *Down Argentine Way* (1940), *I Was an Adventuress* (1940), *The Mark of Zorro* (1940), *That Night in Rio* (1941), *Double Indemnity* (1944), and *Going My Way* (1944).

Jesse Borrego

B: 1962

A San Antonio, Texas, native, Borrego was featured in *Bound by Honor* (1993), *Mi Vida Loca* (1994), and Martin Scorsese's segment of *New York Stories* (1989). He played the Mexican American dancer Jesse for four years on the syndicated "Fame" TV series.

Sonia Braga

B: 1949

A Brazilian-born actress, Braga has gained attention in several American films for her dark beauty, screen sensuality, and acting talent. Her full talent has never been utilized as effectively in her American films as in her Brazilian films. Her Brazilian films have capitalized on her flair for comedy juxtaposed with her smoldering sexuality.

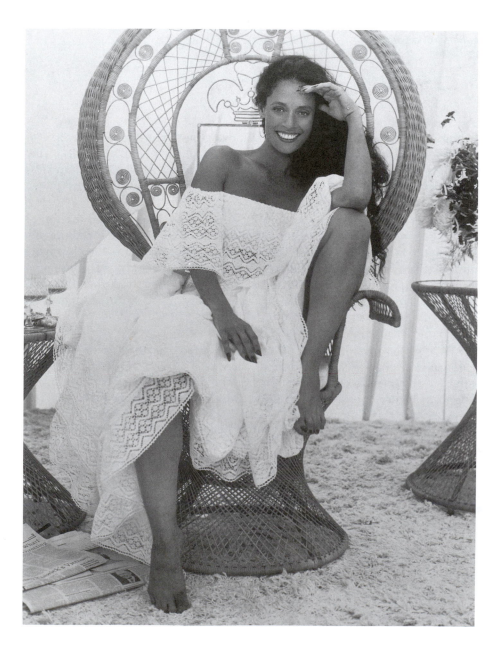

Sonia Braga stars as Madonna, the mistress of the dictator of Parador, in *Moon over Parador*.

366

Kiss of the Spider Woman (1985) was her first English-language film and the one that brought her the greatest international recognition. "When I made the film I still couldn't speak the language well. Sometimes I would say a line and wonder what it meant," the actress admitted during an interview. In the film she essayed three roles, Raul Julia's girlfriend, a French chanteuse who falls in love with a Nazi officer in one of the films within the film, and the mysterious Spider Woman in another of the film's fantasy sequences.

American audiences first became aware of her in the 1977 Brazilian movie *Dona Flor and Her Two Husbands,* directed by Bruno Barreto. She followed this with Arnaldo Jabor's *I Love You* (1981), and Barreto's *Gabriela* (1983), based on Jorje Amado's best-seller, in which she starred opposite Marcello Mastroianni.

In the States, she co-starred in *The Milagro Beanfield War* (1988), directed by Robert Redford, in which she played Ruby Archuleta, and in *Moon over Parador* (1988), directed by Paul Mazursky, in which she co-starred opposite Raul Julia and Richard Dreyfuss as the sensuous mistress of a dictator. Her other films include *Lady on the Bus* (1978) and *The Rookie* (1990).

Braga's rise to international fame began in Marinaga, Paran, in the south of Brazil, where her childhood was shaken by her father's death when she was eight years old. At age 14 she quit school and took a series of clerical jobs. A walk-on part as a little princess in a children's television program began her acting career. By age 18, Braga was working in theater and created a minor sensation by taking her clothes off on stage in a production of *Hair.*

In 1968, Braga starred in a television soap opera, "The Girl of the Blue Sailboat." She followed with a series of soaps for TV Globo, the leading Brazilian network. Two of these, "Gabriela" and "Dancin' Days," made her a star.

Benjamin Bratt [born: Benjamin Bratt Banda]
B: 12/16/1963

The actor stars as Paco in the feature film *Bound by Honor* (1993) and is featured in *One Good Cop* (1991) as Felix, the inexperienced young detective partnered with Michael Keaton's seasoned Artie Lewis. His other film credits are *Bright Angel* (1991), *Rope of Sand* (1991), and *Chains of Gold* (1991). Bratt developed his acting skills as an undergraduate at the University of California at Santa Barbara, continuing in the master's program at San Francisco's prestigious American Conservatory Theater. He starred in the TV series pilot "Juarez" and co-starred in the ABC-TV series "Knightwatch" and NBC's "Nasty Boys."

J. Robert Bren
B: 1903

A film producer and writer, Bren made his film writing debut in 1934 with *Looking for Trouble.* He wrote the screenplays for such films as *In Old California* (1942), *The Great Sioux Uprising* (1953), and *The Siege at Red River* (1954). Bren was born in Guanajuato, Mexico

Romney Brent [born: Romulo Larralde]
B: 1/26/1902
D: 9/24/1976

An actor and writer born in Saltillo, Mexico, Brent was a stage actor in London and New York. He made his screen debut in the British production *East Meets West* in 1936. Other screen credits include *Dreaming Lips* (1937), *The Dominant Sex* (1937), *Under the Red Robe* (1937), and *The Adventures of Don Juan* (1949).

Ruth Britt

An actress of Puerto Rican descent, Britt was one of the last Universal contract players in the late 1970s. She appeared in *The Nude Bomb* (1980) and *Night School* (1981). Britt was a regular on the "Operation Petticoat" television series, playing a native island girl, and has made numerous guest appearances on episodic series and in TV movies.

Georg Stanford Brown

B: 1944

An actor/director born in Havana, Cuba, and raised in New York's Harlem, Brown is perhaps best known for his role as a tough cop on "The Rookies" television series and as the staunch Tom in TV's history-making *Roots* and *Roots: The Next Generation* miniseries. His film credits include *The Comedians* (1967), *Bullitt* (1968), *The Man* (1972), and *Stir Crazy* (1980). Brown has devoted most of his creative energies to directing for television, where his credits include "Family," "Starsky and Hutch," "Charlie's Angels," "Hill Street Blues," and "Cagney & Lacey."

Argentina Brunetti

B: 8/31/1907

This Argentine-born veteran character actress has over 60 motion picture credits. She usually plays dignified Latin donas or mothers. Her credits include such classic motion pictures as *California* (1946); *Miracle on 34th Street* (1947); *Broken Arrow*

Argentina Brunetti plays the care-worn mother role in *The Brothers Rico*.
Photo by Crosby.

(1950), in which she played Cochise's (Jeff Chandler's) Indian squaw; *The Lawless* (1950), as the mother of a Mexican youth on the run from the law; *The Caddy* (1953), in which she played Dean Martin's Italian mother, to whom he sang the famous song "That's Amore"; *King of the Khyber Rifles* (1953), as a Hindu woman; *Three Violent People* (1956); *The Brothers Rico* (1957); and *The Appaloosa* (1966), with Marlon Brando. Brunetti also appeared on the popular daytime television soap opera "General Hospital" for three years. Brunetti's mother was the internationally renowned stage actress Mimi Aguglia, who in the 1930s, late in her career, appeared in several Spanish-language films made in Hollywood.

Luis Bunuel

B: 2/22/1900
D: 7/29/1983

A Spanish filmmaker, Luis Bunuel was a giant of world cinema. In 1929 he collaborated with artist Salvador Dali to make *Un Chien Andalou,* one of the most scandalous films of its time. The movie, which is about dreams, contains unexplained images such as a dead donkey on a grand piano and a scene in which an eyeball is sliced by a razor. In 1940 Bunuel worked as a technical adviser for an uncompleted pro-Spanish Loyalist film at MGM Studios in Hollywood. From 1941 to 1944, he worked in the film department at the Museum of Modern Art in New York City. He was scheduled to direct *The Beast with Five Fingers* (1946), starring Peter Lorre, but the job went to Robert Florey. He returned to France after the war for a short time but then moved to Mexico.

Bunuel's Mexican period, which lasted until 1961, was one of his most prolific. He worked regularly for the first time and directed some 20 productions including *Los Olvidados* (1950), *Robinson Crusoe* (1952), and *El Bruto* (1952), a melodrama about a butcher who falls in love with a rich man's daughter, starring Pedro Armendariz and Katy Jurado. He returned to Spain and made *Viridiana* (1961), which Franco promptly banned. From then on Bunuel worked in France, where he made such films as *Belle de Jour* (1967) and *Tristana* (1970). His final film was *That Obscure Object of Desire* (1977).

Robert Cabal

An actor of Filipino descent, Cabal appeared in such films as *Crisis* (1950), *Mara Maru* (1952) with Errol Flynn, and *The Man Behind the Gun* (1952) with Randolph Scott. He played Hey Soos for two years on the "Rawhide" TV series.

David Cadiente

An actor/stuntman, Cadiente has been featured in such films as *Donovan's Reef* (1963), *Ride the Wild Surf* (1964), *The Sting II* (1983), and *Stick* (1985). His numerous television credits include "Adventures in Paradise," "The Gallant Men," and "The A-Team."

Joseph Calleia

B: 8/4/1897
D: 10/31/1975

Born on the island of Malta, the son of English and Spanish parents, Calleia was a character actor of extraordinary range, best known for his sadistic gun-toting gangster or villain portrayals. He is also closely identified with his many Latin roles in such films as *Juarez* (1939), *For Whom the Bell Tolls* (1943), *Gilda* (1946), *Branded* (1950), *The Treasure of Pancho Villa* (1955), *The Littlest Outlaw* (1955), *Serenade* (1956), *Touch of Evil* (1958), *Cry Tough* (1959), and *The Alamo* (1960). In 1936 he wrote a film script for MGM called *The Robin Hood of El Dorado,* which starred Warner Baxter.

Jacqueline Cambas

This film editor has collaborated with director Richard Benjamin on *City Heat* (1984), *Racing with the Moon* (1984), *The Money Pit* (1986), *Little Nikita* (1988), *My Stepmother Is an Alien* (1988), *Downtown* (1990), *Mermaids* (1990), and *Made in America* (1993). Cambas was born in New York. She originally was a teacher but left the profession to enroll in UCLA's Film School. Her first film job was as an apprentice editor on *Billy Jack* (1971). Her other film credits include *School Ties* (1992), *Zoot Suit* (1981), and *Cat People* (1982) as co-editor.

Rafael Campos

B: 5/13/1936
D: 7/9/1985

A smiling and ebullient actor, Campos is best known for his role as the young Puerto Rican boy, Pete Morales, in the classic 1955 MGM film *Blackboard Jungle*, starring Glenn Ford as a besieged inner-city schoolteacher. He followed this with the role of a Mexican American boy accused of murder in MGM's *Trial* (1955), with Ford and Katy Jurado. Campos played Native American youths in Disney's

Rafael Campos shortly before he appeared in *This Could Be the Night*.

The Light in the Forest and *Tonka* (both 1958). Later in his career, he played character roles in such films as *The Appaloosa* (1966) with Marlon Brando and *Oklahoma Crude* (1973) with George C. Scott. His other films include *The Sharkfighters* (1956) and *This Could Be the Night* (1957).

Campos worked consistently on television in such distinguished early series as "Studio One," "Playhouse 90," and "Alcoa Theatre." He was a regular as Ramon Diaz on "Rhoda," starring Valerie Harper. The epic miniseries *Centennial* (1978) provided Campos an important role as Nacho Gomez, a trail cook.

A native of the Dominican Republic, Campos came to the States in 1949 with his family. He attended the High School for the Performing Arts in New York City where he was spotted by film writer and director Richard Brooks, who cast him, along with such other little-known actors as Vic Morrow, Paul Mazursky, Jamie Farr, and Sidney Poitier, in *Blackboard Jungle*. Campos was reunited with Brooks for his last film, *Fever Pitch* (1985). Campos died of cancer at age 49.

Victor Campos

An actor who co-starred in *Newman's Law* (1974) and *Five Days from Home* (1978), opposite George Peppard, and *The Master Gunfighter* (1975) with Tom Laughlin, Campos also co-starred in the television series "Doctors' Hospital" and "Cade's County."

Larry Cano

Cano was the executive producer of the 1983 feature film *Silkwood*.

Cantinflas [born: Mario Moreno]

B: 8/12/1911
D: 4/20/1993

Charlie Chaplin once said, "Cantinflas is the world's greatest comedian." Cantinflas made people laugh throughout the Spanish-speaking world for over 50 years and at times held the position of number-one box-office star. He became a hero figure for the common man, a symbol and idol for the people of Mexico and Latin America.

He appeared in only two English-language motion pictures, *Around the World in 80 Days* (1956) as Passepartout, Phileas Fogg's (David Niven's) valet and traveling companion in the Academy Award–winning film, and *Pepe* (1960), in which he portrays a peon ranch hand whose love for his horse involves him with many celebrities. Cantinflas had first come to Hollywood in 1944 under an arrangement with RKO Studios for a series of pictures, but the details were never worked out to the satisfaction of Cantinflas or the studio.

Michael Todd, the producer of *Around the World in 80 Days,* said in an interview at the time, "I picked him for the part because he is an expert in pantomime. This picture will be as international as we can possibly make it and therefore securing players from different countries, if they fit into the screenplay, will be the thing to do." He also said, "The fact that Cantinflas always liked the Passepartout character makes him doubly desirable. It is easy to change Phileas Fogg's servant into a Mexican in this modern time, and thus the character can be perfectly tailored to his needs."

Cantinflas stated, "Mr. Todd demonstrated his excellent intentions about the Jules Verne story when he permitted me to see a treatment. He also permitted me to portray the character as a Mexican rather than a French character. So I was still Cantinflas to my audiences in Latin America." In an *L.A. Times* interview many years later, Cantinflas pointed out that it took some convincing on his part to make Michael Todd see it the way he expressed it in those interviews.

Cantinflas.

Cantinflas was born Mario Moreno in 1911, in a poverty-ridden district of Mexico City called Tenampa. He ran away from home as a young man in order to join a *carpas,* a traveling circus. To avoid bringing shame on his family, he adopted the name Cantinflas.

Over the years the name has come to mean "the little guy with the funny two-piece moustache and the baggy droopy pants, barely held up by a rope." The character always wants to help his fellow man, even though he himself can use some help.

The Cantinflas character represents the common man who battles hunger, suffering, sickness, and injustice, still finding goodness, love, and hope in man-kind and life. Cantinflas, like Chaplin, is a comedian who represents the under-dog. Cantinflas once remarked that the main difference between his tramp and Chaplin's is that Chaplin's tramp is helpless before the blows of fate while his tramp, with luck, wit, and unparalleled flexibility of character, can and does do something about those blows. Chaplin's tramp is a figure of semi-tragedy, while Cantinflas plays a figure of hope.

Cantinflas the artist always conveyed a social and humanistic message. He showed a positive road for people in all his films. Cantinflas made such inroads in the affection of all Spanish-speaking peoples that his name has become part of the Spanish language, meaning "to talk much, say little, and indulge in frenetic speech."

Cantinflas made his motion picture debut in 1936 and starred in 49 Mexican films. Two years after he began making films, he established his own production company, which gave him complete ownership of most of his films and made him a multimillionaire.

Irene Cara

B: 3/18/1959

A versatile actress, singer, and dancer, Cara co-starred in *Aaron Loves Angela* (1975), *Sparkle* (1976), *Fame* (1980), *City Heat* (1984), and *Certain Fury* (1985). In 1984 she won an Academy Award for co-writing the Best Original Song, "Flashdance . . . What a Feeling," the title song to the film *Flashdance* (1983). Cara also recorded the song, which became a Top 40 hit. Born of Cuban/Puerto Rican parents Cara has been performing since the age of seven on the Broadway stage and in TV and films.

Irene Cara.

Elsa Cardenas

B: 8/3/1935

Born in Tijuana, Mexico, and raised in Mexico City, Cardenas made her Mexican film debut in March 1954 in *Magdalena*. Her first American film was *The Brave One* in 1956. She followed this with a role in *Giant* (1956), in which she played Juana Benedict, wife of the son of an oil rancher. Cardenas was off the American screen for six years until 1963 when she played opposite Elvis Presley in *Fun in Acapulco* as a lady bullfighter. In 1964 the actress was cast in a minor western for Universal called *Taggart*.

Annette Cardona

A multitalented actress, Cardona was featured as Cha Cha in the film *Grease* (1978). She also co-starred in Haskell Wexler's *Latino* (1985).

Ismael ("East") Carlo

B: 1/19/1942

A Puerto Rican–born, New York–raised character actor, Carlo usually plays corrupt officials, drug kingpins, and concerned fathers or merchants on television and in feature films. His credits include the films *A Piece of the Action* (1977) and *Defiance* (1980) and on television such episodic series as "The A-Team," "Murder, She Wrote," and "Crime Story."

Julie Carmen

B: 4/4/1960

Carmen won the Best Supporting Actress prize at the Venice Film Festival for her role as the young mother in John Cassavetes's 1980 film *Gloria*. She starred opposite Raul Julia and Armand Assante in *The Penitent* (1988) and played the strong-willed wife of a New Mexico farmer in *The Milagro Beanfield War* (1988). Carmen most recently played a beautiful and outlandish vampire in *Fright Night II* (1988).

Born in New York City, she graduated from the State University of New York and studied acting with Uta Hagen, Sanford Meisner, and Jose Quintero. Soon she was playing leading roles on stage and in television movies like *Can You Hear the Laughter? The Story of Freddie Prinze* (1979) and *Fire on the Mountain* (1981), opposite Ron Howard. She made her film debut in Robert Butler's *Night of the Juggler* (1980). Her other film credits include *Blue City* (1986) and *Last Plane Out* (1983).

Carlos Carrasco

A native of Panama, Carrasco has appeared in feature films including *"Crocodile" Dundee II* (1988), *The Fisher King* (1991), and *Bound by Honor* (1993).

Barbara Carrera

B: 12/31/1945

A Nicaraguan-born fashion model turned actress, Carrera has put her exotic look to good use in a variety of leading roles in several major film and television productions, usually playing strong-willed women.

Carrera came to the States at age 10 and attended the St. Joseph Academy in Memphis, Tennessee. At age 15 she moved to New York City and just a few months later was spotted on Fifth Avenue by designer Lily Daché, who suggested that Carrera had a fresh face and an ideal figure for modeling. She signed with the Eileen Ford Agency, but after several attempts to conform to the requisite fashion, she decided to go with her own unique, indigenous look; within a year she had her first magazine cover on *Harper's Bazaar* and within four years, she was one of the highest-paid models in the world.

She made her major motion picture debut in 1975 as a Spanish senorita in *The Master Gunfighter* opposite Tom Laughlin, who spotted her picture on a magazine cover and arranged a screen test for her.

Carrera was soon cast in another film, *Embryo* (1976), which starred Rock Hudson. Next followed roles as a mysterious island woman opposite Burt Lancaster in *The Island of Dr. Moreau* (1977), a Hawaiian in the all-star *When Time Ran Out* (1980), followed by the female lead in *I, the Jury* (1982), starring Armand Assante as Mickey Spillane's Mike Hammer.

She received praise from critics and the public for her role as Fatima Bush, the villainess and assassin in the James Bond adventure *Never Say Never Again* (1983), starring Sean Connery.

On television she portrayed the Indian woman Clay Basket in the epic 24-hour miniseries *Centennial* (1978–1979), starring opposite Robert Conrad and Richard Chamberlain. She portrayed a beautiful Jewish woman in the miniseries *Masada* (1981), starring Peter O'Toole.

Edward Carrere

B: 1905
D: 1979

An art director/production designer born in Mexico City of a Spanish mother and a French father, Carrere won an Academy Award for *Camelot* (1967), and worked on a number of films during his long tenure at Warner Bros., including *The Adventures of Don Juan* (1949), *The Fountainhead* (1949), *White Heat* (1949), *Sunrise at Campobello* (1960), and *The Wild Bunch* (1969). He worked with Hecht-Hill-Lancaster on *Separate Tables* (1958) and *Run Silent, Run Deep* (1958). He was the brother of Fernando Carrere and the father of Leon Carrere.

Fernando Carrere

B: 12/31/1910

An art director and production designer, Carrere was born in Mexico City of a Spanish mother and a French father. He designed sets for such Hollywood productions as *The Pride and the Passion* (1957), *Birdman of Alcatraz* (1962), *The Great Escape* (1963), and several of the Pink Panther films. In 1961, he was nominated for an Academy Award for William Wyler's *The Children's Hour*. He is the brother of Edward Carrere.

Leon Carrere

B: 2/26/1935

The son of Edward Carrere, Leon Carrere is a television film editor and director who has edited such shows as "Charlie's Angels" (which he has also directed), "The Rookies," and "In the Heat of the Night."

Robert Carricart

B: 1/18/1917

A veteran character actor featured in such films as *Black Orchid* (1959), *Follow That Dream* (1962), *Fun in Acapulco* (1963), *Robin and the Seven Hoods* (1964), *Villa Rides* (1968), and *The Milagro Beanfield War* (1988), Carricart was born in Bordeaux, France, of a Spanish mother and a French father. He worked consistently on the

Broadway stage in such major productions as *Antony and Cleopatra* with Katharine Cornell, *Detective Story* with Ralph Bellamy, *The Rose Tattoo,* and *Annie Get Your Gun,* until 1957 when he turned to film acting and moved to Hollywood. He co-starred in the TV series "T.H.E. Cat."

Elpidia Carrillo [alternate spelling: Elpedia]

B: 8/16/1961

A Mexican actress, Carrillo has become Hollywood's favorite all-purpose native since 1981. She made her film debut opposite Jack Nicholson in *The Border* (1982) as a Guatemalan immigrant whose baby is stolen on the U.S.-Mexico border. She played the love interest of Michael Caine and Richard Gere in *Beyond the Limit* (1983), and a captured Central American rebel in *Predator* (1987), starring Arnold Schwarzenegger. In Oliver Stone's *Salvador* (1986), she was the Salvadoran girl-friend of an American photographer, played by James Woods. Her other feature film credits include *Under Fire* (1983) and *Let's Get Harry* (1987).

Leo Carrillo

B: 8/6/1881
D: 9/11/1961

A versatile character actor who had a long career in stage, films, and television, Carrillo is best known for his role as the loyal and trustworthy sidekick Pancho in a series of Cisco Kid films and television programs. His buffoonish interpretation

Leo Carrillo, "Mr. California."

of Pancho, who was overweight and spoke an accented English full of malapropisms, was so well etched that it endeared him to audiences worldwide and overshadowed his other film and theatrical work.

He was called "Mr. California" because of his deep pride in California's Spanish-Mexican history, and the prominent part his family had played in it. Leo Antonio Carrillo was born in an adobe building in Los Angeles, the fifth of eight children in a family that could trace its lineage back to the colonization of California by Spanish conquistadors. His great-great-grandfather, Joe Reimundo Carrillo, accompanied Father Junipero Serra and explorer Gaspar De Portola on the expedition north from Baja California in 1769 to settle San Diego. His great-grandfather, Carlos Antonio Carrillo, was in 1837 appointed in Mexico as provisional governor of California. Carlos Antonio once controlled a tract of 70,000 acres in what is now West Los Angeles. Carlos Antonio's brother, Jose Antonio Esquivel, was a signer of the Treaty of Cahuenga, in which the Mexican forces capitulated to the Americans in 1847. Leo's grandfather, Pedro C. Carrillo, was an early Los Angeles judge, and the actor's father, Juan Jose, was once mayor of Santa Monica.

Leo Carrillo recalled in a newspaper interview, "In my family, I never needed *The Arabian Nights,* we had our own. It was compounded of the mighty saga of priests, leather jacketed soldiers, grizzly bear hunters, bagueros who rode horses as swift as the wind, ropers who flung a reata with the precision of rifle fire, grandes of the rancheros, and dancing girls with castanets who sang the siren song of California to the tune of a Spanish guitar in a jasmine scented patio" (*L.A. Times Calendar,* 10/29/61).

The future actor received his early education at Santa Monica High School and at St. Vincent's (now Loyola Marymount University). Carrillo decided to pursue a career as an artist. To earn money for additional studies, he took a job in the engineering department of the Southern Pacific Railroad. He was assigned to construction along California's coast. He worked with men of many nationalities and learned the dialects that he was to use later on stage. Carrillo was next hired by the *San Francisco Examiner* as a cartoonist. He made his first stage appearance at an amateur benefit. Then, when an act on the Orpheum circuit didn't show up, Carrillo filled in and was a hit. He remained in vaudeville for several years as a headliner, but his career as a legitimate actor began when, while playing polo at a fashionable Long Island club, he ad-libbed a comic Italian, was overheard by a theatrical producer, and was given the part of an Italian in the Broadway production *Twin Beds* (1914).

This led to his appearance in a number of Broadway hits after World War I. His greatest success in the theater was in *Lombardi, LTD,* written especially for him by Frederic and Fanny Hatton, in which he starred in 1917.

Carrillo made his screen debut in *Mr. Antonio* in 1929. He appeared in over 100 motion pictures, the most notable being *Girl of the Rio* (1932), *Viva Villa!* (1933), *Love Me Forever* (1935), *The Gay Desperado* (1936), *Twenty-Mule Team* (1940), *Crazy House* (1943), *Follow the Band* (1943), *Frontier Badmen* (1943), *Phantom of the Opera* (1943), *Bowery to Broadway* (1944), *Gypsy Wildcat* (1944), *Moonlight and Cactus* (1944), *Crime, Inc.* (1945), *The Girl from San Lorenzo* (1950), and *Pancho Villa Returns* (1950).

Lynda Carter

B: 7/24/1951

An Arizona-born actress of German-Hispanic heritage, Carter is best known for the title role of the 1970s television series "Wonder Woman."

Movita Castenada

See Movita.

Antonio Castillo

A Spanish-born Parisian fashion and theatrical costume designer, Castillo won an Academy Award for his work on *Nicholas and Alexandra* (1971).

Enrique Castillo [aka: E.J. Castillo]
    B: 12/10/1949

A Mexican American actor, Castillo was featured in *Borderline* (1980), *Losin' It* (1983), and *Bound by Honor* (1993). His television credits include "The Waltons" and the telefilm *Fighting Back: The Rocky Bleier Story* (1980) with Robert Urich.

Eduardo Castro

A film and stage costume designer, Castro designed the period costumes for the film *Shout* (1991) and was co-designer on *Bird on a Wire* (1990). In 1987, he designed a full season of the television series "Miami Vice." He holds a master of fine arts in scenic and costume design from Carnegie-Mellon University and was an in-house assistant at the Western Costume Company in Hollywood, working with major film costume designers.

Larry Ceballos
    B: 10/21/1887
    D: 9/12/1978

One of Hollywood's foremost dance directors during the late 1920s and early 1930s, the Chilean-born and -raised Ceballos worked on numerous Vitaphone shorts and feature films at Warner Bros. and RKO. The dance sequences that he choreographed were typical 1920s stage dance arrangements adapted directly to the screen. Some of his credits include *Gold Diggers of Broadway* (1929), *On with the Show* (1929), *Show of Shows* (1929), *Hold Everything* (1930), *No, No Nanette* (1930), and *Sally* (1930).

Gary Cervantes

A Mexican American character actor, Cervantes usually plays heavies and criminal felons. He holds the distinction of having been killed on screen by such stars as Al Pacino in *Scarface* (1983), Arnold Schwarzenegger in *Commando* (1985), Burt Reynolds in *Stick* (1985), Nick Nolte in *Extreme Prejudice* (1987), and Whoopi Goldberg in *Fatal Beauty* (1987). His other film credits include *Boulevard Nights* (1979), *Walk Proud* (1979), *Colors* (1988), and *Grand Canyon* (1991). Cervantes also has many episodic television credits.

Jorge Cervera, Jr.

This actor has appeared in *Papillon* (1973), *The Big Fix* (1978), *Black Marble* (1979), *True Confessions* (1981), and *¡Three Amigos!* (1986). His extensive television work includes 13 episodes as a co-star of "Viva Valdez."

Damian Chapa

A young actor of Mexican American and German heritage, Chapa plays the leading role of Miklo in *Bound by Honor* (1993). He also appeared in *Under Siege* (1992) with Steven Seagal.

Charo
B: 1/15/1951

This vivacious Spanish-born singer, actress, and comedienne has appeared in the films *Airport '79* (1979) and *Moon over Parador* (1988). She received her professional start in the States with Xavier Cugat, to whom she was married. Charo has guest starred in numerous television variety shows and on many situation comedies. She also guest starred in a somewhat serious dramatic role on an episode of the TV series "Fantasy Island," starring Ricardo Montalban.

Richard Chaves

An actor whose Vietnam War experience has been catalytic, Chaves co-wrote the highly successful stage play *Tracers*. He co-stars in the film *Predator* (1987) as Poncho and was also in *Cease Fire* (1985) opposite Don Johnson. He co-starred in the television film *Fire on the Mountain* (1981) with Buddy Ebsen and has guest starred on numerous popular series.

Linda Christian [born: Blanca Rosa Welter]
B: 11/13/1924

Born in Mexico of Dutch parents, Christian was signed by an MGM talent scout in 1945 for *Holiday in Mexico* (1946) and *Green Dolphin Street* (1947). Afterward, she decided to freelance and appeared in the made-in-Mexico *Tarzan and the Mermaids* (1948) and *The Happy Time* (1952), with Louis Jourdan. Christian became best known when she married actor Tyrone Power in 1949. After her marriage to Power ended in divorce in 1955, she resumed her film acting career in Europe.

Cynthia Cidre
B: 1957

A Cuban-born screenwriter, Cidre's credits include *Fires Within* (1991) and *The Mambo Kings* (1992). She also co-scripted *In Country* (1989), starring Bruce Willis and directed by Norman Jewison.

Alex Colon
B: 1/26/1941

A Puerto Rican–born actor, Colon was raised in New York. He has worked extensively in theater, television, and film. Colon appeared on Broadway in Neil Simon's *The Gingerbread Lady* (1970) with Maureen Stapleton.

He can be seen in such films as *Invasion, U.S.A.* (1952), *The Cross and the Switchblade* (1970), *The Hospital* (1971), *Harry and Tonto* (1974), *The Super Cops* (1974), *The Taking of Pelham 1,2,3* (1974), *The Ultimate Warrior* (1975) with Yul Brynner, *Special Delivery* (1976), *When You Comin' Back, Red Ryder?* (1979), *Back Roads* (1981), *Deal of the Century* (1983), *Death of an Angel* (1985), *Deep Cover* (1988), *The Mighty Quinn* (1989), and *Red Scorpion* (1989). Television films include *The Law* (1974), *Hustling* (1975) with Jill Clayburgh, *Raid on Entebbe* (1977), *Women of San Quentin* (1983), and the 24-hour epic miniseries *Centennial* (1978–1979).

Miriam Colon
B: 1925

A Puerto Rican–born actress, Colon has appeared as a Mexican in such films as *One-Eyed Jacks* (1961) and *The Appaloosa* (1966), both starring Marlon Brando. She had an important and strong role as Tony Montana's (Al Pacino's) mother in Brian

De Palma's *Scarface* (1983). Her other films include *The Possession of Joel Delaney* (1972), *Back Roads* (1981), and *The House of the Spirits* (1994).

Spotted as a serious talent while she was a drama student at the University of Puerto Rico, Colon was admitted to New York's prestigious Actors Studio on her first audition. After studying under Lee Strasberg and Elia Kazan, she appeared on the New York Stage in *In the Summer House, The Innkeepers, The Wrong Way Light Bulb,* and *The Oxcart.*

Colon guest starred in more than 100 television shows and is the founder and artistic director of New York's Puerto Rican Traveling Theatre, which she established over 20 years ago.

Anjanette Comer

A talented actress, Comer has co-starred in such films as *Quick, Before It Melts* (1964), *The Loved One* (1965), *The Appaloosa* (1966), *Banning* (1967), *Guns for San Sebastian* (1968), *Lepke* (1975), and *Fire Sale* (1978).

James Contreras

    B: 1923
    D: 1990

A film sound man for over 40 years, Contreras's credits include *Easy Rider* (1969) and *The Night of the Iguana* (1964). In television, he worked on such series as "Kung Fu" and "The Streets of San Francisco." He was the brother of actor Roberto Contreras.

Luis Contreras

    B: 9/18/1950

A Mexican American character actor, Contreras usually plays unsavory characters and heavies in films and episodic television shows. Among his multitude of film credits are *Coming Home* (1978), *Borderline* (1980), *The Long Riders* (1980), *Barbarosa* (1982), *Pee-Wee's Big Adventure* (1985), *Red Heat* (1985), *Blues City* (1986), *Extreme Prejudice* (1987), *Walker* (1987), and *Bound by Honor* (1993). His television work includes such shows as "Gunsmoke" (his first appearance in 1969), the original "Mission: Impossible," "Hill Street Blues," "Dallas," the new "Adam 12," and "MacGyver." He is the son of actor Roberto Contreras.

Roberto Contreras

Born in St. Louis and raised in Mexico City, Contreras, son of director Jaime Contreras, began his acting career at age eight, appearing in Mexican films and television productions. His film credits include *The Sun Also Rises* (1957), *The Magnificent Seven* (1960), *Ship of Fools* (1965), *The Appaloosa* (1966), *The Professionals* (1966), *Topaz* (1969), *Barbarosa* (1982), *Scarface* (1983), and *Streets of Fire* (1984). Among his numerous television credits was a regular role as a ranch hand on "The High Chaparral" series. His son, Luis Contreras, is also an actor.

Caesar Cordova

    B: 5/16/1936

A Puerto Rican–born character actor, Cordova's film credits include *Shark's Treasure* (1975), starring and directed by Cornel Wilde, *Where the Buffalo Roam* (1980), *Nighthawks* (1981), and *Scarface* (1983) opposite Al Pacino. His television credits include "East Side/West Side" and "Kojak."

Mapy Cortes [born: Maria del Pilar; aka: Mapy Cortez]

B: 3/1/1919

Born in Puerto Rico, Cortes entered musical comedy in Spanish theater, performing throughout Latin America and Spain. She made films in Spain and Mexico, where she was enormously popular. The Latin star came to Hollywood in 1942, where at RKO she made *Seven Days Leave* (1942), an entertaining all-star musical extravaganza with Victor Mature and Lucille Ball. She basically played herself, a Puerto Rican singing and dancing star, with Les Brown and his Band of Renown.

Ricardo Cortez [born: Jacob Krantz]

B: 9/19/1899

D: 4/28/1977

Born in Vienna, Cortez immigrated to New York City with his family at age three. He started as an extra in movies when he was 17 in New York. In 1922, Jesse Lasky, head of Paramount Studios, spotted him because of his dark good looks, and Lasky's secretary picked the name Ricardo Cortez when it was decided he needed a Latin name. Ricardo was on his way to stardom as a screen Latin lover and successor to Valentino, who was Lasky's big star then. Valentino was threatening to leave the studio, and Lasky cast Cortez in the next movie intended for him and let Valentino go his own way, allowing Ricardo to achieve prominence. He stayed with Lasky for six more years and then moved to MGM, where he was the only star billed above Garbo in her first American motion picture, *The Torrent* (1926, silent). Cortez's career waned with the coming of sound.

Cortez is included here because, even though not a Latin, he was closely identified as one and had adopted a Latin name.

Stanley Cortez [born: Stanley Krantz]

B: 11/4/1908

Stanley Cortez adopted the stage surname of his actor brother, Ricardo Cortez. As a cinematographer he created powerful images in *The Magnificent Ambersons* (1942) for Orson Welles, for which he received an Oscar nomination; *Since You Went Away* (1944), *The Night of the Hunter* (1955), and *The Three Faces of Eve* (1957).

He worked as a young portrait photographer in New York City in the 1920s and entered motion pictures as a camera assistant to D.W. Griffith on two of his last films. He is recognized as having played a key role in defining cinematography as an art form by the powerful example of his body of work. Cortez is a life member of the American Society of Cinematographers.

Manny Cota

A writer and director, Cota directed the 1992 theatrical feature film *Dr. Giggles*. For television he has directed episodes of HBO's "Tales from the Crypt" and the syndicated series "Monsters." Cota was born in Havana, Cuba, and was raised in Orlando, Florida.

Linda Cristal [born: Marta Luis Moya Burgess]

B: 2/24/1935

An Argentine-born actress, Cristal achieved popularity in the States during the late 1950s and early 1960s. Her most important film role was in *The Alamo* (1960), starring John Wayne (however, in theatrical reissues and on television her part has been considerably edited), and she later starred in the NBC television series "The High Chaparral" as the strong-willed and beautiful Victoria Cannon.

The actress was born in Buenos Aires, Argentina. She was orphaned at age 13, and at age 17, while vacationing in Mexico, she was noticed by Mexican film producer/director Raul de Anda during a concert. He persuaded her to do a screen test. Upon seeing the results he put her under contract and gave her a leading role in his next production, *Genio y Figura*. She starred for six years in Spanish-language films and was then signed to a Hollywood contract by Universal-International, which exploited her Latin background, as this press release indicates: "Universal-International's best bet for stardom is an Argentinian beauty with more zing than a chili pepper, more beauty than a Buenos Aires sunset and more curves than a roadmap of the Andes."

Cristal began the U.S. phase of her career playing virginal senoritas and Indian maidens in a number of films. She played a Mexican girl in *The Last of the Fast Guns* (1958), an Italian movie star in *The Perfect Furlough* (1958) with Tony Curtis, a Cuban dance hall hostess in *Cry Tough* (1959), and a Mexican woman captured by Indians in John Ford's *Two Rode Together* (1961). Her last major motion picture role to date was in *Mr. Majestyk* (1974), starring Charles Bronson, as a socially concerned Chicana activist. Her other films include *Comanche* (1956) and *The Fiend Who Walked the West* (1958).

Her role as Victoria Cannon on the long-running TV series "The High Chaparral" demonstrated acting ability and a maturity that brought her great popularity. She received two Emmy Award nominations as Best Actress in a Drama Series.

Xavier Cugat

B: 1/1/1900
D: 10/27/1990

A Spanish-born orchestra leader, Cugat was instrumental in popularizing Latin American music in the United States during the 1930s and 1940s. Through night-club performances, radio, recordings, motion pictures, and television, Cugat became a household name in America. More than any other person, he is credited with starting the rumba craze in the States. His flair for featuring beautiful singers with his band helped launch the careers of Lina Romay, Margo, Abbe Lane, and Charo.

While under contract to MGM, Cugat was featured in several musicals of the late 1930s and the 1940s in sumptuous production numbers that spotlighted him and his band. *Go West, Young Man* (1936), *Bathing Beauty* (1944), *Two Girls and a Sailor* (1944), *Holiday in Mexico* (1946), *No Leave, No Love* (1946), *This Time for Keeps* (1947), *A Date with Judy* (1948), *Luxury Liner* (1948), *On an Island with You* (1948), and *Neptune's Daughter* (1949).

Xavier Cugat and Carmen Miranda supply the chili-flavored romantic doings in the musical *A Date with Judy*.

Born in Barcelona, Spain, on New Year's Day, Cugat discovered at an early age that all the members of his artistic family were expected to help to support the group. His three brothers were struggling artists, his parents, musicians. His father became a political refugee from Spain, and the family moved to Cuba when Xavier was three years old. They lived across the street from a violin maker, and he was given one as a present and quickly mastered the instrument. At age 12, Xavier's violin playing with a symphony orchestra in Havana earned enough to support his entire family. Eventually, the talents of his brothers were recognized also, and all achieved success.

Later, back in Spain, Cugat studied under Tullio Serafin. He then came to America and enrolled at the Frank Damrosch School, studying under Frank Kneisel. In Italy he became acquainted with Enrico Caruso, who engaged him to play his violin between Caruso's numbers on concert tours. It was Caruso who started Cugat drawing, an endeavor that brought the bandmaster as much fame as his music.

Returning to America, Cugat found the concert field far from lucrative. Stowing his fiddle in its case, he went to southern California, where he became a cartoonist on the staff of the *Los Angeles Times* from 1924 to 1925. Music was his first love, however, and he soon found work as a composer for a motion picture studio. He also found six other musicians to play commercial music with him. "Well, almost commercial," remarked Cugat in an interview quoted in the *L.A. Times* obituary (10/28/90). "They were a Latin Music combo, and in the 1920's (Rudolph Valentino notwithstanding) such rhythms were considered 'gigolo music' and demand was limited."

This led to the organization of a small band, with which he made a short subject with Rita Cansino (later to become Rita Hayworth). He took the same band to Hollywood's Montmartre Cafe, and they caused a sensation whenever they played. His big break came when he was booked into the Starlight Roof of New York City's famed Waldorf-Astoria Hotel. There followed long engagements at the Waldorf-Astoria for almost a decade. In 1941, Louis B. Mayer's limousine drew up in front of Hollywood's Palladium, a famous dance palace frequented by the younger generation. He took notice of Cugat's name on the marquee and the excitement of the crowd and signed Cugat to a contract. Hayworth and Cugat were reunited in 1942 for his appearance in the musical *You Were Never Lovelier* (1942), in which Hayworth co-starred with Fred Astaire. Cugat usually played himself, along with his band, in these film appearances.

Bertila Damas

A Cuban–Puerto Rican actress, Damas co-starred opposite Jimmy Smits in *Fires Within* (1991) and was featured in *Nothing But Trouble* (1991) with Chevy Chase and in *Stop! Or My Mom Will Shoot* (1992).

Henry Darrow [born: Henry Delgado]
B: 1931

A New York–born Puerto Rican actor, Henry Delgado grew up in the Washington Heights area of northern Manhattan. He decided to seek opportunities in California and studied at the Pasadena Playhouse. Producer David Dortort saw him in a production of Ray Bradbury's *The Wonderful Ice Cream Suit* at the Coronet Theatre; a year later Dortort remembered the young actor's spirited performance and felt he might be right for the role of Manolito on a television show he was creating called "The High Chaparral." A casting call for Delgado went out, but he could not be found, for Delgado had changed his name to Darrow to further his acting opportunities. He finally got word that Dortort was looking for him, and he landed the role that would lead him to television stardom, as the rascally son of a wealthy Mexican cattle baron on the long-running series. He later co-starred with David Janssen on the "Harry-O" series and on "The New Dick Van Dyke Show." He made his feature film debut in a small role in *Holiday for Lovers* (1959) starring Clifton Webb. Darrow has had co-starring roles in such films as *Badge 373* (1973), *Walk Proud* (1979), and *Losin' It* (1983).

Howard da Silva

B: 5/4/1909
D: 2/16/1986

Often cast as a heavy, da Silva, born in Cleveland, Ohio, the son of Benjamin and Bertha da Silva, was of Russian and Portuguese descent. He made his motion picture debut in 1940 in *I'm Still Alive,* and gained recognition as the bartender in Billy Wilder's *The Lost Weekend* (1945) and as the sadistic captain in *Two Years Before the Mast* (1946). His more than 40 motion picture credits include *Duffy's Tavern* (1945), *Unconquered* (1947), *David and Lisa* (1962), *Topkapi* (1964), and *Nevada Smith* (1966). He created the role of Judd in the original Broadway stage production of *Oklahoma!* and starred in the stage and film (1972) versions of the musical *1776* as Ben Franklin. He won an Emmy Award for Outstanding Performance by a Supporting Actor in the TV special "Verna, USO Girl." He also directed the original Broadway production of *Purlie Victorious* (1961) starring Ruby Dee and Ossie Davis.

Francisco ("Chico") Day [born: Francisco Alonso]

B: 1907

Born in Juarez, Mexico, and raised in El Paso and Los Angeles, Day was the first Hispanic American assistant director in Hollywood and worked for over 30 years at Paramount Studios on such films as *The Big Broadcast of 1938* (1938), *Lady in the Dark* (1944), *Whispering Smith* (1948), *Streets of Laredo* (1949), *Samson and Delilah* (1949), *The Ten Commandments* (1956), *Teacher's Pet* (1958), and *One-Eyed Jacks* (1961). He later became a unit production manager on such noted films as *The Magnificent Seven* (1960), *Hello, Dolly!* (1969), and *Patton* (1970). Day is a life member of the Directors Guild of America.

Assistant director Francisco "Chico" Day, Cecil B. De Mille, and second assistant director Mickey Moore on the set of *The Ten Commandments.*

Pedro De Cordoba
B: 9/28/1881
D: 1950

A tall, gaunt-looking character actor who appeared in numerous silent and sound films, De Cordoba was born in New York City to Cuban-French parents. His credits include the silent 1915 version of *Carmen* as Escamillo, *Temptation* (1915, silent), *Ramona* (1936), *The Garden of Allah* (1936), *The Sea Hawk* (1940), *The Mark of Zorro* (1940), *Aloma of the South Seas* (1941), *The Song of Bernadette* (1943), *The Keys of the Kingdom* (1944), *Samson and Delilah* (1949), and *Crisis* (1950).

Arturo De Cordova [born: Arturo Garcia Rodriguez]
B: 1908
D: 11/3/1973

Arturo De Cordova had a likable, pleasant manner on screen, but he never quite clicked with U.S. moviegoing audiences. After starring in a number of films at Paramount, he decided to return to Mexico and South America, where he began his career and became a screen idol, working constantly in leading roles until his death.

Born in Merida, Mexico, he initially worked as a sports writer for UPI and as a radio announcer. While working in Argentina as a sports writer, he met Russian stage director Aready Boytler, who suggested that De Cordova become an actor. De Cordova did not take him seriously until the two met again years later in Mexico City, where Boytler was about to produce a film with Fernando Soler. Boytler asked

Arturo De Cordova.

De Cordova to play the romantic lead. He took the job thinking that it might help his radio announcing career. In 1935 he starred in the hit film *Cielito Lindo,* at which time he formally adopted the screen name of De Cordova.

In 1938, De Cordova made his first Hollywood film, the Spanish-language *Son's Command,* followed by *The Miracle of Main Street,* with Margo, in 1939. De Cordova's first big break in American films came with the role of Augustin in Paramount's adaptation of Ernest Hemingway's *For Whom the Bell Tolls* (1943), with Gary Cooper and Ingrid Bergman.

Under contract to Paramount Pictures, he had important roles in such films as *Duffy's Tavern* (1945), *A Medal for Benny* (1945), *Incendiary Blonde* (1945), and *Masquerade in Mexico* (1945). Paramount gambled and assigned him the leading role opposite Joan Fontaine in the important and expensive film *Frenchman's Creek* (1944). Although it was not a hit, De Cordova turned in an impressive performance as the French pirate. He left Paramount for Mexico, where he starred in a version of *The Count of Monte Cristo* (1934), which became a smash hit and made him the idol of millions of women in 17 Latin countries. De Cordova became one of the stars of Mexico's Golden Age of Cinema (1942–1952) as a romantic leading man in a wide variety of roles. His other U.S. films include *New Orleans* (1947) and *The Adventures of Casanova* (1948).

Frederick De Cordova

    B: 10/27/1910

De Cordova was born in New York City and came to films from the stage in 1944 as a dialogue director at Warner Bros. He directed many routine medium-budget entertainment features through the mid-1960s but has been active mainly in TV since the mid-1950s. From 1971 until May 1992, when he retired, he was the producer of NBC's "The Tonight Show Starring Johnny Carson."

Josie De Guzman

A Puerto Rican Broadway stage actress, De Guzman was featured in the film *F/X* (1986) starring Bryan Brown. Her stage credits include her Tony-nominated starring role in the 1992 revival of *Guys and Dolls.*

Joe (Jose) De La Cruz

    B: 3/19/1892
    D: 12/14/1965

A Mexican-born western film supporting player from the 1920s through the 1940s, De La Cruz usually played a Mexican bandit or *vaquero.* His films include *The Bearcat* (1922, silent) with Hoot Gibson, *A Devil with Women* (1930) with Victor McLaglen and Mona Maris, *The Cactus Kid* (1935) with Jack Perin, *Zorro's Fighting Legion* (1939, 12-chapter serial) with Reed Hadley, and *Oklahoma Frontier* (1939) with Johnny Mack Brown. De La Cruz's final film was *The Black Scorpion* (1957).

Danny De La Paz

    B: 4/13/1957

An intense actor, De La Paz has played starring roles in such films as *Boulevard Nights* (1979) as Chuco, a young and troubled gang member; *Cuba* (1979), as a Cuban rebel; *Barbarosa* (1982), as the Mexican American son who sacrifices himself to the wishes of his father; and *American Me* (1992), as Puppet, a prison gang member who is forced to kill his own brother in order to uphold a deadly code. He was also featured in *Miracle Mile* (1989).

George De La Pena

B: 1958

Born in New York of mixed Russian-Argentinian parentage, De La Pena, a remarkable young dancer from the American Ballet Theatre, portrayed the legendary Russian dancer who electrified the Western world in the 1980 film *Nijinsky*, directed by Herbert Ross.

Marcus De Leon

The director/writer of the independent feature *Kiss Me a Killer* (1991), De Leon is the son of a prominent Mexican American artist and a German-born educator. A native of Los Angeles, he attended UCLA Film School and wrote and directed a short film, *Xavier*, that went on to win the school's prestigious Best Film Award. De Leon and several of his UCLA classmates made a film called *Border Radio* (1988).

Marcel Delgado

B: 1900

D: 1976

With special effects genius Willis O'Brien, Delgado worked on many films, most notably as chief model maker and sculptor on the 1933 RKO production of *King*

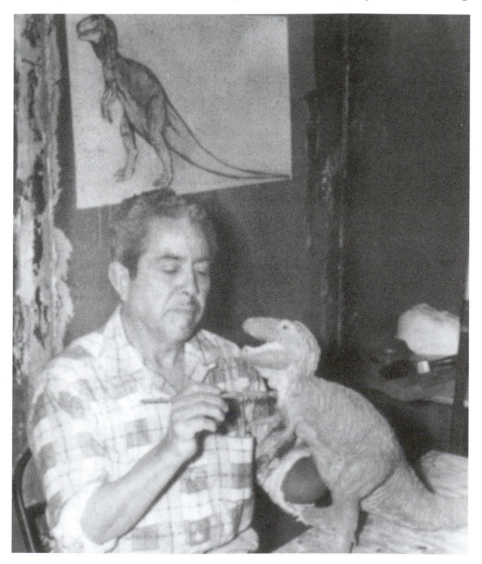

Model maker and sculptor Marcel Delgado at work in the 1930s.

Kong. Born in La Parrita, Mexico, he moved with his family to California in 1909. A self-educated sculptor, he worked on such films as *The Lost World* (1925, silent), *Son of Kong* (1934), *Mighty Joe Young* (1949), *Jack the Giant Killer* (1962), *It's a Mad Mad Mad Mad World* (1963), and *Fantastic Voyage* (1966).

Marcia Del Mar

Del Mar's feature film credits include roles in *Under Fire* (1983) and *Body Double* (1984). She also co-starred on the USA cable TV series "Sanchez of Bel Air."

Pilar Del Rey

An actress, Del Rey made her film debut as a young girl in *The Miracle of Our Lady of Fatima,* starring Gilbert Roland, in 1952. She went on to appear on early dramatic television shows and in such films as *Black Horse Canyon* (1954) with Joel McCrea, *Mark of the Renegade* (1951) with Ricardo Montalban, and *And Now Miguel* (1966) with Michael Ansara. Del Rey played the mother of Sal Mineo and the wife of Victor Millan in George Stevens's *Giant* (1956). Her other film credits include *The Naked Jungle* (1953) and *Lonely Are the Brave* (1962).

Dolores Del Rio [born: Lolita Dolores Martinez Ansunsolo Lopez Negrette]

B: 8/3/1905
D: 3/11/1983

Dolores Del Rio was one of the legendary beauties of the silver screen, and her 50-year career spanned the transition from silent to sound movies and television. Though she starred in a number of silent and early talkie Hollywood film classics, such as *What Price Glory?* (1926, silent), *Resurrection* (1927, silent), *The Loves of Carmen* (1927, silent), *Ramona* (1928, silent), *Flying Down to Rio* (1933), and *Bird of Paradise* (1932), the greater part of her career from 1943 was spent in her native Mexico, where she became a top star after filming *Maria Candelaria* (1943). Her luminous beauty and natural dignity combined with her acting ability gained her a wide range of starring roles in Mexican films.

She was born in Durango, Mexico, where her father was a banker. At age four, Dolores and her family were forced to leave Durango for Mexico City when Pancho Villa threatened them. At age 15 she married Jaime Martinez del Rio and took his name, capitalizing the "D" on the "del" for her career, which began quite casually after she studied dancing and began to perform at various society galas and festivals.

U.S. film director Edwin Carewe, honeymooning in Mexico in the early 1920s, saw Del Rio dancing a tango at a party in his honor and was immediately struck by her beauty and dancing ability. The Del Rios and the Carewes became friends, and eventually Dolores acceded to his request to come to Hollywood in 1925. "He told me I was the female Valentino," said Del Rio in a 1981 interview. "He kept sending me wires and eventually my husband and I decided to go. I didn't know what would happen but I thought it would be fun to meet all the people I idolized like Chaplin and Valentino," Bridget Byrne, *San Francisco Chronicle* (11/20–27/81).

Del Rio played her first small part, as a vamp society girl, in Carewe's minor jazz tale *Joanna* (1925, silent). She followed this with a second film for Carewe, *High Steppers* (1926, silent), in which her role was subordinate to star Mary Astor. Her first lead was in *Pals First* (1926, silent), and then she filmed *The Whole Town Is Talking* (1926, silent). Her first real success, however, was as the provocative

French flirt Charmaine in Raoul Walsh's *What Price Glory?* that same year. The film brought her wide praise and immediate fame. It also proved not only that she was beautiful but that she could handle comedy as well, especially opposite two scene-stealing leading men like Edmund Lowe and Victor McLaglen.

Del Rio's next film was *Resurrection* (1927, silent) from the novel by Tolstoy, for her director friend Edwin Carewe and with Rod La Rocque as her leading man. She portrayed Katusha, who is forced into prostitution after an unhappy affair with a married man. That same year she starred in *The Loves of Carmen* for Raoul Walsh, and the following year she played the first in a series of native roles as a half-caste girl in love with a tough railroad manager (Walter Pidgeon) in *The Gateway of the Moon* (1928, silent). In 1928 she was also directed by Carewe in *Ramona,* the famous love story of an Indian girl and a Spaniard, which became one of her most successful films. Her leading man was Warner Baxter. With her great success, a studio released a quickie she had made two years before with Don Alvarado called *No Other Woman* (1926, silent), and she followed her success with *Revenge* (1928, silent) also for Carewe. Raoul Walsh directed her again in *The Red Dance* (1928), in which she played the role of the Red Dancer of the Russian Revolution. She played the part of a dance hall girl in *The Trail of '98* (1928, silent) opposite Harry Carey. *Evangeline* in 1929 with Roland Drew was a tearjerker, the story of youthful lovers who are reunited in old age. Del Rio sang two songs and spoke one line of dialogue at the end of this otherwise silent film.

Her first all-talking picture was *The Bad One* (1930) with Don Alvarado and Edmund Lowe, with Del Rio as an inmate of a brothel. After the film she broke her contract with Carewe and signed with Joseph Schenck of United Artists. Following the signing she suffered a nervous breakdown, which kept her away from the cameras for almost two years. She returned in 1931 to RKO with a new contract and filmed *Girl of the Rio* (1932), in which she played a cantina performer opposite Leo Carrillo and Norman Foster. The film was later banned in Mexico for its unflattering portrayals of Mexican and Latin characters.

She played Luana, a native girl of the Hawaiian Islands, in *Bird of Paradise* (1932), directed by King Vidor mostly on location in Hawaii. Producer David O. Selznick later reportedly told Vidor: "I don't care what story you use as long as we call it *Bird of Paradise* and Del Rio jumps into a flaming volcano at the finish." Her leading man was Joel McCrea, at the time the epitome of the new athletic leading man and much in demand. The film was a tremendous hit with the public, the photography was outstanding, and Vidor's direction kept a strong hand on the flimsy plot contrivances of love and uprising in the South Seas.

In 1933 she accepted a role in the musical *Flying Down to Rio.* On paper she had the lead opposite Gene Raymond, but Fred Astaire and Ginger Rogers danced away with the film. Her tango to "Orchids in the Moonlight" with Astaire was seen in the picture before his now more famous dances with Ginger Rogers in the landmark musical. In an interview many years later she said, "For the first time I was to play the part of a smart modern woman with plenty of music and comedy around me. I knew it was a sign that I could play a sophisticated role. I was no longer little Luana or Ramona. The picture was a great success. The credit mainly belonged to others, but my private battle was partly won," *Film Weekly* (July 1972).

In 1934 she made three pictures for Warner Bros. that, according to her contract (located at the Warner Bros. Archives at the University of Southern California Library), earned her a total of $100,000—not a bad sum for the middle of the Depression, when the average worker, if lucky enough to have a job, was earning only $12 a week. In *Wonder Bar* (1934) she was the dance partner of Ricardo Cortez. She starred in *Madame du Barry* (1934) with Reginald Owen and Anita Louise. This bedroom comedy proved a disappointment to the star, who

Dolores Del Rio—1945.

considered it her best work of that period. The film suffered at the hands of the censors, and the public was not interested. *In Caliente* and *I Live for Love* (both 1935) marked the change in image that she had strived for, but she was used more for decorative purposes in these musical fantasies. Del Rio continued working in such films as *The Widow from Monte Carlo* (1936), *Accused* (1936), *Ali Baba Goes to Town* (1937), *Devil's Playground* (1937), *Lancer Spy* (1937), *International Settlement* (1938), and *The Man from Dakota* (1940).

By the early 1940s, between program pictures and marital difficulties, both her career and her personal life were in distress. She had already divorced her first husband, and her marriage to famed MGM art director Cedric Gibbons was now on the rocks. Meanwhile, she was engaged in a close relationship with Orson Welles and appeared as a nightclub dancer in the first two reels of his *Journey into Fear* (1942), an espionage thriller starring Joseph Cotten. Dissatisfied with her work and life in Hollywood, Del Rio returned to Mexico. She recalled in a 1981 interview, "I didn't want to be a star anymore, I wanted to be an actress and with all of those gowns they put on me, all of those millions of feathers, I couldn't be. I chose instead the chance to be a pioneer in the movie industry of my country, an exciting new challenge," Herb Michelson, *Variety* (10/15/81).

The Mexican film industry had developed tremendously since she had left in 1926 and was technically as proficient and accomplished as Hollywood. In Mexico, Del Rio found a director, Emilio Fernandez, who realized her full potential as an actress and star. *Flor Silvestre,* her first film for him in 1943, established her as Mexico's top star and gained her the first of the four Ariels (Mexico's Oscar) she was to receive as Best Actress. Pedro Armendariz, director Fernandez, cameraman Gabriel Figueroa, and Del Rio became known as "The Team" of the Mexican film industry. *Maria Candelaria,* directed by Emilio Fernandez, showcased Del Rio at her finest, as a peasant girl of simplicity and deep spirituality who is stoned to death by her fellow villagers, who mistrust and fear her. As a result of its showing at the Cannes Film Festival, it was the first Mexican film to make an impact on the international film community following World War II. In a folkloric style enhanced by Gabriel Figueroa's brilliant black-and-white photography, the film reflected a national identity rooted in the Mexican culture. The Team stayed together for several more films, including *Bugambilia* (1944), *Las Abandonadas* (1944), and *La Malquerida* (1949).

John Ford's *The Fugitive* (1947), though an American film, was shot largely in Mexico by Figueroa and starred Henry Fonda as an alcoholic priest on the run;

Dolores Del Rio—1965.

it featured Pedro Armendariz, Del Rio, and Leo Carrillo. She continued starring in Mexican films as a top star during and beyond the so-called Golden Age of Mexican Cinema (1942–1952).

In 1960 she returned to Hollywood to play Elvis Presley's Indian mother in Don Siegel's *Flaming Star.* Critics noted her moving performance and her enduring beauty. She had planned an earlier return to Hollywood to act with Spencer Tracy in *Broken Lance* (1954), but the State Department delayed her visa until they were satisfied that she had not been affected by her association with communists in the Mexican film industry, and by that time production had gone ahead with then-popular Mexican actress Katy Jurado, fresh from her success with *High Noon.*

In 1964 she played an Indian woman in John Ford's *Cheyenne Autumn.* As the character called Spanish Woman, Del Rio with little dialogue stood out in a cast that included Gilbert Roland, Richard Widmark, Sal Mineo, and James Stewart. While in the States she made several television guest appearances on such shows as "I Spy," and "Marcus Welby, M.D.," "Schlitz Playhouse of Stars" (1957), "U.S. Steel Hour" (1958), and her own special "Dolores Del Rio's Mexico" (1968). She also followed her aspirations for the stage, where she received more accolades as the "First Lady of the Mexican Theater," having appeared in numerous stage productions in Mexico City. Her last film appearance was in a brief role as the grandmother in Hall Bartlett's little-seen 1978 *The Children of Sanchez,* in which the essence of Del Rio's dignity and beauty were captured by her longtime cinematographer and collaborator Gabriel Figueroa. At a tribute in her honor at the San Francisco Film Festival in 1981, she remarked, "I gave 50 years to my career. It was number one, two and three in my life, the thing I lived for. Everything I did was with my career in mind. I was very honest with my career but there was a lot of personal sacrifice which I had to undergo." She died at her Newport Beach, California, home of natural causes in 1983.

Benicio Del Toro

B: 1967

A Puerto Rican–born actor, Del Toro was featured in *Christopher Columbus: The Discovery* (1992), as Indian slave master Alvaro. He also played in *Fearless* (1993) as Carla Rodrigo's husband; in *Licence to Kill* (1989), as Dario, a henchman; and in *Big Top Pee-wee* (1989). His television credits include "Miami Vice," the miniseries *Drug Wars: The Camarena Story.*

Nick De Ruiz

De Ruiz appeared in 27 feature films from 1920 to 1930 in a variety of roles ranging from Mexican bandits to sultans. Some of his better-known credits are *The Hunchback of Notre Dame* (1923) with Lon Chaney, *Old Ironsides* (1926), and *The Unknown* (1927) with Lon Chaney, all of which are silent.

Rosana De Soto

B: 1947

Having made the transition from repertory theater to television to feature films, De Soto received critical acclaim for her role as Ritchie Valens's mother in the hit film *La Bamba* (1987). She co-starred in *Stand and Deliver* (1988) as Fabiola Escalante and had the pivotal role of the translator in *The Ballad of Gregorio Cortez* (1983). De Soto played Dustin Hoffman's wife in *Family Business* (1989) and a Klingon princess in *Star Trek VI: The Undiscovered Country* (1991). Her other films include *The In-Laws* (1979) and *Cannery Row* (1982). On television she has guest starred in many

Rosana De Soto as Ritchie Valens's mother in *La Bamba*.

series and appeared in many TV movies. She was a regular in two series, "The Redd Fox Show" and "A.E.S. Hudson Street." Born in San Jose, California, De Soto studied drama at San Jose University and joined the Northern California Light Opera Company.

Steven E. De Souza

De Souza is a writer of Spanish and Portuguese background whose screenplays include *48 HRS.* (1982), *Die Hard* (1988), and *Die Hard 2* (1990). He spent years at Universal Studios as a contract writer on many television series.

Carlos J. de Valdez

B: 3/19/1894
D: 10/30/1939

A Peruvian-born stage and screen actor, de Valdez was featured in such films as *The Robin Hood of El Dorado* (1936), *Conquest* (1937), *Lancer Spy* (1937), *Suez* (1938), *The Girl from Mexico* (1939), *Juarez* (1939), and *The Llano Kid* (1940).

Jose De Vega, Jr.

B: 1935
D: 1991

Jose De Vega, Jr., played Chino in the Broadway and film versions of *West Side Story.* His other film credits include a role as one of Elvis Presley's Hawaiian backup singers in *Blue Hawaii* (1962). His other films include *The Spiral Road* (1962), *A Covenant with Death* (1966), and *Ash Wednesday* (1973). He was born in San Diego to a Filipino father and a Colombian mother.

Don Diamond

B: 1917

Brooklyn-born Don Diamond played El Toro, Bill Williams's Mexican sidekick, on the TV series "The Adventures of Kit Carson" (1951–1955). He also portrayed Corp. Reyes on Walt Disney's "Zorro" (1958–1959) and Crazy Cat on the "F Troop" series (1965–1967).

Edith Diaz

A Puerto Rican–born actress, Diaz was featured as one of the singing nuns in *Sister Act* (1992). Her other film credits include *Scenes from the Class Struggle in Beverly Hills* (1989) and *Born on the Fourth of July* (1989). She starred on the "Popi" television series in the 1970s and played Desi Arnaz's mother in the telefilm *Lucy and Desi: Before the Laughter* (1991).

Ken Diaz

A makeup artist, Diaz was nominated for an Academy Award for his work on *Dad* (1989), which starred Jack Lemmon. Through makeup, Diaz turned Lemmon into an aged and terminally ill man.

Placido Domingo

B: 1/21/1941

A Spanish-born, Mexican-raised international opera and recording star, Domingo was encouraged in his youthful interest in music by his parents, as other family members were professional practitioners of the Zarzuela, a three-century-old operatic form from Spain. He starred in Franco Zeffirelli's 1982 film production of *La Traviata* as Alfredo, and in 1986 as Verdi's tragic Moor in *Otello*. He also starred in *Bizet's Carmen* (1984) as Don Jose opposite Julia Migenes Johnson, directed by Francisco Rosi.

Marta Du Bois

An actress of French Panamanian heritage, Du Bois grew up in the United States. She co-starred as Shady in *Boulevard Nights* (1979) and has guest starred on numerous episodic series including "Magnum, P.I."

Larry Duran

B: 7/26/1925

A Mexican American actor/stuntman born in Los Angeles, Duran had featured roles in *Viva Zapata!* (1952), *The Magnificent Seven* (1960), and *One-Eyed Jacks* (1961). His father worked as an extra and as a runner (a person who recruited extras) for the studios, and Duran worked occasionally as an extra as a young man before he entered the military, where he became an amateur boxer. After military service he continued to box, and then met Marlon Brando at a bout. They took an immediate liking to each other, and Marlon offered him a job as his stand-in. Soon Duran began doing bit parts, and with his athletic and boxing abilities, he learned to do stunt work. He learned movie fistfighting, horsefalls, car crashes, and explosions, doubling for Brando on the motorcycle fall in *The Young Lions* (1958). After that, he did most of Brando's film stunt work. Duran was even employed as one of the background dancers on *Guys and Dolls* (1955), which starred Brando. As he met producers and other stuntmen, he began to work on films not associated with Brando. His son, Larry Duran, Jr., has followed in his father's footsteps and is currently a stuntman.

"I wasn't looking to be a movie star," remarked Duran during a 1992 interview with Luis Reyes. "Not bad for a guy who only completed junior high school with no skills. I was able to travel the world and now I'm retired and own my own home but I owe everything to Marlon Brando."

Chuy Elizondo
B: 12/25/1942

This renowned American television and film cinematographer was born in Torreon, Mexico, and was brought to the States at age 12. He learned about photography at a commercial production house and started as a camera assistant at Universal Studios. He developed an association with cinematographer John Alonzo, with whom he worked as a camera operator on such films as *Chinatown* (1974), *Conrack* (1974), *Farewell, My Lovely* (1975), and *The Bad News Bears* (1976). Elizondo became a director of photography on the feature *Shadow of Kilimanjaro* (1987). His extensive TV credits include *La Pastorela* (1991), *Bodies of Evidence* (1992), and *Terror in the Towers* (1993).

Hector Elizondo
B: 12/22/1936

Well known for his supporting character portrayals in both films and television, the Puerto Rican–born Elizondo was raised in New York City.

Elizondo is best known for his featured role as the warmhearted hotel manager Mr. Thompson in the hit film *Pretty Woman* (1990), starring Richard Gere and Julia Roberts. He made his film debut in 1971 as a Mexican bandit in *Valdez Is Coming*, and in that same year also appeared in *Born to Win*. He followed with diverse, memorable portrayals such as a psychopathic killer in *The Taking of Pelham 1, 2, 3* (1974); a police captain in *Report to the Commissioner* (1975); a military officer in *Cuba* (1979); and Inspector Andrews in *The Fan* (1981). Elizondo portrayed a mafioso forced to dress as a woman in order to elude assassins in Garry Marshall's comedy *Young Doctors in Love* (1982), and in Marshall's *The Flamingo Kid* (1984), he played a concerned father who doesn't understand his son's fascination with cars. He portrayed Detective Sunday in *American Gigolo* (1980), opposite Richard Gere. Elizondo's other feature film credits include roles in *Thieves* (1977), *Leviathan* (1989), *Taking Care of Business* (1990), *Frankie and Johnny* (1991), and *Necessary Roughness* (1991).

Elizondo has starred in five television series, "Freebie and the Bean"; "Popi"; "Casablanca"; "A.K.A. Pablo," on which he made his television directorial debut; and "Foley Square." He has made guest appearances on numerous television shows. The actor has appeared in such telefilms as *Wanted: The Sundance Woman* (1976), in which he played Pancho Villa; *The Dain Curse* (1978), *Honeyboy* (1982); *Casablanca* (1983); and *Women of San Quentin* (1983).

With an extensive theater background, Elizondo has been featured in such Broadway productions as *The Great White Hope* (1967); *Sly Fox* (1976), opposite George C. Scott; and Neil Simon's *Prisoner of Second Avenue* (1989). Off-Broadway, he created the role of God in *Steambath* (1973).

Rene Enriquez

B: 11/25/1933
D: 3/23/1990

An actor, born in San Francisco and raised in Nicaragua, Enriquez is best known for his role as Lt. Ray Calletano on the long-running "Hill Street Blues" television series. His film credits include *Bananas* (1971), *Under Fire* (1973), and *The Evil That Men Do* (1984).

Moctezuma Esparza

B: 3/12/1949

An award-winning film and television producer, Esparza produced *The Milagro Beanfield War* (1988) and *Only Once in a Lifetime* (1979). Esparza has an impressive record of achievement as both a filmmaker and a political activist.

Born in Los Angeles, he attended public schools and UCLA, where he received his BA and MFA in film. During his college years, Esparza became involved in many antiwar and civil rights groups and was a founder of the Chicano Research Center at UCLA. While still a graduate student, he produced bilingual films for "Sesame Street." His master's thesis took the form of a 1973 documentary film for NBC entitled *Cinco Vidas* (*Five Lives*), a poignant look at five people living in the barrio of East Los Angeles. *Cinco Vidas* won Esparza an Emmy in 1973. After that, Esparza was hired as producer for a PBS children's series called "Villa Alegre" ("Happy Village") and did a series of documentaries for the McGraw-Hill broadcasting series "La Raza" ("The People"), for which he won the John F. Kennedy Journalism Award. Forming Moctezuma Esparza Productions in 1974, he continued to work in the documentary and children's film fields. In 1977, he produced his first feature, Alejandro Grattan's *Only Once in a Lifetime,* the story of a down-on-his-luck Chicano painter. That same year, Esparza was nominated for an Academy Award in the Best Documentary Short category for *Agueda Martinez,* a portrait of an old woman from northern New Mexico.

Deciding to focus his energies on feature films, Esparza teamed up with the National Council of La Raza, a civil rights group, to develop a series of films exploring the literature and history of Chicanos in the United States. The first was Robert M. Young's *The Ballad of Gregorio Cortez* (1983), the true story of a young Chicano cowhand (Edward James Olmos) who kills a Texas sheriff in self-defense and is pursued by the Texas Rangers. The film was released theatrically by Embassy Pictures in 1983 and aired on PBS's "American Playhouse" series. The second was *The Milagro Beanfield War* (1988), to which Esparza had optioned the film rights in 1979. Through his Esparza/Katz Productions, he is active in producing films and television, including the Turner Entertainment theatrical release *Gettysburg* (1993) and the Turner Network Television movie *The Cisco Kid* (1994).

Richard Espinoza

B: 4/4/1948

A Texas-born assistant director, Espinoza rose through the ranks of the Directors Guild of America Training Program and has worked on such films as *North Dallas Forty* (1979), *The Border* (1982), *Remo Williams* (1985), *American Me* (1992), and *Dr. Giggles* (1992). His television credits include "Jake and the Fatman," "Baywatch," and "Beauty and the Beast."

Emilio Estevez
B: 5/12/1962

The son of actor Martin Sheen (whose real name is Ramon Estevez), Emilio chose to use the family's real surname, and within a few years established himself as a young star. Upon graduation from Santa Monica High School, Estevez made his professional acting debut in an after school television special and was soon featured in several television film dramas, including *In the Custody of Strangers* (1982), in which he worked opposite his father.

Estevez made his feature film debut in *Tex* (1982), based on the novel by S.E. Hinton, starring Matt Dillon. The film adaptation of Hinton's *The Outsiders* (1983), directed by Francis Ford Coppola, provided him with a second screen role as Two Bit Matthews. He then played a young punker who becomes involved with automobile repossessors and alien beings in the cult film *Repo Man* (1984).

His additional acting credits include a driven video-game champion in *Nightmares* (1983), a high school jock in John Hughes's *The Breakfast Club* (1985), and a law student obsessed with an older woman in *St. Elmo's Fire* (1985).

Estevez wrote the screenplay and starred in *That Was Then . . . This Is Now* (1985), which he adapted from an S.E. Hinton story, and *Wisdom* (1987), in which he also

Emilio Estevez.

starred and made his directorial debut, becoming at age 23 the youngest person ever to write, direct, and star in a major motion picture.

Estevez co-starred in the enormously successful comedy *Stakeout* (1987) with Richard Dreyfuss, and its far less successful sequel, *Another Stakeout* (1993), and in the hit youth westerns *Young Guns* (1988) and *Young Guns II* (1990) as Billy the Kid. *Young Guns* also provided the actor his first opportunity to star alongside his brother, actor Charlie Sheen. They followed this by starring together in *Men at Work* (1990), which Estevez also directed. In 1992, he starred in *The Mighty Ducks;* a sequel, *D2: The Mighty Ducks,* was released in 1994.

Angelina Estrada

B: 2/28/1932

A veteran character actress, Estrada started her career as a small child working as an extra in films. She had her first line in *Only Angels Have Wings* (1939), as a child tortilla vendor who says, "Tortillas," to Cary Grant. Estrada is an accomplished Hawaiian dancer, and she danced with Elvis Presley in *Blue Hawaii* (1961). Her film credits include *Aloma of the South Seas* (1941), *The Jungle Book* (1942) with Sabu, *Tortilla Flat* (1942), *A Medal for Benny* (1945), *One-Eyed Jacks* (1961), *Paint Your Wagon* (1969), and *Ghost* (1990) with Patrick Swayze.

Erik Estrada

B: 3/16/1949

Born in Spanish Harlem, New York, of Puerto Rican parents, Estrada was catapulted to television stardom with his role as Ponch Poncherello, an extroverted motorcycle officer, during the six-year run, from 1978 to 1983, of the successful and popular series "CHiPs."

Estrada's first break came when actor/director Don Murray was looking for a new face to co-star opposite Pat Boone in *The Cross and the Switchblade* (1970), in which he landed the co-starring role of a gang leader.

When Estrada heard that director Richard Fleischer was in New York to cast his new film, *The New Centurions* (1972), he knew, having read the book, that the important co-starring role of the Mexican American rookie policeman was exactly right for him and that a film credit opposite George C. Scott and Stacy Keach would be extremely beneficial to his career. The director didn't agree and told him he was much too young for the part. Undaunted, Estrada pursued the director to Hollywood and landed the role.

Estrada kept busy with roles in such films as *Airport 1975* (1974) and *Midway* (1976). He starred in *Trackdown* (1976) opposite James Mitchum. His most recent film credit is *A Show of Force* in 1990 with Robert Duvall.

Antonio Fargas

Flashy nightclub owner, malicious villain, pathetic barfly, powerful witch doctor— all these characters are within the creative province of Antonio Fargas, who has appeared in such films as *Shaft* (1971), *Across 110th Street* (1972), *Conrack* (1974), *Car Wash* (1976), *Next Stop, Greenwich Village* (1976), *Pretty Baby* (1978), *I'm Gonna Get You Sucka* (1989), and *Whore* (1991).

Born and raised in New York's Spanish Harlem, Fargas was first drawn to an acting career during his days at Fashion Industries High School, which led to study with several New York theater groups. His big break came when he landed a role as a witch doctor in the Broadway production of *The Great White Hope,* starring James Earl Jones.

Joao Fernandes

A Brazilian-born cinematographer, Fernandes has photographed a number of international Hollywood productions, including *Invasion, U.S.A.* (1952), *Missing in Action* (1984), and *Red Scorpion* (1989).

Abel Fernandez

> B: 7/14/1930

Fernandez is best known for his portrayal of American Indian Treasury Agent Youngfellow on "The Untouchables" television series from 1959 to 1963. Born and raised in East Los Angeles of Mexican American ancestry, Fernandez appeared on many classic TV series of the 1950s including "Rin-Tin-Tin" and "Lassie," usually as an Indian or a Mexican.

Emilio "El Indio" Fernandez

> B: 3/26/1904
> D: 8/6/1986

The single most important Mexican director of the 1940s, Emilio "El Indio" Fernandez's cinematic vision of Mexico forged a national identity for its people, folklore, and country. In later years his work became a caricature of itself, with his larger-than-life portrayals of stereotypical Mexican bandidos or generals in American films, in which he worked as an actor from the early 1960s.

Emilio Fernandez, director/actor/screenwriter, was born in a mining town called El Hondo in the Sabinas area of Coahuila, Mexico, the son of a Spanish-Mexican father and an Indian mother (hence the nickname "El Indio"). When his father left to join one of the revolutionary armies, Emilio, at age nine, became head of the family. Almost immediately he shot and killed a man for molesting his mother. Placed in a reform school, he escaped and joined the revolution. He fought under General Carranza against Pancho Villa, was captured, was sentenced to die at dawn, but escaped from a drunken guard. Later, he fought with Obregon against Carranza, then against Obregon for General de la Huerta. Jailed again, he blew up his cell with smuggled dynamite, appropriated a horse, and galloped north to the border.

In San Antonio he worked by day and studied English at night school. He picked cotton, herded sheep, stuck pigs, whatever he could to make a living. One day, the sharp-eyed Emilio saved a girl from drowning off a Chicago beach. She turned out to be an Earl Carroll dancer. Indio was picked up by the Edgewater Beach theatrical crowd, and his proficiency at Latin dances attracted the attention of Rudolph Valentino, who became his friend. After Valentino's death, El Indio rode the funeral train to Los Angeles, where he arrived broke and jobless. He got a job at United Artists Studios as a busboy, worked occasionally as an extra, and did bit parts as a heavy in westerns. He returned to Mexico with the desire to make films and found work as an actor.

He made his film debut in *Janitzio* (1934) as an Indian who loses his lady love to a Spaniard. The film served as a major influence for two films he later directed. His directing career began in 1943 with *Isla de la Pasion* (Of Passion Island). He quickly became the single most important Mexican film director of Mexico's Golden Age (1942–1952).

The Mexican film industry had been established as both a creative and commercial force since the late 1920s and, along with Argentina and Cuba, it was one of the three predominant motion picture producers of the Spanish-speaking world.

Maria Candelaria (1943) won the Grand Prize at the Cannes Film Festival in 1947, *Flor Silvestre* (1943) won at Locarno that same year, and *La Perla* (*The Pearl*)

(1945) won at San Sebastian in 1946. He recalled at a University of California symposium, "I worked with John Steinbeck on the screenplay for *The Pearl*, which I directed in Spanish. It was released in an English version as well with the same actors' voices dubbed in."

Fernandez's films were immediately seen as uniquely Mexican, both in style and subject matter. Although Fernandez and his ever-present cameraman, Gabriel Figueroa, had both worked on American films while in Hollywood for a time early in their careers, El Indio resolved to divorce himself from their influence and to bring a sense of Mexican social consciousness, nationalism, and a glorification of poetic populism to his films. Mexico's colorful folklore, expansive landscapes, coastlines, dramatic skies, vibrant cloud patterns, and, most importantly, the ethereal presence and passionate indigenous beauty of the actors, most notably Dolores Del Rio, Pedro Armendariz, Maria Felix, and Maria Elena Marques, were captured by Gabriel Figueroa's stunning photography. Fernandez and co-writer Mauricio Magdaleno synthesized and depicted a unique and identifiable Mexican cinematic vision.

He assisted director John Ford, whom he greatly admired, on the production of *The Fugitive* (1947), which was shot in Mexico.

It is ironic that Emilio Fernandez, who as a director gave the Mexican cinema an identity forged on images of its people and its past, as an actor in his later career in American films usually played despicable Mexican generals or bandidos. He will perhaps remain best known for his role as the drunken, excessive, and vicious General Mapache in Sam Peckinpah's *The Wild Bunch* (1969). His other American film credits include *The Reward* (1965), *A Covenant with Death* (1966), *Return of the Seven* (1966), *Pat Garrett and Billy the Kid* (1973), *Bring Me the Head of Alfredo Garcia* (1974), and *Under the Volcano* (1984).

In later years, alcoholism, violent, irrational behavior, poor health, political disagreements, and an alleged murder charge hindered his ability to direct films in Mexico. The last film he wrote and directed in Mexico was *La Choca*, made in 1973. Fernandez died in 1986.

Esther Fernandez
B: 4/23/1920

Born in Mexico City, where she achieved tremendous success in films, Fernandez was brought to the States under contract to Paramount Studios in 1941. In a year and a half, no suitable roles were found, due largely to her poor English. She went over to RKO for six months, but nothing happened. She then left for Mexico but returned to the States a year later, after her success in the Mexican film *Santa* (1943), which was directed by Norman Foster and which co-starred Ricardo Montalban. Paramount quickly found her a role as Maria Dominguez y Peralta, the Spanish beauty who becomes a passenger on the hellship *Pilgrim* in *Two Years Before the Mast* (1946), in which she falls in love with star Alan Ladd. She returned to Mexico after the film and never made another Hollywood film.

Evelina Fernandez
B: 4/28/1954

With Edward James Olmos, Fernandez co-starred as Julie in *American Me* (1992). Fernandez has been featured in such films as *Downtown* (1989), *Flatliners* (1990), and *Postcards from the Edge* (1990). On television she had a recurring role as Juanita Herrera, a factory co-worker, on the first season of the long-running series "Roseanne."

Juan Fernandez

Fernandez has played sinister character roles in such films as *Kinjite: Forbidden Subjects* (1989) with Charles Bronson and Oliver Stone's *Salvador* (1986) opposite James Woods. He had featured roles in *Uncommon Valor* (1983), *Fear City* (1984), *"Crocodile" Dundee* (1986), and *Cat Chaser* (1990) with Kelly McGillis.

Jose Ferrer

B: 1/8/1912
D: 1/26/1992

Jose Ferrer in his tripartite career as actor, director, and writer received three New York Drama Critics Circle Awards, five Tony Awards, two Oscar nominations for Best Actor and one for Best Supporting Actor, and one Academy Award as Best Actor for *Cyrano de Bergerac* (1950). He was the first Hispanic American actor to receive an Academy Award.

Ferrer was born in Puerto Rico in 1912. His father was an attorney, his mother's family owned sugar cane land. Ferrer called his father "Perhaps the most important influence in my life. He and his friends inculcated a thirst for knowledge, inquisitiveness, the desire to grow and develop to the utmost, to be as good as you can be."

What's in a nose? Jose Ferrer turns on an impish grin as the lead character in *Cyrano de Bergerac* (1950) for which he won the Academy Award for Best Actor.
Photo by Acme Photo.

All three children were taught French and English, as well as Spanish, and were educated in private schools in the United States. Ferrer attended Princeton University, majoring in architecture and graduating in 1933. In his last year at Princeton, however, Ferrer was asked to be in a play. "I began to hang around with some theater people. Eventually I realized that the only thing that made any sense to me was to be an actor. It really was an obsession. Sure, my parents took me to the theater from early on, six or seven, and I still remember those first shows. But without the play at Princeton, I'd never have focused on a theatrical career."

Ferrer is reported to have said that he'd have been no good as an architect, and so he went on to Columbia University to study modern languages, intending to become a college professor instead.

However, for Ferrer, there were no fledgling actor's struggles. "I couldn't believe it. In the beginning I was getting jobs right and left. It got tougher when I was successful. Then I had to be more careful. I had to select; when you're young, you just want to be seen and to learn, you know."

Although *Brother Rat* (1936) was Ferrer's first critical success, his professional stage debut had actually come one year earlier (the same year he joined Actors' Equity) with *A Slight Case of Murder* (1935), in which he had one line. He had his first major role in a revival of *Charley's Aunt* (1940). In 1941, he made his directorial debut with *The Admiral Had a Wife,* but it was his portrayal of Iago opposite Paul Robeson's Othello in 1942 that first brought him wide public attention.

Jose Ferrer's other theater credits included *Cyrano de Bergerac* (1947), *The Silver Whistle* (1948), and *Man of La Mancha* (1970).

He produced, directed, and starred in a revival of *Twentieth Century* (1951) and directed *The Four Poster* (1952), for each of which he won a Tony Award. He produced, directed, and starred in *The Shrike* (1955), Joseph Kramm's Pulitzer Prize–winning play, for which he received three New York Drama Critics Circle Awards and two Tony Awards. He also directed *My Three Angels* (1952), *Stalag 17* (1952), and *The Andersonville Trial* (1959).

Joan of Arc (1948), in which he played the Dauphin to Ingrid Bergman's Joan of Arc, marked his first screen appearance as well as his first Oscar nomination. He next played a con man and killer in *Whirlpool* (1949) with Gene Tierney and a small part in *The Secret Fury* (1950). Ferrer then played a Latin American dictator, Raoul Farrargo, in *Crisis* (1950), written and directed by Richard Brooks.

For the film version of *Cyrano de Bergerac,* Ferrer won an Academy Award as Best Actor of 1950. "My life was changed by that. We did [the movie] with very little money in four six-day weeks. Michael Gordon directed it. I think it was done for something like $400,000," Ferrer said in an interview. He received another Oscar nomination for Best Actor for the role of the famed diminutive French painter Toulouse Lautrec in *Moulin Rouge* (1952), directed by John Huston.

Additional films through the years included *Miss Sadie Thompson* (1953), *The Caine Mutiny* (1954), *Deep in My Heart* (1954), *Lawrence of Arabia* (1962), *Nine Hours to Rama* (1963), *The Greatest Story Ever Told* (1965), *Ship of Fools* (1965), *Enter Laughing* (1967), *Behind the Iron Mask* (1977), *Fedora* (1978), and *The Big Brawl* (1980).

He entered the ranks of film directors by directing such films as *Cockleshell Heroes* (1955), *Return to Peyton Place* (1961), and *State Fair* (1962). He served as both director and star of *The Shrike* (1955), *The Great Man* (1957), *The High Cost of Loving* (1958), and *I Accuse* (1958).

Among his many television credits are the original "Kojak" pilot, "The Marcus Nelson Murders," "Kismet," "A Case of Libel," "Gideon," "The Return of Captain Nemo," "The Dream Merchant," *Evita Peron*, "Fame," and the miniseries *Blood & Orchids.*

Directing remained Ferrer's preferred craft and theater his preferred form. Despite the range of his work and despite those honors accorded him, Ferrer viewed with a certain rue the things he hadn't yet done in an interview several years before his death. "Really, in twenty years or more, I haven't played so many of the roles I think I should have played. In a sense, it was a series of bad judgments. I went to California with my wife, Rosemary Clooney, who was successful in films and recordings and I stayed there about fifteen years. My agent told me I'd have a career there too, but my kind of actor didn't suit the studio casting system as it was then. I either did not deliver the goods or I made bad choices. When I finally returned to New York, I found I'd lost the position I'd had there. My career went downhill and has remained fairly downhill for a long time," David Galligan, *Drama Logue* (10/8/87).

Ferrer's later film credits include Woody Allen's *A Midsummer Night's Sex Comedy* (1982), *To Be or Not to Be* (1983), and *Dune* (1984).

"I'm grateful for the work I have received in the last twenty or thirty years, I appreciate the fact that I've been able to survive and live very well," said the actor. Ferrer has six children, and one, Miguel, is an actor. Jose Ferrer directed a national tour of a production of *The Best Man* (1987) starring his friend and colleague Mel Ferrer. Jose Ferrer died on January 26, 1992, after a short illness.

Mel Ferrer [born: Melchior Gaston Ferrer]
   B: 8/25/1917

Director/actor/producer Mel Ferrer has displayed his talents in such diverse theatrical mediums as screen, stage, radio, and television.

He was born and raised in New York City of Spanish-Cuban parents and attended Princeton University. A writing award led to a trip to Mexico. Ferrer began his career as an actor on Broadway and in radio, where he later became a producer. In 1945 Ferrer was signed as a dialogue supervisor and director at RKO. His first directorial effort was *The Girl of the Limberlost* (1945). Ferrer also co-founded the La Jolla Playhouse near San Diego.

After two years he returned to Broadway and landed the lead in *Strange Fruit* (1947) and directed Jose Ferrer in the stage production of *Cyrano de Bergerac* (1947).

Ferrer went to Mexico as John Ford's assistant on *The Fugitive* (1947). He directed two plays in Mexico with Margo and Eddie Albert. As an actor he has starred in such films as *The Brave Bulls* (1951), in which he was quite effective as a Mexican peasant who rises to eminence and idol status in the bullring as a matador; *Scaramouche* (1952); *Lili* (1953), as a lame puppeteer; *Knights of the Round Table* (1953); and *War and Peace* (1956), with Henry Fonda and Audrey Hepburn. He has directed such films as *The Secret Fury* (1950), *Vendetta* (1950), and *Green Mansions* (1959), starring Audrey Hepburn. He also produced the hit thriller *Wait Until Dark* (1967), starring Audrey Hepburn and Alan Arkin. On television, Ferrer had a recurring role as Phillip Erikson on the series "Falcon Crest" and directed a number of episodes.

Miguel Ferrer

The son of actor/director Jose Ferrer and singer Rosemary Clooney, Miguel Ferrer has been featured in such films as *Heartbreaker* (1983), *RoboCop* (1987), *Valentino Returns* (1987), and *Revenge* (1990). On television he starred in two short-lived series, "Broken Badges" and "UnSub," and made an impression with his occasional role on the series "Twin Peaks," as the quirky FBI agent Albert Rosenfield.

Pablo Ferro
   B: 1/15/1935

Born in Havana, Cuba, and raised in New York City, Ferro is a leading optical special effects director for films and television commercials. His special visual optical effects have been seen in *The Thomas Crown Affair* (1968), in which Ferro pioneered split-screen images; *A Clockwork Orange* (1971), in which Ferro used split-second intercutting; and *Midnight Cowboy* (1969). More recent credits include *Darkman* (1990) and *Mobsters* (1991). In 1991 he directed his first film, the intimate comedy *Me, Myself, and I,* starring George Segal.

Efrain Figueroa

An actor, Figueroa was featured in *Tequila Sunrise* (1988) and *Pretty Woman* (1990).

Gabriel Figueroa

B: 4/24/1907

A world-renowned master Mexican cinematographer, Figueroa studied for a short time under Gregg Toland at RKO Studios. He photographed John Ford's *The Fugitive* (1947), John Huston's *The Night of the Iguana* (1964), and *Under the Volcano* (1984), for which he was nominated for an Academy Award. He also photographed *Two Mules for Sister Sara* (1970) in Mexico for director Don Siegel and *Kelly's Heroes* (1971) in Yugoslavia.

He started in the film business in 1932 as an assistant to Alex Phillips, the leading Mexican cameraman. A few years later he went to RKO Studios in Hollywood to be a pupil of the American cinematographer Gregg Toland for four months. He returned to Mexico and began a prolific career as a cameraman on over one hundred films. His first film as director of photography, *Alla en el Rancho Grande* (1936), was also the first Mexican film to become an international hit.

Figueroa ranks among the leading directors of photography in the world and is considered one of the greatest interpreters of black-and-white photography.

He is noted for his unforgettable images of indigenous Mexican landscapes highlighted against white cloud-filled skies, men in big sombreros, and women in black shawls. He made his reputation with a remarkable series of films he collaborated on with Mexican director Emilio Fernandez beginning with *Flor Silvestre* in 1943 and including such classics as *Maria Candelaria* (1943) and *The Pearl* (1945). These films gave Mexican cinema a national identity and raised it to an unprecedented level of aesthetic sophistication and international acclaim.

William Fraker

B: 1923

A six-time Academy Award–nominated cinematographer, William Fraker was born in Los Angeles of a Mexican mother and an American father.

He is a graduate of the University of Southern California Film School. Following extensive work in television, Fraker entered feature films as a camera operator and an assistant to the famed cinematographer Conrad Hall.

Fraker is one of the few cinematographers who has also directed films. He made his directorial debut with *Monte Walsh* (1970), and followed with *A Reflection of Fear* (1973) and later with *The Legend of the Lone Ranger* (1981). He has worked as a director of photography on such films as *Rosemary's Baby* (1968), *Bullitt* (1968), *Paint Your Wagon* (1969), *Looking for Mr. Goodbar* (1977), and *Heaven Can Wait* (1978).

Abel Franco

B: 1922

A Pasadena, California, schoolteacher and an actor, Franco has credits on such films as *The Searchers* (1956), *Zoot Suit* (1981), *El Norte* (1984), *The Falcon and the Snowman* (1985), and *¡Three Amigos!* (1986). He won an Emmy Award for writing the PBS daytime drama "Cancion de la Raza."

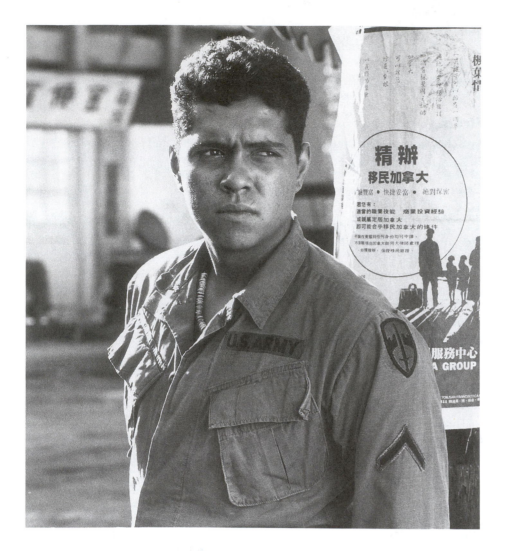

Ramon Franco

B: 1963

Born in Caguas, Puerto Rico, Franco began his acting career at age 14. His films include *Boardwalk* (1979), *Heartbreak Ridge* (1986), and *Bulletproof* (1988). He is best known for his role as Private Ruiz on the "Tour of Duty" Vietnam War television series.

Hugo Fregonese

B: 4/8/1909
D: 1/25/1987

An Argentine-born director of international thrillers and westerns, Fregonese worked in Hollywood in the late 1940s and throughout the 1950s.

The son of a winemaker from Venice who settled in Mendoza near Buenos Aires, Fregonese studied economics in college. He became a sportswriter for an Argentine magazine, and shortly thereafter moved to New York City to become a press agent.

While in New York he acted as a technical adviser for a producer on a movie script with a South American background. He came to Hollywood, but the film was never made, and Fregonese then worked as an extra in movies. That career was short-lived because he kept getting fired, as he could never keep the place the assistant director assigned him. Instead, he was always near the camera, trying to find out how movies were made. As an extra he worked as a prisoner in *The Hurricane* (1937) and as a pirate in *The Buccaneer* (1938) with Fredric March.

In Los Angeles he went to a film trade school to learn editing. Fregonese returned to Argentina, where he began a career as an assistant director in the film industry there. He got the opportunity to co-direct a film called *Pampa Barbara* in 1943. He then directed *Hardly a Criminal* (1949), the story of a clerk's attempt to hide and hold a half-million dollars he has stolen. The film was purchased for release in the States with dubbed English dialogue. Fregonese made another film, *Where Words Fail* (1948), entirely on location and then had the actors' voices and sound effects "looped in," or added, during post-production. On the strength of this he was signed at MGM. They kept him around for a year but gave him nothing to do. Universal International signed him to a contract to direct the thriller *One Way Street* (1950), starring James Mason. He followed by directing several westerns, including *Saddle Tramp* (1950) with Joel McCrea, *Apache Drums* (1951), *Mark of the Renegade* (1951) with Ricardo Montalban and Gilbert Roland, and *Untamed Frontier* (1952).

He moved to Columbia Pictures and directed the prison comedy *My Six Convicts* (1952), produced by Stanley Kramer and starring Gilbert Roland. Though mainly known for his B pictures, Fregonese also made some films with top stars, among them *Blowing Wild* with Barbara Stanwyck, Gary Cooper, and Anthony Quinn in 1953.

Director Hugo Fregonese (left) discusses a love scene between co-stars Cyd Charisse and Ricardo Montalban during the filming of *Mark of the Renegade*, a story of adventurous early California.

During the remainder of the 1950s he made several pictures for Twentieth Century–Fox, including *Man in the Attic* (1953), starring Jack Palance, a well-regarded version of the Jack the Ripper tale.

Fregonese's career became international at this time and included all-star projects such as *Decameron Nights* (1953) for RKO, the Italian epic *The Beast of Marseilles* (1957), and the Italian *Marco Polo* (1962) with Rory Calhoun. During the 1960s he directed the European western *Old Shatterhand* (1964) with Lex Barker, *Secrets of Dr. Mabuse* (1964), and *Savage Pampas* (1966), a remake of his debut *Pampa Barbara*, with Robert Taylor, filmed on location in Argentina.

In the 1970s he directed *La Mala Vida* (1973) and *Mas Alla del Sol* (1975). Fregonese married actress Faith Domergue. He died of a heart attack at age 77 in Buenos Aires.

Jenny Gago

Gago's film credits include *Under Fire* (1983), *No Man's Land* (1987), *Irreconcilable Differences* (1984), *Innerspace* (1987), *Best Seller* (1987), and *Old Gringo* (1989). She has guest starred on such shows as "Cagney & Lacey" and "Falcon Crest" and landed recurring roles on "Dallas" and "Knots Landing," in which she played the character Maria for three years.

Nacho Galindo

D: 6/22/1973

A character actor, Galindo appeared in films from the 1940s through the 1960s, including *Tycoon* (1946), *South of St. Louis* (1949), *Borderline* (1950), *Border River* (1954), *Broken Lance* (1954), *One-Eyed Jacks* (1961), and *El Dorado* (1967).

Silvana Gallardo

B: 1/13/1953

An actress born in New York City of Venezuelan-Cuban parents, Gallardo was featured in *Windwalker* (1980), *Death Wish II* (1982), and *Solar Crisis* (1993). Her television credits include the TV movies *Copacabana* (1986) and *The Calendar Girl Murders* (1984) and guest appearances on episodic series.

Gina Gallego

B: 10/30/1959

An actress born and raised in Los Angeles of Mexican heritage, Gallego's feature film credits include *The Men's Club* (1986) with Treat Williams, *My Demon Lover* (1987) with Scott Valentine, and *Lust in the Dust* (1985) with Cesar Romero. She is perhaps best known for her two years as a regular on the daytime soap opera "Santa Barbara" as Santana and for her work on the soap opera "Rituals." Gallego was also a regular on the TV series "Flamingo Road" and co-starred in the Showtime movie *Keeper of the City* (1991).

Joaquin Garay II

B: 1911
D: 1990

A veteran vaudeville song and dance man, Garay shared the bill with such performers as Jack Benny and later Martin and Lewis and provided the voice of Panchito (the pistol-packin' parrot) for Walt Disney's *The Three Caballeros* (1944). He was also one of the featured singers on the bus in *It Happened One Night* (1934). His son, Joaquin Garay III, starred as an 11-year-old street urchin in the Disney feature film *Herbie Goes Bananas* in 1980.

Allan Garcia

B: 3/18/1887

D: 9/4/1938

Credited with working as a casting director at Chaplin Studios, Garcia had his first major role in Chaplin's *The Circus* (1923, silent) as the circus proprietor. He played the butler in Chaplin's *City Lights* (1931, silent) and appeared in Chaplin's *Modern Times* (1936, silent) as the factory boss. His other film credits include *The Idle Class* (1921, silent), *Pay Day* (1922, silent), *Morgan's Last Raid* (1929), *Under the Tonto Rim* (1933), *The California Trail* (1933) at Columbia, and *The Gay Desperado* (1936).

Andy Garcia

B: 4/12/1956

Andy Garcia became an international star with the role of Italian American rookie cop George Stone in Brian De Palma's hit film *The Untouchables* (1987), which followed Garcia's noted performance as the treacherous but suave cocaine king-pin Angel Maldonado in Hal Ashby's *8 Million Ways to Die* (1986). De Palma wanted Garcia to play Capone's murderous sidekick Frank Nitti, but Garcia persuaded the director to let him play Stone, against type. His star continued to ascend with his roles as Michael Douglas's detective partner in *Black Rain* (1989) and as the inter-

Andy Garcia stars as Vincent Mancini in *The Godfather, Part III*, the epic story of the Corleone family.

Photo by Fabian.

409

nal affairs police investigator Ray Avila opposite Richard Gere in *Internal Affairs* (1990). Full-fledged stardom was reached in Francis Ford Coppola's epic *The God-father, Part III* (1990), in which his portrayal of Sonny Corleone's illegitimate son Vincent Mancini earned him Best Supporting Actor nominations for the Golden Globe Award and the Academy Award. He also co-starred in a smaller but pivotal role in Kenneth Branagh's *Dead Again* (1991). Garcia's recent films include *Hero* (1993) opposite Dustin Hoffman and *Jennifer 8* (1993). Garcia made his film debut as a police detective in the Phillip Borsos film *The Mean Season* (1985) opposite Kurt Russell and Mariel Hemingway. On HBO he starred in the telefilm *Clinton and Nadine* (1988). His other film credits include *Stand and Deliver* (1987), *American Roulette* (1988), and *A Show of Force* (1990).

Born in Cuba, Garcia came to the United States with his parents when he was five years old. He grew up in Miami Beach, Florida, where he began his acting career performing in regional theater productions. After moving to Los Angeles, Garcia made his television acting debut in the pilot for the TV series "Hill Street Blues" and made guest appearances in other series and telefilms.

Rick Garcia

An American-born actor with numerous screen and television credits, Garcia is best known for uttering Alfonso Bedoya's immortal line from *The Treasure of the Sierra Madre*, "Badges? We don't need no stinkin' badges," as a Mexican bandit in Mel Brooks's spoof *Blazing Saddles* (1974), and as the Mexican border official who gets kicked in the crotch by Kirk Douglas in *Tough Guys* (1986), also starring Burt Lancaster.

Ron Garcia

This noted cinematographer's feature film credits include *Disorganized Crime* (1989), *Side Out* (1990), and *Twin Peaks: Fire Walk with Me* (1992). In television, Garcia's credits include the series "Crime Story" and "Hunter." He was nominated for an Emmy Award in 1993 for his work on the television miniseries *Murder in the Heartland*.

Stella Garcia

An actress, Garcia co-starred in the films *The Last Movie* (1971) with Dennis Hopper and *Joe Kidd* (1972) with Clint Eastwood.

Carlos Gardel
   B: 12/11/1890
   D: 6/24/1935

An Argentine singer, composer, and movie star, Gardel had an immense reputation in the Spanish-speaking world and in France and popularized the tango. He was actually born in France but was raised from the age of one in Argentina, where he was exposed to the musical form that he would make world famous. He made four Spanish-language films in New York for Paramount in 1934 and 1935. Prior to that he made several films at Paramount Studios in Joinville, France. His meteoric career was cut short when he was killed in a plane crash in Colombia in 1935.

Martin Garralaga

B: 11/10/1898

D: 6/12/1981

A Spanish-born singer and actor, Garralaga portrayed many Spanish and Mexican characters in films. He began his career in Barcelona as a singer, and this talent carried him to the concert and opera stages of South and North America and eventually to the motion picture studios of Hollywood.

He made his motion picture debut in the Spanish version of *The King of Jazz* (1930), in which he played the master of ceremonies, and thereafter appeared in many Spanish-language films, both in heavy and comedic parts. Garralaga had his first important English-speaking role in 1936 in *A Message to Garcia*. His other films include *Rose of the Rio Grande* (1938), *Starlight over Texas* (1938), *The Fighting Gringo* (1939), *Juarez* (1940), *Rhythm of the Rio Grande* (1940), *Stage to Chino* (1940), *In Old California* (1942), *The Lady Has Plans* (1942), *For Whom the Bell Tolls* (1943), *Man in the Shadow* (1957), *The Left-Handed Gun* (1958), and *The Last Angry Man* (1959). He played the Cisco Kid's sidekick, Pancho, in several films with Duncan Renaldo.

John Gavin [born: John Anthony Golenar]

B: 4/8/1931

Born in Los Angeles, Gavin is the Stanford University–educated son of a Mexican mother and an American father. He joined the Navy and became interested in acting through a friend while he was on leave. He was put under contract at Universal Pictures. The young actor made his motion picture debut in *Behind the High Wall* (1956) with Sylvia Sidney. Two of his most important film credits are Alfred

John Gavin as Julius Caesar in *Spartacus*.

Hitchcock's *Psycho* (1960) and as Julius Caesar in *Spartacus* (1960) opposite Charles Laughton and Sir Laurence Olivier. Gavin is a tall, dark, and handsome Ivy League–looking leading man in the Rock Hudson tradition. His other films include *Back Street* (1961), *Tammy, Tell Me True* (1961), and *The Madwoman of Chaillot* (1969).

In the late 1970s he left films for politics and was appointed U.S. Ambassador to Mexico.

Tony Genaro

A supporting actor, Genaro's credits include *The Milagro Beanfield War* (1988), *Tremors* (1989), and *Bound by Honor* (1993).

Mike Gomez

B: 4/18/1951

A Dallas-born and -raised character actor, Gomez has appeared in such films as *The Border* (1982) as a greaser Mexican type, opposite Jack Nicholson; *Heartbreak Ridge* (1986) as a Marine recruit, opposite Clint Eastwood; and *Zoot Suit* (1981) as Joey, one of the pivotal Pachuco characters.

Panchito Gomez

B: 1964

A New York–born actor, Gomez has been acting since age four. For over 25 years he has played a tough-talking urban or rural Latino youth on many network television shows, dramatic and comedic. He received attention for his role as the teenage Santana in Edward James Olmos's 1992 Universal film *American Me*. His television credits include "Barney Miller," "CHiPs," "Simon and Simon," and "Baretta." His film credits include *Uncle Joe Shannon* (1978), *Run for the Roses* (1978), *Walk Proud* (1979), and *Borderline* (1980).

Thomas Gomez [born: Sabino Thomas Gomez]

B: 7/10/1905
D: 6/20/1971

A versatile character actor, Gomez was adept at playing every type of character role, from assorted urban types to period and classical types. In 1942 the actor signed with Universal International following a notable stage career highlighted by seven years with Alfred Lunt and Lynn Fontanne. In addition, Gomez opened the Guild Theater in 1925, with Helen Hayes.

Gomez's paternal grandfather came to the States from Santander, Spain, in 1842 to run a coffeehouse and an oyster boat fleet in New Orleans. His paternal grandmother was born in Gibraltar and came to New Orleans about the same time as her future husband. Gomez's maternal grandfather, Frank Thomas, commanded a ship under Admiral David Farragut when the famed naval officer captured New Orleans for the Union in the American Civil War.

Born in New York City, he attended Public School 77, and later went to Jamaica High School on Long Island. There he won a citywide speech contest. Gomez went on to study acting and joined a theater troupe, making his professional debut in *Cyrano de Bergerac* in 1924. After playing a variety of roles over the next seven years, Gomez joined a stock company in Cleveland, Ohio. In three years there he did 40 leading character roles. He then went on the road, and the following year, 1934, he joined the Lunts.

The actor's cumulative performances on the stage attracted attention from studio scouts. His screen bow came in *Sherlock Holmes and the Voice of Terror* in 1942. He then turned in some of his finest character portrayals in such films as *Ride the*

Thomas Gomez as Louvain, chief of the French police, in *Casbah*.

Pink Horse, which earned him an Oscar nomination in 1947 for Best Supporting Actor, *Pittsburgh* (1942), *White Savage* (1943), *Captain from Castile* (1947), and *Casbah* (1948), to name just a few.

Gomez's other film credits include *Phantom Lady* (1944), *Key Largo* (1948), *Kim* (1950), *The Magnificent Matador* (1955), *Summer and Smoke* (1961), *Stay Away, Joe* (1968), and *Beneath the Planet of the Apes* (1970).

Vicente Gomez

B: 1915

Gomez, who was strumming flamenco melodies in his father's cafe in Madrid when he was only 10, is one of the few composers of Spanish Gypsy music. In 1941, at age 26, after touring Europe and South and Central America as a soloist and with symphony orchestras, he was brought to Hollywood by director Rouben Mamoulian to compose Gypsy music and play guitar for motion pictures.

Myrtle Gonzales

B: 9/23/1891
D: 10/22/1918

Gonzales grew up in Los Angeles and was a rapidly rising player at Vitagraph Studios in 1913. She co-starred with William Duncan in many westerns and appeared also in other types of films. Her career was cut short when she died unexpectedly at age 27.

Peter Gonzales [born: Peter Gonzales Falcon]

A Texas-born actor, Gonzales played the Young Fellini in *Fellini's Roma* (1972). He also appeared in Burt Reynolds's *The End* (1973).

Jose Gonzalez-Gonzalez

B: 12/21/26

Identical twin brother of Pedro, who followed his brother to Hollywood and pursued a successful acting career by assuming his brother's characterization of the short, comical Mexican. His film credits include *Cha-Cha-Cha Boom* (1956), *Panama Sal* (1957), and television appearances.

Pedro Gonzalez-Gonzalez

B: 12/21/1926

A San Antonio comic, Gonzalez-Gonzalez was propelled by his appearance on the 1950s TV game show "You Bet Your Life" with Groucho Marx into a film and nightclub career. On the half-hour show, Pedro hilariously topped every line that expert funnyman Groucho said to him, with his exaggerated comedic stereotypical "Si, Senor" dumb Mexican characterization. After the original telecast, young Pedro was flooded with offers from nightclubs and film studios. He finally settled on a personal contract with John Wayne. Pedro made his screen debut as a comic revolutionary in *Wings of the Hawk* (1953). There then followed *The High and the Mighty* (1954), *I Died a Thousand Times* (1955), *Strange Lady in Town* (1955), *The Sheepman* (1958), *Rio Bravo* (1959), and *Hostile Guns* (1967). Gonzalez-Gonzalez also made numerous television and nightclub appearances.

Jose Greco

B: 1919

The Italian-born, Brooklyn-raised master of Spanish dance, Greco made film appearances as a Spanish Gypsy pimp in *Ship of Fools* (1965) and in a Spanish dance sequence in *Around the World in 80 Days* (1956) and a dance sequence in *Sombrero* (1953).

He was brought to the United States at age eight and began learning Spanish dance steps at age ten. "My neighborhood had ethnic diversity, but from the beginning I was drawn to things Spanish," he recalled in an interview (Walter Price, *L.A. Times Calendar* [10/19/86]). Performing in nightclubs in New York, he was noticed and was asked to be the touring partner of "La Argentinita," the greatest Spanish woman dancer of modern times, from 1941 until her untimely death in 1945. He later went to Spain, where he became a sensation, and formed his own dance troupe. In the same interview, Greco recounted, "They couldn't believe I wasn't Spanish, they just dismissed the idea that an Italian from Brooklyn could master this Spanish art form. No one had ever done it before and they thought I was lying."

In 1946 Greco was invited to choreograph and lead a Spanish dance sequence in a Spanish film called *Manolete,* based on the life of Spain's greatest bullfighter. Every time the film was shown, the theater patrons stopped the show and asked the manager to rerun the reel with the dance sequence. Greco toured throughout Europe and returned triumphantly to the States in 1948. Currently, he performs and tours the world to international acclaim.

Castulo Guerra

A professional actor in Argentina until 1971, Guerra came to the United States on a Fulbright scholarship to do theater research in New York City. He appeared as an underworld kingpin in *Stick* (1985) and as a desert inhabitant in *Terminator 2: Judgment Day* (1991). He has guest starred on a number of weekly TV series and was a regular for a season on "Falcon Crest."

Evelyn Guerrero

B: 2/24/1949

A Mexican American actress, Guerrero was featured as Cheech Marin's dream girl, the sexy, unpredictable, and elusive Donna, in *Cheech and Chong's Next Movie* (1980), *Cheech and Chong's Nice Dreams* (1981), and *Things Are Tough All Over* (1982).

Born in East Los Angeles, Guerrero moved to Hollywood at age three, when her mother became a teacher at a Hollywood dancing school. She was motivated by her mother and her aunt, Sally Marr. She also appeared in *Lenny* (1974), in Ralph Waite's *On the Nickel* (1980), and in *Bound by Honor* (1993). She played Dora's sister Marisol on the television series "I Married Dora," and also starred as Lupe Cordero in the Luis Valdez–directed TV series pilot "Fort Figueroa" (1988).

Tito Guizar

B: 4/8/1908

Tito Guizar, famed Latin American singing star, and Martha Raye in preparation for a scene in the musical *Tropic Holiday*.

A Latin singer, songwriter, and recording and film star, Guizar made a dozen American films in the 1930s and 1940s. He is best remembered for his colorful

Tito Guizar, Mexican tenor, guitarist, and film star.

roles in numerous musicals at Paramount Pictures, where he was under contract, beginning with *The Big Broadcast of 1938* (1938) with Bob Hope and *Tropic Holiday* (1938). He is responsible for solidifying the romantic screen image of the Mexican *vaquero* or *charro* (cowboy) in both Mexican and American cinema.

Guizar was born in Mexico City of French and Italian ancestry. After training there, he studied voice in Milan, Italy, and later made his stage debut at the Hippodrome in New York City with the Chicago Opera Company. He performed at the Central Park Casino and the Ritz Carlton and became a popular radio soloist. When Guizar switched from classical to popular music, he made a number of musical short subjects. He later returned to his native Mexico and starred in the first successful musical motion picture in Mexican cinema, *Rancho Grande* (1936), creating a genre of musical that became closely identified with Mexican cinema for over 50 years.

His career received a brief boost at Paramount Pictures from 1938 through 1940. Besides *The Big Broadcast of 1938,* he also filmed a western, *The Llano Kid* (1940). He later went to Republic, where he appeared in *Brazil* (1944), *On the Old Spanish Trail* (1947), and *The Gay Ranchero* (1948) with Roy Rogers. He appeared in American musical all-star extravaganzas throughout the 1940s, making guest appearances as himself.

Vincent R. Gutierrez

A writer of television dramas, Gutierrez had a long association with Michael Landon Productions, for which he wrote a number of "Little House on the Prairie" episodes as well as many of the episodes of Landon's subsequent series, "Highway to Heaven."

Claudio Guzman

B: 1931

Guzman produced and directed four years of the popular hit series "I Dream of Jeannie," starring Barbara Eden and Larry Hagman. He also directed episodes of "The Wackiest Ship in the Army," "Love on a Rooftop," "The Flying Nun," and "The Iron Horse."

Born in Santiago, Chile, he attended the University of Chile's school of architecture. He came to the United States in 1952 to continue his studies at the University of Southern California and later at the Chouinard Art Institute. An instructor at USC was so impressed with the student's work that he suggested Claudio do work on film sets, and thus a new career was born. At Desilu Studios, Guzman acted as art director on "The Life of Riley," "The Danny Thomas Show," "Official Detective," "Wyatt Earp," "December Bride," "I Love Lucy," and "Our Miss Brooks." During his Desilu tenure, he created, produced, and directed "The Victor Borge Comedy Hour." He also directed segments of "I Love Lucy," "The Dick Van Dyke Show," "The Fugitive," "The Patty Duke Show," and "The Untouchables." He is the brother of Pato Guzman.

Luis Guzman

Guzman appeared in Sidney Lumet's *Q & A* (1990) as a streetwise Puerto Rican detective. His other feature credits include *Short Eyes* (1977), *Family Business* (1989), *True Believer* (1989), *Rooftops* (1989), *Black Rain* (1989), *Cadillac Man* (1990), and *Carlito's Way* (1993).

Pato Guzman

B: 1934
D: 1/2/1991

A producer and production designer on 11 films with Paul Mazursky, Guzman's association with the director began in 1967: "I was designing *I Love You, Alice B. Toklas*, which Paul wrote with Larry Tucker. Paul was on the set a lot, and we talked about what we'd do when we made a movie together. When *Bob & Carol & Ted & Alice* [1969] came along we hooked up," recalled Guzman during an interview with publicist Vic Heutschy while making *Enemies, a Love Story* (1989), on location in New York.

Born in Santiago, Chile, Guzman studied architecture and came to the United States in the late 1950s. After a summer of stock and a three-month stint with the MGM design department, he began to work in television. He worked happily for many years at Desilu, doing all its pilots as well as "The Danny Thomas Show," "The Dick Van Dyke Show," and others, including "Star Trek," which tickled his fancy and hinted at the design possibilities of the film medium.

He left television and traveled, later returning to Los Angeles to visit his brother Claudio and got a job on *The President's Analyst* (1967), directed by social satirist Ted Flicker. "I tend to be very serious," says Guzman. "The Weidman house in *Down and Out in Beverly Hills* [1986], for example, was so outsized it became monumental and funny." Guzman cited a special chemistry with Mazursky as the key to their 20 years of enormously successful collaboration. "We guide all our energy into the project," said Guzman. "There are no battling egos, and it's fun." Their other hits include *Blume in Love* (1973), *An Unmarried Woman* (1978), *Tempest* (1982), *Moscow on the Hudson* (1984), and *Enemies, a Love Story* (1989). Guzman also designed *The In-Laws* (1979) and *Hide in Plain Sight* (1990).

Daniel A. Haro

B: 5/27/1955

A Los Angeles–born actor, Haro has played a prison gang member in *American Me* (1992), a classroom teacher in *Stand and Deliver* (1988), and the baseball player Burns in *Talent for the Game* (1993).

Dick Haymes

B: 9/13/1916

D: 1980

Born in Buenos Aires, Argentina, of Scottish-English descent, he was educated in France and England before coming to the United States in 1936. Haymes began his show business career as a radio announcer, band vocalist, and occasional film extra and bit player. In the early 1940s he became a highly successful nightclub and recording artist and developed into one of the leading crooners of his time. In 1943, he was signed to a film contract by Twentieth Century–Fox and enjoyed great popularity during 1944–1947. His singing personality, however, didn't quite come across on the screen. In 1953, he married Rita Hayworth, but they divorced in 1955.

Among Haymes's film credits are *Four Jills in a Jeep* (1943), *State Fair* (1945), *Diamond Horseshoe* (1945), *Do You Love Me?* (1946), *The Shocking Miss Pilgrim* (1947), *Carnival in Costa Rica* (1947), and *One Touch of Venus* (1948).

Rita Hayworth [born: Margarita Cansino]

B: 10/17/1918

D: 5/14/1987

Called "The Love Goddess," Rita Hayworth was one of the most beautiful and exciting talents ever to grace the Silver Screen.

Rita Hayworth is truly one of the first Hispanic American stars, having been able to transcend her ethnic origins and become the ethereal all American girl to a generation of moviegoers worldwide. Her popularity reached its zenith during the 1940s through a succession of roles that began with such films as *Only Angels Have Wings* (1939), *Blood and Sand* (1941), *The Strawberry Blonde* (1941), *You Were Never Lovelier* (1942), and *Cover Girl* (1944), and was capped off by *Gilda* (1946).

She was born Margarita Cansino in Brooklyn, New York, to Eduardo Cansino, a noted Spanish dancer, and his Irish wife, Volga Haworth. Eduardo was one of seven children of the famous Andalusian dance master Don Antonio Cansino. Eduardo was a vaudeville headliner in a Spanish dance act with his sister Elisa, and they performed throughout the United States and Europe. By the time Margarita was four years old, she was already learning dance steps from her father. The family performed and traveled as The Dancing Cansinos. Settling in California, Eduardo opened a dance school in Hollywood and picked up work from the film studios whenever they needed a Spanish or Mexican dance number.

He saw potential in his teenage daughter and teamed with her in a dance act that played in nightclubs south of the border in Tijuana and Agua Caliente. These bordertowns were filled with gaming, free-flowing liquor, loose women, and drugs. The rich and Hollywood's elite would cross the border for a weekend or a night of fun. The artistry of the father-and-daughter dance act immediately drew attention. Winfield S. Sheehan, vice president in charge of production at Fox Studios, was taken by Margarita's looks and dance movements and felt she had some quali-

Rita Hayworth
(as Rita Cansino, 1935; 1944; 1964).

ties that might photograph well for the movies. She began taking acting and elo-cution lessons at the studio, and within a month she worked in her first film, a Spanish-language short subject.

She made her screen debut in *Dante's Inferno* (1935) in a dance sequence cho-reographed by her father. Of this period she recalled in an interview years later, "I developed a burning ambition, as only a too-fat 17 year old can burn, to become a good actress." She followed her debut with *Under the Pampas Moon* (1935) and then began to work steadily in movies. She had parts in *Charlie Chan in Egypt* (1935), *Paddy O'Day* (1935), and *Human Cargo* (1936).

When Fox combined with Twentieth Century, Darryl Zanuck dropped her con-tract even though she was set to star in *Ramona* (1936). "I cried and screamed. I vowed that I would show those men. I would become famous and they would be sorry," she said in a 1940s magazine interview.

She got leading roles as Mexican senoritas in several B pictures and then was put under contract by Columbia Pictures. She toiled in run-of-the-mill films, but she was being groomed for stardom by the studio. She shortened her name to Rita and adopted a surname similar to her mother's, Hayworth. The actress underwent a weight-loss program and painful electrolysis treatments in order to broaden her forehead and to accentuate a widow's peak. Her raven hair was changed to au-burn and still later to the famous coppery red.

She continued in undistinguished roles until she was loaned to Warner Bros., where she worked opposite James Cagney in the turn-of-the-century romance *The Strawberry Blonde* (1941).

Rita was catapulted to stardom as a result of her role as the temptress Dona Sol, opposite Tyrone Power, in *Blood and Sand* (1941), directed by Rouben Mamoulian. Twentieth Century–Fox paid Harry Cohn, the head of Columbia, five times the salary she was receiving at Columbia for her services. "You don't have to be a vengeful person to taste the sweetness of that," commented Rita, who, appearing for the Technicolor cameras for the first time, realized an ambition that had been thwarted by Fox years before. *The Hollywood Reporter* (5/20/41) commented in its review of the film, "To us there were two standouts, Rita Hayworth and Rouben Mamoulian. In her performance, Miss Hayworth, who has been widely cheered for her beauty, comes through with a well defined artistry that must win for her some of the top acting roles." *Daily Variety* (5/20/41) commented, "Miss Hayworth takes another stride toward her assured position among the stars in demand. Her unforgettable performance as the luscious but heartless Dona Sol is among her finest screen achievements."

It was impossible to pick up a magazine at that time without finding Hayworth either on the cover or featured in an article. Columbia, realizing what they had, teamed her with Fred Astaire for a Cole Porter musical, *You'll Never Get Rich* (1941), in which she utilized her dance talent with the supreme master of film dance. She was loaned to 20th for *My Gal Sal* (1942) with Victor Mature. Hayworth couldn't sing, so her singing voice was dubbed; she could dance, however, and she was teamed with Fred Astaire again in *You Were Never Lovelier* (1942), and with Gene Kelly in *Cover Girl* (1944).

"Dancing," she once said, "is my natural heritage and I have always loved it, but I have also always hated to practice. When I was younger I used to study ballet, Spanish and tap dancing for four and five hours a day, and it was no cinch, especially having a father who was so strict. It was hard and tedious work and there were times when I didn't think I could go on. But I did and, of course, as it turned out, the effort was worth it."

In 1946 Hayworth attained her greatest success in the role with which she is now most identified, the beautiful adventuress Gilda, a woman lost in a Latin country who vies for the affections of Glenn Ford and George Macready. The ads for the film proclaimed: "There never was a woman like Gilda!" In a low-cut black satin dress with elbow-length gloves, she did a sensuous striptease number as she sang "Put the Blame on Mame."

She went to Acapulco with her then husband Orson Welles, to film *The Lady from Shanghai* (1948), which he directed and in which they co-starred. The film did not do well at the box office. Columbia then cast her as Carmen in *The Loves of Carmen* (1948), opposite Glenn Ford as Don Jose. Her father choreographed many of the dance sequences. She was next teamed with Glenn Ford in *Affair in Trinidad* (1952), an attempt to recapture the magic of *Gilda*. The film didn't work as well as the original, but it was popular with audiences and was a box-office hit, taking in more money than *Gilda*. Some of the best of her later work includes the title role in *Miss Sadie Thompson* (1953), *Pal Joey* (1957), and *Separate Tables* (1958)

During the 1960s her career faltered, and sporadic appearances in second-rate films did little to revive it. There were reports of public drunkenness, and she often seemed lost and would turn down roles. Her behavior became erratic, and no one could figure out what was wrong. Her daughter was surprised when her mother had memory lapses during which she could not recall the names of her closest friends. After visiting several doctors, she was diagnosed as having Alzheimer's disease. Her last film was *The Wrath of God* in 1972.

Hayworth died from complications arising from the disease on May 14, 1987, at her home in New York under the care of her daughter Yasmin. Her daughter said at a tribute to her mother at the Deauville Film Festival in France, "Had we known the early stages of Alzheimer's disease, we could have saved her notoriety and adverse publicity. But at least her suffering was a catalyst for more knowledge and research about the disease."

Pepe Hern [born: Pepe Hernandez]

Born in Spain, Hern came to the United States at an early age. He appeared in many films of the 1950s, including *Borderline* (1950) and *The Ring* (1952).

George F. Hernandez

    B: 6/6/1863
    D: 12/19/1922

A screen and stage actor from 1912 to 1922, Hernandez had major roles in such silent films as *When Helen Was Elected* (1912), *Arabia* (1922), and *Flaming Hearts* (1922). In 1917 he co-starred in five silent films at Universal: *Mutiny, God's Crucible, Southern Justice, The Showdown,* and *The Greater Law.*

Juano Hernandez

    B: 1898
    D: 7/19/1970

A Puerto Rican actor, Juano Hernandez usually played African American or African characters in films. His deep, resonant voice and dignified presence were used effectively in his 1949 film debut in MGM's *Intruder in the Dust.*

Juano Hernandez as the Mau Mau leader Njogu in *Something of Value* is a man torn by his own convictions of right and wrong in this dramatic story of modern Africa.

Hernandez was born in Puerto Rico, the son of a Puerto Rican seaman, and was orphaned as a small child. He went to live with his aunt in Rio de Janeiro, where he acquired his Portuguese first name. As a boy he joined a little group of street urchins who sang, danced, and did acrobatics. He ran away with a carnival that toured Latin America and the Caribbean, and he wound up in New Orleans in 1915. Although lacking any formal education, Hernandez taught himself to read and write in several languages. "One thing I learned very soon," said the actor, "was that if you speak English with any kind of accent people are inclined to laugh at you," Gladwin Hill, *New York Times* (5/28/50).

As a result, he cultivated perfect diction and along the way acquired a knowledge of Shakespeare's works and other dramatic classics. He worked in carnivals, circuses, and minstrel shows, appeared in vaudeville comedy sketches, and performed dramatic readings. He settled in New York City and found work as an actor in the theater. He played his first Broadway role in *Show Boat*, followed by *Strange Fruit* and *Let My People Free*. A keen interest in exotic foreign chants, languages, and customs developed into work on radio.

For his film debut as the poor southern black sharecropper in *Intruder in the Dust*, Hernandez won praise. He turned in a moving portrayal as an aging jazz musician in *Young Man with a Horn* (1950), starring Kirk Douglas. In *The Breaking Point* (1950), he was John Garfield's buddy, and in *Trial* (1955), he was an African American judge, while in *Something of Value* (1957), he portrayed an African Mau Mau leader.

He continued to work in featured roles in such films as *Stars in My Crown* (1950), *Kiss Me Deadly* (1955), *St. Louis Blues* (1958), *The Sins of Rachel Cade* (1960), *Sergeant Rutledge* (1960), and *Uptight* (1968).

Laura Martinez Herring [alternate spelling: Harring]

B: 3/3/1967

A former Miss USA, Herring starred in the film *Lambada—The Forbidden Dance* (1990). She has guest starred on many episodic series including "Baywatch" and the TV films *The Alamo: 13 Days to Glory* (1987), *Desperado 2* (1991), and *Rio Diablo* (1993). Born in Los Mochis, Sinaloa, Mexico, she moved with her family to Texas when she was 11.

Lance Hool

An independent producer for over two decades, Hool was born in Mexico City and educated in Mexico and the United States. Hool has produced, written, or directed a variety of feature films on location all over the world. His credits include *Missing in Action* (1984) and *Missing in Action II* (1985), both starring Chuck Norris; *The Evil That Men Do* (1984) and *10 to Midnight* (1983), both starring Charles Bronson; and *Steel Dawn* (1987), starring Patrick Swayze. He also produced the comedy *Pure Luck* (1991), starring Martin Short and Danny Glover.

Rodolfo Hoyos, Sr. [alternate spelling: Rudolfo]

B: 1896
D: 5/24/1980

Long regarded as Mexico's best baritone, Hoyos first came to the States in the late 1920s to perform with New York's Metropolitan Opera. During the 1930s and 1940s, Hoyos both appeared in films and coached such actors as Nelson Eddy and Paul Lukas. Movies in which Hoyos sang included *A Night at the Opera* (1935), which starred the Marx Brothers, and *One Night of Love* (1934), with Grace Moore. Fans of the Golden Age (1950s) of television will remember Hoyos's portrayal of Ricky Ricardo's uncle in an episode of "I Love Lucy." His son, Rudolfo Hoyos, Jr., became an actor in Hollywood.

Rudolfo Hoyos, Jr. [alternate spelling: Rodolpho Hoyas, Jr.]

B: 3/14/1916
D: 4/15/1983

A Mexican character actor, Hoyos usually made his presence felt as a heavy or stern father in such films as *The Americano* (1955) and *The Brave One* (1956).

He was the son of Rudolfo Hoyos, Sr., the famous Mexican opera singer who appeared later in his career singing in such films as *A Night at the Opera* (1935) starring the Marx Brothers and *One Night of Love* (1934) with Grace Moore.

Rudolfo, Jr., was born in Mexico City and was brought to the States in the late 1920s. He made his film debut as a 14-year-old boy in Howard Hughes's *Hell's Angels* (1930) with Jean Harlow.

As an adult, Rudolfo couldn't get a role as a Mexican until he grew a mustache. Casting directors said he didn't look the part. Hoyos played Pancho Villa in an undistinguished film called *Villa!* produced in 1958.

Among his many motion picture credits are *The Fighter* (1952), *Second Chance* (1953), *Timetable* (1956), *The First Texan* (1956), *The Three Outlaws* (1956), *Operation Eichmann* (1961), and *Return of the Gunfighter* (1967). Hoyos also appeared in over 300 TV shows.

Leon Ichaso

B: 1949

The Cuban-born director of the award-winning independent films *El Super* (1979), *Crossover Dreams* (1985), and *Sugar Hill* (1994). Ichaso's career began with commercials, documentaries, and industrial film production. He was raised in the world of radio, television, and cinema—his father, Justo Rodriguez Santos, having been a well-known television and film director and writer in Cuba. Leon left Cuba at age 14 and finished his education in the States. He has since directed episodes of such TV hits as "Miami Vice," "Crime Story," and "The Equalizer."

Eugene Iglesias

B: 12/3/1926

A character actor during the 1950s, Iglesias appeared as the lighthearted Pepe Bello in *The Brave Bulls* (1951) and in such films as *The Naked Dawn* (1955), *War Cry* [aka: *Indian Uprising*] (1952), *The Mask of the Avenger* (1951) with John Derek, and *East of Sumatra* (1953) in a Gilbert Roland–type role opposite Jeff Chandler.

He was born in San Juan, Puerto Rico, and at age seven he became a child actor in radio dramas. He left Puerto Rico and attended Columbia University. Iglesias acted with theater companies in Puerto Rico, New York, and Mexico City before entering films.

Gloria Irrizary

A Puerto Rican character actress, Irrizary was featured as Maria Holly's Puerto Rican mother in *The Buddy Holly Story* (1978) and as another Puerto Rican mother in *Q & A* (1990). She has many other motion picture and television credits.

Isabelita

See Lita Baron.

Al Israel

An actor and musician, Israel was born in New York City. His film credits include *Scarface* (1983), *Body Double* (1984), and *Carlito's Way* (1993).

Jose Iturbi [born: Jose De Iturbi]

    B: 11/28/1895
    D: 6/28/1980

A world-famous pianist and conductor, Iturbi appeared as himself in several MGM musical films during the 1940s, including *Thousands Cheer* (1943) and *Two Girls and a Sailor* (1944). He did all the piano playing for actor Cornel Wilde as Chopin on the soundtrack for the movie *A Song to Remember* (1945). His recording of Chopin's "A-flat Polonaise" from the movie was the first classical record to become a million-seller.

During the mid-1940s, Iturbi was one of the most famous pianists, rivaling Oscar Levant.

Born in Valencia, Spain, Iturbi was a child prodigy. By age seven, he was teaching piano and supporting his entire family. His first steady job was playing piano in the first movie theater in his native Valencia. He started at two in the afternoon and played until two in the morning, a steady 12-hour job. In the Basque language the name Iturbi means "twin fountains." His original name was De Iturbi, but he dropped the De. The people of Valencia took up a collection to send him to Barcelona to study under Joaquin Malats.

He played piano in cafes at night to earn room and board. Graduating with honors at age 17, he was eventually offered a post vacated by Liszt at the Zurich Conservatory. He stayed four years and then embarked on a career as a virtuoso. He performed in concert in all the leading world capitals and toured extensively throughout South America.

Later in his career, he was criticized for his work in movies. Some charged he had sold out to commercialism. Iturbi commented, "I would not go that way again if I had to do it over. My critics misunderstood. They thought I abandoned serious pursuits, but others thought it was good that I exposed a whole new audience to a music they would have been ignorant of."

At age 83, a year before his death, Iturbi drew rave reviews for a packed concert at the Ambassador Auditorium in Pasadena, California.

Neal Jimenez
    B: 5/22/1960

Scriptwriter Neal Jimenez launched himself as a director in 1992 with his autobiographical film *The Waterdance,* co-directed with Michael Steinberg. The film dealt with Jimenez's own experiences after a serious hiking accident in 1984 left him permanently paralyzed and confined to a wheelchair. He has also written the screenplay for *River's Edge* (1987) and co-scripted *For the Boys* (1991), starring Bette Midler and James Caan.

Soledad Jimenez [aka: Solidad]
    B: 1872
    D: 10/17/1966

Soledad Jimenez was a character actress who appeared in many silent and sound films including *In Old Arizona* (1929) with Warner Baxter, the first outdoor sound western, and *The Robin Hood of El Dorado* (1936) also with Warner Baxter.

Raul Julia
    B: 3/9/1940

After proving himself on stage in Shaw (*Arms and the Man*), Shakespeare (*Othello*), Coward (*Design for Living*) and Pinter (*Betrayal*), as well as the title roles in *Dracula* and *Where's Charley?,* Raul Julia has come full circle as an actor with his recent return to the Broadway stage portraying Cervantes and Don Quixote in the musical *Man of La Mancha* (1991) and with the enormous success of his film portrayal of Gomez Addams in *The Addams Family* (1991) and *Addams Family Values* (1993).

Julia is one of the most respected and sought-after performers on both stage and screen. He portrayed a South American political prisoner in the highly acclaimed *Kiss of the Spider Woman* (1985); a Hispanic detective in *Compromising Positions* (1985); the title role of the Salvadoran martyr in *Romero* (1989); and the attorney Sandy Stern in *Presumed Innocent* (1990).

He arrived in New York City from Puerto Rico in 1964. "I came [to the U.S.] to be an actor," stated Julia during an interview with Luis Reyes during a press conference for the movie *Romero.* "I didn't come here to be a stereotype. So I always looked for the opportunity to do something that was challenging. I never wanted to take the easy route.

"An actor must be regarded as an actor and he must be given the opportunity to prove that he can play any role, whether it's part of his background or not. Unfortunately, many of the people in casting and producing and directing see actors only as types. So the actor must constantly fight the limitations others want to put on him."

Raul Julia in *Romero*.

A native of San Juan, Puerto Rico, Julia is the oldest of four children of a prominent restaurateur. After graduating from high school, and at the behest of his parents, he enrolled at the University of Puerto Rico to study law. But after earning a bachelor's degree in liberal arts, he opted to work in several local theater troupes and in an occasional nightclub revue.

After arriving in New York, he studied drama at the American Place Theatre and began a long and fruitful association with theatrical producer Joseph Papp and the New York Shakespeare Festival in 1966. He made his Broadway debut in 1968 in a short-lived drama about the Castro revolution called *The Cuban Thing*. He was nominated for Broadway's Tony Award for his roles in *Two Gentlemen from Verona, Where's Charley?, The Threepenny Opera,* and *Nine.*

Julia's motion picture career began in 1971 with roles in *The Organization* and *The Panic in Needle Park*. Since then his films have included *Eyes of Laura Mars* (1978), *The Escape Artist* (1982), Francis Ford Coppola's *One from the Heart* (1982), *The Morning After* (1986), and *The Penitent* (1988). For director Paul Mazursky, he starred in *Moon over Parador* (1988) and *Tempest* (1982). More recent credits include *Presumed Innocent* (1990) and *The Rookie* (1990), as well as the Addams Family movies.

On television Julia's credits include the miniseries *Mussolini* (1985); the TV movie *Onassis: The Richest Man in the World* (1988), in which he played the title role; *The Alamo: 13 Days to Glory* (1987), in which he played General Santa Anna; and the HBO movie *Florida Straits* (1986).

Katy Jurado [born: Maria Cristina Estela Marcela Jurado Garcia]
B: 1/16/1927

A Mexican actress, Jurado is best known for her strikingly dark beauty and for her many strong roles in such classic western dramas as *High Noon* (1952) and *Broken Lance* (1954).

Born in Mexico City, she was the daughter of a rancher and an opera singer. As a teenager, despite her parents' objections, Jurado became an actress and made her first film, *No Mataras*. Her friendship with famed Mexican director Emilio

Katy Jurado.

Katy Jurado and Rita Moreno at a party given after Ed Sullivan's "Toast of the Town." Jurado had recently won Mexico's Ariel Award, the equivalent of Hollywood's Oscar.

Photo by Mel Traxel.

Fernandez helped her entry into the Mexican film industry, in which she became an overnight sensation. For her third motion picture, *La Vida Inutil de Pito Perez* (1943), she was honored with many awards.

In Mexican films she was always cast as a glamour girl or wealthy socialite, and sometimes sang and danced. In American films she almost always played a sultry Mexican beauty, Indian squaw, or suffering mother.

She made her American film debut in 1951 in *The Bullfighter and the Lady,* as the wife of an aging bullfighter played by Gilbert Roland. Later, Stanley Kramer hired her for the role of Helen Ramirez in *High Noon* (1952) opposite Gary Cooper, which brought her attention from critics and audiences alike. Knowing very little English, she learned her lines phonetically. She followed this with a role as a "half-breed" Apache-Mexican squaw in *Arrowhead* (1953) starring Charlton Heston. Jurado played Spencer Tracy's Indian wife in *Broken Lance,* for which she was an Academy Award nominee for Best Supporting Actress in 1954. Her many motion picture credits include *San Antone* (1953); *The Racers* (1955); *Trial* (1955); *The Man from Del Rio* (1956); *Trapeze* (1956); *The Badlanders* (1958); *One-Eyed Jacks* (1961), starring and directed by Marlon Brando; *Barabbas* (1962); *A Covenant with Death* (1966); *Stay Away, Joe* (1968); *Pat Garrett and Billy the Kid* (1973); and *Under the Volcano* (1984). She has made guest appearances on American television.

Tichi Wilkerson Kassel

An innovative businesswoman, Tichi Wilkerson Kassel was publisher emeritus of the trade newspaper *The Hollywood Reporter* until 1991.

She acquired the newspaper after her husband's death in 1963. Under her guidance and leadership, the newspaper expanded and became an internationally respected and read entertainment publication. Through the Wilkerson Foundation and her many civic efforts, she distinguished herself for her continuing devotion and service to the entertainment industry. She has a star on the Hollywood Walk of Fame.

Born in Los Angeles, California, a daughter of the Verdugo family, whose ancestors came to Latin America in 1520 with Cortes, Tichi was raised in Mexico City and returned to Los Angeles as a teenager.

Pancho Kohner

B: 1/7/1939

Son of agent Paul Kohner and Mexican actress Lupita Tovar, and the brother of actress Susan Kohner, Pancho produced such films as *St. Ives* (1976), *The White Buffalo* (1977), *The Evil That Men Do* (1984), *Death Wish 4: The Crackdown* (1987), and *Kinjite: Forbidden Subjects* (1989).

Susan Kohner

B: 11/11/1936

As the daughter of Mexican actress Lupita Tovar and Hollywood agent Paul Kohner, it is not surprising that Susan Kohner became an actress. She was nominated for an Oscar for Best Supporting Actress for her role as a young black woman who tries to pass for white in Universal's 1959 remake of *Imitation of Life*.

She made her film debut as Maria in *To Hell and Back* starring Audie Murphy in 1955. Her other films include *Trooper Hook* (1957), *All the Fine Young Cannibals* (1960), *By Love Possessed* (1961), and *Freud* (1962). She semi-retired in 1964 when she married designer John Wurtz. The actress is a graduate of UCLA and has appeared on the Broadway stage.

Apollonia Kotero

A Mexican American actress/singer/dancer, Kotero co-starred with Prince in the hit film *Purple Rain* (1984) and played a character called Apollonia on TV's "Falcon Crest" for a season.

Carlos LaCamara

B: 1957

LaCamara plays Paco, the orderly who is tapped into the hospital grapevine, on the NBC-TV series "Nurses." Born in Havana, Cuba, LaCamara moved with his family to Washington, D.C., at age two, when Fidel Castro came to power. He credits his interest in theater, which he says began in elementary school, to the influence of his father, a graphic artist, and his mother, who was an opera singer in Cuba. At age seven, his family moved to Los Angeles. He attended the University of California at Los Angeles, where he earned a bachelor of arts degree.

Fernando Lamas

B: 1/9/1915
D: 10/8/1982

A handsome, virile, athletic MGM star of the 1950s, Lamas played opposite some of the most beautiful actresses in Hollywood, including Lana Turner, Elizabeth Taylor, Esther Williams, Arlene Dahl, and Rhonda Fleming.

He was born in Buenos Aires, Argentina, the son of electrical engineer Emelio Lamas and his wife, Maria, who died when Fernando was only four years old. He was subsequently raised by an aunt and a grandmother. He joined the local theater group as a young boy, and became a major film star in Europe and in Argentina before coming to MGM in 1950.

In an interview with Burt Prelutsky in the *L.A. Times* (3/19/78), Lamas described his early years at MGM: "I couldn't break the Latin Lover image, hard as I tried. It was a great image to have off screen, but a pain in the ass in the movies." He spent 10 years under contract to MGM, where he earned $2,500 a week and an occasional $25,000 bonus.

In another interview, with Paul Rosenfield of the *L.A. Times* in 1977, Lamas remarked, "I was the Technicolor boy; get me the guitar, the horse, the girl, and get it over with. We were bottled and sold as products. Audiences then were buying trips not truth."

After his contract was up, Lamas starred in and directed a number of unsuccessful films in Europe. He directed more than 60 episodic television shows over

Smooth, suave, sophisticated Fernando Lamas starred as a smooth, suave, sophisticated French patriot seeking refuge from the Nazis during the 1940s in *The Cheap Detective* (1978).

the years, including several episodes of the popular series "Falcon Crest," which starred his son Lorenzo, born of his marriage to actress Arlene Dahl. Lamas later married Esther Williams. He died of cancer in 1982 shortly after beginning work as Robert Urich's co-star in a new television series called "Gavilan." A caricature of his personality was made famous for a new generation by comedian Billy Crystal on the TV show "Saturday Night Live" with a character whose catch phrase was "You look maaahvelous!"

His films include *The Law and the Lady* (1951), *Rich, Young and Pretty* (1951), *The Merry Widow* (1952), *Dangerous When Wet* (1953), *The Girl Who Had Everything* (1953), *Rose Marie* (1954), *The Girl Rush* (1955), *The Lost World* (1960), *100 Rifles* (1969), and *The Cheap Detective* (1978).

Lorenzo Lamas

B: 1/20/1958

Best known for his role as Lance Cumson on the long-running CBS-TV series "Falcon Crest," Lamas has appeared in numerous television shows and feature films including *Grease* (1978), *Take Down* (1979), *Body Rock* (1984), and *Final Impact* (1991).

Born in Santa Monica, California, he is the son of Fernando Lamas and Arlene Dahl. He starred in a syndicated TV series, "Renegade" (1992).

Dorothy Lamour

B: 12/10/1914

The dark, alluring, blue-eyed beauty Lamour is of French, Scots-Irish, and Spanish descent and was born in New Orleans. She played a Latin in *A Medal for Benny* (1945), *Masquerade in Mexico* (1945), and *The Road to Rio* (1947). She played a Spaniard in *The Last Train from Madrid* (1937).

Her first picture was *The Jungle Princess* in 1936. She became an overnight star at Paramount Pictures when it was released, and the abbreviated costume she wore, the sarong, became her trademark as a native island siren and started an international fashion trend. Lamour's first outstanding screen success was in Samuel Goldwyn's *The Hurricane* (1937). Her singing and comedic talents were put to good use as the female co-star in a series of successful *Road to . . .* pictures with Bob Hope and Bing Crosby. In some of her other 52 films, she co-starred with Ray Milland, Alan Ladd, Tyrone Power, William Holden, and Fred MacMurray.

William Douglas Lansford

B: 7/13/1922

A film and television writer, Lansford was born and raised in East Los Angeles of a Mexican mother and an Anglo father. His credits include such series as "Bonanza," "The Virginian," "The High Chaparral," "Fantasy Island," "The Rookies," "Matt Houston," and "CHiPs." He wrote a best-selling book on Pancho Villa, for which he wrote a film treatment from which Sam Peckinpah wrote a script. Peckinpah was fired from the project, which he had planned to direct, and Robert Towne reworked the script. The film was eventually shot in Spain by producer Ted Richmond with Yul Brynner as Villa. Lansford also wrote the television movies *The Deadly Tower* (1975) and *Don't Look Back: The Story of Leroy "Satchel" Paige* (1981).

Mario Larrinaga

A native Californian, Larrinaga was a background effects scenic artist. He worked at RKO and was a significant contributor to the classic 1933 production *King Kong*. He was also a noted painter and artist.

John Leguizamo

A rising young actor/writer of Colombian heritage, Leguizamo has appeared as a Mexican mountain boy in *Revenge* (1990), a street hood in *Regarding Henry* (1991), and a kinky Soho artist in *Whispers in the Dark* (1992). His first major role was as a Puerto Rican youth in *Hangin' with the Homeboys* (1991). He produced, wrote, and starred in his own one-man Off-Broadway show, called *Mambo Mouth*, in 1990, which was later taped and aired on the HBO cable network (1991). *Mambo Mouth* is an incisive, funny, vicious satire on Latino stereotypes presented through different characters impersonated by Leguizamo. He followed this in 1992 with another, equally biting satirical one-man stage show, *Spic-O-Rama*, which was also taped for HBO. In 1993 he co-starred with Bob Hoskins in *Super Mario Brothers*, and also appeared in *Carlito's Way*.

George J. Lewis

B: 12/10/1904

A veteran character actor born in Guadalajara, Mexico, Lewis has over 250 American feature film credits, beginning in 1924 with *Captain Blood* for Vitagraph and ending with *The Comancheros* in 1961. He is perhaps best remembered as Zorro's father in the Walt Disney TV series starring Guy Williams.

Lewis appeared in countless B westerns and serials for such studios as Monogram, Republic, and Columbia. He also appeared in many Spanish-language features produced in Hollywood in the 1930s. His better-known feature film credits include *Gilda* (1946), *Crisis* (1950), *Branded* (1951), *The Bad and the Beautiful* (1952), *The Iron Mistress* (1952), *Viva Zapata!* (1952), *Shane* (1953), and *Hell on Frisco Bay* (1956).

Luis Llosa

A Peruvian filmmaker, Llosa made his American theatrical motion picture directing debut in 1993 with *Sniper,* starring Tom Berenger.

Gerry Lopez

B: 1948

A surfer/actor/entrepreneur, Lopez was featured in *Big Wednesday* (1978) as himself and co-starred in *Conan the Barbarian* (1982) as Subotai the Mongol, Conan's loyal partner. He was also featured in *North Shore* (1987) and *Farewell to the King* (1989).

Lopez was born and raised in Honolulu. His father is a New Yorker of Cuban-German descent who first went to Hawaii as a soldier in World War II. His mother is of Japanese descent.

Kamala Lopez [aka: Kamala Lopez Dawson]

B: 1965

An actress, Lopez was featured as Dolores, the female lead, in *Born in East L.A.* (1987). She was born in New York City of an Indian mother and a Venezuelan father. She made her professional debut on television's "Sesame Street," where she spent two seasons before entering Yale University. Her television credits include guest-starring roles on "Spenser: For Hire," "Miami Vice," and "The Cosby Show."

Perry Lopez [born: Julius Caesar Lopez]

B: 7/31/1931

In a career that spans over 40 years, Lopez has worked for such distinguished and legendary directors as Roman Polanski, who gave him his most notable role, as Detective Luis Escobar in the classic *Chinatown* (1974); John Ford in *Mister Roberts* (1955); and Raoul Walsh, who directed him in his film debut as Spanish Joe in *Battle Cry* (1954).

Warner Bros. put Lopez under term contract in 1953, and the actor subsequently appeared in *Drum Beat* (1954) and *The McConnell Story* (1955). He starred as a young ex-con in *The Steel Jungle* (1956) and a gang tough who menaces James Dean in *Rebel Without a Cause* (1955), and he co-starred with Tony Curtis and Yul Brynner in *Taras Bulba* (1962).

The son of Puerto Rican parents, Esther and Alphonso Lopez, he was born in New York City and christened Julius Caesar. However, a few years later his parents relented and renamed him Perry. He was educated at Public Schools 57 and 172 and George Washington High School in New York, and then attended New York University.

Perry kept busy after school doing odd jobs to add to the family income. He sold newspapers near Madison Square Garden and had his first contact with the show world when he shined the shoes of the famous in Shubert Alley.

He later became a top amateur lightweight boxer, a career that was short-lived because he decided there were easier ways to make a living. The actor was attending New York University when a chance meeting with director Joshua Logan in 1950 started him on an acting career. He stopped by the theater at which Logan was rehearsing the national company of *South Pacific* to pick up actress Diosa Costello for a lunch date. The director spotted Perry and asked him to read, and he got a role as a Seabee.

He left NYU and toured with *South Pacific* for three years. Lopez left the musical, returned to New York, and toured in summer stock productions. Then, in 1953, an automobile accident almost ended his life. While recuperating from his injuries with relatives in Los Angeles, an interview at Warner Bros. brought him a screen test that resulted in a contract, and the role in *Battle Cry*. More recently, he reprised the role of Detective Luis Escobar in *The Two Jakes* (1990), the sequel to *Chinatown*, and co-starred with Charles Bronson in *Kinjite: Forbidden Subjects* (1989). His other films include *I Died a Thousand Times* (1955), *Hell on Frisco Bay* (1956), *The Young Guns* (1956), *Omar Khayyam* (1957), *Cry Tough* (1959), *Flaming Star* (1960), *McLintock!* (1963), *Bandolero!* (1968), *Che!* (1969), and *Deadlock* (1969)

Priscilla Lopez

Born in the Bronx and raised in Brooklyn, Lopez is a dancer, singer, and actress. She won an Obie Award and was nominated for a Tony for her performance on Broadway in *A Chorus Line*, and won the Tony for Featured Actress in a Musical in 1980 for *A Day in Hollywood, A Night in the Ukraine*. On television she was a regular on the series "In the Beginning" as Sister Agnes and "Kay O'Brien" as nurse Rosa Villanueva. She has also guest starred on "All in the Family," "Trapper John, M.D.," and "Family."

Rafael Lopez [alternate spelling: Raphael]
B: 1948

Lopez was a juvenile actor in Hollywood films of the 1960s. His film credits include *The Young Savages* (1961), *Dime with a Halo* (1963), and *Trackdown* (1976).

Sal Lopez
B: 11/8/1954

A Mexican American actor, Lopez played a young recruit in Stanley Kubrick's *Full Metal Jacket* (1987) and played Santana's (Edward James Olmos's) father in *American Me* (1992). He made his feature film debut in the film version of Luis Valdez's *Zoot Suit* (1981).

Sylvia Lopez

A Spanish-born actress, Lopez worked in Italian sand-and-spear epics of the 1960s that were dubbed into English and released in the States. Her credits include *Hercules* (1960) and *Herod the Great* (1961).

Trini Lopez

B: 5/15/1937

A Dallas-born Mexican American singer and recording artist, Lopez played a major role as Private Pedro Ramirez, one of the Dirty Dozen in the hit 1967 World War II action film of the same name. Lopez played himself in the films *Marriage on the Rocks* (1965) and *The Poppy Is Also a Flower* (1960). In 1964 he signed a five-picture contract with Twentieth Century–Fox, but no suitable film roles were found for him.

Lopez grew up in a Dallas ghetto in a one-room house with his parents, four sisters, and a brother. He didn't finish high school, but his father taught him to play guitar and to sing. Lopez was discovered by Frank Sinatra, who signed him to his label, Reprise Records, for whom Lopez went on to record a number of million-sellers. Lopez quickly became an international recording star with such hit records as "If I Had a Hammer" and "La Bamba."

Jose Lopez Rodero

B: 10/20/1937

Born in Madrid, Spain, the oldest of four children, Rodero entered films at age 15 and since that time has worked on over 100 movies in a range of capacities, largely in Europe. Among the better known of the international films on which he served as either first or second assistant director are *Solomon and Sheba* (1959), *Spartacus* (1960), *King of Kings* (1961), *55 Days at Peking* (1963), *Cleopatra* (1963), *Patton* (1970), *Papillon* (1973), *The Boys from Brazil* (1978), and *Conan the Barbarian* (1982). He was also associate producer of *Dune* (1984).

Linda Loredo [born: Herlinda Loredo]

B: 1908
D: 8/11/1931

Born in Los Angeles to a prominent Mexican American family, Loredo did bit parts in silent films and appeared prominently in several Spanish-language Laurel and Hardy and Charley Chase comedy short subjects. She appeared in the English-language version of *Come Clean* (1931), as Stan Laurel's wife. She died at an early age after a long illness.

Barbara Luna

B: 1939

A beautiful, raven-haired actress, Luna has played a Latin in so many films and television shows throughout the 1950s, 1960s, and 1970s that she has become closely identified with Mexican or Latin dancer, cantina girl, spitfire, and senorita roles. Her father is Filipino-Spanish, her mother Hungarian-Italian and Jewish, and she was reared in a Puerto Rican neighborhood in New York City. Her father supported the family by working as a waiter at the Copacabana nightclub. She first came to public attention as a child actress in the original Broadway production of *South Pacific* (1949).

Her exotic good looks took her into an active film and television career in which she played Japanese Geisha girls, island girls, or Chinese and Mexican maidens. Luna made her television debut as a guest star on "Desilu Playhouse." As a young adult she scored as a blind nurse who helps Frank Sinatra in the film *The Devil at 4 O'Clock* (1961). She was also featured in *Ship of Fools* (1965) and *Dime with a Halo* (1963). Other credits include *Five Weeks in a Balloon* (1962), *Firecreek* (1968), *Che!* (1969), *Synanon* (1965), and *The Concrete Jungle* (1982). Her television credits include over 400 roles on episodic series and in Movies of the Week.

Julio Macat

An Argentine-born cinematographer, Macat immigrated with his family to the United States at age 14. Macat shot *Home Alone,* the 1990 box-office hit, for director Chris Columbus, and *Only the Lonely* (1991).

Bill Maldonado

B: 5/25/1921

Maldonado was construction coordinator and supervisor on a number of films for the Mirisch brothers, including such large-scale international film productions as *Some Like It Hot* (1959), *The Great Escape* (1963), *Kings of the Sun* (1963, filmed in Mexico), *Hawaii* (1966), *Hour of the Gun* (1967, filmed in Mexico), *Gaily, Gaily* (1969), and *Fiddler on the Roof* (1971).

Maldonado served in the Armed Forces during World War II, and after his discharge went to work as a carpenter at one of the studios, where it was some time before he was admitted to the union. He landed work as a propmaker, which led to construction. His first film was a Gary Cooper western called *Man of the West* (1958). He is now retired; his last film was *The Milagro Beanfield War* (1988).

Luis Mandoki

B: 8/17/1954

Mandoki is the Mexican-born director of such films as *Gaby* (1987), *White Palace* (1990), and *Born Yesterday* (1993).

Adele Mara [born: Adelaide Delgado]

B: 4/28/1923

Born in Dearborn, Michigan, Mara was a starlet at Republic Pictures and co-starred in two major hits with John Wayne in the late 1940s, *Wake of the Red Witch* (1949) and *Sands of Iwo Jima* (1949).

At the close of World War II, she was crowned Hollywood's new pinup girl over reigning Betty Grable by the service magazine *Yank.*

In 1941, Harry Cohn spotted her with Xavier Cugat's band at the Waldorf-Astoria in New York City and cast her as Rita Hayworth's younger sister in *You Were Never Lovelier* (1942). Later she was put under contract by Republic Pictures, where she appeared in many B westerns such as *Bells of Rosarita* (1945) with Roy Rogers, *Girls of the Big House* (1945), *The Tiger Woman* (1945), and *Vampire's Ghost* (1945). She also starred for the studio in the big-budget *The Avengers* (1950) and *California Passage* (1950).

Margo [born: Maria Margarita Guadalupe Teresa Estella Castilla Bolado y O'Donnell]

B: 5/10/1918
D: 7/17/1985

Margo will always be remembered as the girl in Frank Capra's *Lost Horizon* (1937) who withered and died a centuries-old woman as she fled the idyllic valley of Shangri-La.

Born in Mexico City and reared in the United States, Margo was taught dance by Eduardo Cansino, father of Rita Hayworth, and at age 10 began her professional career dancing and singing at various community affairs.

Her aunt married Xavier Cugat, and Margo joined them in Cugat's band where for a year and a half they played at the Waldorf-Astoria in New York.

Margo in *Lost Horizon*

She was spotted by a talent scout in New York and made her film debut at age 16 playing Carmen Brown, the discarded mistress of a middle-aged district attorney, in the Ben Hecht–Charles MacArthur production *Crime Without Passion* (1934). She went to Hollywood and made *Rumba* (1935) with George Raft and Carole Lombard and *The Robin Hood of El Dorado* (1936) with Warner Baxter.

On Broadway she did *Winterset* (1935), a performance for which she received fantastic notices and which she repeated in the memorable 1936 film version.

She took a brief respite from acting and then appeared in films throughout the 1940s and early 1950s, most notably in *Cat People* (1942), *The Leopard Man* (1943), *A Bell for Adano* (1945), and *Viva Zapata!* (1952). She recalled in an interview with Luis Reyes, "I was exposed to a great amount of ignorant prejudice and it hurt me." She continued, "I was frightened by the whole situation at the studios. I didn't seem to fit in, in that environment. I was terribly young and inexperienced. People thought I was much older as I had registered on the screen as mature in my first picture but nobody realized I was then only 18."

Margo married actor Eddie Albert in 1945 and devoted herself largely to raising a family. She was deeply involved in Mexican American community affairs and founded Plaza De La Raza, a theater and cultural center in East Los Angeles. She was the mother of actor Edward Albert.

Cheech Marin

B: 7/13/1946

Cheech Marin and his partner, Tommy Chong, as Cheech and Chong, were one of the most successful comedy duos of the 1970s with their drug and counterculture humor.

Cheech (short for "chicharron," a Mexican delicacy made of deep-fried pork skins) was born in Central Los Angeles. He was one of four children of a Los Angeles police officer and was raised in the San Fernando Valley.

A straight-A student in high school, Cheech also took the time to sing with neighborhood rock bands. After putting himself through college working as a dishwasher and janitor, he earned a bachelor of arts degree in English from the California State University at Northridge.

Cheech's break in comedy came when he drove to Vancouver, B.C., to audition for an improvisational comedy group called City Works, run by Tommy Chong. When the troupe broke up in 1970, Cheech and Chong formed their own comedy duo. Their first album, *Cheech and Chong,* went gold. Their second, *Big Bamboo,* was voted the number-one comedy album of 1972. Their third, *Los Cochinos,* brought them a Grammy Award.

Cheech and Chong teamed together in eight feature films. The first, *Cheech and Chong's Up in Smoke,* was the highest-grossing comedy of 1979, generating more than $100 million at the box office. Their other films are *Cheech and Chong's Next Movie* (1980), *Cheech and Chong's Nice Dreams* (1981), *Cheech and Chong: Things Are Tough All Over* (1982), *Cheech and Chong: Still Smokin'* (1983), and *Cheech and Chong's The Corsican Brothers* (1984). They also made cameo appearances in *Yellowbeard* (1983) and in Martin Scorsese's *After Hours* (1985).

In 1985, after 15 years together, Cheech and Chong decided to branch out into other projects and pursue their own creative ideas. Two years later Cheech wrote, directed, and starred in *Born in East L.A.* for Universal Pictures. He also starred in *Shrimp on the Barbie* (1990) and did the voice of Tito the streetwise chihuahua in Disney's animated film *Oliver and Company* (1988). In 1992, he was one of the stars of the TV sitcom "The Golden Palace." Marin also portrayed Pancho in TNT's *The Cisco Kid* (1994).

Ada Maris

B: 6/13/1963

Maris has starred for three seasons as Gina Cuevas, an immigrant nurse, on the NBC-TV series "Nurses." Maris was born and raised in East Los Angeles, and she began her performing career after attending Boston University and the University of California at Los Angeles. She co-starred with Tony Orlando in a series pilot that aired as an episode of "The Cosby Show."

Mona Maris

B: 11/8/1908
D: 3/22/1992

Born in Buenos Aires, Argentina, to a Spanish family, Maris made her screen debut in England in 1926. In Europe, she met Dolores Del Rio, who encouraged her to go to Hollywood. After a brief time at United Artists, she made *Romance of the Rio Grande* (1929) opposite Warner Baxter, followed by *Under the Texas Moon* (1930) and *The Arizona Kid* (1930), also with Baxter. She filmed *One Mad Kiss* (1930) simultaneously in English and Spanish, which marked the first screen appearance of Jose Mojica, lyric tenor for the Chicago Opera Company. Maris made many Spanish-language films, frequently appearing as a sophisticated woman. Her later films include *I Married an Angel* (1942), *The Falcon in Mexico* (1944), *Tampico* (1944), *Heart-*

beat (1946), *Monsieur Beaucaire* (1946), and *The Avengers* (1950). She died in 1992, having retired from the screen many years earlier.

William Marquez

B: 3/14/1943

A Cuban-born actor, Marquez played General Cordosa in *Deal of the Century* (1983). He has appeared in many major television series from "Hart to Hart" to "Quincy, M.E." and "CHiPs."

Chris-Pin Martin

B: 11/19/1893
D: 6/27/1968

A famed character actor, Martin usually played lackadaisical Mexicans. He was best known for his role as Cisco's sidekick in a series of Cisco Kid films starring Cesar Romero.

Martin began in the motion picture business in 1911. For a time he was an extra, and then he became what is known as a runner, recruiting Mexican and Indian extras. When a studio wanted any given number of these types rounded up, they'd call on Chris. When the formation of Central Casting ended this business, he turned to acting. His first part of any consequence was in *The Gay Desperado* in 1936. His other films include *Under the Pampas Moon* (1935), *The Cisco Kid and the Lady* (1939), *Frontier Marshall* (1939), *The Return of the Cisco Kid* (1939), *Stagecoach* (1939), *The Mark of Zorro* (1940), *Romance of the Rio Grande* (1941), *Robin Hood of Monterey* (1947), and *The Beautiful Blonde from Bashful Bend* (1949).

Martin was born in Tucson, Arizona, to Toro ("Bull") Martin, a Yaqui Indian, and his wife, Florence Morales Martin, a Mexican. His father rejoined his tribe during the Mexican-Yaqui troubles at the beginning of the century and is believed to have died in battle.

Exposed to very little education, Martin early learned a lot about life through working at Silver Bell and other Arizona mining camps. Somewhere along the line he picked up a knowledge of the barber's trade and served in the Army as a barber at Fort Snelling, Minnesota. In 1911 he returned to Arizona and joined a group of Indians whom Universal Studios was bringing to Hollywood for picture work. The wages were $5 a week and a ration of meat. Martin led an uprising when it was discovered that the meat was horse meat. In 1912, he married Margaret Avell in Pomona, California, and he lived near Chavez Ravine in Los Angeles.

Richard Martin [born: Herbert Pinney]

B: 12/12/1918

Born in Spokane, Washington, of Scots-Irish descent, Martin is best known for his role as Chito Jose Gonzales Bustamante Rafferty, Mexican-Irish sidekick to B western hero Tim Holt in 29 films at RKO in the late 1940s and early 1950s. Chito was tall and handsome and had wit, and could fight any man and win any senorita's heart. Martin actually created the role in the World War II film *Bombardier* (1943), with Randolph Scott and Pat O'Brien, as a character named simply Chito Rafferty. The character was transferred to an Old West setting for several westerns that starred Robert Mitchum and James Warren, and then Chito was successfully paired up with Tim Holt.

He was typecast in the role, and when the film series ended in 1952, he decided to leave films. Instead, he became a successful insurance agent.

Martin grew up in the predominantly Mexican American area of Los Angeles, where the family moved from Washington during the Great Depression. He picked up the accent he used so well in his film characterizations from the people in the neighborhood. Though not Latin, Martin is included here because he is so identified with the role of Chito and because he made Chito different from the stereotypical sidekick. In fact, Chito was taller and much better looking than his western hero buddy, though perhaps not as smart.

A Martinez [born: Adolpho Martinez]
B: 9/27/1948

A native Californian, Martinez was age 12 when he made his professional singing debut at the Hollywood Bowl, where he won a talent competition. Later, while attending UCLA, he got his first feature film experience in *Born Wild* (ca. 1971). He made his motion picture debut as the young Mexican American cowhand, Cimarron, in *The Cowboys* (1972), starring John Wayne.

He followed this in quick succession with *Once upon a Scoundrel* (1973), *Joe Panther* (1976), *Shoot the Sundown* (1981), *Beyond the Limit* (1983) starring Michael Caine, and *Walking the Edge* (1983), among others. In the last few years, in addition to taping the daytime soap "Santa Barbara," he has appeared in *She-Devil* (1989) as Meryl Streep's butler turned lover, and starred as a Native American political activist in *Powwow Highway* (1989), which earned acclaim at several international film festivals.

A Martinez on "L.A. Law."

Among Martinez's television movie credits are NBC's *Manhunt: Search for the Night Stalker* (1989), as a Los Angeles Police detective trailing a serial killer; *Seguin* (1982), for PBS's "American Playhouse," as a Texas folk hero; *Death Among Friends* (1975); *Not of This World* (1991); and the recent *Criminal Behavior* (1992) opposite Farrah Fawcett. His many TV guest starring credits include "Barney Miller," "Quincy, M.E.," "Police Story," "The Streets of San Francisco," and an important role in the epic miniseries *Centennial (1978)*. Martinez starred for eight years as Cruz Castillo, a romantic hero on the daytime TV soap opera "Santa Barbara." He won a Daytime Emmy Award for Best Actor in a Daytime Drama in 1990 for his role on the series. In the fall of 1992, Martinez joined the cast of the Emmy Award–winning television series "L.A. Law" as attorney David Morales.

Alma Martinez

B: 3/18/1953

An actress, Martinez has appeared in such films as Luis Valdez's *Zoot Suit* (1981), as Della, the younger sister; Roger Spottiswoode's *Under Fire* (1983), as an unassuming secretary who is really a rebel; and Fred Schepisi's *Barbarosa* (1982), in the role of Willie Nelson's daughter. On television, Martinez was featured in over 50 episodes as a police sergeant in the syndicated series the new "Adam 12."

Carmen Martinez

B: 1933

Featured in *Heartbreaker* (1983) and *Fires Within* (1992), Martinez has also appeared in countless episodic TV series.

Joaquin Martinez

B: 11/5/1932

A Mexican-born actor, Martinez left Mexico to work in American films. Martinez played the title role of the Indian renegade in *Ulzana's Raid* (1972), starring Burt Lancaster and directed by Robert Aldrich. He also appeared in *Joe Kidd* (1972), starring Clint Eastwood, and co-starred as the friendly Mexican peasant Mauro in *Revenge* (1990), starring Kevin Costner. His credits include guest appearances in dozens of television shows over the years.

Patrice Martinez [aka: Patrice Camhi]

B: 6/12/1963

Born in Albuquerque, New Mexico, Martinez is best known for her role as Carmen in *¡Three Amigos!* (1986). As Patrice Camhi, she starred for four seasons on the new "Zorro" TV series starring Duncan Regehr. Her first film appearance was in *Convoy* (1978), directed by Sam Peckinpah, who encouraged her to study drama. Upon graduation from high school, she obtained a scholarship to study at the Royal Academy of Dramatic Art in London. Martinez guest starred twice on "Magnum, P.I." opposite Tom Selleck and appeared in the film *Beetlejuice* (1988).

Ron Martinez

B: 11/17/1943

Born in Santa Ana, California, first assistant director Martinez worked his way up at Universal Studios, where he worked on such films as *Red Sky at Morning* (1971), *Dillinger* (1973), *Walk Proud* (1979), *Little Miss Marker* (1980), and *The Yakuza* (1975).

His episodic television credits include "Quincy, M.E." and "Little House on the Prairie." He is currently executive production manager for Universal Television, where he has been responsible for such shows as "Murder, She Wrote," "Major Dad," "Coach," and "Quantum Leap."

Tony Martinez

A Puerto Rican comedic character actor, Martinez is best known for his portrayal of Pepino the Mexican farmworker on the 1950s television series "The Real McCoys" for six years. He toured in stage productions of *Man of La Mancha* as Sancho Panza with Richard Kiley in the late 1970s and Raul Julia in 1992, and with ten other actors since 1967.

Patricia Medina

B: 7/19/1920

The daughter of the Spanish-born English barrister Laureano Medina and English-woman Gouda Strode, Patricia attended school in England and France. This brunette beauty made her American film debut in MGM's *The Secret Heart* in 1946. She has more than 40 film appearances to her credit, including *The Foxes of Harrow* (1947), *Fortunes of Captain Blood* (1950), *Valentino* (1951), *Desperate Search* (1952), *Botany Bay* (1953), *Snow White and the Three Stooges* (1961), and *The Killing of Sister George* (1968).

Bill Melendez [born: Jose Cuauhtemoc (Bill) Melendez]

B: 1917

Animator Jose Cuauhtemoc (Bill) Melendez is best known as the producer of the "Peanuts" TV specials. He has produced 49 specials and is considered one of the top independent animators in the industry.

A native of Mexico, Melendez started working for Walt Disney in 1938 during the production of the film *Fantasia* (1940) and has been in Hollywood ever since.

Tina Menard

A character actress and bit player for over 50 years, Menard is most noted for her participation in George Stevens's *Giant* (1956), in which she was responsible for the coordination of Mexican extras and bit players.

John Mendoza

B: 1953

A half–Puerto Rican, half-Irish stand-up comedian, Mendoza was born in the Bronx, New York. He stars in the situation comedy "The Second Half," which premiered on NBC in 1993.

Ramon Menendez

The Cuban-born Menendez directed the celebrated 1988 film *Stand and Deliver,* his only major film to date. He studied at the American Film Institute, where he made several short films.

Hector Mercado

B: 1953

A Puerto Rican actor, Mercado can be seen in *Slow Dancing in the Big City* (1978) and *Delta Force 2: Operation Stranglehold* (1990).

Ricardo Mestres

B: 1/23/1958

The former president of Disney's Hollywood Pictures, Mestres is a graduate of Harvard University. Mestres started as a production assistant and became a creative executive at Paramount Pictures in 1981. In 1982, he was promoted to executive director of production, Paramount; in 1984, vice president of production, Motion Picture Group; in 1985, vice president of production, Walt Disney Pictures; in 1986, senior vice president of motion picture production, Walt Disney Pictures; in 1988, head of Hollywood Pictures, a position he held until 1994.

Mestres was born in New York City.

Tomas Milian

B: 3/3/1937

A Cuban-born actor, Milian immigrated to the United States in the mid-1950s. He has appeared in such American films as *Cat Chaser* (1989), *Revenge* (1990), and *Havana* (1990). Milian has starred in over 100 Italian films and worked almost exclusively in Europe for almost two decades. He is the recipient of the Nastro d'Argento, Italy's equivalent to the Oscar, for his role as the schoolteacher in Bernardo Bertolucci's *Luna* (1979). He co-starred with Rod Steiger and Shelley Winters in Francesco Maseli's *Time of Indifference* (1965) and starred in Michelangelo Antonioni's *Identification of a Woman* (1983).

Victor Millan

B: 8/1/1920

A Mexican American actor, Millan has given dignified portrayals in such classic films as Raoul Walsh's *Battle Cry* (1954), George Stevens's *Giant* (1956), and Orson Welles's *Touch of Evil* (1958). His other film credits include *Drum Beat* (1954), *Walk the Proud Land* (1956), *The Ride Back* (1957), in which he co-starred with Anthony Quinn, *The FBI Story* (1959), and *Boulevard Nights* (1979).

Born and raised in East Los Angeles, Millan served in World War II and always had the desire to be an actor. He used the G.I. Bill to study at the Pasadena Playhouse and at UCLA, where he attended classes with James Dean. He made his professional acting debut in 1951 co-starring in a "Schlitz Playhouse" production entitled *A Pair of Shoes*. For over 40 years he has guest starred in most of the major television series. He was a series regular on the "Ramar of the Jungle" program and on the "Broken Arrow" series he played Taza, son of Cochise. He served for 30 years as a drama professor and department head at Santa Monica College.

Yvette Mimieux

B: 1/8/1939

A beautiful blonde actress, Mimieux specialized in ingenue roles under a long-term MGM contract in the early 1960s. Her father, Rene Mimieux, of French parentage, was born in London. Her mother, Carmen, was born in Mexico. She made her film debut in 1960 in the science fiction classic *The Time Machine* opposite Rod Taylor. Her other credits include *Where the Boys Are* (1960), *The Four Horsemen of the Apocalypse* (1962), *Light in the Piazza* (1962), *Diamond Head* (1962), and *Toys in the Attic* (1963).

Aurora Miranda

The younger sister of Carmen Miranda, Aurora appeared in the films *Phantom Lady* (1944), *Brazil* (1944), and *The Three Caballeros* (1944).

Carmen Miranda

    B: 2/9/1909
    D: 8/5/1955

"The Brazilian Bombshell," Miranda combined her radiant smile and personality with gyrating hips and samba rhythms to become one of the best-remembered performers of the 1940s. Her act was punctuated by extravagant fruit-topped headdresses, colorful skirts, and platform shoes. Her success in Hollywood was instantaneous, and she was often imitated and parodied.

Miranda appeared in 14 Hollywood films, many of which were Technicolor musicals designed to encourage the Good Neighbor Policy between the United States and Latin America. She made many guest appearances on early television shows and was a top attraction at nightclubs throughout the States.

Carmen Miranda in *The Gang's All Here.*

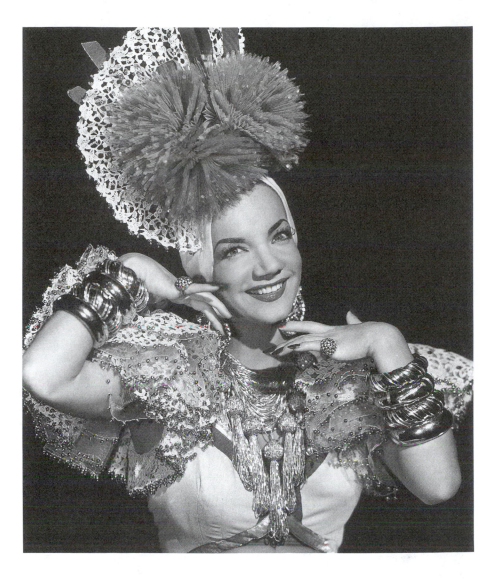

From 1932 to 1939, she was the most popular female performer in all of South America, where she sang on the radio, performed in nightclubs, made nine concert tours throughout the region, and starred in four movie musicals. She was brought to the United States by theatrical producer Lee Shubert and made her Broadway debut in 1939 with an appearance in the musical *The Streets of Paris.* She also performed a show at the Waldorf-Astoria Hotel and made her first American film appearance in *Down Argentine Way* in 1940. Although identified as a Brazilian, Miranda was actually born near Lisbon, Portugal. Her parents moved to Rio de Janeiro, Brazil, when she was a baby. The singer, actress, and dancer died of a heart attack after taping a mambo dance number for U.S. television's "The Jimmy Durante Show" in 1955. Her film credits include *That Night in Rio* (1941), *Weekend in Havana* (1941), *Springtime in the Rockies* (1942), *The Gang's All Here* (1943), *Doll Face* (1945), *If I'm Lucky* (1946), *Copacabana* (1947), *A Date with Judy* (1948), *Nancy Goes to Rio* (1950), and *Scared Stiff* (1953).

Robert Miranda

A former University of South Carolina student, Miranda began acting in college when a teacher prescribed it as a way of compensating for previously undiagnosed dyslexia. He then decided to move to New York to pursue an acting career.

Miranda's feature film credits include *The Untouchables* (1987), *Midnight Run* (1988), *My Blue Heaven* (1990), *The Rocketeer* (1991), *Stop! Or My Mom Will Shoot* (1991), *Sister Act* (1992), and *Lost in Yonkers* (1993). He has garnered a sizable list of television credits, including a recurring role on the series "Roseanne."

Susan Miranda

B: 1949

Born in East Los Angeles, Miranda made her film debut at age 21 in *Flap* (1970), co-starring opposite Anthony Quinn. Miranda danced with the Jose Greco company and on the TV series "Rowan and Martin's Laugh-In."

Miroslava [born: Miroslava Stern]

B: 1928
D: 3/10/1955

Born in Prague, Czechoslovakia, Miroslava and her family immigrated to Mexico after escaping the Nazi occupation at the beginning of World War II. She learned to speak Spanish fluently, and after a beauty pageant victory she entered the Mexican film industry as an actress in 1946. She quickly ranked with Dolores Del Rio as one of the leading ladies of Mexican cinema. Miroslava co-starred in two Hollywood films, *The Brave Bulls* (1951), starring Mel Ferrer and Anthony Quinn and directed by Robert Rossen, and the western/adventure *Stranger on Horseback* (1955) opposite Joel McCrea. Miroslava committed suicide by taking poison after a disastrous affair with famed Spanish bullfighter Luis Miguel Dominguin.

Jose Mojica

B: 1896
D: 9/20/1974

An Argentine-born, internationally renowned opera singer, Mojica starred in Spanish-language film musicals in the 1930s produced in Hollywood, including *One Mad Kiss* (1930).

Victor Mojica

B: 7/15/1940

A New York–born Puerto Rican actor, Mojica was featured in the films *The Final Countdown* (1980), *Ghost Dance* (1983), and *Bound by Honor* (1993). His television credits include guest starring roles on "Murder, She Wrote," "Hill Street Blues," "The Streets of San Francisco," and "The Six Million Dollar Man."

Carlos Montalban

B: 3/28/1904
D: 4/4/1991

The older brother of actor Ricardo Montalban, Carlos worked as an actor in the early 1930s in such films as *Flying Down to Rio* (1933). He later had a role in *The Harder They Fall* (1956), with Humphrey Bogart, and is perhaps best known as the general in Woody Allen's *Bananas* (1971). He did Spanish-language commercials and voice-overs for many years.

Ricardo Montalban
B: 11/25/1920

Actor, caballero, and star: these words aptly describe Ricardo Montalban, who has become a living symbol of the endurance and longevity of the Hispanic American artist in Hollywood. Few actors today can look back at a successful career during the heyday of MGM Studios as a contract player, through the exciting infancy of television, and on into the present.

Besides the success of his seven-year run as the mysterious Mr. Roarke on the television series "Fantasy Island," and his Emmy Award–winning portrayal of Chief Satangkai in the miniseries *How the West Was Won* (1977), Montalban enjoyed tremendous public and critical acclaim for his role as Khan in *Star Trek II: The Wrath of Khan* (1982), a role he re-created from a previous appearance on the "Star Trek" series, and as the villain in *Naked Gun* (1988). Both films were box-office smashes.

When asked to describe his most positive attribute, Montalban replied, "Tenacity." This, along with a devotion to his craft, his family, and his Catholic faith, has been his touchstone. His steadfastness has allowed him to survive during the lean years when roles were scarce, which fostered his growth as a person and an actor.

Ricardo Montalban.
Portrait by Clarence Bull.

If film roles were not available, Montalban went to the stage, following the axiom: An actor is not an actor when he is not acting.

On stage, Montalban starred as Don Juan in George Bernard Shaw's *Don Juan in Hell,* a role he still considers the most challenging of his career. Top critics called him "superb," "awesome," "compelling," and "dashing." He went on the road with the production on three separate occasions from 1972 to 1976, on tours that lasted several months and visited over 150 cities, in collaboration with such talents as Agnes Moorehead and director John Houseman. He also won critical acclaim for his performance in the L.A. Music Center production of *The King and I* (1967) and the Broadway musical *Jamaica* (1957), which he starred in for two years with Lena Horne.

Born in Mexico City, the son of Jenaro and Ricarda Montalban, he is the youngest of four children. The family moved to Torreon in northern Mexico and away from the teeming city that had been Ricardo's early home. The young Ricardo learned to ride and swim, with the great outdoors as his playground.

After receiving his basic education in Mexico City, he was brought to the United States by his older brother Carlos. Ricardo finished his schooling at Fairfax High School in Hollywood, where he also made his theatrical debut in a number of school productions. It was there that he attracted the attention of studio talent scouts and was offered an MGM screen test after graduation. However, his brother convinced him to join him in New York to continue his studies. In New York, Ricardo was dazzled by the legitimate stage and talked his brother into letting him take a year's absence from college so that he might attempt to seek out acting opportunities.

He found himself among hundreds of aspiring young actors, making the rounds of talent agents, auditioning with dozens of others for the same role. But his break finally came when he was cast in a small part opposite Tallulah Bankhead in the stage play *Her Cardboard Lover.* From that point on, he became a much employed stage actor.

In 1941, he returned to his native Mexico and made 13 Spanish-language films in four years. Montalban was nominated for the Ariel, the Mexican equivalent of the Academy Award, for the film *Santa* (1943), in which he played a bullfighter. He was the most important leading man in Mexico at the time, and Louella Parsons, a noted columnist of the time, called him the "Tyrone Power of Mexico."

Montalban was then rediscovered by MGM through producer Jack Cummings, who went to Mexico looking for a young Mexican actor for a leading role opposite Esther Williams in *Fiesta* (1947). After the picture was released, Montalban was immediately put under contract for a 10-year period. He made three pictures with Esther Williams and danced with Cyd Charisse in several musicals.

In *Neptune's Daughter* (1949), he and Esther Williams introduced the hit song "Baby, It's Cold Outside." Several major dance numbers with Cyd Charisse in *On an Island with You* (1948) and *The Kissing Bandit* (1948) convinced audiences that Montalban was a dancer, when in actuality he had never before danced professionally.

Soon after, Montalban starred in another film, *Two Weeks with Love* (1950), with Jane Powell, and the cover of *Life* magazine proclaimed him the "New Romantic Star!"

Montalban co-starred in three William Wellman films, *Battleground* (1949), *Across the Wide Missouri* (1951) with Clark Gable, and *My Man and I* (1952) with Shelley Winters. While filming *Across the Wide Missouri,* he suffered a serious injury on location in the Colorado Rockies. A horse he was riding was spooked by the noise of a cannon firing and took off down a mountain trail. Montalban fell on some rocks, seriously injuring part of his spine. The injury left him in constant pain, with one leg partially paralyzed for many years, but through exercise, therapy, and sheer will power, he recovered the full use of his leg.

In his early MGM films, Montalban often portrayed the archetypal Latin lover; he even starred in a film called *Latin Lovers* (1953) with Lana Turner. The actor also turned in some solid dramatic work in such films as *Border Incident* (1949), *Right Cross* (1950) with June Allyson and Dick Powell, and *Mystery Street* (1950). He was released from his MGM contract (along with other big MGM stars) in 1953.

As a freelance star, Montalban appeared in *A Life in the Balance* (1955) with Anne Bancroft and Lee Marvin; as a Japanese Kabuki dancer in *Sayonara* (1957) with Marlon Brando; *Adventures of a Young Man* (1962) for director Martin Ritt; *The Money Trap* (1966) with Glenn Ford and Rita Hayworth; *The Singing Nun* (1966) with Debbie Reynolds; and *Sol Madrid* (1968).

His co-starring role with Shirley MacLaine as a Latin movie idol in *Sweet Charity* (1969), directed by Bob Fosse for Universal, was a great success. "It was really a satire on the Latin Lover," recalled Montalban during an interview with Luis Reyes. "The role was basically comedic and the circumstances that developed were quite hilarious."

Montalban had a co-starring role as Little Wolf in John Ford's western epic *Cheyenne Autumn* (1964), in which he also worked for the first and only time with both Dolores Del Rio and Gilbert Roland.

His other films (English-language) include *Mark of the Renegade* (1951), *Sombrero* (1953), *The Saracen Blade* (1954), *The Queen of Babylon* (1956), *Let No Man Write My Epitaph* (1960), *The Reluctant Saint* (1962), *Love Is a Ball* (1963), *The Longest Hundred Miles* (1967), *Blue* (1968), *The Deserter* (1971), and *The Train Robbers* (1973).

His TV credits start with varied roles in such vintage series as "Playhouse 90," "Climax," "Wagon Train," "Ben Casey," "Riverboat," "Combat," "The Name of the Game," and over 300 more, including made-for-television films. Prior to the "Fantasy Island" series, Montalban attained new success after several years of film and television inactivity as a spokesperson for the Chrysler Cordova automobile in a series of national television commercials and print ads, making the car a top-seller. After "Fantasy Island," he co-starred as a Greek tycoon on "The Colbys" series, a spin-off from the successful "Dynasty."

Conchita Montenegro

B: 9/11/1912

An actress, Montenegro appeared in silent and sound films and in Spanish-language films produced in Hollywood in the 1930s. Her credits include *Caravan* (1934), *Grenadiers of Love* (1934), *Handy Andy* (1934), *Hell in the Heavens* (1934) with Warner Baxter, and *Insure Your Wife* (1935) with Raul Roulien.

Maria Montez [born: Maria Garcia Van Dahl de Santa Silas]

B: 6/6/1919
D: 9/7/1951

One of Universal's most beautiful and top money-making stars during the 1940s, Maria Montez is renowned for reducing the dance of the seven veils to one veil in *Arabian Nights* (1942), and she amused her public in *Ali Baba and the Forty Thieves* (1944) by her sinuous actions in a harem bubble bath. Montez made 18 films for Universal, 14 of them in color. Her name became synonymous with exotic adventures as Universal's "Queen of Technicolor Epics."

She was born in Ciudad Trujillo, Barahona, in the Dominican Republic. Her father was a Spanish consul, and she was educated in the Canary Islands, where she attended the Sacred Heart Convent. In her teens, Maria traveled in Europe. Her father held consular posts in South America, France, England, and Ireland. After some minor stage experience in Ireland and a short-lived marriage, Montez came to New York. She was discovered in Manhattan in 1940 by a talent scout who had seen her picture in a magazine. Her progress in films was gradual. Universal offered her a movie contract at $150 a week, and the young actress began her Hollywood career with small roles in *The Invisible Woman* (1941) and in a Johnny Mack Brown western, *Boss of Bullion City* (1941).

Her Spanish accent caused casting problems, and Universal loaned her to Fox for a small role as a Latin-spitfire type in *That Night in Rio* (1941), which was in color and featured Alice Faye, Don Ameche, and Carmen Miranda.

The beautiful starlet captured public attention in *South of Tahiti* (1941), in which she played a jungle beauty, and *White Savage* (1943). Universal soon discovered that, in a sarong, Montez could be serious competition for Paramount's Dorothy Lamour. Montez knew the value of publicity, and she was soon acting like a genuine movie star, receiving more publicity than better-established stars. She became a favorite pinup girl of servicemen during World War II. She was given an important role in *Arabian Nights* (1942), an escapist exotic entertainment, and she looked stunning as Scheherazade. One critic's description of her role in the film applies to almost her entire career: "Maria Montez comes through ably in a role that consists chiefly of looking ravishing in scanty oriental costumes."

In *Cobra Woman* (1944), Montez had two roles as twin sisters, one good and one bad, involved in a snake cult. She followed with *Ali Baba and the Forty Thieves* and *Gypsy Wildcat* (1944). Her limitations as an actress became apparent when Universal cast her in *Bowery to Broadway* (1944) and *Tangier* (1946). Her last Universal film under contract was *Pirates of Monterey* in 1947, in which she was cast as a Spanish lady in an early California western drama.

Her other films include *Moonlight in Hawaii* (1941), *Raiders of the Desert* (1941), *Bombay Clipper* (1942), *The Mystery of Marie Roget* (1942), *Follow the Boys* (1944), *Sudan* (1945), *The Exile* (1947), and *Siren of Atlantis* (1948).

She married French actor Jean-Pierre Aumont, and she lived for several years in Europe, where she made a couple of French-Italian films. Montez died in September 1951 of an apparent heart attack.

Sarita Montiel [born: Antonia Maria Abad]

    B: 3/10/1928

Sarita Montiel was born in a small town near La Mancha, Spain, to a Spanish mother and a Moorish father. Early in her teens she won a beauty contest, which led to Madrid and work in films. Due to her success in Spanish films, she was signed for an American film, *That Man from Tangiers* (1953). In Mexico she made 14 films between 1951 and 1954.

Warner Bros. brought her to Hollywood for a co-starring role with Mario Lanza in *Serenade* in 1956. She was introduced to American film audiences in 1954 in *Vera Cruz,* opposite Gary Cooper and Burt Lancaster. She also starred as an Indian maiden opposite Rod Steiger in Sam Fuller's *Run of the Arrow* (1957).

Alex Montoya

    B: 10/19/1907
    D: 9/25/1970

A character actor, Montoya was featured in scores of films and TV shows, usually as a heavy or bandit. He was born in El Paso, Texas, and among his feature film credits are *Conquest of Cochise* (1953), *Escape from Fort Bravo* (1953), *Apache Ambush* (1955), *Escape to Burma* (1955), *The Magnificent Seven* (1960), and *The Flight of the Phoenix* (1965) as Carlos Reyes, a Mexican oilfield worker.

Danny Mora

A stand-up comedian and comedy writer, Mora began his writing career on the "Laverne and Shirley" television series.

Esai Morales

B: 1963

Esai Morales is best known for his intense performance as Bob Morales, Ritchie Valens's half-brother, in *La Bamba* (1987), and as Sean Penn's Latin nemesis in *Bad Boys* (1983).

Born in Brooklyn, New York, Morales ran away from home at age 15 because his mother would not let him study acting. He attended New York's prestigious High School of the Performing Arts while living in a group home as a voluntary ward of the state. He recalls, "I never graduated from school because I stopped going to any classes except my acting classes."

He appeared as a misfit in the stage production *Short Eyes* and in Paul Morrissey's *Forty Deuce* (1982), his first film. He was also seen on screen in *Rainy Day Friends* (1985) and *Bloodhounds of Broadway* (1989).

Among his proudest accomplishments is his role opposite Burt Lancaster in the television miniseries *On Wings of Eagles* (1986), in which he played an Iranian. Additional television appearances include a role in the Emmy Award–winning After School Special "The Great Love Experiment" and guest appearances on "The Equalizer," "Fame," and "Miami Vice."

Jacobo Morales

A Puerto Rican–born actor, writer, and director, Morales appeared in brief acting assignments in *Up the Sandbox* (1972) with Barbra Streisand and Woody Allen's *Bananas* (1971).

Morales starred in many television soap operas and theater productions in Puerto Rico. He directed his first film, *Dios los Cria,* a critical and satirical look at the new modern Puerto Rico, in 1980, and his second, *Nicolas y los Demas,* a romantic triangle involving two old friends, in 1985. *Whatever Happened to Santiago* (1989), the story of a widowed accountant whose life begins anew upon his retirement, was Morales's first feature in 35mm; it was nominated for the Best Foreign Language Film Oscar in 1990.

Santos Morales

B: 6/1/1935

A Puerto Rican–born character actor, Morales is noted for his roles as the Marine drill instructor in the Vietnam War drama *The Boys in Company C* (1978) and as Joseph and Mary Rivas in *Cannery Row* (1982). He also has appeared in numerous television productions.

Antonio Moreno [born: Antonio Garcia Moreno Mantaugudo]

B: 9/27/1887

D: 2/15/1967

The first of Hollywood's suave Latin leading men of the silent movie era, Moreno had his greatest success in the 1920s, when he was ranked second only to Rudolph Valentino as the great lover of the screen.

Born in Madrid, Spain, he was destined to be a baker in the family business and began apprenticing at age nine. One day, two American tourists entered the baker's shop and were impressed with the boy. When they asked him his name, he replied, "Antonio Garcia Moreno Mantaugudo at the service of you and god."

His mother permitted the two men to take the young Moreno to New York and place him in a school. Moreno began his acting career on the New York stage several years later but eventually gave up the New York stage for Hollywood. While playing bit parts on stage in Hollywood he was seen by D.W. Griffith, who launched him on his screen career.

Making his first screen appearance in 1914 in the two-reeler *The Voice of Millions,* the actor went on to star with Gloria Swanson in *My American Wife* (1923, silent), with Mary Miles Minter in *The Trail of the Lonesome Pine* (1923, silent), with Pauline Starke in *Love's Blindness* (1926, silent), and with Dorothy Gish in *Madame Pompadour* (1927, silent). Other movies included *Mare Nostrum* (1926, silent) with Alice Terry and directed by Rex Ingram, and *Romance of the Rio Grande* (1929). He starred with Greta Garbo in her second film, *The Temptress* (1926, silent).

Though Moreno made the transition to sound movies, he could not do it as a leading man and became a character actor in films such as *Rose of the Rio Grande* (1938), *Captain from Castile* (1947), *Thunder Bay* (1953), *Creature from the Black Lagoon* (1954), and *The Searchers* (1956). He directed some films in Mexico during the early 1930s and starred in that country's first sound film, *Santa* (1932). He died in 1967 at the age of 79.

Rita Moreno [born: Rosa Dolores Alverio; aka: Rosita Moreno]
B: 12/11/1931

Her career as an actress, singer, dancer, and comedienne has brought Rita Moreno the distinction of being one of only a few women to win an Oscar, an Emmy, a Grammy, and a Tony, the four most prestigious awards a performer can receive.

She was born in Humacao, Puerto Rico; after her parents divorced, she came to New York City with her mother at age five. Recognizing her daughter's talent, her mother held down two jobs in New York so that Rita could start dancing lessons. "Whenever I heard music," she recalls, "I used to dance around the room and show off for my grandmother." By age seven, she was performing professionally in local clubs. At age 13, she made her Broadway debut in *Skydrift* (1945) with Eli Wallach, and by age 15 she had abandoned her formal education to work as a singer and dancer in Spanish Harlem and anywhere else that offered a booking.

It's a period of her life on which she still looks back with a shudder. "Often the only audience we had were the waiters. Even if there were no customers the management paid us and we had to give value for money," she recalled in a 1993 interview with Luis Reyes. Two days in a Broadway play and a handful of radio shows later, she was given the cinema seal of approval in the form of a contract with MGM from Louis B. Mayer, who saw her upon the insistence of an MGM talent scout who had discovered Moreno a few years earlier but felt her too young for movies at the time.

She made her film debut in an independent film called *So Young, So Bad* (1950), in which she was billed as Rosita Moreno. MGM changed her name, and her first film there was *The Toast of New Orleans* (1950), followed by *Pagan Love Song* (1950), and a bit part in the classic musical *Singin' in the Rain* (1952). After two years her contract was dropped. "I was shattered. I had visions of being the next Lana Turner. And then at 19, I was through. I couldn't go back to New York, I was ashamed," she said in an interview with Reyes. "So I stayed on in Hollywood and did what every other actor did to survive. I worked in B movies and did TV shows. I played all those roles the same way. Barefoot with my nostrils flaring."

She went to Twentieth Century–Fox where she became the resident "Latin Inferno." In 11 years she made 14 films, among them, *Garden of Evil* (1954), *The Yellow Tomahawk* (1954), *Seven Cities of Gold* (1955), and *Untamed* (1955), in which

Rita Moreno co-stars with Dennis Morgan in *Cattle Town* (1952).

she played mainly Indian squaws, Mexican dancers, and handmaidens. "I did it because I needed the money for basics, like rent, food, and analysis."

Rita began to be referred to in the press as "Rita the Cheetah." "One reporter claimed I had a necklace made from the teeth of my boyfriends. So with an image like that I wasn't offered many passive or interesting parts."

She won excellent notices for her performance as Tuptim in the film adaptation of *The King and I* (1956), and in 1960 Jerome Robbins cast her as Anita, the fiery Puerto Rican in *West Side Story* (1961). She auditioned for co-director/producer Robert Wise and screen tested and won approval from the Mirisch brothers, who were the producers. She gave a memorable performance that won her an Academy Award in 1961 for Best Supporting Actress. "I couldn't believe it. I had just turned 30 and thought I had finally broken through as an actress. I was sure the Oscar would change everything, but I soon found out that it made no difference." She did not work for seven years in films because all the roles offered her were the conventional Rosita and Pepita type roles and she refused to demean her talent any longer.

The following year she went to London. There she starred in *She Loves Me,* which led to her return to Broadway as the star of Lorraine Hansberry's last play, *The Sign in Sidney Brustein's Window* (1964).

In the 1960s and 1970s she was seen on Broadway as the female lead in the musical *Gantry* starring Robert Shaw, in Neil Simon's *The Last of the Red Hot Lovers* with James Coco, in *The National Health,* and in *The Ritz* as Googie Gomez, a role written especially for her by Terrence McNally. She won a Tony Award on Broadway for her Googie portrayal and re-created the role in Richard Lester's film version. "By playing Googie Gomez, I was thumbing my nose at all those Hollywood writers responsible for lines like, 'Ju Yankee Peeg, ju rape my seester. I keel ju!'" said Moreno in a 1993 interview with Luis Reyes.

Among her other films are *The Ring* (1952), *Latin Lovers* (1953), *Jivaro* (1954), *The Lieutenant Wore Skirts* (1956), *The Vagabond King* (1956), *The Deerslayer* (1957), *This Rebel Breed* (1960), *Summer and Smoke* (1961), *Marlowe* (1969), *The Night of the Following Day* (1969) with Marlon Brando, *Popi* (1969), *Carnal Knowledge* (1971) with Jack Nicholson, *The Boss's Son* (1978), and *The Four Seasons* (1981).

On television, Moreno won her Emmy for a performance in an episode of the series "The Rockford Files" starring James Garner, in which she played a free-spirited Polish hooker. Moreno starred for two seasons on "9 to 5" as Violet and had a recurring role as Burt Reynolds's estranged wife on the "B.L. Stryker" series for two seasons. She won a Grammy Award for her contributions on the album recording of "The Electric Company," a popular children's educational TV series in which she appeared regularly.

Rosita Moreno

> B: 1904
> D: 4/25/1993

A dancer from Buenos Aires, Moreno starred in many films during the late 1920s and 1930s, including *Her Wedding Night* (1930) with Richard Arlen, and *Walls of Gold* (1933) with Norman Foster. In 1945, she returned to Paramount for a small part in *A Medal for Benny*. She married a theatrical agent and remained in the States.

Ruben Moreno

A veteran character player, Moreno was usually cast as an Indian or a Mexican bandit in westerns such as *El Dorado* (1967) and television shows including "Bonanza" and "The Big Valley."

Alberto Morin

> B: 1903
> D: 5/5/1989

A character actor, Morin portrayed many different nationalities during his 55-year career. Among his credits were *Gone with the Wind* (1939), *Casablanca* (1942), several John Ford films, *Two Mules for Sister Sara* (1970), and Robert Redford's *The Milagro Beanfield War* (1988).

A native of Puerto Rico, Morin moved to Europe at an early age and in the 1920s went to Mexico, where he studied acting. He moved to Hollywood in the 1930s to work in Spanish-language versions of films. Aside from acting, he was Errol Flynn's riding double in several films.

Morin appeared frequently in the theater and acted in many TV shows, including "I Love Lucy," "Hopalong Cassidy," and "The Jack Benny Show." He also worked as a technical director and dialogue coach.

Michael Moroff

A towering Mexican American character actor, Moroff was featured in the film *La Bamba* (1987) and played Pancho Villa in an episode of TV's "The Young Indiana Jones Chronicles."

Bob Morones

> B: 1/6/1943

Morones was casting director and associate producer on Oliver Stone's *Salvador* (1986) and casting director on Stone's Academy Award–winning *Platoon* (1986). He was also casting director on Edward James Olmos's *American Me* (1992).

Movita [born: Maria Luisa Castenada]
B: 4/12/1917

A Mexican actress, born in Nogales, Arizona, known simply as Movita. She co-starred in MGM's classic 1935 production of *Mutiny on the Bounty* as the native girl who falls for Byam (Franchot Tone); the film also starred Clark Gable and Charles Laughton. She was also seen to good effect in John Ford's *The Hurricane* (1937), again as a native island girl.

While visiting friends in San Francisco, Movita attended a party where she was seen by Pandro S. Berman, who was then in charge of production at RKO Studios. He signed her to a contract, and she made her film debut in *Flying Down to Rio* (1933). Later, she made a film in Mexico and then appeared in *Mutiny on the Bounty*. In an interview with Luis Reyes, she reflected that, despite the attention she received for the film, MGM lost interest in promoting her after boy genius producer Irving Thalberg, who had been a supporter, died.

She went to Monogram Studios for a series of four westerns in which she played the female lead. Movita later toured Europe in a musical/comedy review and made one film in England, *The Tower of Terror* (1942). Upon her return to the States in

Movita in *Mutiny on the Bounty*.

1948, she appeared in minor roles in such films as *Fort Apache* (1948), *Red Light* (1949), *Kim* (1950), *Wagon Master* (1950), *Saddle Legion* (1951), and *Last of the Comanches* (1952). She has remained active in the film industry, doing both extra and featured work in recent years.

Corrina Mura [born: Corinna Wall]

Born in San Antonio, Texas, where she worked as a singer and an entertainer, Mura played Andrea, the French singer, at Rick's Cafe in the classic 1942 film *Casablanca*, starring Humphrey Bogart and Ingrid Bergman. She also appeared in *Call Out the Marines* (1942).

Karmin Murcelo

A Cuban-born actress, Murcelo co-starred with Charles Bronson in *Borderline* (1980). Her film credits include *Walk Proud* (1979), *Stir Crazy* (1980), *The Big Score* (1983), *Revenge* (1990), and *Bound by Honor* (1993). She has appeared in hundreds of television series episodes as well as the miniseries *Centennial (1978)* and *The Blue Knight* (1973).

Daniel Nagrin
B: 1922

A Bronx-born Broadway dancer-choreographer, Nagrin was featured in a Mexican ballet sequence in *Just for You* (1952), starring Bing Crosby and Jane Wyman. He also choreographed the native Fijian dance sequences for *His Majesty O'Keefe* (1953), starring Burt Lancaster.

J. Carroll Naish
B: 1/21/1897
D: 1/31/1973

A consummate character actor, Naish portrayed every nationality and ethnic type over his long Hollywood career. With his dark complexion, black hair, and mustache, he was closely identified with the many Latin roles he portrayed in films. He was nominated for an Academy Award as Best Supporting Actor for his role as a Mexican American father in *A Medal for Benny* (1945).

Some of the other films in which he portrayed a Latin include *The Kid from Spain* (1932), *The Robin Hood of El Dorado* (1936), *Down Argentine Way* (1940), *Blood and Sand* (1941), *That Night in Rio* (1941), *The Fugitive* (1947), and *The Last Command* (1955).

In actuality Naish was an Irish American born in New York City, but he explained in an *L.A. Herald Examiner* interview (1/27/73): "When the part of an Irishman comes along, nobody thinks of me, they call Barry Fitzgerald." Naish received two Oscar nominations and amassed over 200 film credits.

Gregory Nava
B: 4/10/1949

A director and writer, Nava was nominated for an Academy Award along with Anna Thomas for their original screenplay for the film *El Norte* (1984), which Nava also directed. Shot on a limited budget, this moving and often harrowing film about two young Guatemalan refugees who endure numerous hardships in order to reach the American border was one of the first contemporary films to address honestly and compassionately the state of the immigrant experience in America today. Nava also directed the film *A Time of Destiny* (1988), starring William Hurt. Born in San Diego of Mexican-Basque heritage, Nava is a graduate of UCLA Film School and was interested in filmmaking from an early age.

Taylor Negron
B: 1958

An actor/comedian of Puerto Rican–Italian heritage, born in Glendale, California, Negron was notable in several roles as an oversexed Latin party boy. He made his motion picture debut in 1982 as a love-struck, eye-popping intern in director Garry Marshall's *Young Doctors in Love*. He has since appeared as Rodney Dangerfield's Puerto Rican son-in-law, Julio, in *Easy Money* (1983), and in *Fast Times at Ridgemont High* (1982), *Bad Medicine* (1985), *Punchline* (1988), *Nothing But Trouble* (1991), and as a psychotic hitman in *The Last Boy Scout* (1992).

Barry Norton [born: Alfredo Biraben]
B: 6/16/1905
D: 8/24/1956

A supporting actor, Norton worked in films from the 1920s until the mid-1950s. He was born in Buenos Aires, Argentina, and began his career in silent film productions like *The Lily* (1926) and *What Price Glory?* (1926). His Spanish-speaking ability came in handy when sound films arrived, and he appeared alternately in many Hollywood-produced English- and Spanish-language productions.

Ramon Novarro [born: Jose Ramon Gil Samaniegos]
B: 2/6/1899
D: 10/31/1968

A leading man of silent films and early talkies, Mexican-born Novarro was one of Hollywood's first great Latin lovers, a forerunner of a generation of darkly handsome young men with flashing eyes who were considered surefire box-office successes for a time during and after Valentino.

His fame crested in silent films, and he never achieved the same heights of popularity in talking pictures; however, he did co-star with Greta Garbo in *Mata Hari* in 1931. In later years he continued his career as a character actor in films and television.

Novarro was born in Durango, Mexico, in 1899 into a well-to-do family. In 1913, his dentist father brought his wife, five sons, and four daughters to California to escape from Pancho Villa and the Mexican Revolution.

When Ramon and his brother Mariano arrived in Los Angeles looking for work, they had just $100 between them. Young Ramon worked as a grocery clerk, theater usher, piano teacher, cafe singer, and bit player until he was finally spotted by Marion Morgan, a dance instructor, who gave him a place in her vaudeville act. She sent him to New York, and Novarro's job for Miss Morgan led to a real break when Ferdinand Pinney Earle signed him to play the lead in *Omar Khayyam* on the West Coast. Rex Ingram, the famous silent screen director, heard about Novarro, saw him dance in a pantomime called *The Royal Fandango* at the Hollywood Community Theater, and engaged him to play Rupert of Hentzau in the 1922 version of *The Prisoner of Zenda*.

Novarro was an immediate hit. He followed this success with roles in *Trifling Women* (1922, silent), *Scaramouche* (1923, silent), *Where the Pavement Ends* (1923, silent), and *The Arab* (1924, silent), which ultimately rocketed him to stardom and international fame. However, it was as Ben-Hur in the classic 1926 epic of the same name that the actor's popularity crested.

Ramon Novarro, John Gilbert, and Roy D'Arcy, on the set of *A Certain Young Man* (1928), pose for a publicity shot.

By 1934 Novarro had given up on Hollywood but kept busy with concert and theater performances. He made one film in Italy and another in his native Mexico. In 1948, he accepted a role in John Huston's *We Were Strangers* (1949) and followed this with an important part in *The Big Steal* (1949) at RKO. Next came *The Outriders* (1950) and *Crisis* (1950), both at MGM, the studio at which he gained his greatest fame. He received good reviews for his work in a small role in *Heller in Pink Tights* (1960) with Sophia Loren and Anthony Quinn, directed by George Cukor. His other films include *The Red Lily* (1924, silent), *Thy Name Is Woman* (1924, silent), *The Midshipman* (1925, silent), *Ben-Hur* (1926, silent), *Lovers?* (1927, silent), *The Road to Romance* (1927, silent), *The Student Prince in Old Heidelberg* (1927, silent), *A Certain Young Man* (1928, silent), *Devil May Care* (1929), *The Flying Fleet* (1929, silent), *The Pagan* (1929, silent), *Call of the Flesh* (1930), *In Gay Madrid* (1930), *Daybreak* (1931), *Son of India* (1931), *Huddle* (1932), *The Son-Daughter* (1932), *The Barbarian* (1933), *The Cat and the Fiddle* (1934), *Laughing Boy* (1934), and *The Night Is Young* (1935).

Novarro made occasional guest appearances on such television shows as "Bonanza." He was beaten to death during an apparent robbery at his Hollywood Hills home on October 31, 1968.

Danny Nunez

A veteran character actor and bit player, Nunez appeared in such films as *Viva Zapata!* (1952), *The Professionals* (1966), *Close Encounters of the Third Kind* (1977), and *The Legend of the Lone Ranger* (1981). His numerous television credits date back to the mid-1950s.

Maria O'Brien

The daughter of actor Edmond O'Brien and actress Olga San Juan, Maria appeared in the 1975 film *Smile* as a pushy beauty pageant contestant who sells her Mexican American heritage for all it's worth.

Edward James Olmos
B: 2/21/1946

Edward James Olmos has become one of the most important Hispanic American actors of his generation with work in such films as *Zoot Suit* (1981), *The Ballad of Gregorio Cortez* (1983), and his Academy Award–nominated role as the teacher Jaime Escalante in *Stand and Deliver* (1988). Olmos seeks out roles that both satisfy a performer's natural artistic desires and realistically dramatize socially relevant themes or incidents.

Olmos became a household name through his sullen, no-nonsense role as Lt. Martin Castillo on the innovative police TV series "Miami Vice," which ran for five years and won Olmos an Emmy Award and the Hollywood Foreign Press Association's Golden Globe Award for Best Supporting Actor in a Continuing Drama Series. Olmos made his directorial debut with a "Miami Vice" episode entitled "Bushido," which was the highest-rated show of the entire series according to the A.C. Nielsen ratings.

Olmos spent most of his youth in the Boyle Heights section of East Los Angeles, the son of a Mexican father and a mother born of three generations of Mexican American heritage.

Music had a profound effect upon him as a youth, and it was his immersion in the worlds of performers like James Brown and Little Richard that led him, at age 13, to announce to his parents that he wanted to pursue a career as a singer and dancer.

Following his graduation from Montebello High School, Olmos formed a band that he named Eddie and the Pacific Ocean. For several years, the group played various Sunset Strip clubs until, in 1968, it became the house band at the private club The Factory.

While music occupied Olmos's evenings, studies at East Los Angeles College and later California State University more than filled his daytime hours. Although he was initially interested in the social sciences of psychology and criminology, his later education leaned more toward dance and the theater.

In the early 1970s, he began acting in various small theater productions around Los Angeles and landed several bit parts in episodic television shows like "Kojak" and "Hawaii Five-O" while continuing to sing (and deliver antique furniture) to support himself and his family. He made his motion picture debut in a bit part in Floyd Mutrux's *aloha, bobby and rose* (1975).

At age 31, Olmos auditioned for and won the role that would alter his life, that of El Pachuco in Luis Valdez's *Zoot Suit*. The street theater musical, described by Olmos as "the first real play about Latinos," opened in 1978 for what was originally scheduled to be a mere 10-day run in Los Angeles. Instead, it ran a year and a half and then enjoyed a short but well-deserved run on Broadway, for which Olmos was nominated for a Tony and for which he won the prestigious Theatre World Award.

As a result of his work in the show, Olmos received accolades as a performer and became recognized as a positive role model for Latinos. He was honored by the American Theatre Wing for creating "one of three definitive performances in the history of the American Stage." He later reprised his stage role in the 1981 screen version of the successful musical for Universal Pictures.

When *Zoot Suit* closed on Broadway, Olmos was offered the role of an American Indian high beam steelworker in *Wolfen* (1981), starring Albert Finney, but he turned the part down, insisting that the producers cast a real Native American. When such efforts proved futile and the filmmaker returned to Olmos, he ultimately accepted the role, but only after securing the full approval and blessing of the American Indian Movement. Several years later, Olmos received a humanitarian award from the group.

Edward James Olmos proudly holds his well-deserved Emmy Award for "Miami Vice."

He went on to play the title role in Robert M. Young's *The Ballad of Gregorio Cortez* (1983), a true turn-of-the-century story about a Mexican American farmhand unjustly accused of murder who became the object of the largest manhunt in Texas history.

The film debuted on the Public Broadcasting Service in the summer of 1982 and was then picked up for theatrical release by Embassy Pictures. For his work as an actor and associate producer on the film, Olmos was honored by the American Historical Association. Olmos and co-star Tom Bower devoted the next two years to promoting the film across the country. During this extensive national tour, Olmos coordinated his work on behalf of the film with personal appearances at public schools and prisons, enhancing Hispanic pride throughout the country.

Olmos appeared as a multiracial police detective in Ridley Scott's *Blade Runner* (1982) opposite Harrison Ford and in *Saving Grace* (1986) opposite Tom Conti.

In 1984, Olmos was invited by series creator Michael Mann to join the regular cast of NBC-TV's "Miami Vice." He declined the offer several times on the basis that he preferred to continue to seek out projects of a more personal nature, but eventually worked out an arrangement with Mann in which the actor would be allowed time off from the series with 90 days' advance notice if a project arose about which he felt strongly. Under those conditions, Olmos accepted the part of the austere, intense Lt. Castillo.

From the moment he first became aware of the project, Olmos's enthusiasm for *Stand and Deliver* extended well beyond playing the lead role; it resulted in his involvement as a member of the production team as well.

For his portrayal of the stout, dynamic Bolivian-born teacher, Olmos was nominated for an Academy Award as Best Actor. During an interview with Luis Reyes, Olmos recalled his feelings when he heard he had been nominated: "It's like getting the best news and getting it thrown at your stomach. It's given to you at such a high dosage that it ends up making you queasy." He was in very good company that year, for his fellow nominees were Gene Hackman, Tom Hanks, Dustin Hoffman, and Max von Sydow.

In 1992 Olmos made his theatrical feature film directorial debut with *American Me,* which he also starred in and produced. His other films include *Alambrista!* (1977), *Virus* (1980), *Triumph of the Spirit* (1989), and *Talent for the Game* (1991).

On television, Olmos has made guest appearances on such shows as "Police Story" and "Hawaii Five-O." He co-starred along with Tony Orlando and Pepe Serna in the made-for-television film *Three Hundred Miles for Stephanie* (1981), and he co-starred in the miniseries *The Fortunate Pilgrim* (1988) opposite Sophia Loren. On PBS, he also made a guest appearance as General Santa Anna in *Seguin* (1982), an "American Playhouse" presentation written and directed by Jesus Trevino.

Lupe Ontiveros

A versatile Mexican American character actress, Ontiveros was featured in such films as *Zoot Suit* (1981), *The Border* (1982), *El Norte* (1982), *The Goonies* (1985), and *Born in East L.A.* (1987). She has numerous television and stage credits.

Tony Orlando
B: 4/12/1944

A Greek–Puerto Rican singer, songwriter, and actor, Orlando hosted his own musical variety television show on CBS, "Tony Orlando and Dawn." He starred in the television film *Three Hundred Miles for Stephanie* (1981) as a Mexican American

Tony Orlando and Freddie Prinze.

police officer and made a guest appearance as a social worker on several episodes of "The Cosby Show."

Kenny Ortega

Considered the foremost choreographer for modern popular music, Ortega is equally accomplished in film, stage, and television work. Ortega pioneered and set the standards of excellence for dance and form in music videos. He has worked with Madonna, Cher, Diana Ross, Billy Joel, Smokey Robinson, the Pointer Sisters, and Miami Sound Machine. Ortega is best known for his choreography for the 1987 smash hit movie *Dirty Dancing*. For the movie *Salsa* (1989), he served as choreographer and as associate producer. Ortega's unique blend of dance and film was developed through his association with the American screen's living dance master, Gene Kelly, an association that began during the making of *Xanadu* (1980), starring Olivia Newton-John, for Universal Pictures.

Kenny Ortega was born in Palo Alto, California, of Spanish parents. He grew up in Redwood City, and at an early age he developed an interest in music and dance, earning scholarships to several dance academies in the San Francisco area.

As a teenager, his interest in the arts expanded beyond dance to legitimate theater.

At age 13, he began working as an actor in local repertory theater, which quickly became his passion. While still in high school, he began associations with the Hyatt Music Theatre in Burlingame, California, and the Circle Star Theatre in San Carlos, where as a company member he appeared in such shows as *Oliver!* with the late Georgia Brown.

In 1968, he enrolled in Canada College, majoring in theater arts and dance. The following year he landed the role of George Berger in the San Francisco company of *Hair.* This was followed by a featured role in *The Last Sweet Days of Isaac* for the American Conservatory Theatre. He then played the role of Berger again in the national touring company of *Hair.* After three years of touring, he returned to the San Francisco area, where he began working with The Tubes, a multimedia recording group. This began a new phase of his career; he staged and performed in five world tours with The Tubes.

At a Tubes performance at the Pantages Theater in Los Angeles, Cher approached Ortega to choreograph a television special. This marked the beginning of his successful choreography career and of a professional relationship with Cher that still continues. This association also led to his assisting Toni Basil on *The Rose* (1979), starring Bette Midler.

Following that film, Ortega served as co-choreographer on *Xanadu* and had the unforgettable experience of working with dancer/director/choreographer/actor Gene Kelly, who co-starred with Olivia Newton-John. Ortega credits Kelly with teaching him the art of choreographing for the camera. In the following years, he choreographed for television, stage shows, films, and music videos.

Ortega's film credits as choreographer include *One from the Heart* (1982), *St. Elmo's Fire* (1985), *Ferris Bueller's Day Off* (1986), and *Pretty in Pink* (1986).

The choreographer's television directing debut came in 1988 with the short-lived series "Dirty Dancing." In 1990 he directed the pilot and several episodes of the series "Hull High," a program he also co-executive produced and choreographed. *Newsies,* a Walt Disney Pictures presentation released in 1992, a musical about turn-of-the-century newsboys in New York, marked Ortega's feature film directorial debut, which he followed with *Hocus Pocus* (1993), starring Bette Midler.

Dyana Ortelli

B: 5/1/1961

Born in Nuevo Laredo, Mexico, and raised in California, Ortelli played a tough-talking Zoot Suiter in *American Me* (1992), a Tijuana beggar girl in *Born in East L.A.* (1987), a hooker in *La Bamba* (1987), and a Mexican village girl in *¡Three Amigos!* (1986). She co-starred as the wacky maid, Lupe Lopez, in the short-lived syndicated television series "Marblehead Manor."

Humberto Ortiz

B: 10/12/1979

Born in Laredo, Texas, and raised in California, this child actor has been featured in such films as *¡Three Amigos!* (1986), *Salsa* (1989), and *Kickboxer II* (1991). Ortiz co-starred with his mother, Dyana Ortelli, on the "Marblehead Manor" TV series.

Manuel Padilla, Jr.

B: 1956

A juvenile actor of the 1960s and 1970s, Padilla had important roles in *Dime with a Halo* (1963), *The Young and the Brave* (1963), *Robin and the Seven Hoods* (1964), *Tarzan and the Great River* (1967), and as a low-riding Mexican American teenager in *American Grafitti* (1973). He co-starred in the NBC-TV series "Tarzan," starring Ron Ely, which was produced in Mexico. Padilla has been inactive in recent years, except for a small role in *Scarface* (1983).

Anita Page [born: Anita Pomares]
B: 8/4/1910

An actress born of Spanish descent in Flushing, New York, the blonde, sexy Page was a leading lady of Hollywood silent films in the transition period from silent to sound. She began as an extra in 1924 and reached her peak in *The Broadway Melody* in 1929.

Joy Page [born: Joanne Page]
B: 1921

The daughter of actor Don Alvarado and Ann Boyer (who later married Jack Warner), Page's best-known role is as the young Hungarian girl who offers herself to Colonel Renault in the 1942 Warner Bros. classic *Casablanca*. Her other film credits include *Kismet* (1944), *The Shrike* (1955), and *The Bullfighter and the Lady* (1951).

Nestor Paiva
B: 6/30/1905
D: 9/9/1966

A character actor born in Fresno, California, of Portuguese descent, Paiva appeared in 117 motion pictures, playing every type of role from comics to heavies. A flair for dialects and mimicry made him sought after to play characters of different nationalities. He became so skillful at these kinds of roles that he was often referred to as "that foreign actor."

Paiva decided from early boyhood that he wanted to become an actor. He attended St. John's School in Fresno, the University of San Francisco, and later the University of California at Berkeley, where he received his degree.

He made his stage debut at the Greek Theatre in Berkeley in *Antigone.* Following graduation, he did a series of plays in Oakland and San Francisco.

In 1934, he appeared in the L.A. Staging Company's production of *The Drunkard,* playing the role of Squire Cribbs, the villain. He continued in the role for 11 years and combined the work with film roles. Finally, Paiva's work load became so heavy that he was forced to resign from the production. Paiva made his film debut at Paramount in 1936. Among his many films are *Hold Back the Dawn* (1941), in which he played a hotel manager, *The Song of Bernadette* (1943), *Road to Utopia* (1945), *A Thousand and One Nights* (1945), *Badman's Territory* (1946), *Humoresque* (1946), *Carnival in Costa Rica* (1947), *Mighty Joe Young* (1949), *The Great Caruso* (1951), *Jim Thorpe—All American* (1951), *Comanche* (1956), and *Girls, Girls, Girls* (1962). His last film was *Caper of the Golden Bulls* in 1965.

His television credits include appearances on "I Love Lucy," "The Red Skelton Show," "The Loretta Young Show," and "Perry Mason."

Virginia Paris

Although best known for her role as Chairwoman Ortega, who opposes teacher Jaime Escalante in *Stand and Deliver* (1988), Paris has made over 100 appearances on such television shows as "Have Gun Will Travel," "Ironside," "Medical Center," "Police Story," and "Quincy, M.E."

Gil Parrondo

B: 1921

A two-time Academy Award–winning Spanish production designer and art director, for his work on *Patton* (1970) and *Nicholas and Alexandra* (1971), Parrondo also received an Oscar nomination for *Travels with My Aunt* (1972). His film credits as production designer include *The Wind and the Lion* (1975), *The Boys from Brazil* (1978), *Cuba* (1979), *Lionheart* (1987), and *Farewell to the King* (1989).

Born in Luarca, Spain, he began as an assistant director in 1945 in the Spanish film industry but quickly became more interested in using his architectural skills. He worked on many Spanish films, but his international film career as an art director began with *Mr. Arkadin* (1962) and such epic classics as *El Cid* (1961) and *Doctor Zhivago* (1965).

Pele [born: Edison Arantes de Nascimento]

B: 1940

A popular, charismatic, internationally renowned Brazilian soccer star, Pele played Luis Hernandez, a British soldier from Trinidad who joins the Allied POW soccer team, in John Huston's 1981 World War II drama *Victory* opposite Sylvester Stallone and Michael Caine. He has made other film appearances in European and Brazilian productions. Pele was born in an impoverished village in Brazil.

Pina Pellicer

B: 1940

D: 12/10/1964

A Mexican stage and screen actress, Pellicer starred as Luisa, opposite Marlon Brando, in the only film he directed as well as starred in, *One-Eyed Jacks* (1961). She won the Best Actress award at the San Sebastian Film Festival for her work in the film.

She was discovered for the role while she was performing the lead in a Mexican stage production of *The Diary of Anne Frank,* which was later televised throughout Mexico. In 1963, she returned to the States, where she starred in "The Life Work of Juan Diaz" episode of Universal TV's "The Alfred Hitchcock Hour." Suffering from depression, she committed suicide in her home in Mexico City in 1964.

Elizabeth Pena

B: 9/23/1959

A Cuban-born actress, Pena has contributed a gallery of vivid characterizations, including a tempestuous Latina in *Vibes* (1988) with Cyndi Lauper and Peter Falk; a murderously jealous ex-girlfriend in Peter Bogdanovich's *They All Laughed* (1981), starring Audrey Hepburn; Carmen, the sultry maid, in the hit *Down and Out in Beverly Hills* (1986); the jilted Rosie in Luis Valdez's *La Bamba* (1987); and Marissa in Steven Spielberg's *batteries not included* (1987). Pena also starred in the ABC series "I Married Dora" and the John Sayles series "Shannon's Deal" on NBC.

Her first major film role was in the highly acclaimed *El Super* (1979), followed by a co-starring role in *Crossover Dreams* (1985) with Ruben Blades. More recently, she appeared as Jezzie in *Jacob's Ladder* (1990).

Jose Perez

B: 1940

A diminutive Puerto Rican actor, Perez began as a child actor on the Broadway stage and has worked in motion pictures and television for over 40 years. His film credits include *A Life in the Balance* (1955), in which he plays a young boy, and *The Sting II* (1983) and *Stick* (1985), in which he is featured as an adult.

Manuel Perez

An animator for Warner Bros. Cartoon Studios, Perez was active during the 1940s and 1950s.

Pepito Perez

A famous clown, Pepito was born in Barcelona, Spain, and started his circus career with the Circo Parisch in Madrid, where he became a favorite of King Alfonso. He toured Europe and appeared in the United States at the New York Hippodrome and in vaudeville. He was also featured in the 1929 *Ziegfeld Follies*. Later, in Hollywood films, he performed in the circus sequence in *Lady in the Dark* (1944) and appeared in *A Medal for Benny* (1945). Perez coached Desi Arnaz and Lucille Ball in slapstick vaudeville routines for the pilot episode of the "I Love Lucy" TV series, in which he also appeared.

Rosie Perez

B: 1966

Perez is the first Puerto Rican actress since Rita Moreno to make an impact in co-starring roles in contemporary motion pictures that project her unique comic and ethnic personality as a sassy, smart-mouthed but vulnerable inner-city Hispanic American woman.

One of 11 children of Lydia and Ismael Perez, Rosie is a sixth-generation, 100 percent Puerto Rican native New Yorker. She made her motion picture debut and won recognition in Spike Lee's controversial hit film *Do the Right Thing* (1989) as

Rosie Perez as Gloria Clemente in the comedy *White Men Can't Jump*.

Tina, who is the lover of Mookie, played by Lee. She followed with a co-starring role as Gloria, an ex–disco queen from Brooklyn who aspires to become a contestant on the game show "Jeopardy" in writer/director Ron Shelton's *White Men Can't Jump* (1992). In Tony Bill's *Untamed Heart* (1993) she plays a waitress, and in *Fearless* (1993) she plays a young mother who loses her baby. For her performance in *Fearless,* she was nominated for an Academy Award as Best Supporting Actress. She played a young Hispanic crack addict in the HBO film *Criminal Justice* and has made appearances on such television series as "21 Jump Street" and "WIOU."

She is also a noted choreographer and was nominated for an Emmy for her choreography of the Fox television series "In Living Color."

Severo Perez

Perez directed the "American Playhouse" presentation of *Tierra* (1994) and produced *Seguin* (1982), another "American Playhouse" presentation.

Alex Phillips, Jr.

Born in Mexico, the son of Hollywood cinematographer Alex Phillips, Sr., the younger Alex's 50 films as cinematographer are such Hollywood productions as *Buck and the Preacher* (1972), *Bring Me the Head of Alfredo Garcia* (1974), *The Savage Is Loose* (1974), *Caboblanco* (1980), *Fade to Black* (1980), *Little Treasure* (1985), and the television miniseries *Evita Peron* (1981).

Lou Diamond Phillips
B: 1962

This young actor rose to stardom in the role of the late rock 'n' roll legend Ritchie Valens in the hit film *La Bamba,* directed by Luis Valdez in 1987. Phillips has since starred in such films as *Stand and Deliver* (1988), *Young Guns* (1988), *The First Power* (1989), *Renegades* (1989), *A Show of Force* (1990), *Young Guns II* (1990), and *Ambition* (1991). He is Dallas-born and -raised of Scots-Irish and Cherokee Indian background on his father's side and Filipino with strains of Chinese and Spanish on his mother's side.

Miguel Pinero
B: 12/19/1946
D: 6/17/1988

A Puerto Rican–born playwright and actor, Pinero usually portrayed drug-addicted felons in films and television during the late 1970s and the 1980s. His award-winning play, *Short Eyes,* a searing portrayal of violent prison life, written while he was serving prison time in 1973 in Sing Sing, went on to win an Obie Award and the New York Drama Critics Circle Award as Best American Play in 1974. It was later made into a film, directed by Robert M. Young, for which he wrote the screenplay and in which he appeared. Pinero wrote scripts for the "Baretta" TV series starring Robert Blake as well as several scripts for the "Kojak" and "Miami Vice" series. No one knew or wrote the terse, colorful, and realistic language of the streets, drug dealers, pimps, and prison inmates better than Pinero. Most of his writing was based on his own life experiences; this eventually hampered his creativity and productivity, and ultimately ended in his untimely death. His acting credits include *Times Square* (1980); *Fort Apache, The Bronx* (1981); *Breathless* (1983 Richard Gere version); *Deal of the Century* (1983); *Alphabet City* (1984); and *The Pick-up Artist* (1987).

Tony Plana

B: 4/19/1954

A Cuban-born actor, Plana has established himself as one of the most effective character actors in feature films. His varied film roles include the mohawked cadet Dellaserra in *An Officer and a Gentleman* (1982), Major Max in Oliver Stone's *Salvador* (1986), the long-haired zany caricature of a Mexican bandit in *¡Three Amigos!* (1986), and the ratlike golden-toothed nemesis Feo in *Born in East L.A.* (1987). In addition, he starred as the gung ho Green Beret in Haskell Wexler's *Latino* (1985), the covetous waiter in the Oscar-nominated *El Norte* (1984), the guerrilla priest in *Romero* (1989), and the journalist in *Havana* (1990).

His television appearances include three Emmy Award–winning special telecasts: the miniseries *Drug Wars: The Camarena Story,* the PBS drama *Sweet 15,* and an episode of "L.A. Law."

Begonia Plaza

B: 1962

Plaza has worked with some of the film industry's most popular leading men, including Chuck Norris, Clint Eastwood, Nick Nolte, Eddie Murphy, and Tom Cruise. Her feature films include *48 HRS.* (1982), *Heartbreak Ridge* (1986), *Maid to Order* (1987), *Born on the Fourth of July* (1989), and *Delta Force 2: Operation Stranglehold* (1990). Born in Colombia, Plaza also lived in Spain before moving with her family at age nine to Los Angeles, where she developed an interest in acting.

Rose Portillo

B: 11/7/1953

A Mexican American actress, Portillo was featured in such films as *Walk Proud* (1979) and *Zoot Suit* (1981). On television, her credits include the series "Eisenhower and Lutz," the "American Playhouse" presentation of *Seguin* (1982) opposite A Martinez, and guest-starring roles on "Police Story."

The Los Angeles–born actress has also appeared in such films as *Exorcist II: The Heretic* (1977), *Where the Buffalo Roam* (1980), and *The Mean Season* (1985).

Jaime Prades

A native of Uruguay, Prades pioneered filmmaking in virtually every Spanish-speaking country, becoming an expert in production and global distribution. He served as vice president of Samuel Bronston Productions and was associate producer on such Bronston films as *El Cid* (1961) and *King of Kings* (1961).

Victoria Principal

B: 1/3/1950

An actress and television producer, Principal was born in Japan of an American career Army officer. She lived in many diverse places around the globe but began her dramatic studies with Max Croft in Springfield, Massachusetts, and in Miami. Principal went to New York to pursue an acting career and, earning her living as a model, decided to move to Hollywood. While studying with drama coach Estelle Harmons, Principal was picked by director John Huston for the role of Paul Newman's Mexican mistress in *The Life and Times of Judge Roy Bean* (1972). The films that followed were mostly forgettable, including *The Naked Ape* (1973), *Earthquake* (1974), *I Will, I Will . . . for Now* (1976), and *Vigilante Force* (1976).

In 1975, unhappy with her career, Principal quit for three years to become an agent. Producers told her repeatedly that she didn't have the right look. In a *TV*

Guide interview (3/14/87), she recalled a producer candidly telling her, "You don't look American. Are you Latin or Eurasian?" Principal found that she did not fit the studio's image of a leading lady at that time.

In 1978, as a result of her successful work as an agent, she was asked to read for a part on a new television series called "Dallas." She won the role of Pamela Ewing on the hit long-running series, which brought her national and international fame. Principal played the role for nine years and left to pursue new career opportunities, forming her own television production company. Since then she has starred in the television films *Mistress* (1987), *Naked Lie* (1989), *Blind Rage* (1990), and *Don't Touch My Daughter* (1991).

Freddie Prinze
B: 6/22/1954
D: 1/29/1977

Prinze was born in New York City of Puerto Rican–Hungarian heritage. The comedian's brilliant career was cut short by his growing dependence on drugs and alcohol and his inability to cope with the pressures of Hollywood success. Prinze, a stand-up comedian who starred in major nightclubs as well as in the hit television series "Chico and the Man," died by his own hand, when, under the influence of drugs, he put a gun to his head and accidentally fired it.

Prinze's only dramatic role was in the telefilm *The Million Dollar Rip-Off* (1976), in which he starred as an ex-con electronics whiz who, with the aid of four females, attempts a robbery. He also made guest appearances on "Tony Orlando and Dawn." Prinze was the first Puerto Rican or Hispanic American comedian and television performer whose personality and special brand of street humor were able to cross over into mainstream America. Had he lived, it is possible that he would have had a career similar to that of black superstar comedian Eddie Murphy, who also came out of stand-up comedy and television.

Tito Puente
B: 4/23/1920

Known as "The King of Latin Music," Tito Puente has contributed to the recognition and popularity of Latin music around the world. He was born in New York City of Puerto Rican parents and grew up in Spanish Harlem during the flowering of the big band era in the late 1930s, which led him to attend the New York School of Music. Puente was drafted into the Navy in 1942; after the war he expanded his knowledge of composition and arranging but got sidetracked into becoming a bandleader.

Prior to his screen appearance as himself in *The Mambo Kings* (1992), Puente appeared in Woody Allen's *Radio Days* (1987) as a Xavier Cugat–like bandleader, *Salsa* (1989) as himself, and *Armed and Dangerous* (1986) with John Candy. He also appeared in early soundies, the predecessors to today's music videos, with several Latin bands of the period. Puente also provided the opening theme music for several seasons of the long-running television series "The Cosby Show."

Luis Puenzo
B: 1946

An Argentinian, Puenzo directed and co-wrote *Old Gringo* (1989) for Columbia Pictures, starring Gregory Peck and Jane Fonda, following his Academy Award–winning film *The Official Story* (1985). This acclaimed film, which Puenzo directed, produced, and co-wrote, received more than 35 international awards, starting with the award for Best Actress and the Ecumenical Jury Award at the Cannes Film

Festival in 1985 and culminating in the Academy Award for Best Foreign-Language Film in 1985. *The Official Story* also received an Oscar nomination for Best Original Screenplay.

Puenzo directed commercials from the age of 19 in his native Argentina and has been awarded almost all the international prizes in this field. He had his own film production services company, Cinemania, in Buenos Aires for almost 20 years. In addition to *Old Gringo* and *The Official Story,* Puenzo's feature credits include the 1973 film *Luces de Mis Zapatos* (Lights of My Shoes) and *Cinco Anos de Vida* (Five Years of Life), an episode of the 1975 film *Las Sorpresas* (Surprises).

Frank Puglia

B: 3/9/1892

D: 10/25/1975

A Sicilian-born actor, Puglia frequently played Latin types over a 60-year career that included roles in a number of silent and sound films as well as stage and TV productions. Among his many film credits are D.W. Griffith's silent masterpiece *Orphans of the Storm* (1922), *Viva Villa!* (1934), *The Gay Desperado* (1936), *For Whom the Bell Tolls* (1943), *The Road to Rio* (1947), and *Serenade* (1956).

Anthony Quinn

B: 4/21/1916

Anthony Quinn's career spans more than 50 years, beginning with his first screen appearance in 1936 as a convict in *Parole* to his latest starring role as Tiburon Mendes, a charming but dangerous powerbroker in *Revenge* (1990), opposite Kevin Costner. He most recently assumed a trio of important character roles as an Italian don in *Mobsters* (1991), a domineering Italian father in Spike Lee's *Jungle Fever* (1991), and a romantic Greek widower in Chris Columbus's *Only the Lonely* (1991), opposite Maureen O'Hara.

Born during the Mexican Revolution in Chihuahua, Mexico, to an Irish-Mexican father and a Mexican mother, Quinn was raised in the slums of East Los Angeles, where his father found work at a film company. Though still young when his father died, he worked odd jobs to help support his mother, sister, and grandmother.

Quinn has garnered two Academy Awards for Best Supporting Actor, one in 1952 for his portrayal of Zapata's troubled brother Eufemio in Elia Kazan's *Viva Zapata!* opposite Marlon Brando, the other in 1956 for his interpretation of artist Paul Gauguin in Vincente Minnelli's *Lust for Life.* He also received Oscar nominations as Best Actor for his portrayal of an Italian American rancher in George Cukor's *Wild Is the Wind* (1957) and for the role he has come to be so closely identified with, Zorba in *Zorba the Greek* (1964). He returned to that role in the musical stage version, *Zorba,* which ran for a year on Broadway and toured over 70 U.S. cities.

Quinn first appeared on a credit sheet when he was enrolled as a student at Polytechnic High School in Los Angeles. After nearly becoming a student of the great architect Frank Lloyd Wright, Quinn instead went to acting school to help correct a speech impediment and ended up playing stereotypical Hollywood roles as an Indian, a Mexican, a Pacific Islander, or a villain. In 1935 he gained his first professional acting job in the Los Angeles stage presentation of *Clean Beds,* which starred Mae West. It carried with it a weekly paycheck of $15. Quinn's big-screen break came in 1936 when he was signed to portray a Cheyenne Indian in Cecil B. DeMille's *The Plainsman* (1937), starring Gary Cooper. He vows he won his interview by claiming to be a member of the Black Foot tribe and speaking the "doggonnest Cheyenne gibberish you've ever heard." His early credits include such films

Anthony Quinn.

as *Waikiki Wedding* (1937), *Blood and Sand* (1941), *They Died with Their Boots On* (1942), *Guadalcanal Diary* (1943), *The Ox-Bow Incident* (1943), *Buffalo Bill* (1944), *Black Gold* (1947), and *Tycoon* (1947).

In 1947 Quinn left Hollywood for the stage and appeared on Broadway in *The Gentleman from Athens*. Elia Kazan offered him the part of Stanley Kowalski in the road company of *A Streetcar Named Desire,* and he later followed Marlon Brando in the role in the Broadway production. In 1951, he returned to films in *The Brave Bulls,* as the manager of a gored torreador who fears a return to the bullring. Despite winning the Oscar for Best Supporting Actor in *Viva Zapata!* he continued to be cast in the usual character parts: a Portuguese sailor in *The World in His Arms* (1952), a Madagascan pirate in *Against All Flags* (1952), a Seminole chief in *Seminole* (1953), and a Javanese despot in *East of Sumatra* (1953). He even played a Mexican bandit in *Ride, Vaquero!* (1953) to good reviews.

With no change in sight, Quinn left for Europe in search of better acting opportunities. Things did not fare well for him until he played the role of the brutish, gigantic circus strongman Zampano in Fellini's *La Strada* (1954). An internationally acclaimed film, it won the Best Foreign-Language Film Academy Award in

1956. Quinn's performance was hailed by critics worldwide and established him as an international actor and star. Quinn said to Luis Reyes during a 1988 interview, "My life really started all over again when I did *La Strada*. I think *La Strada* really convinced people I was an actor."

In 1956, Quinn took on the challenge of directing the remake of the Cecil B. DeMille production of *The Buccaneer* (1958), at the request of his ailing father-in-law (Quinn had married DeMille's adopted daughter, Katherine DeMille, in 1938). Quinn had appeared in a small part in the original 1938 version. Featuring an all-star cast headed by Yul Brynner and Charlton Heston, the film did not measure up with critics or the public.

Back on Broadway, he and Laurence Olivier starred in the American production of *Becket* (1960), in which Quinn played King Henry II. About seven months after the opening, theatrical history was made when the two famous actors switched roles for the remainder of the play's year-long run, to the same high critical acclaim received on opening night. Shortly after that, Quinn co-starred with Margaret Leighton in *Tchin-Tchin* (1962) for nearly a year.

He entered into a period of rich characterizations in the 1960s with a series of roles beginning with *The Guns of Navarone* (1961) as a Greek resistance fighter, *Lawrence of Arabia* (1962) as an Arab leader, *Barabbas* (1962) in the title role in the biblical spectacle, and in two smaller dramas, *Requiem for a Heavyweight* (1962) as the washed-up fighter Mountain Rivera and *Zorba the Greek* (1964) as the uneducated, life-affirming Greek peasant. He recalled in an interview with Luis Reyes, "We did *Zorba the Greek* for $400,000 on location in Crete and in *Requiem* I changed the character of the boxer to a Mexican and played him inarticulate. I even changed my voice for it."

In 1971 Quinn starred in the television series "The Man and the City" for ABC, in which he portrayed the Mexican American mayor of a southwestern city.

In 1972 he published his autobiography, *The Original Sin,* which became a best-seller.

Quinn's later films include *Guns for San Sebastian* (1968), *The Shoes of the Fisherman* (1968), *The Secret of Santa Vittoria* (1969), *The Don Is Dead* (1973), *The Greek Tycoon* (1978), and *The Lion of the Desert* (1981).

Acting and writing are not Quinn's only achievements. He is a recognized collector of paintings and sculptures and in 1982 his own talent as a sculptor and painter was publicly unveiled when the Center Art Galleries of Hawaii held an exhibition of his original artworks. The complete collection was sold out in three days, and enough back orders were on hand to occupy him full time as an artist for years.

However, in January 1983, he could not resist an offer to once again return to the stage to star in the musical version of *Zorba,* based on the Academy Award–winning motion picture. Far surpassing everyone's expectations, the production ran on the road and in New York until August 1986. Quinn never missed even one of the 1,240 performances during the entire run of the play.

In 1986, the Hollywood Foreign Press Association gave Quinn one of its highest honors, the Cecil B. DeMille Award for Lifetime Achievement.

He was nominated for television's Emmy Award as Best Supporting Actor in a Miniseries for his portrayal of the father of Aristotle Onassis in *Onassis: The Richest Man in the World* (1988).

"Out of the 250 pictures I've done I've only worked with what I'd consider five or six great directors. I've had the joy of working with Kazan, Minnelli, Cukor and Fellini, who is one of the geniuses, and David Lean," remarked the actor in an interview with Reyes. "I started working when I was a year and a half old and it's a way of life for me. I get bored doing nothing."

For television, in 1990 Quinn played the role of Santiago, the old Cuban fisherman, in an adaptation of Ernest Hemingway's *The Old Man and the Sea.* "I felt I was serving Santiago and not serving Anthony Quinn at any time in the picture. Each man, each actor has a soul, and he can only be guilty of what his soul wants to say. What my soul wanted to say about *The Old Man and the Sea* was very simple: You can be destroyed but not defeated." *This Can't Be Love,* a 1994 television movie, paired Quinn and Katharine Hepburn for the first time.

Ana Maria Quintana

Born in Chile, Quintana is a script supervisor on Hollywood films whose credits include *The Formula* (1980), *The Falcon and the Snowman* (1985), *Remo Williams: The Adventure Begins* (1985), and *Jurassic Park* (1993).

Jose Quintero

> B: 1925

An acclaimed Panamanian-born director, Quintero etched his career in the American theater interpreting the works of Tennessee Williams and Eugene O'Neill. He directed only one film, the 1961 Warner Bros. film *The Roman Spring of Mrs. Stone,* starring Vivien Leigh and Warren Beatty, based on a Tennessee Williams novel. Quintero has received two Tony Awards, two Drama Desk Awards, an Emmy, and a Eugene O'Neill Gold Medal for his work in the theater and television direction.

Victoria Racimo

> B: 12/26/1950

The dark-haired, dark-eyed Racimo has an extensive background in motion pictures, television, and the theater and has portrayed a variety of roles, including a Vietnamese, a Hawaiian, a Mexican, and a Native American. Racimo is of Filipino, English, Irish, and Native American descent. She began her career on the New York stage appearing in several award-winning productions at Joseph Papp's Public Theatre. The actress was featured in *Red Sky at Morning* (1971), *The Magic Garden of Stanley Sweetheart* (1971), *Prophecy* (1979), and *The Mountain Men* (1980). Her TV credits include roles on "The Doctors" series and in the telefilms *Green Eyes* (1973), *Brave New World* (1980), and *The Rhineman Exchange* (1977).

Carlos Ramirez

> B: 1915
> D: 12/11/1988

A Colombian baritone, Ramirez appeared in various MGM musical films of the 1940s and 1950s in specialty musical numbers. He performed in *The Barber of Seville* at Carnegie Hall and at the Colon Theatre in Buenos Aires. He was discovered by MGM in 1943 during a successful singing engagement at New York's Waldorf-Astoria and was signed to a seven-year contract. His film credits include *Bathing Beauty* (1944), *Two Girls and a Sailor* (1944), *Anchors Aweigh* (1945), *Where Do We Go from Here?* (1945), *Easy to Wed* (1946), *Night and Day* (1946), and *Latin Lovers* (1953), for which he dubbed vocals for actor Ricardo Montalban.

Loyda Ramos

> B: 11/5/1958

A New York–born Puerto Rican actress, Ramos has been featured in such films as *¡Three Amigos!* (1986), *Deal of the Century* (1983), and *Best Seller* (1987).

Rudy Ramos
B: 1950

Born in Lawton, Oklahoma, Ramos was introduced as a regular cast member of the television series "The High Chaparral" during its last season. Among his film credits are *Defiance* (1980) and *Colors* (1988).

Vic Ramos

A longtime New York–based casting director, Ramos has been responsible for the casting of major television shows and feature films made in New York since the 1960s, including *The Godfather: Part II* (1974).

Donald Reed
B: 1905
D: 2/28/1973

Born in Mexico City, Reed was a leading man in a number of Hollywood films late in the silent era. He turned to supporting roles when sound came, usually playing a Latin lover or gigolo. His film credits include *Evangeline* (1927), *Show Girl* (1928), and *Naughty But Nice* (1939).

George Regas
B: 1900
D: 12/13/1940

Born in Sparta, Greece, George Regas along with his brother, Pedro, came directly to America in a theatrical production of a Greek play that toured the United States. He appeared in the English-language plays *The Jade God* and *Zombie on Broadway*. In 1922 Mary Pickford brought him to Hollywood to play in *Lovelight*. His success was immediate. His brother, Pedro, followed with a role opposite Bebe Daniels in *Senorita* (1927). Among George Regas's many fine film credits are *Riptide* (1934), *Rose Marie* (1936), *Waikiki Wedding* (1937), *Beau Geste* (1939), *The Oklahoma Kid* (1939), and his last film, *The Mark of Zorro* (1940). He died on December 13, 1940, of throat cancer.

Pedro Regas
B: 1899
D: 8/10/1974

Pedro Regas carried on in many character roles. Five of his films were directed by Howard Hawks: *Scarface* (1932), *Tiger Shark* (1932), *Viva Villa!* (1934), *Only Angels Have Wings* (1939), and *To Have and Have Not* (1944). Among his other films are *Waikiki Wedding* (1937), *Juarez* (1939), *Viva Zapata!* (1952), *Lonely Are the Brave* (1962), *Flap* (1970), and *High Plains Drifter* (1973). He appeared in over a hundred episodic television shows over the years. He died at age 74.

Duncan Renaldo
B: 1904
D: 9/3/1980

Best known for his role as the Cisco Kid in films and on television during the late 1940s and throughout the 1950s, Renaldo was born in Spain. He was orphaned and came to the United States in 1921 at age 17. He landed in New York and worked in silent films as a studio artist, producer, and assistant director. Soon, Renaldo became interested in acting and started securing parts in Hollywood films.

In 1929, he played the leading role of Esteban in the MGM classic *The Bridge of San Luis Rey*. The picture was a success, and MGM decided to star Renaldo with Harry Carey in *Trader Horn* (1931). Renaldo said, "I spent two years in Africa making *Trader Horn*, 1929 and 1930. This was the first time a Hollywood studio ever went on location in Africa. It was a wonderful safari, and Africa was so much different than it is today. It was still unspoiled. We shot over five million feet of exciting jungle footage, with fantastic shots of the wild animals." *Trader Horn* was a huge success, and Renaldo became one of the hottest stars in Hollywood. Then the federal government prosecuted Renaldo for being an illegal alien (he claimed various citizenships). For the next four years he was involved in difficult litigation and court trials, after which he spent a year at McNeill Island detention center before being granted an unconditional presidential pardon in 1936 from Franklin Roosevelt. Renaldo became a U.S. citizen in 1941.

Renaldo found it difficult to get work and finally landed a job as a janitor at Republic Pictures. When studio president Herbert J. Yates, an old friend, found out, he ordered that Renaldo be paid as an actor and put him back in pictures. From 1936 until 1940, Renaldo played in a number of westerns and serials.

"I had an idea for a cowboy hero from Latin America. I told Mr. Yates that if we did the character right, he would be able to sell his westerns all over Mexico and South America. We came up with the Three Mesquiteers and I played the Latin member of the trio, named Rico. I was right and those pictures were big hits in Latin America." John Wayne was one of the trio in later films.

In 1941, when Fox dropped the Cisco Kid series, Renaldo, an associate producer, bought the rights to the character from Doubleday and came up with the idea of basing the Cisco Kid on Don Quixote and Pancho on Sancho Panza. Renaldo subsequently starred in four Cisco Kid westerns with Martin Garralaga as Pancho, and the films were extremely popular. Renaldo entered the war effort, and the series continued with Gilbert Roland.

After the war, Renaldo continued the film series and decided that the best man to play Pancho was Leo Carrillo, a top character actor who had started out in silent films and had made over 79 sound features. Renaldo and Carrillo made six features as the Cisco Kid and Pancho for United Artists. Carrillo was the perfect balance to Renaldo. The Duncan Renaldo–Leo Carrillo team became the screen's most popular and best-known Cisco Kid and Pancho.

The movies were so successful that Renaldo and Carrillo decided to start the Cisco Kid television series in 1950. The TV series was a great success and was the first western to be produced especially for television in color. A total of 156 episodes were produced, the last filmed in 1955. Renaldo retired to a ranch in Santa Barbara and continued to make personal appearances until 1970.

Alejandro Rey

B: 2/8/1930
D: 5/21/1987

An Argentine-born actor, Rey appeared in American films and television shows. He was perhaps best known for his role as the swinging playboy Carlos Ramirez on the popular "The Flying Nun" television series from 1967 until 1970, opposite Sally Field.

Born in Buenos Aires, Rey appeared in such films as *Solomon and Sheba* (1959), *Fun in Acapulco* (1963), *Blindfold* (1966), *Mr. Majestyk* (1974), *Breakout* (1975), *Cuba* (1979), and *Moscow on the Hudson* (1984), in which he co-starred as a Cuban lawyer opposite Robin Williams.

His television work included guest-star appearances on such series as "Naked City," "Gunsmoke," "Bob Hope Presents the Chrysler Theatre," "The High Chap-

Alejandro Rey and Sally Field in a scene from "The Flying Nun."

arral," "Fantasy Island," and "The Love Boat." He played Rita Hayworth's father, Eduardo Cansino, in the TV movie *Rita Hayworth: The Love Goddess* (1983).

Fernando Rey

B: 9/20/1918
D: 3/9/1994

An internationally recognized Spanish-born actor, Fernando Rey appeared in over 150 films and is noted for his work with director Luis Bunuel yet is best known to

Fernando Rey as Charnier, the Mr. Big
of the French drug underworld,
in *The French Connection II*.

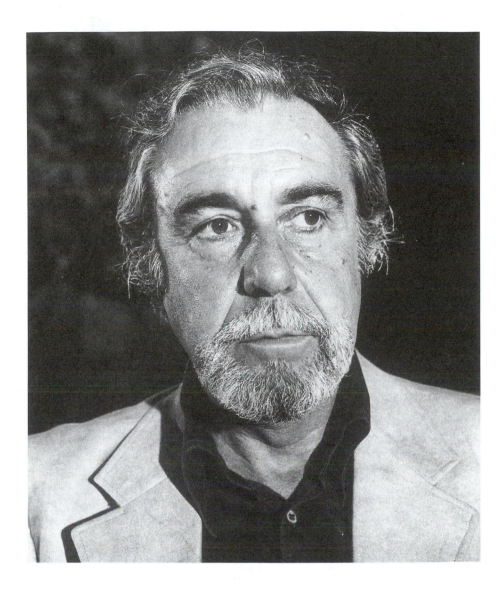

American audiences for his role as the French drug dealer in the Academy Award–
winning *The French Connection* (1971) and its sequel, *The French Connection II* (1975).

Born in Galica, Spain, Rey had planned to be an architect until the Spanish
Civil War interrupted his plans. He fought on the side of the Loyalists alongside
his father, and the war brought them financial ruin. This led to work in the movies
as an extra and later in bit parts. His knowledge of several languages soon gained
him employment dubbing foreign films. Dubbing films proved to be good voice
and acting training for the young Rey, who had never attended an acting school.

He worked consistently in Spanish films over a 50-year period in supporting
roles and in American or international productions filmed in Spain.

His association with Luis Bunuel brought him worldwide critical acclaim, beginning with his role as Don Lope, the elderly guardian obsessed with his beautiful ward, in *Tristana* (1970). His other films for Bunuel include *Viridiana* (1961), *The
Discreet Charm of the Bourgeoisie* (1972), and *That Obscure Object of Desire* (1977).

Ernie Reyes, Jr.
B: 1/15/1972

Born in San Jose, California, of Filipino heritage, since age eight Reyes has been
competing in martial arts competitions under the tutelage of his father and has
earned a black belt. He is the first child in the United States ever rated in the top 10

in professional adult forms competition. The young actor starred in his own TV series, "Sidekicks," and has appeared in four theatrical feature films, *The Last Dragon* (1985), *Red Sonja* (1985), *Teenage Mutant Ninja Turtles II: The Secret of the Ooze* (1991), and *Surf Ninjas* (1993).

Julian Reyes

A New York–born Puerto Rican actor, Reyes was featured in *Die Hard 2* (1990) and in *Point Break* (1991) as an FBI agent. On television he has guest starred on "Miami Vice" and was a regular on the syndicated series "What a Country."

Burt Reynolds
B: 1936

A popular leading man of part Native American heritage, Reynolds was born in Waycross, Georgia, and grew up in the area of Palm Beach, Florida. Because of his dark good looks, Reynolds began his career playing Indians and Mexican bandits in films and television shows, initially as a stuntman. Reynolds appeared on television in such series as "Riverboat" (1959–1960), "Gunsmoke" (three seasons as an Indian), "Hawk" (as an Indian detective), and "Dan August" (1970). In the theatrical film *100 Rifles* (1969) he co-starred as Mexican bandit Yaqui Joe. His ascent to superstardom began with his performance in *Deliverance* (1972). The huge success of *Smokey and the Bandit* in 1977 took his career in new directions, and he has played a wide variety of roles. Reynolds has also directed a number of feature films and television shows, and currently co-stars on the television series "Evening Shade."

David Reynoso

A popular star in Mexico, Reynoso has worked in his native country for over three decades as an actor in 130 Mexican films. He has appeared in the American films *Rage* (1966), starring Glenn Ford, and *Stick* (1985), starring Burt Reynolds.

Alfonso Ribeiro
B: 1968

A young actor, Ribeiro plays Carlton Banks on the hit NBC-TV series "Fresh Prince of Bel Air." Ribeiro was also a regular as a teenager on the "Silver Spoons" series. He made his television debut at age eight on the PBS series "Oye Willie," and he created the leading role in the Broadway production of *The Tap Dance Kid*. His family is from the Dominican Republic.

Branscombe Richmond
B: 1955

A stuntman and actor, Richmond has appeared in more than 300 television shows and 100 feature films. His recent film credits include *Star Trek III: The Search for Spock* (1984), *Thief of Hearts* (1984), *Commando* (1985), *Licence to Kill* (1989), *Hard to Kill* (1990), *Grand Canyon* (1991), and *Batman Returns* (1992). He is part French, Hawaiian, Spanish, and Aleutian Indian.

Maria Richwine

A Colombian-born, California-raised actress, Richwine co-starred as Maria Elena Holly, Buddy Holly's Puerto Rican wife, in the Academy Award–nominated film *The Buddy Holly Story* (1978). She also co-starred on the short-lived ABC-TV series "A.K.A. Pablo."

Lalo Rios

B: 2/7/1927
D: 3/14/1973

Rios played what could be considered the quintessential Mexican American or Chicano teenager of the 1950s in two films, *The Lawless* (1950) and *The Ring* (1952).

Rios was born in Sonora, Mexico, and moved to Los Angeles at an early age. While working as a carpenter, he was asked by some friends to play a role in a church drama. Director Joseph Losey discovered him on a construction job site in 1950, and he made his film debut in a major role in *The Lawless* as a Mexican youngster falsely accused of a crime in a small agricultural community in central California.

The following year he starred in the role of a young Mexican American boxer from East Los Angeles in *The Ring*, produced by the King Brothers.

Rios received good notices for his work from the critics, but was never able to land a leading role again due to the rigid Hollywood casting system of the time. (That he played those two leads had more to do with the director and the producers, who worked outside the established Hollywood mainstream.)

Rios played small roles in *Mark of the Renegade* (1951) and *City Beneath the Sea* (1970) for Universal and had a featured role in *Giant* (1956) for Warner Bros. and in Orson Welles's *Touch of Evil* (1958). After his small role in *City Beneath the Sea*, Rios never appeared in another film. He died of a liver ailment in 1973.

Carlos Rivas

B: 2/16/1925

A Mexican-born leading man and supporting actor, Rivas was popular during the mid-1950s and early 1960s. Rivas has appeared in numerous American motion pictures, including *The King and I* (1956) as Tuptim's lover, *The Deerslayer* (1957) as an Indian, John Huston's *The Unforgiven* (1960) as an Indian chief, Alfred Hitchcock's *Topaz* (1969) as a Cuban, and *The Undefeated* (1969) and *True Grit* (1969), both with John Wayne. Rivas has guest starred on almost all the major television series of the past 35 years. He has starred in over 20 Mexican films. His other American film credits include *The Beast of Hollow Mountain* (1956) and *The Big Boodle* (1957).

Carlos Rivas

D: 1/15/1967

A sound technician who won three Academy Awards for technical advancements in sound, Rivas worked for MGM from 1943 until his retirement in 1965.

Geoffrey Rivas

Actor Geoffrey Rivas's film credits include *La Bamba* (1987), *Born in East L.A.* (1987), and *Bound by Honor* (1993).

Chita Rivera [born: Dolores Conchita del Rivero]

B: 1/23/1933

Broadway actress and dancer Chita Rivera made her motion picture debut in *Sweet Charity* (1969) as Shirley MacLaine's best friend. She created the role of Anita on Broadway in the original stage production of *West Side Story*, but the role in the film version went to Rita Moreno. Rivera also created the role of Dick Van Dyke's Latin secretary in the Broadway musical *Bye, Bye Birdie*, but the film role went to Janet Leigh.

A native of Washington, D.C., Rivera is of Puerto Rican descent.

Geraldo Rivera

   B: 1943

A sometimes-controversial award-winning TV broadcast journalist, television producer, and syndicated talk show host for over 20 years, Rivera is half-Jewish and half–Puerto Rican. Though not an actor, he has played himself or a character like himself in several network TV movies and specials.

Jose Rivera

   B: 3/24/1955

A Puerto Rican–born screenwriter/playwright, Rivera has written mostly for television. He was a staff writer on the short-lived "A.K.A. Pablo" series. His play *The House of Ramon Iglesias* was filmed for the PBS "American Playhouse" series in 1986. He has written episodes of the situation comedy "Family Matters" and was co-creator and producer of the 1991–1992 series "Eerie, Indiana."

Jorge Rivero

   B: 1940

A popular Mexican leading man, Rivero has appeared opposite some of the American cinema's biggest stars in a number of American films shot in Mexico. Yet, despite his good looks, athletic physique, and charming demeanor, the actor has never stirred much interest in the States.

He made his Hollywood film debut as an Indian chief in *Soldier Blue* (1970). He received co-star billing with John Wayne in *Rio Lobo* (1970), directed by Howard Hawks, in which he played a young cavalry officer. He also worked with Charlton Heston and James Coburn in *The Last Hard Men* (1976) and starred in *Fist Fighter* (1988).

Julian Rivero

   B: 7/25/1891
   D: 2/24/1976

A veteran character actor born in San Francisco, California, of Spanish-Mexican parents, Rivero left home at age 16 to pursue a career as an actor in the theater in New York. He worked on the Broadway stage before arriving in Hollywood in 1920. He directed a few comedies and westerns for World Film Co. and Canadian film companies. His first film appearance was in *The Bright Shawl* (1923, silent) for First National, which was filmed in Cuba.

Rivero appeared in dozens of B westerns throughout the 1920s and 1930s with Harry Carey, Bob Steele, Tim McCoy, Gene Autry, and Roy Rogers, usually as a Mexican bandit, a sidekick to the hero, or a don. His feature films include *The Night Rider* (1932) with Harry Carey, *The Westerner* (1940) with Gary Cooper, *The Outlaw* (1943), *The Treasure of the Sierra Madre* (1948) as the man who gives Bogart a haircut, *Broken Lance* (1954) with Spencer Tracy, *Don't Go Near the Water* (1957) with Glenn Ford, and *The Reward* (1965) as El Viejo. On television he appeared on episodes of "The Cisco Kid," "The Lone Ranger," "Wyatt Earp," "Marcus Welby, M.D.," and "The Bold Ones."

Victor Rivers [born: Victor Rivas]
B: 1956

A Cuban-born actor, Rivers made his film debut in *8 Million Ways to Die* in 1986 playing a gang member. Rivers co-starred with Eddie Murphy and Sheryl Lee Ralph in *The Distinguished Gentleman* (1992) as Amando, one of a trio of scam artists who plot to get Murphy elected to Congress. He is also featured in *Bound by Honor* (1993).

Estelita Rodriguez [aka: Estelita]
B: 1930
D: 1966

Born in Juanara, Cuba, Rodriguez started her career at age nine singing on Cuban radio, where she was called "the Cuban Shirley Temple." While appearing at the National Theater in Havana at age 14, she was signed by an agent to appear at the famous Copacabana nightclub in New York City. She performed at the Copacabana for a season and was then signed by MGM. She lost the MGM contract when she had to return unexpectedly to Cuba and could not reenter the States for months.

She was put under contract by Herbert J. Yates, the head of Republic Studios, where she worked for almost 10 years. She appeared in many westerns and was a frequent co-star of Republic's singing cowboy star, Roy Rogers, in such films as *Along the Navajo Trail* (1945), *On the Old Spanish Trail* (1947), *Santa Susanna Pass* (1949), and *The Golden Stallion* (1949). She starred in *Belle of Old Mexico* (1950) and *Havana Rose* (1951). She was planning to star in a film about the life of actress Lupe Velez when she died in 1966 under mysterious circumstances.

Marco Rodriguez
B: 7/10/1953

Rodriguez has played heavies in such feature films as *The Baltimore Bullet* (1980) and *The Rookie* (1990). He played Smiley in the film version of *Zoot Suit* (1981) and has appeared on many episodic television shows.

Paul Rodriguez
B: 1955

A stand-up Mexican American comedian with three television series and seven feature films to his credit, Rodriguez was born in Mexico and raised in California, the son of migrant workers. He came to the attention of producer Norman Lear while doing comedy warm-ups for Lear's show "Gloria." Lear ultimately wrote and developed a weekly series for him, "A.K.A. Pablo," focusing on the life of a Mexican American family in East L.A. Although the ABC series was short-lived, it focused attention on Rodriguez's talents and was followed by series "Trial and Error" and "Grand Slam," in which he starred opposite John Schneider.

His feature film credits include *D.C. Cab* (1984), *The Whoopee Boys* (1986), *Miracles* (1986), *Quicksilver* (1986), *Born in East L.A.* (1987), and *Made in America* (1993). Rodriguez's HBO and Fox comedy specials have attracted large viewing audiences. In 1994 he directed and starred in the comedy *A Million to Juan*, released by the Samuel Goldwyn Company.

Paul Rodriguez in *Quicksilver*.

Percy Rodriguez

Born in Montreal, Canada, the son of Maria and Juan Rodriguez, Percy plays dignified black American characters in films and episodic television programs in the United States. His film credits include *The Plainsman* (1966), *The Sweet Ride* (1968), and *The Heart Is a Lonely Hunter* (1968). His television work includes guest starring roles on such series as "Naked City," "Peyton Place," "Route 66," "The Man from U.N.C.L.E.," "Benson," and "Dynasty."

Robert Rodriguez

B: 1968

The Texas-born Rodriguez directed the $7,000 independent feature film *El Mariachi* (1993), which was picked up for distribution by Columbia Pictures, with whom Rodriguez has been under contract since 1992.

Jaime Rogers

B: 1935

A Puerto Rican choreographer/director, Rogers was featured as an actor/dancer in the film *West Side Story* (1961). He has worked as a director/choreographer on many television shows with most of the top performing artists over the years. He directed episodes of the syndicated television series "Fame" and directed the musical numbers for the film *Breakin'* (1984).

Gilbert Roland [born: Luis Antonio Damaso Alonso]

B: 12/11/1905
D: 5/15/1994

Gilbert Roland's career spans over 60 years from silent movies to his last screen role to date in *Barbarosa* (1982).

A resonant voice, athletic build, ever-present wristband, mustache, and cigar or cigarette in hand are Roland's identifying on-screen trademarks. First as a romantic leading man, then later in supporting character roles, he became synonymous with action, adventure, and romance as one of Hollywood's greatest stars. He has survived from silent films through the transition to sound, television, 3-D, CinemaScope, and now video laser discs and cable television.

Roland was one of six children, born in Juarez, Mexico. His family moved to El Paso, Texas, during the Mexican Revolution when Pancho Villa threatened the lives of all Mexicans of Spanish ancestry (both his parents were Spanish-born.)

At an awards ceremony held by the organization Nosotros in his honor in 1980, Roland remarked, "As a child living near the Rio Grande, a great love came into my life. All my life I have loved all the people on the screen. It became an obsession."

He grew up in the barrios of El Paso, selling newspapers in 1913 in the plaza in front of Paso del Norte Hotel. He drifted to Hollywood during his teens with only $2.60 in his pocket, arriving in Los Angeles at age 14. Broke and desperate to get into the movies, he had to sleep on a park bench. A man who owned a shop near the park gave the boy $5, a lot of money in those days, to get something to eat. When Roland secured a job and was receiving a steady income, he returned and paid the man for his generosity.

After a few years of working at whatever jobs he could find, Roland found work as an extra in countless motion pictures, including *The Phantom of the Opera* (1925, silent) and *Blood and Sand* (1922, silent). "I worked as an extra for $2 a day and a box lunch alongside such would-be stars as Clark Gable," Roland recalled during an interview with Luis Reyes in 1982. "We all had something in common; we believed in ourselves while waiting for the chance to be discovered." He doubled for Ramon Novarro in *The Midshipman* (1925, silent). He remembers, "I was thrown into the icy waters of Chesapeake Bay at 2 A.M. for a scene."

Roland was discovered in a mob scene by agent Ivan Kahn, and he was signed for the second lead in *The Plastic Age* (1925, silent), opposite Clara Bow. "An extra girl who was very beautiful asked if I would get a glass of water for her. In those days, things were so simple. The extra girls wanted only water. The set was a big Venetian square, and the water was on the other side of it. Ordinarily I would have walked around the set. But this time for some reason I took a shortcut. There I was in a fine costume all alone on the set, which was brilliantly lighted. When I reached the other side a man said, 'What is your name?' I said, 'Luis Antonio Damaso Alonso.' 'Well, come to my office tomorrow,' he said. He signed me to a contract and sold me to B.P. Schulberg for *The Plastic Age*."

At age 19, Roland chose his screen name by combining those of two of his favorites, John Gilbert and serial queen Ruth Roland. He attained stardom in 1927 with his next picture, *Camille* (silent), playing the young Frenchman Armand op-

Gilbert Roland and Mae West in
She Done Him Wrong.

posite Norma Talmadge. Now one of the most sought-after leading men, he starred opposite Mary Astor in *Rose of the Golden West* (1927, silent) and with Billie Dove in *The Love Mart* (1927, silent). He again starred opposite Norma Talmadge in *New York Nights* (1929). Other silent films include *The Blonde Saint* (1926, silent), *The Campus Flirt* (1926, silent), *The Dove* (1927, silent), and *The Woman Disputed* (1928, silent)

He had the looks associated with the fiery Latin lover, and although he was cast in the role frequently, he also played a variety of international types. "If you seem to be a Latin lover, they expect you'll be on screen a tough guy. But I am not a tough man. I have sentiment." Noting a difference between the private Roland and the public image he created in movies, he added, "My screen image never bothers me, but I have never tried to contradict it either."

Roland's career as a leading man waned during the early 1930s, although he was one of the few actors to survive the transition from silent to sound films. He went to Metro for both the English and Spanish versions of *Men of the North* (1930), and was cast opposite Clara Bow in *Call Her Savage* (1932) as a "half-breed." Roland starred in the English version of *Resurrection* (1931) opposite Lupe Velez. He was cast as a South American gigolo in Mae West's *She Done Him Wrong* (1933). Leading parts became fewer and far between for a while, though occasionally he made a few Spanish-language features.

Films he appeared in during the 1930s and 1940s include *Life Begins* (1932), *No Living Witness* (1932), *A Parisian Romance* (1932), *The Passionate Plumber* (1932), *The Woman in Room 13* (1932), *After Tonight* (1933), *Gigolettes of Paris* (1933), *Our Betters* (1933), *Elinor Norton* (1935), *Ladies Love Danger* (1935), *Mystery Woman* (1935), *Midnight Taxi* (1937), *Gambling on the High Seas* (1940), *Isle of Destiny* (1940), *Rangers of Fortune* (1940), *Angels with Broken Wings* (1941), *My Life with Caroline* (1941), *Enemy Agents Meet Ellery Queen* (1942), *Isle of Missing Men* (1942), *Captain Kidd* (1945), *Beauty and the Bandit* (1946), *The Gay Cavalier* (1946), *South of Monterey* (1946), *High Conquest* (1947), *The Other Love* (1947), *Pirates of Monterey* (1947), *Riding the California Trail* (1947), *Robin Hood of Monterey* (1947), *The Dude Goes West* (1948), and *King of the Bandits* (1949).

In 1937 he scored a good role in a western at Paramount, *Thunder Trail,* and received good notices for his lead in *The Last Train from Madrid* (1937) opposite Lew Ayres, Dorothy Lamour, and Anthony Quinn. A supporting role in *Gateway* (1938) was followed by the Columbia Pictures Spanish *La Vida Bohemia* (1937), and then by roles in Warner Bros.' *Juarez* (1939) and *The Sea Hawk* (1940).

Roland enlisted in the U.S. Army during World War II. After the war, he starred in a series of popular Cisco Kid films at Monogram Studios.

Gilbert Roland.

In 1949 his career took an upward turn when director John Huston picked him to play a cynical guitar-plucking Cuban revolutionary in *We Were Strangers*. "The producer said, 'not that so and so,' and Huston said 'that so and so is going to be in the picture,' and I was. The funny thing is that I scarcely knew Huston. Why he insisted on having me in the film, I don't know. The picture wasn't a success, but the critics, particularly in New York, gave me wonderful notices. Now I was back in business, after being buried in the Cisco Kid series for years."

This was the beginning of a new career period that was to see Roland successively appear in strong supporting character roles in above-average films throughout the 1950s. He appeared in Richard Brooks's *Crisis* (1950) opposite Cary Grant with several of his contemporaries, including Ramon Novarro and Antonio Moreno. He gave a moving and much-talked-about performance as an aging bullfighter in *The Bullfighter and the Lady* (1951), and played a Latin lover opposite Lana Turner in Vincente Minnelli's *The Bad and the Beautiful* (1952). He also starred with James Stewart in *Thunder Bay* (1953), with Robert Wagner in *Beneath the 12-Mile Reef* (1953), and with Jane Russell in *Underwater!* (1955). He played the role of the prison kingpin Punch Pinero in *My Six Convicts* (1952).

Roland's screen characters were always dashing, romantic, and sly. No matter how roguish a character he played, however, audiences knew he would always do the right thing by the last reel. Good examples of such portrayals are his role in *The Miracle of Our Lady of Fatima* (1952) and the role of the circus aerialist who walks a tightrope over Niagara Falls in *The Big Circus* (1959).

His other films of the period include *The Desert Hawk* (1950), *The Furies* (1950), *Malaya* (1950), *The Torch* (1950), *Mark of the Renegade* (1951), *Ten Tall Men* (1951), *Apache War Smoke* (1952), *Glory Alley* (1952), *The Diamond Queen* (1953), *The French Line* (1954), *The Racers* (1955), *That Lady* (1955), *The Treasure of Pancho Villa* (1955), *Bandido* (1956), *Three Violent People* (1956), *Around the World in 80 Days* (1956), *The Midnight Story* (1957), *The Last of the Fast Guns* (1958), *Catch Me if You Can* (1959), and *The Wild and the Innocent* (1959).

Roland has worked occasionally on television on such shows as "Zorro"; "Wagon Train," for which he wrote the script and guest starred in an episode titled "The Bernal Sierra Story"; "Medical Center"; "The High Chaparral"; "Kung Fu"; "Hart to Hart"; and "The Sacketts." In 1959 he starred in a pilot program for MGM television called "Amigo" in which he played the title role of a police detective in the bordertowns of El Paso and Juarez.

In the 1960s he had an important role in John Ford's *Cheyenne Autumn* (1964) as Chief Dull Knife with Dolores Del Rio, Ricardo Montalban, and Sal Mineo. He went to Italy and made several "spaghetti westerns" and also made a film in the Philippines. The films of this period include *Guns of the Timberland* (1960), *Samar* (1962), *The Reward* (1965), *The Poppy Is Also a Flower* (1966), *Any Gun Can Play* (1968), *The Christian Licorice Store* (1971), *Johnny Hamlet* (1972), *Running Wild* (1973), and *The Black Pearl* (1977).

In 1977 Roland played Captain Ralph in Ernest Hemingway's *Islands in the Stream*, starring George C. Scott. Unfortunately, the role was small and not sufficiently developed. He had a cameo role as a doctor in Charles Bronson's *Caboblanco* (1981). In 1980 Roland returned to the big screen in fine form to play a Mexican patriarch in the western *Barbarosa* (1982), starring Willie Nelson.

Lina Romay [born: Elena Romay]

B: 1/16/1921

Born in Brooklyn, New York, Lina Romay was the daughter of Mexican diplomat Porfirio A. Romay and his wife, Lillian. She was the lead singer for Xavier Cugat before being signed to an MGM contract by producer Joe Pasternak. She was featured in a number of MGM musicals singing with Cugat's orchestra. She made her film debut in *You Were Never Lovelier* (1942), in which she appeared with Cugat and the film's stars, Fred Astaire and Rita Hayworth. Her initial dramatic role was in 1945's *Adventure* starring Clark Gable. In the small role of Gable's seaport girlfriend, Romay got to kiss Gable. Her other films include *The Heat's On* (1943), *Stage Door Canteen* (1943), *Bathing Beauty* (1944), *Two Girls and a Sailor* (1944), *Weekend at the Waldorf* (1945), *Honeymoon* (1947), *Embraceable You* (1948), and *The Lady Takes a Sailor* (1949)

Carlos Romero

B: 1927

A character actor born in Los Angeles to a vaudeville family, his credits include *They Came to Cordura* (1959) and *The Professionals* (1966). On television he has guest starred in "Wagon Train," "The F.B.I.," and "Maverick." He was featured in a recurring role on the series "Falcon Crest" and "Wichita Town."

Cesar Romero

B: 2/15/1907
D: 1/1/1994

Tall, Dark and Handsome was the title of one of his early films and best describes the essential screen image of Cesar Romero.

Romero, in a career that spanned over 60 years as a leading man and supporting player, amassed an amazing array of screen portrayals. Whether playing a

Cesar Romero and Tyrone Power on a Latin American goodwill tour.

gangster, Latin lover, rogue, Indian prince, or Frenchman, he had a sophisticated style, charm, and manner that made him a favorite, especially with female moviegoers.

"I've had a long and fruitful career; who could ask for anything more?" Romero said during a 1990 interview with Luis Reyes. "I can't really complain. I was never a superstar in this business. I've always had a good steady position and that's a damn sight more than a lot of them have had that have come and gone."

Cesar Romero was born in New York City to an Italian-born sugar exporter and concert pianist Maria Mantilla. Cesar's grandfather was the great Cuban patriot and writer Jose Marti y Perez (1853–1895).

Romero started his career in show business in 1927 as a ballroom dancer in New York theaters and nightclubs, where he generated much attention with fancy footwork and dark good looks. He later began working as an actor in the legitimate theater and soon replaced an actor in a leading role in a touring production of *Strictly Dishonorable,* which led him to other stage work and inevitably to Hollywood.

In 1934, the young actor made his film debut with a small role in *The Thin Man,* with William Powell at MGM. He followed this with a leading role in *British Agent* (1934) at Warner Bros. and then *Clive of India* (1935) with Ronald Colman. At Universal, he did *Love Before Breakfast* (1936), opposite Carole Lombard.

He signed a long-term contract in 1937 with Twentieth Century–Fox and appeared in such films as *Wee Willie Winkie* (1937), *The Little Princess* (1939), *Frontier Marshall* (1939), and *Coney Island* (1943). During this time, Cesar became the first Hispanic American actor to portray the Cisco Kid in a series of popular films at Fox.

In the 1940s, he was cast in a series of musicals opposite such actresses as Betty Grable, Alice Faye, and Carmen Miranda. These films included *The Great American Broadcast* (1941), *Dance Hall* (1941), *Weekend in Havana* (1941), *Springtime in the Rockies* (1942), *Wintertime* (1943), and *Tales of Manhattan* (1942).

World War II interrupted his career, and he joined the U.S. Coast Guard. He returned from the service in 1946 and made *Carnival in Costa Rica* (1947).

In 1946, Fox sent Romero and Tyrone Power on a goodwill tour of South America. Romero's fluency in Spanish came in handy, and the tour was a resounding success. They were greeted officially in every Latin American country they visited and were mobbed by fans everywhere.

One of his best roles (his own personal favorite) came in 1947 in the film *Captain from Castile,* as the conquistador Hernando Cortez, a role that allowed Romero the rare opportunity to showcase his talent as a mature actor in a bravura performance that suggested the vigor, fire, and complexity of the legendary Spanish conquistador.

Romero's Fox contract came to an end in 1950, which coincided with the early days of television. He immediately went to work in the new medium in a variety of roles in comedies, dramas, and westerns. He starred in his own TV series, "Passport to Danger," and made guest appearances on most of the popular television series over the years, including "Bonanza" and "Zorro." The veteran actor's best-known and best-loved television role was as the comic villain the Joker on the "Batman" series of the mid-1960s. He appeared in a recurring role as Greek shipping magnate Nick Stavros in the long-running series "Falcon Crest" opposite Jane Wyman for several seasons, alternating easily between film and television.

During the 1950s as a freelance actor, Romero appeared in such films as *Vera Cruz* (1954) opposite Burt Lancaster and Gary Cooper, *The Americano* (1955) opposite Glenn Ford, *The Racers* (1955) opposite Kirk Douglas, and the all-star *Around the World in 80 Days* (1956).

Cesar Romero.

His later film credits include *Ocean's Eleven* (1960), *Donovan's Reef* (1963), *The Castillan* (1963), *Two on a Guillotine* (1965), *Marriage on the Rocks* (1965), *Batman* (1966), *Skidoo* (1969), *The Computer Wore Tennis Shoes* (1969), *The Strongest Man in the World* (1975), *Won Ton Ton, the Dog Who Saved Hollywood* (1976), and *Lust in the Dust* (1985).

Romero was a romantic symbol to several generations of moviegoers and television watchers. In a business where long-lasting popularity is difficult to achieve, Romero continued working in films and television throughout his life. In 1992, Romero celebrated his eighty-fifth birthday and appeared as a guest star along with Mickey Rooney on an episode of the TV series "Jack's Place" starring Hal Linden. Romero died on January 1, 1994.

George A. Romero
B: 1940

A screenwriter, director, and producer, Romero has been one of America's most distinctive and original regional moviemakers since 1969, when he made his explosive debut with the low-budget horror classic *Night of the Living Dead*. From his adopted home base in Pittsburgh, Romero has consistently explored the dark underside of uniquely American subjects.

The most conspicuous example, before *The Dark Half* (1993), is probably *Dawn of the Dead*, the 1979 sequel in which the zombies of *Night* gather for a flesh-eating orgy in an enormous suburban shopping center.

Raised in the Bronx, New York, Romero left home in the 1950s to enroll in the drama department of prestigious Carnegie-Mellon University in Pittsburgh. After graduation, he founded a film production company and quickly became the leading local producer of commercials, reeling in high-profile Pittsburgh-based clients like Calgon, Alcoa, and U.S. Steel.

His other films include *Martin* (1977), *Knightriders* (1981), *Creepshow* (1982), *Day of the Dead* (1985), *Monkey Shines: An Experiment in Fear* (1988), and *Two Evil Eyes* (1991).

Ned Romero

A Louisiana-born actor, Romero is known for the many Native American roles he plays in films and television. He played Burt Reynolds's Hispanic detective partner in the TV series "Dan August" in 1970.

Thomas Rosales, Jr.

A stuntman and actor, Rosales has worked in countless motion pictures and television shows from 1977 until the present. His film credits include *Walk Proud* (1979), *Hunter* (1980), *Commando* (1985), *The Bedroom Window* (1987), *Extreme Prejudice* (1987), *Kindergarten Cop* (1990), and *American Me* (1992), to name just a few.

Bert Rosario
B: 11/7/1945

A Puerto Rican character actor, Rosario has a long list of television credits and feature films. His films include Blake Edwards's *S.O.B.* (1981), *Who's That Girl* (1987), and *Stick* (1985) starring Burt Reynolds. Rosario co-starred in the television series "Sword of Justice," "A.K.A. Pablo," and "Black Jack Savage." Among his guest starring appearances are roles on such episodic series as "Baretta," "Murder, She Wrote," "Hill Street Blues," "Paradise," and "Knight Rider."

Raul Roulien
B: 10/8/1905

A Brazilian-born actor and singer, Roulien appeared in such films as *Delicious* with Janet Gaynor at Fox in 1931 and in *Flying Down to Rio* at RKO in 1933 with Dolores Del Rio. He also appeared in various Spanish-language productions at Fox during the 1930s and 1940s. Roulien was a popular entertainer who performed on the stage in his native Brazil and all over South America.

Mercedes Ruehl

An Academy Award–winning actress in the supporting category for *The Fisher King* (1991), Ruehl first gained attention for her role as a Mafia wife in the film *Married to the Mob* (1988). She won a Tony Award on Broadway in 1991 for Neil Simon's *Lost in Yonkers* in the role of Aunt Bella, which she reprised in the 1993 film version. She is of Spanish-Irish descent.

Jose Luis Ruiz

A producer and director in the film and television industry since 1970, Ruiz's television programs have garnered 11 Emmy nominations and 4 Emmy Awards. He has been most recognized for his documentary films and his articulation of a vision for institutionalizing a Latino presence in television. Ruiz is currently director of the National Latino Communications Center, headquartered in Los Angeles, which is a media arts and production center and provider of Latino programming to public television.

Juan Ruiz Anchia

B: 1949

A Spanish-born cinematographer, Ruiz Anchia graduated from the Escuela Oficial Cinematografia in 1972 and from the American Film Institute in 1981. His credits as a cinematographer on U.S. films include *Reborn* (1978), *That Was Then . . . This Is Now* (1985), *The Stone Boy* (1984), *Maria's Lovers* (1984), and *At Close Range* (1986). Ruiz Anchia worked with writer/director David Mamet on two theatrical features, *House of Games* (1987) and *Things Change* (1988).

Andy Russell [born: Andres Robago]

B: 9/16/1919
D: 4/16/1992

Born in East Los Angeles, Russell became a crooner of the 1940s and popularized such classic songs as "Besame Mucho" and "What a Difference a Day Makes." He made several musical film appearances as himself, in such films as *The Stork Club* (1945), *Breakfast in Hollywood* (1946), and *Copacabana* (1947).

Theresa Saldana

Of part Hispanic extraction, Saldana was adopted at five days old and raised by an Italian American couple in Brooklyn. Her feature film credits include *I Wanna Hold Your Hand* (1978), *Defiance* (1980), *Raging Bull* (1980), *The Evil That Men Do* (1984), and *Angel Town* (1989). She co-stars on the ABC television series "The Commish" and has made numerous episodic series guest appearances. Saldana starred as herself in the TV movie *Victims for Victims: The Theresa Saldana Story* (1984).

Jaime Sanchez

B: 12/19/1938

This Puerto Rican–born actor is best known for his portrayal of Angel, an idealistic Mexican member of the group known as the Wild Bunch in Sam Peckinpah's *The Wild Bunch* (1969). He made his film debut in *David and Lisa* (1963) and had an important co-starring role as Jesus Ortiz in Sidney Lumet's *The Pawnbroker* (1965), for which he won a Screen World Award and the Laurel Award. His other film credits include *Beach Red* (1967) and *Bobby Deerfield* (1977). Sanchez began his show business career in his native Puerto Rico at age 14 as a radio actor on local island stations. He came to the States and got his first big break in the smash Broadway production of *West Side Story* in the role of Chino.

Mark Sanchez

B: 1955

A Los Angeles–born makeup artist, Sanchez began his career as an assistant on the television series "Sanford and Son" and on "Chico and the Man" (1976–1978). He also worked on "The Tonight Show Starring Johnny Carson" from 1976 to 1986. Sanchez won an Emmy Award for his makeup work on "The Joan Rivers Show" in 1992. Sanchez's artistry has been featured on many television specials, dramatic series, sitcoms, and daytime soap operas.

Miguel Sandoval

B: 1/16/1951

A New Mexico–born actor, Sandoval has appeared in *Repo Man* (1984), *Walker* (1987), *Ricochet* (1991), and *Jurassic Park* (1993).

Bel Sandre [aka: Bel Hernandez]

B: 12/20/1956

A Mexican American actress, Sandre was featured in *Losin' It* (1983) and *Colors* (1988). On television she was featured in the PBS "American Playhouse" presentation *La Carpa* (1993) and in the miniseries *The Alamo: 13 Days to Glory* (1987).

Olga San Juan

B: 3/18/1927

A contract player for a short time at Paramount Pictures during the mid-1940s, San Juan, at age 18, co-starred in *Blue Skies* (1946) with Bing Crosby and Fred Astaire. In the film, she and Fred Astaire performed "Heat Wave," a torrid dance number that remains a classic.

She was born in Brooklyn, New York, the oldest daughter of Puerto Rican parents, Mercedes and Luis San Juan. The family moved to Puerto Rico when she was three years old and later returned to New York. There she started to establish a reputation as a teenage nightclub performer, appearing at many important clubs of the period, including El Morocco, the Copacabana, and the Astor Hotel. While San Juan was featured on a radio show, a Paramount scout had her screen tested in New York. She flew to Hollywood, where, because of her age, she found herself attending school with such starlets as Mona Freeman and Gail Russell.

Olga San Juan and Fred Astaire in *Blue Skies*.

San Juan made her film debut in *Rainbow Island* (1944) opposite Dorothy Lamour and appeared as a blonde in Paramount's all-star *Variety Girl* (1947). She later went to Universal to star with Ava Gardner and Dick Haymes in *One Touch of Venus* (1948). She found success on Broadway in Lerner and Loewe's musical *Paint Your Wagon* (1951).

She retired from active involvement in the industry when she married actor Edmond O'Brien and raised three children.

Emily Santiago [alternate spelling: Emile; born: Emily Richardson]
B: 1902

Santiago shared with Charles LeMaire an Academy Award for costume design for the biblical motion picture *The Robe* (1953), starring Victor Mature and Richard Burton, the first movie filmed in CinemaScope. She specialized in period costumes for the stars. Beginning in 1928, she worked for 18 years at Hollywood's Western Costume house and then decided to go to work for various studios. Her film credits include *Wells Fargo* (1937), *The Prince and the Pauper* (1937), *The Adventures of Robin Hood* (1938), *One Million B.C.* (1940), *Quo Vadis* (1951), and *Strange Lady in Town* (1955). Santiago provided many costume sketches for Cecil B. DeMille. She was born in Bloomburg, Pennsylvania, and she married Santiago, a construction engineer, in 1923.

Reni Santoni
B: 4/21/1940

Born in New York of a Corsican father and a Spanish mother, Santoni was raised in a Puerto Rican neighborhood in the Bronx. He made his major film bow starring in 1967's *Enter Laughing*. He has also appeared in *Anzio* (1968), *Dirty Harry* (1971), *I Never Promised You a Rose Garden* (1977), *Dead Men Don't Wear Plaid* (1982), and *Bad Boys* (1983). He has numerous television guest star credits including "Life Goes On," "Owen Marshall, Counselor at Law," and "The Senator." He starred in the USA cable channel comedy series "Sanchez of Bel Air."

Joe Santos
B: 6/9/1933

Brooklyn-born of Italian and Puerto Rican parents, Santos began his acting career while in his mid-30s after years of odd jobs and traveling between the United States and the Caribbean. Accompanying a friend to an audition in Brooklyn, he was asked to read for the part of a boxer and was cast in the role.

Santos is a character actor best known for his work on television in the long-running series "The Rockford Files" and many guest appearances on such shows as "Police Story" and "Magnum, P.I." Among his many feature film credits are roles in *Blue Thunder* (1983), *The Detective* (1985), *Shamus* (1973), *The Gang That Couldn't Shoot Straight* (1971), *Revenge* (1990), and *Mo' Money* (1992).

John Saxon [born: Carmen Orrico]
B: 11/5/1935

Born in Brooklyn, New York, the son of Italian immigrants, Saxon has endured as a successful and versatile film and television actor since the mid-1950s. He has played ethnics, "half-breeds," and Mexican bandits in a number of films, including *Cry Tough* (1959), as Puerto Rican Miguel Estrada; *The Plunderers* (1960), as Rondo, a young Mexican *vaquero*; *The Unforgiven* (1960), as half-breed Johnny Portugal; *The Appaloosa* (1966), as Chuy, a Mexican bandit; and *Joe Kidd* (1972), as Luis Chama. His other film credits include *Enter the Dragon* (1973), *The Electric Horseman* (1979), *Wrong Is Right* (1982), and *Nightmare on Elm Street* (1984).

Lalo Schifrin

B: 6/21/1932

An outstanding Argentinian-born composer and jazz musician with more than 60 feature film scores and television series themes to his credit, Schifrin is also a six-time Oscar-nominated composer, for the films *Cool Hand Luke* (1967), *The Fox* (1968), *Voyage of the Damned* (1976), *The Amityville Horror* (1979), *The Competition* (1980), and *The Sting II* (1983). He also scored such films as *Dirty Harry* (1971), *Magnum Force* (1973), *Bullitt* (1968), *The Cincinnati Kid* (1965), and *The Mean Season* (1985).

Schifrin was born in Buenos Aires, where his father was a concert master for the Buenos Aires Symphony. He developed a strong interest in American jazz, and he became a film buff at age 16. He studied at the Paris Conservatory of Music, where he met famed jazz musician Dizzy Gillespie, who was so impressed with the young man's talents that he helped Schifrin to enter the United States. He worked as a pianist for Gillespie for over two years, and then he secured a job at Universal Television. As a composer he is best known for his theme for the "Mission: Impossible" TV series, among many other memorable scores.

Pepe Serna

B: 7/23/1944

A talented supporting character actor, Serna usually portrays a sort of "modern Chicano everyman." His career encompasses the early prerequisite gang-tough roles to more recent diverse portrayals. Movie audiences will best remember Serna as Al Pacino's Cuban refugee buddy who meets an untimely demise from a chainsaw in Brian De Palma's *Scarface* (1983).

Pepe Serna.

Born in Corpus Christi, Texas, Serna got his start in films at a casting audition, where the legendary producer Hal Wallis was so impressed with the young actor's talent that he offered him an important role in the film *Red Sky at Morning* (1971). Soon, Serna found himself acting opposite such stars as Gregory Peck in *Shootout* (1971) and Karen Black in *Day of the Locust* (1975).

His credits include *Deal of the Century* (1983), as an illegal arms dealer; *The Adventures of Buckaroo Banzai* (1984), a science fiction cult classic in which he portrayed Reno, a member of Buckaroo's elite squad; *Red Dawn* (1984), as the patriotic father of one of the rebellious boys; Lawrence Kasdan's super-western *Silverado* (1985), as Scruffy, a hired gun; Clint Eastwood's *The Rookie* (1990), as Eastwood's police superior; and *Postcards from the Edge* (1990), as a revolutionary. The actor received critical acclaim for his portrayal of Atif, Egyptian president Sadat's brother, opposite Lou Gossett, Jr., in the television miniseries *Sadat* (1983). He has had the distinction of appearing in four PBS "American Playhouse" presentations: *Seguin* (1982), *The Ballad of Gregorio Cortez* (1983), *Break of Dawn* (1989), and *Hot Summer Wind* (1991). Among his feature film credits are *Johnny Got His Gun* (1971), *Car Wash* (1976), *A Force of One* (1979), *Walk Proud* (1979), *Honeysuckle Rose* (1980), *Inside Moves* (1980), *Vice Squad* (1982), and *American Me* (1992).

Carmen Sevilla

B: 1930

One of Spain's leading actresses of the 1960s, Sevilla was featured in Samuel Bronston's *King of Kings* (1961) as Mary Magdalene, and in *Spanish Affair* (1958).

Carmen Sevilla, known as the First Lady of the Screen in Spain, as Mary Magdalene in *King of Kings*.

Charlie Sheen.

Charlie Sheen [born: Carlos Irwin Estevez]

B: 9/3/1966

Since his first starring role in 1984's *Red Dawn,* Charlie Sheen has seen his career skyrocket through a succession of motion pictures including *Lucas* (1986), *The Wraith* (1986), and the film that established him as a major talent, the Academy Award–winning *Platoon* (1986), directed by Oliver Stone. His performance as the young soldier helped define the Vietnam War experience for the generation of the 1980s, as his father Martin Sheen previously had in the 1970s with his portrayal of Captain Willard in Francis Ford Coppola's *Apocalypse Now* (1979).

Born in New York and raised in California along the shores of Malibu, Charlie Sheen spent his childhood alternating between sports, making super-8 movies, and going on location shoots with his father. He made his acting debut at age nine in the haunting TV movie *The Execution of Private Slovik* (1974), which starred his father. But eight years passed before he played his second role, in the 1982 film *Grizzly II.*

Eight months in the Philippines with his father during the filming of *Apocalypse Now* provided a lasting impression that made him decide to pursue acting and working in films. After *Platoon,* Sheen starred as Bud Fox, a young stockbroker, in Oliver Stone's *Wall Street* (1987). Martin Sheen played his father in the movie, and they worked in several scenes together. His other feature film credits include *No Man's Land* (1987); *Three for the Road* (1987); *Young Guns* (1988), in which he played opposite his brother Emilio Estevez; *Eight Men Out* (1988), in which he played a young baseball player; *Major League* (1990), as another baseball player; *The Rookie* (1990) with Clint Eastwood; *Men at Work* (1990), which co-starred and was directed by Emilio Estevez; and *Cadence* (1991), which co-starred and was directed by Martin Sheen. Charlie has also made cameo appearances in Emilio Estevez's *Wisdom* (1986) and *Ferris Bueller's Day Off* (1986).

More recent roles include leads in the spoofs *Hot Shots!* (1991) and its sequel, *Hot Shots! Part Deux* (1993), and *The Chase* (1994).

Martin Sheen [born: Ramon Estevez]
B: 8/3/1941

A well-respected, critically acclaimed actor, Sheen has starred in such major motion pictures as *Apocalypse Now* (1979), *Badlands* (1974), and *Gandhi* (1982), but hasn't really achieved real star status or box-office clout.

Born in Dayton, Ohio, Sheen is the seventh son of 10 children born to his Irish mother and Spanish father. As soon as he graduated from high school, he left for New York to begin his training at the Off-Off Broadway Living Theater. He changed

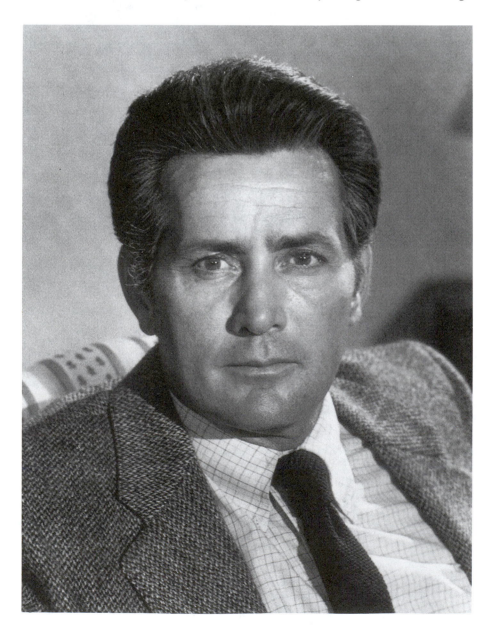

Martin Sheen is Captain Hollister in *Firestarter*.

his given name at the beginning of his career when he discovered that New York casting directors had difficulty pronouncing it. "I looked Irish," he recollects, "so I thought of Bishop Sheen. Martin? It went with Sheen."

After making his Off-Broadway debut in *The Connection* (1959) and his Broadway bow in the short-lived *Never Live Over a Pretzel Factory* (1964), Sheen starred as a returning Army veteran confronted by his parents' personal war in the Pulitzer Prize–winning play *The Subject Was Roses* (1964). That led to his film debut as one of a pair of punks terrorizing subway passengers in the 1967 film *The Incident.*

In 1968, he reprised his role in the film version of *The Subject Was Roses* opposite Patricia Neal and Jack Albertson for MGM. He went on to appear in such films as *Catch-22* (1970), *No Drums, No Bugles* (1971), and *Rage* (1972). He stunned critics and filmgoers with his work in Terrence Malick's *Badlands,* in which he performed opposite Sissy Spacek as a roving youngster on a killing spree. Sheen was named Best Actor at the San Sebastian Film Festival for his work in the film.

He won the pivotal role of Captain Willard, an Army captain sent on a secret military operation at the height of the Vietnam conflict, in Francis Ford Coppola's classic *Apocalypse Now.* Since then, Sheen has alternated between television and motion pictures, winning special praise for his moving work in the 1974 TV movie *The Execution of Private Slovik.* He also scored on television as JFK in *Kennedy* (1983), as RFK in *Missiles of October* (1974), as John Dean in *Blind Ambition* (1979), and as the star of *The Atlanta Child Murders* (1985).

Sheen's other film credits include *Pickup on 101* (1972), *The Cassandra Crossing* (1977), *Eagle's Wing* (1979), *In the King of Prussia* (1982), *That Championship Season* (1982), *The Dead Zone* (1983), *Man, Woman and Child* (1983), *Firestarter* (1984), *A State of Emergency* (1986), *Wall Street* (1987), *Beyond the Stars* (1989), and *Gettysburg* (1993). He played an American journalist who reports on the activities of the religious and spiritual leader of India in Richard Attenborough's *Gandhi* (1982), starred in John Schlesinger's *The Believers* (1987), and made his motion picture directing debut with the film *Cadence* (1989), in which he and his son Charlie Sheen both appeared.

Gregory Sierra
B: 1/25/1937

Born and raised in New York City, Sierra began his career as a singer while in the Air Force. Sierra's first professional appearance was with the prestigious National Shakespeare Company, with whom he performed *Macbeth* and *The Taming of the Shrew.*

In 1969, after nearly 10 years of working exclusively in New York theater, Sierra relocated to California to break into films and television. His transition to the West Coast proved beneficial, as he soon landed a role on "The Flying Nun" TV series starring Sally Field. Sierra went on to appear in numerous television shows, including a recurring role as Julio Fuentes, Fred Sanford's Puerto Rican neighbor, on "Sanford and Son," and as a series regular on "Barney Miller" as Detective Chano. He starred in his own short-lived series, "A.E.S. Hudson Street," and today makes regular guest appearances on episodic television series. His feature film credits include *The Wrath of God* (1972), *The Towering Inferno* (1974), and *The Prisoner of Zenda* (1979) with Peter Sellers.

Geno Silva

Silva is a New Mexico–born character actor seen in *The Cheyenne Social Club* (1970) with James Stewart and Henry Fonda, Steven Spielberg's *1941* (1979), Brian De Palma's *Scarface* (1983), Blake Edwards's *Sunset* (1988), and Robert Towne's *Tequila Sunrise* (1988). His many episodic television guest appearances include "Murder, She Wrote," "Miami Vice," "Hunter," and "Simon and Simon."

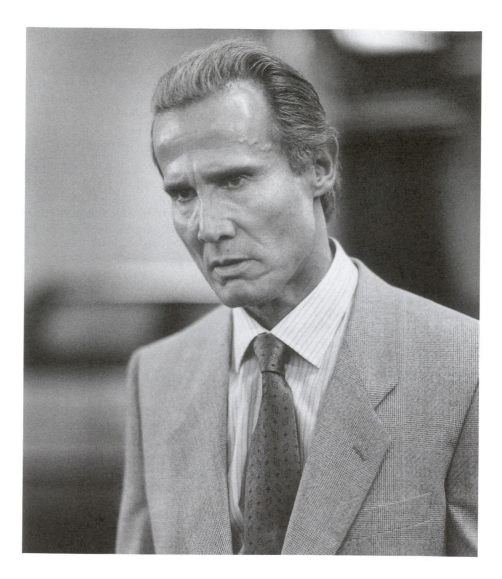

Henry Silva

B: 1927

Henry Silva has carved out a career playing a variety of villainous characters in a number of films, including *The Bravados* (1958), *Green Mansions* (1959), *The Manchurian Candidate* (1962), and *Sharkey's Machine* (1982). He has menaced such movie tough guys as Burt Reynolds, Gregory Peck, Chuck Norris, and Frank Sinatra.

Born in Brooklyn, New York, of Italian–Puerto Rican parents, Silva left home at age 13 to pursue his acting dreams. A variety of jobs eventually introduced Silva to a group of actors who sent him to study acting at the Harris and Lewis School. He auditioned for the Actors Studio, and when that company's production of *A Hatful of Rain* went to Broadway in 1956, Silva went with it and was nominated for a Tony Award for his role of Mother, a drug dealer.

He made his film debut in 1952's *Viva Zapata!* and has appeared in such films as *The Law and Jake Wade* (1958), *The Last of the Fast Guns* (1958), *Ocean's Eleven* (1960), *Sergeants 3* (1962), *A Gathering of Eagles* (1963), *The Hills Run Red* (1967), *The Italian Connection* (1973), *Buck Rogers in the 25th Century* (1979), *Wrong Is Right* (1982), and *Megaforce* (1982). Silva starred in *Johnny Cool* (1963), a film about a young Sicilian mobster that has attained cult status through the years. *Above the Law* (1989) and *Dick Tracy* (1990) are his most recent screen credits.

Trinidad Silva

B: 1950
D: 7/31/1988

A diminutive, charismatic character actor, Silva appeared in supporting roles in a number of films in the late 1970s and throughout the 1980s until his untimely death. He was born in Mission, Texas, and grew up in the Rio Grande valley. In his teens, Silva drifted to Los Angeles, where he met a hometown friend who was working as an actor. Silva visited him on the set of Tom Laughlin's *The Master Gunfighter* (1975) and was immediately hired as an extra. That marked the beginning of a promising career that was cut short by a drunk driver who killed Silva on impact.

Silva made his film debut in a major role in *Alambrista!* (1978), Robert M. Young's feature about the exploitation of illegal Mexican immigrants. He had roles in *Walk Proud* (1979), a story of urban youth gang rivalry, as Dagger; in *El Norte* (1983) as a friendly illegal; and in *Crackers* (1984), a caper film directed by Louis Malle and starring Donald Sutherland. He received good notices for his role as the older streetwise gang member Frog in *Colors* (1988), starring Robert Duvall and Sean Penn.

On television, Silva was featured in a recurring role as gang member Jesus Martinez on the critically acclaimed, Emmy Award–winning "Hill Street Blues" cop series.

Frank Silvera

B: 7/24/1917
D: 6/11/1970

A character player on stage, screen, and television, Silvera worked for over two decades with scarcely anyone realizing he was a black man. The actor recalled in

Frank Silvera as a Mexican bandit in a scene from *Hombre*.

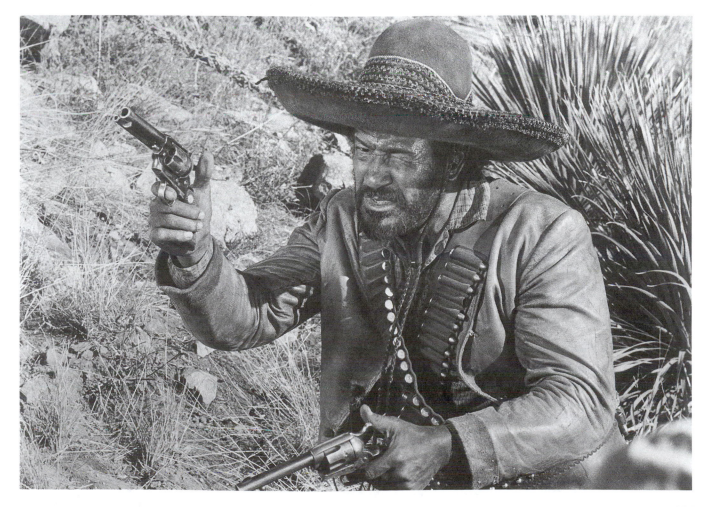

an interview, "I didn't hide it, I simply made no point of it. I agreed with my agent that I wanted to realize myself as an actor, per se, not a negro actor. In my profession, the word negro meant death." Because of the lack of diverse roles available to black actors, "unless one wanted to play servants or slaves for the rest of a career," he continued, "I was accepted as a Latin, [and] I let it go at that," Cecil Smith, *L.A. Times* (10/2/66).

He played a Mexican general in *Viva Zapata!* (1952), a Portuguese policeman in *The Miracle of Our Lady of Fatima* (1952), a Chinese general in *The Mountain Road* (1960), a Tahitian chieftain in the 1962 version of *Mutiny on the Bounty*, and a Mexican outlaw with a surprising wit in *Hombre* (1967).

Silvera was born in Kingston, Jamaica, the son of a Spanish Jewish father and a Jamaican mother. He was raised in Boston and originally intended to become a lawyer, studying for two years at Northwestern University. But his secret desire to act took hold, and he eventually turned to drama studies at Boston University.

Silvera appeared in the first two movies directed by Stanley Kubrick, *Fear and Desire* (1953) and *Killer's Kiss* (1955). Among his other film credits are *Heller in Pink Tights* (1960), *Key Witness* (1960), *The Appaloosa* (1966), *The St. Valentine's Day Massacre* (1967), *Uptight* (1968), *Guns of the Magnificent Seven* (1969), and *Valdez Is Coming* (1971). He achieved great success on television with his role of Don Sebastian Montoya in the popular western series "The High Chaparral." With the success he achieved Silvera was able to organize a black actors' workshop, a place where black actors and writers were free to develop their talents. He died unexpectedly in Los Angeles in a freak electrical accident at his home.

Jimmy Smits
B: 7/9/1955

Jimmy Smits is best known for his role as the idealistic young Hispanic attorney Victor Sifuentes on the popular, long-running television series "L.A. Law," though he made a bid for screen stardom in the role of the fiery young Mexican general Arroyo in the epic *Old Gringo* (1989) co-starring Jane Fonda and Gregory Peck. "The role of Victor Sifuentes was so appealing to me as a chance to establish an alternative image of Hispanics in the U.S.," he remarked during a 1993 interview with Luis Reyes.

An education major at Brooklyn College, he studied drama and the classics and went on to earn an MFA degree from Cornell University. Smits is at home on stage, in films, and on television. He has appeared Off-Broadway and with the New York Shakespeare Festival under the direction of Joseph Papp.

Smits made his major film debut as a crime czar in *Running Scared* (1986) opposite Billy Crystal and Gregory Hines. He was a police detective gripped with the fear of voodoo in John Schlesinger's *The Believers* (1987) with Martin Sheen. His most recent film credit is Blake Edwards's *Switch* (1991) in a change-of-pace role as a young advertising executive. Smits guest starred on such shows as "Spenser: For Hire" and "Miami Vice." He played the title role in Luis Valdez's *The Cisco Kid* (1994), for cable television's TNT.

Luis Soto

A Puerto Rican–born, New York–raised television director, Soto has worked on such episodic series as "The Equalizer" and "Miami Vice."

Richard Soto

An award-winning producer with extensive credits in public television, Soto began his career as a documentary filmmaker. He produced two acclaimed episodes for the PBS "WonderWorks" series, *Maricela* and *Sweet 15*, which won an Emmy Award.

He was associate producer as well as supervising film editor of the film *The Ballad of Gregorio Cortez* (1983).

Talisa Soto

A Brooklyn-born Puerto Rican fashion model turned actress, Soto co-starred as Lupe Lamora, a James Bond girl in *Licence to Kill* (1989). She was also featured in *The Mambo Kings* (1992). She made her film debut in *Spike of Bensonhurst* (1988) as India, a Puerto Rican girl who falls in love with an aspiring Italian boxer.

Charles Stevens

B: 1893
D: 8/22/1964

A character actor, Stevens specialized in villainous character roles, usually as an Indian or a Latin. He worked in Hollywood from the silent era through talkies and television. His father was a Welshman who turned lawman, and his mother, a Mexican Indian named Eloisa, was a daughter of the Apache warrior Geronimo. Stevens was born in Arizona and was a great friend of Douglas Fairbanks, Sr., appearing in all of his films, including *The Mark of Zorro* (1940). He played Spanish Ed in *The Virginian* (1929) opposite Gary Cooper and Diabolito in *Ambush* (1949). His last film credit was *Sergeants 3* (1962), opposite Frank Sinatra.

Madeleine Stowe

B: 1964

The daughter of a Costa Rican mother and an American father, Stowe was born in Los Angeles. She played the daughter of an English officer in Michael Mann's *The Last of the Mohicans* (1992) and a Latin American woman in *Revenge* (1990) opposite Kevin Costner. Stowe made her film debut as a Hispanic American woman, Maria McGuire, in *Stakeout* (1987) starring Richard Dreyfuss and Emilio Estevez. She has also acted in *The Two Jakes* (1990) opposite Jack Nicholson; *Unlawful Entry* (1992), a thriller co-starring Kurt Russell; *Short Cuts* (1993), directed by Robert Altman; *Blink* (1994), a thriller co-starring Aidan Quinn; and *China Moon* (1994), with Ed Harris. She was in the television miniseries *Blood & Orchids* (1986).

Miguelangel Suarez

A Puerto Rican–born actor, Suarez co-starred as Jesus Ramirez, a prison convict, in the 1980 hit comedy *Stir Crazy,* opposite Richard Pryor and Gene Wilder. His other motion picture credits include featured roles in *Che!* (1969) and Woody Allen's *Bananas* (1971). On television he starred in the PBS series "Mundo Real."

Carlos Thompson

B: 6/7/1923
D: 10/10/1990

A tall, green-eyed Argentine-born actor, Thompson starred in several major films during the 1950s. Born a blond, Thompson's hair was dyed dark for his U.S. film roles, which were usually villains or the second romantic lead. He spent his formative years in New York, and his boyhood ambition was to become a novelist. His father was a newspaper editor and a Latin American correspondent for CBS Radio. He returned to Argentina to attend the University of Buenos Aires, and there he was introduced to a movie producer who urged him to try acting.

Thompson's acting studies led to a top role in an Argentine film, *Men of Tomorrow,* which resulted in his securing the role of Armand in the Argentine version of

Camille. Both he and the film were popular successes throughout Latin America in 1952. That same year, he met American actress Yvonne De Carlo at the Uruguay Film Festival, and she convinced him to come to the United States, where he co-starred with De Carlo in *Fort Algiers* in 1953. MGM offered him a contract, and he co-starred with Lana Turner as a young Italian in *Flame and the Flesh* (1954) and with Robert Taylor in the adventure/drama *Valley of the Kings* (1954). In 1958 he co-starred with Jeff Chandler and Esther Williams in *Raw Wind in Eden.*

Rachel Ticotin

B: 11/1/1958

Rachel Ticotin made her film debut in *Fort Apache, The Bronx* (1981), starring Paul Newman, in the role of a heroin-addicted nurse with whom Newman falls in love. The actress also starred as Melina the mystery woman with Arnold Schwarzenegger in *Total Recall* (1990) and as a policewoman in *Falling Down* (1993) with Michael Douglas. She starred with Bryan Brown in *F/X 2: The Deadly Art of Illusion* (1991) and in *Critical Condition* (1986) with Richard Pryor.

Born in New York of Dominican parents, Ticotin is one of six children. She attended the High School of Music and Art and the Professional Children's School. As a teenager she joined the Ballet Hispanico of New York. She began to work in motion pictures as a production assistant on *The Wanderers* (1979), *Dressed to Kill* (1980), and *Raging Bull* (1980). On television she appeared as a regular on the series "For Love and Honor," "Ohara," and "Crime and Punishment."

Edwin Torres

B: 1930

New York State Supreme Court Justice Edwin Torres is the author of the novel *Carlito's Way* and its sequel, *After Hours,* both of which formed the basis for the feature film *Carlito's Way* (1993), starring Al Pacino. Another of his novels was adapted for Sidney Lumet's film *Q & A* (1990).

Born and raised in New York's Spanish Harlem, Torres studied for the bar at City College of New York and Brooklyn Law School, becoming the city's first assistant district attorney of Puerto Rican descent. From 1961 to 1977, he was in private practice, defending indigent clients without fee. He was elevated to the post of judge of the criminal court in 1977.

In 1979 he was named an acting justice of the New York State Supreme Court, and became a fully elected justice the following year.

Liz Torres

A Puerto Rican actress/comedienne, Torres was featured on television's "All in the Family" and co-starred on the popular television series "Phyllis" and on "The John Larroquette Show." Torres has guest starred on many episodic series.

Raquel Torres [born: Paula Marie Osterman]

B: 11/11/1908
D: 8/10/1987

A dark-haired Mexican-born actress, Torres starred in a number of early sound films through the early 1930s.

She was born in Hermosillo, Mexico, and moved with her parents to Los Angeles and studied at a convent. At age 19 she was chosen to co-star in W.S. Van Dyke's *White Shadows in the South Seas,* a 1928 MGM release that was the studio's first feature with fully synchronized dialogue, music, and effects. She played Pepita

Raquel Torres.

in *The Bridge of San Luis Rey* (1929) and was in *The Desert Rider* (1929, silent). She also appeared in *The Sea Bat* (1930), *Under a Texas Moon* (1930), *Aloha* (1931), *Duck Soup* (1933), *So This Is Africa* (1933), and *The Woman I Stole* (1933). After a British feature, *The Red Wagon,* in 1934, she retired from the screen, but later made an occasional film appearance, as in *Tampico* (1944).

Jose Torvay
B: 2/18/1910

A Mexican-born character actor, Torvay worked in both Mexican films and Hollywood films shot in Mexico. His credits include *The Fugitive* (1947), *The Treasure of the Sierra Madre* (1948), *Border Incident* (1949), *Borderline* (1950), and *Untamed* (1955).

Lupita Tovar
B: 1915

A Mexican-born actress, Tovar starred in the first Mexican sound film, *Santa* (1932). She came to Hollywood in 1931 and starred in many of the Spanish-language films produced in Hollywood, including the 1931 Universal Pictures Spanish version of *Dracula, The Cat Creeps* (1930), and *The King of Jazz* (1930), produced by Paul Kohner, who at that time was a young, ambitious producer and later became a noted talent agent. He and Lupita were married a few years later. She appeared in numerous films throughout the 1930s and 1940s, including *East of Borneo* (1931), *Yankee Don* (1931), *Border Law* (1931), *Mr. Robinson Crusoe* (1932), *The Fighting Gringo* (1939), *South of the Border* (1939), and *The Westerner* (1940).

Bill Travilla

> B: 1923
> D: 11/2/1990

An Academy Award–winning fashion designer, Travilla was under contract at Warner Bros. and then Twentieth Century–Fox, where he designed costumes for the studio's most important films. Travilla was born in Avalon, Santa Catalina, an island 25 miles off the southern California coast. Travilla worked on 11 films with Marilyn Monroe; costumed *Viva Zapata!* (1952), with Marlon Brando; and worked on TV's "The Loretta Young Show." With Leah Rhodes and Marjorie Best, he won the Academy Award in 1949 for Best Costume Design for *The Adventures of Don Juan,* starring Errol Flynn. Travilla is known for his classic, glamorous designs for women and men of the Hollywood period of the 1930s, 1940s, and 1950s. His best-known creation is the white chiffon dress worn by Marilyn Monroe in *The Seven Year Itch* (1955).

In the 1980s Travilla worked for television, winning Emmy Awards for his costume designs for the series "Dallas" in 1985 and for the miniseries *Moviola* in 1980. He also designed costumes for such other miniseries as *The Thorn Birds* (1983), *Evita Peron* (1981), *Jacqueline Bouvier Kennedy* (1981), and *My Wicked, Wicked Ways* (1985).

Jesus Trevino

> B: 3/26/1946

A Mexican American director, Trevino began in documentaries at public television station KCET in Los Angeles. He directed the feature film *Raices de Sangre* (Blood Roots) (1979) and the "American Playhouse" presentation of *Seguin* (1982). He won the Directors Guild of America Award for Best Daytime Drama directing for the television film *Gangs* (1988). Trevino directed episodes of the TV series "Gabriel's Fire," "Life Stories," and "NYPD Blue."

Felipe Turich [aka: Felipe Turriche]

> B: 12/5/1898
> D: 3/9/1992

A veteran character player, Turich's film career lasted from the 1930s till the late 1970s. Some of his film credits include *We Were Strangers* (1949), *Crisis* (1950), *The Lawless* (1950), *My Favorite Spy* (1951), *Giant* (1956), *One-Eyed Jacks* (1961), *Hook, Line and Sinker* (1969), and *Walk Proud* (1979).

Rosa Turich

A veteran character actress, Rosa Turich, along with her husband, Felipe, appeared in many westerns at Republic Pictures from 1937 until 1965, usually as a Mexican mamacita or dona. Some of her film credits include *Starlight over Texas* (1938), *Rangers of Fortune* (1940), *Bowery Buckaroos* (1947), *The Loves of Carmen* (1948), *On the Isle of Samoa* (1950), and *Tripoli* (1950).

Natividad Vacio

B: 9/8/1912

Born in El Paso, Texas, Vacio started his career as a teacher and musician. He made his film debut in *The Loves of Carmen* (1948) at Columbia with Rita Hayworth. He has worked in countless motion pictures, including *Branded* (1951), *The Magnificent Seven* (1960), and *The Milagro Beanfield War* (1988).

David Valdes

The executive producer of Clint Eastwood's *Unforgiven* (1992) and *White Hunter, Black Heart* (1990), and *Bird* (1988), Valdes also served as producer of *Pink Cadillac* (1988). He was also producer of *The Dead Pool* (1988), the fifth in the *Dirty Harry* series, and associate producer of *Pale Rider* (1985).

Valdes rose through the ranks of film production, beginning his career with Francis Ford Coppola as an assistant director on *The Outsiders* (1983) and *Rumble Fish* (1983). He then moved to Clint Eastwood's Malpaso Company and worked as first assistant director on *Any Which Way You Can* (1980), *Firefox* (1982), *Sudden Impact* (1983), *City Heat* (1984), and *Tightrope* (1984) before becoming a producer.

Valdes also worked with Brian Grazer, co-producing the feature *Like Father, Like Son* (1987), which followed a co–executive producer assignment with producer/director Francis Ford Coppola on *Gardens of Stone* (1987). He was also associate producer of *Ratboy* (1986), starring and directed by Sondra Locke.

Daniel Valdez

B: 1949

The brother of Luis Valdez, Daniel is an actor, singer, songwriter, and composer and starred as Henry Reyna in the 1981 film *Zoot Suit*. His other film credits include *Which Way Is Up?* (1971), *The China Syndrome* (1979), *La Bamba* (1987), and *Born in East L.A.* (1987). He was an associate producer on *La Bamba*.

Luis Valdez

B: 6/12/1940

Luis Valdez triumphed in Hollywood in 1987 with the motion picture *La Bamba*, which he wrote and directed for Columbia Pictures. The film was one of the biggest box-office successes of that year and made its lead actor, Lou Diamond Phillips, a star. The main title song shot to the top of the charts and, 30 years after its original release, became an international hit once again.

In 1981 Valdez wrote and directed the motion picture version of his hit play *Zoot Suit*, garnering a Golden Globe nomination for Best Musical Picture.

For television he wrote and directed the Christmas fantasy *La Pastorela*, starring Paul Rodriguez and Cheech Marin, for PBS's "Great Performances" series. Valdez adapted his stage play *Corridos! Tales of Passion and Revolution* for PBS. It starred Linda Ronstadt and offered a striking visual history of Mexican folklore and songs, winning acclaim and a George Peabody Award. Valdez directed an unsold series pilot for Warner Bros. Television, *Fort Figueroa*, starring Charles Haid.

Valdez founded El Teatro Campesino (The Farmworkers Theatre) on the strike lines in the fields of Delano, California, during its great grape strike of 1965. He created "actos"—short plays that were performed to dramatize the cause of the farmworkers and urban Chicanos. The Teatro toured these "actos" across the country, garnering for Valdez and the company national attention and acclaim with an Off-Broadway Obie Award in 1969 and the Los Angeles Drama Critics Circle Award in 1969 and 1972. In the course of five major European tours, Valdez and ETC earned international plaudits from the World Theatre Festival in France, the

Festival of Nations in Paris, and numerous other prestigious European festivals. *Zoot Suit*, a play that he wrote and directed, became one of the most critically acclaimed productions ever to originate in Los Angeles. Mounted on the New York stage by the Shubert Organization and the Mark Taper Forum, *Zoot Suit* became the first play by a Chicano playwright to be presented on Broadway. His latest play, *I Don't Have to Show You No Stinking Badges,* completed a successful national tour that originated at the Los Angeles Theater Center. In the spring of 1994, a new musical melodrama, *Bandido,* written by Luis Valdez premiered at the Mark Taper Forum in Los Angeles.

Harry Vallejo [born: Enrique Juan Vallejo]

B: 1883
D: 1950

Born and raised in Mexico City in a well-to-do family, Vallejo left home at age 19 and came to the United States, where he found work as a film cameraman for Charlie Chaplin, Mack Sennett, Douglas Fairbanks, Sr., and Mary Pickford. In 1927 he returned to Mexico to make a series of promotional films for the oil industry.

Victor Vallejo

B: 1907

The son of Harry Vallejo, Victor worked as a costumer at Warner Bros. from 1937 to 1957. He became a second assistant director, then a first assistant, and later unit manager at Warner Bros. For the next 20 years he was assigned to such episodic film television series as "Cheyenne," "Maverick," "Hawaiian Eye," and "77 Sunset Strip."

Nina Varela

B: 1908
D: 2/12/1982

A Mexican character actress, Varela appeared in numerous westerns at Republic Pictures in the 1940s and 1950s, usually as a mamacita or dona. Some of her film credits include *Viva Zapata!* (1952), *Niagara* (1953), *Jubilee Trail* (1954), and *Madigan* (1968).

Jacob Vargas

B: 8/18/1970

Vargas's film credits include important roles in *Ernest Goes to Camp* (1987), *The Principal* (1987), *American Me* (1992), *Gas, Food, Lodging* (1992), and *Mi Vida Loca* (1994).

John Vargas

B: 4/24/1955

A New York–born Puerto Rican actor, Vargas has been featured in such films as *Only When I Laugh* (1981), *Star Trek II: The Wrath of Khan* (1982), *Mass Appeal* (1984), and *Hanoi Hilton* (1987). He was a regular on the television series "At Ease" for ABC and guest starred in the TV movie *The Jesse Owens Story* (1984) and on many episodic series.

Joseph B. Vasquez

B: 1963

From age 12, when a family friend gave him an 8mm camera, writer/director Joseph B. Vasquez has been on a nonstop quest to make movies. Vasquez is both black and Puerto Rican, and his low-budget films include *Street Story* (1989) and *Bronx War* (1991), in which he also acted. He directed the critically acclaimed film *Hangin' with the Homeboys* (1991).

Isela Vega

B: 1940

The beautiful Isela Vega was a number-one film sex symbol and box-office attraction in Mexico and Latin America. She capitalized on her beautifully sculptured face and body in revealing wardrobe and nude sequences in her films.

Born in Sonora, Mexico, Vega, by the late 1960s, began to be cast opposite such prominent Mexican leading men as Jorge Rivero, Mauricio Garces, Jorje Luke, and even Cantinflas.

Vega made her American film debut in a small role in *The Deadly Trackers* (1973). She followed with a co-starring role as Elita, a wiped-out, curvaceous, outspoken woman, in director Sam Peckinpah's *Bring Me the Head of Alfredo Garcia* (1974).

Isela Vega starred as Elita, a Mexican girl who becomes involved in a head-hunting search in *Bring Me the Head of Alfredo Garcia*.

She proved herself a capable actress without the sexy glitter with co-starring roles in *Drum* (1976) as a southern woman and in *Barbarosa* (1982) as an aristocratic Mexican wife, opposite Willie Nelson. She played a suffering Mexican mother in the television film *The Streets of L.A.* (1979).

Sylvia Vega Vasquez

A costume designer, Vega Vasquez worked on such films as *La Bamba* (1987) and *American Me* (1992).

Jerry Velasco

B: 1/31/1953

A Mexican-born actor, Velasco has appeared in such films as *The Jerk* (1979), *Boulevard Nights* (1979), and *Heartbreaker* (1983).

Eddie Velez

A native of New York City, Velez attended the High School of Art and Design and served in the U.S. Air Force.

Velez had a major supporting role in the cult film *Repo Man* (1984). His other film credits include a role as a boxer in *Split Decisions* (1988), co-starring Gene Hackman, and *The Women's Club* (1987) with Michael Pare. Velez made his television debut in the NBC series pilot film *For Love and Honor* (1983) and was a regular on such series as "Bay City Blues," "Berenger's," "Charlie & Co.," and the final season of "The A-Team" as Frankie Santana. Velez starred as a young lawyer in the series "Trial and Error."

Lupe Velez [born: Guadalupe Villalobos Velez]

B: 1909

D: 12/14/1944

Born in the Mexican town of San Luis Potosi, the daughter of an opera singer and an army colonel, Velez received her formal education in a convent in San Antonio, Texas. The veteran stage actor Richard Bennett discovered Velez in Mexico City appearing in a musical. After a series of dancing jobs in Mexico and Hollywood, she landed her first motion picture assignment in a series of comedies for Hal Roach.

In 1927, at age 18, Velez got her start in films by accepting a role as a wild mountain girl opposite Douglas Fairbanks in the silent film *The Gaucho* when Dolores Del Rio turned it down. She received good notices and the film was a hit. She played a girl of dubious morals in D.W. Griffith's *Lady of the Pavements* (1928, silent), set in 1868 Paris.

She co-starred in *Wolf Song* (1929) with a young Gary Cooper, who was smitten with Velez. They had an affair that lasted three years, until Cooper's family dissuaded him from marrying her because she was Mexican. In MGM's *Where East Is East* (1929), she played the half-caste daughter of Lon Chaney. In 1931 she did the talkie version of the Del Rio success *Resurrection* with John Boles. She appeared in DeMille's sound remake of *The Squaw Man* (1931), as an Indian maiden. After *Cuban Love Song* in 1931, she turned from heavy dramatics to comedy roles, for which she was more suited. Velez had a stormy five-year marriage to Johnny Weissmuller (the Olympic Gold Medal swimmer and a screen Tarzan), which ended in divorce. She gained new fame in 1939 when she returned in the B comedy *Mexican Spitfire* series for RKO, which proved successful. Her dynamic energy, coupled with rapid-fire line delivery and hot Latin temperament, led Velez to become known

Lupe Velez in the 1940s.

as the "Mexican Wildcat" or "Hot Tamale" as a result of these popular comedies. Despondent over a broken love affair that left her pregnant, Velez committed suicide in 1944.

Elena Verdugo

B: 4/20/1927

Elena Verdugo received two Emmy Award nominations as Best Supporting Actress while co-starring for seven years on the top-rated television series "Marcus Welby, M.D." as Nurse Consuelo Lopez.

Born in Paso Robles, California, Elena was raised in Los Angeles. She is a fifth-generation Californian and a direct descendant of Don Jose Maria Verdugo, to whom the King of Spain gave one of the first California land grants over 200 years ago.

As a child, Verdugo displayed a talent for dancing, so she was enrolled at a dance academy. Her first professional appearances were as a child dancer at several of the large downtown Los Angeles movie theaters. At age 17 she recorded "Tico Tico" with Xavier Cugat's Orchestra. Elena was spotted by a Twentieth Century–Fox talent scout and signed to a contract. She completed her schooling by attending classes with Anne Baxter, Roddy McDowall, and Linda Darnell.

She made her film debut when she was only age 13, appearing in *Down Argentine Way* (1940) with Don Ameche and Betty Grable. This led to her first major role as a Tahitian beauty opposite George Sanders's Gauguin in the memorable *The Moon and Sixpence* (1942). She later appeared in *House of Frankenstein* (1944), the Abbott and Costello feature *Little Giant* (1946), and *Cyrano de Bergerac* (1950) with Jose Ferrer. In the early 1950s, Verdugo starred in one of CBS-TV's biggest hit series, "Meet Millie," which aired for four years and firmly established her as a major talent. She played a secretary in New York with a very blonde-haired, loud-mouthed mother. Following the series she became a popular guest star on numerous shows including "The Red Skelton Show" and "The Bob Cummings Show" and co-starred in "The Phil Silvers Show."

Noah Verduzco

A child actor, Verduzco gained experience and exposure by appearing in commercials. His screen credits include *Radio Flyer* (1992) and *Bound by Honor* (1993).

James Victor

    B: 7/27/1939

Born in the Dominican Republic, Victor immigrated with his family to New York City at age four. His important motion picture work includes *Rolling Thunder* (1977), as Lopez, a barroom brawler; *Boulevard Nights* (1979), as an auto shop owner; *Defiance* (1980), as a Puerto Rican priest; *Borderline* (1980), a Charles Bronson thriller in which he co-starred as Mirandez, the truck driver importing more than tomatoes across the border; and *Losin' It* (1983), in which he played a shady lawyer opposite Shelley Long. In 1976, Victor starred in "Viva Valdez," the first prime-time network series to feature a Hispanic family. In 1982, he was signed for his second series, "Condo," an ABC situation comedy, as a 75-year-old grandfather, which required a 45-minute makeup job. He spent four seasons in Spain in the role of the bumbling Sergeant Garcia in New World Television's "Zorro" starring Duncan Regehr. Victor also has extensive theater credits in New York and Los Angeles.

Christina Vidal

A Puerto Rican child actress, Vidal starred in *Life with Mikey*, opposite Michael J. Fox, in 1993.

Reynaldo Villalobos

Villalobos has created memorable images for a remarkably diverse list of films, among them *9 to 5* (1980), *The Ballad of Gregorio Cortez* (1983), *Risky Business* (1983), *Punchline* (1988), *Major League* (1989), *Coupe de Ville* (1990), *American Me* (1992), and *A Bronx Tale* (1993).

He has also directed episodes of several TV series, including "Tour of Duty" and "Midnight Caller." Villalobos directed the Turner Network Television film western *Conagher* (1991).

The Los Angeles–born cinematographer was raised in Los Angeles, where his father was a standby painter on movie sets before running several studio paint departments. After high school, the younger Villalobos attended El Camino College and Dominican State College, majoring in art and design. He then enlisted in the Navy, where he worked as a photographer.

Returning to civilian life, Villalobos was employed as a studio laborer, painting and hauling equipment, before being hired as an assistant cameraman for *The Young Lawyers* in 1969.

Director of photography Reynaldo Villalobos (at camera) shooting a scene from *Punchline*, the bittersweet story about making it in the world of comedy.

After only eight months of camera crew experience, Villalobos was promoted to first assistant cameraman. He worked in that capacity for eight years before becoming an operator. He began his career as a cinematographer on *Urban Cowboy* (1980).

Carlos Villar [born: Carlos Villarias]

Born in Cordoba, Spain, the actor Carlos Villar starred in the Spanish-language version of Universal's *Dracula* in 1931. He occasionally worked in English-language film roles throughout the 1930s and 1940s. He also appeared in the part of the head waiter in *Bordertown* (1935).

He lived in Cuba for many years and then went to Spain and was never heard of again. It is supposed that he is dead, for he could not be located in 1992 to be invited to attend a screening of the restored Spanish *Dracula* in Spain.

Daniel Villarreal

B: 11/19/1960

Villarreal played an unreachable gang tough in *Stand and Deliver* (1988) and a young prison gang member in *American Me* (1992).

Mike Vitar

B: 1979

A native of the Los Angeles area, Vitar played Benny Rodriguez in the film *The Sandlot* (1993). On television he appeared on CBS's acclaimed "Brooklyn Bridge" series.

Sam Vlahos

B: 8/10/1935

Born in San Diego, California, of a Greek father and a Mexican mother, Vlahos has appeared in such feature films as *Summer and Smoke* (1961), *The Milagro Beanfield War* (1988), *Powwow Highway* (1989), and *Kiss Me a Killer* (1991). He has made many episodic television appearances on such series from "Hawaiian Eye" in the early 1960s to "Hill Street Blues" in the 1980s. Vlahos also guest starred on the Fox series "Key West."

Ethan Wayne

B: 1962

The youngest son of actor John Wayne and his Peruvian-born wife, Pilar, Ethan was featured as the young boy who is kidnapped in *Big Jake* (1971), starring his father. He starred as an adult on the new "Adam 12" syndicated TV series and has guest starred on several episodic series.

Raquel Welch [born: Raquel Tejada]

B: 9/5/1940

The last of the studio-manufactured screen sex goddesses, Raquel Welch reached the heights of popularity during the mid-1960s and early 1970s. She was born in Chicago, the daughter of Armand C. Tejada, a Bolivian-born engineer, and Josephine Sarah Hall. In over 35 films she has played opposite such leading actors as Richard Burton, Burt Reynolds, Dudley Moore, James Stewart, Frank Sinatra,

Raquel Welch.

Raquel Welch in 1993.

Dean Martin, Vittorio De Sica, Jean-Paul Belmondo, and Bill Cosby. She has worked with such directors as Stanley Donen, Richard Lester, Herbert Ross, Peter Yates, and James Ivory.

Welch made her film debut in a small role as a college student in the Elvis Presley film *Roustabout* (1964) and soon after landed another small role, as a bordello girl in *A House Is Not a Home* (1964), starring Shelley Winters. A contract starlet at Twentieth Century–Fox, she was groomed for stardom after she gained attention as a beautiful loincloth-clad prehistoric woman in *One Million Years B.C.* (1967). In 1965 *Time* magazine called her "The Nation's Number One Sex Symbol." In that one year, she was cast in four major productions, *The Biggest Bundle of Them All* (1968), *The Lovely Ladies* (1966), *Shoot Loud, Louder, I Don't Understand!* (1966) opposite Marcello Mastroianni, and the title role in *Fathom* (1967). The response to her publicity photos and the attention drawn to her prompted the studio to cast her opposite important male stars in big-budget films such as *Fantastic Voyage* (1966) with Stephen Boyd, *Bandolero!* (1968) with Dean Martin and James Stewart, and *Lady in Cement* (1968) with Frank Sinatra.

Her roles in these films capitalized on her physical beauty and screen presence. She was cast as Maria, a Mexican woman, in *Bandolero!,* and as Sarita, a Mexican Yaqui Indian, in *100 Rifles* (1969). Among her other film credits are *Bedazzled* (1967), *Kansas City Bomber* (1972), *The Last of Sheila* (1973), *The Wild Party* (1975), and *Mother, Jugs & Speed* (1976). As she matured, critics recognized her acting ability, beginning with Richard Lester's *The Three Musketeers* (1974). However, by this time her screen sex goddess image was so etched in the public mind that she could not escape it, and the box-office response to her films dipped. She did utilize her screen image to her advantage when she gambled and took over for Lauren Bacall in the Broadway musical *Woman of the Year* (1981). Audience curiosity over seeing the legendary body beautiful in person boosted ticket sales, and critics and audiences alike were surprisingly pleased with her live performing and acting abilities. Welch continued her live performing in Las Vegas and Atlantic City as well as in concert halls in London, Paris, and Rio de Janeiro. On television she gave a critically acclaimed performance in the telefilm *Right to Die* (1987), as a victim of Lou Gehrig's disease, and followed with *Scandal in a Small Town* (1988). In a *New York Times* interview on October 7, 1987, she remarked of her role in the television film, "I was letting go of everything I had ever used before in a part, everything that was the public Raquel Welch. It was a big relief. There was a great freedom in knowing for myself how much there was, without all that, and what a range of things I can look forward to personally, as well as for myself as an actress."

She is currently a woman's fitness guru, with herself as a stunning example.

Tahnee Welch

The daughter of Raquel Welch, Tahnee has appeared in the films *Cocoon* (1985) and *Cocoon: The Return* (1988).

Guy Williams [born: Armando Catalano]

    B: 1924
    D: 5/8/1989

An actor whose name became a household word, Guy Williams became an over-

Guy Williams, who starred in the Walt Disney TV series as Zorro.

© WALT DISNEY PRODUCTIONS WORLD RIGHTS RESERVED

night star with his role in the popular 1950s television series "Zorro." The 6-foot, 3-inch second-generation Italian American was born in New York City. He was chosen by Walt Disney to portray Zorro on television, the role having been made famous in motion pictures by Douglas Fairbanks, Sr., and later by Tyrone Power. The series ran for two years on ABC, from 1957 until 1959.

He could never quite equal the early success of "Zorro" and was forever identified as the "Masked Avenger of Early California." He went on to guest star on a number of episodes of the TV series "Bonanza" as a cousin to the Cartwright family. Williams starred in two theatrical films, *The Prince and the Pauper* in 1962 and *Captain Sinbad* in 1963.

From 1965 through 1968 Williams starred as Professor John Robinson in the television series "Lost in Space." He was offered the role of Zorro for the short-lived "Zorro and Son" comedy series for Disney, but he turned down the role. He remained inactive in films and television until his death of a heart attack in Buenos Aires, where he had resided off and on for several years.

David Yanez

A child actor, Yanez appeared in many episodic TV series and films during the late 1970s and throughout the 1980s, usually as a Native American or Hispanic youth. His credits include the miniseries *Centennial (1978)* and the film *Born in East L.A.* (1987).

Alfred Ybarra

B: 1907

An art director, Ybarra has worked on such films as *The High and the Mighty* (1954) and the 1960 epic *The Alamo* for Batjac, John Wayne's production company.

A native-born Californian and a direct descendant of the original founding families of Los Angeles, Ybarra was an architect before entering the movie industry and spent two years on the plans for the Empire State Building in New York City. He entered the motion picture business as a set designer in 1935 at the Samuel Goldwyn Studios and became an art director in 1943. Ybarra worked for RKO Radio Pictures and oversaw the construction of their Churubusco Studios facility in Mexico City during the mid-1940s. He was production designer and art director on a number of films shot in Mexico during this period. Among his many credits as an art director are *The Fugitive* (1947), *The Bullfighter and the Lady* (1951), *Track of the Cat* (1954), *Blood Alley* (1955), and *The Comancheros* (1961). He retired in 1967.

Rocky Ybarra

B: 1900
D: 1965

A cowboy actor and stuntman, Ybarra worked in countless motion pictures, including *Viva Zapata!* (1952).

Richard Yniguez

B: 12/8/1946

A handsome Mexican American leading man, Yniguez starred in *Boulevard Nights* (1979) and *Raices de Sangre* (Blood Roots) (1979). Yniguez has had major roles in such films as *Zandy's Bride* (1974) and *Cancel My Reservation* (1972). He starred in the TV movies *Tribes* (1970), *The Deadly Tower* (1975), *River of Promises* (1977), and *Shark Kill* (1976).

Born in Firebaugh, California, and raised in Sacramento, Yniguez moved with his family to Mexico, where he spent his early teenage years and considered a vocation in the priesthood. But at age 17 he returned to California and served in the United States Navy for three years. Later, he attended East Los Angeles College, supporting himself as a night attendant at a mortuary. Considering his career options, he began writing songs and acting in local theater and aspired to start his own theater group. In 1968, Yniguez won his first daytime TV role in "Cancion de la Raza" for PBS. It was the first Chicano-written and -produced series on television. Many guest appearances followed on such shows as "The Lucy Show," "Marcus Welby, M.D.," "Bonanza," "Hawaii Five-O," "The Streets of San Francisco," and "Simon and Simon."

Joe Yrigoyen

A veteran Basque stuntman, Yrigoyen doubled for Roy Rogers in many westerns and worked at Republic Pictures from 1935 to 1958.

Del Zamora

Born in Roswell, New Mexico, Zamora was featured as one of the Castillo brothers in *Repo Man* (1984). He has also acted in *Private School* (1983), *Sid and Nancy* (1986), *Born in East L.A.* (1987), *RoboCop* (1987), and *Walker* (1987).

Carmen Zapata

B: 1927

During more than 40 years in the industry, Zapata has enjoyed a highly diversified career as an actress, producer, translator, and lecturer/narrator. Her career began in 1946 on the Broadway stage in the musical *Oklahoma!* She followed in other musicals such as *Bells Are Ringing* (1956), *Guys and Dolls* (1957), and many others. The Mexican American actress has been featured in many film roles including *Sol Madrid* (1968), *Hail, Hero!* (1969), *Pete and Tillie* (1972), *Boulevard Nights* (1979), and as one of the nuns in the chorus in *Sister Act* (1992), starring Whoopi Goldberg. She has appeared in recurring roles on "Flamingo Road" and "The Dick Van Dyke Show." She was seen for three years on the daytime soap "Santa Barbara" as Carmen Castillo. Zapata starred in a short-lived prime-time series, "Viva Valdez," and for nine seasons starred in PBS's bilingual children's series, "Villa Alegre." She is a co-founder of the Bilingual Foundation of the Arts, a resident theater company in Los Angeles.

Zeppy Zepulveda

A longtime property master at Universal Studios, Zepulveda propped many movies during Universal's Golden Age from the late 1930s through the early 1970s.

Daphne Zuniga

B: 10/28/1962

Zuniga has co-starred in such films as Rob Reiner's comedy *The Sure Thing* (1985), as a traveling college student; Mel Brooks's *Spaceballs* (1987), as a Mercedes-riding space princess; and *The Fly II* (1989), as a computer programmer who falls in love with the ill-fated son of The Fly.

Born in San Francisco and raised in Berkeley, California, Zuniga lived briefly with her family in Vancouver, B.C. It was there at age 12 that she first appeared on stage, performing in a production of *H.M.S. Pinafore*. She performed in school and community stage productions and studied at the American Conservatory Theatre in San Francisco. Zuniga enrolled in UCLA's theater arts program, and in

1984, the actress made her professional debut in the thriller *The Initiation.* Among her other feature film credits are *Vision Quest* (1985) opposite Matthew Modine, *Modern Girls* (1986), and *Last Rites* (1988), as a Mexican temptress opposite Tom Berenger. Her television credits include the films *Stone Pillow* (1985) opposite Lucille Ball and *Quarterback Princess* (1983). Zuniga stars as Jo Reynolds, a beautiful strong-willed photographer in the Fox series "Melrose Place."

Frank Zuniga

> B: 3/20/1936

A film director, Zuniga's credits include the Goldwyn Company's *The Golden Seal* (1983), *Heartbreaker* (1983), and *Fist Fighter* (1988). Born in New Mexico, Zuniga began his career at Walt Disney Studios, where he was a cameraman and later a director on a number of wildlife films.

DIRECTOR BIOGRAPHIES

Robert Aldrich

> B: 1918
>
> D: 1983

Aldrich made films in almost every major genre, but his greatest successes were with such action features as *Vera Cruz* (1954), *The Dirty Dozen* (1967), and *The Longest Yard* (1972).

He worked as an assistant director at RKO from 1941 to 1950 and made his directorial debut in 1953 with the film *The Big Leaguer* at MGM. Producer Harold Hecht and actor/producer Burt Lancaster were impressed by Aldrich's ability and ambition and hired him as director of their productions of *Apache* and *Vera Cruz* in 1954, which were commercial successes.

Vera Cruz, filmed on location in Mexico in CinemaScope and Technicolor, fueled the imagination and filled the screen with slam-bang action and excitement. It is a rugged story of American soldiers of fortune in Mexico right after the American Civil War, who are transporting a shipment of gold for Emperor Maximilian while trying to outdo one another and eluding Juaristas, who seem to be waiting at every turn. The film was the only teaming of action stars Gary Cooper and Burt Lancaster, in roles ideally suited to their screen personas. Ben Trane (Cooper), who lost everything fighting for the South in the Civil War, intends to work for Maximilian but in the end sides with the freedom-loving underdog Juaristas and falls in love with the native Mexican girl.

Aldrich's use of the actual Mexican landscapes, including the pyramids at Teotihuacan and Chapultepec Castle against a sweeping romantic historical panorama, etched a memorable image of Mexico as a last frontier where Americans can find adventure, romance, and spiritual renewal.

Budd Boetticher

> B: 7/29/1916

Boetticher's passion for bullfighting and Mexico expressed itself in his direction of such notable films as *The Bullfighter and the Lady* (1951) and *The Magnificent Matador* (1955). He began his career as a technical consultant on Rouben Mamoulian's 1941 version of *Blood and Sand* and went on to direct *Wings of the Hawk* (1953), *Seven Men from Now* (1956), *The Tall T* (1957), *Ride Lonesome* (1959), and *Comanche Station* (1960). He wrote the original story for *Two Mules for Sister Sara* (1970), which

Don Siegel directed and in which Clint Eastwood co-starred with Shirley MacLaine. He also directed, wrote, and produced a documentary film on the life of famed Spanish bullfighter Carlos Arruza titled *Arruza* (1972). He also directed a number of adventure films at Universal during the 1950s.

Richard Brooks

B: 5/8/1912

D: 3/11/1992

A director and writer, Brooks offered three distinct cinematic views of Hispanics: a Latin American country in dictatorial political turmoil was presented in *Crisis* (1950); teenage Puerto Rican slum dwellers and the conditions of urban American high schools were featured in *Blackboard Jungle* (1955); and American soldiers of fortune battling bandits in 1917 revolutionary Mexico in *The Professionals* (1966).

Brooks was known for hard-hitting dramatic films that also addressed social themes and for his skillful adaptations of literary material for the screen in such films as *Elmer Gantry* (1960) and *In Cold Blood* (1967).

He started his screen career as a dialogue writer at Universal in 1942. Earlier, he had sold articles to newspapers and magazines before becoming a radio news writer. Brooks spent three years in the U.S. Marines and wrote a novel, *The Brick Foxhole,* which later became RKO's *Crossfire* (1947), one of the first films to deal with anti-Semitism. He wrote the scripts for *Swell Guy* (1946) and *Brute Force* (1947).

Brooks collaborated with John Huston on the screenplay of *Key Largo* (1948) and Huston invited Brooks to stay on the set during shooting to learn the filmmaking process. Huston's influence may have prompted Brooks to strive for filmmaking autonomy, and when he moved over to MGM he was contracted as a writer/director. *Crisis*, a political thriller starring Cary Grant and Jose Ferrer, was the first of his many films at MGM. The film that really established him as a director was the controversial hit film *Blackboard Jungle.* The screenplay he developed from Evan Hunter's novel was nominated for an Academy Award.

John Ford

B: 2/1/1894

D: 8/31/1973

One of America's greatest directors, John Ford won four Academy Awards for Best Direction, though none for a western, a genre he helped to define. In his career he directed more than 140 feature films.

Ford portrayed Mexicans as people with evident strength and dignity, using their identifying dress, music, and language in movies such as *Stagecoach* (1939) and *The Searchers* (1956). He used African Americans, Indians, and Mexicans as part of his cinematic canvas of the American West, a romantic panorama in which these groups took part.

He was the first to acknowledge on screen the participation of black Americans in the winning of the West in *Sergeant Rutledge* (1960), yet he subscribed in his earlier work to the accepted and popular eye-popping, dancing Negro image. Though he portrayed Indians as savages impeding the way of white civilization in many westerns, he gave a thoughtful nod to their humanity in *Fort Apache* (1948), *She Wore a Yellow Ribbon* (1949), and most poetically in *Cheyenne Autumn* (1964). Ford featured a Mexican outlaw in his first western, *Straight Shooting*, in 1917.

In *Stagecoach,* Mexicans are seen in the background as we hear their musical strains. In *Three Godfathers* (1948), Pedro Armendariz plays Pete, a bilingual Mexican American outlaw from Texas who is the equal of the two Anglo cowboys he rides with. He is identified by his *charro* (cowboy) saddle, Mexican blanket, his sombrero, and his etiquette. Though the character played by John Wayne ribs him about his speaking Spanish in front of the baby, whom they have named William

Antonio Moreno and John Wayne in *The Searchers*.

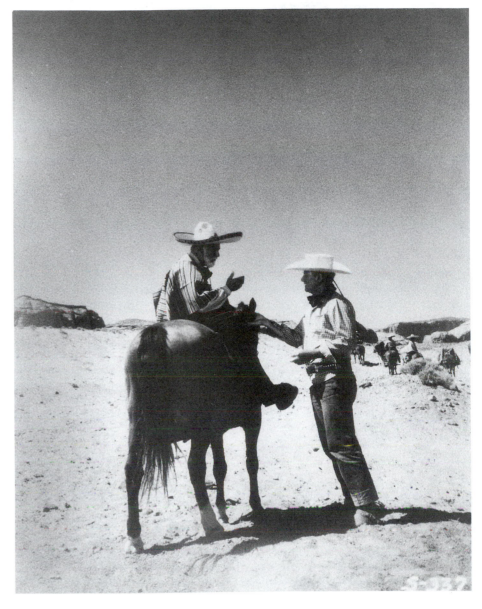

Robert Pedro Hightower, Wayne apologizes to Pete, and honors his friend by his last words to the baby, which are in Spanish, "Adios, compañero."

In *The Searchers,* Antonio Moreno is Emilio Figueroa, a Mexican *vaquero* (cowboy) who takes John Wayne as Ethan Edwards and Jeffrey Hunter as Martin Pauley to find Chief Scar. Ford presents the spitfire and mamacita stereotypes but does not dwell on them, as innocent and childlike Pauley cries, "Mamacita, mas frijoles!" What makes the portrayal of the mamacita go beyond the stereotype of the life-sustaining earth mother is that we find her equivalent in the Anglo family.

The self-sufficient loner Ethan (Wayne) uses the help of the Mexican to find Sicatriz (Spanish for "scar"), the Indian chief who abducted his niece and massacred her family. Ford remarked in an interview, "[*The Searchers*] is the tragedy of a loner. He's the man who came back from the Civil War, probably went into Mexico, became a bandit, probably fought for Juarez or Maximilian."

Ford made his most profound statements on the American West and what it turned into with *The Man Who Shot Liberty Valance* (1962). Mexican Americans in the film are segregated in the southern end of the town of Shinbone and in their own, rather boisterous and lively cantina. The cowardly Anglo sheriff is married to a Mexican woman with many offspring. Mexicans are shown in the cantina with identifying wardrobe and music. In the scenes when the people of the town are voting for representation, there are no Mexicans present.

The only place where everyone seems to find equality is in the schoolhouse, where Ransom Stoddard (James Stewart) is teaching the values of the American system. The people in the class, Mexican Americans, women, children, blacks, and immigrants, come to represent the disenfranchised of American society who believe in the American Dream.

In *Two Rode Together* (1961), Ford explored themes of racial prejudice against Indians and the more familiar contrasts of civilization and the wilderness. A sheriff, McCabe (James Stewart), and an Army officer, Lt. Jim Gary (Richard Widmark), go on a rescue mission to retrieve white captives from a Comanche tribe. They return with only a boy and a Spanish Mexican woman, Elena de la Madriaga (Linda Cristal), who for five years was the squaw of a Comanche chieftain, Stone Calf. Upon her return, Elena is subjected to constant insults by the white women at the fort, who ostracize her because she did not kill herself rather than mate with an Indian.

Elena is Mexican and a Catholic, a religion which forbids suicide. What's more, she shows affection for her former mate, Stone Calf, despite what he subjected her to at first. In a damning scene, Elena explains to the prim and upright women of the fort that she was treated better by the Indians in her captivity than she has been by them in her "freedom."

At the end of the film, McCabe falls in love with Elena and rides off to start a new life with her, but they are both outcasts, set apart from this new civilization that falls far short of its ideals.

John Huston

B: 8/5/1906
D: 8/28/1987

John Huston was a vital creative force in the film industry for over 50 years and was still making movies right up to the time of his death in 1987. He won two Academy Awards for *The Treasure of the Sierra Madre* (1948), for Best Direction and Best Screenplay, and was nominated 11 other times for such films as *The Maltese Falcon* (1941), *The African Queen* (1952), and *Prizzi's Honor* (1985). Not only was he a director, he was a writer and an actor as well as a strong personality, espousing an Ernest Hemingway–like philosophy of macho lifestyle combined with keen artistic insight.

In a 1984 interview with Luis Reyes, Huston revealed his feelings about Mexico. "I never wanted to make a travelogue of cliches about Mexico. Usually, Americans see only one aspect of Mexico, the tourism. Mexico is a country with so many faces, and only through living there and going around can you get to know anything about its heart or hearts, I should say."

He continued, "There's a savage face to Mexico, and another, benign and gentle, a deep humanity. There's the history too."

Huston spent part of his youth in Mexico, and it became his adopted home from 1974 until his death. Mexico was the location for three of his films, *The Treasure of the Sierra Madre*, *The Night of the Iguana* (1964), and *Under the Volcano* (1984). In Huston's films, Mexicans are in control of their own universe. Americans in Mexico are not superior beings as in other films, but fragile, vulnerable, often flawed creatures in a harsh but hospitable environment. The insecure and distrustful Fred C. Dobbs and his gold seekers of *The Treasure of the Sierra Madre*; the defrocked minister who conducts tours for lonely spinsters, and the proprietress of a run-down Mexican hotel who frolics with the natives, in *The Night of the Iguana*; Fermin, the alcoholic, self-destructive British consul who meets a violent death in *Under the Volcano* are all characters Huston found in literature (two of the movies

John Huston directs Emilio Fernandez in *Under the Volcano.*

were based on novels; the third was based on a stage play) and shaped for the screen. John Huston's Mexico is not a place for Anglos to go for spiritual renewal. These Anglos carry their demons with them, and whoever they are or whatever they did in their place of origin across the border eventually destroys them in Mexico.

By filming on location, and with the help of famed Mexican cameraman Gabriel Figueroa, Huston captured in his films a feeling of the real Mexico that no other American filmmaker has been able to capture.

Sam Peckinpah
B: 2/21/1925
D: 12/28/1984

As a writer and director, Peckinpah was one of the key figures responsible for the revival of the western genre during the 1960s and 1970s with such films as *The Deadly Companions* (1961), *Ride the High Country* (1962), *Major Dundee* (1965), *The Wild Bunch* (1969), and *Pat Garrett and Billy the Kid* (1973).

Peckinpah began writing scripts for such television series as "Gunsmoke," and he helped to create "The Rifleman" and "The Westerner" series. It was not his first feature, *The Deadly Companions,* but *Ride the High Country,* starring Joel McCrea and Randolph Scott (in his last film) as two aging gunfighters, that gained him critical attention.

Peckinpah first discovered Mexico after World War II, when he enrolled in a summer school in theater in Mexico City. He wanted to return to China, where he had been sent at the close of World War II, but the Bamboo Curtain had dropped and he went for the next best place. Most of his wives were Mexican, and he listed Huston's *The Treasure of the Sierra Madre* among his favorite films. Peckinpah was quoted in the February 1975 issue of *Game Magazine*, in a story by Tony Crawley: "Everything important in my life has been linked with Mexico in one way or another."

In Peckinpah's films, Mexico is a place where gringos can play out their fantasies, a never-never land of sex, violence, and ultramachismo. It is a place to escape from American law and a place of spiritual renewal. With the closing of the American West, Mexico became an extension of the lawless frontier and an oasis for those who had outlived their usefulness. Women were there to serve the needs, usually sexual, of the men. Most Mexican women in Peckinpah's films are portrayed as whores, or as easily available sexual creatures of one type or another.

Yet Peckinpah is able to capture images of the turmoil and violence of a country in the midst of a revolution, as he did in *The Wild Bunch,* which stings with accuracy and a hint of truth.

The Wild Bunch is considered by some to be Peckinpah's finest effort (though others cite *Ride the High Country*), and one French critic correctly described his films as a universe of violence and nostalgia. Other Peckinpah films that have Mexican elements are *Major Dundee, Bring Me the Head of Alfredo Garcia* (1974), and *Pat Garrett and Billy the Kid.*

Peckinpah was the perfect Hemingwayesque/John Huston character in Mexico, with his violent nature, bouts with alcohol, and fights with studio executives over the final cuts of his films. His death from a heart attack was clearly brought on by his self-abusive lifestyle.

Director Sam Peckinpah sizes up a set for *The Wild Bunch.*

Raoul Walsh

B: 3/11/1887

D: 12/31/1980

Raoul Walsh was noted for his fast-moving direction of rugged and masculine action/adventure movies and roustabout comedies, while women fared well as strong, independent, pioneering types integral to his stories.

Born in New York City of a Spanish mother and an Irish father, Walsh spent his late teens as a cowboy and traveled through Mexico and the American West. He worked as a seaman en route to Cuba on his uncle's ship. One of his first assignments as a filmmaker was working for D.W. Griffith, who sent him to Mexico to film the real-life exploits of Pancho Villa.

Walsh directed and shaped the exploits of the Cisco Kid in the early outdoor sound film *In Old Arizona* (1929). He had intended to play the leading role himself, but an unfortunate accident on location resulted in the loss of one eye, which ended his career as an actor. Walsh had directed most of the outdoor action sequences, and director Irving Cummings guided actor Warner Baxter, who replaced Walsh, into an Academy Award–winning role as the Cisco Kid.

Walsh also directed Dolores Del Rio in her first major screen role as the French farm maiden in the hit silent film *What Price Glory?* (1926), and as Carmen in *The Loves of Carmen* (1927), but his critical acclaim now rests primarily with his directorial work for Warner Bros., from 1939 through 1951.

He directed Cornel Wilde in an important role as hotel clerk Victor Mendoza in the classic *High Sierra* (1941) starring Humphrey Bogart. He directed Anthony Quinn as Chief Crazy Horse in *They Died with Their Boots On* (1941) starring Errol Flynn, and 15 years later in a starring role as a Portuguese sailor opposite Gregory Peck in the two-fisted nineteenth-century Barbary Coast drama *The World in His Arms* (1952). Walsh also directed Joel McCrea as a cowboy on the run and Virginia Mayo as a "half-breed" Mexican girl in *Colorado Territory* (1949). In *Distant Drums* (1951), he directed Gary Cooper in a tale of Yankee soldiers fighting Indians in the Everglades and Spanish soldiers along the Florida coast. In *Captain Horatio Hornblower* (1951), Walsh directed a romantic seafaring tale with Gregory Peck in the title role of a British naval captain at war with the French and the Spanish.

INDEX

Underscored page numbers indicate main entries; **boldface** page numbers indicate illustrations. Entries for awards (Academy Award, Emmy Award, etc.) refer only to Hispanic nominees and winners. Dates and other descriptive information (e.g., "stage," to indicate a theatrical performance) are provided only where necessary to distinguish between identical titles and names.

"A.E.S. Hudson Street," <u>269</u>, 394, 499
"A.K.A. Pablo," <u>269</u>, 396, 478, 480, 481, 490
Aaron Loves Angela, <u>27</u>, 373
Abad, Antonia Maria. *See* Montiel, Sarita
Abbott, Bud, 157, 198, 512
Abbott, George, 225, 357
ABC, 27, 269–304 *passim*, 309, 310, 316, 317, 319, 465, 478, 481, 491, 512
ABC Afterschool Specials, 310, 317
Abdah, Mario, 248
Above the Law, 500
Abrahams, Derwin, 343
Academy Award, 14, 21, 22, 28, 34, 53, 97, 100, 111, 381, 395, 397, 402, 403, 405, 410, 413, 428, 429, 451, 452, 453, 456, 459, 461, 465, 467, 469, 470, 471, 479, 491, 494, 495, 506
"Acapulco," <u>269</u>
Acaraz, Luis, 73
Accused, 391
ACE Award, 365
Ace in the Hole, 204
Acierto, Tony, 282
Ackerman, Robert Allan, 314
Acosta, Enrique, 323, <u>347</u>
Acosta, Ivan, 97, 98
Acosta, Rodolfo [Rodolpho, Rudolpho, Rodolfa], 36, 42, **42**, 66, 145, 146, 147, 151, 171, 174, 178, 193, 197, 224, 254, 282, <u>347–48</u>
Across 110th Street, 399
Across the Wide Missouri, 448
Actors Studio, 380, 500
"Adam 12," 380, 441, 514
Adames, John, 118
Adams, Brooke, 86
Adams, Gerald Drayson, 254
Adams, Julia, 254
Adams, Lee, 67
Addams, Charles, 27, 269
Addams Family, The, <u>27</u>, 269, 425, 427

"Addams Family, The," <u>269</u>
Addams Family Values, 425, 427
"Adios," 139
"Adios Mi Amor," 153
Adler, Hans, 220
Adler, Lou, 237
Adler, Luther, 148
Admiral Had a Wife, The, 403
Adorf, Mario, 151, 152
Adreon, Franklyn [Franklin], 324, 326, 327
Adventure, <u>27</u>, 487
Adventurers, The, <u>28</u>, 350
"Adventures in Paradise," 369
Adventures of a Young Man, 449
Adventures of Buckaroo Banzai, The, 496
Adventures of Casanova, The, 147, 387
Adventures of Don Juan, The, 14, <u>28</u>, 367, 375, 506
"Adventures of Kit Carson, The," <u>270</u>, 395
"Adventures of Ozzie and Harriet, The," 285, 359
Adventures of Robin Hood, The, 326, 494
Affair in Havana, <u>29</u>
Affair in Trinidad, 116, 420
African Queen, The, 522
After Hours, 438
After Hours (novel), 504
After Tonight, 485
Against All Flags, 471
Against All Odds, 3, 137
Age-Scarpelli, 119
Agricultural and Industrial Development Bank of Cuba (BANFAIC), 29
Agueda Martinez, 397
Aguero, Juan Manual, 218
Aguglia, Mimi, 369
Aguilar, Tony, 235, **235**, <u>348</u>
Aherne, Brian, 132
Aidman, Charles, 258
Ainslee, Marian, 64
Airport 1975, 399
Airport '79, 379

Akins, Claude, 193, 197
Aladjem, Norman, 103
Alambrista!, 23, <u>29</u>, 353, 461, 501
Alamo, The, 2, 4, 14, <u>30–31</u>, **31**, 140, 317, 369, 381, 517
Alamo, The: 13 Days to Glory, <u>301</u>, 422, 427, 493
Alaniz, Rico, 36, 68, 102, 140, 207, 233, 292
Alberghetti, Anna Maria, 140
Albert, Eddie, 54, 218, 348, 404, 437
Albert, Edward, 301, <u>348</u>, 437
Albertson, Jack, 273, 499
Alcala, Felix Enriquez, <u>348</u>
Alcaniz, Luana, 11
"Alcoa Theatre," 371
Aldrich, Robert, 89, 239, 441, <u>519</u>
Aleandro, Norma, 22, 111, 315, <u>348</u>, **349**
Alejandro, Miguel, 183, **183**
Alexander, Dick, 324
Alexander, Erika, 280
Alexander, Ronald, 126
Alexander the Great, 354
Alfonso, Kristian, 278
"Alfred Hitchcock Show, The," 465
Ali Baba and the Forty Thieves, 354, 449, 450
Ali Baba Goes to Town, 391
Alicia, Ana, 200, 277, 316, <u>349</u>
Alive, <u>32</u>
"All in the Family," <u>270</u>, 273, 434, 504
All Star Fiesta at Ford's, <u>301</u>
All Story, 321
All the Fine Young Cannibals, 429
All the President's Men, 236
Alla en el Rancho Grande, 405
Alland, William, 189
Allen, Corey, 133
Allen, Debbie, 278
Allen, Karen, 190
Allen, Steve, 298
Allen, Woody, 41, 42, 404, 446, 451, 469, 503

Allende, Fernando, 123, 279, 301, 318, 349–50
Allied Artists, 29, 93, 103, 123, 179, 182
Allyson, June, 194, 195, **195**, 449
Almanzar, James, 74
Almeida, Laurindo, 28, 85, 350
Almendros, Nestor, 350
Almodovar, Pedro, 362
Aloha, 505
aloha, bobby and rose, 33, 459
Aloma of the South Seas, 386, 399
Along the Navajo Trail, 481
Alonso, Chelo, 350
Alonso, Francisco. *See* Day, Francisco ("Chico")
Alonso, Maria Conchita, 2, 23, 79, 80, 98, **99**, 107, 185, 227, 293, 350–51
Alonzo, John, 151, 329, 351, 396
Alonzo, Luis. *See* Roland, Gilbert
Alperson, Edward L., 149
Alphabet City, 467
Altman, Robert, 163, 503
Alvarado, Angela, 202
Alvarado, Carlos, 14, 351, 352
Alvarado, Don, 10, 14, 49, 64, 71, 139, 197, 198, 201, 351–52, **352**, 390, 464
Alvarado, Fernando, 100, 140, 156, 234, 352
Alvarado, Magali, 202, 353
Alvarado, Trini, 353
Alvaranga, Tony, 246, **246**
Alvarez, Abraham, 270
Alvarez, Edmundo Rivera, 184
Alvarez, Felix, 308
Alvarez, Lily, 308
Alvarez Guedes, Guillermo, 48
Alvarez Kelly, 32
Alverio, Rosa Dolores. *See* Moreno, Rita
Alvin Ailey American Dance Theatre, 308
Always in My Heart, **356**, 357
Amado, Jorje, 367
Amalio, Sonia, 254
Amaral, Nestor, 126, 222
Ambition, 467
Amboy Dukes, The, 78
Ambriz, Domingo, 29, 245, 246, 353
Ambush, 503
Ameche, Don, 17, 90, 190, 191, 220, 450, 512
"America," 250
American Ballet Theatre, 388
American Blue Note, 353
American Conservatory Theatre, 463, 518
American Film Distribution, 57
American Film Institute, 442, 491
American Gigolo, 396
American Grafitti, 464
American Indian Movement, 460
American International Pictures, 88, 123
American Me, 23, 25, 32–34, **33**, 60, 80, 353, 359, 387, 397, 401, 412, 418,

434, 454, 461, 463, 490, 496, 508, 510, 512, 513
American Place Theatre, 311, 426
"American Playhouse," 41, 97, 216, 313, 314, 317, 360, 397, 441, 461, 467, 468, 480, 493, 496, 506
American Roulette, 410
American Society of Cinematographers, 381
American Theatre Wing, 460
Americano, The, 20, 34–35, 62, 423, 488
Ames, Leon, 47
Ames, Ramsay, 339, 353–54, **353**
Ames, Stephen, 165, 194, 234
"Amigo," 270, 486
Amityville Horror, The, 495
Anchors Aweigh, 473
And Now Miguel, 35, 389
Anders, Allison, 353
Anders, Chris, 123
Anderson, John, 258
Anderson, Judith, 234, 295
Anderson, Maxwell, 79
Anderson, Melody, 103
Anderson, Michael, 37
Anderson, Robert J., 27
Anderson, William H., 327
Andersonville Trial, The, 403
Andress, Ursula, 109
Andrews, Dana, 177
Andrews, Edward, 257
Andrews, Robert, 45
Andrews Sisters, The, 37
Angel, Heather, 323
Angel, Jonathan, 296
Angel Town, 491
Angeli, Pier, 213, **214**
Angels with Broken Wings, 485
Angustain, Ira, 300, 302, 303, 354
Anhalt, Edna, 185
Anhalt, Edward, 127, 185, 257
Aniov, Mario, 191
Ankrum, Morris, 239
Annie Get Your Gun, 376
Ann-Margret, 67, 188
Another Stakeout, 399
Ansara, Michael, 35, 81, 389
Anspach, Susan, 49, 301
Antonio, Lou, 314
Antonio and the Mayor, 302
Antonioni, Michelangelo, 443
Antony and Cleopatra, 376
Any Gun Can Play, 486
Any Which Way You Can, 507
Anzio, 494
Aoki, Tsuru, 123, **124**
Apache Ambush, 450
Apache Drums, 407
Apache War Smoke, 486
Apocalypse Now, 497, 498, 499
Apold, Raul, 248
Apollonia. *See* Kotero, Apollonia
Appaloosa, The, 35–36, 172, 369, 371, 379, 380, 494, 502

Appointment in Honduras, 36
"Aquarela do Brazil," 204
Aquarius Theatre, 258
Arab, The, 457
Arabia, 421
Arabian Nights, 449, 450
Aragon, Art, **195**
Arantes de Nascimento, Edison. *See* Pele
Arau, Alfonso, 199, 200, 207, 221, 247, 252, 254, 291, 318, 354
Arce, Manuel, 84, 97, 311
Archer, Ann, 228
"Archie Bunker's Place." *See* "All in the Family"
Arco, 216
Arden, Eve, 177
Ardrey, Robert, 108, 255
Argentine Love, 36
Argentine Nights, 16, 37
Argenziano, Carmen, 215, 217
Argosy Pictures, 355
Arias, Jose, 101
Ariel Award (Mexican Oscar), 348, 392, 448
Arizmendi, Yareli, 343, 354
Arizona Kid, The, 336, **336**, 438
Arkin, Alan, 109, 121, 130, 183, **183**, 184, 317, 404
Arlen, Michael, 100
Arlen, Richard, 454
Armed and Dangerous, 469
Armendariz, Pedro, 17, 18, 19, 48, 56, **56**, 109, 147, 154, 180, **180**, 222, 223, **223**, 225, 248, 249, 255, 354–56, **355**, 369, 392, 393, 401, 520
Armendariz, Pedro, Jr., 119, 145, 151, 168, 169, 187, 235, 247, 308, 343, 356
Armida, 101, 235, 236, 339, 342, 356–57, **356**,
Armillita, 53
Arms and the Man, 425
Armstrong, Gillian, 102
Armstrong, R.G., 179
Arnaud, Georges, 214
Arnaz, Desi, 3, 45, 86, 106, 140, 152, 167, 225, 261–62, **262**, 267, 284–86, **285**, 288, 357–58, **358**, 358, 359, 466
Arnaz, Desi, Jr., 152, 191, 358–59
Arnaz, Lucie, 288, 358, 359
Arness, James, 301
Arnold, Danny, 271
Arnold, Elliott, 32, 134
Arnold, Jack, 153
Arnold, Roseanne, 295
Around the World in 80 Days, 37, 181, 371, 414, 486, 488
Arriaga, Dolly, 70
Arrowhead, 428
Arroyo, Don, 171
Arroyo, Luis, 257
Arruza, Carlos, 30

Arruza, 66, 520
Artenstein, Isaac, 63, <u>359</u>
Arthur, George M., 141
Arthur, Jean, 175
Arthur, Karen, 319
Arthur, Robert, 124, 157, 219
Ash Wednesday, 395
Ashby, Hal, 409
Askew, Luke, 151
Askin, Peter, 311
Asner, Edward, 107, 298
Assante, Armand, 108, 152, 181, 187, 188, 374, 375
Association of Motion Picture Producers, 8
Astaire, Fred, 17, 104, **104**, 105, 173, 256, 384, 390, 420, 487, 493, **493**
Astin, John, 27, 241, 269
Astor, Mary, 101, 139, 323, 389, 484
At Close Range, 491
"At Ease," <u>270</u>, 508
At Play in the Fields of the Lord, <u>38</u>, 361
"A-Team, The," 263, <u>270</u>, 369, 374, 510
Atkins, Tom, 305
Atlanta Child Murders, The, 499
Atlas Theaters, 17
Attenborough, Richard, 499
Atwater, Gladys, 37, 229
Atwill, Lionel, 73, 88
Aubel, Joe, 34, 160, <u>359</u>
Audience Award (Sundance Film Festival), 95
Audley, Nancy, 314
Auer, John H., 177
Aumont, Jean-Pierre, 450
Auntie Mame, 14, 352
Aurtes, Islin, 167
Authentic Death of Hendry Jones, The, 171
Autobiography of Miss Jane Pittman, The, 264
"Automan," 358
Autry, Gene, 3, 344, 480
Avalon, Frankie, 30
Avalos, Luis, 39, 40, 275, 277, 280, 282, 284, 301, 315, <u>359–60</u>, **360**
Avco Embassy, 245
Avell, Margaret, 439
Avengers, The, 436, 439
Avila, Carlos, 313, <u>360</u>
Aviles, Angel, <u>360</u>
Aviles, Rick, <u>361</u>
Ayars, Anne, 101
Ayres, Gerald, 78
Ayres, Lew, 141, 142, 485
Azteca Films, 188, 225

"B.L. Stryker," <u>270</u>, 454
Babe, The, 353
Babenco, Hector, 38, 135, 136, **136**, <u>361</u>
"Baby, It's Cold Outside," 448
Baca, Jimmy Santiago, 60
Baca, Patrick, **216**
Bacall, Lauren, 516

Bach, Catherine, 264, 267, <u>361</u>
Bacher, William A., 72
Back Roads, 379, 380
Back Street, 412
Back to Bataan, <u>38</u>
Bacon, Irving, 51
Bacon, Lloyd, 128
Bad and the Beautiful, The, <u>38–39</u>, 433, 486
Bad Boys, <u>39</u>, 451, 494
Bad Day at Black Rock, 220
Bad Man, The, <u>39</u>
Bad Medicine, 457
Bad News Bears, The, 396
Bad One, The, 390
Badge of Evil, 227
Badge 373, <u>39–40</u>, 80, 359, 384
Badger, Clarence, 39
Badham, John, 207
Badillo, Robert, 312
Badlanders, The, 428
Badlands, 498
Badman's Territory, 464
Baer, Willi, 71
Baez, Rafael, 200
Baguez, Salvador, 34, 56, 60, 103, 210
"Baia," 222
Baker, Carroll, 49, 75
Baker, Elliot, 64, 241
Baker, Phil, 112
Baker, Stanley, 328
"Bakersfield P.D.," <u>270</u>
Bakula, Scott, 277
Baldwin, Alec, 301
Balin, Ina, 74, 80, 81, 306
Ball, Lucille, 106, 152, 225, 262, **262**, 284–86, **285**, <u>288</u>, 357, 358, 359, 381, 466, 519
Ballad of an Unsung Hero, 63, 359
Ballad of Gregorio Cortez, The, 23, 25, <u>40–41</u>, 163, 217, 393, 397, 459, 461, 496, 503, 512
Ballard, Kaye, 198
Ballet Hispanico, 504
Ballhaus, Michael, 152
Balsam, Martin, 86, 127
Baltimore Bullet, The, 481
Bananas, <u>41–42</u>, 251, 397, 446, 451, 503
Bancroft, Anne, 145, 146, **146**, 314, 449
Banda, Benjamin Bratt. *See* Bratt, Benjamin
Banda de Lua, 220
Banderas, Antonio, 152, 181, <u>362</u>
Bandido, 20, <u>42</u>, **42**, 348, 486
Bandido (stage), 508
Bandolero!, <u>43</u>, **43**, 434, 515
Bankhead, Tallulah, 448
Banning, 380
Bannon, Fred C., 326, 327
Bannon, Jim, 114
Bar, Jacques, 119
Bara, Nina, 114
Barabbas, 428, 472

Barbarian, The, 458
Barbarosa, <u>44</u>, **44**, 380, 387, 441, 486, 510
Barbash, Bob, 182, 219
Barbeau, Adrienne, 307
Barber of Seville, The, 473
Barcena, Catalina, 11
Barefoot Contessa, The, <u>45</u>
"Baretta," 263, 412, 467, 490
Bari, Lynn, 64, 219, 338
Barker, Lex, 408
"Barnaby Jones," 266
"Barney Miller," <u>271</u>, 412, 441, 499
Baron, Lita [Isabelita], 114, 178, <u>362</u>
Barr, Nancy, 314
Barrat, Robert, 220
Barreto, Bruno, 212, 367
Barrett, James Lee, 43, 235
Barrett, Michael, 193
Barroso, Ary, 63
Barry, Tom, 334
Barrymore, John, 11, 28, 357
Barrymore, Lionel, 71, 91
Barsocchini, Peter, 102
Bart, Hank, 110
Bartel, Paul, 92, 93
Barthelmess, Richard, 139, 175, 336
Bartholomew, Freddie, 71
Bartlett, Hall, 76, 213, 393
Bartlett, Lanier, 139
Bartlett, Sy, 49, 74
Barton, Charles T., 157, 327
Barzman, Ben, 38
Basehart, Richard, 134
Basevi, James, 70
Basil, Toni, 463
Bassler, Robert, 219
Bataan, 17, <u>45</u>, 357
Bataille, Henri, 186
Bates, Cary, 78
Bates, Kathy, 38
Bathing Beauty, 17, 383, 473, 487
Batista, Lloyd, 141
Batjac, 30, 517
Batman, 489
"Batman," 488
Batman Returns, 478
Batnik, Aida, 168
*batteries not included, 465
Battle Cry, <u>45–46</u>, **46**, 433, 434, 443
Battle Stripe. *See* Men, The
Battleground, 17, <u>47</u>, 448
Battleship Potemkin, The, 142
Bauer, Fred, 65
Bauer, Ralph, 7, 8
Bauer, Steven, 208, 209, 280, 293, 300, 307, <u>362–63</u>, **363**
Baum, Martin, 64
Baxter, Anne, 511
Baxter, Charles, 311
Baxter, Warner, 11, 190, 199, 236, 334, 335, **335**, 336, 337, 338, 344, 369, 390, 425, 437, 438, 449, 525

"Bay City Blues," <u>271</u>, 510
"Baywatch," 397, 422
Beach Red, 154, 492
Beacham, Stephanie, 296
Bean, Henry, 130
Bearcat, The, 387
Beast, The, 363
Beast of Hollow Mountain, The, <u>47</u>, 140, 479
Beast of Marseilles, The, 408
Beast with Five Fingers, The, 369
Beatty, Warren, 473
Beau Geste, 474
Beauchamp, Richard, 272
Beautiful Blonde from Bashful Bend, The, 439
Beauty and the Bandit, <u>339</u>, 354, 485
"Beauty and the Beast," 348, 397
Because You're Mine, 210
Beck, Michael, 247, 284
Becker, Stephen, 82
Beckerman, Sidney, 131
Becket, 472
Beckner, Michael Frost, 213
Beckworth, 148
Bedazzled, 515
Bedelia, Bonnie, 49, 87
Bedford, Patrick, 238
Bedoya, Alfonso, 49, 56, **56**, 68, 180, 194, 213, 214, 230, 232, **232**, <u>363</u>, 410
Bedroom Window, The, 490
Beebe, Ford, 342, 343
Beery, Noah, 235, 324
Beery, Noah, Jr., 175
Beery, Wallace, 12, 241, 242, 336
Beetlejuice, 441
Bega, Leslie, 281
Behind the High Wall, 411
Behind the Iron Mask, 403
Behold a Pale Horse, <u>47</u>
Beirute, Yerye, 211
Belasco, David, 201
Belden, Charles S., 339, 341
Belgard, Arnold, 177
Bel Geddes, Barbara, 276
Believers, The, <u>48</u>, 499, 502
Bell, Geoffrey, 6
Bell for Adano, A, 437
Bellamy, Earl, 306
Bellamy, Ralph, 186, 376
Bellaver, Harry, 170
Belle de Jour, 369
Belle of Old Mexico, 481
Bellini, Nino, 224
Bellisario, Don P., 141
Bells Are Ringing, 518
Bells of Rosarita, 436
Bellwood, Pamela, 304
Belmondo, Jean-Paul, 515
Beloin, Edmund, 198
Below Zero, 13
Belson, Jerry, 110

Beltran, Alma, 125, 177, 178, 191, 214, 258, 274, 295, 310, <u>363</u>
Beltran, Orlando, 56
Beltran, Ray, 155
Beltran, Robert, 92, 93, 111, 135, 142, 147, 258, 278, 308, <u>363</u>
Belushi, James, 205, 206
"Ben Casey," 263, 449
Ben-Ami, Yoram, 147
Benard, Maurice, 314
Benchley, Robert, 177
Bend of the River, 19
Bender, Jack, 315
Bendix, William, 49, 119
Beneath the Planet of the Apes, 413
Beneath the 12-Mile Reef, 486
Benedek, Laslo, 29, 137
Benedict, Dirk, 270
Benedict, Richard, 78, 79
Benenson, Bill, 59
Ben-Hur (1926), 8, 10, 457, 458
Ben-Hur (1959), 93
Benitez, Tomas, 202
Benjamin, Richard, 370
Bennet, Spencer, 326
Bennett, Bruce, 230
Bennett, Richard, 510
Benny, Jack, 408
"Benson," 482
Benson, Robby, 245, 246, **246**, 298
Benton, Jack, 342
Berenger, Tom, 38, 141, 213, 433, 519
"Berenger's," 510, <u>271</u>
Berg, Benjamin, 142
Berger, Senta, 151
Bergman, Andrew, 130
Bergman, Ingrid, 105, **106**, 122, 168, 387, 403, 456
Beristain, Gabriel, <u>363–64</u>
Beristain, Luis, 363
Berke, William, 100
Berkeley, Busby, 112, 129
Berlin Film Festival, 363
Berman, Pandro S., 49, 198, 455
Bernard, Judd, 53
Bernerd, Jeffrey, 341
Bernsen, Corbin, 287
Bernstein, Armyan, 172
Bernstein, Elmer, 151
Bernstein, Leonard, 3, 249, 250
Berry, John, 312
Bertolucci, Bernardo, 443
Bertrand, Rafael, 187
"Besame Mucho," 491
Best, Marjorie, 28, 506
Best, Willie, 114
Best Man, The, 404
Best Seller, 408, 473
Best Years of Our Lives, The, 19
Betancourt, Anne, 278
Betrayal, 425
Bettinson, Ralph, 339
"Beverly Hillbillies, The," 295

Beverly Hills Cop III, 354
"Beverly Hills, 90210," 266
Beyer, Troy, 200
Beymer, Richard, 249
Beyond All Limits, 147
Beyond the Border. See Mexicana
Beyond the Limit, <u>48</u>, 376, 440
Beyond the Stars, 499
Biberman, Herbert, 203
Bickford, Charles, 49, 60, 91, 201
Biddell, Sidney, 223
Bieri, Ramon, 214, 239
Big Bamboo, 438
Big Bird, 297
Big Boodle, The, <u>48</u>, 356, 479
Big Brawl, The, 403
Big Broadcast of 1938, The, 14, 385, 416
Big Carnival, The, 204
Big Circus, The, 486
Big Country, The, <u>49</u>, 363
Big Fix, The, <u>49</u>, 378
Big House, The, 12
Big Jake, 514
Big Leaguer, The, 519
Big Score, The, 456
Big Steal, The, 20, <u>49</u>, 458
Big Top Pee-wee, 393
"Big Valley, The," 348, 454
Big Wednesday, 433
Biggers, Earl Derr, 73
Biggest Bundle of Them All, The, 515
Biggs, Roxann, 291
Bilingual Foundation of the Arts, 518
Bill, Tony, 59, 60, 467
"Bill Dana Show, The," <u>271–72</u>, **272**, 276
Bill Haley and the Comets, 50
Billingsley, Barbara, 342
Billy Bathgate, 350
Billy Jack, 156, 370
Billy Jack Enterprises, 155
Billy Two Hats, 358
Binyon, Claude, 129, 181
Biraben, Alfredo. *See* Norton, Barry
Bird, 507
Bird of Paradise, 389, 390
Bird on a Wire, 378
Birdman of Alcatraz, 375
Birinski, Leo, 113
Biros, Lajos, 186
Birth of a Nation, The, 7
Bishop, William, 189
Bisset, Jacqueline, 237
Bixby, Bill, 264, 318
Bizet, Georges, 148
Bizet's Carmen, 395
Black, Karen, 78, 496
Black, Ralph, 128
Black, Todd, 255, 308
Black Alibi, 144
Black Beauty, 351
Black Camel, The, 73
Black Gold, 471
Black Horse Canyon, 389

"Black Jack Savage," 490
Black Marble, 378
Black Orchid, 375
Black Pearl, The, 486
Black Rain, 409, 417
Black Rose, The, 363
Black Scorpion, The, 387
Black Sunday, 351
Black Widow, 354
Blackboard Jungle, 20, <u>49–50</u>, 217, 238, 245, 257, 370, 371, 520
Blackburn, Richard, 92
Blackman, Honor, 118
Blackmer, Sidney, 82
Blackschleger, Janis, 304
Blade Runner, 461
Blades, Ruben, 84, 100, 147, 159, 160, 185, 188, 218, 305, 315, <u>364–65</u>, **364**, 465
Blair, Janet, 266
Blake, Bobby, 230
Blake, Pamela, 326
Blake, Robert, 224, 467
Blame It on Rio, <u>50</u>
Blanc, Mel, 215
Blanchard, Mari, 148
Blanke, Henry, 45, 132, 210, 230
Blasco Ibanez, Vicente, 36, 51, 52, 108, <u>365</u>
Blatt, Daniel H., 145
Blaustein, Julian, 83, 108
Blazing Saddles, 410
Blessed, Brian, 302
Blind Ambition, 499
Blind Rage, 469
Blindfold, 475
Blink, 503
Blinn, Holbrook, 201
Block, Ralph, 166, 336
Blockade, <u>50–51</u>
Blonde Saint, The, 484
Blondie Goes Latin, <u>51</u>
Blood Alley, 517
Blood & Orchids, 403, 503
Blood and Sand (1922), 7, <u>51</u>, 211, 483
Blood and Sand (1941), 7, <u>52–53</u>, 66, 70, 211, 365, 418, 420, 456, 471, 519
Blood In . . . Blood Out . . . . See *Bound by Honor*
Blood Roots. See *Raices de Sangre*
Bloodhounds of Broadway, 451
Bloom, Claire, 176, 191
Bloom, Verna, 39
Blowing Wild, 20, <u>53</u>, 239, 407
Blue, <u>53</u>, 363, 449
Blue City, 374
Blue Hawaii, 395, 399
Blue Knight, The, 456, 350
Blue Skies, 17, 493, **493**
Blue Thunder, 351, 494
Blues City, 380
Blum, Deborah, 239
Blumberg, Lewis F., 48

Blume in Love, 418
"Boa Noite," 220
Boardwalk, 406
Bob & Carol & Ted & Alice, 417
"Bob Cummings Show, The," 512
"Bob Hope Presents the Chrysler Theatre," 475
Bobby Deerfield, 492
Bochco, Steven, 271, 283, 287
Bodies of Evidence, 396
Bodrero, James, 222
Body Double, 389, 423
Body Rock, 431
Boehm, Sydney, 60, 165, 210
Boetticher, Budd, 53, 66, 149, 234, 254, 255, <u>519–20</u>
Bogart, Humphrey, 2, 19 20, 45, 120, 230, **232**, 237, 446, 456, 480, 525
Bogart, Peter, 314
Bogdanovich, Peter, 465
Bogeaus, Benedict, 36, 64, 178
Bolado y O'Donnell, Maria Margarita Guadalupe Teresa Esella Castillo. *See* Margo
Bold Caballero, <u>323</u>, 323, 324
"Bold Ones, The," 480
Boles, John, 197, 198, 201, 510
Bologna, Joseph, 50, 304
Bolt, Robert, 162
Bolton, Guy, 197
Bombardier, 17, <u>54</u>, 439
Bombay Clipper, 450
Bonanova, Fortunio, 63, 101, 105, 109, 166, 210, 220, 325, <u>365</u>
"Bonanza," 154, 263, 281, 431, 454, 458, 488, 517, 518
Bond, Ward, 197
Bonfiglio, Lois, 168
Bonilla-Gianini, Roxanna, 188, 189
Bonnie and Clyde, 144
Boone, Pat, 399
Boone, Richard, 30, 127, 197, 248
Boorman, Charley, 98
Boorman, John, 98
Booth, Charles G., 149, 163
Boothe, Powers, 2, 98
Borack, Carl, 49
Borcosque, Carlos, 11
Borden, Bill, 137
Border, The, 22, <u>54</u>, **54**, 376, 397, 412, 461
Border Cafe, 357
Border Incident, 20, <u>55–56</u>, 55, 362, 449, 505
Border Law, 506
Border Radio, 388
Border River, <u>56</u>, **56**, 355, 363, 408
Border Romance, 357
Borderline (1950), <u>57</u>, 408, 421, 505
Borderline (1980), <u>57</u>, 378, 380, 412, 456, 512
Bordertown, 20, <u>57–58</u>, **58**, 82, 513
Boretz, Allen, 82

Borgnine, Ernest, 28, 89, 140, 239, 252, 253
Born in East L.A., 1, 25, 26, <u>58–59</u>, **59**, 343, 433, 438, 461, 463, 468, 479, 481, 507, 517, 518
"Born in the USA," 58
Born on the Fourth of July, 3, 395, 468
Born to Win, 396
Born Wild, 440
Born Yesterday, 436
Borofsky, Mickey, 308
Borrego, Jesse, 60, 278, <u>366</u>
Borrelli, Jim, 72
Borsos, Phillip, 410
Boryea, Jay M., 200
Bosch, Roselyne, 108
Boss of Bullion City, 450
Bosson, Barbara, 283
Boss's Son, The, 454
Botany Bay, 442
Boudu Sauvé des Eaux, 89
Boudu Saved from Drowning, 89
Boulevard Nights, <u>59–60</u>, 378, 387, 395, 443, 510, 512, 517, 518
Boulting, Roy, 202
Bound by Honor, 26, <u>60</u>, 364, 366, 367, 374, 378, 380, 412, 415, 446, 456, 479, 481, 512
Bourguignon, Serge, 193
Bow, Clara, 11, 483, 484
Bower, Tom, 40, 461
Bowery Buckaroos, 506
Bowery to Broadway, 377, 450
Bowie, Jim, 30
Box, Muriel, 77
Box, Sydney, 77
Boy and the Turtle, The, <u>302</u>
Boyd, Stephen, 515
Boyer, Ann, 464
Boyer, Charles, 126
Boyle, Richard, 205
Boys from Brazil, The, 435, 465
Boys in Company C, The, 23, 451
Boytler, Aready, 386
Brabin, Charles, 64
Bracco, Lorraine, 157
Brach, Houston, 213
Bracken, Eddie, 225
Brackett, Charles, 112, 126, 201
Brackett, Leigh, 197
Bradbury, Ray, 384
Bradford, Richard, 191
Bradna, Olympe, 142
Braga, Sonia, 22, 135, 136, 159, 160, 163, 265, 314, <u>366–67</u>, **366**
Brahm, John, 160
Brams, Richard, 307
Branagh, Kenneth, 410
Branded, <u>60</u>, 369, 433, 507
Brando, Marlon, 20, 35, 36, 78, 171, 172, **172**, 242, 243, **243**, 244, 245, 348, 369, 371, 379, 395, 396, 428, 449, 454, 465, 470, 471, 506

Brandon, Henry, 75
Bratt, Benjamin, 60, 173, 286, 287, 291, 367
Bravado, The, 61
Bravados, The, 500
Brave Bulls, The, 20, 61, 66, 404, 423, 446, 471
Brave New World, 473
Brave One, The, 61–62, 62, 374, 423
Brazil, 63, 416, 444
"Brazil," 63
Brazzi, Rossano, 45
Break of Dawn, 25, 63–64, 359, 496
Breakfast at Sunrise, 351
Breakfast Club, The, 398
Breakfast in Hollywood, 491
Breakin', 483
Breaking Point, The, 422
Breakout, 64, 475
Breathless, 467
Brecher, Irving, 67
Brecher, Kenneth, 258
Breen, Richard L., 211
Bregman, Martin, 71, 208
Bregman, Michael S., 71
Bren, J. Robert, 37, 229, 367
Bren, Milton H., 57
Brennan, Frederick Hazlitt, 27
Brennan, Terence, 200
Brennan, Walter, 164, 197, 294
Brenner, Alfred, 133
Brenon, Herbert, 118
Brent, Romney, 28, 327, 367
Bresler, Jerry, 151
Brice, Monte, 158
Brick, Richard, 120
Brick Foxhole, The, 520
Brickman, Paul, 87
Bridge of San Luis Rey, The (1929), 64, 351, 475, 505
Bridge of San Luis Rey, The (1944), 64
Bridges, Beau, 281
Bridges, James, 35
Bridges, Jeff, 100
Bridges, Lloyd, 125, 125, 281
Bridges, Tom, 112
Bright, John, 61, 78
Bright Angel, 367
Bright Shawl, The, 64, 480
Brightman, Homer, 204, 222
Brimley, Wilford, 311
Brimmer, Gabriela, 111
Brinckerhoff, Burt, 302, 318
Bring Me the Head of Alfredo Garcia, 64–65, 401, 467, 509, 509, 524
Briones brothers, 66
British Agent, 488
Britt, Ruth, 368
Britton, Barbara, 189
Broadway Magic, 181
Broadway Melody, The, 464
Broccoli, Albert R., 118, 145
Brock, Lou, 104, 220, 221

Brodney, Oscar, 157
Broken Arrow, 19, 368
"Broken Arrow," 443
"Broken Badges," 404
Broken Lance, 21, 393, 408, 427, 428, 480
Broken Wing, The, 11
Brolin, James, 290, 290
Bronco Billy and the Greaser, 5
Bronfman, Edgar, Jr., 54
Bronson, Charles, 57, 64, 89, 119, 135, 149, 150, 163, 239, 240, 240, 277, 382, 402, 422, 434, 456, 486, 512
Bronston, Samuel, 931, 496
Bronx Tale, A, 512
Bronx War, 509
"Brooklyn Bridge," 513
"Brooklynonga," 37
Brooks, James L., 294
Brooks, Leslie, 256
Brooks, Mel, 410, 518
Brooks, Richard, 49, 50, 83, 84, 148, 165, 186, 187, 371, 403, 486, 520
Brother Rat, 403
Brotherhood of the Gun, 302
Brothers Rico, The, 368, 369
Brower, Otto, 338
Brown, Bryan, 387, 504
Brown, Cecil, 251
Brown, Clancy, 304
Brown, David, 101
Brown, Garrett M., 300
Brown, Georg Stanford, 368
Brown, Georgia, 463
Brown, Hiram S., Jr., 324
Brown, James, 459
Brown, Jim, 89, 94, 173, 174, 197
Brown, Johnny Mack, 387, 450
Brown, Lloyd, 190
Browne, Porter Emerson, 39
Browne, Roscoe Lee, 83
Browning, Kirk, 308
Bruce, George, 101
Bruce, Virginia, 63
Bruckheimer, Jerry, 88
Brunetti, Argentina, 140, 143, 158, 233, 234, 249, 368–69, 368
Brute Force, 520
Brynner, Yul, 73, 120, 134, 149, 150, 151, 193, 240, 240, 379, 431, 433, 472
Buccaneer, The (1938), 406
Buccaneer, The (1956), 472
Buccella, Grazia, 240
Buchanan, James David, 305
Buchholz, Horst, 149, 150
Buchinsky, Charles. *See* Bronson, Charles
Buchman, Harold, 338
Buck, Jules, 230
Buck and the Preacher, 467
Buck Rogers in the 25th Century, 500
Buckner, Robert, 153, 316
Buddy Holly Story, The, 65, 65, 137, 423, 478

Buena Vista, 60, 124, 147, 173, 204, 207, 327
Buenos Aires Symphony, 495
Buffalo Bill, 4
Buffalo Bill, 471
Buffington, Adele, 341
Buford, Gordon, 124
Bugambilia, 392
Bull, Sheldon, 275
Bulldog Drummond in Africa, 365
Bulletproof, 406
Bullfighter and the Lady, The, 20, 66, 126, 428, 464, 486, 517, 519
Bullfighters, The, 66
Bullitt, 368, 405, 495
Bullock, Sandra, 255
Bullock, Walter, 112, 338
Buloff, Joseph, 220
Bundy, A. Frank, 77
Bunuel, Luis, 15, 25, 247, 361, 363, 369, 476, 477
Buono, Victor, 255
Burbridge, Betty, 339, 342
Burden of Proof, 302
Burgess, Dorothy, 334, 335
Burns, Allan, 277, 294
Burns, George, 363
Burns, Walter Noble, 199
Burr, Raymond, 29
Burrell, Christine, 314
Burrell, Peter, 87, 258
Burroughs-Tarzan Pictures, 324
Burrud, L.M., 147
Burton, Richard, 167, 167, 168, 494, 514
Busch, Niven, 91, 111, 229
Busey, Gary, 44, 65, 65, 137, 145, 185, 350
Bush, Barbara, 301
Bush, George, 301
Bush-Fekete, Ladislas, 181
Butch Cassidy and the Sundance Kid, 2, 67, 151, 245
Butcher's Wife, The, 359
Butler, David, 245
Butler, Frank, 67, 129, 156
Butler, Michael, 79
Butler, Robert, 207, 374
Butterflies Are Free, 348
By Love Possessed, 429
Bye, Bye Birdie, 67, 219
Bye, Bye Birdie (stage), 479
Byrnes, Jim, 316

Caan, James, 109, 425
Cabal, Robert, 153, 294, 369
"Caballero's Way, The," 333
Cabanne, Christy, 341
Caboblanco, 467, 486
Cabot, Bruce, 199
Cabot, Sebastian, 220
Cactus Kid, The, 387
Caddy, The, 369
Cadence, 498, 499

"Cade's County," 272, 371
Cadiente, Dave, 187, 369
Cadillac Man, 417
Cadman, Joshua, 287
Cady, Jerry, 119, 158, 159, 220
Caffrey, Stephen, 299
Cagney, James, 19, 114, 226, 419
"Cagney & Lacey," 368, 408
Cain, Christopher, 256
Cain, James M., 210
Caine, Michael, 48, 50, 239, 376, 440, 465
Caine Mutiny, The, 403
Cains, Ruth, 148, 149
Calderon, Antonio, 264, 305, 319
Calderon, Paul, 188
Caldwell, Anne, 104
Calendar Girl Murders, The, 408
Calhern, Louis, 49, 64, 106
Calhoun, Rory, 20, 229, **229**, 248, 408
"Caliente," 128
California, 67, 368
California Conquest, 68, 363
California Motion Picture Corporation, 7
California Passage, 436
California Trail, The, 409
Californian, The, 68
Californio, The, 173
Calihan, William A., 151
Call Her Savage, 484
Call of the Flesh, 458
Call Out the Marines, 456
Callahan, Pepe, 32, 149
Calleia, Joseph, 30, 60, 85, 105, 116, 132, 133, 147, 199, 210, 227, **228**, 229, 237, 369
Callejo, Cecilia, 100
Calvelli, Joseph, 87
Calvin, Henry, 302, 327, 329
Calvo, Jose, 103
Camacho, Manuel Avila, 16
Camacho, Miguel, 257
Cambas, Jacqueline, 370
Camelot, 350, 359, 375
Cameron, Rod, 182
Camhi, Patrice. *See* Martinez, Patrice
Camille (1927), 10, 483
Camille (1952), 504
Campana, Nina, 226
Campanella, Joseph, 290
Campbell, Bill, **46**
Campos, Rafael, 35, 49, 50, 232, 233, 294, 303, **303**, 304, 370–71, **370**
Campos, Victor, 155, 156, 208, 272, 277, 371
Campus Flirt, The, 484
Camus, Amy. *See* Sumac, Yma
Can You Hear the Laughter? The Story of Freddie Prinze, 302–3, 354, 374
Canaan, Christopher, 307
Cancel My Reservation, 517
"Cancion de la Raza," 405, 518
Candy, John, 469

Cannan, Denis, 126
Cannell, Stephen J., 270, 300
Cannery Row, 68, 393, 451
Cannery Row (novel), 68
Cannes Film Festival, 18, 29, 155, 162, 400, 469–70
Cannon (film company), 103, 135, 202
Cannon, Pomeroy, 108
Cannonball Run, The, 361
Cannonball Run II, 361
Cano, Larry, 371
Cansino, Don Antonio, 418
Cansino, Eduardo, 14, 148, 418, 420, 436
Cansino, Elisa, 418
Cansino, Rita [Margarita]. *See* Hayworth, Rita
Cantin, Marie, 247
Cantinflas, 37, 181, 271, 371–73, **372**, 509
Cantor, Eddie, 13, 134
Canutt, Yakima, 324
Caper of the Golden Bulls, 464
Capetanos, Leon, 89, 163
Caplan, Harry, 74
Capp, Al, 87
Capra, Frank, 19, 436
Captain Blood, 81, 433
Captain from Castile, 2, 20, 69–71, 69, 218, 413, 452, 488
Captain Horatio Hornblower, 525
Captain Kidd, 485
Captain Sinbad, 356, 517
Captain Thunder, 71, 351
Captains Courageous, 71, 170
Car Wash, 399, 496
Cara, Irene, 27, 277, 373, 373
Carabatsos, Jim, 122
Carabatsos, Steven, 94
Caravaggio, 363
Caravan, 449
Carbajol, Henry. *See* Carr, Henry
Cardenas, Elsa, 61, 62, **62**, 109, 110, 115, **115**, 116, 219, 374
Cardi, Pat, 35
Cardiff, Jack, 62
Cardinale, Claudia, 186, 187
Cardona, Annette, 142, 374
Cardona, Rene, 11, 211
Carewe, Edwin, 190, 389, 390
Carey, Harry, 390, 475, 480
Carey, Harry, Jr., 222, **223**
Carey, Macdonald, 143
"Carioca, The," 105, 173
Cariou, Len, 292
Carliner, Mark, 241
Carlito's Way 71–72, 417, 423, 432, 504
Carlo, Ismael ("East"), 88, 295, 374
Carlson, Richard, 140
Carmen, Julie, 118, 135, 141, 159, 160, 181, 275, 278, 302, 305, 307, 309, 311, 314, 319, 374
Carmen, 386

Carmen (stage), 365
Carmichael, Hoagy, 63
Carmona, Pedro, 8
Carnal Knowledge, 454
Carnegie Hall, 473
Carner, Charles Robert, 145
Carnival in Costa Rica, 72, 418, 464, 488
Carnival Story, 61
Carpenter, John, 308
Carr, Henry, 8
Carr, Richard, 153
Carr, Vikki, 301
Carradine, David, 147, 187, 219
Carradine, Keith, 318
Carradine, Robert, 275, 307
Carrasco, Ada, 61
Carrasco, Carlos, 374
"Carrascolendas," 273
Carreno, Zarco, 56
Carrera, Barbara, 147, 155, 156, 276, 303, 374–75
Carrere, Edward, 28, 375
Carrere, Fernando, 375
Carrere, Leon, 375
Carricart, Robert, 89, 109, 110, 159, 240, 298, 375–76
Carrière, Jean-Claude, 38
Carrillo, Elpidia [Elpedia], 22, 48, 54, **54**, 145, 185, 205, 206, 376
Carrillo, Leo, 18, 50, 51, 109, 113, **113**, 114, 118, 128, 129, 159, 241, 263, 341, 342, 343, 344, **345**, 376–77, **376**, 390, 393, 475
Carroll, Gordon, 179
Carroll, John, 10, 198, 324
Carroll, Madeleine, 50
Carter, Lynda, 264, 267, 316, 377
Carter, Mike, 315
Carter, Thomas, 300
Carthay Continental, 94
Caruso, Enrico, 384
Caruso, Fred, 72
Carvajal, Tony, 229
Carvalho, Betty, 59
Carver, Steve, 147
"Casa de Locos." *See* "Marblehead Manor"
Casablanca (1942), 8, 81, 121, 122, 454, 456, 464
Casablanca (1983), 396
"Casablanca," 396
Casados, Eloy, 301
Casbah, 413, **413**
Case, Carroll, 234
"Case of Libel, A," 403
Casey, Bernie, 120, 271
Casey, James, 159
Cassandra Crossing, The, 499
Cassavetes, John, 29, 89, 118, 374
Cassidy, Hopalong, 3, 344
Cassidy, Joanna, 236
"Cassie and Company," 273
Castenada, Movita. *See* Movita

Castillan, The, 489
Castillejo, Chris, 23
Castillion, Chuy, 178
Castillo, Antonio, <u>378</u>
Castillo, Enrique [E.J.], 57, 60, 95, 148, 264, 313, 317, <u>378</u>
Castillo, Sol, 301
Castle, William, 34, 35
Castro, Eduardo, <u>378</u>
Castro, Isabel Beth. *See* Baron, Lita
Casualties of War, <u>72</u>
Cat and the Canary, The, 114
Cat and the Fiddle, The (1934), 458
Cat Chaser, <u>72</u>, 402, 443
Cat People (1942), 437
Cat People (1982), 370
Catalano, Armando. *See* Williams, Guy
Catch Me If You Can, 486
Catch-22, 499
Catlow, <u>73</u>
Cattle Town, **453**
Cavens, Albert, 326, 331
CBS, 270–302 *passim,* 309, 313, 314, 315, 316, 318, 331, 512, 513
CBS Radio, 284, 503
Cease Fire, 379
Ceballos, Larry, <u>378</u>
Cecil B. DeMille Award, 472
Celi, Teresa, 56
Centennial, <u>303</u>–4, **303**, 371, 375, 379, 441, 456, 517
Centeno, Lia, 248
Center Art Galleries, 472
Central Casting, 8, 439
Central Park Casino, 416
Century Pictures, 191
Certain Fury, 373
Certain Young Man, A, 458, **458**
Cervantes, Carlos, 98
Cervantes, Gary, 246, **246**, <u>378</u>
Cervantes, Miguel de, 154, 339
Cervera, Jorge, 221
Cervera, Jorge, Jr., 147, 299, 302, 318, <u>378</u>
Cha-Cha-Cha Boom, <u>73</u>, 414
Chacon, Juan, 203
Chadwick, June, 280
Chains of Gold, 367
Chair, The, 353
Chakiris, George, 134, 249, 250, **250**
Chaliapin, Feodor, 365
Chamberlain, Richard, 303, 375
Champagne for Two, 362
Chandler, Jeff, 153, 182, 369, 423, 504
Chaney, Lon, 393, 510
Chanslor, Roy, 167
Chapa, Damian, 60, <u>378</u>
Chaplin, Charlie, 11, 271, 322, 371, 372, 389, 409, 508
Chaplin Studios, 409
Charisse, Cyd, 101, 137, 213, **407**, 448
Charley's Aunt, 403
"Charlie & Co.," 510

Charlie Chan in Egypt, 419
Charlie Chan in Panama, <u>73</u>
Charlie Chan in Rio, <u>73</u>
"Charlie's Angels," 171, 368, 375
Charo, 163, 274, <u>379</u>, 383
Charro!, <u>74</u>
Chartoff, Robert, 64
Chase, Borden, 191, 234, 239
Chase, Charley, 435
Chase, Chevy, 87, 221, 384
Chase, The, 359, 498
Chaves, Richard, 185, <u>379</u>
Chavez, Jose, 187
Chavez, Oscar, 63
Che!, <u>74</u>, 434, 435, 503
Cheap Detective, The, **430**, 431
"Checking In," <u>273</u>
Cheech and Chong, 58, 237, 278, 438
Cheech and Chong's Next Movie, 238, 415, 438
Cheech and Chong's Nice Dreams, 238, 415, 438
Cheech and Chong's Still Smoking, 238, 438
Cheech and Chong's The Corsican Brothers, 438
Cheech and Chong's Things Are Tough All Over, 438
"Cheech Show, The," <u>273</u>
Cher, 462, 463
Cherback, Cynthia, 314
"Chevy Show, The," 266
"Cheyenne," 263, 508
Cheyenne Autumn, 21, <u>75</u>–76, **75**, 393, 449, 486, 520
Cheyenne Social Club, The, 499
"Chica, Chica, Boom, Chica," 220
Chicago Opera Company, 416, 438
Chicano Research Center, 397
Chicanos and Film, 6
Chickens Come Home, 13
"Chico and the Man," 261, 266, <u>273</u>–74, 363, 469, 492
Children of Sanchez, The, <u>76</u>, 393
Children of the Dark, 85
Children's Hour, The, 375
Children's Television Workshop, 277, 297
Childs, Herbert, 248
"China Beach," 264, 299
China Moon, 503
China Syndrome, The, 507
Chinatown, <u>77</u>, 77, 351, 396, 433, 434
"CHiPs," 8, 261, <u>274</u>–75, **274**, 399, 412, 431, 439
Chisholm Trail, The, 191
Choices of the Heart, <u>304</u>
Chomsky, Marvin J., 308
Chong, Rae Dawn, 81
Chong, Tommy, 58, 237, 278, 438
Chorus Line, A, 434
Christian, Linda, <u>379</u>
Christian Licorice Store, The, 486

Christie, Howard, 140
Christopher Columbus, <u>77</u>–78
Christopher Columbus: The Discovery, <u>78</u>, 393
Churubusco Studios, 18, 19, 120, 135, 162, 169, 181, 239, 517
Chuy Reyes and his Orchestra, 178
CIAA, 15, 37, 204
Ciannelli, Eduardo, 149
Cidre, Cynthia, 102, 152, <u>379</u>
Cielito Lindo, 387
Cilento, Diane, 127
Cimarron, 8
Cincinnati Kid, The, 495
Cinco Anos de Vida, 470
Cinco Vidas, 397
Cinecom, 95, 142
Cinemania, 470
CinemaScope, 61, 112, 126, 494, 519
Cintron, Humberto, 294
Circle Star Theatre, 463
Circo Parisch, 466
Circus, The, 409
Cisco Kid, 7, 321, <u>333</u>–45, 376–77, 411, 439, 474, 475, 485, 486, 488
Cisco Kid (1931), <u>336</u>
Cisco Kid, The (1914–16), <u>333</u>–34, **334**
Cisco Kid, The (1994), <u>343</u>–44, **343**, 354, 397, 438, 502
"Cisco Kid, The," 261, 263, <u>344</u>–45, **345**, 475, 480
Cisco Kid and the Lady, The, <u>337</u>, 439
Cisco Kid Returns, The, <u>339</u>
Cisco Pike, <u>78</u>
Cisneros, Evelyn, 304
Citizen Kane, 365
"CITY," <u>275</u>
City Across the River, <u>78</u>–79
City Beneath the Sea, 479
City Heat, 370, 373, 507
City Lights, 409
City Works, 438
Clark, Angela, 160
Clark, Dick, 304
Clark, Greydon, 139
Clark, Harry, 223
Clark, James B., 35, 213, 240
Clark, L. Travis, 299
Clark, Susan, 238
Clark, Walter Van Tilburg, 177
Clarke, Robert, 99
Clarkson, Patricia, 315
Clayburgh, Jill, 379
Clean Beds, 470
Cleopatra, 435
Clift, Montgomery, 20, 191
"Climax," 263, 449
Clinton and Nadine, 410
Clive of India, 488
Clockwork Orange, A, 405
Clohessy, Robert, 293
Clooney, Rosemary, 404
Close, Glenn, 318

Close Encounters of the Third Kind, 359, 459
Clothier, William H., 30, 76
Clouzot, Henri-Georges, 214
Club Havana, 362
Clune, 190
Clune, W.H., 190
"Coach," 442
Cobb, Lee J., 69, 102, 108, 119, 149, 233
Cobra Woman, 450
Coburn, James, 90, 126, 149, 150, 151, 179, 256, 269, 480
Coca, Richard, 32, 295
Cochran, Steve, 82, 114
Cockeyed World, The, <u>79</u>
Cockleshell Heroes, The, 403
Coco, James, 154, 453
Cocoon, 516
Cocoon: The Return, 516
Code of Silence, 79
Coe, Fred, 144
Coen, Franklin, 32, 135
Cohen, Albert J., 56
Cohen, Bennett R., 341
Cohen, Larry, 94, 187, 193
Cohen, Ronald M., 53
Cohn, Alfred, 336
Cohn, Harry, 420, 436
"Colbys, The," 264, 449
"Cold Blooded Penguin, The," 222
Coldrosen, John, 65
Cole, Gary, 315
Cole, Lester, 101
Cole, Royal, 326
Coleman, Cy, 219
Collins, Joan, 61
Collins, Richard, 135
Collins, Robert, 245
Colman, Ronald, 488
Colomby, Harry, 227
Colon, Alex, 87, 88, 304, 316, 317, <u>379</u>
Colon, Miriam, 35, 171, 172, 184, 208, 209, **209**, 288, 306, 316, <u>379–80</u>
Colon, Willie, 203, 294, 308
Colon Theatre, 473
Color Purple, The, 160
Colorado Territory, 525
Colors, <u>79–80</u>, **80**, 107, 350, 378, 474, 493, 501
Colton, John, 86
Columbia Pictures, 3, 13, 27, 32, 47, 51, 61, 64, 65, 67, 68, 72, 73, 78, 83, 94, 95, 101, 110, 114, 116, 118, 120, 137, 139, 148, 149, 151, 168, 172, 175, 176, 181, 186, 188, 192, 193, 201, 223, 224, 239, 248, 256, 280, 354, 407, 409, 419, 420, 433, 469, 482, 485, 507
Columbia Television, 363
"Columbo," 266, 356
Columbo, Arrigo, 103
Columbus, Chris, 436, 470
Colvig, Pinto, 204

Comanche, 382, 464
Comanche Station, 519
Comancheros, The, <u>80–81</u>, 433, 517
"Combat," 50, 264, 299, 449
Come Clean, 435
Comedians, The, 368
Comer, Anjanette, 35, 36, 119, <u>380</u>
Comfort, Bob, 294
Coming Home, 380
"Coming to America," 59
Commando, <u>81</u>, 378, 478, 490
"Commish, The," 491
Commonwealth United Release, 241
Competition, The, 495
Compromising Positions, <u>81</u>, 425
Computer Wore Tennis Shoes, The, 489
CONACINE, 188, 189
Conagher, 512
Conan the Barbarian, 433, 435
Concorde, 135
Concrete Jungle, The, 435
Conde, Rita, 194
"Condo," <u>275</u>, 360, 512
Coney Island, 488
Congressional Medal of Honor, 17, 23
Connection, The, 499
Connell, Del, 222
Connell, Richard, 198, 202
Connelly, Marc, 71
Connery, Sean, 86, 118, 122, 157, 356, 375
Connors, Chuck, 49, 178
Conqueror, The, 355
Conquest, 394
Conquest of Cochise, 450
Conquistador, 338
Conrack, 396, 399
Conrad, Michael, 283
Conrad, Robert, 275, 282, 303, 375
Conrad, Steve, 255
Conrad, William, 82, 166
Conroy, Kevin, 292
Considine, John W., Jr., 199
Constantine, Michael, 308
Conte, Richard, 102, 189
Conte, Robert, 224
Conti, Tom, 461
Contreras, Jaime, 211, 380
Contreras, James, <u>380</u>
Contreras, Luis, 98, <u>380</u>
Contreras, Robert(o), 32, 187, 208, 225, 282, <u>380</u>
Convoy, 441
Conway, Jack, 241
Conway, Kevin, 173
Conway, Tom, 100
Coogan, Jackie, 269
Cool Hand Luke, 359, 495
Coolidge, Rita, 179
Coon, Gene L., 153
Cooper, Dennis, 78
Cooper, Gary, 10, 11, 53, 105, **106**, 112, 125, **125**, 126, 239, 336, 387, 407,

428, 436, 450, 470, 480, 488, 503, 510, 519, 525
Cooper, Inez, 341
Cooper, Jackie, 167
Cooper, Merian C., 109, 222
Cooper, Paul, 309
Copacabana (1947), <u>82</u>, 445, 491
Copacabana (1986), <u>304</u>, 408
Copland, Aaron, 3, 101
Coppola, Francis Ford, 172, 358, 398, 410, 427, 497, 499, 507
Cordova, Caesar, <u>380</u>
Cordova, Fabian Gregory, 258
Cordova, Margarita, 171, 295
Cordova, Victoria, 220
Corey, Wendell, 111, 165
Corman, Roger, 123
Corn Is Green, The, 61
Cornall, Jack, 36
Cornell, Katharine, 365, 376
Coronet Theatre, 384
Corporacion Nacional Cinematografica. *See* CONACINE
Corporation for Public Broadcasting, 26, 216
Corraface, George, 78
Corral, Dolores, 187
Corri, Nick, 312
Corridos! Tales of Passion and Revolution, <u>304</u>, 507
Corrigan, Lloyd, 139
Cortes, Mapy, <u>381</u>
Cortez, Maria, 194
Cortez, Mary. *See* Cortes, Mapy
Cortez, Ricardo, 10, 36, 68, 338, <u>381</u>, 390
Cortez, Stanley, <u>381</u>
Corwin, Norman, 166
Cosby, Bill, 277, 515
"Cosby Show, The," 265, 433, 438, 462, 469
Coslow, Sam, 82
Costa-Gavras, Constantin, 161, 162
Costello, Diosa, 220, 434
Costello, Lou, 157, 158, 198, 512
Coster, Nicolas, 313
Costner, Kevin, 193, 441, 470
Cota, Manny, <u>381</u>
Cotten, Joseph, 91, **91**, 391
Cottrell, William, 222
Couderc, Pierre, 71
Count of Monte Cristo, The (1934), 387
Count of Monte Cristo, The (1941), 147
Coupe de Ville, 512
"Courtship of Eddie's Father, The," 264
Cousins, 348, **349**
Covenant with Death, A, <u>82</u>, 395, 401, 428
Cover Girl, 418, 420
Coward, Noel, 176, 425
Cowboy, <u>83</u>
Cowboys, The, <u>83</u>, 275, 440
"Cowboys, The," <u>275</u>
Cowen, Will, 86

Cox, Alex, 191, 247
Cox, Jack, 141
Cox, Morgan, 324
Cox, Ronnie, 296
"CPO Sharkey," 272
Crackers, 501
Craig, Yvonne, 256, 257
Crawford, Joan, 279, 336
Crazy from the Heart, 305, 365
Crazy House, 377
Creature from the Black Lagoon, 452
Creepshow, 490
Crenna, Richard, 73, 191, 294, 298
Crime, Inc., 377
"Crime and Punishment," 275, 504
"Crime Story," 374, 410, 423
Crime Without Passion, 437
Criminal Behavior, 441
Criminal Justice, 467
Crisis, 83–84, **84**, 369, 386, 403, 433,
    458, 486, 506, 520
Crisp, Donald, 190, 323
Cristal, Linda, 30, **31**, 85, **85**, 140, 163,
    261, 263, 281, 381–82, **382**, 522
Critical Condition, 364, 504
Crockett, Davy, 30–31
"*Crocodile*" *Dundee*, 402
"*Crocodile*" *Dundee II*, 374
Cromwell, James, 284
Crosby, Bing, 198, 199, 431, 456, 493
Crosby, Floyd, 61
Crosby, Mary, 141
Crosland, Alan, 71
Cross and the Switchblade, The, 379, 399
Crossfire, 520
Crossover Dreams, 25, **84**, 364, 423, 465
Crothers, Scatman, 273
Crowley, Pat, 133
Croyden, John, 126
Cruise, Tom, 101, 148, 468
Cruz, Alexis, 200, 311
Cruz, Brandon, 264
Cruz, Carlina, 314
Cruz, Celia, 29, 203
Cruz, Raymond, 309
Cruz, Socorro, 308
Cry Tough, 20, 85–86, **85**, 369, 382, 434,
    494
Crystal, Billy, 431, 502
Cuba, **86**, 122, 387, 396, 465, 475
Cuban Cultural Center, 98
Cuban Love Song, **86**, 510
Cuban Pete, **86**, 358
Cuban Thing, The, 426
Cue, Baltazar Fernandez, 39
Cuesta, Mike, 308
Cugat, Xavier, 3, 17, 127, 166, 256, 300,
    357, 362, 379, 383–84, **383**, 436,
    469, 486, 487
Cukor, George, 458, 470, 472
Cullingham, Mark, 311
Culver, Carmen, 314
Cummings, Irving, 90, 220, 334, 336,
    525

Cummings, Jack, 101, 213, 448
Cummings, Ruth, 64
Cunningham, Jack, 323
Curacao, 305
Curry, Mark, 280
"Curse of Capistrano, The," 321, 322
Curtin, Valerie, 292
Curtis, Ken, 327
Curtis, Tony, 78, 79, 382, 433
Curtiz, Michael, 80, 81, 235
Cusick, John, 211
Cypher, Jon, 238
Cyrano de Bergerac, 402, **402**, 403, 512
Cyrano de Bergerac (stage), 403, 404, 412

"D.A., The," 275
D.C. Cab, 481
D2: The Mighty Ducks, 399
Daché, Lily, 374
Dad, 395
Da Gradi, Don, 207
Dahl, Arlene, 430, 431
Dailey, Dan, 181
Dailey, Dan, Jr., 177
Dain Curse, The, 396
Dali, Salvador, 369
"Dallas," 276, 380, 408, 469, 506
Dalmas, Herbert, 28
Dalton, Timothy, 145
Daly, Tyne, 258
Dalya, Jacqueline, 230
Damas, Bertila, 384
Dames, Rob, 289
Damita, Lily, 64, 79
"Dan August," 276, 354, 478, 490, 271,
    272, **272**, 276, 298, 331
Dance Hall, 488
"Dance of Fury," 137
"Dancin' Days," 367
Dancing Cansinos, The, 418
Dancingers, Oscar, 180
D'Andre, Dante, 125
Dangerfield, Rodney, 457
Dangerous When Wet, 431
Daniel, Rod, 218
Daniel, Sean, 32, 187
Daniels, Bebe, 36, 197, 198, 474
Daniels, Harold, 220
"Danny Thomas Hour, The," 359
"Danny Thomas Show, The," 271, 276,
    357, 417
Danova, Cesare, 74
Dante's Inferno, 419
Darcel, Denise, 239
D'Arcy, Roy, **458**
Dare, Daniel, 198
Daring Caballero, The, 342
Dark Half, The, 490
Darkman, 405
Darling, W. Scott, 66
Darnell, Linda, 21, 52, 164, **164**, 210,
    325, 326, 511
Darren, James, 224

Darrow, Henry, 24, 39, 40, 127, 148,
    245, 246, 261, 264, 276, 281, **282**,
    291, 292, 293, 296, 304, 317, 331,
    332, 333, 384
Darwell, Jane, 21, 191
da Silva, Howard, 55, 176, 385
Date with Judy, A, 383, **383**, 445
Daughters of the Republic of Texas, 241
Daves, Delmar, 83, 230, 256
Davi, Robert, 145
David and Lisa, 385, 491
Davidson, Boaz, 202
Davidson, Donald, 327
Davidson, Ronald, 324, 326
Davidson, Royal, 327
Davies, Lane, 295
Davis, Andy, 79
Davis, Bette, 57, 58, **58**, 132
Davis, Clyde Brian, 27
Davis, Jim, 275, 276
Davis, John, 185
Davis, Luther, 126
Davis, Ossie, 270, 385
Davis, Peter S., 72
Davis, Sammy, Jr., 219
Davis, Tony, 120
Davison, Bruce, 212
Davitt, Hal, 71
"Davy Crockett," 331
Dawn of the Dead, 490
Dawson, Gordon, 64
Dawson, Kamala Lope. *See* Lopez,
    Kamala
Day, Doris, 20
Day, Francisco ("Chico"), 13–14, 134,
    142, 151, 385, 385
Day, Laraine, 234
Day, Richard, 249
Day, Robert, 219
Day Breakers, The, 316
*Day in Hollywood, A Night in the Ukraine,
    A*, 434
Day of the Dead, 490
Day of the Locust, 496
Daybreak, 458
Days of Heaven, 350
"DEA—Drug Enforcement Agency," 276
Dead Again, 410
Dead and Buried, 359
Dead Man Out, 305, 365
Dead Men Don't Wear Plaid, 494
Dead Pool, The, 507
Dead Zone, The, 499
Deadlock, 434
Deadly Companions, The, 523
Deadly Tower, The, 264, 305–6, **306**, 431,
    517
Deadly Trackers, The, 509
Deal of the Century, 87, 379, 439, 467,
    473, 496
De Almeida, Joaquin, 48
Dean, James, 20, 115, 116, 433, 443
de Anda, Raul, 382

Dearholt, Ashton, 324
Death Among Friends, 441
Death of a Gunfighter, <u>87</u>
Death of an Angel, <u>87</u>–88, 379
Death of Billy the Kid, The, 144, 311
"Death on a Side Street," 174
Death Wish II, 408
Death Wish 4: The Crackdown, 429
De Bar, Irene, 314
De Bote en Bote, 13, 347
Decameron Nights, 408
De Carlo, Yvonne, 56, 105, 178, 213, 504
"December Bride," 417
De Cordoba, Pedro, 72, 83, 100, 105, 114, 132, 133, 143, 153, 157, 190, 201, 325, 338, 339, 341, 342, <u>386</u>
De Cordova, Arturo, 17, 19, 105, **106**, 129, 130, 155, 156, **156**, 157, <u>386</u>–<u>87</u>, **386**
De Cordova, Frederick, <u>387</u>
de Cordova, Leander, 114
Dee, Ruby, 385
Deep Cover, 379
Deep in My Heart, 403
Deerslayer, The, 454, 479
Defiance, <u>88</u>, 374, 474, 491, 512
De Guzman, Josie, <u>387</u>
de Havilland, Olivia, 28, 52, 126
Dehn, Paul, 118
Dehner, John, 144
de Hoyos, Juan Martin, 151
Dein, Edward, 144
Deitch, Donna, 315
De Iturbi, Jose. *See* Iturbi, Jose
Dekker, Albert, 148
De La Cruz, Jose (Joe), 190, <u>387</u>
de la Madrid, Roberto, 257
de Landa, Juan, 12
De La Paz, Danny, 32, 34, 44, **44**, 59, 86, 111, 317, <u>387</u>
De La Pena, George, <u>388</u>
De la Pena, Gilbert, 228
de la Torre, Dale, 207
Del Campo, Rudy, 250
de Lemos, Lou, 293, 294, 308
De Leon, Marcus, 135, <u>388</u>
De Leon, Walter, 114
Delgado, Adelaide. *See* Mara, Adele
Delgado, Emilio, 297
Delgado, Henry. *See* Darrow, Henry
Delgado, Jose, 308
Delgado, Marcel, 14, <u>388</u>–<u>89</u>, **388**
Delgado, Victor, 14
Delicious, 490
Deliverance, 478
Del Mar, Marcia, 295, <u>389</u>
Delon, Alain, 328
De Lorenzo, Michael, 101, 281
del Pilar, Maria. *See* Cortes, Mapy
del Rey, Nita, 99
Del Rey, Pilar, 35, 56, 115, 116, 214, 233, <u>389</u>

Del Rio, Dolores, 9, 10–11, 18, 20, 21, 75–76, **75**, 104, **104**, 105, 109, 112, 118, 128, 129, **129**, 154, 190, 266, 290, 351, 355, <u>389</u>–<u>93</u>, **391**, **392**, 401, 438, 446, 449, 486, 490, 510, 525
Del Rio, Jack, 56
del Rivero, Dolores Conchita. *See* Moreno, Rita
Delta Force 2: Operation Stranglehold, <u>88</u>, 443, 468
Del Toro, Benicio, 78, 100, 307, <u>393</u>
DeMarco, Tony, 24, 112
DeMille, Cecil B., 5, 201, **385**, 470, 472, 494, 510
DeMille, Katherine, 68, 191, 241, 472
Demme, Jonathan, 181
De Niro, Robert, 162
Dennehy, Brian, 302
Dennis, Sandy, 238
Dennison, Rachel, 292
De Palma, Brian, 71, 72, 208, 209, 362, 380, 409, 495, 499
Depardieu, Gerard, 108, 187
Derek, John, 423
Dern, Bruce, 83
De Ruiz, Nick, 199, <u>393</u>
de Santa Silas, Maria Garcia Van Dahl. *See* Montez, Maria
Desert Hawk, The, 486
Desert Rider, The, 505
Deserter, The, 449
De Sica, Vittorio, 515
Design for Living, 425
"Desilu Playhouse," 299, 435
Desilu Productions, 357
Desilu Studios, 106, 262, 286, 417
Desilva, Noel, 219
De Soto, Rosana, 22, 40, 68, 137, 215, 217, 269, 291, 294, <u>393</u>–<u>94</u>, **394**
De Souza, Steven E., 81, <u>394</u>
Desperado 2, 422
Desperados, 307
Desperate Mission, The, <u>306</u>
Desperate Search, 442
De Sylva, B.G., 177, 236
Detective, The, 494
Detective Story, 376
Detmers, Maruschka, 152
de Toth, Andre, 94
Deutsch, Armand, 194
Deutsch, Helen, 106, 148
de Valdez, Carlos J., 50, 51, 199, 323, <u>394</u>
Devane, William, 280
De Vargas, Valentin, 24, 102, 227
De Vega, Jose, Jr., 250, <u>394</u>–<u>95</u>
Devil at 4 O'Clock, The, 89, 435
Devil Is a Woman, The, <u>88</u>
Devil May Care, 458
Devil with Women, A, 387
Devil's Playground, 391
De Vito, Danny, 199

Devon, Laura, 82
De Wolf, Karen, 36, 51
Dexter, Brad, 149, 150, 151
Dexter, Maury, 102
Dey, Susan, 287
Diamond, Don, 270, <u>395</u>
Diamond, Neil, 59, 359
Diamond, Peter, 333
Diamond Head, 443
Diamond Horseshoe, 418
Diamond Queen, The, 486
Diane, 356
Diary of Anne Frank, The, 465
Diaz, Edith, 293, <u>395</u>
Diaz, Ken, <u>395</u>
Diaz, Manny, 132, 133
Diaz, Ruby, 43, 74, 149
Diaz, Sully, 311
Dick Tracy, 500
"Dick Van Dyke Show, The," 417, 518
Dickey, Basil, 326
Dickey, Paul, 114
Dickinson, Angie, 197, 273
Die Hard, 394
Die Hard 2, 394, 478
Diehl, John, 310
Dieterle, William, 50, 132, 133
Dietrich, Marlene, 88, 227
Dietrich, Ralph, 338
Dilello, Richard, 39, 79, 276
Dillinger, 61, 441
Dillon, Matt, 398
Dime with a Halo, <u>89</u>, 434, 435, 463
Dingle, Charles, 156
Dino, Desi, and Billy, 358
Dios los Cria, 251, 451
Directors Guild of America, 148, 385, 397
Directors Guild of America Award, 309, 506
Dirty Dancing, 462
"Dirty Dancing," 463
Dirty Dozen, The, <u>89</u>, 151, 435, 519
Dirty Harry, 494, 495, 507
Discreet Charm of the Bourgeoisie, The, 477
Disney, Walt, 16, 204, 292, 327, 329, 395, 408, 433, 442, 517
"Disney Presents the 100 Lives of Black Jack Savage," <u>276</u>
Disorganized Crime, 364, 410
DiSpina, Teresa, 309
Distant Drums, 525
Distant Water, 360
Distinguished Gentleman, The, 364, 481
Dix, Richard, 113, 153
Dmytryk, Edward, 32, 38
"Do Not Forsake Me, Oh My Darlin'," 126
Do the Right Thing, 466
Do You Love Me?, 418
Dr. Giggles, 381, 397

Doctor Zhivago, 74, 465
"Doctors, The," 473
"Doctors' Hospital," <u>277</u>, 371
Dodge, David, 182
Dog of Flanders, A, 35
Dolenz, George, 254
Doll Face, 445
"Dolores Del Rio's Mexico," 393
Dom Juan, 28
Domasin, Larry, 109
Domergue, Faith, 408
Dominant Sex, The, 367
Domingo, Placido, <u>395</u>
Dominguez, Beatrice, 108
Dominguez, Joe, 60, 111, 144, 194, 213, 224, 226, 234, 237, 255
Dominguez, Jose, 83, 137, 174, 210
Dominguin, Luis Miguel, 37, 446
Don Daredevil Rides Again, <u>327</u>
Don Giovanni, 28
Don Is Dead, The, 472
Don Juan, 365
Don Juan in Hell, 448
Don Q, Son of Zorro, <u>323</u>, 347
"Don Q's Love Story," 323
Don Quixote, 154
Dona Flor and Her Two Husbands, 367
Donati, Sergio, 90
Donde, Manuel, 230
Donen, Stanley, 50, 137, 515
Donlevy, Brian, 128
Donnelly, Thomas Michael, 88
D'Onofrio, Vincent, 102
Donovan's Reef, 369, 489
Don't Go Near the Water, 480
Don't Look Back: The Story of Leroy "Satchel" Paige, 431
Don't Touch My Daughter, 469
Dor, Karin, 225
Dorso, Richard, 313
Dortort, David, 281, 384
Dos Passos, John, 88
Dotrice, Roy, 280
Double Crossed, <u>307</u>
Double Indemnity, 365
Doud, Gil, 123
Doug, Doug E., 120
Douglas, Diana, 275
Douglas, Gordon, 197, 207
Douglas, Kirk, 38, 204, 410, 422, 488
Douglas, Michael, 199, 409, 504
Douglas, Robert, 28
Dove, Billie, 484
Dove, The, 118, 484
Down and Out in Beverly Hills, 22, <u>89–90</u>, 417, 465
Down Argentine Way, 17, <u>90</u>, 220, 365, 445, 456, 512
Downs, Cathy, 164
Downtown, 370, 401
Doyle, Laird, 57
Doyle-Murray, Brian, 270
Dracula (1931; English-language version), 12

Dracula (1931; Spanish-language version), 12, 513
Dracula (stage), 425
Dracula, The Cat Creeps, 506
"Dragnet," 263
Drago, Billy, 88
Drake, Larry, 287
Drama Desk Award, 473
"Dream Merchant, The," 403
Dreaming Lips, 367
Dreifuss, Arthur, 114
Dresher, Beatrice, 178
Dresner, Hal, 328
Dressed to Kill, 504
Drew, Roland, 390
Drexell, Oliver, Jr., 313
Dreyfuss, Richard, 49, 89, 163, 367, 399, 503
Drug Wars: The Camarena Story, 264, <u>307</u>, 362, 363, 393, 468
Drug Wars: The Cocaine Cartel, 264, <u>307</u>
Drum, 510
Drum Beat, 433, 443
Drums in the Deep South, 61
Drunkard, The, 464
Dryer, Fred, 284
Du Bari, Irene, 246
Du Bois, Marta, 59, <u>395</u>
Dubrow, Donna, 157
Duchow, Peter K., 309
Duck Soup, 505
Duck, You Sucker!, <u>90</u>
Dude Goes West, The, 485
"Dudley," <u>277</u>
Dudley Pictures, 29
Duel in the Sun, 21, <u>91–92</u>, **92**
Duff, Howard, 279
Duff, Warren, 128, 140
Duffey, Jesse, 326
Duffy, Albert, 338
Duffy, Patrick, 276
Duffy's Tavern, 385, 387
Duggan, Pat, 257
Duigan, John, 200
Duke, Bill, 185
"Dukes of Hazzard, The," 264, 267, 361
Duna, Steffi, 139, 149
Dunaway, Faye, 77, 245, 308
Duncan, David, 130
Duncan, Steve, 299
Duncan, William, 413
Dune, 404, 435
Dunlap, Dawn, 123
Dunlap, Scott R., 339, 341
Dunn, Herbert Stanley, 333, 334, **334**
Dunn, Steve, 73
Dunne, Philip, 248
Duran, Larry, 36, 151, 171, 172, <u>395–96</u>
Duran, Larry, Jr., 396
Durante, Jimmy, 86
Durell, Marina, 39, 40, 312
Durning, Charles, 72
Duron, Gilbert, 299

Durrell, Marina, 218
Duryea, Dan, 174, 219
Dutton, Charles, 187, 188
Duvall, Robert, 39, 40, 64, 79, 80, **80**, 131, 145, 212, 255, 350, 399, 501
Dvorak, Ann, 155
Dwan, Allan, 36, 128, 178
Dyal, H. Kaye, 147
"Dynasty," 264, 449, 482
Dysart, Richard, 287

"E/R," <u>277</u>
Eagle-Lion, 225
Eagle's Wing, 499
Earle, Ferdinand Pinney, 457
Earthquake, 356, 468
East Meets West, 367
East of Borneo, 506
East of Eden, 14
East of Sumatra, 423, 471
"East Side/West Side," 263, 380
Eastwood, Clint, 103, 105, 119, 122, 131, 234, 294, 410, 412, 441, 468, 496, 498, 507, 520
Easy Money, 457
Easy Rider, 380
Easy to Wed, 473
Eating Raoul, <u>92–93</u>, 363
Eaton, Shirley, 118
Eberhard, Jude, 63
Ebsen, Buddy, 220, 266, 379
Echevarria, Gerald, 341
Echevarria, Rocky. *See* Bauer, Steven
Echevarria Alvarez, Luis, 188
Eclair Films, 333
Eddie and the Pacific Ocean, 459
Eddy, Nelson, 422
Edelman, Louis F., 256
Eden, Barbara, 417
Edington, Harry E., 225
Edward, Paul, 228
Edwards, Anthony, 308
Edwards, Blake, 490, 499, 502
Edwards, Gus, 357
Edwards, Vince, 87
"Eerie, Indiana," 265, 480
Egan, Eddie, 39–40
Egan, Richard, 211, 237, 277
Eight Men Out, 498
8 Million Ways to Die, 409, 481
Eikenberry, Jill, 287
Eileen Ford Agency, 374
"Eisenhower and Lutz," <u>277</u>, 468
Eisenstein, Sergei, 142
Eisinger, Jo, 48, 116
Eisner, Michael, 317
El Baquine de Angelitos Negros, <u>308</u>
El Bruto, 369
El Burlador de Sevilla, 28
El Cid, <u>93–94</u>, 465, 468
El Condor, <u>94</u>
El Corrido: La Gran Carpa de los Rasquachis, <u>308</u>

El Diablo, <u>308</u>
El Dorado, 408, 454
"El Gaucho Goofy," 204
El Greco, 52
El Gringo Viejo [The Old Gringo], 168
El Mariachi, <u>94–95</u>, **95**, 482
El Norte, 25, 63, <u>95–97</u>, **96**, 405, 456, 461, 468, 501
El Presidio, 12
"El Salon Mexico," 101
El Super, 25, <u>97–98</u>, 423, 465
El Teatro Campesino, 24, 251, 294, 304, 308, 313, 507–8
El Teatro de la Esperanza, 24
El Topo, 354
Elam, Jack, 165
Eldard, Ron, 270
Eldridge, Florence, 77
"Electric Company, The," <u>277</u>, 454
Electric Horseman, The, 494
Elias, Hector, 155, 156
Elias, Michael, 281
Elinor Norton, 485
Eliot, Mark, **216**
Eliscu, Edward, 114
Elizondo, Chuy, <u>396</u>
Elizondo, Hector, 23, 86, 238, 269, 279, 280, 293, 302, 309, 312, 314, 319, <u>396</u>
Ellington, E.A., 116
Elliott, Robert, 71
Elliott, Sam, 100, 301, 316
Elliott, Shawn, 84, 212
Ellis, Robert, 338
Ellis, Terry, 313
Ellison, James, 220
Elmer Gantry, 520
Ely, Ron, 89, 298, 464
Embassy Pictures, 40, 41, 98, 148, 397, 461
Embraceable You, 487
Embryo, 375
Emerald Forest, The, <u>98</u>
Emerson/Monorex, 123
Emery, Gilbert, 86
Emigrants, The, 258
Emmy Award, 34, 264, 288, 290, 291, 296, 305, 318, 365, 382, 385, 397, 405, 410, 441, 447, 452, 454, 459, 472, 473, 491, 492, 502, 506, 511
"Empire," <u>277</u>
Enamorada, 225
End, The, 414
Endore, Guy, 202
Enemies, a Love Story, 417, 418
Enemy Agents Meet Ellery Queen, 485
Engel, Peter, 296
Engel, Samuel G., 73, 164, 338
English, John, 324
English, Richard, 63
Englund, George, 318
Enric Madriguera and his Orchestra, 223

Enriquez, Rene, 41, 183, 236, 261, 283, **283**, 304, 316, 317, <u>397</u>
Enter Laughing, 403, 494
Enter the Dragon, 494
Epstein, Julian, 128
Epstein, Mel, 60, 210
"Equal Justice," 348
"Equalizer, The," 423, 451, 502
Equinox, 360
Erickson, C.O., 328
Ericson, Leif, 281
Ernest Goes to Camp, 508
Ernst, Jessie, 220
Errol, Leon, 158, 159
Erskine, Charles, 255
Erwin, Stuart, 241, 242
Escalante, Henry, 36
Escalante, Jaime, 215, **215**, 217
Escape Artist, The, 358, 427
Escape from Fort Bravo, 450
Escape to Burma, 450
Esparza, Moctezuma, 23, 41, 159, 160, 175–76, 343, <u>397</u>
Esparza, Phil, 308
Esparza/Katz Productions, 397
Espinosa, Carmen, 211
Espinoza, Richard, 34, <u>397</u>
Espinoza, Robert, 174
Esposito, Giancarlo, 270
Estabrook, Howard, 39, 64, 178
Estelita. *See* Rodriguez, Estelita
Estevez, Carlos Irwin. *See* Sheen, Charlie
Estevez, Emilio, 191, 256, <u>398–99</u>, **398**, 498, 503
Estevez, Ramon. *See* Sheen, Martin
Estrada, Angelina, 8, <u>399</u>
Estrada, Erik, 8, 212, 228, 261, 274, **274**, 275, 284, 312, **312**, 344, <u>399</u>
Eugene O'Neill Gold Medal, 473
Eustis, Rich, 281
Evangeline (1927), 474
Evangeline (1929), 390
Evans, David Mickey, 207
Evans, Robert, 77, 218
"Evening Shade," 478
Everybody's, 333
Evil That Men Do, The, 397, 422, 429, 491
Evita Peron, <u>308</u>, 403, 467, 506
Execution of Private Slovik, The, 497, 499
Exile, The, 450
Exorcist II: The Heretic, 468
Exterminating Angel, The, 363
Extreme Prejudice, 2, <u>98–99</u>, **99**, 350, 378, 380, 490
Eyes of Laura Mars, 427

"F Troop," 395
"F.B.I., The," 487
FBI Story, The, 443
F/X, 387
F/X 2: The Deadly Art of Illusion, 504
Fabares, Shelley, 282

Fabian, Laura, 301
Fabulous Senorita, The, <u>99</u>
Fade to Black, 467
Fairbanks, Douglas, Jr., 323
Fairbanks, Douglas, Sr., 11, 112–13, 186, 322, **322**, 323, 325, 326, 331, 503, 508, 510, 517
Fairchild, Morgan, 279, 312, **312**
Falcon, Peter Gonzales. *See* Gonzales, Peter
Falcon and the Snowman, The, <u>99–100</u>, 405, 473
"Falcon Crest," <u>277–78</u>, 349, 404, 408, 415, 429, 431, 487, 488
Falcon in Mexico, The, <u>100</u>, 438
Falk, Harry, 303
Falk, Peter, 130, 239, 465
Falkenburg, Jinx, 114
Falling Down, 504
Fame, 27, 373
"Fame," 264, <u>278</u>, 366, 403, 451, 483
"Family," 368, 434
Family Business, 22, 393, 417
Family Channel, 333
"Family Martinez, The," <u>278</u>
"Family Matters," 480
Famous Players–Lasky, 51
Fan, The, 396
Fantasia, 442
"Fantasia Mexican," 101
Fantastic Voyage, 389, 515
"Fantasy Island," 263, 264, **265**, <u>278</u>, 379, 431, 447, 449, 476
Fante, John, 165
Farah, Jameel. *See* Farr, Jamie
Faraldo, Daniel, 278
Farentino, James, 308
Farewell, My Lovely, 396
Farewell to Arms, A, 105
Farewell to Manzanar, 264
Farewell to the King, 433, 465
Fargas, Antonio, 78, <u>399</u>
Farina, Dennis, 307
Farr, Felicia, 103
Farr, Jamie, 50, 371
Farrell, Mike, 304
Farrow, John, 37, 67, 182, 194
Fast Times at Ridgemont High, 457
Fatal Beauty, <u>100</u>, 364, 378
"Father Knows Best," 134, <u>279</u>
Father Takes a Wife, 357
Fathom, 515
Fauchois, Rene, 89
Fawcett, Farrah, 441
Fay, Frank, 235
Faye, Alice, 10, 112, 220, 249, 450, 488
Fear and Desire, 502
Fear City, 402
Fearless, <u>100</u>, 393, 467
Fedora, 403
Fehmiu, Bekim, 28
Feins, Bernard, 86
Feist, Felix, 153

Feitshans, Buzz, 98
Feldberg, Mark, 145
Feldman, Phil, 252
Feliciano, Jose, 27, 266
Felix, Maria, 225, 401
Fellini, Federico, 219, 414, 471, 472
Fellini's Roma, 414
Fellows, Robert, 38, 54, 182
Felton, Earl, 42
Fender, Freddy, 159, 212
Fennelly, Vincent M., 120
Fenton, Frank, 112, 194
Ferber, Edna, 115
Ferguson, Norman, 222
Fernandes, Joao, 400
Fernandez, Abel, 140, 210, 299, 400
Fernandez, Emilio "El Indio," 18, 35, 36,
    64, 82, 109, 154, 155, 179, 180,
    180, 193, 225, 237, 252, 254, 348,
    355, 392, 400–401, 405, 427–28,
    523
Fernandez, Esther, 401
Fernandez, Evelina, 23, 32, 33, 34, 295,
    401
Fernandez, Jose, 233
Fernandez, Juan, 72, 135, 205, 206, 402
Fernandez, Peter, 78, 79
Ferrara, Abel, 72
Ferrer, Jose, 83, 245, 308, 402–4, **402**,
    512, 520
Ferrer, Lupita, 76
Ferrer, Mel, 61, 109, 119, 218, 276, 404,
    404, 446
Ferrer, Melchior Gaston. *See* Ferrer, Mel
Ferrer, Miguel, 123, 193, 307, 404
Ferris, Walter, 149
Ferris Bueller's Day Off, 463, 498
Ferro, Dan, 278
Ferro, Pablo, 404–5
Fessier, Michael, 256
Fever Pitch, 371
Few Good Men, A, 101
Fiddler on the Roof, 436
Field, Sally, 279, 475, **476**, 499
Field, Shirley Anne, 134
Fielder, Richard, 319
Fields, Dorothy, 219
Fields, Freddie, 239
Fields, Herbert, 177
Fields, Joseph A., 117, 158
Fiend Who Walked the West, The, 382
Fierro, Paul, 102, 255
Fiesta (1941), 101
Fiesta (1947), 101, 214, 448
Fifteenth Pelican, The, 279
55 Days at Peking, 435
Figgis, Mike, 130
Fighter, The, 62, 102, 423
Fighting Back: The Rocky Bleier Story, 378
Fighting Gringo, The, 411, 506
Figueroa, Efrain, 284, 405
Figueroa, Gabriel, 18, 76, 109, 154, 155,
    167, 168, **180**, 181, 225, 234, 237,
    254, 355, 392, 393, 401, 405

Figueroa, Ruben E., 183, **183**, 316, 317
Film Festival of International Cinema
    Students (Tokyo, Japan), 360
Film festivals. *See also under* Berlin,
    Cannes, Locarno, San Sebastian,
    etc.
Film League, 212
Filmhaus, 29
Final Countdown, The, 446
Final Impact, 431
Finch, Scot, 73
Finding the Way Home, 309
Fine, Morton, 179
Fine Mess, A, 350
Fink, Agustin J., 154
Fink, Harry Julian, 151
Finnegan, Bill, 301
Finnegan, Pat, 301
Finney, Albert, 237, 460
Fiorello, Tom, 107
Fire on the Mountain, 374, 379
Fire Sale, 380
Firebrand, The, 102
Firecreek, 435
Firefox, 507
Fires Within, 102, 359, 379, 384, 441
Firestarter, **498**, 499
Firewalker, 103
First National, 39, 64, 128, 480
First Power, The, 467
First Texan, The, 103, 423
First Time, The. *See* Fighter, The
Fisher, Frances, 314
Fisher, Marc, 139
Fisher, Terry Louise, 287
Fisher King, The, 374, 491
Fiskin, Jeffrey, 193
Fist Fighter, 480, 519
Fistful of Dollars, A, 103, 105
Fistful of Dynamite, A. *See* Duck, You
    Sucker!
Fistful of Revolution, A. *See* Duck, You
    Sucker!
Fitzgerald, Barry, 456
Fitzgerald, F. Scott, 10
Fitzgerald, Geraldine, 179
Fitzgerald, Michael, 181, 237
Fitzsimmons, Cortland, 101
Five Days from Home, 371
Five Weeks in a Balloon, 89, 435
Flaherty, William Barby, 119
Flaiano, Ennio, 219
Flame and the Flesh, 504
Flaming Hearts, 421
Flaming Star, 21, 74, 76, 393, 434
Flamingo Kid, The, 396
Flamingo Road, 279
"Flamingo Road," 279, 408, 518
Flanagan, Markus, 292
Flanery, Sean Patrick, 319
Flap, 446, 474
Flashdance, 373
"Flashdance . . . What a Feeling," 373

Flatliners, 401
Fleischer, Richard, 42, 74, 163, 399
Fleming, Eric, 294
Fleming, Ian, 145
Fleming, Rhonda, 233, 430
Fleming, Victor, 27, 71, 226
Flicker, Theodore J., 271, 417
Flight of the Phoenix, The, 450
Flor Silvestre, 18, 154, 392, 400, 405
Flores, Iris, 194
Flores Brothers, 220
Florey, Robert, 149, 369
Florida Straits, 309, 427
Flournoy, Richard, 51
Fly II, The, 518
Flying Down to Rio, 104–5, **104**, 173, 221,
    389, 390, 446, 455, 490
Flying Fleet, The, 458
"Flying Gauchito, The," 222
"Flying Nun, The," 279, 417, 475, **476**,
    499
Flynn, Errol, 14, 28, 48, 52, 135, 218,
    321, 323, 325, 326, 332, 369, 454,
    506, 525
Flynn, John, 88
Flynn, John Perrin, 302
Flynn, Sean, 321
Fodor, Ladislas, 219
"Foley Square," 279, 396
Follow That Dream, 375
Follow the Band, 377
Follow the Boys, 450
Follows, Megan, 296
Folsey, George, Jr., 221
Fonda, Henry, 18, 50, 109, 164, 177,
    233, 354, 392, 404, 499
Fonda, Jane, 9, 110, 168, 169, **169**, 288,
    469, 502
Fontaine, Joan, 19, 153, 210, 387
Fontana, Gilda, 140
Fontanne, Lynn, 412
Foote, John Taintor, 325
For a Few Dollars More, 105
For Love and Honor, 510
"For Love and Honor," 279, 504
For the Boys, 425
*For the Love of My Child: The Anissa Ayala
    Story*, 309
For Whom the Bell Tolls, 17, 105–6, **106**,
    141, 365, 369, 387, 411, 470
Force of One, A, 496
Ford, Francis, 177
Ford, Glenn, 20, 34, 35, 36, 49, 83, 108,
    116, 148, 182, 232, 272, 316, 370,
    420, 449, 478, 480, 488
Ford, Harrison, 190, 319, 461
Ford, John, 18, 19, 66, 75, 76, 109, 164,
    164, 165, 222, 231, 327, 348, 354,
    355, 382, 392, 393, 401, 404, 405,
    433, 449, 454, 455, 486, 520–22
Ford, Patrick, 256
Ford, Wallace, 103
Ford Foundation, 216
Ford's Theater, 301

Foreman, Carl, 125, 149
Foreman, John, 67
Forester, C.S., 185
Forever Darling, <u>106</u>, 357
Forgotten Village, The, 102
Formula, The, 473
Forrest, Frederic, 72, 172, 173
Forrest, Sally, 165
Forrest, Steve, 319
Forsythe, Henderson, 277
Forsythe, John, 225
Forsythe, William, 32, 98, 247
Fort, Garrett, 325
Fort Algiers, 504
Fort Apache, 354, 456, 520
Fort Apache, The Bronx, <u>107</u>, **107**, 467, 504
"Fort Figueroa," <u>279</u>, 415
Fort Lee Studios, 365
Fortunate Pilgrim, The, 461
Fortune, Jan, 153
Fortunes of Captain Blood, 442
Forty Deuce, 451
48 HRS., 394, 468
Fosse, Bob, 219, 449
Foster, David, 245
Foster, Lewis R., 233, 327
Foster, Meg, 98
Foster, Norman, 73, 118, 213, 214, 292, 327, 331, 338, 390, 401, 454
Foster, Preston, 119
Fountainhead, The, 375
Four Horsemen of the Apocalypse, The (1921), 7, 51, <u>108</u>
Four Horsemen of the Apocalypse, The (1962), <u>108</u>, 443
Four Horsemen of the Apocalypse, The (novel), 365
400 Blows, The, 361
Four Jacks and a Jill, 358
Four Jills in a Jeep, 418
Four Poster, The, 403
Four Seasons, The, 454
Four Seasons Entertainment, 200
1492: Conquest of Paradise, <u>108</u>
Fox, Elsie, 141
Fox, Finis, 190
Fox, Frederic Louis, 74
Fox, Michael J., 72, 147, 512
Fox, Paul Hervey, 86, 141
Fox, Wallace, 341, 342
Fox, William, 79, 334
Fox, The, 495
Fox Classics Division, 92
Fox Studios, 11, 13, 79, 129, 191, 236, 334, 336, 418, 450, 475, 490
Fox Television, 270, 276, 482, 514, 519
Foxes of Harrow, The, 442
Foxx, Redd, 294, 295
Foy, Bryan, 119, 160
Fraker, William, <u>405</u>
Franchina, Basilo, 118
Franciosa, Anthony, 166, 197

Francis, Anne, 45, 49, 50, 178
Francis of Assisi, 356
Franco, Abel, 87, 88, 95, 213, 221, 258, <u>405</u>
Franco, Ramon, 122, 299, <u>406</u>, **406**
Frank, Frederic M., 93
Frank, Harriet, Jr., 83, 127
Frank Damrosch School, 384
Frankenheimer, John, 257, 351
Frankie and Johnny, 396
Franklin, Don, 287, 291, 296
Franklin, Jeff, 280
"Frannie's Turn," <u>279</u>
Franquelli, Fely, 38
Franz, Dennis, 271, 291
Fraser, Bob, 289
Frawley, William, 284
Frederick, Pauline, 191
Frederickson, Gary, 172
Freebie and the Bean, <u>109</u>
"Freebie and the Bean," <u>280</u>, 396
Freed, Arthur, 83, 177
Freed, Rona, 181
Freedman, Jerrold, 57, 318
Freeland, Thornton, 104
Freeman, Al, Jr., 284
Freeman, David, 54
Freeman, Devery, 57, 223
Freeman, Mona, 60, 493
Freeman, Morgan, 217, 277
Fregonese, Hugo, 53, 174, 348, <u>406–8</u>, **407**
Freiberger, Fred, 112
French, Victor, 74
French Connection, The, 39, 477
French Connection II, The, 477
French Line, The, 486
Frenchman's Creek, 19, 387
Frenke, Eugene, 201
"Fresh Prince of Bel-Air," 264, 478
Freud, 429
Frida and Diego, 22
Friedkin, David, 179
Friedkin, William, 87, 214
Friedman, Bruce Jay, 318
Friedman, Stephen, 227
Fright Night II, 374
Frings, Ketti, 126
Frobe, Gert, 118
Frohman, Clayton, 236
Frohman, Mel, 307
From Here to Eternity, 280
"From Here to Eternity," <u>280</u>, 363
From Russia with Love, 356
Frontier Badmen, 377
"Frontier Frenzy," 256
Frontier Marshall, 164, 439, 488
Frost, Mark, 48
Frost, Sadie, 343
Fruit of the Poppy, 213
Fryer, Robert, 245
Fuentes, Carlos, 3, 168
Fuentes, Julio, 363

Fugitive, The, 18, 76, <u>109</u>, 231, 348, 354, 355, 392, 401, 404, 405, 456, 505, 517
"Fugitive, The," 266, 359, 417
Fuisz, Robert, 315
Full Metal Jacket, 23, 434
Fuller, Robert, 193
Fuller, Samuel, 145, 450
Fun in Acapulco, <u>109–10</u>, **110**, 374, 375, 475
Fun with Dick and Jane, <u>110</u>
Funny Girl, 74
Furie, Sidney J., 23, 35, 36, 172
Furies, The, <u>111</u>, 486
Furthman, Jules, 175, 197
Fusco, John, 256

Gabaldon, Guy, 123–24, **124**
Gable, Clark, 10, 20, 27, 448, 455, 483, 487
Gabriel, Gilbert, 149
Gabriela, 367
"Gabriela," 367
"Gabriel's Fire," 506
Gaby—A True Story, 22, <u>111</u>, 348, 436
Gago, Jenny, 276, 318, <u>408</u>
Gaiety. See Fiesta (1941)
Gaily, Gaily, 436
Galindo, Eileen, 218
Galindo, Nacho, 56, 57, 101, 173, 234, <u>408</u>
"Gallant Men, The," 264, 369
Gallardo, Camilo, 280
Gallardo, Carlos, 94, **95**
Gallardo, Silvana, 304, <u>408</u>
Gallego, Gina, 279, <u>408</u>
Gallian, Ketti, 236
Gallo, Guy, 237
Galton, Ray, 295
Galvan, George, 304
Galvan, Pedro, 211
Gambling on the High Seas, 485
Gamboa, Elisa, 144, 155
Gamet, Kenneth, 219
Gammon, James, 40, 193
Gandhi, 498, 499
Gang. *See Walk Proud*
Gang That Couldn't Shoot Straight, The, 494
Gangs, <u>309</u>, 506
Gang's All Here, The, <u>112</u>, 445, **445**
Gantry, 453
Ganz, Lowell, 239
Ganz, Tony, 239
Garay, Joaquin, 142, 222
Garay, Joaquin, II, <u>408</u>
Garay, Joaquin, III, 124, 408
Garber, Victor, 284
Garbo, Greta, 11, 365, 381, 452, 457
Garces, Mauricio, 509
Garcia, Allan, 113, <u>409</u>
Garcia, Andy, 23, 130, 212, 217, 283, <u>409–10</u>, **409**

Garcia, Aurelio, 36
Garcia, Irma, 87
Garcia, Juan, 182, 202
Garcia, Rick, 98, <u>410</u>
Garcia, Ron, <u>410</u>
Garcia, Stella, 131, **131**, <u>410</u>
Garcia, Stenio, 38
Garcia Pena, Pascual, 165
Gardel, Carlos, 11, <u>410</u>
Garden of Allah, The, 92, 386
Garden of Evil, 20, <u>112</u>, 239, 452
Gardenia, Vincent, 218
Gardens of Stone, 507
Gardner, Ava, 45, 166, 167, **167**, 168,
    194, 218, 494
Garfield, John, 132, 226, **226**, 248, 312,
    422
Garland, Beverly, 309
Garner, James, 127, **128**, 264, **266**, 454
Garnett, Tay, 45
Garr, Teri, 172, 173
Garralaga, Martin, 56, 83, 99, 105, 129,
    132, 144, 153, 155, 156, 194, 196,
    210, 211, 219, 224, 230, 234, 237,
    339, 340, 341, 342, <u>411</u>, 475
Garrett, Oliver H.P., 91
Garrison, Miranda, 202
Garson, Greer, 27
Gas, Food, Lodging, 508
Gassman, Vittorio, 213
Gateway, 485
Gateway of the Moon, The, 390
Gathering of Eagles, A, 500
Gaucho, <u>310</u>, **310**
Gaucho (novel), 310
Gaucho, The, 11, <u>112–13</u>, 510
Gautier, Dick, 110
Gavaldon, Roberto, 147
"Gavilan," <u>280</u>, 431
Gavin, John, <u>411–12</u>, **411**
Gay, John, 108, 302
Gay Amigo, The, <u>342</u>
Gay Caballero, The, <u>338</u>
Gay Cavalier, The, <u>339–41</u>, 485
Gay Defender, The, <u>113</u>
Gay Desperado, The, <u>113–14</u>, **113**, 377,
    439, 470
Gay Ranchero, The, 416
Gay Senorita, The, <u>114</u>, 362
"Gay Senorita, The," 256
Gaynor, Janet, 490
Geary, Paul, 298
Gedrick, Jason, 200
Geer, Will, 203
Gelbart, Larry, 50
Gelsey, Erwin, 104
Genaro, Tony, <u>412</u>
General Crack, 357
"General Hospital," 369
Genio y Figura, 382
Genovese, Mike, 79
Gentleman from Athens, The, 471
Gentleman from California, The. See
    Californian, The

Gentleman of the Jungle, 233
Gentleman's Agreement, 19, 144, 195, 242
Geraghty, Gerald, 100
Geraghty, Maurice, 100
Gerber, David, 316
Gere, Richard, 23, **48**, 130, 376, 396,
    410, 467
Gering, Marion, 201, 202
Geronimi, Clyde, 222
Gerould, Katherine Fullerton, 338
Gershwin, Jerry, 60
Gerstad, Henry, 126
Gerzo, Gunther, 237
"Get Smart," 272
Getty, Estelle, 280
Gettysburg, 397, 499
Ghia, Fernando, 162
Ghost, 361, 399
Ghost Breakers, The, <u>114</u>
Ghost Dance, 446
Ghost of Zorro, <u>326</u>
Ghosts, 6
Giant, 20, 62, <u>115–16</u>, **115**, 374, 389,
    442, 443, 479, 506
Gibbons, Cedric, 391
Gibbs, Marla, 273
Gibson, Brian, 307
Gibson, Hoot, 387
"Gideon," 403
Giglio, Sandro, 48
Gigolettes of Paris, 485
Gilbert, Billy, 249
Gilbert, John, **458**, 483
Gilbert, Lewis, 28
Gilbert, Lou, 244
Gilbert, Melissa, 304
Gilbert, Ron, 314
Gilda, <u>116–17</u>, **117**, 148, 369, 418, 420,
    433
Giler, David, 110
Gill, Frank, Jr., 63, 159
Gill, Tom, 233
Gillespie, Dizzy, 495
Gillum, Vern, 302
Gilmore, William S., 207
Gilmore, William S., Jr., 88
Gilroy, Bert, 159
Gimbel, Roger, 302
Gimpel, Erica, 278
Gindoff, Bryan, 148
Gingerbread Lady, The, 379
Ginsberg, Henry, 115
Girard, William, 66
Girl from Mexico, The, <u>117</u>, 158, 394
Girl from Monterey, The, 357
Girl from San Lorenzo, The, <u>343</u>, 377
"Girl of the Blue Sailboat, The," 367
Girl of the Limberlost, The, 404
Girl of the Rio, <u>118</u>, 377, 390
Girl Rush, The, 431
Girl Who Had Everything, The, 431
Girls, Girls, Girls, 464

Girls of the Big House, 436
Gish, Dorothy, 452
Gish, Lillian, 20, 91, 92
Gittler, Robert, 65
Glaser, Benjamin, 226
Glass, Ron, 271, 291
Gleaming the Cube, 363
Gleason, Adda, 190
Gleason, Jackie, 192
Glen, John, 78, 145
Glenville, Peter, 217
Glimcher, Arne, 152
Glitz, <u>310</u>
Globus, Yoram, 88, 103
Gloria, <u>118</u>, 374
"Gloria," 481
Glory Alley, 486
Glover, Danny, 160, 185, 187, 305, 350,
    422
Glover, John, 307
Gluck, Marvin A., 318
G-Men Never Forget, 354
Go West, Young Man, 383
Goddard, Charles W., 114
Goddard, Paulette, 114, 126, 225
Godfather, Part III, The, **409**, 410, 474
God's Crucible, 421
Goff, Ivan, 210
Goin' South, 350
Going My Way, 365
"Going to Extremes," <u>280</u>, 348
Golan, Menahem, 103, 202
Gold, Jack, 318
Gold, Lee, 312
Gold Diggers of Broadway, 378
Goldberg, Whoopi, 100, 160, 364, 378,
    518
Goldblum, Jeff, 239
Golden, Annie, 312
Golden, Ray, 37
Golden Gate and the Silver Screen, The, 6
"Golden Girls, The," 280
Golden Globe Award, 291, 410, 459
Golden Lion Award (Venice Film
    Festival), 118
"Golden Palace, The," <u>280</u>, 438
Golden Seal, The, 519
Golden Stallion, The, 481
Goldfinger, <u>118</u>
Goldman, Alain, 108
Goldman, Albert, 139
Goldman, Shepard, 202
Goldman, William, 67, 123
Goldsmith, Ken, 37
Goldstein, Leonard, 145, 174
Goldstone, James, 191, 316
Goldstone, Richard, 29
Goldwyn, Samuel, 134, 431
Goldwyn, Tony, 111
Goliath and the Barbarians, 350
Gomez, Angela, 7–8
Gomez, Consuelo, 94
Gomez, Inez, 190, 235

Gomez, Jaime, 313
Gomez, Maria, **186**, 187
Gomez, Mike, 54, 122, 258, 273, <u>412</u>
Gomez, Panchito, 32, 57, 246, 283, 309, 310, **310**, 318, <u>412</u>
Gomez, Sabino Thomas. *See* Gomez, Thomas
Gomez, Thomas, 69, 71, 111, 149, 194, 217, 218, <u>412</u>–13, **413**
Gomez, Vicente, 14, 52, 83, 137, <u>413</u>
Gomez Cruz, Ernesto, 95, 188, 189
Gone with the Wind, 21, 92, 105, 106, 111, 226, 454
Gonzales, Gabriel, 309
Gonzales, Mark, 36
Gonzales, Myrtle, 6–7, <u>413</u>–14
Gonzales, Peter, 123, <u>414</u>
Gonzalez, Gloria, 310
Gonzalez-Gonzalez, Jose, 73, 177, <u>414</u>
Gonzalez-Gonzalez, Pedro, 124, 197, 201, 254, 255, 257, <u>414</u>
Good, the Bad, and the Ugly, The, 105, <u>119</u>, 350
Good Neighbor Policy, 10, 15–19, 21, 47, 73, 100, 127, 130, 140, 195, 230, 444
Goodman, Benny, 112
Goodman, John, 295, 353
Goodman Theatre, 311
Goodwins, Leslie, 117, 158, 159, 220
Goonies, The, 461
Gordon, Bernard, 178
Gordon, Charles A., 218
Gordon, Harold, 244
Gordon, James B., 73
Gordon, Lawrence, 185, 247
Gordon, Leo V., 134
Gordon, Mack, 220
Gordon, Michael, 403
Gore Vidal's Billy the Kid, <u>311</u>
Goring, Marius, 45
Gorney, Jay, 114
Gorney, Karen Lynn, 207
Goros, Tomas, 307
Gosnell, Robert, 103
Gosselaar, Mark-Paul, 296
Gossett, Louis, Jr., 103, 308, 496
Gotay, Will, **216**, **309**
Gottlieb, Alex, 102
Gottlieb, Carl, 251
Gould, Elliott, 277
Gould, Heywood, 107, 173
Goulding, Edmund, 64
Goya, Francisco Jose de, 52
Goya, Tito, 107, 212, 291
Grable, Betty, 10, 17, 90, 436, 488, 512
Graham, Carroll, 57
Graham, James, 255
Graham, William A., 311
Grahame, Gloria, 38, 39
Grainger, Edmund, 119, 229
Gramercy Pictures, 184
Grammy Award, 350, 438, 452, 454

Gran Concho de Oro (San Sebastian Film Festival), 29
Grand Canyon, 378, 478
Grand Hotel, 141
"Grand Slam," <u>280</u>, 481
Granet, Bert, 225
Grant, Cary, 2, 8, 83, 168, 175, 185, 399, 486, 520
Grant, James Edward, 30, 66, 80
Grant, Joe, 204
Grant, John, 157, 198
Grapes of Wrath, The, 21
Grattan, Alejandro, 175–76, 397
Gray, Linda, 276
Gray, Mike, 79
Grayco, Helen, 73
Grayson, Kathryn, 137
Grazer, Brian, 507
Grease, 374, 431
Grease (stage), 359
Greaser's Revenge, The, 5
Great American Broadcast, The, 488
Great Caruso, The, 464
Great Courage, The, 207
Great Escape, The, 375, 436
"Great Love Experiment, The," 451
Great Man, The, 403
"Great Performances," 313, 507
Great Sioux Uprising, The, 367
Great White Hope, The (stage), 396, 399
Greater Law, The, 421
Greatest Story Ever Told, The, 403
Greco, Jose, 37, 126, 213, <u>414</u>, 446
Greek Tycoon, The, 472
Green, Alfred E., 82
Green, Bruce Seth, 314
Green, Gerald, 205
Green, Howard, 202
Green, Janet, 29
Green, Johnny, 101
Green, Walon, 54, 214, 252, 254
Green Berets, The, 142
Green Dolphin Street, 379
Green Eyes, 473
Green Ice, 353
Green Mansions, <u>119</u>, 404, 500
Greene, Graham, 48, 109, 176
Greene, Lorne, 140
Greer, Jane, 49, 202
Greisman, Gordon, 307
Grenadiers of Love, 449
Grey, Virginia, 66, 157, 158
Grice, Grimes, 184
Grier, Pam, 107
Grier, Roosevelt, 306
Gries, Tom, 64, 173
Griffith, D.W., 5, 7, 146, 147, 190, 322, 381, 452, 470, 510, 525
Griffith, J.J., 73
Griffith, Raymond, 325
Grimaldi, Alberto, 105, 119
Grisell, Wallace, 326
Grizzly II, 497

Grossberg, Jack, 41
Grot, Anton, 133
Group Theater, 244
Gryphon, <u>311</u>
Guadalajara Trio, 101, 155
Guadalcanal Diary, 17, <u>119</u>, 471
Guardino, Harry, 191
Guerra, Blanca, 247
Guerra, Castulo, 278, <u>415</u>
Guerrero, Evelyn, 279, <u>415</u>
Guerrero, Lalo, 259, 313
Guild Theater, 412
Guillermin, John, 94
Guinness, Alec, 176
Guiol, Fred, 115
Guiry, Tom, 207
Guizar, Tito, 51, 63, 159, 223, **224**, 233, <u>415</u>–16, **415**, **416**
Gulager, Clu, 35
Gun, The, 185
Gunga Din, 8
Gunn, Joe, 314
Gunn, Moses, 122
Guns for San Sebastian, <u>119</u>–20, 380, 472
Guns of Navarone, The, 472
Guns of the Magnificent Seven, <u>120</u>, 151, 502
Guns of the Rio Conchos, 197
Guns of the Timberland, 486
"Gunsmoke," 263, 327, 380, 475, 478, 523
Gunter, Robert, 207
Gurry, Eric, 39
Guss, Jack, 306
Gutierrez, Andres, 308
Gutierrez, Vincent R., 264, <u>417</u>
Gutierrez, Vincente, 123
Gutierrez, Zaide Silvia, 95, **96**, 103
Gutierrez Alea, Tomas, 25
Guys and Dolls, 396
Guys and Dolls (stage), 387, 518
Guzman, Claudio, 264, 299, <u>417</u>
Guzman, Luis, 71, 72, 187, 188, 200, 291, <u>417</u>
Guzman, Pato, <u>417</u>–18
Gypsy Wildcat, 377, 450

H.M.S. Pinafore, 518
Haber, Carl, 311
Hackel, Dave, 295
Hackford, Taylor, 3, 23, 60, 137, 364
Hackman, Gene, 78, 82, 236, 258, 461, 510
Haddad, Ava, 287
Hadley, Reed, 324, 387
Hagen, Uta, 374
Hagman, Larry, 276, 417
Haid, Charles, 507
Hail, Hero!, 518
Haines, Randa, 255
Hair, 367, 463
Hale, Alan, Jr., 153
Hale, Jonathan, 319

Halevy, Julian, 178
Haley, Jackie Earle, 148
Hall, Alexander, 106
Hall, Conrad, 405
Hall, Jane, 166
Hall, Norman Shannon, 256
Hall, Thurston, 114
Hallet, Jack, 270
"Hallmark Hall of Fame," 318
Hamel, Veronica, 283
Hamill, Pete, 39, 40
Hamilton, George, 328, **328**, 329
Hamilton, Guy, 118
Hamlin, Harry, 287, **287**
Hamlisch, Marvin, 359
Hammer, Earl, 277
Hammett, Dashiell, 103
Hammond, Victor, 339
Hampton, Christopher, 48
"Hands Across the Border," 63
Handy Andy, 449
Hanemann, H.W., 104
"Hangin' with Mr. Cooper," 280, 360
Hangin' with the Homeboys, 1, 26, 120, 432, 509
Hanks, Tom, 181, 461
Hannah, Daryl, 38
Hanoi Hilton, 508
Hansberry, Lorraine, 453
Hansen, Peter, 60
Hanson, Curtis, 148
Happy Time, The, 379
Hard to Kill, 478
Harder They Fall, The, 120–21, 446
Hardin, Melora, 139
Harding, Bertita, 132
Harding, John Briard, 137
Hardly a Criminal, 407
Hardwicke, Sir Cedric, 234
Hardy, Oliver, 13, **13**, 16, 66, 347, 435
Harkness Ballet, 308
Harlow, Jean, 423
Harmon, David P., 140
Harmon, Mark, 145, 279
Harmons, Estelle, 468
Haro, Daniel A., 418
Harold and Maude, 351
Harper, Valerie, 50, 109, 275, 294, 371
Harper's Bazaar, 375
Harrelson, Woody, 251
Harring, Laura Martinez. *See* Herring, Laura Martinez
Harris, Burt, 187
Harris, Ed, 57, 236, 247, 503
Harris, Fox, 191
Harris, Howard, 82
Harris, Lay, 113
Harris, Lewis, 212
Harris, Mel, 302
Harris, Richard, 151, 255
Harris, Susan, 292
Harris, Timothy, 187
Harrison, Jim, 193

Harrison, Joan, 194
Harry and Tonto, 379
"Harry O," 281, 384
Hart, Lorenz, 221
Hart, William S., 5
"Hart to Hart," 263, 439, 486
Harte, Bret, 4
Harvey, Laurence, 30, **31**, 176, 217
Harvey, Rodney, 202
Harwood, Ronald, 126, 308
Haskin, Byron, 103, 166
Hasso, Signe, 83
Hastings, Michael, 28
"Hat Squad, The," 281
Hatfield, Hurd, 93, 144
Hatful of Rain, A, 500
Hathaway, Bri, 102
Hathaway, Henry, 112
Hatton, Fanny, 377
Hatton, Frederic, 377
Hauser, Lionel, 117
Hausman, Michael, 29, 40
Havana, 26, 86, 121–22, 121, 443, 468
Havana Rose, 481
"Have Gun Will Travel," 348, 464
Hawaii, 436
"Hawaii Five-O," 459, 461, 518
"Hawaiian Eye," 508, 514
"Hawk," 478
Hawk, The. *See Phantom of Santa Fe, The*
Hawke, Ethan, 32
Hawks, Howard, 175, 191, 197, 208, 209, 241, 474, 480
Hawley, Lowell S., 327
Hayakawa, Sessue, 119, 123
Hayden, Sterling, 140, 220
Hayes, Helen, 412
Haymes, Dick, 72, 418, 494
Hays Office, 100
Hayward, Leland, 170, 171
Hayward, Lillie, 189
Hayward, Susan, 112
Hayworth, Rita, 14, 17, 20, 45, 52, 116, 117, **117**, 128, 148, 175, 191, 237, 255, 256, 384, 418, 418–20, 419, 436, 449, 487, 507
HBO, 305, 307, 308, 309, 311, 315, 365, 381, 410, 427, 432, 467, 481
HBO Comedy Hour: John Leguizamo's Spic-O-Rama, 311
HBO Comedy Hour: Mambo Mouth, 311
"Head of the Class, " 281
Heard, Charly, 279
Heart Is a Lonely Hunter, The, 482
Heart of the West, 333
Heartbeat, 438
Heartbreak Ridge, 122, 406, 412, 468
Heartbreaker, 123, 350, 404, 441, 510, 519
Heartland, 63
"Hearts of the West," 281
Heat, 123

"Heat Wave," 17, 493
Heat's On, The, 487
Heaven Can Wait (1978), 405
Hecht, Ben, 168, 194, 208, 241, 437
Hecht, Harold, 519
Hecht-Hill-Lancaster, 375
Heckart, Eileen, 122, 238
Hedaya, Dan, 81
Hedison, David, 145
Heerman, Victor, 336
Heffron, Richard T., 228
Heflin, Van, 45, 254
Hegyes, Robert, 299
Heinemann, Arthur, 310, 319
Hell in the Heavens, 449
Hell on Frisco Bay, 433, 434
Hell to Eternity, 123–24, **124**
Heller, Lukas, 89
Heller in Pink Tights, 458, 502
Hellfighters, 124
Hellinger, Mark, 226
Hellman, Sam, 164, 182
Hello Dolly!, 14, 385
Hell's Angels, 423
Hell's Heroes, 222
Hell's Hinges, 5
Hemdale, 205, 206
Hemingway, Ernest, 3, 10, 105, 170, 171, 218, 315, 387, 473, 486, 522
Hemingway, Mariel, 410
Hempstead, Hannah, 148
Hendrix, Wanda, 194
Henkin, Hilary, 100
Henning, Carlos, 202
Henreid, Paul, 108
Henriquez, Ron, 79, 276
Henry, Buck, 118
Henry, Mike, 219
Henry, Will, 149
Henson, Jim, 297
Hepburn, Audrey, 119, 404, 465
Hepburn, Katharine, 351, 473
Her Cardboard Lover, 448
Her Wedding Night, 454
Herbie Goes Bananas, 124–25, 363, 408
Hercules, 434
Hereford, Kathryn, 133
"Here's Lucy," 358, 359
Hergesheimer, Joseph, 64
Hern, Pepe, 36, 57, 111, 131, 140, 196, 217, 421
Hernandez, Bel. *See* Sandre, Bel
Hernandez, George F., 421
Hernandez, Juano, 148, 232, 233, 421–22, **421**
Hernandez, Pepe. *See* Hern, Pepe
Hernandez, Richard, 24
Hernandez, Rogelio, 48
Hernandez, Tom, 140
"Hernandez, Houston P.D.," 281
Hero, 410
Herod the Great, 434
Herrera, Chris, 218

Herrera, George, 14
Herrera, Joe, 14
Herring, Laura Martinez, 139, 301, <u>422</u>
Hershey, Barbara, 280
Hesseman, Howard, 281
Heston, Charlton, 49, 93, 151, 166, 210, 227, 228, **228**, 428, 472, 480
Heyman, Norma, 48
Hickman, Gail Morgan, 307
Hidalgo-Gato, Raymundo, 97
Hide in Plain Sight, 418
Higgins, John C., 55, 211
High and the Mighty, The, 14, 414, 517
"High Chaparral, The," 40, 127, 261, 263, <u>281</u>–<u>82</u>, **282**, 331, 348, 356, 380, 381, 382, 384, 431, 474, 475–76, 486, 502
High Conquest, 485
High Cost of Loving, The, 403
"High Mountain Rangers," <u>282</u>
High Noon, 21, 53, <u>125</u>–<u>26</u>, **125**, 220, 393, 427, 428
High Plains Drifter, 474
High School of Art and Design, 510
High School of Music and Art, 504
High School of the Performing Arts, 451
High Sierra, 525
High Steppers, 389
High Wind in Jamaica, A, <u>126</u>
"Highcliffe Manor," <u>282</u>
"Highway to Heaven," 264, 417
Hijuelos, Oscar, 152
Hill, George Roy, 67, 245
Hill, James, 239
Hill, Mariana, 94
Hill, Robert, 47
Hill, Walter, 98, 247
"Hill Street Blues," 261, 263, 271, <u>283</u>, **283**, 317, 363, 368, 380, 397, 410, 446, 490, 501, 514
Hiller, Arthur, 130, 154, 183
Hills Run Red, The, 500
Hillyer, Lambert, 339
Hines, Gregory, 87, 502
Hinton, S.E., 398
Hippodrome, 416, 466
Hirson, Roger O., 315
His Majesty O'Keefe, 456
Hitchcock, Alfred, 168, 225, 411–12, 479
Hively, Jack, 220
Hochberg, Victoria, 318
Hocus Pocus, 463
Hodge, Stephanie, 292
Hodges, Mike, 309
Hodiak, John, 47
Hoffenstein, Samuel, 72, 220
Hoffman, Dustin, 22, 393, 410, 461
Hoffman, Herman, 120
Hogan, James, 141
Holcomb, Rod, 309
Holcomb, Sarah, 245
Hold Back the Dawn, 14, <u>126</u>, 464
Hold Everything, 378

Holden, William, 32, 252, **253**, 254, 431
Holiday for Lovers, <u>126</u>–<u>27</u>, 384
Holiday in Mexico, 17, <u>127</u>, 379, 383
Holland, Tom, 100
Holliman, Earl, 82
Holloway, Sterling, 222
Holly, Buddy, 65
Hollywood Bowl, 440
Hollywood Community Theater, 457
Hollywood Pictures, 443
Hollywood Reporter, The, 429
"Hollywood Television Playhouse," 318
Hollywood Walk of Fame, 429
Holm, Celeste, 72
Holmes, Preston, 184
Holt, Tim, 54, 189, 230, 439
Hombre, <u>127</u>, **501**, 502
Home Alone, 436
"Home Free," <u>284</u>
Home of the Brave, 144, 195
"Homefront," 348
Homes, Geoffrey, 49, 143, 144
Homrich, Junior, 98
Hondo, 182, 348
Honeyboy, <u>312</u>, **312**, 396
Honeymoon, 487
Honeysuckle Rose, 496
Honorary Consul, The, 48
Hook, 333
Hook, Line and Sinker, 506
Hooker, Brian, 201
Hooks, Kevin, 27, 300, 302
Hooks, Robert, 27
Hool, Lance, 187, <u>422</u>
"Hopalong Cassidy," 454
Hope, Anthony, 163
Hope, Bob, 114, 198, 199, 416, 431
Hopkins, Anthony, 315
Hopkins, Robert E., 86
Hopkins, Stephen, 185
Hopper, Dennis, 79, 115, **115**, 116, 133, 256, 257, 307, 410
Hopper, Jerry, 210
Horman, Arthur T., 37
Hornblow, Arthur, Jr., 114, 126, 233
Horne, Lena, 87, 177, 448
Horner, Harry, 145, 153
Hoskins, Bob, 48, 432
Hospital, The, 379
Hostile Guns, 414
"Hot L Baltimore," <u>284</u>
Hot Shots!, 498
Hot Shots! Part Deux, 498
Hot Stuff, 359, **360**
Hot Summer Wind, 496
Hough, Stanley L., 43, 235, 319
Hour of the Gun, <u>127</u>–<u>28</u>, **128**, 436
House Is Not a Home, A, 515
House of Frankenstein, 512
House of Games, 491
House of Ramon Iglesias, The, <u>312</u>–<u>13</u>, 480
House of the Spirits, The, 362, 380
Houseman, John, 38, 448

"Houston Knights," <u>284</u>
How the West Was Won (1962), 348
How the West Was Won (1977), 264, 447
Howard, Jeff, 238
Howard, Ken, 300
Howard, Ron, 374
Howard, Trevor, 202
Howard, Willie, 201
Howe, James Wong, 61, 127, 171, 351
Hoyos, Rodolfo [Rudolfo], Sr., 155, <u>422</u>
Hoyos, Rodolfo [Rodolpho], Jr., 24, 34, 61, 62, **62**, 83, 102, 103, 155, 210, 240, 299, 316, <u>423</u>
Hubbard, John, 66
Huddle, 458
Hudson, Rock, 115, 235, **235**, 375, 412
Hudson, W.H., 119
Huemer, Dick, 204
Huffaker, Clair, 80, 124, 173, 197
Hughes, Dorothy B., 194
Hughes, Howard, 423
Hughes, John, 398
Hughes, Mary Beth, 73, 177, 338
Hughes, Richard, 126
Hugh-Kelly, Daniel, 276, 286
Hulce, Tom, 100
"Hull High," 463
Human Cargo, <u>128</u>, 419
Humberstone, H. Bruce, 338
Humbert, George, 64, 226
Hume, Cyril, 60, 104
Humoresque, 464
Hunchback of Notre Dame, The, 393
Hunnicutt, Arthur, 140
Hunt, Helen, 247
Hunter, Evan, 49, 245, 257, 520
Hunter, Jeffrey, 123, 133, 163, 211, 521
Hunter, Tab, 45
Hunter, 490
"Hunter," 263, <u>284</u>, 410, 499
Hunter, The, 359
Hurd, Gale Ann, 247
Hurricane, The, 406, 431, 455
Hurt, William, 135, 136, **136**, 361, 457
Hussein, Waris, 184, 304, 309
Hustle, 361
Hustling, 379
Huston, Anjelica, 27
Huston, John, 3, 19, 48, 64, 77, 132, 167, **167**, 168, 230, 231, 232, 237, 239, 248, 363, 403, 405, 458, 465, 468, 479, 486, 520, **522–23**, **523**, 524
Huston, Walter, 39, 91, 111, 230
Hutchinson, Ron, 305
Hutton, Betty, 129
Hutton, Brian G., 213
Hutton, Jim, 124
Hutton, Timothy, 99, 100, 187, 188
Hyatt Music Theatre, 463
Hyer, Martha, 135
Hyland, Frances, 337
Hyman, Kenneth, 89

I, the Jury, 375
I Accuse, 403
I Died a Thousand Times, 414, 434
I Don't Have to Show You No Stinking Badges, 508
"I Dream of Jeannie," 264, 417
"I Had Three Wives," <u>284</u>
I Live for Love, 391
I Live for You, 11
"I Love Lucy," 140, 152, 261–62, **262**, 267, <u>284</u>–86, 357, 358, 417, 422, 454, 464, 466
I Love You, 367
I Love You, Alice B. Toklas, 417
I Married an Angel, 438
"I Married Dora," <u>286</u>, 415, 465
I Never Promised You a Rose Garden, 494
"I Spy," 262, 393
I Wanna Hold Your Hand, 491
I Was an Adventuress, 365
I Will, I Will . . . for Now, 468
I Will Be Faithful, 128
Iacone, Jeremy, 60
Ichaso, Leon, 84, 97, 98, 364, <u>423</u>
Identification of a Woman, 443
Idle Class, The, 409
Idolmaker, The, 137
"If I Had a Hammer," 435
If I'm Lucky, 445
Iglesias, Eugene, 61, 68, 83, 166, 237, <u>423</u>
Iglesias, Rafael, 100
"I'll Fly Away," 348
I'm Gonna Get You Sucka, 399
I'm Still Alive, 385
Imitation of Life (1959), 429
In Caliente, 11, <u>128</u>–<u>29</u>, **129**, 391
In Cold Blood, 520
In Country, 379
In December the Roses Will Bloom Again. See Choices of the Heart
In Gay Madrid, 458
In-Laws, The, **130**, 393, 418
"In Living Color," 467
In Old Arizona, <u>334</u>–36, **335**, 336, 425, 525
In Old California, 367, 411
In Old New Mexico, <u>339</u>
"In the Beginning," 434
In the Custody of Strangers, 398
"In the Heat of the Night," 375
In the King of Prussia, 499
In the Summer House, 380
Incendiary Blonde, <u>129</u>–<u>30</u>, 387
Incident, The, 499
Inclan, Miguel, 109, 211
Inclan, Rafael, 18
Inda, Stella, **69**, 70
Indian Uprising. See War Cry
Ingram, Rex, 108, 452, 457
Ingster, Boris, 67
Initiation, The, 519
Innerspace, 408

Innkeepers, The, 380
Inside Moves, 496
Insure Your Wife, 449
Internal Affairs, **130**, 410
International Prize (San Sebastian Film Festival), 181
International Settlement, 391
International Union of Mine, Mill, and Smelter Workers, 203
Intolerance, 7
Intruder in the Dust, 421, 422
Invasion, U.S.A., 379, 400
Invisible Woman, The, 450
Invitation to a Gunfighter, 351
IPC Distributors, 203
Ireland, Jill, 64
Ireland, John, 164
"Iron Horse, The," 417
Iron Mistress, The, 433
Irons, Jeremy, 162
"Ironside," 29, 266, 354, 464
Ironweed, 361
Irreconcilable Differences, 408
Irizary, Gloria, 65, 107, 187, 188, <u>423</u>
Irving, Amy, 212
Isaacs, Susan, 81
Isabelita. *See* Baron, Lita
Isla de la Pasion, 400
Island Alive, 95, 135
Island of Dr. Moreau, The, 375
Island of the Blue Dolphins, 35
Islands in the Stream, 486
Isle of Destiny, 485
Isle of Missing Men, 485
Israel, Al, 71, <u>423</u>
It Happened One Night, 408
Italian Connection, The, 500
Italian Network Commentators, 118
It's a Mad Mad Mad Mad World, 389
It's All True, 16
Iturbi, Jose, 17, 127, <u>424</u>–25, **424**
Ives, Burl, 49
Ivey, Judith, 81
Ivey, Lela, 292
Ivory, James, 515

Jabor, Arnaldo, 367
Jaccard, Jacques, 324
"Jack Benny Show, The," 454
Jack the Giant Killer, 389
Jackée, 273
Jacks, Robert L., 42, 43, 153, 235
"Jack's Place," 489
Jackson, Helen Hunt, 190
Jackson, Henry, 236
Jackson, Michael, 203
Jackson, Wilfred, 204
Jacobo Timerman: Prisoner Without a Name, Cell Without a Number, <u>313</u>
Jacobs, Lawrence-Hilton, 299
Jacob's Ladder, 23, 465
Jacqueline Bouvier Kennedy, 506
Jade God, The, 474

Jaeckel, Richard, 78, 79
Jaffe, Sam, 119
"Jake and the Fatman," 397
Jamaica, 448
James, Polly, 189
James, Rian, 90
Jameson, Jerry, 305
Janitzio, 400
Janssen, David, 123, 281, 303, 304, 384
Jara, Maurice, 103, 115, 116, 210, 233
Jarman, Derek, 363
Jarrico, Paul, 203
Jarrott, Charles, 314
Jason, Rick, 213
Jaws, 154
Jazz Singer, The (1927), 10
Jazz Singer, The (1980), 359
"Jeffersons, The," 273, 295
Jencks, Clinton, 203
Jencks, Virginia, 203
Jenkins, Daniel, 309
Jennifer 8, 410
Jennings, Talbot, 166
Jennings, William Dale, 83
"Jeopardy," 251
Jerk, The, 510
Jesse Owens Story, The, 508
Jewison, Norman, 379
Jim Thorpe—All American, 464
Jimenez, Neal, 247, <u>425</u>
Jimenez, Soledad [Solidad], 57, 83, 105, 129, 199, 236, 336, 339, <u>425</u>
Jimenez-Leal, Orlando, 97, 98
"Jimmy Durante Show, The," 445
Jivaro, **130**, 454
Joan of Arc, 403
"Joan Rivers Show, The," 492
Joanna, 389
Joe Kidd, <u>131</u>, **131**, 410, 441, 494
Joe Panther, 440
Joel, Billy, 462
Joffe, Charles H., 41
Joffé, Roland, 162
John F. Kennedy Journalism Award, 397
"John Larroquette Show, The," <u>286</u>, 504
Johnny Cool, 500
Johnny Got His Gun, 496
Johnny Hamlet, 486
Johnson, Ben, 171, 252, 316
Johnson, Brad, 315
Johnson, Don, 291, 379
Johnson, Eli, 309
Johnson, Gilbert, 17
Johnson, Julia Migenes, 395
Johnson, Julian, 338
Johnson, Lamont, 82
Johnson, Nunnally, 89
Johnson, Rafer, 219
Johnson, Van, 47
Jones, Buck, 3
Jones, Carolyn, 269
Jones, Evan, 239
Jones, F. Richard, 112

Jones, James, 280
Jones, James Earl, 399
Jones, Jennifer, 21, 91, **91**, 92, 248
Jones, Martin, 315
Jones, Paul, 156
Jones, Robert Edmond, 139
Jones, Shirley, 181
Jordan, Richard, 200, 314
Jory, Victor, 76, 148
Joseph, Ron, 318
Josephine Baker Story, The, 365
Joslyn, Allyn, 223
Jourdan, Louis, 379
Journey into Fear, 331, 391
Joyner, Mario, 120
Juarez, 132–33, **132**, 144, 369, 394, 411, 474, 485
"Juarez," 286, 367
Juarez & Maximilian, 132
Jubilee Trail, 508
Judels, Charles, 71
Julia, Raul, 22, 23, 27, 81, 121, **121**, 122, 135, 136, **136**, 163, 172, 173, 181, 200, 269, 301, 302, 309, 349, 361, 367, 374, 425–27, **426**
Juncos, Victor, 42, **42**, 211
Jungle Book, The, 399
Jungle Fever, 470
Jungle Goddess, 357
Jungle Princess, The, 141, 431
Jurado, Katy, 21, 36, 66, 76, 82, 125, **125**, 126, 153, 171, 172, **172**, 179, 232, 233, 237, 269, 302, 308, 369, 370, 393, 427–28, **427**, **428**
Jurassic Park, 2, 333, 473, 492
Just for You, 456

Kagan, Jeremy Paul, 49
Kahlo, Frida, 22
Kahn, Ivan, 483
Kalember, Patricia, 286
Kalmar, Bert, 134
Kandel, Aben, 102
Kane, Bob, 321
Kane, Frank, 133
Kane, Michael, 343
Kane, Robert, 52
Kanin, Michael, 176
Kansas City Bomber, 515
Kaplan, Gabriel, 299
Kaplan, Marvin, 99
Kardos, Leslie, 224
Karlson, Phil, 123, 133
Karp, David, 74, 213
Kasdan, Lawrence, 190, 496
Kashfi, Anna, 83
Kassel, Tichi Wilkerson, 429
Katz, Robert, 343
Katzin, Lee, 316
Katzka, Gabriel, 99
Katzman, Sam, 68, 73, 201, 224
Kaufman, Bel, 238
Kaufman, David, 314

Kaufman, Philip, 190
Kaufman, Robert, 109
Kay, Gordon, 219
"Kay O'Brien," 286, 434
Kaye, Lila, 288
Kazan, Elia, 242, 243, 244, 245, 380, 470, 471, 472
Kazan, Lainie, 298
KCET-TV (Los Angeles), 137, 318, 506
Keach, Stacy, 399
Kean, E. Arthur, 316
Keaton, Buster, 284
Keaton, Diane, 353
Keaton, Michael, 173, 227, 350, 367
Kedrova, Lila, 126
Keel, Howard, 194
Keenen, Mary Jo, 292
Keeper of the City, 408
Keighley, William, 226
Keitel, Harvey, 54
Keith, Brian, 207, 213, 240, 301
Keith, Robert, 60
Kellard, Rick, 294
Keller, Harry, 227
Kelly, April, 295
Kelly, Gene, 420, 462, 463
Kelly, Grace, 125, **125**
Kelly's Heroes, 234, 405
Kemmer, Edward, 177
Kennedy, 499
Kennedy, Arthur, 166, 232
Kennedy, Burt, 193, 301
Kennedy, George, 43, 120
Kennedy, Kathleen, 32
Kennedy, William, 361
Kent, Robert E., 68
Kermit the Frog, 297
Kerr, Deborah, 167
Kerr, Laura, 63
Kerry, Norman, 324
Key Largo, 413, 520
"Key West," 514
Key Witness, 133, 502
Keyes, Evelyn, 223
Keys of the Kingdom, The, 386
Kibbee, Roland, 35, 238, 239
Kickboxer II, 463
Kid from Spain, The, 13, 134, 456
Kieser, Ellwood E., 200
Kiley, Richard, 49
Kilian, Victor, 191
Killer's Kiss, 502
Killing a Mouse on Sunday, 47
Killing Fields, The, 162
Killing of Sister George, The, 442
Kilmer, Val, 311
Kim, 413, 456
Kimble, Lawrence, 174, 177
Kimmel, Anne, 92
Kindergarten Cop, 490
King, Bradley, 139, 236
King, Frank, 61, 62, 196, 316, 479
King, Henry, 61, 69, 190, 218

King, Herman, 61, 62, 144, 196, 479
King, Maurice, 61, 62, 144, 196, 316, 479
King, Perry, 184
King and I, The, 453, 479
King and I, The (stage), 21, 448
King Kong, 14, 187, 388–89, 431
King of Jazz, The, 411, 506
King of Kings, 435, 468, 496
King of the Bandits, 341, 485
King of the Khyber Rifles, 369
King of the Night, The, 361
Kings of the Sun, 2, 134–35, 201, 436
Kingsley, Dorothy, 119, 181
Kinjite: Forbidden Subjects, 135, 402, 429, 434
Kinney, Jack, 204, 222
Kinoy, Ernest, 318
Kinski, Nastassia, 172, 173
Kipling, Rudyard, 71
Kirby, Bruno, 57
Kirkland, Sally, 193
Kismet, 464
"Kismet," 403
Kiss Me a Killer, 135, 388, 514
Kiss Me Deadly, 365, 422
Kiss of Fire, 135
Kiss of the Spider Woman, 135–36, **136**, 361, 367, 425
Kissing Bandit, The, 137, 448
Kleiner, Harry, 85, 98
Kline, Benjamin H., 73
Kline, Herbert, 102
Kline, Steve, 57
Klove, Jane, 35
Klugman, Jack, 233, 301
Kneisel, Frank, 384
Knight, Wayne, 297
"Knight & Daye," 287
"Knight Rider," 356, 490
Knightriders, 490
Knights of the Round Table, 404
"Knightwatch," 287, 367
Knoblock, Edward, 201
"Knots Landing," 408
Knowles, Patric, 49, 155
Knox, Terence, 299
Koch, Howard W., 39
Koch, Howard W., Jr., 200
Koch, Marianne, 103
Koepp, David, 71
Kohlmar, Fred, 67, 220
Kohner, Frederick, 166, 177
Kohner, Pancho, 135, 429
Kohner, Paul, 11, 12, 429, 506
Kohner, Susan, 429
"Kojak," 171, 263, 380, 403, 459, 467
Komack, James, 273
Korda, Alexander, 186
Korvin, Charles, 327
Koster, Henry, 166
Kotcheff, Ted, 110
Kotero, Apollonia, 277–78, 429

Kotto, Yaphet, 279
Kovacs, Ernie, 176
Kowalski, Frank, 64
Kozlenko, William, 127
Kozoll, Michael, 283
KQED/San Francisco, 304
Kramer, Stanley, 125, 126, 185, 188, 407, 428, 434
Kramer, Stepfanie, 284
Kramer vs. Kramer, 350
Kramm, Joseph, 403
Krantz, Jacob. *See* Cortez, Ricardo
Krantz, Stanley. *See* Cortez, Stanley
Krantz, Steve, 251
Krasne, Philip N., 339, 341, 342, 343
Krasner, Milton, 94
Krasny, Paul, 303, 307
Kreitsek, Howard B., 64
Kristofferson, Kris, 78, 179
Kroll, Leonard, 100
Krumgold, Joseph, 35
Kubrick, Stanley, 23, 502
Kuder, Leo, 133
Kulik, Buzz, 240, 241
Kuller, Sid, 37
Kung Fu, 264
"Kung Fu," 380, 486
Kung Fu: The Legend Continues, 264
Kurnitz, Barry, 28
Kurosawa, Akira, 103, 149, 176
Kwapis, Ken, 239
Kyne, Peter B., 222

"L.A. Law," 261, 287-88, 287, 343, 440, 441, 468, 502
L.A. Music Center, 448
L.A. Staging Company, 464
"La Argentinita," 414
La Bamba, 1, 22, 25, 26, 65, 137-38, 138, 152, 217, 260, 343, 393, 394, 451, 454, 463, 465, 467, 479, 507, 510
"La Bamba," 435
La Barraca, 147
La Carpa, 313, 360, 493
La Cava, Gregory, 113
La Chèvre, 187
La Choca, 401
La Conga Nights, 357
La Cucaracha, 14, 139, 352
"La Cucaracha," 87, 139
La Immaculada, 365
La Jolla Playhouse, 404
La Mala Vida, 408
La Malquerida, 392
La Opinion, 11
La Otra, 147
"La Paloma," 153
La Pastorela, 313, 396, 507
La Perla, 18, 400-401. *See also Pearl, The*
"La Raza," 317, 397
La Rosa Blanca, 147
La Strada, 471-72
La Traviata, 395

La Vida Bohemia, 485
La Vida Inutil de Pito Perez, 428
Labiosa, David, 309
Labyrinth of Solitude, 3
LaCamara, Carlos, 292, 429
Lachman, Harry, 73
Ladd, Alan, 60, 207, 401, 431
Ladies Love Danger, 485
Ladrones, 347
Lady from Shanghai, The, 20, 420
Lady Has Plans, The, 411
Lady in Cement, 515
Lady in the Dark, 14, 385, 466
"Lady in the Tutti Frutti Hat, The," 112
Lady of the Pavements, 510
Lady on the Bus, 367
Lady Sings the Blues, 351
Lady Takes a Sailor, The, 487
Lahti, Christine, 305
Lake, Arthur, 51
Lake, Stuart N., 164
"Lake Titicaca," 204
Lamarr, Hedy, 226, **226**
Lamas, Fernando, 10, 130, 173, **174**, 263, 277, 280, 430-31, **430**
Lamas, Lorenzo, 277, 349, 431, 431
Lambada, 139
Lambada—The Forbidden Dance, 139, 422
Lamm, Karen, 228
Lamour, Dorothy, 141, 142, 155, 156, 157, 198, 199, 233, 431, 450, 485, 494
L'Amour, Louis, 73, 219, 316
Lancaster, Burt, 186, 238, 239, 257, 375, 410, 441, 450, 451, 456, 488, 519
Lancelot and Guinevere, 154
"Lancer," 354
Lancer Spy, 391, 394
Lanchester, Elsa, 165
Landau, Richard, 38
Landers, Lew, 68
Landham, Sonny, 185
Landis, John, 221
Landon, Joseph, 197
Landon, Michael, 154, 264, 417
Lane, Abbe, 34, 35, 154, 254, 255, 300, 383
Lane, Burton, 29
Lane, Charles, 184
Lane, Mike, 120
Lane, Nathan, 147
Lane, Nora, 336
Lang, Charles, 149
Lang, Daniel, 72
Lang, Hal, 338
Lang, Walter, 249
Langella, Frank, 255, 331
Langner, Philip, 179
Langton, Paul, 89
Lansburgh, Larry, 147
Lansford, William Douglas, 240, 305, 431
Lanza, Mario, 210, 450

LaPaglia, Anthony, 173
Lapine, James, 147
Lapland, Harold, 155
Lara, Augustin, 233
Larkin, John, 72, 73, 338
La Rocque, Rod, 390
Larralde, Romulo. *See* Brent, Romney
Larrinaga, Mario, 14, 431
Larroquette, John, 286
Las Abandonadas, 363, 392
Las Surpresas, 470
Lash, The, 139-40
Lasky, Jesse L., 113, 381
Lasky Company, 201
Lasser, Louise, 41
"Lassie," 400
Last Angry Man, The, 411
Last Boy Scout, The, 457
Last Command, The, 4, 30, 140, 456
Last Dragon, The, 478
Last Hard Men, The, 480
Last Movie, The, 410
Last of Sheila, The, 515
Last of the Comanches, 456
Last of the Fast Guns, The, 140, 382, 486, 500
Last of the Mohicans, The, 23, 503
Last of the Red Hot Lovers, The, 453
Last Plane Out, 141, 374
Last Prostitute, The, 314
Last Rites, 141, 519
Last Sweet Days of Isaac, The, 463
Last Train from Madrid, The, 14, 141-42, 431, 485
Latimer, Jonathan, 182
Latimore, Frank, 321
Latin Lovers, 10, 142, 449, 454, 473
Latino, 142, 363, 374, 468
Laughing Boy, 458
Laughlin, Frank. *See* Laughlin, Tom
Laughlin, Tom, 155, 371, 375, 501
Laughton, Charles, 412, 455
Lauper, Cyndi, 239, 465
Laurel, Stan, 13, **13**, 16, 66, 347, 435
Laurel Award, 491
Laurents, Arthur, 249
Laurie, Piper, 255
Lava, William, 331
"Laverne and Shirley," 451
Lavi, Daliah, 73
Lavin, Linda, 314
Law, Lindsay, 216
Law, The, 379
Law and Jake Wade, The, 500
Law and the Lady, The, 431
Lawless, The, 20, 143-44, **143**, 197, 204, 369, 479, 506
Lawrence, Gertrude, 10
Lawrence, Marc, 147, 219
Lawrence, Vincent, 27
Lawrence of Arabia, 74, 162, 403, 472
Lawson, John Howard, 50
Lazar, Ava, 295

Lazarus, Paul N., III, 44
Lazo, Lilia, 29
Lea, Tom, 61, 255
Leachman, Cloris, 124
Leachman, Phyllis, 293
League of United Latin American
    Citizens (LULAC), 20
Leal, Pete, 273
Lean, David, 472
Lean on Me, 217
Lear, Norman, 269, 270, 481
"Leave It to Beaver," 342
LeBaron, William, 112, 197, 201, 202,
    249
Lederer, Charles, 194
Lederer, Francis, 64, 154
Lee, Dorothy, 197
Lee, Lila, 51
Lee, Rowland V., 64
Lee, Spike, 364, 466, 467, 470
Leeds, Herbert I., 337, 338
Left-Handed Gun, The, <u>144</u>, 311, 411
Legend of the Lone Ranger, The, 405, 459
Leguizamo, John, 71, 72, 120, 193, 311,
    <u>432</u>, **432**
Lehman, Ernest, 249
Lehman, Gladys, 198
Lehrer, James, 241
Leibman, Ron, 328, 329
Leigh, Janet, 67, 219, 227, 479
Leigh, Vivien, 473
Leighton, Margaret, 472
"Leiningen Versus the Ants," 166
Leisen, Mitchell, 14, 126, 155
LeMaire, Charles, 494
Lemmon, Jack, 83, 161, 395
Lennart, Isobel, 127, 137, 142
Lenny, 415
Lenox, John, 314
Leonard, Elmore, 72, 127, 131, 163, 238,
    310
Leonard, Herbert B., 183
Leonard, Jack, 165
Leonard, Kay, 254
Leonard, Robert Z., 166
Leonard, Sheldon, 226, 249
Leone, Sergio, 90, 103, 105, 119, 350
Leopard Man, The, <u>144</u>, 437
Lepke, 380
Lerner, Alan Jay, 494
Lerner, Irving, 201
Lerner, Michael, 57, 316
LeRoy, Mervyn, 142
Les Brown and his Band of Renown, 381
Lesser, Sol, 68
Lester, David, 251
Lester, Mark, 81
Lester, Richard, 86, 198, 453, 515, 516
Let My People Free, 422
Let No Man Write My Epitaph, 449
Let's Get Harry, <u>145</u>, 376
Levant, Oscar, 424
Leviathan, 396

Levien, Sonya, 181
Levin, Henry, 126
Levin, Irving H., 123
Levin, Rachel, 111
Levine, Nat, 323
Levinson, Art, 305
Levitt, Saul, 82
Levy, David, 269
Levy, Melvin, 199
Lewis, Dawnn, 280
Lewis, Edward, 161
Lewis, George J., 56, 100, 103, 174, 182,
    189, 237, 326, 327, 329, 339, <u>433</u>
Lewis, Jerry, 408
Lewis, Joseph H., 220
Lewis, Oscar, 76
Lewis, Roger, 179
Lewis, Ruth, 76
Lewton, Val, 144
Leyland, Crash, 213
Leytes, Joseph, 178
Leyva, Frank, 134, 142, 144, 155, 234
Libertini, Richard, 87, 130
Licence to Kill, <u>145</u>, 356, 393, 478, 503
Lieberman, Rob, 310
Lieutenant Wore Skirts, The, 454
Life and Times of Judge Roy Bean, The, 468
Life Begins, 485
"Life Goes On," 265, 494
Life in the Balance, A, <u>145–46</u>, 146, 348,
    449, 465
"Life of Riley, The," 417
Life of Villa, The, <u>146–47</u>
"Life Stories," 506
Life with Mikey, <u>147</u>, 512
"Life Work of Juan Diaz, The," 465
Lifetime Cable, 314
Light in the Forest, The, 371
Light in the Piazza, 443
Lighton, Louis D., 71
Like Father, Like Son, 507
Like Water for Chocolate, 354
Lili, 404
Lily, The, 457
Linden, Hal, 271, 489
Lindfors, Viveca, 28, 189
Lindsay, Margaret, 57
Linero, Jeannie, 284
Linson, Art, 72
Lion of the Desert, The, 472
Lionheart, 465
Lipton, James, 304
Lithgow, John, 38
"Little Engine That Could, The," 204
Little Giant, 512
"Little House on the Prairie," 264, 417,
    442
Little Miss Marker, 441
Little Nikita, 370
Little Princess, The, 488
Little Richard, 459
Little Savage, The, 356
Little Treasure, 467

Littlest Outlaw, The, <u>147</u>, 348, 356, 369
Lively, William, 326
Living Theater, 498
Livingston, Robert, 323
Llano Kid, The, 394, 416
Llosa, Luis, 213, <u>433</u>
Lloyd, Christopher, 27
Lloyd, Euan, 73
Lloyd, Frank, 139, 140
Lloyd, Harold, 252
Lloyd, Lauren, 102
Lloyd, Norman, 318
Locarno Film Festival, 18, 400
Locke, Sondra, 507
Loewe, Frederick, 494
Loews, 15
Logan, Helen, 338
Logan, Joshua, 434
Loggia, Robert, 48, 74, 111, 208, 292,
    298
Lom, Herbert, 93
Lombard, Carole, 202, 336, 437, 488
Lombardi, LTD, 377
Lombardo, Goffredo, 166
Lombardo, Leon, 155
Lombardo, Lou, 237
Lomond, Britt, 327, 329, 330
London, Jack, 102
"Lone Ranger, The," 480
Lone Star International, 76
Lone Wolf McQuade, <u>147</u>, 363
Lonely Are the Brave, 389, 474
Long, Audrey, 177
Long, Hal, 220
Long, Shelley, 148, 512
Long, Long Trailer, The, 106, 357
Long Riders, The, 380
Longest Hundred Miles, The, 449
Longest Yard, The, 519
Lonsdale, Frederick, 186
Looking for Mr. Goodbar, 405
Looking for Trouble, 367
Lopez, Estrellita, 175
Lopez, Fernando, 293
Lopez, Gerry, <u>433</u>
Lopez, Jennifer, 296
Lopez, Julius Caesar. *See* Lopez, Perry
Lopez, Kamala, 58, 59, 305, 309, <u>433</u>
Lopez, Manny, 73
Lopez, Manuel, 226
Lopez, Mario, 296
Lopez, Perry, 43, 45, 46, 74, 77, 77, 85,
    135, 213, <u>433–34</u>
Lopez, Primo, 155, 187
Lopez, Priscilla, 286, 309, <u>434</u>
Lopez, Rafael [Raphael], 89, 228, 257,
    <u>434</u>
Lopez, Sal, 23, 32, 34, 258, 304, <u>434</u>
Lopez, Sylvia, <u>434</u>
Lopez, Trini, 89, <u>435</u>
Lopez Neri, Efrain, 97
Lopez Rodero, Jose, 94, <u>435</u>
Lord, Marjorie, 276

Mary Kaye Trio, 73
Mary Pickford Company, 201
"Mary Tyler Moore Show, The," 293, 294
Mas, Carlos, 48
Mas Alla del Sol, 408
Masada, 375
Maseli, Francesco, 443
"M*A*S*H," 50, 264, 299
Mask of the Avenger, The, 423
Mason, James, 106, 174, 245, 348, 407
Mason, Marsha, 122
Mason, Tom, 276, 280
Masquerade in Mexico, 155, 387, 431
Mass Appeal, 508
Massey, Ilona, 127
Master Gunfighter, The, 155–56, 371, 375, 501
Masterson, Whit, 227
Mastrantonio, Mary Elizabeth, 208, 209, **209**
Mastroianni, Marcello, 367, 515
Masur, Richard, 284
Mata Hari, 457
Mate, Rudolph, 60, 210
Mateos, Julian, 193
Mathis, June, 51, 108
Matlin, Marlee, 247
Matofsky, Harvey, 258
"Matt Houston," 431
Matter of Conviction, A, 257
Matthews, DeLane, 277
Matthiessen, Peter, 38
Mature, Victor, 164, **164**, 381, 420, 494
Maura, Corinna, 114
Maurer, Joshua, 299
"Maverick," 263, 487, 508
Maverick Gold. See Catlow
Max Mambru Films Ltd., 97
Mayer, Edwin Justus, 155
Mayer, Louis B., 241, 384, 452
Mayo, Archie, 57
Mayo, Frank, 324
Mayo, Virginia, 525
Mazursky, Paul, 23, 49, 50, 89, 149, 163, 350, 367, 371, 417, 427
Me, Myself, and I, 405
Mean Season, The, 410, 468, 495
Medak, Peter, 328
Medal for Benny, A, 144, 156–57, 156, 352, 362, 387, 399, 431, 454, 456, 466
"Medical Center," 266, 464, 486
Medicine Man, 157
Medina, Julio, 299, 304, 316
Medina, Ofelia, 49
Medina, Patricia, 47, 182, 442
Medina, Raynaldo, 97
Medium Cool, 142
Meehan, Elizabeth, 118
"Meet Millie," 177, 290, 512
Megaforce, 500
Meins, Gus, 68
Meisner, Sanford, 374

Melendez, Bill, 442
Melendez, Jose Cuauhtemac (Bill). *See* Melendez, Bill
Melgar, Gabriel, 274
Melgar, Gilbert, 65
Melody Top Theatre, 359
"Melrose Place," 519
Memories of Underdevelopment, 25
Men, The, 19
Men at Work, 399, 498
Men of the North, 12, **12**, 484
Men of Tomorrow, 503
Menard, Tina, 89, 115, 116, 125, 144, 168, 210, 249, 274, 442
Mendes, Lothar, 219
Mendoza, John, 297, 442
Mendoza, Victor Manuel, 112, 255
Menendez, Ana Margarita, 293
Menendez, Ramon, 215, 216, 217, 442
Menges, Chris, 162
Menjou, Adolphe, 256
Men's Club, The, 408
Menudo, 202
Menzies, William Cameron, 106
Mercado, Hector, 88, 308, 443
Mercury Theater, 331
Merediz, Olga, 218
Meredyth, Bess, 86, 220, 325
Mérimée, Prosper, 148
Mermaids, 370
Merrill, Dina, 257
Merry Widow, The, 431
Message to Garcia, A, 411
Mestres, Ricardo, 443
Metcalf, Laurie, 130
Metro Pictures Corp., 86, 108
Metropolitan Opera, 113, 422
Metzer, Howard, 309
Mexican, The, 5
"Mexican, The," 102
"Mexican Fiesta," 266
Mexican Hayride, 157–58
Mexican Spitfire, 21, 158, 510
Mexican Spitfire at Sea, 158
Mexican Spitfire Out West, 158
Mexican Spitfire Sees a Ghost, 158
Mexican Spitfire's Baby, 159
Mexican Spitfire's Blessed Event, 159
Mexican Spitfire's Elephant, 159
Mexican Village, A, 213
Mexicana, 159
MGM, 11, 13, 15, 17, 19, 27, 38, 45, 47, 49, 55, 56, 64, 68, 71, 73, 83, 86, 88, 89, 100, 101, 106, 108, 119, 127, 133, 137, 142, 154, 165, 166, 167, 176, 177, 179, 194, 198, 199, 213, 214, 222, 226, 232, 241, 242, 255, 357, 369, 370, 379, 381, 383, 391, 407, 417, 424, 430, 442, 443, 447, 448, 449, 452, 455, 458, 473, 475, 479, 481, 484, 486, 487, 488, 499, 504, 510, 519, 520
MGM/Pathé, 102
MGM-TV, 270, 486

MGM/UA, 141, 145
Mi Vida Loca, 353, 360, 366, 508
Miami Sound Machine, 462
"Miami Vice," 34, 209, 261, 291, 307, 378, 393, 423, 433, 451, 459, 461, 467, 478, 499, 502
Michael Landon Productions, 417
Michaels, Lorne, 221
Michaels, Sidney, 133
Michelena, Beatriz, 6
Michener, James A., 303
Midler, Bette, 89, 353, 425, 463
"Midnight Caller," 512
Midnight Cowboy, 405
Midnight Run, 446
Midnight Story, The, 486
Midnight Taxi, 485
Midshipman, The, 458, 483
Midsummer Night's Sex Comedy, A, 404
Midway, 399
Mighty Ducks, The, 399
Mighty Joe Young, 389, 464
Mighty Quinn, The, 379
Milagro Beanfield War, The, 22, 23, 68, 159–60, 359, 364, **364**, 367, 374, 375, 397, 412, 436, 454, 507, 514
Milan, Lita, 144
Milchan, Arnon, 152, 187
Mildred Pierce, 81
Miles, Vera, 124
Milian, Tomas, 72, 121, 122, 193, 279, 288, 307, 443
Milicevic, Djordje, 239
Milius, John, 98, 236
Millan, Victor, 45, 46, **46**, 115, 116, 196, 208, 220, 227, **228**, 389, 443
Milland, Ray, 67, 233, 431
Millard, Oscar, 193, 210
Miller, Alan, 35
Miller, Alice Duer, 64
Miller, Ann, 137, 223, 225
Miller, Dan, 251
Miller, Earl, 302
Miller, J.P., 47, 257
Miller, Penelope Ann, 71
Miller, Ron, 124
Miller, Seton I., 67
Miller, Winston, 130, 164
Million Dollar Rip-Off, The, 469
Million to Juan, A, 481
Mimieux, Yvette, 108, 193, 443
Minardos, Nico, 126
Mineo, Sal, 75, 76, 116, 389, 393, 486
Minnelli, Vincente, 38, 108, 470, 472, 486
Minns, Byron Keith, 276
Minter, Mary Miles, 452
Mintz, Sam, 113
Miracle Mile, 387
Miracle of Main Street, The, 387
Miracle of Our Lady of Fatima, The, 160, **161**, 389, 486, 502
Miracle on 34th Street, 368

Miracles, 481
Miramax, 84
Miranda, Aurora, 63, 222, <u>444</u>, **444**
Miranda, Carmen, 2, 10, 17, 21, 82, 90, 112, 166, 167, 199, 220, 249, **383**, <u>444</u>–45, **445**, 450, 488
Miranda, Robert, <u>445</u>–46
Miranda, Susan, <u>446</u>
Mirelez, Tony, 187
Mirisch, Walter, 62, 103, 163
Mirisch Brothers, 436, 453
Miroslava, 61, <u>446</u>
Miss Sadie Thompson, 403, 420
Miss Teenager of the World, 351
Miss USA, 422
Miss Venezuela, 351
Missiles of October, 499
Missing, 97, <u>161</u>–62
Missing in Action, 400, 422
Missing in Action II, 422
Mission, The, <u>162</u>
"Mission: Impossible," 264, 380, 495
Mr. Antonio, 377
Mr. Arkadin, 465
Mr. Majestyk, <u>163</u>, 382, 475
Mister Roberts, 433
Mr. Robinson Crusoe, 506
Mr. T., 270
Mistress, 469
Misty, 35
Mitchell, Cameron, 112, 281
Mitchell, Thomas, 27, 45, 210
Mitchum, James, 228, 399
Mitchum, Robert, 42, 210, 240, 255, 348, 439
Mitz, Rick, 269
Mix, Tom, 5
Mo' Better Blues, 364
Mo' Money, 494
Mobley, Roger, 89
Mobsters, 405, 470
Moctezuma Esparza Productions, 397
"Mod Squad, The," 359
Modern Girls, 519
Modern Times, 409
Modine, Matthew, 519
Moffat, Ivan, 115
Mohr, Gerald, 190, 196, **196**
Mojica, Jose, 438, <u>446</u>
Mojica, Victor, <u>446</u>
Mola, Laura, 312
Moliere, 28
Molieri, Lillian, 339
Molina, Carmen, 222
Molina Campos, F., 204
Monash, Paul, 67
Monclova, Rene, 251
Money Pit, The, 370
Money Trap, The, 449
Monkey Shines: An Experiment in Fear, 490
Monogram Studios, 3, 337, 339, 341, 354, 433, 455, 485
Monoson, Lawrence, 111

Monroe, Marilyn, 14, 20, 506
Monsieur Beaucaire, 439
"Monsters," 381
Montalban, Carlos, 41, 120, 181, <u>446</u>, 448
Montalban, Ricardo, 10, 20, 24, **24**, 25, 47, 53, 55, **55**, 56, 75–76, 101, 137, 142, 145, 146, **146**, 165, 194, **195**, 213, 214, **214**, 219, 263, 264, **265**, 266, 278, 301, 306, 317, 331, 379, 389, 401, 407, **407**, 446, <u>447</u>–49, **447**, 473, 486
Montana, Karla, **216**, 278, 313, 318
Monte Walsh, 405
Montenegro, Conchita, 336, <u>449</u>
Montero, Zully, 97
Monteros, Elsa, 151
Monteros, Rosenda, 240
Montes, Lola, 114
Montes, Vira, 32
Montez, Maria, 17, 21, 182, 220, <u>449</u>–50
Montgomery, Robert, 194
Monti, Carlotta, 199
Montiel, Sarita, 21, 35, 210, 239, <u>450</u>
Montmartre Cafe, 384
Montoya, Alex, 68, 101, 140, 158, 178, 224, 326, 339, 341, <u>450</u>
Montoya, Eustachio, 6
Montoya, Julia, 174
Moody, Jim, 39
Moon and Sixpence, The, 512
Moon over Parador, 22, 149, <u>163</u>, 366, 367, 379, 427
Moonlight and Cactus, 377
Moonlight in Hawaii, 450
Moore, Clayton, 326
Moore, Constance, 37, 159
Moore, Demi, 50, 101
Moore, Dudley, 277, 514
Moore, Grace, 422, 423
Moore, Joanna, 227
Moore, Mickey, **385**
Moorehead, Agnes, 448
Mora, Danny, 274, <u>451</u>
Morales, Esai, 22, 39, 137, 138, 291, <u>451</u>
Morales, Jacobo, 41, 42, 251, <u>451</u>
Morales, Santos, 23, 68, 88, 148, 183, 208, 221, <u>451</u>
Moreno, Antonio, **6**, 10, 39, 69, 70, 83, 84, **84**, 101, 126, 168, 219, 220, 254, <u>451</u>–52, 486, 521, **521**
Moreno, Jorge, 125
Moreno, Mario. *See* Cantinflas
Moreno, Rita [Rosita], 20, 21–22, 99, 112, 130, 142, 183, 184, 196, 198, 211, 217, 218, 219, 249, 250, **250**, 263, 264, **266**, 270, 277, 292, 294, 301, 308, **428**, 466, 479, <u>452</u>–54, **453**
Moreno, Rosita, 11, 156, <u>454</u>
Moreno, Ruben, 125, <u>454</u>
Morgan, Dennis, **453**
Morgan, Harry, 275
Morgan, Marion, 457

Morgan-Witts, Max, 245
Morgan's Last Raid, 409
Morheim, Lou, 224
Moriarty, Cathy, 152
Moriarty, Michael, 187
Morin, Alberto, 105, 110, 124, 137, 140, 159, 220, 234, 249, <u>454</u>
Morison, Patricia, 149, 338
Morita, Pat, 292
Moritz, Louisa, 86
Morley, Karen, 142
Morning After, The, 427
Morning Glory, 352
Moro, Nick, 101
Moroff, Michael [Mike], 307, 319, <u>454</u>
Morones, Bob, 34, <u>454</u>
Morosco, Walter, 338
Morricone, Ennio, 103
Morrill, Norman Mcleod, 301
Morris, Gordon, 236
Morris, Phillip, 289
Morrison, Shelley, 279
Morrissey, Paul, 451
Morrow, Jeff, 103
Morrow, Vic, 49, 50, 371
Morsella, Fulvio, 90
Mortensen, Viggo, 71, 72
Moscow Film Festival, 63
Moscow on the Hudson, 23, 350, 351, 418, 475
Mosel, Tad, 238
Moser, James E., 254
Mosquiz (Musquiz), Carlos, 211, 229, 240
Moss, Arnold, 148
"Most Dangerous Game, The," 202
Mostel, Zero, 358
Mother, Jugs & Speed, 515
"Mothers-in-Law, The," 357, 358
Motion Picture Group, 443
Motion Picture Society for the Americas, 15
Moulin Rouge, 403
Mountain Men, The, 473
Mountain Road, The, 502
Movie Time Films, 175
Moviola, 506
Movita, 20, 111, 194, <u>455</u>–56, **455**
Mozart, Wolfgang Amadeus von, 28
Mrs. Cage, <u>314</u>
Mrs. Soffel, 353
"Mucho Money," 202
Mule for the Marquesa, A, 186
Mulkey, Chris, 270
Mulligan, Robert, 238
Mulroney, Dermot, 256
"Mundo Real," 503
Muni, Paul, 20, 57, **58**, 82, 132, **132**, 133, 208
Munier, Ferdinand, 323
Muniz, Pedro, 251
Muniz, Tommy, 251, 305
Muppets, 297

Mura, Corrina, <u>456</u>
Murcelo, Karmin, 57, 303, 304, <u>456</u>
"Murder, She Wrote," 356, 374, 442, 446, 490, 499
Murder in the Heartland, 410
Murdock, George, 300
Murieta, <u>163</u>
Murillo, Bartolomé Esteban, 52
Murphy, Audie, 429
Murphy, Ben, 271
Murphy, Eddie, 354, 364, 468, 469, 481
Murphy, Geoff, 256
Murphy, George, 45, 47, 55, 56, 167
Murphy, Michael, 205
Murray, Don, 399
Murray, Forrest, 305
Musca, Tom, 215, 216
Museum of Modern Art (New York), 15, 369
Music for Millions, 17
Mussolini, 427
Mutiny, 61, 421
Mutiny on the Bounty (1935), 20, 455, **455**
Mutiny on the Bounty (1962), 502
Mutrux, Floyd, 32, 33, 60, 109, 459
Mutual Film Corporation, 146
My American Wife, 452
My Blue Heaven, 446
My Darling Clementine, 21, <u>164–65</u>, **164**
My Demon Lover, 408
"My Favorite Husband," 284, 357
My Favorite Spy, 506
My Gal Sal, 420
My Life with Caroline, 485
My Man and I, 20, <u>165</u>, 448
My Six Convicts, 407, 486
My Son, the Hero, 356
My Stepmother Is an Alien, 370
My Three Angels, 403
My Wicked, Wicked Ways, 506
Mystery of Marie Roget, The, 450
Mystery Street, <u>165</u>, 449
Mystery Woman, 485

Nadine, 350
Nagrin, Daniel, <u>456</u>
Naidu, Ajay, 227
Naish, J. Carroll, 52, 72, 90, 109, 134, 137, 140, 156, **156**, 157, 190, 199, 220, 231, 232, 236, <u>456</u>
Nakano, Desmond, 32, 59, 60
Naked Ape, The, 468
"Naked City," 263, 475, 482
Naked City, The, 19
Naked Dawn, The, <u>166</u>, 423
Naked Gun, 447
Naked Jungle, The, <u>166</u>, 389
Naked Lie, 469
Naked Maja, The, <u>166</u>
Naked Prey, The, 154
Naldi, Nita, 51
"Name of the Game, The," 449

Nancy Goes to Rio, <u>166–67</u>, 445
"Nango," 249
Narizzano, Silvio, 53
Nash, Clarence, 204, 222
Nassour, Edward, 47
Nassour, William, 47
Nastro d'Argento, 443
"Nasty Boys," <u>291</u>, 367
Nathan, Vivian, 257
Nathanson, E.M., 89
National Council of La Raza, 41, 397
National General, 74, 94, 201
National Health, The, 453
National Hispanic Scholarship Fund, 301
National Latino Communications Center, 491
National Science Foundation, 216
National Shakespeare Company, 499
National Theatre (England), 201
National Variety Artists, 336
National Vaudeville Association, 336
Naughton, David, 270
Naughty But Nice, 474
Nava, Gregory, 95, 96, 97, <u>456–57</u>
Navarro, Carlos, 61
Navarro, Mario, 47
Navy Comes Through, The, <u>167</u>, 358
Nayfack, Nicholas, 55
Nazarro, Ray, 66
Nazimova, Alla, 52, 64
NBC, 264, 266, 269–319 passim, 442, 464
Neal, Patricia, 499
Nebe, Chris D., 123
Nebenzal, Harold, 135
Necessary Roughness, 396
"Ned Blessing," 360
Ned Blessing: The Story of My Life and Times, <u>315</u>
Neeson, Liam, 162
Negrete, Jorje, 101
Negron, Taylor, <u>457</u>
Neider, Charles, 171
Neilson, James, 316
Nelson, B.J., 147
Nelson, Craig T., 307
Nelson, David, 141
Nelson, Grant, 326
Nelson, James, 57
Nelson, Ralph, 192, 255
Nelson, Ricky, 197
Nelson, Willie, 44, 441, 486, 510
Neptune's Daughter, 383, 448
Nestor Amaral and his Orchestra, 126
Nestor Amaral and his Samba Band, 178
Netter, Douglas, 316
Neumann, Kurt, 61, 148, 196
Neumeyer, Fred, 252
Nevada Smith, 385
Never Live Over a Pretzel Factory, 499
Never Say Never Again, 375

"Never Trust a Jumping Bean," 101
New Centurions, The, 399
New Century–Vista, 123, 181, 200
"New Dick Van Dyke Show, The," <u>291</u>, 384
New Land, The, 258
New Line Cinema, 22, 120
"New Odd Couple, The," <u>291</u>
New Orleans, 387
New Visions, 137
New World Television, 332, 512
New York Drama Critics Circle Award, 402, 403, 467
New York Film Critics Award, 348
New York Nights, 484
New York School of Music, 469
New York Shakespeare Festival, 426, 502
New York Stories, 366
New Yorker, The, 27, 269
Newell, Gordon, 68
Newman, Alfred, 70, 326, 331
Newman, Joseph M., 135
Newman, Paul, 67, 107, **107**, 127, 144, 176, 468, 504
Newman, Randy, 221
Newman, Walter, 237
Newman's Law, 371
Newmar, Julie, 149
Newsies, 463
Newton-John, Olivia, 462, 463
Next Stop, Greenwich Village, 399
Niagara, 508
Niblo, Fred, 51, 322, 323
Niblo, Fred, Jr., 219
Nicholas and Alexandra, 378, 465
Nicholls, George, 153
Nichols, Dudley, 105, 109, 202
Nichols, John, 159, 160
Nicholson, Jack, 22, 54, **54**, 77, **77**, 101, 361, 364, 376, 412, 454, 503
Nicita, Wallis, 102
Nicolas y los Demas, 251, 451
Nicole, Lydia, **216**
Nieto, Lucila, 211
Niggli, Josefina, 213
Nigh, William, 339, 341
Night and Day, 473
Night at the Opera, A, 422, 423
Night Is Young, The, 458
Night of the Following Day, The, 454
Night of the Hunter, The, 381
Night of the Iguana, The, 3, <u>167–68</u>, 167, 237, 380, 405, 522
Night of the Juggler, 374
Night of the Living Dead, 490
Night Rider, The, 480
Night School, 368
Nighthawks, 380
"Nightingales," <u>291</u>
Nightmare on Elm Street, 494
Nightmares, 398
Nijinsky, 388
Nine, 426

Nine Hours to Rama, 403
"Nine Lives of Elfeco Baca, The," 292
9 to 5, 512
"9 to 5," 292, 454
1941, 499
Niven, David, 37, 371
No, No Nanette, 378
No Drums, No Bugles, 499
No Leave, No Love, 383
No Living Witness, 485
No Man's Land, 408, 497
No Mataras, 427
No Other Woman, 390
Nolan, Lloyd, 119, 149, 207
Nolte, Nick, 2, 68, 89, 98, 99, 187, 188, 236, 378, 468
Noriega, Chon, 6
Noriega, Eduardo, 140, 182, 211
Noriega, Felix, 46
Noriega, Inigo de Martino, 225
Norma Rae, 351
Norman, Marc, 64, 258
Norris, Aaron, 88
Norris, Chuck, 79, 88, 103, 147, 422, 468, 500
North, Edmund H., 83
North, Richard, 63
North, Sheree, 175, 176
North Dallas Forty, 397
North Shore, 433
Northern California Light Opera Company, 394
Norton, B.W.L., 78, 148
Norton, Barry, 11, 457
Nosotros, 24–25, 264
Not of This World, 441
Nothing But Trouble, 384, 457
Notorious, 168
Notti de Cabiria, 219
Nouri, Michael, 271
Novarro, George, 140
Novarro, Ramon, 8, 9, 10, 49, 83, 84, 84, 248, 249, 457–58, 458, 483, 486
Now, Voyager, 61
Nucci, Danny, 278, 274, 309
Nude Bomb, The, 368
Nugent, Frank, 222
Nunez, Daniel [Danny], 187, 459
Nunez, Miguel, 299
"Nurses," 292, 429, 438
"NYPD Blue," 506
Nyswaner, Ron, 181

O. Henry, 333, 334, 336, 338, 339, 340
Oates, Warren, 54, 64, 65, 193, 252
Oberon, Merle, 186
Obie Award, 311, 434, 467, 507
Objective, Burma!, 14
O'Brian, Clay, 275
O'Brien, Edmond, 45, 252, 459, 494
O'Brien, George, 3
O'Brien, Lorenzo, 247
O'Brien, Marian, 459

O'Brien, Pat, 54, 128, 167, 226, 439
O'Brien, Willis, 14, 47, 388
Ocean's Eleven, 489, 500
O'Connell, Arthur, 82
O'Connor, Carroll, 270
Odd Couple, The, 291
O'Dea, John, 190
O'Dell, Dennis, 198
Office of the Coordinator of Inter-American Affairs (CIAA), 15, 37, 204
Officer and a Gentleman, An, 23, 137, 468
"Official Detective," 417
Official Story, The, 22, 111, 168, 348, 469–70
Oh God! Book II, 363
O'Hanlon, James, 160, 163
"Ohara," 23, 292, 504
O'Hara, Maureen, 149, 176, 220, 221, 470
Ojeda, Manuel, 199, 200
O'Keefe, Dennis, 144
Oklahoma!, 385, 518
Oklahoma Crude, 371
Oklahoma Frontier, 387
Oklahoma Kid, The, 474
Oland, Warner, 73
Old Gringo, 2, 9, 168–69, 169, 288, 356, 408, 469, 470, 502
Old Gringo, The (novel), 3
Old Ironsides, 393
Old Man and the Sea, The (1958), 14, 105, 170–71, 170, 350, 352
Old Man and the Sea, The (1990), 315, 473
Old Shatterhand, 408
Olin, Lena, 121, 121, 122
Oliu, Ingrid, 216
Olivari, Carlos, 256
Oliveira, Aloysio, 204
Oliveira, Jose, 222
Oliver!, 463
Oliver and Company, 438
Olivier, Laurence, 412, 472
Olmos, Edward James, 32–34, 33, 40, 41, 60, 80, 215, 215, 216, 216, 217, 258, 259, 259, 261, 291, 316, 317, 319, 397, 401, 412, 434, 454, 459–61, 460
Olsen, Leila Hee, 300
Olson, Gerald T., 315
Omar Khayyam, 434, 457
On an Island with You, 383, 448
On the Border, 357
On the Isle of Samoa, 506
On the Nickel, 415
On the Old Spanish Trail, 416, 481
"On the Rocks," 292
On Wings of Eagles, 451
On with the Show, 378
Onassis: The Richest Man in the World, 427, 472
Once upon a Scoundrel, 440

One-Eyed Jacks, 36, 171–72, 172, 348, 379, 385, 395, 399, 408, 428, 465, 506
One from the Heart, 172–73, 427, 463
One Good Cop, 173, 367
"100 Centre Street," 292–93
100 Rifles, 173, 174, 431, 478, 515
One Mad Kiss, 438, 446
One Man's War, 315
One Million B.C., 494
One Million Years B.C., 515
One Night of Love, 422, 423
"One of the Boys," 293
One Touch of Venus, 418, 494
One Way Street, 174, 348, 407
O'Neal, Patrick, 94
O'Neal, Ron, 155, 156
O'Neill, Eugene, 473
Only Angels Have Wings, 2, 175, 175, 399, 418, 474
Only Once in a Lifetime, 175–76, 397
Only the Lonely, 436, 470
Only When I Laugh, 508
Ontiveros, Asuncion, 162
Ontiveros, Lupe, 58, 95, 258, 277, 317, 318, 461
Operation Eichmann, 423
"Operation Petticoat," 368
Oppenheimer, George, 28
Oquendo, Luis, 293
"Orchids in the Moonlight," 104, 390
Ordinary People, 160
Organization, The, 427
Original Sin, The (book), 472
Orion Pictures, 48, 79, 99, 147, 221, 236
Orlando, Tony, 265, 266, 298, 319, 438, 461, 461–62, 462
Ormsby, Alan, 227
Orona, Moon, 202
O'Rourke, Frank, 61, 186
Orphans of the Storm, 470
Orpheum circuit (vaudeville), 357, 377
Orrico, Carmen. *See* Saxon, John
Ortega, Kenny, 203, 462–63
Ortega, Tony, 118
Ortelli, Dyana, 289, 289, 304, 463
Ortiz, Humberto, 289, 289, 463
Ortiz, John, 71
Osborne, Madolyn Smith, 218
Osmond, Cliff, 181
Osterhage, Jeff, 316
Osterloh, Robert, 196
Osterman, Paula Marie. *See* Torres, Raquel
Otello, 395
Othello, 403, 425
Other Love, The, 485
Othon, Yvonne, 250, 250. *See also* Wilder, Yvonne
O'Toole, Annette, 304
O'Toole, Peter, 154, 375
Ottero, Victor, 36
Our Betters, 485

Our Man in Havana, <u>176</u>
"Our Miss Brooks," 417
Out of the Past, 3
Outer Critics Circle Award, 311
Outlaw, The, 480
Outrage, The, <u>176</u>
Outriders, The, 458
Outsiders, The, 398, 507
Owen, Reginald, 390
Owen, Seena, 202
"Owen Marshall, Counselor at Law," 494
Ox-Bow Incident, The, <u>177</u>, 471
Oxcart, The, 380
"Oye Willie," <u>293</u>, 478

Pacheco, Johnny, 40
Pacino, Al, 33, 71, 208, **208**, **209**, 293, 362, 378, 379, 380, 495, 504
Paddy O'Day, 419
Padilla, Frank, 6
Padilla, Manuel, Jr., 89, 219, 298, 302, <u>463</u>–64
Padilla, Margaret, 102
Padilla, Miguel, 178
Padilla, Ruben, 255
Padilla Sisters, 178
Padula, Vincent, 140
Pagan, The, 458
Pagan Love Song, 452
Pagano, Ernest, 256
Page, Anita, <u>464</u>
Page, Ann, 352. *See* Boyer, Ann
Page, Carlos. *See* Alvarado, Carlos
Page, Don. *See* Alvarado, Don
Page, Geraldine, 217
Page, Harrison, 272
Page, Joanne. *See* Page, Joy
Page, Joy, 66, 352, <u>464</u>
Paint Your Wagon, 399, 405
Paint Your Wagon (stage), 494
Pair of Shoes, A, 443
Paiva, Nestor, 99, 100, 103, 126, 130, 144, 156, 198, 199, 219, 244, 292, 341, <u>464</u>
Pakula, Alan J., 238
Pal, George, 166
Pal Joey, 420
Palance, Jack, 74, 135, 186, **186**, 187, 192, 210, 256, 408
Palange, Inez, 338
Pale Rider, 507
Palevsky, Max, 110
Palladium (Hollywood), 384
Pallenberg, Rospo, 98
Pallette, Eugene, 57, 325
Palme d'Or (Cannes Film Festival), 29, 162
Palmer, Ernest, 52
Pals First, 389
Pampa Barbara, 407, 408
Pan, Hermes, 220
Pan-Americana, <u>177</u>–78, **178**, 362

Panama Hattie, <u>177</u>
Panama Sal, <u>177</u>, 414
Panavision, 241
Pancho Villa, <u>178</u>, 240
Pancho Villa Returns, 348, 377
Panic in Needle Park, The, 427
Pantages Theater, 463
Panzer, William, 72
Paper Bullets, 61
Papi, Giorgio, 103
Papillon, 378, 435
Papp, Joseph, 353, 426, 473, 502
Pappas, George, 123
"Paradise," 490
Paramor, E.E., Jr., 153
Paramount Pictures, 7, 8, 11, 14, 17, 27, 28, 36, 39, 40, 48, 51, 53, 60, 67, 77, 81, 88, 105–14 *passim,* 126, 129, 130, 141, 142, 143, 149, 154, 155, 156, 166, 171, 184, 190, 198, 201, 202, 204, 207, 210, 212, 214, 217, 219, 233, 237, 239, 240, 247, 362, 381, 385, 386, 387, 401, 410, 416, 431, 443, 450, 454, 464, 485, 493, 494
Pardon Us, 13
Pare, Michael, 284, 510
Paredes, Americo, 40, 41
Paris, Jerry, 241
Paris, Manuel, 224
Paris, Virginia, 215, 217, <u>464</u>
Paris Conservatory of Music, 495
Parisian Romance, A, 485
Parker, Dorothy, 10
Parker, Eleanor, 166
Parker, Fess, 46, **46**, 331
Parker, Jefferson, 128
Parks, Gordon, Jr., 27
Parrish, Robert, 255
Parrondo, Gil, <u>465</u>
Parslow, Philip, 155
Parsonnet, Marion, 116
Parsons, Louella, 448
Partos, Frank, 201, 202
Pasadena Playhouse, 348, 384, 443
Pascal, Ernest, 236
Pass, Dira, 98
Passion, <u>178</u>
Passionate Plumber, The, 485
"Passport to Danger," <u>293</u>, 488
Pasternak, Joe, 127, 137, 142, 166, 486
Pat Garrett and Billy the Kid, <u>179</u>, 348, 401, 428, 523, 524
Pathé, 252
Patten, Lewis B., 87
Patton, 14, 385, 435, 465
"Patty Duke Show, The," 417
Paul, Rodrick, 331
Pawnbroker, The, <u>179</u>–80, **179**, 491
Paxinou, Katina, 105, **106**
Pay Day, 409
Payne, Bruce, 343
Payne, John, 190, 249

Paz, Octavio, 3
Pazos, Felipe, 170, **170**, 171
PBS, 23, 29, 41, 63, 97, 137, 273, 277, 293, 294, 297, 299, 302, 304, 308, 311–18 *passim,* 441, 461, 468, 480, 493, 502, 503, 507, 518
"Peanuts," 442
Pearce, Christopher, 88
Pearce, Richard, 305
Pearl, The, 166, <u>180</u>–<u>81</u>, **180**, 242, 355, 363, 405. *See also La Perla*
Peck, Gregory, 9, 47, 49, 61, 91, 149, 168, 169, **169**, 358, 469, 496, 500, 502, 525
Peck, J. Eddie, 139
Peckinpah, Sam, 64, 151, 152, 179, 221, 240, 252, 253, 254, 401, 431, 441, 491, 509, <u>523</u>–24, **524**
"Pedro," 204
Pedroza, Inez, 188
Peet, Bill, 222
Pee-Wee's Big Adventure, 380
Pele, 239, <u>465</u>
Pellicer, Pina, 36, 171, **172**, <u>465</u>
Pena, Elizabeth, 22, 23, 84, 89, 90, 97, 137, 239, 247, 286, 297, **297**, 298, 307, **362**, <u>465</u>
Pena, Pascual Garcia, 49, 130, 229
Pena, Sergio, 29
Penitent, The, <u>181</u>, 374, 427
Penn, Arthur, 144
Penn, Sean, 39, 71, 72, 79, 80, 99, 100, 350, 451, 501
Pepe, <u>181</u>, 371
Peppard, George, 270, 277, 371
Perelman, S.J., 37
Perez, Anthony, 293
Perez, Jose, 145, 146, **146**, 212, 248, 257, 292, 318, <u>465</u>
Perez, Livia, 308
Perez, Manuel, <u>466</u>
Perez, Olivia, 293
Perez, Pepito, 155, 156, 284, <u>466</u>
Perez, Rosie, 23, 100, 251, <u>466</u>–<u>67</u>, **466**
Perez, Severo, 317, <u>467</u>
Perez, Tony, 309
Perez Prado's Orchestra, 89
Perfect Furlough, The, 382
Perin, Jack, 387
Perkins, Anthony, 119
Perlman, Ron, 343
Peron, Eva, 18
Peron, Juan, 18, 248
Perrin, Nat, 201
Perrine, Valerie, 54, 318
Perry, Ben L. *See* Trumbo, Dalton
Perry, Frank, 81
Perry, Pinchas, 111
"Perry Mason," 464
Persoff, Nehemiah, 80, 81, 191
Pesci, Joe, 218
"Pete and Gladys," 354
Pete and Tillie, 518

Peters, Brock, 179
Peters, Charles, 50
Peters, Jean, 69, 242, 244
Petersen, William, 256, 305
Petracca, Joseph, 211
Petrie, Daniel, 107
Pettet, Joanna, 53
Pevney, Joseph, 182
"Peyton Place," 482
Pfeiffer, Michelle, 208
Phantom Crown, The, 132
Phantom Lady, 413, 444, **444**
Phantom of Santa Fe, The, <u>324</u>
Phantom of the Opera, The (1925), 483
Phantom of the Opera (1943), 377
"Phil Silvers Show, The," 512
Philadelphia, <u>181</u>, 362
Philips, Lee, 319
Phillips, Alex, Jr., <u>467</u>
Phillips, Alex, Sr., 213, 240, 405, 467
Phillips, Bill, 308
Phillips, Lou Diamond, 22, 137, 138, **138**, 212, 215, **216**, 217, 256, 291, <u>467</u>, 507
Phillips, Michael, 68
Phillips, Michelle, 296
"Phyllis," <u>293</u>, 504
Picerni, Paul, 299
Pichel, Irving, 156
Pichon, Edgcumb, 241, 242
Pickens, Slim, 179, 306
Picker, Sidney, 99
Pickford, Mary, 11, 18, 113, 201, 322, 474, 508
Pickup, Ronald, 162
Pick-up Artist, The, 467
Pickup on 101, 499
Pidgeon, Walter, 127, 390
Piece of the Action, A, 374
Pielmeier, John, 304
Pinal, Silvia, 119, 234
Pinchuk, Sheldon, 301
Pine, Lester, 183, 293
Pine, Tina, 183, 293
Pine, William H., 130, 143, 233
Pinero, Miguel, 107, 212, 291, <u>467</u>
Pink Cadillac, 507
Pinky, 195
Pinney, Herbert. *See* Martin, Richard
Pinter, Harold, 425
Pioncela, Jardiel, 11
Pirates of Monterey, <u>182</u>, 450, 485
Pirosh, Robert, 47
Pittsburgh, 413
Pixote, 136, 361
Place in the Sun, A, 203
Places in the Heart, 350
Plainsman, The, 470, 482
Plana, Tony, 23, 63, 87, 95, 121, 122, **142**, 173, 200, 205, 206, 221, 270, 288, 307, 318, <u>468</u>
Plastic Age, The, 483
Platform Releasing, 63

Platoon, 23, 206, 454, 497
"Playhouse 90," 233, 263, 371, 449
Plaza, Begonia, 88, <u>468</u>
Plaza De La Raza, 437
Pleshette, Suzanne, 291
Pliego, Eduardo, 211
Plotnick, Jonathan, 313
Plummer, Amanda, 311
Plummer, Christopher, 201
Plunder of the Sun, <u>182</u>
Plunderers, The, <u>182</u>, 494
Plymmer, Elmer, 222
Podesta, Rossanna, 207
Poe, James, 37, 217
Poggi, Grace, 219
Poinc, Eugene, 302
Point Break, 478
Pointer Sisters, 462
Poitier, Sidney, 49, 50, 371
Poland, Joseph, 326
Polanski, Roman, 77, 433
"Police Story," 263, 441, 461, 464, 468, 494
Politiquerias, 13, 347
Poll, Martin, 184
Pollack, Sydney, 121, 122
Pomares, Anita. *See* Page, Anita
Ponce, LuAnne, 275
Ponelli, Tullio, 219
Poole, Douglas, 248
Popescu, Petru, 87
Popi, <u>183</u>–84, **183**, 293, 317, 454
"Popi," <u>293</u>, 395, 396
Poppy Is Also a Flower, The, 435, 486
Porcasi, Paul, 134, 139, **226**, 237
Porcel, Jorje, 71
Porter, Cole, 3, 177, 420
Porter, William Sidney. *See* O. Henry
Portillo, Rose, 246, 258, 277, 316, 317, <u>468</u>
Portrait of Maria. *See* Maria Candelaria
Posse, <u>184</u>, 354
Possession of Joel Delaney, The, <u>184</u>, 380
Post, Markie, 310
Postcards from the Edge, 401, 496
Postman Always Rings Twice, The, 135
Potts, Cliff, 279
Powell, Ann, 307
Powell, Dick, 38, 194, 195, **195**, 449
Powell, Jane, 127, 166, 448
Powell, William, 64, 488
Power, Tyrone, 2, 16, 18, 52, 69, 218, 243, 323, 325, **325**, 326, 330, 331, 379, 420, 431, **487**, 488, 517
Power and the Glory, The, 109
Powers, Stephanie, 302
Powwow Highway, 440, 514
Prades, Jaime, <u>468</u>
Prado, Perez, 3, 73, 89
Pratt, James, 292
Predator, <u>185</u>, 376, 379
Predator 2, <u>185</u>, 350, 364
President's Analyst, The, 417

Presley, Elvis, 21, 74, 76, 109, 110, **110**, 374, 393, 394, 399, 515
Presnell, Robert, Jr., 145
Presnell, Robert, Sr., 86
Pressburger, Emeric, 47
Pressman, Michael, 59
Preston, J.A., 292
Presumed Innocent, 302, 425, 427
Pretty Baby, 399
Pretty in Pink, 463
Pretty Woman, 396, 405
Prichard, Hesketh, 323
Prichard, Kate, 323
Pride and the Passion, The, <u>185</u>, 375
Prieto, Antonio, 103
Prince, 429
Prince and the Pauper, The (1937), 494
Prince and the Pauper, The (1962), 517
Prince and the Pauper, The (novel), 163
Prince of the City, 187
Princess Bride, The, 333
Principal, Victoria, 276, 302, <u>468</u>–69
Principal, The, 217, 508
Prinz, Leroy, 101, 233
Prinze, Freddie, 261, 273, 274, 363, **462**, <u>469</u>
Prison Stories: Women on the Inside—"Esperanza," <u>315</u>
Prisoner of Second Avenue, 396
Prisoner of Zenda, The (1922), 457
Prisoner of Zenda, The (1979), 499
Prisoner of Zenda, The (novel), 163
Private Life of Don Juan, The, <u>186</u>
Private School, 518
Prizzi's Honor, 522
Production Code Administration (PCA), 15
Professional Children's School, 353, 504
Professionals, The, <u>186</u>–87, **186**, 380, 459, 487, 520
Promises, Promises, 359
Prophecy, 473
Prosperi, Georgio, 166
Proud Ones, The, 348
Pryor, Richard, 251, 364, 503, 504
Psycho, 412
Public Theatre, 473
Puente, Tito, 152, 203, 265, 301, <u>469</u>
Puenzo, Luis, 168, <u>469</u>–70
Puerto Rican Traveling Theatre, 24, 380
Puglia, Frank, 63, 103, 105, 220, 226, 241, 325, <u>470</u>
Puig, Manuel, 135, 136
Punchline, 457, 512, **513**
Pure Luck, <u>187</u>, 422
Purlie Victorious, 385
Purple Rain, 429
Pustin, Bruce, 318
Puttnam, David, 162
Puzo, Mario, 78

Q, <u>187</u>
Q & A, <u>187</u>–88, 364, 417, 423, 504

Quaid, Randy, 64
"Quantum Leap," 442
Quarterback Princess, 519
"Que Bonita Bandera," 251
"Que Pasa, U.S.A.?," <u>293</u>, 363
Queen of Babylon, The, 449
Quick, Before It Melts, 380
Quicksilver, 481, **482**
Quijada, John, 257
"Quincy, M.E.," 439, 441, 442, 464
Quinn, Aidan, 38, 162, 503
Quinn, Anthony, 5, 7, 17, **24**, 38, 47, 52,
    53, 61, 67, 76, 114, 119, 126, 141,
    149, 153, 177, 188, 192, 193, 194,
    211, 234, 242, 243, **243**, 244, 245,
    265, 288, 315, 407, 443, 446, 458,
    <u>470–73</u>, **471**, 485, 525
Quinn, Francesco, 23, 291, 315, 319
Quinn, Frank, 7
Quinn, Valentina, 315
Quinones, Adolfo "Shabba Doo," 139
Quintana, Ana Maria, <u>473</u>
Quintero, Jose, 374, <u>473</u>
Quo Vadis, 494

R.P.M., <u>188</u>
Rabe, David, 72
Racers, The, 428, 486, 488
Rachmil, Lewis J., 134
Racimo, Victoria, 191, 277, <u>473</u>
Racing with the Moon, 370
Rackin, Martin, 54, 207, 234
Radford, James Q., 166
Radio Days, 469
Radio Flyer, 512
Radnitz, Robert B., 35
Raft, George, 114, 202, 437
Rage, 478, 499
Raging Bull, 491, 504
Raices de Sangre, 23, 25, <u>188–89</u>, 506,
    517
Raid on Entebbe, 379
Raiders, The, <u>189</u>
Raiders of the Desert, 450
Raiders of the Lost Ark, 2, <u>190</u>
Raiders of the Seven Seas, <u>190</u>
Rainbow Island, 494
Rains, Claude, 132, 168
Rainy Day Friends, 451
Raisbeck, Kenneth, 113
Ralph, Sheryl Lee, 481
"Ramar of the Jungle," 443
Rambo, Dack, 298
Ramirez, Carlos, 17, 101, <u>473</u>
Ramona (1916), <u>190</u>
Ramona (1928), <u>190</u>, 389, 390
Ramona (1936), <u>190–91</u>, 386, 419
Ramos, Loyda, 87, 202, 221, 301, <u>473</u>
Ramos, Rudy, 79, 88, 282, 284, <u>474</u>
Ramos, Vic, 118, <u>474</u>
Ramus, Nick, 277
Rancho Grande, 416
Randell, Ron, 148

Rangel, A. Soto, 230
Rangers of Fortune, 485, 506
Rapper, Irving, 61
Rascoe, Judith, 121
Rash, Steve, 65
Rashomon, 41, 176
Rasumny, Mikhail, 156
Ratboy, 507
Rathbone, Basil, 325, 326
Rathmell, John, 324
Ratoff, Gregory, 72
Ravens, Rupert, 295
Ravetch, Irving, 83, 127
Raw Wind in Eden, 504
"Rawhide," <u>294</u>, 369
Ray, Aldo, 45, **46**
Ray, Gene Anthony, 278
Ray, Michel, 61, 62, **62**
Raye, Martha, 233, **415**
Rayfiel, David, 121, 238
Raymond, Gary, 93
Raymond, Gene, 104, 390
Raymond, Paula, 83
Reagan, Ronald, 233
"Real McCoys, The," <u>294</u>
"Realidades," <u>294</u>, 308
Reason, Rex, 135
Rebel Without a Cause, 352, 433
Reborn, 491
Red Dance, The, 390
Red Dawn, 496, 497
Red Harvest, 103
Red Heat, 380
Red Light, 456
Red Lily, The, 458
Red Pony, The, 242
Red River, 19, <u>191</u>
Red Scorpion, 379, 400
Red Shoes, The, 62
"Red Skelton Show, The," 464, 512
Red Sky at Morning, <u>191</u>, 358, 363, 441,
    473, 496
Red Sonja, 478
Red Wagon, The, 505
"Redd Foxx Show, The," <u>294</u>, 394
Redford, Robert, 23, 67, 121, 122, 159,
    160, 367, 454
Reed, Alan, 242
Reed, Sir Carol, 176
Reed, Donald, <u>474</u>
Reed, Donna, 190
Reed, John, 5
Reed, Luther, 197
Reed, Philip, 182
Reed, Theodore, 233
Reese, John, 256
Reeves, George, 37
Reeves, Harry, 204
Reeves, Steve, 350
Reflection of Fear, A, 405
Regarding Henry, 432
Regas, George, 199, 226, 241, 325, <u>474</u>
Regas, Pedro, 32, 105, 241, 339, <u>474</u>

Regehr, Duncan, 311, 332–33, **332**, 441,
    512
Regin, Naja, 118
Regina, Paul, 331
Reid, Alan, 244
Reid, Carl Benton, 140
Reid, Cliff, 117, 158, 159
Reid, Wallace, 114
Reiner, Rob, 101, 270, 518
Reinhardt, Elizabeth, 72
Reinhardt, Wolfgang, 132, 133
Rekant, Stuart B., 309
Reluctant Saint, The, 449
Remo Williams, 397
Remo Williams: The Adventure Begins, 473
Remsen, Bert, 57
Renaldo, Duncan, 7, 64, 105, 263, 324,
    334, 339, 340, 341, 342, 343, 344,
    345, 411, <u>474–75</u>
Renaldo, Tito, 27, 68, 99, 105, 174, 194,
    226, 339
Renan, Sheldon, 139
Renavent, Georges, 197, 198
"Renegade," 431
Renegades, 467
Renna, Patrick, 207
Rennahan, Ray, 52, 106
Rennie, James, 36, 139
Rennie, Michael, 211
Renoir, Jean, 89
Repo Man, <u>191–92</u>, **192**, 247, 398, 492,
    510, 518
Report to the Commissioner, 396
Reprise Records, 435
Republic Studios, 3, 30, 63, 66, 99, 140,
    153, 159, 177, 323, 324, 326, 327,
    330, 331, 354, 416, 433, 436, 475,
    481, 506, 508, 518
Requiem for a Heavyweight, **192**, 472
Resurrection (1927), 389, 390
Resurrection (1931), 484, 510
"Return of Captain Nemo, The," 403
Return of the Cisco Kid, The, <u>338</u>, 439
Return of the Gunfighter, <u>316</u>, 423
Return of the Seven, 151, <u>193</u>, 348, 401
Return to Fantasy Island, 278
Return to Peyton Place, 403
Revenge (1928), 390
Revenge (1990), 23, <u>193</u>, 404, 432, 441,
    443, 456, 470, 494, 503
Revueltas, Rosaura, 203, 214
Reward, The, <u>193</u>, 401, 480, 486
Rexer, Fred, 98
Rey, Alejandro, 64, 86, 109, 110, 120,
    163, 279, 298, 316, <u>475–76</u>, **476**
Rey, Antonio, 183
Rey, Fernando, 28, 163, 193, 240, 245,
    <u>476–77</u>, **477**
Rey, Robert, 11
Rey, Rosa, 210
Reyes, Ernie, Jr., <u>477–78</u>
Reyes, Julian, 300, <u>478</u>
Reyes, Luis, 246, **246**
Reyguera, Francisco, 140

Reynolds, Burt, 123, 173, **174**, 270, 276, 378, 414, 454, <u>478</u>, 490, 500, 514

Reynolds, Debbie, 181, 449

Reynolds, Lee, 88

Reynoso, David, <u>478</u>

Rhineman Exchange, The, 473

"Rhoda," 109, <u>294</u>, 371

Rhodes, Leah, 28, 506

Rhythm Inn, 357

Rhythm of the Rio Grande, 411

Ribeiro, Alfonso, 264, 293, <u>478</u>

Ricard, Eduardo, 87

Rich, John, 275

Rich, Robert. *See* Trumbo, Dalton

Rich, Young and Pretty, 431

Rich Kids, 353

Richard, Pierre, 187

Richards, Martin, 107

Richards, R.M., 123

Richardson, Emily. *See* Santiago, Emily

Richardson, John S., 64

Richardson, Ralph, 176

Richardson, Sy, 184

Richardson, Tony, 54

Richler, Mordecai, 110

Richmond, Branscombe, <u>478</u>

Richmond, Ted, 193, 240, 241, 431

Richwine, Maria, 65, **65**, 269, <u>478</u>

Rickles, Don, 272

Ricochet, 492

Ride, Vaquero!, <u>194</u>, 471

Ride Back, The, 443

Ride Lonesome, 519

Ride On, Vaquero, <u>338</u>

Ride the High Country, 523, 524

Ride the Pink Horse, <u>194</u>, 412–13

Ride the Wild Surf, 369

Riding the California Trail, <u>341</u>, 485

Riesner, Dean, 100

"Rifleman, The," 266, 523

Rigby, Gordon, 71, 235

Right Cross, 10, 20, <u>194–96</u>, **195**, 449

Right to Die, 516

"Rin-Tin-Tin," 400

Ring, The, 20, 61, 144, <u>196–97</u>, **196**, 204, 421, 454, 479

Rintels, David W., 304

Rio Bravo, <u>197</u>, 414

Rio Conchos, <u>197</u>

Rio Diablo, 422

Rio Lobo, 480

Rio Rita (1929), <u>197–98</u>

Rio Rita (1942), <u>198</u>

Rios, Guillermo, 145

Rios, Lalo, 143, **143**, 144, 196, **196**, 197, 227, <u>479</u>

Rios, Sixto Pondal, 256

Rios, Tere, 279

Rios-Bustamente, Antonio, 6, 7

Riptide, 474

Riquelme, Carlos, 159, 160

Risky Business, 512

Rita Hayworth: The Love Goddess, <u>316</u>, 476

"Rita Moreno Show, The," <u>294</u>–95

Ritt, Martin, 127, 176, 449

Ritter, Thelma, 78

"Rituals," 408

Ritz, The, 22, <u>198</u>, 295, 453

Ritz, The (stage), 453

Ritz Brothers, 37

Ritz Carlton Hotel, 416

Rivas, Carlos (actor), 24, 47, 48, 148, 177, 225, 235, <u>479</u>

Rivas, Carlos (sound technician), <u>479</u>

Rivas, Geoffrey, 307, <u>479</u>

Rivas, Victor. *See* Rivers, Victor

River of Promises, <u>316</u>, 517

Rivera, Chita, 67, 219, 291, <u>479</u>

Rivera, Diego, 22

Rivera, Fermin, 62

Rivera, Geraldo, 265, <u>480</u>

Rivera, Jose, 265, 312, 313, <u>480</u>

"Riverboat," 449, 478

Rivero, Carlos, 210

Rivero, Jorge, <u>480</u>, 509

Rivero, Jose Antonio, 29

Rivero, Julian, 36, 100, 134, 137, 155, 156, 158, 177, 193, 194, 230, 241, 249, 341, <u>480</u>

Rivers, Victor, 72, <u>481</u>

River's Edge, 425

Rivkin, Allen, 223

RKO Radio Pictures, 14, 18, 34, 35, 36, 38, 49, 54, 61, 100, 104, 105, 109, 117, 118, 139, 144, 158, 159, 167, 168, 177, 178, 180, 181, 189, 197, 210, 220, 221, 222, 225, 229, 234, 237, 286, 331, 357, 358, 362, 371, 378, 381, 388, 390, 401, 404, 405, 408, 431, 439, 455, 458, 490, 510, 517, 519, 520

Roach, Hal, 53, 101, 252, 510

Road to Rio, The, <u>198–99</u>, 431, 470

Road to Romance, The, 458

Road to Utopia, 464

Robago, Andres. *See* Russell, Andy

Robards, Jason, 127, **128**, 179

Robards, Sam, 313

Robbins, Harold, 28

Robbins, Jerome, 249, 250, 453

Robe, Mike, 302

Robe, The, 494

Robelo, Miguel, 175, 176

Roberti, Lyda, 134

Roberts, Ben, 210

Roberts, Bill, 204, 222

Roberts, Charles E., 99, 158, 159

Roberts, Cyril, 77

Roberts, Francesca, 315

Roberts, Julia, 396

Roberts, Marguerite, 191

Roberts, Meade, 53, 217

Roberts, William, 149, 150

Robeson, Paul, 403

Robin, Dany, 225

Robin and the Seven Hoods, 375, 463

Robin Hood of El Dorado, The, <u>199</u>, 369, 394, 425, 437, 456

Robin Hood of Monterey, <u>341</u>, 439, 485

Robinson, Edward G., 219

Robinson, Holly, 280

Robinson, Matt, 184

Robinson, Sally, 157

Robinson, Smokey, 462

Robinson Crusoe, 369

RoboCop, 404, 518

Robson, Mark, 120, 232

Rock Around the Clock, 73

"Rock Around the Clock," 50

Rockefeller, Norman, 221

Rocketeer, The, 446

"Rockford Files, The," 264, **266**, 363, 454, 494

Rocky, 246

Rodgers, Richard, 221

Rodman, Howard, 281, 302

Rodriguez, Abelardo, 241

Rodriguez, Arturo Garcia. *See* De Cordova, Arturo

Rodriguez, Beatriz, 308

Rodriguez, Diane, 308

Rodriguez, Estelita, 99, 159, 197, 233, <u>481</u>

Rodriguez, Gladys, 251

Rodriguez, Ismael, 47

Rodriguez, Jose, 238

Rodriguez, Marco, 271, <u>481</u>

Rodriguez, Paul, 58, 59, 261, 269, 280, 299, 301, 313, <u>481</u>, **482**, 507

Rodriguez, Percy, <u>482</u>

Rodriguez, Robert, 94, **95**, <u>482</u>

Rodriguez, Steve, 218

Rodriguez Santos, Justo, 423

Rogell, Albert S., 37

Rogers, Charles "Buddy," 159

Rogers, Ginger, 104, 105, 173, 390

Rogers, Jaime, 250, 264, 278, <u>483</u>

Rogers, Jean, 73, 338

Rogers, Roy, 3, 63, 344, 416, 436, 480, 481, 518

Roizman, Owen, 122

Rojas, Manuel, 149

Rojo, Maria, 63

Roland, Gilbert, 5, 7, 9, 10, 11, 12, **12**, 13, 14, **24**, 37, 38–39, 42, **42**, 44, **44**, 51, 66, 75, **75**, 83, 84, 111, 132, 133, 140, 141, 142, 160, **161**, 182, 191, 193, 225, 229, **229**, 237, 248, 249, 266, 270, 282, 302, 316, 329, 331, 339, 340, **340**, 341, 344, 389, 393, 407, 423, 428, 449, 475, <u>483–86</u>, **484**, **485**

Roland, Ruth, 483

Rolling Thunder, 512

Roman, Ric, 36

Roman, Ruth, 53

Roman Spring of Mrs. Stone, The, 473

Romance in the Dark, 365

Romance of the Rio Grande (1929), 336, 438, 452

Romance of the Rio Grande (1941), <u>338</u>, 439

Romancing the Stone, <u>199–200</u>, 354

Romay, Elena. *See* Romay, Lina

Romay, Lina, 17, 27, 153, 256, 383, <u>486–87</u>

Romeo and Juliet, 249

Romero, <u>200</u>, 349, 425, **426**, 468

Romero, Carlos, 187, <u>487</u>

Romero, Cesar, 2, 10, 17, 18, 20, 34, 35, 37, 69, **69**, 70, 72, 88, 164, 239, 240, 249, 257, 266, 278, 293, 300, 329, 336, 337, **337**, 338, 339, 340, 344, 408, 439, <u>487–89</u>, **487**, **489**

Romero, Ernesto A., 326

Romero, George A., <u>490</u>

Romero, Ned, 275, 276, <u>490</u>

Ronstadt, Linda, 304, 313, 507

Rooftops, <u>200</u>, 417

Rookie, The, 367, 427, 481, 496, 498

"Rookies, The," 368, 375, 431

Rooney, Mickey, 192, 489

Roos, Fred, 172

Roosevelt, Franklin D., 10, 21

Roosevelt, Theodore, 4

Root, George, Jr., 112

Root, Wells, 153, 323

Roots, 264, 368

Roots: The Next Generation, 368

Rope of Sand, 367

Ropes, Bradford, 182

Rory, Rossana, 48

Rosa, Robby, 202

Rosales, Thomas, Jr., <u>490</u>

Rosaly, Johanna, 251

Rosario, Bert, 276, 298, <u>490</u>

Rose, Jack, 198

Rose, Mickey, 41

Rose, Reginald, 233

Rose, The, 463

Rose Marie (1936), 474

Rose Marie (1954), 431

Rose of the Golden West, 484

Rose of the Rancho, <u>201</u>

Rose of the Rio Grande, 411, 452

Rose Tattoo, The, 376

"Roseanne," <u>295</u>, 401, 446

Rosemary's Baby, 405

Rosen, Phil, 339

Rosen, Robert L., 213

Rosenbaum, Jeffrey, 103

Rosenberg, Aaron, 193, 254

Rosenberg, Frank, 171

Rosenberg, Mark, 100

Rosenberg, Stuart, 87, 245

Rosenthal, Richard, 39

Rosi, Francisco, 395

Rosita, <u>201</u>

Rosner, Rick, 275

Ross, Diana, 462

Ross, Herbert, 388, 515

Ross, Jeff, 311

Ross, Katharine, 67, 124, 319

Ross, Lillian Bos, 258

Rossellini, Isabella, 100

Rossen, Robert, 61, 66, 446

Roth, Joe, 256

Roth, Richard, 121

Rotman, Keith, 123

Rough Sketch, 248

Roulien, Raul, 11, 104, 449, <u>490</u>

Roundtree, Richard, 187

Roustabout, 515

"Route 66," 82, 482

"Rowan and Martin's Laugh-In," 446

Rowe, Arthur, 151

Rowlands, Gena, 118

Royal, Charles, 324

Royal Academy of Dramatic Art, 441

Royal Fandango, The, 457

Royal Hunt of the Sun, The, <u>201</u>

Rubin, Stanley, 193

Rubio, Lopez, 11

Ruby, Harry, 134

Rudin, Scott, 27

Rudolph, Alan, 360

Ruehl, Mercedes, <u>491</u>

Ruffino, Mercedes, 226

Ruiz, Brunilda, 308

Ruiz, Francisco, 207

Ruiz, Jose Carlos, 206

Ruiz, Jose Luis, 294, <u>491</u>

Ruiz Anchia, Juan, <u>491</u>

Rule, Janice, 32

Rumba, <u>202</u>, 437

Rumble Fish, 507

"Rumboogie," 37

Run for the Roses, 412

Run for the Sun, <u>202</u>

Run of the Arrow, 450

Run Silent, Run Deep, 375

Runaway Train, 351

Runaways, 353

Running Man, The, 350

Running Scared, 363, 502

Running Wild, 486

Rush, Barbara, 135

Rush, Richard, 109

Ruskin, Harry, 202

Russ, William, 305

Russek, Jorge, 119, 127, 128, 179, 254

Russell, Andy, <u>491</u>

Russell, Gail, 143, 493

Russell, Jane, 237, 486

Russell, John, 36, 197

Russell, Kurt, 305, 306, **306**, 410, 503

Russo, Mario, 166

Russo, Rene, 173

Ruttan, Susan, 287, 318

Ryan, Catherine, 135

Ryan, Robert, 54, 89, 127, 186, 252

Rydell, Mark, 83, 122

S.O.B., 490

Sabu, 399

Sackett, 316

Sacketts, The, <u>316</u>

"Sacketts, The," 486

Sackheim, William, 56, 130

Sacks, Alan, 299

Sacramento Music Circus, 359

Sadat, 496

Saddle Legion, 456

Saddle Tramp, 407

Sagal, Boris, 89

Sager, Carole Bayer, 359

St. Clair, Malcolm, 66

St. Elmo's Fire, 398, 463

St. Ives, 429

St. John, Betta, 166

St. John, Jill, 126

St. Louis Blues, 422

Saint of Fort Washington, The, 361

St. Valentine's Day Massacre, The, 502

Sainz de Vicuna, Jose, 163

Sakata, Harold, 118

Salazar, Angel, 209, 246, **246**

Saldana, Theresa, 88, 319, <u>491</u>

Salinas, Jose Luis, 344

Salinas, Martin, 111

Salinger, Matt, 296

Salisbury, Monroe, 190

Salkind, Ilya, 78

Salkow, Sidney, 190

Sally, 378

Salomy Jane, 7

Salón México, 348

Salsa, <u>202–3</u>, 353, 462, 463, 469

Salt of the Earth, 20, <u>203–4</u>, 214

Saltzman, Harry, 118

Saludos Amigos, 16, <u>204</u>

Salvador, 141, <u>205–6</u>, **205**, 236, 376, 402, 454, 468

Salzer, Albert J., 307

Samar, 486

Sampson, Will, 103, 280

Samson and Delilah, 14, 385, 386

Samuel Bronston Productions, 468

Samuel Goldwyn Company, 247, 481, 517, 519

San Antone, 428

San Antonio, 14

San Francisco Examiner, 377

San Giacomo, Laura, 22

San Juan, Olga, 17, 459, <u>493–94</u>, **493**

San Sebastian Film Festival, 18, 29, 181, 401, 465, 499

Sanchez, Elvira, 226

Sanchez, Jaime, 71, 72, 179, **179**, 180, 252, 254, 312, 316, <u>491–92</u>, **492**

Sanchez, Marcelino, 247

Sanchez, Marco, 296

Sanchez, Mark, <u>492</u>

Sanchez, Raymond, 89

"Sanchez of Bel Air," <u>295</u>, 363, 389, 494

Sanchez Tello, Alfonso, 42

Sand, Bob, 227

Sanders, George, 512

Sandler, Buddy, 292

Sandlot, The, <u>207</u>, 513
Sandor, Anna, 309
Sandoval, Miguel, 276, <u>**492**</u>
Sandoz, Mari, 75
Sandre, Bel, 301, 313, <u>**493**</u>
Sands of Iwo Jima, 436
Sanford, Gerald, 27
"Sanford and Son," <u>295</u>, 363, 492, 499
Sangre y Arena, 51, 52, 365
Santa, 401, 448, 452, 505
Santa Anna, 30, 31
"Santa Barbara," 264, <u>295</u>–96, 408, 440, 441, 518
Santa Susanna Pass, 481
Santana, Arnaldo, 209
Santell, Alfred, 159, 336
Santiago, <u>207</u>
Santiago, Emily [Emilie], <u>**494**</u>
Santiago, Saundra, 291
Santiago's America, 316–17
Santiago's Ark, 316, <u>317</u>
Santley, Joseph, 63
Santoni, Reni, 39, 120, 295, <u>**494**</u>
Santos, Bert, 125
Santos, Edmundo, 204
Santos, Joe, 193, 258, 264, 316, <u>**494**</u>
Saphier, Peter, 208
Saracen Blade, The, 449
Sarandon, Chris, 86
Sarandon, Susan, 81
Sarecky, Barney A., 324
Sargent, Joseph, 304
Satan's Cradle, <u>342</u>
Satisfaction, 353
Saturday Night Fever, 202, <u>207</u>
"Saturday Night Live," 431
Saul, Oscar, 151, 166
Savage Is Loose, The, 467
Savage Pampas, 408
Savalas, Telly, 149, 178, 269
"Saved by the Bell," <u>296</u>
"Saved by the Bell: The College Years," <u>296</u>
"Saved by the Bell: The New Class," <u>296</u>
Saving Grace, 461
Savoca, John, 233
Saxon, Edward, 181
Saxon, John, 35, 85, **85**, 87, 131, **131**, 182, <u>**494**</u>, 297, 465
Sayonara, 10, 449
Scacchi, Greta, 102
Scala, Gia, 48
Scandal in a Small Town, 516
Scandalous John, <u>207</u>, 354
Scaramouche, 404, 457
Scardapone, Dario, 184
Scared Stiff, 445
Scarface (1932), 208, 474
Scarface (1983), 33, 71, <u>208</u>–9, **208**, 209, 293, 351, 363, 378, 380, 423, 464, 495, 499
Scarlet Pimpernel, The, 321

Scenes from the Class Struggle in Beverly Hills, 363, 395
Schacht, Rose, 307
Schary, Dore, 47
Scheider, Roy, 214, 296, 313
Scheiman, Andrew, 101
Schell, Maximilian, 300
Schenck, Joseph, 390
Schepisi, Fred, 44, 441
Schiff, Paul, 256
Schiffer, Michael, 79
Schifrin, Lalo, 264, <u>**495**</u>
Schindler's List, 333
Schlamme, Thomas, 305, 311
Schlesinger, John, 48, 99, 499, 502
"Schlitz Playhouse of Stars," 393, 443
Schmidt, Walter Roeber, 123
Schnee, Charles, 38, 39, 111, 191, 194, 232
Schneider, Herman, 166
Schneider, John, 280, 481
Schneider, Nina, 166
School Ties, 370
Schrader, Leonard, 135, 136
Schrader, Paul, 60
Schroeder, Doris, 342
Schulberg, B.P., 483
Schulberg, Budd, 120
Schulman, Tom, 157
Schultz, Barbara, 308
Schultz, Carl, 305, 319
Schultz, Dwight, 270
Schultz, Michael, 251
Schwartz, Bernard, 228
Schwartz, Marvin, 173
Schwartz, Ted, 147
Schwarzenegger, Arnold, 81, 185, 350, 376, 378, 504
Scoggins, C.E., 234
Scorsese, Martin, 366, 438
Scotia International, 178
Scott, George C., 305, 309, 371, 396, 399, 486
Scott, Gordon, 321
Scott, Oz, 278
Scott, Randolph, 54, 153, 369, 439, 523
Scott, Ridley, 108
Scott, Tony, 193
Scott, Zachary, 36, 42
Screen Extras Guild, 14, 246
Screen World Award, 491
Sea Bat, The, 505
Sea Hawk, The, 386, 485
Seagal, Steven, 378
"seaQuest DSV," <u>296</u>
Searchers, The, 75, 405, 452, 520, 521, 521
Sears, Fred F., 73
Sears, Ted, 222
Seaton, George, 220
Second Chance, 62, <u>210</u>, 423
"Second Chances," <u>296</u>

"Second Half, The," <u>297</u>, 442
Second Thoughts, 359
Seconds, 351
Secret Fury, The, 403, 404
Secret Heart, The, 442
Secret of Santa Vittoria, The, 472
Secret of the Incas, <u>210</u>
Secrets of Dr. Mabuse, 408
Seduction of Mimi, The, 251
Segal, Erich, 188
Segal, George, 110, 405
Segall, Pamela, 294
Seguin, 25, <u>317</u>, 441, 461, 467, 468, 496, 506
Seiler, Lewis, 119
Seiter, William A., 57, 256
Selander, Lesley, 189
Selig Studios, 7
Sellecca, Connie, 296
Selleck, Tom, 78, 316, 441
Sellers, Arlene, 86
Sellers, Peter, 499
Seltzer, Frank N., 220
Selznick, David O., 91, 92, 241, 390
Selznick, Joyce, 65
Selznick International, 91
Seminole, 471
"Senator, The," 494
Sennett, Mack, 140, 508
Senorita, 474
Separate Tables, 375, 420
Serafin, Tullio, 384
Serenade, 140, <u>210</u>–11, 369, 450, 470
Sergeant Rutledge, 422, 520
Sergeants 3, 500, **503**
Serling, Rod, 192
Serna, Pepe, 32, 34, 40, 63, 87, 123, **188**, 189, 191, 208, 209, 245, 246, **246**, 276, 279, 291, 296, 307, 317, 318, 319, 461, <u>495</u>–96, **495**
Serrano, Luis, 168
Serrano, Nestor, 120, 281
Sertner, Robert M., 311
"Sesame Street," <u>297</u>, 397, 433
Seurat, Pilar, 257
Seven Cities of Gold, <u>211</u>, 452
Seven Days Leave, 381
Seven Men from Now, 519
Seven Samurai, The, 149
Seven Year Itch, The, 506
1776, 385
"77 Sunset Strip," 508
Sevilla, Carmen, <u>**496**</u>, **496**
sex, lies and videotape, 22
Shaber, David, 247
Shadow of Kilimanjaro, 396
Shaffer, Peter, 201
Shaft, 399
Shagan, Steve, 245
Shakespeare, William, 249, 425
Shamus, 494
Shane, 14, 433

Shane, Maxwell, 78
Shane, Sara, 29
Shanley, John Patrick, 32
Shannon, Elaine, 307
"Shannon's Deal," 465, 297–98, 297
Shapiro-Glickenhaus, 141
Sharif, Omar, 47, 74, 149
Shark Kill, 517
Sharkey's Machine, 500
Sharkfighters, The, 371
Shark's Treasure, 154, 380
Sharp, Alan, 72
Sharpe, Dave, 331
Shaw, George Bernard, 425, 448
Shaw, Robert, 201, 453
Shawn, Wallace, 87
"She Doesn't Say Yes and She Doesn't Say No," 224
She Done Him Wrong, 484, **484**
She Loves Me, 453
She Wore a Yellow Ribbon, 520
Shearer, Norma, 118, 336
She-Devil, 440
Sheehan, Winfield S., 418
Sheekman, Arthur, 201
Sheen, Charlie, 256, 399, 497–98, 497, 499
Sheen, Martin, 48, 264, 267, 304, 398, 497, 502, 498–99, **498**
Sheepman, The, 414
Sheik, The, 7
Sheldon, Gene, 327, 329, 330
Sheldon, Sidney, 166
Shellabarger, Samuel, 69
Shelton, Ron, 236, 251, 467
Shepard, Kathleen, 128
Shepard, Peter, 139
Shepherd, Cybill, 301
Sherdeman, Ted, 35, 123, 154
Sheridan, Ann, 36, 226
Sheridan, Jamey, 297, **297**
Sherin, Edwin, 238
Sherlock Holmes and the Voice of Terror, 412
Sherman, Bobby, 295
Sherman, George, 56, 80, 140, 163, 229
Sherman, Harry R., 319
Sherman, Vincent, 28
Ship of Fools, 380, 403, 414, 435
Shipman, Barry, 324
Shocking Miss Pilgrim, The, 418, 472
Shoot Loud, Louder, I Don't Understand!, 515
Shoot the Sundown, 440
Shootout, 496
Shor, Sol, 324, 326
Short, Martin, 187, 221, 422
Short Cuts, 503
Short Eyes, 212, 417, 467
Short Eyes (stage), 107, 467, 451, 467
Shout, 378
Show Boat, 422
Show Girl (1928), 474

Show of Force, A, 212, 399, 410, 467
Show of Shows, 235, 378
Showdown, The, 421
Showtime Cable, 305, 408
Shrike, The, 403, 464
Shrike, The (stage), 403
Shrimp on the Barbie, 438
Shryack, Dennis, 79
Shubert, Lee, 445
Shubert Organization, 508
Shulman, Irving, 78, 85, 196
Shumate, Harold, 153
Sickner, Roy N., 252, 254
Sid and Nancy, 247, 518
Side Out, 410
"Sidekicks," 478
Sidney, George, 67, 127, 181, 191
Sidney, Robert, 148
Sidney, Sylvia, 411
Siege at Red River, The, 367
Siegel, Don, 87, 234, 393, 405, 520
Siegel, Sol C., 32, 153, 324
Siemaszko, Casey, 256
Sierra, Gregory, 145, 255, 269, 271, 291, 295, 302, 316, 319, 331, 499
Sierra, Martinez, 11
Sierra, Melissa, 175
Sierra Baron, 213
Sign in Sidney Brustein's Window, The, 453
Sign of the Gladiators, 350
Sign of Zorro, The, 327, **330**
Silberg, Joel, 139
Silkwood, 371
Silva, David, 103
Silva, Geno, 310, 499
Silva, Henry, 61, 79, 119, 193, 242, 244, 500, **500**
Silva, Trinidad, 29, 79, **80**, 95, 245, 246, **246**, 283, 284, 318, 501
Silveira, Mario, 36
Silver, David, 306
Silver, Joel, 81, 185
Silver Bear (Berlin Film Festival), 363
"Silver Spoons," 264, 478
Silver Whistle, The, 403
Silvera, Frank, 74, 102, 120, 127, 133, 160, 238, 242, 244, 281, 282, 501–2, **501**
Silverado, 496
Silverheels, Jay, 69, 70
Silvestre, Armando, 134, 234
Simenon, Georges, 145
Simmons, Jean, 49
Simmons, Richard, 327
Simms, Larry, 51
Simon, Neil, 219, 291, 359, 379, 396, 453
Simon, Robert F., 292
Simon, Roger L., 49
Simon, S. Sylvan, 198, 223
Simon, Sam, 218
"Simon and Simon," 412, 499, 518
Simpson, Alan, 295

Sinatra, Frank, 89, 137, 185, 435, 500, 503, 514, 515
Since You Went Away, 381
Sinclair, Madge, 292
Singer, Robert, 145
Singerman, Berta, 11
Singin' in the Rain, 452
Singing Nun, The, 449
Singleton, Penny, 51
Sins of Rachel Cade, The, 422
Siren of Atlantis, 450
Sisk, Robert, 153
Sisowath, Monirak, 162
Sister Act, 395, 446, 518
Sistroms, Joseph, 129
"Six Million Dollar Man, The," 446
Sixteenth Mountain Brigade, Argentina, 248
Skelton, Red, 177
Skidoo, 489
Skinner, Ann, 315
Skouras, Plato A., 213, 240
Skydrift, 452
Slammer, The. *See Short Eyes*
Slater, Christian, 256
"Slattery's People," 298
Slight Case of Murder, A, 403
Slightly Scandalous, 362
Slow Dancing in the Big City, 443
Sly Fox, 396
Smile, 459
Smirnoff, Yakov, 300
Smith, Bernard, 75
Smith, Charles Martin, 65, 124
Smith, Constance, 230
Smith, Cotter, 314
Smith, Irby, 256
Smith, Lane, 286
Smith, Wallace, 57, 113
Smithee, Alan. *See* Rosenberg, Stuart
Smits, Jimmy, 9, 23, 48, 102, 168, 169, **169**, 261, 287, **287**, 288, 310, 343, **343**, 384, 502
Smokey and the Bandit, 478
Sniper, 213, 433
Snipes, Wesley, 247, 251
Snow White and the Three Stooges
So This Is Africa, 505
So Young, So Bad, 452
"Soap," 292
Society for the Prevention of Cruelty to Animals, 66
Sol Madrid, 213, 449, 518
Solar Crisis, 408
Solas, Humberto, 25
Soldier Blue, 480
Soler, Fernando, 386
Solo, Robert, 39, 79
Solomon and Sheba, 435, 475
Sombrero, 213–14, **214**, 414, 449
Some Like It Hot, 436
Something of Value, **421**, 422
Son-Daughter, The, 458

Son of Fury, 230
Son of India, 458
Son of Kong, 389
Son of the Sheik, 323
Son of Zorro, 326
Sondergaard, Gale, 325
Sondheim, Stephen, 249, 250
Song Is Born, A, 350
Song of Bernadette, The, 92, 386, 464
Song to Remember, A, 424
Sonnenfeld, Barry, 27
"Sons and Daughters," 359
Son's Command, 387
Sons of Katie Elder, The, 348
Soo, Jack, 271
Sophie's Choice, 350
Sorcerer, 214
Soria, Alberto, 204
Sorkin, Aaron, 101
Sorolla (artist), 52
Sosa, GeoAnn, 156
Sothern, Ann, 166, 177
Soto, Luis, 293, 312, 502
Soto, Richard, 40, 313, 314, 318, 502–3
Soto, Talisa, 145, 152, 281, 315, 503
Soul, David, 301
Sounder, 35, 351
"South Beach," 348
South of Monterey, 341, 485
South of St. Louis, 408
South of Tahiti, 450
South of the Border, 506
South of the Rio Grande, 339
South Pacific, 89, 434, 435
Southern Justice, 421
Southside 1-1000, 61
Souto, Gilberto, 204
Spaceballs, 518
Spacek, Sissy, 161, 499
Spalding, Harry, 102
Spanish Affair, 496
Spano, Vincent, 32
Sparhawk, Lynn, 134
Sparkle, 373
Sparks, Robert, 51
Spartacus, 411, 412, 435
Sparv, Camilla, 149
Special Delivery, 379
Speedy Gonzalez, 215
Speight, Johnny, 270
Spelling, Aaron, 278
Spence, Ralph, 90
Spencer, Franz, 155
"Spenser: For Hire," 433, 502
Sperling, Milton, 53, 338
Spic-O-Rama, 432. See also *HBO Comedy Hour: Spic-O-Rama*
Spiegel, Sam, 248
Spielberg, Steven, 2, 160, 190, 333, 465, 499
Spigelgass, Leonard, 165, 181
Spike of Bensonhurst, 503
Spindola, C., 248

Spiral Road, The, 395
Split Decisions, 510
Spottiswoode, Roger, 236, 441
Springsteen, Bruce, 58
Springsteen, R.G., 99, 219
Springtime in the Rockies, 445, 488
Squaw Man, The (1931), 510
Stack, Robert, 66, 299
Stade, O.B., 241
Stafford, Frederick, 225
Stage Door Canteen, 487
Stage to Chino, 411
Stagecoach, 439, 520
Stahl, Jorje, 211
Stakeout, 22, 399, 503
Stalag 17, 403
Stallings, Laurence, 79, 222
Stallone, Sylvester, 239, 246, 465
Stamp, Terence, 53, 256
Stand and Deliver, 1, 23, 25, 26, 34, 152, 215–17, 215, 216, 393, 410, 418, 442, 459, 461, 464, 467, 513
Stanley, Chris, 276
Stanley, Paul, 85
Stanton, Harry Dean, 191
Stanwyck, Barbara, 53, 67, 111, 407
Stapleton, Jean, 270
Stapleton, Maureen, 67, 379
"Star Trek," 262, 263, 286, 357, 417, 447
Star Trek II: The Wrath of Khan, 447, 508
Star Trek III: The Search for Spock, 478
Star Trek IV: The Voyage Home, 22, 359
Star Trek VI: The Undiscovered Country, 393
Star Wars, 333
Stark, Ray, 167, 168
Starke, Pauline, 452
Starlight over Texas, 411, 506
Starr, Irving, 45
Stars and Guitars. See *Brazil*
Stars in My Crown, 422
"Starsky and Hutch," 263, 368
State Fair (1945), 418
State Fair (1962), 403
State of Emergency, A, 499
State of Siege, 161
Stay Away, Joe, 74, 413, 428
Steambath, 318
Steambath (stage), 396
Steel Dawn, 422
Steel Jungle, The, 433
Steel Magnolias, 351
Steele, Bob, 480
Steele, Jim, 184
Steiger, Rod, 90, 120, 179, 179, 180, 443, 450
Stein, Gertrude, 10
Steinbeck, John, 68, 156, 180, 181, 226, 242, 243, 355, 401
Steinberg, Michael, 247, 425
Steiner, Ira, 238
Stella, 353
Stephenson, Carl, 166

Stephenson, Henry, 90
"Steptoe and Son," 295
Sterling, Jan, 120
Sterling, Linda, 326
Stern, Daniel, 58
Stern, Miroslava. See Miroslava
Stern, Sandor, 310
"Steve Allen Show, The," 271, 276, 298
Stevens, Charles, 503
Stevens, George, 19, 115, 389, 442, 443
Stevens, Leslie, 144
Stevens, Louis, 56, 141
Stevens, Stella, 213
Stevens, Warren, 45
Stevenson, McLean, 275
Stewart, Donald, 161
Stewart, James, 19, 43, 393, 486, 499, 514, 515, 522
Stewart, Michael, 67
Stewart, Peggy, 326
Stewart, Ramona, 184
Stick, 369, 378, 415, 465, 478, 490
Stigwood, Robert, 207
Stiller, Jerry, 198
Stillman, Robert, 34
Sting, The, 68, 160
Sting II, The, 369, 465, 495
Stir Crazy, 368, 456, 503
Stockwell, Guy, 35
Stockwell, John, 148
Stoddard, Brandon, 317
Stolen Jools, The, 336
Stoltz, Eric, 247
Stone, John, 337
Stone, Oliver, 3, 23, 205, 206, 208, 209, 376, 402, 454, 468, 497
Stone, Peter, 219
Stone Boy, The, 491
Stone Pillow, 519
Stoner, Joy, 224
Stones for Ibarra, 318
Stop! Or My Mom Will Shoot, 384, 446
Stork Club, The, 491
Storke, Bill, 315
Stowaway Girl, 356
Stowe, Madeleine, 22, 23, 193, 503
Straight Shooting, 520
Strange Fruit, 404, 422
Strange Lady in Town, 414, 494
Stranger, The, 258
Stranger on Horseback, 446
Strasberg, Lee, 380
Strassman, Marcia, 299
Strauss, Theodore, 67
Strawberry Blonde, The, 418, 419
Strayer, Frank R., 51
Streep, Meryl, 361, 440
Street Story, 509
Streetcar Named Desire, A, 244, 471
Streets of Fire, 380
Streets of L.A., The, 318, 350, 510
Streets of Laredo, 14, 363, 385
Streets of Paris, The, 445

"Streets of San Francisco, The," 380, 441, 446, 518
Streisand, Barbra, 451
Strickland, Gail, 300
Strictly Dishonorable, 488
Strode, Woody, 74, 186
Strong, John, 212
Strongest Man in the World, The, 489
Stroud, Don, 65
Strouse, Charles, 67
Struthers, Sally, 270
Student Prince in Old Heidelberg, The, 458
Studi, Wes, 315
"Studio One," 371
Sturges, John, 127, 131, 149, 150, 165, 170, 171, 194, 237
Suarez, Miguelangel, 41, 503
Subject Was Roses, The, 499
Subject Was Roses, The (stage), 499
Sudan, 450
Sudden Impact, 507
Suez, 394
Sugar Hill, 423
Sullivan, Barry, 166
Sullivan, Francis L., 77
Sullivan, Gardner, 86
Sumac, Yma, 210
Summer and Smoke, 217–18, 413, 454, 514
Sun Also Rises, The, 140, 218, 380
Sundance Film Festival, 95
Sunday in New York, 359
Sundays and Cybèle, 193
Sunrise at Campobello, 375
Sunset, 499
Super, The, 218
Super Cops, The, 379
Super Mario Brothers, 432
Superfly, 156
Superman, 78
Sure Thing, The, 518
Surf Ninjas, 478
Susskind, Andrew, 316
Susskind, David, 192
Sutherland, A. Edward, 167
Sutherland, Donald, 501
Sutherland, Kiefer, 256
Sutton, John, 69
Svanoe, Bill, 100
Swan, Socorro, 175
Swanson, Gloria, 365, 452
Swanton, Scott, 309
Swarthout, Gladys, 201
Swayze, Patrick, 361, 399, 422
Sweet Charity, 10, 219, 449, 479
Sweet 15, 318, 468, 502
Sweet Lorraine, 353
Sweet Ride, The, 482
Sweet Thursday, 68
Swell Guy, 520
Swerling, Jo, 52
Swing High, Swing Low, 141
Switch, 502

Swope, Henry B., Jr., 61
"Sword of Justice," 298, 490
Sylva, Marguerita, 114
Sylvester, Robert, 48, 248
Synanon, 435

"T.H.E. Cat," 298, 376
"T.J. Hooker," 263
Tabori, George, 83
Taeger, Ralph, 269
Taggart, 219, 374
Taggert, Brian, 331
Tahse, Martin, 310
Tait, Don, 124
Take Down, 431
Takei, George, 123
Taking Care of Business, 396
Taking of Pelham 1, 2, 3, The, 379, 396
Talavera, Frank, 203
Talent for the Game, 418, 461
"Tales from the Crypt," 381
Tales of Manhattan, 488
Tall, Dark and Handsome, 487
Tall T, The, 519
Talmadge, Constance, 351
Talmadge, Norma, 11, 484
Talton, Alix, 73
Taming of the Shrew, The, 499
Tamiroff, Akim, 64, 105, 149, 226, 227
Tammy, Tell Me True, 412
Tampico, 219, 438, 505
Tangier, 450
Tap Dance Kid, The, 478
Taplin, Jonathan, 236
Taras Bulba, 433
"Tarzan," 89, 298, 464
Tarzan and the Great River, 219, 463
Tarzan and the Mermaids, 379
Tass, Nadia, 187
Tatelman, Harry, 202, 237
Taylor, Don, 47
Taylor, Elizabeth, 115, 168, 234, 430
Taylor, Frank E., 165
Taylor, Jud, 315
Taylor, Kent, 102, 190, 191
Taylor, Robert, 45, 194, 316, 357, 408, 504
Taylor, Rod, 443
Taylor, Roderick, 309
Taylor, Sam, 252
Taylor, Samuel, 225
Tchin-Tchin, 472
Teacher's Pet, 385
Technicolor, 17, 21, 28, 34, 35, 52, 56, 60, 61, 69, 70, 77, 90, 101, 112, 127, 139, 148, 149, 182, 191, 210, 213, 218, 220, 230, 233, 235, 241, 249, 255, 352, 362, 420, 444, 449, 519
Teenage Mutant Ninja Turtles II: The Secret of the Ooze, 478
Tello, Sanchez, 211
Tempest, 418, 427

Temptation, 386
Temptress, The, 365, 452
Ten Commandments, The, 14, 93, 385, **385**
Ten Tall Men, 486
10 to Midnight, 422
Ten Wanted Men, 363
Tenney, Jon, 275
Tequila Sunrise, 405, 499
Terminator 2: Judgment Day, 415
Terrazzas, Ernest, 222
Terror in a Texas Town, 220
Terror in the Towers, 396
Terry, Alice, 108, 452
Terry, Phillip, 177
Terry, Ruth, 51
Tessari, Duccio, 103, 328
Tetzloff, Ted, 256
Tex, 398
Thalberg, Irving, 455
That Championship Season, 499
That Lady, 486
That Man from Tangiers, 450
That Midnight Kiss, **424**
That Night in Rio, 220, 365, 445, 450, 456
That Obscure Object of Desire, 369, 477
That Was Then . . . This Is Now, 398, 491
"That's Amore," 369
That's My Baby, 362
Thayer, Frank M., 146
Theatre World Award, 460
They All Laughed, 465
They Came to Cordura, 487
They Died with Their Boots On, 471, 525
They Met in Argentina, 220–21
They're Playing Our Song, 359
Thief of Bagdad, The, 7
Thief of Hearts, 363, 478
Thiess, Ursula, 34, 42
Thiessen, Tiffani-Amber, 296
Thieves, 396
Thin Man, The, 488
Things Are Tough All Over, 238, 415
Things Change, 491
This Can't Be Love, 473
This Could Be the Night, 371
This Rebel Breed, 454
This Time for Keeps, 383
Thomas, Anna, 95, 97, 456
Thomas, Betty, 283
Thomas, Danny, 276
Thomas, Diane, 199
Thomas, Elton. *See* Fairbanks, Douglas, Sr.
Thomas, Gordon, 245
Thomas, James, 185
Thomas, John, 185
Thomas, Phillip Michael, 291
Thomas, Richard, 191
Thomas, William C., 130, 143, 233
Thomas Crown Affair, The, 404
Thomerson, Tim, 343
Thompson, Carlos, 503–4

Thompson, Caroline, 27
Thompson, Fred, 197
Thompson, Harlan, 149, 201
Thompson, J. Lee, 103, 134, 135, 149, 201
Thompson, Marshall, 47
Thompson, Robert C., 331
Thorn Birds, The, 506
Thorpe, Jerry, 281, 302
Thorpe, Richard, 101, 109
Thorson, Linda, 289
Thousand and One Nights, A, 464
Thousands Cheer, 424
¡Three Amigos!, 221, 254, 354, 378, 405, 441, 463, 468, 473
Three Caballeros, The, 204, 222, 408, 444
Three Faces of Eve, The, 381
Three for the Road, 497
Three Godfathers, 222–23, **223**, 354, 520–21
Three Godfathers, The, 222
Three Hundred Miles for Stephanie, 264, 319, 461, 461–62
Three Mesquiteers, 475
Three Musketeers, The (1974), 516
Three Outlaws, The, 423
Three Violent People, 369, 486
Threepenny Opera, The, 426
Thrill of Brazil, The, 223–24, **224**
Thunder Bay, 452, 486
Thunder Trail, 485
Thunderbolt and Lightfoot, 361
Thy Name Is Woman, 458
Tibbett, Lawrence, 86
"Tico Tico," 511
Ticotin, Rachel, 23, 107, **107**, 173, 275, 279, 292, 315, 504
Tidyman, Ernest, 141
Tiembla y Titubea, 13, 347
Tierney, Gene, 248, 403
Tierra, 467
Tiger Shark, 474
Tiger Woman, The, 436
Tightrope, 507
Tijuana Story, The, 224, 348
"'Til Death Do Us Part," 270
Tilton, Charlene, 276
Time Machine, The, 443
Time of Destiny, A, 457
Time of Indifference, 443
Times Square, 353, 467
Timetable, 62, 423
Tinling, James, 236
Tiomkin, Dmitri, 171, 126
Tirso de Molina, 28
TNT [Turner Network Television], 305, 311, 343, 354, 365, 397, 438, 502, 512
To Be or Not to Be, 404
To Have and Have Not, 474
To Hell and Back, 429
Toast of New Orleans, The, 452
Tobias, George, 226

Todd, Michael, 37, 371
Toland, Gregg, 405
Toledo, Sergio, 315
Toler, Sidney, 73
Tolstoy, Leo, 390
Tomlin, Lily, 292
Tone, Franchot, 455
Tone Lōc, 184
"Tonight Show Starring Johnny Carson, The," 387, 492
Tonka, 371
Tony Award, 198, 258, 294, 309, 387, 402, 403, 426, 434, 452, 453, 460, 473, 491, 500
"Tony Orlando and Dawn," 298, 461, 469
Too Many Girls, 225, 357
Topaz, 225, 380, 479
Topkapi, 385
Tora, Lia, 11
Torch, The, 225, 356, 486
Toren, Marta, 174
Torena, Juan, 155
Torn, Rip, 213
Torrent, The, 365, 381
Torres, Claudio, 248
Torres, Edwin, 71, 188, 504, 504
Torres, Liz, 270, 273, 275, 286, 291, 293, 318, 504
Torres, Raquel, 11, 64, 235, 504–5, **505**
Torrid Zone, 226
Tortilla Flat, 170, 226–27, **226**, 399
Torvay, Jose, 56, 57, 67, 109, 145, 147, 165, 211, 230, 234, 505
Total Recall, 23, 504
Totten, Robert, 87, 316
Touch and Go, 227, 350
Touch of Evil, 227–28, **228**, 369, 443, 479
Touchstone Films, 32, 89
"Tough Cookies," 298
Tough Guys, 410
"Tour of Duty," 264, 299, 406, **406**, 512
Tourneur, Jacques, 36, 144, 248
Tovar, Lupita, 11, 12, 50, 51, 429, 505–6
Tovares, Arthur, 190
Tower of Terror, The, 455
Towering Inferno, The, 499
Towne, Robert, 77, 240, 431, 499
Townley, Jack, 99, 158
Townsend, Leo, 145
Toys in the Attic, 443
Tracers, 379
Track of the Cat, 517
Tracy, Lee, 241, 242
Tracy, Spencer, 21, 71, 170, **170**, 171, 226, **226**, 315, 393, 428, 480
Trader Horn, 334, 475
Tragedy in the Life of General Villa, A. See Life of Villa, The
Trail of '98, The, 390
Trail of the Lonesome Pine, The (1923), 452

Train Robbers, The, 449
Trapeze, 428
"Trapper John, M.D.," 434
Travanti, Daniel J., 283, **283**
Travels with My Aunt, 465
Traven, B., 230
Travilla, Bill, 14, 28, 506
Travis, Nancy, 130
Travolta, John, 207, 299
Treasure of Pancho Villa, The, 229, **229**, 369, 486
Treasure of the Golden Condor, 230
Treasure of the Sierra Madre, The, 2, 18, 19, 166, 230–32, **231**, **232**, 237, 363, 410, 480, 505, 522, 524
Tregaskis, Richard, 119
Tremors, 412
Trevino, George, 140
Trevino, Jesus, 23, 188, 189, 294, 309, 317, 461, 506
Trevor, Claire, 57, 128, 165
Trial, 232–33, 370, 422, 428
"Trial and Error," 299, 481, 510
Triana, Luisita, 114
Tribes, 517
Trifling Women, 457
Trintignant, Jean-Louis, 236
Tripoli, 506
Tristana, 369, 477
TriStar Pictures, 98, 111, 145, 181, 187, 213, 227, 333
Triumph of the Spirit, 461
Troell, Jan, 258
Trooper Hawk, 429
Tropic Holiday, 233, 365, **415**, 416
Tropic Zone, 233
Trosper, Guy, 34, 171
Trotti, Lamar, 69, 119, 177, 190
True Believer, 417
True Confessions, 378
True Grit, 479
Truffaut, François, 45, 350, 361
Truman, Harry S., 19
Trumbo, Dalton, 61, 62
Trustman, Alan, 310
Truth or Dare, 362
Tubes, The, 463
Tucker, Larry, 417
Tucker, Michael, 287
Tulin, Mark, 88
Tully, Richard Walton, 201
Tulsa, 355
Tunberg, Karl, 90, 155, 249
Tunberg, William, 112
Turich, Felipe, 56, 60, 83, 115, 116, 143, 155, 158, 173, 246, 249, 255, 339, 506
Turich, Rosa, 148, 178, 341, 506
Turman, Lawrence, 245
Turner, George, 326
Turner, Kathleen, 199
Turner, Lana, 38, 142, 430, 449, 452, 486, 504

Turner Entertainment, 397
Turriche, Felipe. *See* Turich, Felipe
TV Globo, 367
12 Angry Men, <u>233</u>
Twentieth Century, 403
Twentieth Century–Fox, 10, 16, 17, 18, 43, 50, 52, 61, 66–74 *passim*, 80, 81, 87, 90, 102, 107, 112, 119, 126, 127, 128, 145, 149, 155, 164, 173, 177, 185, 190, 193, 197, 199, 207, 211, 213, 218, 219, 220, 230, 235, 237, 240, 242, 248, 249, 251, 256, 325, 328, 330, 331, 337, 338, 339, 408, 418, 419, 420, 435, 452, 488, 506, 511, 515
Twenty-Mule Team, 377
"21 Jump Street," 467
"Twilight Zone, The," 262
Twin Beds, 377
"Twin Peaks," 404
Twin Peaks: Fire Walk with Me, 410
Twist, John, 54, 139, 153, 207, 210, 225, 234
Two Evil Eyes, 490
Two Gentlemen of Verona, 426
Two Girls and a Sailor, 383, 424, 473, 487
"Two Gun Man," 235
Two Jakes, The, 77, 364, 434, 503
Two Moon Junction, 363
Two Mules for Sister Sara, <u>234</u>, 405, 454, 519
Two on a Guillotine, 489
Two Rode Together, 382, 522
Two Senoritas from Chicago, 354
"227," 265
Two Weeks with Love, 448
Two Years Before the Mast, 385, 401
Tycoon, <u>234</u>, 352, 408, 471
Tyrell, Susan, 258

U.S. Film Festival, 63
"U.S. Steel Hour," 393
UCLA Film Archives, 66
UCLA Film School, 97, 388, 457
Ullman, Daniel B., 103
Ullmann, Liv, 111, 258, 313
Ulmer, Edgar G., 166
Ultimate Warrior, The, 379
Ulzana's Raid, 441
Un Chien Andalou, 369
Uncle Joe Shannon, 412
Uncommon Valor, 402
Unconquered, 385
Undefeated, The, <u>235</u>, **235**, 348, 356, 479
Under a Texas Moon, <u>235</u>, 357, 505
Under Fire, 26, 97, 141, <u>236</u>, 376, 389, 397, 408, 441
Under Siege, 378
Under the Pampas Moon, <u>236</u>–37, 419, 439
Under the Red Robe, 367
Under the Texas Moon, 438
Under the Tonto Rim, 409

Under the Volcano, 48, <u>237</u>, 401, 405, 428, 522, **523**
Underwater!, 486
Underwood, Blair, 184, 287
Unforgiven, 350, 507
Unforgiven, The, 479, 494
United Artists, 11, 18, 30, 37, 41, 42, 45, 47, 48, 49, 50, 64, 68, 82, 85, 86, 90, 101, 102, 103, 105, 112, 113, 118, 119, 120, 125, 127, 134, 148, 149, 151, 153, 154, 163, 166, 183, 185, 186, 190, 191, 193, 196, 201, 202, 220, 228, 233, 238, 239, 249, 255, 257, 322, 323, 342, 343, 390, 400, 438
United Film Distribution, 187
Universal-International, 382, 407, 412
Universal Pictures, 6, 12, 17, 21, 23, 35, 37, 38, 39, 44, 49, 54, 57, 58, 71, 77, 78, 86, 87, 105, 121, 124, 131, 135, 137, 140, 153, 157, 159, 161, 163, 166, 174, 182, 187, 189, 191, 194, 198, 208, 214, 219, 225, 227, 228, 234, 237, 245, 246, 247, 251, 254, 258, 348, 368, 374, 394, 396, 411, 412, 421, 429, 438, 439, 441, 449, 450, 460, 462, 479, 488, 494, 506, 513, 518, 520
Universal Television, 349, 442, 465, 495
University of Southern California Film School, 405
Unknown, The, 393
Unlawful Entry, 503
Unmarried Woman, An, 418
"UnSub," 404
Untamed, 452, 505
Untamed Frontier, 407
Untamed Heart, 467
Untouchables, The, 409
"Untouchables, The," 262, 286, <u>299</u>, 357, 400, 417
Up in Smoke, <u>237</u>–38
Up the Down Staircase, <u>238</u>
Up the Sandbox, 251, 451
Uptight, 422, 502
Urban Cowboy, 513
Urich, Robert, 280, 378, 431
Uris, Leon, 45, 46, 225
Urrueta, Chano, 254
USA Cable, 295, 389, 494
Used Cars, 354
Ustinov, Peter, 241

Vaccaro, Brenda, 328
Vacio, Natividad, 115, 148, 151, 159, 279, <u>507</u>
Vadnay, Laslo, 82, 89
Vagabond King, The, 454
Vajna, Andrew, 157
Valadez, Carlos, 101
Valadez, Enrique, 155
Valdes, David, <u>507</u>
Valdes, Miguelito, 178, **178**
Valdez, Daniel, 581, 137, 189, 251, 258, 259, <u>507</u>

Valdez, Luis, 8, 22–23, 137, **138**, 251, 258, 260, 279, 294, 343, 344, 415, 434, 441, 465, 467, 502, <u>507</u>–8
Valdez, Socorro, 63
Valdez Is Coming, <u>238</u>, 396, 502
Valens, Ritchie, 22, 65
Valentine, Scott, 408
Valentino, 442
Valentino, Rudolph, 7, 9, 10, 51, 108, 323, 381, 384, 389, 400, 451
Valentino Returns, 404
Valez, Kipper, 342
Valiant Hombre, The, <u>341</u>–42
Vallejo, Enrique Juan. *See* Vallejo, Harry
Vallejo, Harry, <u>508</u>
Vallejo, Victor, 190, <u>508</u>
Valley of the Kings, 504
Vampire's Ghost, 436
Vampire's Kiss, 351
Vance, Vivian, 284, 284
Van Cleef, Lee, 61, 94, 105, 119, 148, 151
Van Dyke, Dick, 67, 291, 479
Van Dyke, W.S., 86, 504
Van Evers, Dale, 71
Van Eyck, Peter, 202
Van Peebles, Mario, 122, 184
Van Rooten, Luis, 78
Van Upp, Virginia, 116
Van Valkenburgh, Deborah, 247
Vara, Sarita, 74
Varconi, Victor, 71
Varela, Ann, 220
Varela, Nina, 244, <u>508</u>
Varela, Trini, 105
Vargas, Jacob, <u>508</u>
Vargas, John, 270, 276, <u>508</u>
Variety, 66
Variety Girl, 494
Vasquez, Dennis, 293
Vasquez, Joseph B., 26, 120, <u>509</u>
Vaughn, Robert, 149, 150
Vega, Isela, 44, 64, 65, 301, <u>509</u>–10, **509**
Vega Vasquez, Sylvia, 34, <u>510</u>
Veiller, Anthony, 167
Velasco, Jerry, <u>510</u>
Velasquez, Andres, 147
Velazquez, Diego Rodriguez de Silva, 52
Velez, Eddie, 191, 192, **192**, 200, 270, 271, 299, <u>510</u>
Velez, Gladys, 183
Velez, Lupe, 11, 20, 21, 86, 112, 117, 158, 159, 484, <u>510</u>–11, **511**
Veloz, Frank. *See* Veloz and Yolanda
Veloz and Yolanda, 63, 223, 237
Vendetta, 404
Venice Film Festival, 118, 374
Vennera, Chick, 159, 160
Venrell, Joaquin, 357
Vera Cruz, 20, <u>239</u>, 450, 488, 519
Vera-Ellen, 72
Verdi, Giuseppe, 395

Verdugo, Elena, 177, 261, 263, 290, **290**, 511–12

Verduzco, Noah, 512

"Verna, USO Girl," 385

Verne, Jules, 37, 371

Verneuil, Henri, 119

Vernon, John, 124, 225

Vestron, 72

Vibes, 239, 465

Vice Squad, 496

Victims for Victims: The Theresa Saldana Story, 491

Victor, James, 57, 275, 299, 333, 512

"Victor Borge Comedy Hour, The," 417

Victory, 239, 465

Vidal, Christina, 147, 512

Vidal, Gore, 144

Vidor, Charles, 116, 148

Vidor, King, 91, 390

Viertel, Peter, 170, 218, 248

Vigilante, The, 354

Vigilante Force, 468

Vigoda, Abe, 271

Viharo, Robert, 240

Vila, Alberto, 220

Vilchez, Ernesto, 11

Villa!, 240, 423

Villa, Francisco "Pancho," 5

Villa, Pancho, 146, 147

"Villa Alegre," 299, 397, 518

Villa Rides, 240–41, **240**, 375

Villa-Lobos, Heitor, 119

Villalobos, Reynaldo, 34, 41, 50, 512–13, **513**

Villalobos Velez, Guadalupe. *See* Velez, Lupe

Villalpando, David, 95, **96**

Villar, Carlos, 12, 513

Villareal, Julio, 182

Villarias, Carlos. *See* Villar, Carlos

Villarreal, Daniel, 32, 34, 513

Villasenor, Victor, 40, 41

Villaverde, Manolo, 293, 300

Villechaize, Herve, 278

Vincent, Jan-Michael, 58, 88, 141

Vincenzoni, Luciano, 90, 105, 119

Virginian, The, 503

"Virginian, The," 431

Viridiana, 369, 477

Virus, 461

Vision Quest, 519

"Visions," 29

Vitagraph Studios, 6, 413, 433

Vital Signs, 348

Vitaphone, 10, 378

Vitar, Mike, 207, 513

Vittes, Louis, 240

Viva Cisco Kid, 338

Viva Max!, 241, 359

"Viva Valdez!," 299, 378, 512, 518

Viva Villa!, 241–42, **242**, 244, 377, 470, 474

Viva Zapata!, 53, 242–45, **243**, 395, 433,
437, 459, 470, 471, 474, 500, 502, 506, 508, 517

Vlahos, Sam, 514

Voice of Millions, The, 452

Volonte, Gian Marie, 105

Von Eltz, Theodore, 336

von Seyfferitz, Gustave, 112

von Sternberg, Josef, 88

von Sydow, Max, 193, 239, 245, 461

Voyage of the Damned, 245, 495

"Wackiest Ship in the Army, The," 417

Wacks, Jonathan, 191

Wages of Fear, The, 214

Wagner, Fernando, 180, 211, 254

Wagner, Jack, 139, 156, 180

Wagner, Raymond, 79

Wagner, Robert, 486

Wagner, Wende, 82, 197

Wagon Master, 456

"Wagon Train," 263, 449, 486, 487

Wahl, Ken, 107, 300

Waikiki Wedding, 471, 474

Wait Until Dark, 404

Waite, Ralph, 415

Waiting for the Light, 364

Waits, Tom, 38

Wake of the Red Witch, 352, 436

Wald, Jerry, 28, 128, 226

Waldorf-Astoria Hotel, 384, 436, 445, 473

Walk Proud, 245–46, **246**, 353, 378, 384, 412, 441, 456, 468, 490, 496, 501, 506

Walk the Proud Land, 443

Walken, Christopher, 159

Walker, 247, 356, 380, 492, 518

Walker, Arnetia, 292

Walker, Clint, 89, 178

Walker, Jimmie, 270

Walker, Marcy, 295

Walker, Robert, 45

Walking the Edge, 440

Wall, Corinna. *See* Mura, Corrina

Wall for San Sebastian, A, 119

Wall Street, 497, 499

Wallace, Dee, 292

Wallace, Jean, 154

Wallace, Richard, 54, 234

Wallace, Tommy Lee, 308

Wallach, Eli, 119, 149, 150, 452

Wallant, Edmund Lewis, 179

Waller, Albert, 316, 317

Wallis, Hal B., 109, 111, 132, 133, 191, 217, 496

Walls of Gold, 454

Walsh, Bill, 147, 207

Walsh, George, 201

Walsh, Raoul, 7, 9, 45, 79, 146, 147, 334, 335, 390, 433, 443, 525

Walt Disney Company, 317

Walt Disney Pictures, 438, 443, 463

Walt Disney Studios, 331, 443, 519

"Waltons, The," 264, 277, 378

Wanamaker, Sam, 73, 271

Wanderers, The, 504

Wanger, Walter, 50

Wanted: The Sundance Woman, 319, 396

War and Peace, 404

War Cry, 423

Ward, David S., 68, 159, 160

Ward, Fred, 309

Ward, Rachel, 78

Ward, Robert, 302

Warden, Jack, 287

Ware, Clyde, 301, 319

Ware, Darrell, 90, 249

Warner, H.B., 201

Warner, Jack L., 57, 133, 352, 464

Warner Bros. Cartoon Studios, 466

Warner Bros. Television, 279, 507

Warner Bros., 10, 11, 13, 14, 15, 20, 23, 28, 45, 46, 52, 53, 57, 59, 61, 62, 71, 75, 78, 82, 83, 87, 100, 109, 115, 122, 128, 130, 132, 139, 144, 152, 153, 160, 162, 163, 170, 171, 182, 197, 198, 207, 210, 215, 217, 226, 230, 235, 238, 252, 255, 258, 312, 352, 375, 378, 387, 390, 419, 433, 434, 450, 464, 473 479, 485, 488, 506, 508, 525

Warren, Charles Marquis, 74, 294

Warren, Harry, 220

Warren, James, 439

Warren, Michael, 283, 284

Warriors, The, 247

Washburn, Deric, 54, 98

Washington, Denzel, 181

Washington, Ned, 126

Wasserman, Dale, 154

Waterdance, The, 247–48, 425

Watts, Robert, 32

Way of a Gaucho, 20, 248

Wayne, Ethan, 514

Wayne, John, 3, 4, 10, 19, 20, 30–31, **31**, 38, 66, 80, 81, 83, 124, 142, 182, 191, 197, 222, **223**, 234, 235, **235**, 275, 317, 348, 354, 381, 414, 436, 440, 475, 479, 480, 514, 517, 520, 521, **521**

Wayne, Patrick, 256, 257

Wayne-Fellows Company, 30, 182

We Were Strangers, 248–49, 355, 458, 486, 506

Weathers, Carl, 185

Weaver, Dennis, 303

Weaver, Marjorie, 68, 337

Weaver, Sigourney, 87, 108

Web, William K., 71

Webb, Clifton, 126, 384

Webb, Jack, 263

Webb, James R., 49, 75, 119, 134, 239

Webb, Robert D., 211

Webster, M. Coates, 86

Wee Willie Winkie, 488

Weekend at the Waldorf, 487

Weekend in Havana, 249, 445, 488

Wehling, Bob, 327
Weil, Sharon, 318
Weingrod, Herschel, 187
Weinstein, Paula, 100
Weintraub, Sy, 219
Weir, Peter, 100
Weisbart, David, 126, 197, 135
Weiss, Allan, 109
Weissman, Herman, 64
Weissmuller, Johnny, 11, 510
Weitz, Bruce, 283
Welch, Raquel, 43, **43**, 68, 173, **174**, 514–16, **514**, **515**
Welch, Tahnee, 516
"Welcome Back, Kotter," 299
Weller, Peter, 72
Welles, Orson, **16**, 17, 153, 227, 228, **228**, 245, 278, 331, 381, 391, 420, 443, 479
Wellman, Paul I., 80
Wellman, William, 47, 165, 177, 199, 448
Wells, John, 103
Wells, William K., 79
Wells Fargo, 494
Welsch, Howard, 86
Welter, Blanca Rose. *See* Christian, Linda
Wendkos, Paul, 120
Werfel, Franz, 132
Werker, Alfred, 182
Werner, Oskar, 245
Wertmuller, Lina, 251
West, Mae, 20, 112, 470, 484, **484**
West Side Arts Theatre, 311
West Side Story, 20, 21, 198, 200, 219, 249–50, **250**, 260, 275, 394, 453, 483
West Side Story (stage), 394, 479, 492
Western Costume Company, 378
Westerner, The, 480, 506
"Westerner, The," 523
Westmore, Perc, 133
Weston, Jack, 198
Westworld, 151
Wexler, Haskell, 142, 374, 468
Wexler, Norman, 207
"What a Country," 300, 478
"What a Difference a Day Makes," 491
What Happened in Santiago, 251
What Price Glory?, 11, 79, 389, 390, 457, 525
Whatever Happened to Santiago, 451
Wheaton, Wil, 314
Wheeler, Bert, 197
When Helen Was Elected, 421
When Time Ran Out, 375
When You Comin' Back, Red Ryder?, 379
Where Do We Go from Here?, 473
Where East Is East, 510
Where the Boys Are, 443
Where the Buffalo Roam, 380, 468
Where the Pavement Ends (1923), 457

Where Words Fail, 407
Where's Charley?, 425, 426
Which Way Is Up?, 251, 507
Whirlpool, 403
Whispering Smith, 14, 385
Whispers in the Dark, 432, **432**
White, Betty, 280
White, Edward J., 177
White, John Sylvester, 299
White, Leslie T., 34
White, Stewart Edward, 235
White Buffalo, The, 429
White Heat, 19, 375
White Hunter, Black Heart, 507
White Men Can't Jump, 23, 251, **466**, 467
White Palace, 436
White Savage, 413, 450
"White Shadow, The," 300, 354
White Shadows in the South Seas, 504
Whitehead, Paxton, 289
Whitman, Stuart, 80, 81, 197
Whitmore, James, 46, **46**, 47, 120
Whitney, John Hay, 15, 37, 204
Whitney, Peter, 153
Whole Town Is Talking, The (1926), 389
Whoopee Boys, The, 481
Whore, 399
Who's That Girl, 490
Why Worry?, 252
"Wichita Town," 300, 487
Widmark, Richard, 30, **31**, 32, 75, 76, 87, 112, 202, 393, 522
Widow from Monte Carlo, The, 391
Wiener, Alitzah, 295
Wiere Brothers, The, 199
Wiesenthal, Sam, 210
Wilbur, Cran, 160
Wilcox, Larry, 274, **274**
Wilcox, Steve, 32
Wild and the Innocent, The, 486
Wild Bunch, The, 2, 151, 221, 252–54, **253**, 354, 359, 375, 401, 491, **492**, 523, 524, **524**
Wild Is the Wind, 470
Wild Party, The, 515
Wilde, Cornel, 68, 135, 154, 178, 230, 380, 424, 525
Wilder, Billy, 126, 204, 385
Wilder, Gene, 503
Wilder, John, 303
Wilder, Margaret Buell, 182
Wilder, Robert, 49, 213
Wilder, Thornton, 64
Wilder, Yvonne, 275. *See also* Othon, Yvonne
Wilderson Foundation, 429
Wilhelm, Hans, 89
Williams, Bill, 270, 395
Williams, Elmo, 126
Williams, Esther, 101, 430, 431, 448, 504
Williams, Guy, 327, 329, **329**, 330, 331, 433, 516–17, **516**
Williams, Hal, 292

Williams, Melvin, 203
Williams, Robert Creighton, 219
Williams, Robin, 350, 475
Williams, Roy, 204, 222
Williams, Steven, 276
Williams, Tennessee, 3, 167, 168, 217, 473
Williams, Treat, 307, 408
Willingham, Calder, 171
Willis, Bruce, 379
Wilson, Demond, 291, 295
Wilson, Larry, 27
Wilson, Michael, 74, 203, 204
Wilson, Michael G., 145
Wilson, Richard, 48
Wilson, Woodrow, 5
Wimperis, Arthur, 186
Winchester '73, 19
Wind and the Lion, The, 465
Windwalker, 408
Winfrey, Oprah, 160
Wingate, William P., 258
Winged Serpent, The. See Q
Winger, Debra, 23, 68
Wings of the Hawk, 254–55, 348, 414, 519
Winitsky, Alex, 86
Winkler, Irwin, 53, 64
Winston, Sam, 88
Winter, Nancy, 112
Winter Garden Theatre, 258
Winters, Jonathan, 241
Winters, Shelley, 165, 229, 257, 443, 448, 515
Winterset, 437
Winterset (stage), 437
Wintertime, 488
"WIOU," 467
Wisdom, 398, 498
Wise, Robert, 200, 249, 250, 453
"Wiseguy," 300, 363
Wiseman, Joseph, 242, 244
Wisnievitz, David, 160
With His Pistol in His Hand, 40, 41
Without Reservations, 352
Witney, William, 177, 324
Wittliff, William D., 44, 315
Wizan, Joe, 255
WNET-TV, 294, 302
Wohl, David, 276
Wolf Song, 510
Wolfen, 460
Woman and the Puppet, The, 88
Woman Disputed, The, 484
Woman I Stole, The, 505
Woman in Room 13, The, 485
Woman of the Year, 516
Women of San Quentin, 379, 396
Women's Club, The, 510
Won Ton Ton, the Dog Who Saved Hollywood, 489
Wonder Bar, 11, 390
"Wonder Woman," 264, 267, 377
Wonderful Country, The, 20, 255, 356

Wonderful Ice Cream Suit, The, 384
"WonderWorks," 311, 314, 318, 502
Wood, Charles, 86
Wood, Natalie, 249
Wood, Sam, 105, 106
Woods, Donald, 64
Woods, James, 205, **205**, 206, 376, 402
Woods, Lotta, 112
Woodward, Joanne, 318, 350
Woolrich, Cornell, 144
Woolsey, Robert, 197
World Film Co., 480
World in His Arms, The, 471, 525
Woronov, Mary, 92
WPBT-TV (Miami), 293
Wraith, The, 497
Wrath of God, The, <u>255</u>, 420, 499
Wray, Ardel, 144
Wray, Fay, 14, 71, 241, 336
Wrestling Ernest Hemingway, <u>255</u>
Wright, Cobina, Jr., 73, 249
Wright, Frank Lloyd, 470
Wright, Gilbert, 68
Wright, Harold Bell, 68
Wright, Joseph, 249
Wright, Ralph, 204, 222
Wright, Teresa, 68
Wrong Is Right, 494, 500
Wrong Way Light Bulb, The, 380
Wurlitzer, Rudy, 179, 247
Wurtz, John, 429
Wurtzel, Sol M., 73, 128, 190, 338
Wyatt, Jane, 279
"Wyatt Earp," 417, 480
Wyatt Earp, Frontier Marshall, 164
Wyler, Robert, 141
Wyler, William, 49, 375
Wyman, Jane, 126, 277, 349, 456, 488
Wymore, Patrice, 153
Wynn, Keenan, 149, 223, 241

Xanadu, 462, 463
Xavier, 388
Xavier Cugat and his Orchestra, 17, 256, 511
"Xavier Cugat Show, The," <u>300</u>

Yablonsky, Yabo, 239
Yaconelli, Frank, 339, 340, 341
Yakuza, The, 441
Yanez, David, 304, <u>517</u>
Yank, 436
Yankee Don, 506
Yarbrough, Jean, 86
Yates, George Worthing, 100
Yates, Herbert J., 30, 140, 475, 481

Yates, Peter, 515
Ybarra, Alfred C., 14, 30, 128, 134, 182, <u>517</u>
Ybarra, Rocky, 255, <u>517</u>
Ybarra, Roque, 83, 155, 158, 226
Yellen, Linda, 313
"Yellow Rose, The," <u>301</u>
Yellow Tomahawk, The, 452
Yellowbeard, 438
Yerkovich, Anthony, 291
Yniguez, Richard, 59, 188, 189, 288, 292, 305, 306, **306**, 316, <u>517–18</u>
Yojimbo, 103
Yordan, Philip, 53, 61, 93, 120, 166, 201
York, Dick, 83
Yorkin, Bud, 87
"You Again," <u>301</u>
"You Bet Your Life," 414
You Were Never Lovelier, <u>256</u>, 384, 418, 420, 436, 487
You'll Never Get Rich, 256, 420
Young, Carroll, 148
Young, Chic, 51
Young, Clarence Upton, 341
Young, Dalene, 302
Young, Gig, 64
Young, Harold, 222
Young, Irwin W., 29
Young, John Sacret, 200
Young, Karen, 123
Young, Loretta, 190, 191
Young, Robert (actor), 134, 210, 279, 290, **290**
Young, Robert M. (director), 23, 29, 32, 40, 41, 163, 212, 353, 397, 461, 467, 501
Young, Roger, 307
Young, Tony, 74, 219
Young and the Brave, The, 89, 463
Young Doctors in Love, 396, 457
Young Guns, <u>256</u>, 399, 467, 497
Young Guns, The, 434
Young Guns II, <u>256</u>, 353, 399, 467
"Young Indiana Jones Chronicles, The," 454
Young Indiana Jones Chronicles: Young Indiana Jones and the Curse of the Jackal, The, <u>319</u>
Young Land, The, <u>256–57</u>
Young Lawyers, The, 512
Young Lions, The, 396
Young Lords, 40
Young Man with a Horn, 422
Young Savages, The, 89, <u>257</u>, 434
Yours, Anne, 353
Yrigoyen, Joe, <u>518</u>

Ysais, Gilbert, 219
Yurick, Sol, 247
Yurka, Blanche, 111

Z, 161, 162
Zaentz, Saul, 38
Zaillian, Steven, 99
Zamora, Del, 191, 192, **192**, <u>518</u>
Zandy's Bride, 517, <u>258</u>
Zane, Billy, 184, 213
Zanuck, Darryl F., 18, 52, 69, 74, 90, 218, 242, 243, 244, 248, 326, 337, 419
Zanuck, Richard D., 74
Zapanta, Michael, 313
Zapata, Carmen, 291, 299, <u>518</u>
Zapata the Unconquered, 242
Zarco, Estelita, 56
Zavattini, Cesare, 76
Zeffirelli, Franco, 395
Zemeckis, Robert, 199
Zepulveda, Zeppy, <u>518</u>
Ziegfeld Follies (1929), 466
Ziegler, Isabelle Gibson, 211
Ziffren, Lester, 73
Zimbalist, Efrem, Jr., 193, 333
Zimbalist, Sam, 27, 226
Zimm, Maurice, 29
Zinnemann, Fred, 47, 125, 171
Zito, Steve, 310
Zmed, Adrian, 319
Zoetrope, 172
Zombie, 474
Zoot Suit, 1, 25, 137, 152, 217, <u>258–60</u>, 259, 343, 363, 370, 405, 412, 434, 441, 459, 460, 461, 468, 481, 507
Zoot Suit (stage), 34, 137, 459–60, 508
Zorba, 470, 472
Zorba the Greek, 470, 472
Zorro, <u>321–33</u>
Zorro, <u>328</u>
"Zorro," 327, <u>329–31</u>, **330**, **332**, 395, 433, 441, 486, 488, 512, 517
Zorro, the Avenger, <u>327</u>
Zorro, the Gay Blade, <u>328–29</u>, **328**
"Zorro, the Legend Continues," <u>332–33</u>
"Zorro and Son," <u>331</u>, 333, 517
Zorro and the Three Musketeers, 321
Zorro Rides Again, <u>324</u>
Zorro's Black Whip, <u>326</u>
Zorro's Fighting Legion, <u>324</u>, 387
Zuckerman, George, 55
Zugsmith, Albert, 153, 227
Zukor, Adolph, 106, 113
Zuniga, Daphne, 141, <u>518–19</u>
Zuniga, Frank, 123, <u>519</u>